W9-CCM-693

MAJ. GEN. ISRAEL PUTNAM.

Israel Putnam

HISTORY

OF

WINDHAM COUNTY,

CONNECTICUT.

BY ELLEN D. LARNED.

" If, when we lay down our pen, we cannot say in the sight of God, 'upon strict examination, I
have not knowingly written anything that is not true' . . . . then study and literature render
us unrighteous and sinful."—*Niebuhr*.

VOLUME II.

1760–1880.

PUBLISHED BY THE AUTHOR.

1880.

WORCESTER, MASS. :
PRINTED BY CHARLES HAMILTON,
311 MAIN STREET.
MDCCCLXXX.

SIGILLUM · COMITATUS · WINDHAMIE ·

PORTRAITS.

PREFACE.

It is perhaps but natural in completing a work of this character, attempting to cover so large a field, that the author should
be more conscious of its omissions than its inclusions. To show
what had been accomplished by WINDHAM COUNTY in the past it
was necessary to include the present—a delicate and difficult
matter, rather within the province of the gazetteer than the
historian. Passing events and conditions have been touched as
briefly as possible and present actors very sparingly introduced.
Critics will note with more asperity of judgment the absence of
statistical details and tabulated statements, especially with reference to the three wars in which Windham bore a part; as also of
genealogical and topographical data, so essential to a thorough
knowledge of any particular section. A future supplement may
supply these facts, which it has been impossible for the author to
collect at the present time. She has achieved, she trusts, a clear
and truthful narrative of the settlement and development of the
towns comprising Windham County, gathered from the archives
of the towns and State and from innumerable other sources—a
narrative which though strictly confined to county limits, very
strikingly sets forth the growth and development of the Nation,
and its institutions. The observing reader will see in how many
ways this little corner has sent out its influence, and how vitally
it is connected with the growth of the body politic. Great
pains have been taken to represent its social character and
changes, and to gather up and collate every possible detail of
the lives and services of those residents most connected with its
development. Undoubtedly with all this care persons worthy

of mention have been omitted, and undue prominence may have been given to others. Mistakes and misapprehensions in a work of this kind cannot be avoided, especially in such matters as were never before brought into history, derived from many independent sources. But it is believed that these defects and errors are comparatively trifling, and that the friends of Windham County have good reason to be satisfied with this record. Especially will they be gratified with the faces of honored citizens, familiar still to some and greatly revered by all, that enrich its pages. Long cherished as priceless treasures by descendants and friends, they will be warmly welcomed in many Windham County homes, and will give to future generations a more vivid realization of the days and scenes with which they were connected. The public will join with the writer in thanks to the kind friends who have generously aided in the reproduction of these valued portraits ; others which were greatly desired it was impossible for various reasons to secure. As the record of events comes down to the present, it seemed but fitting that our picture gallery should include a living representative—our chief official resident, the present lieutenant-governor of Connecticut—which his friends and constituents will highly value.

Grateful thanks are also due to the many friends who have given valuable information. Especial mention should be made of our efficient State Librarian, Charles J. Hoadly, Esq., who furnished needful material and opened many sources of information. Reports of interesting incidents, not to be found in the County, were sent back from the papers of the late Hon. Ephraim Cutler, Marietta, Ohio. J. R. Simms, Esq., Fort Plain, New York, author of the History of Schoharie County, and other historical works ; Mr. George Webb, Elizabeth, New Jersey ; Mr. Pulaski Carter, Providence, Pa.; Mr. J. Q. Adams, Natick, R. I.—former residents of Windham County—have kindly contributed many valuable notes, incidents and reminiscences. Documents collected by the late William L.

Weaver, Esq., received from Mr. Thomas S. Weaver, and excerpts from his local notes and genealogical papers, preserved by Prof. Cleveland Abbe, of Washington, D. C., were especially helpful. Very valuable papers and pamphlets were found in the collection left by John McClellan, Esq., Woodstock. For these many favors, and the innumerable details furnished by residents of every town, for the sympathy and aid received from so many sources, the writer can only express her appreciative thanks, and her hope that their expectations may be fully realized. In completing a work which has given her a much higher estimate of Windham County's past standing, the writer cannot but hope that it may excite a truer appreciation in others, and by stimulating county feeling and healthy emulation, help to make its onward course yet more prosperous, and its future record yet fairer and more honorable.

F. D. L.

THOMPSON, *June* 30, 1880.

TOPICAL INDEX.

CONTENTS.

BOOK V. 1740–1775.

BOOK VI. 1764–1783.

WINDHAM IN THE REVOLUTION.

D

BOOK VII. 1783–1807.

BOOK VIII. 1807–1820.

BOOK IX. 1820–1845.

BOOK X. 1840–1880.

BOOK V.

I.

POMFRET. BROOKLYN SOCIETY. PUTNAM. MALBONE. RIVAL
CHURCH EDIFICES. GENERAL AFFAIRS.

THE heavy burden borne by Windham County through the wearisome French and Indian war was not without its compensations.
Stringent compulsory demands called out the energies of the towns
and developed their resources. Wider experience, and the stimulating discipline of camp and battle, made stronger men of those engaged
in warfare, and fitted them for greater usefulness at home. No town
was more favored in this respect than Pomfret. Her sons greatly
distinguished themselves in the war, and returned to engage with
equal zeal and fidelity in the service of town and county. At the
annual meeting of the town, December 1, 1760, many of these returned
soldiers were elected to town offices. Deacon Jonathan Dresser served
as moderator. More than fifty men were needed to fill the various
public offices. Ebenezer Williams, Esq., Captain John Grosvenor,
Captain Zachariah Spalding, Deacons Edward Ruggles and David Williams were chosen selectmen ; Timothy Sabin, town clerk and treasurer ;
Ensign Nathaniel Clark, Ephraim Ingalls and Samuel Williams, con-
stables—one for each society ; Rufus Herrick, John Gilbert, William
Allworth, Paul Adams, Solomon Griggs, Daniel Cheney, Jonathan
White, George Sumner, Samuel Cotton, Ebenezer Deming, Ebenezer
Williams, Esq., David Chandler, Amasa Sessions, Jacob Goodell and
Nathaniel Abbott, highway surveyors ; Abijah Williams and John
Weld, fence viewers ; John Parkhurst, Jun., Josiah Sabin, Ephraim
Tucker, Jun., Joseph Scarborough, Thomas Williams, Deacon Samuel
Craft and Ebenezer Goodell, listers ; John Williams, Jun., Adonijah
Fasset and John Williams, grand-jurors ; Jedidiah Ashcraft, James
Copeland, Joseph Philips, Nathaniel Rogers, Ephraim Griggs and John
Holbrook, tithing-men ; William Sabin, John Davison, Jonathan Allen,
Josiah Wheeler and Captain Zachariah Spalding, horse-branders ; Ben-
jamin Smith and Benjamin Sharpe, weight-sealers ; Samuel Carpenter,
excise collector ; Ensign Nathaniel Clark, town-collector ; Benjamin

1

Griffin, key-keeper. Most of these officers will be recognized as descendants of the early settlers of Pomfret. The sole survivor of the first settlers at this date was apparently Mr. Nathaniel Sessions, "a sober man and useful member of society," who forty years before had opened the first cart road from Providence. Now in serene old age, resting from his labors in his pleasant home in Abington, he was ever ready to aid the town with his counsel and suggestions, and passed his leisure hours in the study of the Scriptures, committing a large part of them to memory in fear that he should be deprived of his eyesight.

The mill-site on the Quinebaug had now changed owners. In 1760, the land between the Quinebaug and Mill Rivers, with privilege of the Falls, mills, dwelling-house, malt house, dye-house, and all their appurtenances, was sold by Nathaniel Daniels to Benjamin Cargill, of South Kingston, R. I., a descendant of Rev. Donald Cargill, of Scotland. Mr. Cargill at once took possession of his purchase and by his shrewdness and good management so improved its business facilities that "Cargill's Mills" soon became a noted place of resort for all the surrounding country; malting, dyeing and grinding for parts of Pomfret, Woodstock, Killingly and Thompson Parish.

Town affairs required very little attention. New roads were discussed and other public improvements, but nothing undertaken. The energies of the first society were now wholly absorbed in building the long projected meeting-house. After a year's suspension work was resumed. At a society meeting, December 4, 1761, William Sabin was chosen moderator; John Payson, clerk; Captain John Grosvenor, Gershom Sharpe and Samuel Carpenter, committee. It was then voted to raise money and go forward with the finishing of the house—money to be raised by a tax of ninepence per pound on the list. A stalwart body of seats in the centre of the house had already been erected. Forty-four pews were now ordered —twenty-six against the walls; eighteen ranged behind the body seats. It was also voted, "That those forty-three persons that are highest in the list shall have the liberty of drawing forty-three of the pews; they building each one his own pew and finishing the wall of said house, adjoining to his pew, to the first girth; he that is highest in the list to have the first choice, and so on till they have done drawing; reserving room for one pew for the ministry in said society, where the Rev. Mr. Aaron Putnam shall choose it." The difficulties and differences which delayed so long the initiation of this work had now subsided, and all parties united with great apparent zeal and heartiness in its progress and completion. Thomas Stedman, the skillful architect of the new meeting-house in Canada Parish, was employed as master-builder. Galleries were built around the sides of the house, a high pulpit and massive canopy erected, and the outside "cullered" in the most approved fashion of the day—the body deep orange with doors and bottom-boards of chocolate color, "window-jets," corner and weather-boards, white. This fanciful "cullering" was greatly admired and copied, and the house when completed was probably the largest and finest in the county. The formal dedication of houses of worship was not then in vogue, but a preliminary "lecture sermon" was preached in this by Mr. Putnam, Thursday, January 20, 1763. The old meeting-house and training-field adjacent were sold by order of the society, and liberty granted to build sheds on the east line of the common within four rods of Rev. Mr. Aaron Putnam's house.

Brooklyn society was increasing in strength and numbers. Ebenezer Witter of Preston, John and Israel Litchfield, James and Thomas Eldredge, William and Nehemiah Prince, Stephen Baker, Rufus Herrick and Andrew Lester had become its residents. The original settlers were represented by many thriving families. A remodeling of school districts, in 1762, shows the distribution of the inhabitants :—

"District 1. Containing Captain Spalding, Prince's place, that farm that was the Reverend Mr. Avery's, Nathan Cady, Adonijah Fasset, David Kendall, John Kimball, Rev. Mr. Whitney, Stephen Baker, Ezekiel Cady, Uriah Cady, Daniel Tyler, Thomas Williams, Samuel Cleveland and Joseph Cady.

District 2. All the lands and houses of Colonel Malbone that are in the society, William Earl, Moses Earl, Jonas Frost, Jedidiah Ashcraft, Joseph Hubbard, Abner Adams, Benjamin Fasset, Nehemiah Adams. John Hubbard, Daniel Adams, Noah and Paul Adams and Samuel Wilson.

District 3. To contain Peter and Richard Adams, Widow Allyn, Lieutenant Smith, Sergeant Woodward, Reuben Darbe, Jonas Cleveland, Josiah. James and Joseph Fasset, John Allyn, Lieutenant Spalding, Elijah Monrose, Joseph Dyer, Jonathan Backus, Andrew Lester, Captain Prince, Nehemiah Prince, Thomas Wheeler, William Copeland and Moses Smith.

District 4. To contain Nehemiah Bacon, Joseph Scarborough, Samuel Jacques, James Bennet, Joseph Ross, Widow Barret, Lieutenant Smith, Dr. Walton, Barnabas Wood, Deacon Scarborough, Colonel Putnam and Thomas Eldredge.

District 5. To contain Samuel Williams, Jun., William Williams, Jun., Deacon Williams, Samuel Williams, Ebenezer Weeks, Rufus Herrick, Jedidiah Downing, Widow Davyson, Banjamin Fasset, Jun., and Amoral Chapman.

District 6. To contain John Litchfield, Israel Litchfield, Darius Cady, James Darbe, Senior and Junior, Samuel and Eleazer Darbe, Nathan Kimball, Benjamin Shepard, Nehemiah Cady, Caleb Spalding, Daniel, Nahum, John, Henry and Benjamin Cady.

District 7. John Fasset, James Copeland, Gidion Cady, Samuel Winter, Nathan Witter, Asa Tyler, Lieutenant Hunt, the farm that was Thomas Stanton's, Jacob Staples, Jethro Rogers, James Bidlack and Aaron Fuller."

The central school-house was now moved to a suitable place in one corner of the common, and "fitted up as well as it was before," and school-houses provided as soon as possible for the surrounding districts. A school was kept at least two and one fifth months a year in each district. Faithful men were appointed to take charge of the school money. Innovations in public religious worship next claimed the attention of Brooklyn society. In 1763, the church concluded that the pastor should read the Holy Scriptures for the time to come on Lord's day, viz. : a portion in the morning out of the Old Testament, and in the afternoon out of the New Testament, in course, immediately before first singing; omitting such chapters as should be thought less instructive. The society voted meanwhile, to provide a cushion for the pulpit. Also—

" To mend ye glass and frames and casements of ye meeting-house, and where ye clapboards are off or split to put on more, and put on shingles where they are wanted, and rectify ye under-pinning—Daniel Tyler to be the man to see that ye meeting-house be repaired."

These repairs were unsatisfactory. The house though but thirty years old, was rude and shabby. The elegant church edifices lately erected by the first and third societies of Pomfret excited envy and emulation. Brooklyn was increasing more rapidly than the other societies; its affairs were managed by men of energy and public spirit; its young pastor was eager for progress and improvement, and it could not long rest satisfied with inferior accommodations. In 1766, it was accordingly proposed to build a new meeting-house, but the society declined to consider the question and only voted—

"To put up a new window on the north side of the meeting-house, and board up the window that is broken against the front gallery, and put some new shingles on the roof where the water runs through, and put a new clapboard on the north side where one is off, and give Mr. Joseph Davison 27s. to do the same. "

This vote gave great offence to the " young American " element in the society, especially to Dr. Walton, who berated the conservatives for meanness and lack of public spirit, and declared the present house " old, shaky and not fit to meet in. "

The return of Colonel Putnam to Pomfret in 1765 gave a new impulse to public improvements in town and society. The distinguished success of this gallant officer in the field had greatly changed his position at home. Enemies more formidable than wolves had now been overcome. The obscure Mortlake farmer had proved himself equal to every emergency. His valorous exploits during the war had captivated the popular fancy. His services at Havana and Detroit had brought him prominently before the public and added dignity to his reputation, and no officer in the American ranks was more widely known or applauded. Time had blunted the edge of sectional prejudice, and he was welcomed home after ten years absence as one whom all delighted to honor. His fellow-citizens once so chary of their favors now loaded him with public offices. He was called to preside as moderator at town and society meetings. He was made first selectman, and sent as deputy to the General Assembly. He devised and laid out roads, he set out school-districts, he deliberated upon the great question whether to repair or pull down the meeting-house; nor did he disdain to "hire the master," seat the meeting-house, collect parish rates, nor even to receive crows' heads and pay out the bounty money. Uniting with the church soon after his return he was sent as its "messenger" upon many important occasions, his military experience giving him, it may have been supposed, peculiar aptitude in disentangling and settling ecclesiastic controversies and complications. These various duties were discharged with character-istic heartiness and fidelity. His eye was quick, his judgment sound and practical, and whatever he devised he was sure to carry through with promptitude. Improvements on his house and farm soon bore witness to his untiring energy. Sword and gun were gladly exchanged for plow and pruning-knife. He imported new stock, set out young trees and engaged in various agricultural experiments. But with all his private and public duties he was ever ready to aid his neighbors by advice or service. When an alarm of fire was heard in the neigh-borhood he was the first man on the ground, and with his own brawny arms brought up from the cellar the well-filled pork barrel that was to furnish food for the needy household, and none was more prompt in relieving the wants of the destitute.

But Putnam was not permitted to restrict his energies to his own farm and neighborhood. He returned at a great political crisis. The revolutionary conflict had opened. The Stamp Act had just been pro-mulgated, and all the Colonies were ablaze with indignation. No man was more imbued with the spirit of the times, more resolute in determination to resist farther encroachment upon colonial liberties, and he had the art of infusing his spirit into others. As the avowed opponent of the Stamp Act he was welcomed home with acclamation, and ardent patriots rallied around him as their champion and leader in resistance and aggression. He was called upon to preside at indignation meet-ings in various parts of Windham County. His pungent, pithy words had great effect upon his hearers. The foray upon Ingersoll and other demonstrations of popular feeling were said to have been instigated by Putnam, and the prominence of Windham County in the subsequent struggle was ascribed in great measure to his presence and influence.

Putnam's triumphant return was shadowed by a great domestic affliction—the death of his beloved wife—in the autumn of 1765. She left seven living children—Israel, the oldest, now twenty-five years of age, and the youngest, Peter Schuyler, an infant of a few months. In 1767, Colonel Putnam was married to Madam Deborah Gardiner, a lady long known to him as the wife of Brooklyn's first minister, Rev. Ephraim Avery, and afterwards of John Gardiner, Esq., of Gardiner's

Island. This marriage gave new dignity to his social position, bringing him into connection with many prominent families, and with that ecclesiastic element so potent in Connecticut at this period. Mrs. Putnam had a large circle of friends and much social experience. Her husband was the most popular man of the day. Their hospitable home drew throngs of visitants. Every soldier passing through Windham County would go out of his way to call upon his beloved colonel. Relatives, friends, traveling ministers, distinguished strangers and gushing patriots came in such numbers that their entertainment became very burdensome. A Virginian Jefferson would submit to such an invasion though it made him bankrupt; a Yankee Putnam could contrive to turn it into profit, or at least save himself from ruin. Finding that his estate could not support such an excessive outlay, Putnam met the emergency with one of his sudden strokes, removed his residence to the Avery estate on Brooklyn Green, and opened his house for general public accommodation. A full-length representation of its proprietor as "General Wolf," in appropriate military costume, hung before the door, its outstretched hand inviting all to enter. That Brooklyn tavern, with Putnam for its landlord and Mrs. Avery Gardiner Putnam as mistress, became one of the most noted gathering places in Eastern Connecticut, and witnessed many a thrilling scene of the great Revolutionary drama.

Putnam's return to Pomfret was nearly cotemporary with the advent of another distinguished personage of very different charcter and proclivities—Godfrey Malbone, of Newport. An aristocrat by birth and sympathies ; a loyalist, devoted to the Crown and Church of England—untoward fate brought him to finish his days amid the rude, rebel yeomanry of Pomfret, in the same neighborhood with the great champion of popular rights and liberties. Colonel Malbone was a man of varied experience and accomplishments. He was educated at King's College, Oxford, had traveled much and moved in the first circles of Europe and America. Inheriting a large estate from his father, he had lived in a style of princely luxury and magnificence. His country-house, a mile from Newport state-house, was called "the most splendid edifice in all the Colonies." Completed at great cost after long delay, it was destroyed by fire in the midst of house-warming festivities. Colonel Malbone's financial affairs had become seriously embarrassed. His commercial enterprises had been thwarted by the insubordination of the Colonies. His ships had been taken by privateers, and his property destroyed by Newport mobs, and now that his elegant edifice was consumed, he refused to battle longer with fate and opposing elements, and, early in 1766, buried himself in the wilds of Pomfret. Some three thousand acres of land, bought from Belcher,

Williams and others, had been made over to him at the decease of his father, well stocked with cows, horses, sheep, swine, goats and negroes. These slaves according to common report were a part of a cargo brought from Holland who helped repel a piratical assault, and were retained for life and comfortably supported. Amid such rude, uncongenial surroundings, Malbone made his home, exchanging his palatial residence for a common tenant-house, and renouncing all business interests but the cultivation of his land and the utilization of his negro forces. With the town's people he held as little intercourse as possible. They belonged to a class and world of which he had a very imperfect conception. Such gentlemen as called upon him were received with politeness; poor people asking aid were relieved; town and church rates were paid without demur or question, but all without the slightest personal interest. Of their schools and churches, their town government and projected improvements, he knew or cared nothing. Their political aspirations and declamations he looked upon with scorn beyond expression.

It was not till he discovered that these insignificant country people were concerting a project very detrimental to his own interests that Colonel Malbone was roused from his lofty indifference. Brooklyn Society was bent upon a new meeting house. Putnam's removal to the village had given a new impetus to the movement. With such a famous tavern and troops of fine company, how could the people condescend to attend religious worship in an old shaky house, with patched roof and boarded windows. Again, in the autumn of 1768, a meeting was called to consider this important question. Great efforts were made to secure a full vote, and as an argument for a new building it was currently whispered that the Malbone estate, now rising in value, would pay a large percentage of the outlay. So ignorant was Colonel Malbone of neighborhood affairs that he did not even know that such a question was pending. " A strange sort of notification" affixed to the public sign-post had for him no significance. He paid no heed to town or society meetings, and the vote might have been carried without out his participation or knowledge had not one of his tenants thought it his duty to apprize him on the very day preceding the meeting. Alarmed by the tidings he at once waited upon Mr. Whitney, whom he had ever treated with the respect due to his position and character, and represented to him the imprudence as well as inexpediency of such a step at a juncture when every one complained of the great hardships of the time and extreme scarceness of money. To convince him of its necessity Mr. Whitney took him to the meeting-house, which he had never before deigned to enter, but though joined " by an Esquire, Colonel and farmer," (probably Holland, Putnam and Williams), all their arguments were ineffectual. The primitive meeting-house seemed to him quite good enough for the congregation, a few trifling repairs were all that was needed, and if really too small its enlargement was practicable. So much uneasiness was manifested at the latter suggestion, and such determined resolution to build at all events that Colonel Malbone saw clearly that the measure was likely to be carried, and without returning home galloped over to Plainfield to consult with the only churchman of any note in the vicinity—John Aplin, Esq., a lawyer lately removed from Providence, a staunch loyalist, greatly embittered against the colonists. He assured Malbone that as the laws stood he could not possibly help himself; that if those people had a mind to erect a square building this year and pull it down and build a round one the next, he must submit to the expense unless they had a church of their own, or got relief from England. Convinced of the necessity of vigorous opposition, Colonel Malbone next day attended the society meeting, " debated the question with the Esquire in very regular fashion," and had the satisfaction of seeing it thoroughly defeated— " the odds against building being very great when put to vote. "

Opposition only made the minority more determined. They continued to agitate the matter both in public and private, and were "so extremely industrious and indefatigable, promising to pay the rates for those who could not afford it, " that they gained many adherents. In September, 1769, another society meeting was called, when Colonel Malbone again appeared with the following protest :—

" 1. I deem the present house with a very few trifling repairs altogether sufficient and proper to answer the purpose designed, it being no way antiquated, and with small expense may be made equal to when it was first finished and full as decent as the situation of the parish will allow of, and certainly much more suitable to our circumstances than the superb edifice proposed to be erected—God Almighty not being so much delighted with temples made with hands as with meek, humble and upright hearts.

2. If the building had been really necessary it would be prudent to postpone it rather than to burden the inhabitants at this distressful season, when there is scarce a farthing of money circulated among us, and the most wealthy obliged to send the produce of their lands to markets for distress to raise a sufficiency for payment of taxes for the support of the ministry only, and the generality scarce able, though we pay no province tax, to live a poor, wretched, miserable life.

3. I was born and educated in the principles and profession of the Established National Church, and determine to persevere in those principles to the day of my death; therefore, decline from entering into so great an expense— a full eighth of the whole charge—wherefore, in presence of this meeting, I do publicly repeat my dissent and absolutely protest. "

Upon putting the question to vote a majority of *one* declared against building; but as three of the prominent advocates were absent at a funeral the point was virtually carried. Elated with the prospect of success, the friends of the new house now indulged in some natural expressions of triumph. That Malbone's opposition had increased their spirit and determination is quite probable. While he esteemed his country neighbors as boors and clowns, characterized by " cant, cunning, hypocrisy and lowness of manners," they had sufficient acuteness to detect and reciprocate his ill opinion, and resent his attempt to thwart them in their dearest legal and local privilege. His scornful contempt was now repaid by downright insolence, and these canting clowns did not hesitate to say in the most public manner, "that as churchmen had made them pay in other places, they had the right and would make use of it to make churchmen pay here," and "that by selling off a few of his negroes to pay his building rate, the damage would not be very great." These "insults" added to the "intended oppression" roused the high spirited Malbone to immediate resolution and action. For nearly thirty years his estate had paid for the support of religious worship in this society. Although as non-resident Episcopalians they might have obtained exemption from government, yet as the tax was comparatively light, the value of the property enhanced by the maintenance of this worship, and father and son exceedingly liberal and open handed, they had paid it without protesting. Removing to Brooklyn, Malbone still disdained to question it till confronted by this large impost. As a resident of the parish he would be compelled by law to pay it unless he could attend public worship elsewhere. To help those who had thus insulted him, to yield the point to his opponents, to be instrumental in erecting "what some called a schism-shop," was wholly repugnant to him. The church at Norwich was practically inaccessible. Relief might be obtained by appealing to the King, but this implied negotiation and delay. A more instant and effectual remedy was needed and devised. Malbone was an ardent royalist, devoted heart and soul to the interests of the British Government. The English Church was one with the Crown. By establishing Episcopal worship in his own neighborhood, he could not only secure himself from taxation and discomfit his opponents, but strengthen the hands of his King and country, and bring new adherents to their cause. These considerations were too weighty to be rejected. They appealed to the strongest and deepest sympathies of his nature, and with characteristic impulsiveness he emerged from his retirement and devoted himself with all his energies and resources to the establishment of the Church of England on the very land purchased by Blackwell for a Puritan Colony.

Followers soon rallied around him. The few Tories in the neighborhood were eager to join him. Dr. Walton, who had made himself obnoxious by his political course and was now " debarred from church privileges for rough speaking," came out boldly for Episcopacy and Malbone. Aplin of Plainfield, was ready with aid and counsel. Brook-

2

lyn, like other parishes, had its malcontents, its aggrieved rate-payers, ready to avenge old wrongs and forestall future assessments by uniting with a new organization. A paper circulated by Dr. Walton procured the signatures of nineteen persons, heads of families, agreeing to become members of the Church of England when church edifice and missionary should be provided. To provide these essentials was a matter of great difficulty. Every argument urged by Malbone against the building of the Brooklyn meeting-house applied with greater force to his own project. Times were hard, money scarce, his own pecuniary affairs embarrassed, his proselytes mainly of the poorer classes. The Society for the Propagation of the Gospel in foreign parts, indig nant at the growing insubordination of the colonies, had " determined not to make any new missions in New England." But Malbone had friends and influence abroad, and a ready wit and pen of his own— " himself a host," able to overcome all opposing obstacles. In graceful letters admirably adapted to the various recipients he told his story. To former boon companions, who might " reasonably be surprized that he had undertaken to make proselytes and build churches," he would not pretend that he was induced to this by religious motives merely. That would " border very near upon that damnable sin of hypocrisy and falsehood, from the schools of which he was endeavoring to bring over as many as he should be able by the utmost pains and assiduity." To them he dwelt mainly upon the unpleasantness of his personal position, and the folly of this ridiculous vain people " of Brooklyn, who, from a ridiculous spirit of pride and emulation, were about to demolish a structure as sound and good as when first finished, that they might build one newer, larger, and probably *yellower* than a monstrous great unformed new one that looked like a barn, painted all over a very bright yellow, recently erected in Pomfret." To clerical friends he expressed his repugnance to saddling his estate already too much encumbered with an expense of perhaps two hundred pounds— and for what—to build an Independent meeting-house ! to furnish money for what could only be a considerable prejudice to the cause of their religion, and begged their utmost assistance from principle. Presbyterianism, he averred, so abhorrent to the true principles of the English Constitution that he considered the man who endeavored by every mild and moderate method to propagate the worship of the Church of England, as aiming at a very great national service. In a very able letter addressed to the Bishop of Bangor—his former classmate at Oxford—he declared that " the ministry could not take a more effectual step to humble the overgrown pride of the Independents in these Colonies (who, notwithstanding their much vaunted loyalty, would very gladly exchange monarchy for a republic, so very compatible with their religious system), than to encourage the growth of the church," and he adjured all having any influence with Bishops or dignitaries to endeavor to procure an order from his Majesty, exempting all churchmen "from the shameful necessity of contributing to the support of dissenting worship." These pleas and representations secured from the Venerable Society the promise of aid in the support of a minister, and various sums of money for the church edifice. A hundred pounds was given by Malbone, ten pounds by Dr. Walton and smaller sums by others. An eligible building site on the Adams tract, south of Malbone's land, was given by Azariah Adams. So expeditious were the movements of the churchmen, that before the middle of November, Malbone had already executed a plan for a building, and made arrangements for providing materials.

This unexpected departure and revolt, and the prospect of an Episcopal house of worship, only stimulated the zeal of the friends of the parish meeting-house. Great efforts were made to bring the neutral and wavering to a decision, the leaders of each party offering to pay the building-rate of such poor persons as should declare in its favor. The decisive vote was taken Feb. 6, 1770, "and there were seventy-two voted to build and twenty-one lawful voters against it." It was also voted at a subsequent meeting, that the meeting-house should be built by a rate upon the previous tax-list. The injustice of this attempt to extort a building-rate from the churchmen enlisted public sympathy in their favor, and some of the leading men in the society joined with Malbone in protesting against it. From neighboring towns he received aid and support. Residents of Plainfield and Canterbury, alienated from their own churches by bitter religious dissensions gave him their names and influence, so that with a strong party to uphold him he thus appealed to the General Court for relief and exemption :—

"Your petitioners, desirous of worshipping God in public according to their own sentiments and the direction of their consciences, in the beginning of October, 1769, did assemble themselves together, and enter into engagements for building within said parish of Brooklyn, a house of worship according to the model of the Church of England, and for supplying the same with a minister duly qualified, and have carried the same into execution, so that public worship will be performed therein in a few months. Public meeting-house is of sufficient dimensions and with some few repairs would make a good and decent house; that soon after their purpose was known the inhabitants of Brooklyn, at a society meeting, held Feb. 6, 1770, did vote that said meeting-house should be pulled down and a new one erected, the expense to be paid by an assessment of the parish ; and to precipitate the transaction the society voted on March 9, That the assessment should be completed according to the list of ratable estates given in the September previous, although the said tax by said vote is not made payable till the first of Dec., 1770, by which illegal and unprecedented act, it is manifest that the whole was passed with a design to include such of your petitioners as belonged to Brooklyn in the taxation, although the church should before that time be erected in Brooklyn, and themselves excused by colony statute. Whereupon your memorialists pray, that on condition the church intended to be built shall be by them built, so that public worship be performed at or before the said first day of Dec., they may stand acquitted and discharged from said tax.

Godfrey Malbone.	John Allyn.	Jonathan Wheeler.
Joseph Hubbard.	John Wheeler.	Jacob Geer.
Jerre Cleveland.	Leonard Cady.	William Walton.
Timothy Lowe.	Noah Adams.	Jonas Cleveland.
Jedidiah Ashcroft, Sen.	Henry Cady.	Jabez Allyn.
Ahaziah Adams.	Thomas Adams.	Nehemiah Adams.
Jacob Staple.	Isaac Adams.	Benjamin Cady.
Daniel McCloud.	Samuel Adams.	John Ashcraft.
Caleb Spalding.	Elisha Adams.	Seth Sabin.
Benjamin Jewett.	James Darbe, Jun.	James Eldridge.

Subscribers adjacent to Brooklyn, united in building a church, recommend the petition as reasonable and fit to be granted.

John Pellet.	William Pellet.	Jonathan Downing.
John Tyler.	David Hide.	Caleb Faulkner.
Zebulon Tyler.	Asa Stevens.	Abijah Cady.
Samuel Adams.	Robert Durkee.	Edward Cleveland.
John Aplin.	Richard Smith.	Richard Butts.
Timothy Adams.	Thomas Pellet.	Dudley Wade.
Philemon Holt.	David Pellet.	Samuel Cleveland.
Phineas Tyler.	Joseph Pellet.	Jedidiah Ashcroft, Jun.
Peter Lort.	Morgan Carmans.	

April 10, 1770."

Consideration of this memorial was deferred until October, when it was opposed by Thomas Williams in behalf of the society. Relief was granted to Malbone, as an acknowledged churchman, but denied to his associates, from lack of confidence in the sincerity of their motives.

Meanwhile the rival edifices were in progress. A committee from the County Court, summoned by Joseph Scarborough, and waited upon by Daniel Tyler and Seth Paine, affixed for the society a building spot on the Green, a few rods southeast of the old meeting-house —"its front foreside facing the road." Mr. Daniel Tyler, the supervisor of the first house, again served as master-builder. His experience and judgment, aided perhaps by the pungent strictures of Colonel Malbone, enabled him to construct an edifice far less amenable to criticism than the Pomfret model—pronounced by common consent "a very genteel meeting-house." It was of ample size and graceful proportions, with a convenient porch and handsome steeple, built at their own expense by Daniel Tyler and others. A special vote provided "that our new meeting-house be colored *white*." Five seats eleven feet long were ranged each side the broad alley. The remainder of the floor was occupied by capacious pews. "Forty-three persons that pay the greatest rates that are on that list, which contains no man's poll and ratable estate than what was under their immediate care and occupancy," were allowed the floor to build pews on. The top of the floor of the wall pews was to be nine inches above the top of the floor of the house, that of the body pews to be four-and a-half inches above the same ; all to be neatly finished with banisters. A competent committee was appointed to decide upon the builders of these pews—viz. : Thomas Williams, Daniel Tyler, Seth Paine, Colonel Putnam, Deacon Scarborough, Captain Pierce, Joseph Holland, Samuel Williams, Sen. and Junior. These gentlemen with the society's committee and the pastor were to determine "where each pew as well as the minister's and pulpit should be." By a bequest from Mr. Joseph Scarborough, who died before the house was completed, a bell was provided and hung—the second in the county. Private enterprise placed a convenient clock in the steeple. The progressive spirit of the Brooklyn people was further manifested by their voting, "That an Eleclarick Rod may be set up at the new meeting-house, provided it be done without cost to the society." This house was probably occupied in the summer of 1771, but there is no record of any especial observance of its opening. The formal dedication of church edifices was one of the Papal practices long eschewed by Dissenting churches. The society showed its regard for the meeting-house so hardly obtained by entrusting its care to its most honored public citizen, voting—

"That Colonel Putnam take care of the new meeting-house and ring the bell at three pounds a year."

When the Colonel went to the war, his minister took his place as bell ringer. Only the first men in the society were deemed worthy of such an honor. It was ordered "that the bell should be rung on Sabbaths, Fasts, Thanksgivings and lectures, as was customary in other places where they have bells, also at twelve at noon and nine at night."

The Malbone Church, as it was commonly called, was completed in advance of its rival. It was a neat, unpretentious structure, closely copying its namesake—Trinity Church, of Newport—in its interior arrangement. To prepare his proselytes for participation in the church service, of which he avowed "they were as ignorant as so many of the Iroquois," Malbone himself invaded "the sacred office of priesthood," conducting worship in his own house till the church was ready. The novelty of the service attracted many hearers. The Rev. John Tyler, church missionary at Norwich, ever ready to forward the work of church extension in Eastern Connecticut, preached in Ashcroft's house, in February, to a number of most attentive hearers. April 12, 1771, he officiated at the public opening of the new church edifice. The occasion was felt to be one of unusual interest and importance, confirming and establishing the worship of the Episcopal Church in a section of country long given over to Dissenters. It was also memorable as the first formal dedication service held in Windham County. The Rev. Samuel Peters, church missionary at Hebron, assisted in the service. The sermon, by Mr. Tyler, very appropriately discussed "the Sanctity of a Christian Temple," and offered many sound and scriptural reasons for its outward and visible consecration. Public services on the following Sabbath were conducted by Mr. Tyler, and on various other occasions. No minister was procured till September, when Mr. Richard Mosely offered his services. He had been chaplain in the British Naval service, and brought with him letters from some of Malbone's Boston friends, but no clerical endorsement. His agreeable manners won the favor of Col. Malbone, who retained him in charge throughout the winter, although Dr. Caner and other Boston clergymen declined to sanction his appointment. Notwithstanding their disapproval Mr. Mosely became very popular, and not only conducted the regular service in Trinity Church, but preached and lectured in Plainfield and Canterbury, having "a great audience each time." The popularity of Malbone's minister, and the freedom and openness of his manners, naturally excited much remark and criticism. The ancient church and ecclesiastic society of Brooklyn had been greatly disturbed by the establishment of this English church and the number of proselytes it had secured. The vigorous opposition and stinging sarcasms of Col. Malbone had excited much bitterness, and predisposed them to severity of judgment. Local wits had tried to meet him with similar weapons. The ceremonials at the opening of the church edifice and at the christening of the first child had been ridiculed in sprightly doggerel, but now more earnest action was demanded. They had heard much of the corruption of the Church of England, and the disreputable character and lives of many of its clergy, and here was one officiating in their own parish, and drawing great numbers to hear him, who, it was whispered, was not even endorsed by his own church, and whose ministerial standing and qualifications were extremely doubtful. As the legal censors of religious order and public morality, the committee of the society felt it their duty to inquire into the matter, and accordingly called at the house of Colonel Malbone. That gentleman, who was apprized in advance of their coming, received them with great calmness and composure, and "suffered them to give full discharge of their embassy," which was, he reports, "to inspect Mosely's letters of orders, and find by what right he had placed him as minister." Col. Malbone expressed his entire willingness to satisfy them, provided they would sign a paper he had prepared for them—a most absurd document, setting forth in inflated, ridiculous and Quixotic terms their authority and power, as committee of the society of Brooklyn, town of Pomfret, county of Windham, and colony of Connecticut, for the inspection and transaction of religious concerns, and preventing every possibility of chicanery, fraud, or collusion in those who had seceded from their Independent Congregational meeting," &c. They indignantly refused to sign, Malbone refused to gratify them on any other terms, and "away they went," he writes, "like fools as they came," threatening "vengeance, fire and fagot," and refrained thenceforward from further interference with one so furnished with offensive and defensive weapons.

Mr. Mosely somewhat reluctantly left the field in April, declaring that every man in the parish would gladly have retained him, and it may be added that his subsequent career justified the suspicions of his ministerial unfitness. His successor, Rev. Daniel Fogg, received upon recommendation of clergymen in Boston, in May, 1772, was a man of very different antecedents and character, sober, quiet, discreet and devout. Devoting himself diligently to his pastoral duties, he soon brought his motley flock into more regular order and discipline, and won the esteem and confidence of all. About twenty-five families were enrolled as his parishioners. A stipend of thirty pounds a year was allowed by the English Missionary Society, and a similar amount raised by his people. The "Malbone Church," thus comfortably settled and sustained, pursued its way quietly, slowly increasing in numbers, and suffering no farther inconvenience than occasional trifling " distrainments " upon some of its members.

With all its interest in ecclesiastic and public affairs, Pomfret was not unmindful of its early literary aspirations. The United Library Association retained its hold on popular favor. As older members passed away their places were filled by others. At a meeting of the proprietors of the Library, at the house of Col. Ebenezer Williams, March 20, 1766, Rev. Daniel Ripley was chosen moderator. The society then voted, viz.:—

" 1.   To admit as members of said company the following persons, viz., Nathaniel Carpenter, Samuel Dana, Sen., Dea. Jonathan Dresser, Abijah Williams, Isaac Sabin, Joseph Scarborough, Nathan Frink, Dr. William Walton, Samuel Wilson, Dea. Edward Ruggles.
  2.   To admit Joseph Griffin, instead of John Davison, moved out of town, of whom said Griffin bought his right, as appears by certificate.
  3.   To admit Daniel Waldo to a right, instead of Jonathan Waldo, of whom he purchased said right, as appears by certificate.
  4.   To admit Ensign Samuel Sumner, instead of Joseph Bowman.
  5.   To admit Mr. Ebenezer Weeks to a right in ye Library, instead of William Prince.
  6.   To recall ye vote past on June 10, 1756, and to receive into ye Library, Chambers' Dictionary and Colmett's Ditto.
  7.   That Col. Williams be ye Library-keeper."

Lieut. Joshua Grosvenor, Simon Cotton, Simeon Sessions, William Sabin, Elijah Williams, John Grosvenor, Elijah Dana and Phinehas

Davison were also admitted members of the company in following years. Pope's Essay on Man, the Life of Peter the Great, and Bishop Kidder's Demonstrations of the Messiah were added to the Library. In 1775, a library association was formed in Brooklyn society, and a hundred volumes procured for the foundation of a library.

Roads and bridges demanded the usual care and legislation. In 1770, Pomfret joined with Killingly in rebuilding what was known as "Danielson's Bridge"—Colonel Putnam, Seth Paine, county surveyor, and Samuel Williams, committee. In the following year, "Cargill's Bridge" was rebuilt—John Grosvenor, Samuel Perrin and Benjamin Cargill, committee. Putnam was foremost in a movement for procuring a new road through Pomfret to Norwich and New Haven, but failed to secure it. An attempt to lay out a more direct route from Ashford's east line to Cargill's Bridge was equally unsuccessful. Notwithstanding all the pains taken to secure easy communication with Providence, rendered so needful by intimate business and social relations, the road thither was still very stony and rough, and the journey laborious. So late as 1776, when Mr. S. Thurber drove over it in the first chaise, he "could not ride out of a slow walk but very little of the way, and was near two days in going." Pomfret was much interested in a project for deepening the channel of the Quinebaug, so as to make it passable for boats, Ebenezer and John Grosvenor petitioning with citizens of other towns for this object. One of the first dams upon the Quinebaug was accomplished by Jabez Allen, near the mouth of Beaver's Brook, about 1770. A large grist-mill was here erected by him, and carried on successfully for a few years. A change of county bounds or county seat was one of the public questions in which Pomfret was deeply concerned. A very earnest meeting was held at the house of Colonel Israel Putnam, Feb. 11, 1771, "to consult in regard to some new bound for the county." Delegates from Woodstock, Killingly, Thompson Parish, Plainfield, Canterbury, Ashford, and Union discussed the situation with much spirit, but as both Pomfret and Woodstock aspired to the shireship, and times were unpropitious for any important change, no movement was undertaken.

The taverns of Pomfret enjoyed a high repute during these years with such noted landlords as Putnam, Ebenezer Grosvenor, James Ingalls, Simon Cotton, William Sumner and Joseph Abbott. In these stirring times these resorts were much frequented, and rum and debate flowed with equal freedom. A grocery store opened in Pomfret, in 1762, by Joseph Carter, of Canterbury, enabled families to procure comfortable supplies of vital necessaries. Beside all that was drunk on the premises, or paid for upon delivery, he had *charged* in his first fortnight more than twenty-five gallons of West India rum. Some families carried away each several gallons. A single gallon usually sufficed Rev. Mr. Whitney. This excessive drinking may have contributed to keep Pomfret's physicians in practice. Dr. Lord was handsomely sustained in Abington; Dr. Walton had his friends and patients in Brooklyn and Killingly; and old Dr. Weld ministered to the sick in Pomfret society. Dr. David Hall removed to Vermont, after the loss of his wife and several children. He was succeeded in practice by Albigence, son of Zechariah Waldo, a young man of uncommon energy and promise, who had studied for the profession with Dr. John Spalding of Canterbury. Nathan Frink, as King's attorney, still practiced law in Pomfret and adjoining towns. Thomas, son of John Grosvenor, Esq., after graduation from Yale College in 1765, and preparatory legal studies, also opened a law office on Pomfret street. The young men of this town were still emulous for collegiate education, and its three ministers were much engaged in fitting them for admission. It will be remembered that *eight* Pomfret boys were graduated from Yale in 1759. In 1760, Joseph Dana was graduated; in 1761, John and Ephraim Avery and Jesse Goodell; in 1766, Asa H. Lyon; in 1767, Elisha Williams; in 1769, Daniel Grosvenor; in 1770, Joseph Pope was graduated from Harvard College. It is said that a lady visitant from Massachusetts querying for what purpose they were training so many young men, was told that they were to be sent as missionaries to that State, and it so chanced that very many of them *did* settle as ministers there, and filled positions of honor and usefulness. One Pomfret youth, not a college graduate, engaged in most useful missionary work in Connecticut. Willard, son of Benjamin Hubbard, succeeded Robert Clelland in teaching Mohegan children about 1764, and continued for many years in this most difficult and thankless service. A small salary was allowed by the English Missionary Society, insufficient for the support of his family even by the addition of his own labor out of school-hours, and it was with great difficulty and many urgent appeals that he obtained relief from the Assembly. He was often obliged to supply the hungry children with bread as well as instruction, and to repair with his own hands and means the dilapidated school-house, nor were the apparent results commensurate with the labor and self-sacrifice.

Little of special note occurred in Abington Parish during this period. Rev. David Ripley officiated to public acceptance, and taught a grammar school in his own house till disabled by bodily infirmity. Parochial and school affairs were wholly managed by competent committees. John Holbrook, Amasa Sessions, William Osgood, James Ingalls, Dr. Lord, and many other Abington residents were active in general town affairs.

3

Much of its land was still held by descendants of the original proprietors. Nine hundred acres originally laid out to Thomas Mowry, descended to Miss Elizabeth Pierpont, of Boston, who took personal possession after her marriage with Captain Peter Cunningham, building a substantial dwelling-house near the Mashamoquet. Part of this land was already laid out in farms and occupied by Benjamin Craft and other tenants. Land in the south part of the society, afterwards known as Jericho, was occupied prior to 1760, by descendants of William Sharpe. The venerable Nathaniel Sessions, long the last survivor of the first settlers of Pomfret, died in 1771. The *Providence Gazette* gives this notice :—

" Sept. 25. Died, at Pomfret, Conn., Nathaniel Sessions, in the ninety-sixth year of his age—father of Hon. Darius Sessions, of Providence, Deputy-Governor—one of the first settlers in Pomfret, in 1704 : the first that opened a cart road through the woods from Connecticut to Providence in 1721, and transported the first cart-load of West India goods from Providence thither. His wife died about three months before him with whom he had lived sixty-five years, had nine sons and three daughters. Could repeat the New Testament, Psalms and most of the moral and practical writings of the Old Testament, the greater part of which he committed to memory after he was eighty, from fear that he should be deprived of his eye-sight, which happened two years before his death. A sober man and useful member of society."

The *Worcester Spy*, July 19, 1773, thus records the death of another valued resident of Pomfret :—

" On Saturday last, departed this life in a sudden and affecting manner, the very amiable consort of the Rev. Aaron Putnam, of Pomfret, in the thirty-sixth year of her age. She had been unwell for some years, and for the promoting of health had been riding out a little way, and now returning back she desired Mr. Putnam to stop the chaise and pick her some useful herbs which she observed as they were passing. Accordingly, apprehending no danger, he got out of the chaise and was doing as she proposed, at which time the horse in the carriage took some start and running with one wheel over a rock, she was thrown out of the chaise, which gave her such a shock, as proved her death in about three hours space. She was a daughter of Rev. David Hall, of Sutton. From her very early years a professor of godliness, and of a very serious and exemplary deportment, a person of distinguishing endowment, a good wife, a tender and indulgent mother, one beloved by her acquaintances abroad and by the people among whom she lived.
She hath left her husband in deep affliction and sorrow for his great loss; hath also left three young children. On the next (being Lord's) day, her remains were decently interred a little before sunset. The Rev. Mr. Whitney, of Brooklyn parish, delivered at Pomfret, on that day, two very suitable discourses, that in the afternoon more particularly adapted to the mournful occasion."

Though Pomfret was in many respects so highly favored, she could not retain her increase. Her best land was held by descendants of early settlers and could not easily be purchased. Large families were the fashion. It is said that in the households of three neighbors, Captain Nathaniel Clark, Capt. Stephen Keyes and Ebenezer Grosvenor, there were thirty-three children growing up. To provide food for so many mouths and work for so many hands, was sometimes a difficult matter. New countries were opening where land was cheap and facilities for settlement more abundant. As early as 1735, Deacon Samuel Sumner, Isaac Dana and others from Pomfret, had attempted to purchase a township in the Equivalent Lands. In 1761, Dana received a patent from Governor Wentworth for a township in the New Hampshire Grants on right of land granted to John White. This land was laid out as the township of Pomfret. Its first settler was Benjamin Durkee, with wife and five children, journeying thither from its Connecticut namesake.

II.

ASHFORD. GENERAL TOWN AFFAIRS. WESTFORD SOCIETY. FIRST BAPTIST CHURCH. EASTFORD SOCIETY. CORBIN LAND CLAIM.

ASHFORD, in 1760, was prominent among Windham County townships. Its position on one of the great thoroughfares of the country brought it into constant communication with Boston, Hartford, and other business centres, and kept it awake and stirring. It was especially noted for high military spirit and keen interest in public affairs, and no town was more ready to speak its mind and bear its part whenever occasion demanded. Descendants of many of the first settlers now filled the places of their fathers, and new families of respectability and influence had established themselves in various localities, and identified themselves with the interests of the town. Ebenezer Byles, upon coming of age, settled about a mile west of Ashford Green, on land purchased in 1726 by Josiah Byles of Boston. William Knowlton of Boxford, a relative of Robert Knowlton, purchased a farm of four hundred acres in the west part of Ashford, divided in time between his sons Daniel and Thomas, who, after serving brilliantly in the French War, engaged with equal ardor in cultivating their land and discharging the ordinary civil and military duties of good citizens at that period. Ephraim Lyon removed from Woodstock to the east part of the town, and was greatly esteemed as a man of shrewdness and sound judgment. Daniel Dow of Voluntown, settled north of the Green, with a rising family of great promise. David Bolles of New London, established himself near the present Eastford village, with a license to exercise "the art and mystery of tanning leather," and great skill and experience in working up the same into serviceable shoes. Stephen Keyes, Theophilus Clark and Amos Babcock were admitted freemen prior to 1760. Samuel Woodcock of Dedham, succeeded to the farm once held by Jacob Parker; Jedidiah Dana to that of John Paine. The remaining part of the Stoddard Tract fell to Martha, daughter of Anthony Stoddard, and wife of Captain John Stevens of Boston, who, in 1757, laid it out and divided it into thirty-one lots or farms, which were sold to John Chapin, Abel Simmons, James Parker, Robert Snow and others. A large and valuable farm near the site of the present Phœnixville, known as the Beaver Dam farm, was retained and occupied by Captain and Mrs. Stevens, and brought under very high cultivation. President Stiles, journeying through Ashford, in 1764, was very much interested in Captain Stevens's agricultural operations. He reported him as holding six thousand acres of land in the town. He had thirty acres of hemp growing tended by one man, and employed thirty hands in pulling-time. He expected to harvest twenty tons of hemp and two hundred bushels of seeds. The people of Ashford testified their respect for their distinguished residents by voting, that Capt. John Stevens and his family have liberty to sit in the ministerial pew during the town's pleasure. Captain Benjamin Sumner, Captain Elisha Wales, Elijah Whiton and Amos Babcock were prominent men in town. The latter had "a shop," and engaged quite extensively in trade. Three young physicians—Doctors Joseph Palmer, Nehemiah Howe and Thomas Huntington—cared for the bodily health of the town. The various tavern-keepers licensed in 1762 were Benjamin Sumner, Joseph Palmer, Benjamin Clark, Jedidiah Fay, Ezra Smith, Samuel Eastman and Elijah Babcock. Mills were run by Solomon Mason and others.

Town affairs were managed with the usual formalities. At the annual town meeting, December 1, 1760, Amos Babcock was chosen moderator and first selectman; Ebenezer Byles, Jedidiah Dana, Captain Benjamin Sumner and Ezra Smith, the remaining selectmen; Mr. Byles, town clerk and treasurer; Ezekiel Tiffany, constable and clerk for the west end of the town; Samuel Holmes, constable and collector for the middle of the town; Benjamin Russel, constable and collector for the east end of the town, and also for colony rates; Timothy Eastman, Josiah Spalding, Benjamin Carpenter, Amasa Watkins, Samuel Allen, Jedidiah Dana, Stephen Abbot, John Bicknell, Benjamin Walker, Jonathan Chaffee, Job Tyler, Benjamin Clark, David Chaffee, William Preston, surveyors of highways; Jonathan Burnham, Josiah Eaton, fence-viewers; Benjamin Clark, Josiah Holmes, Benjamin Russel, Jedidiah Blanchard, Asaph Smith, listers; Nehemiah Smith, Jonathan Burnham, grand-jurors; Josiah Rogers, Stephen Snow, William Chub, tithing-men; Benjamin Russel, brander, pound-keeper and collector of excise; Caleb Hende and Josiah Chaffee, branders and pound-keepers; Samuel Snow, sealer of weights and measures; Asaph Smith, sealer of leather.

Though in the main thrifty and prosperous, Ashford still suffered from "providential visitations" of drought and frost, together with land disputes and religious dissensions. The excellent town clerk, Ebenezer Byles, jots down among his records some meteorological items which elucidate the former phenomena:—

"The 5th day of May, 1761—a very stormy day of snow, an awful sight, the trees green and the ground white; the 6th day, the trees in the blow and the fields covered with snow.

The 19th day of May, 1763, a bad storm of hail and rain and very cold, following which froze ye ground and puddles of water.

The 17th day of October, 1763, it snowed, and ye 18th in ye morning the trees and the ground were all covered with ice and snow, which made it look like ye dead of winter."

Religious dissensions were only heightened by the settlement of Rev. Timothy Allen as minister of the town. A devout Christian and a fervent and eloquent speaker, he was erratic, visionary and imprudent in speech and conduct. Earnest efforts were now made for the division of the town into religious societies. "Two months preaching in the winter paid out of the common stock" emboldened the western inhabitants to ask for full society privileges. "The use of their whole ministerial rate to maintain preaching by themselves," granted by the town, only made them more anxious to gain liberty to dispose of it as they pleased. The "great and almost impossible difficulties" of attending worship in the distant centre incited the eastern inhabitants to join in the struggle for territorial division. At the town meeting, April, 1762, Captain Benjamin Sumner was chosen moderator, and after a long and vehement discussion it was voted by a majority of one, That the town will divide in three equal societies. A year later it was further voted, "That each part shall have one-third of all the public money." Captain Sumner, Edward Tiffany, Benjamin Russel, Amos Babcock, Jedidiah Dana, Captain Benjamin Clark and Jedidiah Fay, Samuel Knox and Ezra Smith were appointed a committee "to consult and advise in what form it was best to divide," who agreed and concluded, March, 1764, " that the town shall be divided in the following manner," i. e. :—

"That the east part shall have one-third part of said town for quantity set off to them for an ecclesiastic society, which shall extend west and bound on Bigelow River, provided there is one-third part on the east side of said river, and that the northwest part shall extend from the northwest corner of said township five and one-fourth miles south on the west line of said town, from thence a strait line to the crotch of Mount Hope River, and thence a strait line to John Dimmock's south line, where said line crosses Bigelow River, thence north on said Bigelow River to Union line, and the remaining part remain to the middle society."

As usual in such cases this decision satisfied no one, and all parties hastened to the General Assembly with their objections. Sixty-seven residents of the central and eastern sections, including such men as

Joseph Snow, Thomas Knowlton, Edward Byles, Ebenezer Eaton, Philip Squire, Daniel Dow, Joshua Kendall, Zebulon Marcy, Josiah Spalding and Ephraim Lyon declared :—

"1. That the form of the proposed new society is such that said old society will be seven miles in length and three in width, and that the meeting-house will be left within one mile of the east end, so we shall be put to the expense of building a new one.

2. By the manner of being done at the expense of town. We think it quite sufficient to bear our own expenses and not those of others.

3. For that we are small and poor, being the oldest part of the town, and our land almost all under improvement and so not capable of growing much better by improvement; are not quite four thousand pounds on the list, and would further suggest that the votes of the town in choosing committee to make division, in accepting reports and in choosing agents to prefer a memorial, &c., ought not to have any influence in the affair, because it appears that about two-thirds of the town in the two ends move jointly at one time to be made two societies, and what cante or wont they do as a town towards crowding us, the minor part, into a corner and loading us with cost unless your Honors interfere, and we think the whole town hardly able to bear the necessary expenses by reason of the bitter effects that we yet forcibly feel of a long and tedious war, scorching droughts, blasting frosts, and many strong and unhappy misfortunes which of late befel us, and we would farther suggest that the vote of the town was delayed till near night while many of the voters were retired and obtained but by *one* majority. We pray you to dismiss the memorial, for if it is done, it will make such an uneasiness and so discourage and impoverish us, that the whole design thereof will be defeated. October, 1764."

The western inhabitants objected to the report, in that—

"1. The doings of said committee were not equal. The land in northwest section is not one-third of the town by more than a thousand acres, and some thousands of it are utterly unfit for settlement and destitute of inhabitants.

2. Said northwest society not equal as to list.

3. We think the addition from Willington prayed for will not make it equal to the other societies, nor to the necessary charges of an ecclesiastic society, by reason of the badness of the land and smallness of the list of the inhabitants. Choose rather to enjoy our privileges in one ecclesiastic society but are willing to have a committee sent as prayed for.

Elijah Whiton.	Benjamin Chaffee.	Jedidiah Blanchard.
Abijah Brooks.	Ebenezer Walker.	Joseph Whiton.
Timothy Dimock.	Benjamin Walker.	James Whiton.
Simeon Smith.	John Ware.	Zeph. Davison.
Josiah Rogers.	Ezra Smith.	Christopher Davison.
Samuel Blanchard.	Edmond Drummer.	John Smith.
Samuel Mosely.	Samuel Eastman.	William Preston.
Medinah Preston.	Peter Eastman.	James Atwell.

Oct. 5, 1764."

The "addition from Willington" referred to a petition just presented by some twenty subscribers, inhabitants of the eastern part of that town formerly taken from Ashford, who being very remote from the public worship of God, desired to be joined with the northwest of Ashford in a society. This request was refused and consideration of the other memorials deferred till the following spring, when, upon farther petition from Elijah Whiton and others, Zebulon West, Erastus Wolcott and William Pitkin were appointed a committee to repair to Ashford, view and report. In this task they were aided by the subjoined paper, submitted to them by two clear-headed and public-spirited *women*, residents of northwest Ashford, who, impatient of the long delay, felt moved to state succinctly the " Reasons to be set off " as follows :—

" 1. Our great distance from meeting-house.
2. Large number of inhabitence.
3. Meeting-house too small.
4. No settled minister.
5. Broken and divided surcurmstances which it is not likely can be settled till the town is divided.
6. The town's refusing to do anything about dividing or to let the inhabitences in the northwest part have any preaching as they have done heretofore.
7. Our not taking but one-third of the land and about one-fourth of list.
8. That every person in our place will be considerably nearer to meeting.
9. The town has manifested a necessity for division for eleven years past, as appears by their votes.
10. They have not opposed the new part being set off by anything they have done this spring, they have been warned with the plan and memorial and not opposed it. [*Note.*—We don't know that any person is against a society being set off in the northwest of the town, but only that some don't like this shape, and some another, and those that oppose this plan yet allow that the new part must be a society, even Captain Fay himself and Mr. Walker, the most active opposers of this plan, and the difficult surcurmstances of the town require a division, in which all parties seem to agree."]

These reasons were effectual. The committee after due survey reported that they found the town to contain 40,000 acres of land ; list £13,700. The west society limits would include 13,300 acres, 80 families, £3,500. Families live five, six and seven miles from the town meeting-house, and all very remote from any place of worship, and roads generally bad, and considered it reasonable and expedient that a new society be formed. The report was accepted and a bill granted in October, 1765, erecting Westford Society according to the bounds prescribed by the town's committee, although an attempt was made by Robert Knowlton to include the strip of land "left out on the south."

The rejoicing inhabitants hastened to improve their new privileges. Their first society meeting was held Nov. 23, 1765, at the house of Captain Ichabod Ward, a distant relative of the William Ward so prominent in the early history of Ashford. Benjamin Walker was chosen moderator; Ezra Smith, Manasseh Farnum and Samuel Eastman, committee ; Ezekiel Tiffany, collector. It was agreed to hold society meetings at different private houses, warnings for meetings "to be set up at Solomon Mason's mills and Zephaniah Davison's shop." Dec. 9, it was voted to build a meeting-house, and hire preaching ; to raise a tax of twopence to pay for preaching ; that the meetings should begin the first Sabbath of April ; that Esquire Whiton should procure a minister, and Ebenezer Dimmock, Christopher Davison, Manasseh Farnum and Joseph Barney be a committee to count the cost. A minister was procured according to vote—the

society further voting to meet at Captain Ward's for divine worship
during his pleasure. June 9, it was voted " to choose a committee of
three able and judicious men to fix a place for the meeting-house, also
five more, *i. e.*, Ezra Smith, Samuel Eastman, Benjamin Walker,
Christopher Davison and Samuel Knox, to notify the first and get
them out." By their efforts the Court appointed Nehemiah Lyon of
Woodstock, Prince Tracy of Windham, and John Curtis of Canterbury, who selected a spot near the centre of the society on land
offered by Captain Ward, north of his residence, west side of the
highway leading to Union, "for the public benefit and use of Westford
Society for a meeting-house green, so long as said society should want
it for said use." Negotiations were then opened with certain proprietors in Brimfield, and a convenient meeting-house frame purchased
for thirty pounds, provided the same could be taken down without
damage. Esquire Whiton was now chosen treasurer, a committee
appointed to receive a deed of the meeting-house green from Capt.
Ward, and another to take oversight of the building. Very particular
instructions were given as to the number, size, price and quality of
nails, shingles and clapboards. March 13, 1767, voted that said
society would dig in the ground a suitable depth and fill the same
with stone for laying the foundation of the meeting-house thereon;
June 2, that the meeting-house frame purchased in Brimfield should
be brought to Westford by June 13. This being safely accomplished,
its re-raising was next in order. The character of the *liquor* deemed
needful on this important occasion called out as much discussion as
the fitness of a ministerial candidate. It was first voted "to have gin
to raise the frame with—meeting-house committee to provide gin," but
considering *quantity* of more consequence than quality, it was afterwards decided to provide one barrel of rum, and one quarter of a
barrel of sugar for the raising said frame—Ensign Walker to provide
the same, and money taken out of the treasury to buy said rum and
sugar. It was further stipulated, that West India rum be procured.
Under this potent stimulant the meeting-house was raised without
apparent accident, and hurried on to completion, workmen being
allowed two shillings and sixpence per day, they victualing themselves,
and two shillings during the winter.

After hearing several " supplies," Ebenezer Martin of Canada Parish,
was invited to preach for the winter. A committee was now chosen
to inquire into his character and temporal circumstances, and take
advice of the Reverend Association as to the propriety of giving him
a call. Reports proving favorable, February 11, 1768, was set apart
as a day of solemn fasting and prayer in order to the gathering of a
church and calling of a minister. Rev. Gideon Noble of Willington,

conducted the service, assisted by Deacon Nathaniel Loomis, and Deacons Wright and Dana from the old Ashford church. A suitable covenant was presented and subscribed in the following order :—James Ould, Ezekiel Tiffany, Ezekiel Holt, Elijah Whiton, Joseph Barney, Ezra Smith, James Whiton, Joseph Whiton, Benjamin Walker, Thomas Chapman, Manasseh Farnum, John Smith, Jonathan Abbe, Josiah Chaffee. At a church meeting four days later it was voted to call the Rev. Mr. Ebenezer Martin to settle in the gospel ministry in this place, at which time the covenant was probably signed by the pastor elect and the following brethren, viz. : Joseph Whiton, David Chaffee, Ebenezer Walker, Christopher Davison and Jonathan Chaffee. The wives of many of these brethren—together with Stephen Nott, Daniel Eldredge, Hezekiah Eldredge, Ichabod Ward, David Kendall and Jacob Fuller were ere long added, making a membership of fifty-five.

The society concurred in the call to Mr. Martin, offering sixty pounds salary, rising to seventy, paid half in money, half in produce, viz., wheat, Indian corn, oats, pork and beef. Twenty pounds in land and sixty pounds towards building a dwelling-house secured acceptance of the call, and, on June 15, he was ordained with the usual solemnities. Work on the meeting-house was slowly carried forward. The floor was laid during the year, and twenty pews were ordered, "as like the pews in the meeting-house at Union, as conveniently may be." Capt. Abijah Larned of Union, John Phelps and John Blygt of Stafford were chosen as a disinterested committee "to dignify and price the places for said pews." A large number of the inhabitants received liberty to build stables for their horses on the meeting-house green, provided they were "set so as not to encroach on any road." June 14, 1770, a meeting was held in the meeting-house, to hear the report of the pew committee. Each pew was to be occupied by two families. Forty inhabitants, highest on the list, were to draw said pews according to their list; build the pews and ceil up to the gallery girths. This report was accepted, and the pew-spots thus distributed :—

1. Benjamin Walker, Elijah Whiton.
2. Ebenezer Dimmock, Ichabod Ward.
3. Thomas Chapman, Ebenezer Walker.
4. Joseph Woodward, Zaccheus Hill.
5. Ezra Smith, Ebenezer Walker.
6. David Chaffee, William Thompson.
7. David Robbins, George Smith.
8. Adonijah Baker, Josiah Chaffee.
9. John Warren, Josiah Rogers.
10. Ezekiel Tiffany, Benjamin Chaffee.
11. Jedidiah Blanchard, Benjamin Walker, Jun.
12. William Henfield, James Whiton.
13. Samuel Eastman, Henry Works.

4

14.   James Averill, Job Tyler.
15.   Ezekiel Holt, David Chaffee.
16.   James Ould, Stephen Coye.
17.   Abijah Brooks, Simon Smith.
18.   Ephraim Walker, Jonathan Abbe.
19.   Jacob Fuller, William Preston.

The committee was now ordered to lay the gallery floor, and build a breastwork around the gallery and the fore seat, which being accomplished during another year, David Kendall was employed to sweep the meeting-house "twelve times the year ensuing for six shillings." The society would gladly have enlarged its borders by reannexing the strip ceded years before to Willington, but though many petitions were preferred by its residents, showing that the meeting-house in Westford would much more greatly commode them, they were unable to obtain a hearing.   Among newly arrived citizens bringing them additional strength was Stephen Nott, the father of sons of great promise, and Dr. Thomas Huntington of Lebanon, who proved a most valuable acquisition to society and town.

The inhabitants of the eastern section preferred to delay separation for a season, and shared in the numerous trials and difficulties that beset the first society, in consequence of the increasing number of Baptists and sectarians, and the great unpopularity of Mr. Allen.   Many of his own people declined to hear him preach or to pay for his support, and in attempting to supply the deficit by trading in land he became so involved that his creditors sent him to jail.   This unfortunate affair brought matters to a crisis.   A council was called which dismissed Mr. Allen from his pastorate, though clearing him from every serious charge.   Deacons Jedidiah Dana and John Wright were appointed a committee to supply the pulpit, and it was voted, "To settle a minister as soon as may be," but several years passed before such settlement was effected.   During this interval the church was greatly weakened and scattered, but still continued its efforts to secure a minister and preserve order.   Baptisms were administered from time to time by the neighboring ministers.   Days of fasting and prayer were held in 1766 and '68, "for direction and assistance in the affair of choosing a minister," and church and society at length happily united in choice of Rev. James Messinger of Wrentham, a graduate of Harvard College, who was installed into the pastorate Feb. 15, 1769.   Taught by painful experience the fallibility of ministers and councils the church had previously voted:—

"That this church do believe that the minister of a church has not power from Christ to negative the votes of his church, and we mean not to be subjected to any such power of a minister of the church, any former vote notwithstanding.

That in all cases hereafter we will not be holden to any council of other churches, but such as we shall choose ourselves mutually."

Fortunately in this instance these precautions proved superfluous. Mr. Messinger made no attempt to exercise undue authority, and by his wisdom and piety soon won the confidence of his people and was held in high repute as " a much beloved spiritual guide." Despite the political distractions of the times the church increased in numbers and regained something of its primitive standing. The venerable Isaac Kendall, elected deacon of the church with so much formality at its first organization, continued in office through all the changes and pastorates, and died Oct. 8, 1773, in the 88th year of his age, and fifty-second of his deaconship. Benjamin Sumner, one of the fathers of the town, Jedidiah Dana and John Wright also served as deacons. Deacon Elijah Whiton was dismissed to the church in Westford society.

Baptists had been numerous in Ashford for many years, but suffered greatly for lack of a local church organization. A few were connected with the Baptist Church of South Brimfield, others united with the church at West Woodstock. Amos Babcock and Abraham, son of Robert Knowlton, were among the most prominent of these early Baptists. A notable accession to the Baptist strength was David Bolles, a man of great religious fervor, belonging to a family long distinguished for devotion to Baptist principles and opposition to the church establishment of Connecticut. Other Baptists might obtain release from rate-paying by lodging certificates of their attendance upon some place of public worship, but he, like Backus and the more advanced of his brethren, " had been brought to a stop about paying so much regard to the laws as to give in certificates," and was soon involved in controversy with the town authorities. Two of his cows were seized and sold to pay rates for the minister, and then his household treasures were invaded. The shining array of pewter so dear to the heart of the housewife, was thrust into bags and carried off to the town-post in spite of the tears and remonstrances of Mrs. Bolles, but when put up for sale not a man had the face to bid for it, and the discomfited collector was forced to take it back to its owners with the insulting explanation, " that the pewter was such poor stuff nobody wanted it." His fellow sufferer, Abraham Knowlton, after paying rates for many years, freed himself from further extortions by turning out to the collector a new pair of *buckskin breeches*. The public notification that a pair of breeches were to be sold for a priest-tax, and their actual presentation at the town-post on the day appointed, called out such volleys of indignation and ridicule that no one dared thereafter to approach Mr. Knowlton with a rate-bill, and the buckskins served the purpose of a life-time certificate. It was probably during this period of sectarian strife and bitterness that some incident occurred which gave rise to the famous

" whipping story," thus reported by Barber in his Connecticut Historical Collections:—

" A concourse of people were assembled on the hill, in front of the meeting-house, to witness the punishment of a man who had been convicted of neglecting to go to meeting on the Sabbath for a period of three months. According to the existing law for such delinquency, the culprit was to be publicly whipped at the post. Just as the whip was about to be applied, a stranger on horseback appeared, rode-up to the crowd of spectators, and inquired for what purpose they were assembled. Being informed of the state of the case, the strange gentleman rose upright in his stirrups, and with emphasis, addressed the astonished multitude as follows:
'You men of Ashford serve God as if the *Devil* was in you! Do you think you can *whip* the grace of God into men? Christ will have none but volunteers.'
The people stared, while the speaker, probably not caring to be arraigned for contempt of court, put spurs to his horse, and was soon out of sight; nor was he ever more seen or heard of by the good people of Ashford."

This story like many other popular traditions cannot be authenticated. No law then or ever existed in Connecticut, prescribing the penalty of a public whipping for even total abstinence from meeting-going, and it may be doubted if any justice would dare enforce an illegal punishment. Details of the affair are conflicting and irreconcilable. *Two* men were arraigned, according to one version, one of whom evaded his share of the blows by means of a cloak dexterously thrown over him by Amos Babcock. A report of the whole transaction quickly traveled to Boston, and upon his next trip to the city, Mr. Babcock found himself quite a hero. His fellow-merchants greatly applauded his chivalrous interposition, and declaring that he should not wear " a whipped cloak," made up a purse and presented him with a new one. Another version gives but a single culprit and ascribes his relief to no less a person than Thomas Knowlton, who, observing in the warrant the omission of the usual clause requiring the stripes to be applied to the bare back, " threw his own overcoat over the shoulders of the victim whereby the torture was greatly mitigated." The mysterious visitant of Barber's narrative appearing and vanishing like the " phantom horseman " of romance is transformed upon closer inquiry into an eccentric citizen of Ashford, distinguished for bitter opposition to the standing order, while the party or parties receiving the whipping have become extremely mythical. These various reports are wholly traditional. No allusion to the circumstance has been found in ancient document or newspaper, and thus it is impossible to ascertain the real truth. That some opponent of the established church was whipped under aggravating circumstances, perhaps for resisting or reviling a rate collector, is highly probable. The invention of this story with its minutiæ of detail, and its universal acceptance in the community, would be almost as great a marvel as the whipping, but the bottom facts of the case will probaby never be recovered.

These collisions and extortions greatly weakened the old church of Ashford, and furnished a powerful argument for the Baptists, who, with increasing strength and numbers, were able to establish religious worship within the town borders. A Baptist Society was organized, July 15, 1774, and David Bolles, Josiah Rogers and William Whipple appointed committee "to receive and pay all money that shall be generously given towards maintaining and supporting a Baptist gospel minister." Another committee was chosen in February following, to select "the most proper place to build a meeting-house on." Land in the southwest part of the town was selected, and a committee "to be under the immediate direction of the Baptist Society," was authorized to receive all money and specie that should be given towards building a Baptist meeting-house. Abraham Knowlton, chairman of the committee, and clerk and treasurer of the society, made a liberal offering. His example was quickly followed by others, and soon an ample sum had been subscribed. Materials were procured, a frame raised and covered, so that by the first of June the house was ready for service. The leaders of the society, flushed with their success, had applied to President Manning, of Brown University, for a minister, who thus represented the field to Mr. Thomas Ustick, a young graduate of Brown, then teaching school in New York:—

"This start for a Baptist minister is a new thing, but they subscribed last week near five hundred pounds lawful money, towards building a new meeting-house. Town large and rich, am told that full one-third have declared for the Baptists, and should they get a man of abilities probably much above half the town will attend their meetings. The richest men are on our side, and say they believe in supporting a minister handsomely."

Mr. Ustick was unable to accept at once, and Mr. Ebenezer Lamson of Charlton, was apparently the first minister employed by the society. Arrangements for the transferrence of the church to Ashford, were now in progress. The ancient church in South Brimfield, after many trials and vicissitudes, had reorganized a few years previous upon a basis distasteful to its non-resident members, who now held a council, and in their turn enacted a new departure, viz:—

"STAFFORD, May ye 29th, 1775.
At a meeting of the First Baptist Church of Christ in South Brimfield, legally warned and met and opened by prayer—whereas there is a second church of the same Denomination lately built up in South Brimfield and a minister settled over them, and whereas many of this church consists of inhabitants in the towns of Ashford, Mansfield, and Willington, and for the conveniancy of meeting for worship on the Sabbath, and the question was put whether for the future the place for public meeting for worship should be at Ashford in general, where the new meeting-house now is, and that the

church for the future shall be known by the name of the Baptist Church of Christ in Ashford—voted in the affirmative.

John Wesson and Amos Babcock added to the committee. John Wesson chose church clerk."

How many members were transferred with the church is not recorded but probably not a large number. A part of its membership and both its deacons were non-residents. Public worship was instituted and carried on with a great deal of spirit and enjoyment, but it is doubtful if anything like "half the town" could attend their meetings. David Bolles and many of the Eastern Baptists still found it more convenient to resort to Woodstock. Mr. Ustick succeeded Mr. Lamson as soon as he was at liberty, and was welcomed as a young man of education and promise. At the second recorded "church meeting in the Baptist meeting-house in Ashford," Nov. 26, 1776, their former pastor, Elder Moulton, was present and served as moderator. It was voted to have Mr. Thomas Ustick supply our pulpit for six months, and an unsuccessful attempt was made to choose a deacon. The action of the church in changing its local habitation and name had been entirely independent in accordance with Baptist polity and practice, but now they felt desirous to receive fellowship and recognition from sister churches. Invitations to a conference were accordingly sent out, and, Feb. 19, 1777, a number of Baptist elders and delegates met with the Ashford church to confer as to its state, standing and regularity :—

" And after prayers for Divine direction, proceeded to choose Elder Elijah Codding, moderator, and brother Thomas Ustick, clerk. After mutual conference upon the original and present state and standing of the church, the delegates from the churches of Brimfield, Woodstock and Abington, upon the question whether the body of people that meet now at Ashford under the appellation of the Baptist church there, be a visible church of Christ—determined unanimously in the affirmative, viz : That in our opinion the said body are a visible church of Christ.

The delegates then proceeded in order to gain fellowship with the aforesaid church to query as followeth :—

1. Whether the church believed that it is their duty to search up such members as have absented from church duties for a considerable time, and mean as soon as may be to treat with such? To which the church consented.

2. Whether the church believe that the majority ought to be submitted to by the minority in all matters of rule and determination, yea or nay? Answered in the affirmative.

3. Whether or not the sisters of the church take hold of the sword of discipline, or have any weight in matters of rule and determination with the male members? Answered in the negative, that they may not.

4. Whether or not it is the duty of the church to maintain their minister in such manner as that he, with his family, rise in proportion as the members in general do, as to their temporal estate? Answered in the affirmative.

After which queries the delegates from the aforesaid churches unanimously concluded to give fellowship to the church in Ashford, as a church of Christ in the order and fellowship of the gospel.

Signed in behalf of the whole.

ELIJAH CODDING, *Moderator.*
THOMAS USTICK, *Clerk.*
JOHN WESTON, *Church Clerk.*

Thus established and acknowledged with a new meeting-house and active young minister, it might have been hoped that this church would go prosperously onward, with increasing strength and influence, but it soon became involved in manifold difficulties. Its external relations were unfavorable to growth and harmony. A strong society organized independently of the church and taking the initiative in establishing public worship, was a troublesome factor in the case, and to add to the complication the meeting-house itself was owned by a *third* independent body, *i. e.*, the proprietors who had borne the cost of its erection. Dissatisfaction was first manifested in a vote respecting the minister. It may be that the preaching of the young college graduate was distasteful to the plain, old-fashioned church members who cared so little for human learning, and occasioned the following action : " April 16, 1777, after some conversation the mind of the church was tried whether they would desire Mr. Ustick to preach any longer than the time which we had agreed with him for ; or whether they chose to hear some other man. Voted, to hear some other man, and then voted to send to Mr. Lamson to come and preach with us four Sabbaths if he can be obtained." The society thereupon voted that they did not concur with the church in dismissing Mr. Us- tick, but showed its willingness to provide all needful temporalities by farther instructing a suitable person " to provide bread-corn for Mr. Lamson's family." Both ministers occupied the field for a season, Mr. Ustick employed by the society, Mr. Lamson by the church. The church attempted to exercise what it deemed its lawful prerogative by choosing " Brother Abraham Knowlton as a trustee to take a deed of a certain piece of land in behalf of said church, of Mr. Josiah Chaffee, on which the Baptist meeting-house now stands in Ashford," and also empowering Brother Samuel Johnson " to give a bond to Mr. Josiah Chaffee in behalf of the church for the delivery of the meeting-house spot to said Chaffee when not any longer wanted by said church for a meeting-house spot." These conflicting claims, ministers and services excited much ill-will and animosity. Many hard things were said on both sides, and certain remarks derogatory to the Christian and minis- terial character of Mr. Ustick so aroused the spirit of this young can- didate that he applied to his friends in the Warren Association, R. I., for advice and assistance, who delegated a committee for that service. Amos Babcock, Elnathan Brigham and Abraham Knowlton were there- upon appointed by the church, " to wait upon the honorable committee appointed by the honorable Baptist Association of Warren, to come and look into our difficult circumstances at Ashford, viz., the Honored Elder Manning, Honored Elder Backus and Honored Elder Ledoit." This meeting was held Nov. 6, 1777. Notwithstanding the high char-

acter of the assembly, the session was stormy. The society set forth
its grievances touching meeting-house and minister ; the church maintained its rights with equal firmness and persistence. Mr. Babcock, in
his earnestness, even followed the Honorable Committee to their lodg-
ings, "assuming very high ground in relation to church prerogative,"
taking, indeed, the position of the previous Separates, "that a religious
society could not exist without a church. The committee did not
relish such doctrine nor act upon it," and they exculpated Mr. Ustick
from unfavorable charges. The church was greatly dissatisfied with
the result of this investigation, and appointed a committee to treat
with uneasy members of the society and see what they wanted of the
church to make them easy. This they found to be that they should
"sell their right to the meeting-house," or divide the improvement of
it according to the proprietors' rights. The church after consultation
"thought there was no propriety " in such relinquishment, and proceeded to arrange affairs according to their own pleasure. Having
given Mr. Lamson a call, they further desired him "to relate to them
the work of grace upon his heart, and also his call to the work of the
ministry," which proving satisfactory, they confirmed the call without
apparent reference to the society. In February, 1778, committees were
chosen to hire a place for the minister to live on, give certificates to
those that desire to join with us in worship and in principles, and to
settle with those proprietors of the meeting-house that manifest an uneasiness or submit the affair to indifferent men. Upon recommendation
of the Baptist Church in Charlton, Mr. Lamson was received as a
proper member of the church in Ashford, preparatory to ordination.
Delegates from the Baptist churches in New London, Charlton, Wilbraham and Abington met in council June 9, 1778. After inquiring into the church's standing and calling their candidate to the work, they
found it "scriptural to their satisfaction." They proceeded to inquire
into his experience and call to the ministry, especially to this church,
and were fully satisfied with it.

"Then certain gentlemen cast in a written objection against the church for
breach of covenant which the council closely inquired into, and find it was
not the church only three of their members, which when we had closely examined we conclude it was a misunderstanding in these gentlemen, &c., and
we know not but that the church has been up to their agreement in every particular, therefore we proceeded.   June ye 10 met again, and according to before
appointment we proceeded to ordain Brother Ebenezer Lamson. Elder Joshua
Morse made the first prayer and preached a suitable discourse from 1st Peter,
ye four first verses; then prayed and laid on hands. Elder Nathaniel Green
made the prayer and gave the charge, and Elder William Grow gave the right
hand of fellowship, then concluded with laying on of hands and prayer. Elder
Clark made the prayer, all of which was done decently and in order. After
which there were some exhortations that were to the comforting of saints,
and we hope will prove convicting to sinners.
                                                JOSHUA MORSE, *Moderator*."

Abraham Knowlton and John Hanks were now installed as deacons.
Mr. Ustick, who up to this date had remained in Ashford, preaching at
times though "not statedly" to his particular adherents, was now satisfied that it would not be best for him to continue there, and after his
withdrawal the difficulties gradually subsided, and church and society
resumed harmonious relations. Various cases of discipline claimed the
attention of the church. Some of these might have been settled by an
appeal to the *dictionary*, as for example that of Brother Ezekiel Sibley, who thus defines his position :—

"*To the Baptist Church of Ashford:* In answer why I withdrew from you
is as followeth, relating to your fellowshiping the church at Willington in a
corrupt faith, to wit, they believe they ought to contribute to the gospel expenses according to their abilities and *Previledges*, which word ' Previledges' is
a corrupt faith and never was introduced by the commands of God. Neither
do I think it ever was in any church since the world began it being full of so
many evils. It not only brings contempt upon the divine authority, but would
have broke up all churches.

And your tolerating and fellowshiping them in it, it brings divers from our
professed faith. You have broke your faith with me, and got yourselves
where I cannot follow you. By which unguarded proceedings you have
offended your grieved brother."

The church out of consideration for such conscientious scruples and
the possible heresies that might lurk in the inscrutable "previledges,"
discharged the brother with "a gentle admonition." The support of
the minister occasioned much discussion and trouble. According to
Baptist theory and practice he was to be supported by " free contributions." No precise sum was specified, but he was "to rise in proportion as the members in general do as to their temporal estate." Anything like rate-paying was most abhorrent to the primitive Baptist, but
freedom in supporting the minister was hardly compatible with the
means adopted for making each brother pay his proportion, viz. :—

"Oct. 8, 1781, vote put whether the church mean to *enspect* each member
respecting the support of the Gospel amongst us when it becomes necessary?
Voted in the affirmative."

Despite these various trials and hindrances the Ashford Baptist
Church maintained a respectable standing in town and denomination,
and gained a strong membership though weakened after a few years
by withdrawals to Willington and Mansfield.

The eastern inhabitants delayed separate organization till October,
1777, when upon petition of Benjamin Sumner and others, showing
that they were of ability to support the gospel in two societies, they
were endowed with distinct society privileges, "according to a line
previously agreed upon beginning at Bigelow River at Mansfield's north
line, thence running up said river to the north line of the town." At a
society meeting, Jan. 7, 1778, it was voted, "That Mr. Elisha Hutchinson be our gospel minister." Failing to carry out this enactment, a

5

meeting was held, May 25, at the house of Lieut. John Russel, when
Josiah Spalding, Benjamin Sumner and Jonathan Chapman were chosen
a committee to hire preaching, with instructions "to employ Mr. Andrew Judson of Stratford, with a view of settling among us, provided
he don't stay with us then to hire some other gentleman." Notwithstanding the heavy burden now laid upon all classes by the war, the
number of absent citizens, and the many pressing public duties, the
residents of Eastford Society manifested great spirit and readiness in
establishing public worship. At this same meeting it was also voted,
"To build a meeting-house in Eastford Society, about four or five rods
northwest from where Captain Benjamin Russel's old shop used to
stand." Abiel Simmons was chosen collector; Ingoldsby Work, "agent
to pray out a committee to set a stake for a meeting-house spot; also,
a committee to treat with such committee as the County Court should
send to stick the stake aforesaid." June 30, it was farther voted, "That
the County Court's committee should stick stake on Lieut. John Russel's land." This being accomplished to the satisfaction of all a subscription was circulated, the society first agreeing, "That those that subscribe towards building a meeting-house have liberty to build it of
equal bigness with Woodstock's West Society's meeting-house, i. e.,
45x35."

Mr. Judson consenting to preach as a candidate, public services were
held September 23, 1778, when "Andrew Judson, Benjamin Sumner,
Samuel Snow, Jonathan Chapman, Elisha Wales and Simeon Deane
entered into church covenant in presence of the Reverends Stephen
Williams, John Storrs and Elisha Hutchinson, making a solemn and
fresh dedication of themselves, and being formed into a church." Few
in number, they were all the more zealous for doctrinal soundness and
purity, desiring to embody "according to the word of God, and in particular according to the light of the following texts, i. e., Deut. 29:12,
13; Jer. 50:55; Second Cor. 8:5; Isaiah 44:5; Nehe. 9:38; Isaiah 10:
28, 29, in an evangelical manner, and not in a legal frame of spirit."
Oct. 13, the church unanimously voted Mr. Andrew Judson to be their
gospel minister, the society concurring in the call, and offering £500
settlement, £70 salary. Ordination services were held Dec. 1, when
"it being through kind Providence a very pleasant day, the solemnities
were performed to the pleasure and satisfaction of a large concourse
of people." Rev. Ephraim Judson of Norwich, a relative of the new
pastor, preached the ordination sermon, and neighboring ministers assisted in the other exercises. Benjamin Sumner, Esq., and Jonathan
Chapman were ere long appointed deacons. Various members were
received by a dismissive and recommendatory letter from the First
Church of Ashford.

Work on the meeting-house was greatly impeded by scarcity of men and money. The frame was raised in the summer of 1779, and partly covered so that business meetings were held in it, but religious services were conducted "at the house of Mr. Aaron Tuffts, or Lieut. Russel's, or Captain Josiah Spalding's." It was voted, "To purchase about an acre of land of Lieut. Russel, in addition to the two acres that the same has promised to give the society for a meeting-house spot." A committee was appointed this summer to treat with Mr. Judson how he must have his salary paid in this paper money, which agreed upon "*the rate of twenty pounds for one.*" In 1780, voted, "To sell the pew ground at vendue, and the money used in finishing the meeting-house—the tier of pews within the body of seats." These pew spots were purchased by Dea. Chapman, Ebenezer Eastman, Jonathan Hayward, John Russel, Jabez Ward, Simeon Deane, John Scarborough, John Work, Benj. Sumner, Joseph and Ingoldsby Work, Ebenezer Bosworth, James Sumner, Benjamin Cates, Stephen Foster, Benj. Hayward, Jonathan Bemis, John Frink, John Russel, Jun., Josiah Spalding, Noah Paine, Ensign Joseph Kendall, Peter Tuffts and Samuel Snow, showing it to be a strong society. It was voted, "To purchase half a box of glass to glaze the meeting-house, and hire it under-pinned in the cheapest and best way." Glass being found too expensive the order was countermanded, and the " windows boarded up" till times were more propitious. It was voted, " To abate the rates of all those Baptists that have brought a certificate and those that frequently attend the Baptist meeting." The following certificate procured exemption for two Quakers:—

" Jeremiah Mory belongs to the Friends' meeting, and so Daniel Bartlett doth sup of the same cup with me, and we own him to be one of our brethren, as I take care of my friends. In the presence of us, which we are ready to answer to, this :

JEREMIAH MORY,
THOMAS SMITH,
JOHN BARTLETT.

Gloucester, March 16, 1774."

During these years of sectarian and political agitation, Ashford was also implicated in a prolonged litigation growing out of the ancient " Corbin land claims," and carried on by Benjamin and Ashael Marcy as legal representatives of James Corbin. Elijah Whiton, Ezra Smith, Elisha Wales, Benjamin Clark and Ebenezer Byles were appointed in 1769, " To search the book of records with respect to the town's commons and Corbin's land," who reported that 2500 acres were allowed to Corbin in 1719, and that over 4000 acres had been laid out to him. The Marcys carried their claim to the Assembly, who appointed Joseph Spencer, Benjamin Lowe and Captain Jonathan Welles a committee of investigation. A meeting was held at Clark's tavern, in Ashford, May

4, 1774, Elijah Whiton and Ezra Smith appearing as agents for the town. Full details of the original purchase and subsequent agreements were presented, and a formidable array of deeds and figures showing plainly that Corbin had received some hundred acres more than his due, while the petitioners demonstrated with equal certainty that a still larger number was lacking. The committee in due time reported, " That Corbin's land had not been taken up, that 910 acres still remained due to his heirs; also, that Corbin's partners had failed to pay taxes, and their shares should revert to him." The Assembly, after consideration of the report, was of opinion that 910 acres were due to Corbin under the settlement of 1719, and 375 acres under the patent of 1725, and granted that the petitioners should take them up in the town's commons. They also affirmed, that the patent granted to Corbin in 1725, should be considered as an *addition* to the claim of 1719. The town refused to accept this decision so contrary to the common understanding of the case, and to the facts adduced by Captain Chandler and others when the patent was granted, and when the Marcys entered upon land proceeded " to prosecute those who had got our common land into their possession." The Superior Court gave verdict in favor of the town. Marcy again appealed to the Assembly, complaining of error in the judgment of the Superior Court, whereupon it was resolved by that body :—

" That the said Superior Court in taking cognizance of said petition manifestly erred, and mistook the law, and that the said judgment is hereby reversed and set aside, and the petitioner restored to the cost, and the petition remain as before entered in the docket of said Superior Court."

The town debarred from farther action at court was compelled to yield up its commons. So far as regards the right of *jurisdiction* in this case the decision may have been legal, but with regard to the ownership of the land a careful study of all the facts would give it to the town. That the settlement of 1725 granted Corbin an *addition* to his immense original claim seems especially untenable, and in view of all the circumstances of the case, suggests the query, if the art of lobbying be strictly a *modern* invention. One result of this controversy was the copying of the original " town book" by the faithful town clerk, Ebenezer Byles, in 1770.

In 1771, Ashford appointed a committee to pray for county reconstruction on the following basis: Ashford with Woodstock, Killingly, Pomfret, Union, Stafford, Tolland and Willington to form a new northern county, and " Colchester and Hebron to be added to the remains of Windham."

III.

AFFAIRS IN CANTERBURY. WHITEFIELD'S VISIT. SEPARATES.
BAPTISTS. ORGANIZATION OF WESTMINSTER SOCIETY.

CANTERBURY was much occupied at this date in resettling
her parishes and repairing her bridges. In 1760, her peace
was greatly disturbed by the attempted secession of a number of her
southeast residents, who asked to be incorporated with residents of
adjoining towns into a new religious society. John Hebard, appointed
to oppose this petition, remonstrated :—

"1. That Canterbury had already parted with a mile or two of land on
the north to help form Brooklyn parish, leaving first society in Canterbury
eight miles by five in extent—wisely and cautiously done to accommodate two
parishes within herself when planters should be multiplied.
2. Inhabitants were settled all over said parish from east to west, north
to south bounds; that the distribution of said parish into two parishes within
themselves has been the governing motive to many planters to settle and
build there; that winter preaching was allowed to the north and northwest
quarter, and division to be made when public charges were less heavy; that
dividing parishes into such small ones weakens the whole colony and is
hurtful to its civil and religious interests."

Even this last consideration, usually deemed so weighty, was ineffectual in this instance. The Assembly taking time for deliberation, Mr.
Hebard farther urged, that the scheme would "*destroy one society*
in Canterbury, destroy the *well-being* of one in Newent, and *wound*
and *weaken* a third in Scotland." In spite of these dismal prognos-
tications, the petitioners carried the day, and secured in 1761, the
erection of the new society of Hanover from parts of Canterbury,
Scotland Parish and Newent.

Town affairs required much care and deliberation. Colonel John
Dyer and others of the second generation of settlers were no longer
in active life. At the town meeting, 1761, John Curtis was chosen
moderator; Captain Obediah Johnson, Stephen Frost, Josiah Butt,
Captain Benjamin Price, selectmen; Stephen Frost, town clerk;
Deacon Samuel Huntington, treasurer; Simon Forbes, constable and
collector of excise; Timothy Cleveland, Obediah Johnson, Joseph
Dyer, James Daley, William Bradford, Josiah Morse, Frederic
Curtis, Gideon Cobb, Joseph Safford, John Hebard, Matthew
Button, Zechariah Waldo, highway surveyors; Nathaniel Aspinwall,
Samuel Adams, fence-viewers; Solomon Paine, Asa Cleveland,
Ebenezer Spalding, Robert Herrick, Silas Cleveland, Jedidiah Dodge,
listers, Robert Herrick, Abijah Cady, leather-sealers; John Hebard,
Nehemiah Ensworth, Ezekiel Spalding, Elisha Paine, Isaiah Williams,
grand-jurymen; Shubael Butts, Hezekiah Pellet, Daniel Paine,

William Bradford, tithingmen; Gideon Cobb, gauger and packer; Ahaziah Adams, brander and toller; William Bond, Ezekiel Spalding, key-keepers. Ezra Ensworth, having managed at great cost and labor to construct a dam across the Quinebaug in the south part of the town, was granted liberty to mend and "keep in repair the same, for the benefit of his corn-mill where it now stands, the same highth and length as it now is." This unusual privilege was only obtained by very strenuous efforts. Anything that obstructed the annual ascent of shad and salmon on which they so much depended was most vigorously resisted by all the residents of the Quinebaug valley—and in addition to this great damage and loss this mischievous dam was charged with undermining and greatly damaging Butts Bridge just below it. This most convenient bridge, erected by Samuel Butts in 1733, had been kept in repair by private subscription, and now in 1760, the neighbors had again rebuilt it, "supposing that Canterbury would order the dam removed." Their fears and forebodings were only too quickly realized. The very next winter, ice falling over the dam again carried off the bridge. The dam, it is believed, was also destroyed by the same flood and never rebuilt; but none the less did the aggrieved neighbors refuse to rebuild the bridge. The town, compelled to join with Plainfield in maintaining Nevins Bridge on the great public thoroughfare, and a fordway near Shepard's Hill in the north part of the town, and to keep up other bridges over Rowland's Brook and Little River, positively declined to assist in rebuilding Butts Bridge. So great were the inconveniences and difficulties resulting from this negligence, that a large number of petitioners from Plainfield, Preston and other towns represented the case to the Assembly, and prayed that Canterbury might be compelled to support said bridge, as a place of much travel. A special act of the assembly in 1763, thereupon provided that Canterbury should build and keep in order a bridge at this place, under the direction of a county committee. Seth Paine of Brooklyn Parish, Nathaniel Webb of Windham, and Asa Smith of Woodstock, were accordingly placed in charge of the work.

The increasing travel through the town made it needful to keep its highways in good order. Many of its own citizens were carried away by emigration. Abraham Paine, Elisha Cleveland, and others removed to Nine Partners, New York. Joshua Hide and Joshua Parke were among the early settlers of Vermont. Captain James Bidlack, Samuel Ransom and many other families joined the great out-flow to Wyoming. A jury was ordered by the County Court to meet at the house of Timothy Backus, and lay out a highway from the dividing line between Windham and Canterbury, four-and-a-half miles east, to the highway leading from Norwich to Canterbury, and thence to the Great Bridge over the Quinebaug. This highway, thus relaid and carefully maintained, accommodated a great part of the travel from Providence to Hartford and farther westward. In 1773, Colonel Jabez Fitch was chosen agent by the town to oppose the memorial of Colonel Israel Putnam and others "for an open and public highway to be laid out through the towns of Killingly, Pomfret and Canterbury, in order the better to accommodate traveling from Boston to New Haven and New York,"—a project which its renowned advocate failed apparently to accomplish. A dam was allowed over Rowland's Brook in the north part of the town, and various mills kept in operation. Tannery works were also carried on by Benjamin Morse.

The various taverns needed upon the public roads and other parts of the town, were kept by Timothy Backus, John Park, Ebenezer Spalding, Robert Ransom and David Reed. Dr. Gideon Welles continued his medical practice in Canterbury and Planfield. A son of Canterbury, Dr. John Spalding, also established himself in his native town. Dr. David Adams, son of David Adams, residing in Scotland and afterward in Preston, was often employed in his old home.

Rev. James Cogswell continued in charge of the First church, which though weakened by secession and emigration maintained a respectable standing, and its old dislike of separation. A visit from Mr. Whitefield in 1764, excited much consternation. This distinguished preacher had lost favor with the more rigid churches and pastors. Mr. Cogswell was greatly exercised in spirit by the rumor of his coming, "not knowing how to conduct, viz: whether to desire him to preach,"—but, after deliberation and prayer, determined "to keep about his duty, viz: what would have been his duty if he had heard nothing of his arrival." Tidings of his actual arrival and entertainment at Colonel Dyer's failed to change the decision of the timid divine, whose natural politeness and curiosity were quite overborne by fear of ministerial censure, but at the request of a number of his people he ventured to call upon the great preacher and held considerable discourse, which he thus recorded in his diary :—

"He professed much unconcernedness at ye thought of death. He appeared a great enemy to Sandeman. He was gross in body but poor in health and declined preaching; wish I may be so weaned from the world and ready to die as he professed to be; can't think, however, there is the greatest propriety in being fond of speaking in such a manner to strangers.

Feb. 14, Mr. Whitefield came along; people seemed very fond of gazing on him. He rode in his chariot with a gentleman—had a waiter to attend on him, and Sampson Occum, ye Indian preacher, who rode on one of the horses, there being three to ye chariot. [Reverends] Messrs. Breck and Whitney ...... and .... Mr. Brock told he did not know but I was right in asking Mr. Whitefield to preach; however he believed he should not have done it."

If Mr. Breck of Springfield, always inclined to Arminianism and heterodoxy, could thus scruple, it may be seen that the cautious pastor did indeed run some risk in extending civilities to the great pulpit orator.

Mr. Cogswell's diary gives us a parting glimpse of another once-famed preacher and religious leader—his old antagonist, Elisha Paine, revisiting Canterbury after many years absence:—

"March 26, 1769. Lawyer Paine sent for me in the evening, said that he wanted to see me but did not desire I should tarry lecture, as Stephen Backus told me; however, when I came there the old gentleman said he had nothing special to say, and that he only sent word that he was going to preach, and began lecture soon. But I thought I would not go away immediately—was not sorry I tarried as I have not heard a Separate teacher in a great while. He is much more moderate than formerly and indeed is a dull preacher; some part of his discourse was good but he preached many things erroneous as I thought, as that all religion which was established by civil authority was false; .... that all Christians have assurance, and those who think they have not are to be suspected of knowing nothing of Christ's beauty experimentally. That though men should live peaceably together yet it was a vain and wicked attempt to reconcile converted and unconverted men for they would always have implacable enemity; and tho' they should agree ever so well on an outward plan of church government which he called a *hiarchee*, meaning as I suppose an Hierarchy, it would be of no service unless men were converted—and several other exceptional things.

27th. Mr. Paine visited me. Discoursed in a friendly manner. I mentioned to him his meddling with Connecticut Establishment in his sermon; he said he did not mean so much Connecticut Establishment as all Establishments. I mentioned his notion of saving faith consisting in assurance. He in effect gave up the point, for he said he believed many were good Christians who had not assurance but did not own he was wrong. He discoursed against several practices.—Presbyterian ordination, ministers being supported by a salary, &c., but with a pleasant countenance and to appearance with a temper much less bitter and severe than when he lived in town—but I believe he holds much the same doctrines."*

The Separate church once so flourishing had suffered many losses. The venerable Obadiah Johnson, one of the early settlers of the town, and a pillar of this church, died in 1765. Mary, wife of William Bradford and sister of John and Ebenezer Cleveland,—"an ornament to her sex and indeed to all her Christian friends,"—died the same year upon the birth of her fourteenth child, "in a perfect calm resignation to the will of God and assurance of faith." Her father, Josiah Cleveland, dying some years previous had shown his love to this "Congregational church in Canterbury" (as its members called it), by bequeathing to it his whole part of the meeting-house, and £200 in bills of credit. Deacon Johnson left "the improvement of a farm and buildings for the benefit of said church as for the poor of said church," and also twenty acres to supply firewood for the minister. But money

---

* The remaining years of the great Separate leader were spent in peaceful seclusion, preaching to his beloved flock at Bridgehampton, L. I., until within two weeks of his decease, which occurred Aug. 26, 1775, at the age of eighty-four.

and land could not make up the loss in membership. Emigration and disaffection had carried away many. The vote by which they had gained society privileges and exemption from ratepaying, gave great offence to many ardent brethren, and after many stringent letters from Ebenezer Frothingham of Middletown, the church decided to reconsider the matter ; renewed their covenant one by one—during which God drew near and united their hearts in the love of the gospel—and appointed a committee, who reported :—

"May 21, 1766. 1. The Separate voting or acting with the society was wrong, as that civil body acted in a matter of conscience, or in an ecclesiastic affair."

The church assented to this "as their minds, and what they meant to abide by, and acknowledged their fault in so far as any of them had been active in those things." Its relations with its pastor were next brought under consideration. This good brother was ardent and zealous to a fault, and offended many of his people by bluntness of speech and lack of discretion. After long labor and agitation a council was held, May 29, 1768, which decided "that brother Joseph Marshall be dismissed from the pastoral care of this church, on account of the contentions in church respecting his gifts and ordination, which renders his improvement unprofitable." Mr. Marshall then followed some members of his flock to the new settlements in Western Connecticut, New York and Vermont, where his labors were greatly blessed. The Canterbury Separate church did not succeed in settling another minister and steadily declined in numbers. Some of its members signified their desire to attend worship with the First society, provided they might pay their part of the expenses by way of contributing and not by rate, whereupon that body voted, "That we are willing and desirous that they should attend public worship with us, and will never levy any tax or assessment upon them contrary to their minds, but will leave it with them to give what, and in what manner, they please" The increase of Baptist sentiments was very annoying to the Separates as well as the standing order. Mr. Cogswell heard with great grief "that several of his people and many of the Separates had attended at Mr. Backus's to hear Ebenezer Lyon, the Baptist teacher," and hoped that God would "convince them of their folly." Notwithstanding this opposition, "Lyon, the Baptist," continued his irregular services for many years, edifying a small number of hearers. These Baptists with the Canterbury Separates held to what was called "mixed communion," and often joined in worship and ordinances with Separate churches.

A division of the First society was accomplished during this period. Population had gathered in the western part of the town. Deacon

6

Stephen Frost, sons of Samuel Butts, and other influential families
were among these residents, and in the spring of 1767, petitioned for
society privileges. A measure and survey were ordered and divisional
line run. The society accepted the report and voted to divide into distinct ecclesiastic societies by a north and south line at the centre of the
parish parallel with the line between Windham and Canterbury—line
to leave 11,736 acres on each side; rate on east side £5,759; west
side £4,251. With this vote the western inhabitants, viz:—

Stephen Frost, Robert and John Herrick, Solomon Adams, Ebenezer Deane,
Ezra and Amos Woodward, Ebenezer Goodell, Stephen Downing, Benjamin
and Nathaniel Cleveland, Samuel Parish, Matthias Button, Benjamin and John
Durfee, David Munro, Solomon Allen, Stephen Ford, Jun., Joseph Burgess,
Josiah, Joseph and Sherebiah Butts, Joseph Leach, John Curtis, William
Foster, Benjamin Jewett, David Canada, Eliphalet and Zebulon Farnham,
William Hebard, Frederic Carter, John Lewis, Jonas Bond—

appeared before the Assembly, and secured a committee which
reported in favor of division. A favorable decision was confidently
expected when to the consternation of the petitioners opposition was
manifested. Notwithstanding previous declarations and agreements,
fifty remonstrants headed by Elijah Dyer, Jabez Fitch and John
Bacon now represented:—

"That the vote to divide was hastily passed; that the inhabitants principally settled in the east; that a number of inhabitants settled afterwards in
the west, and, not considering that the contemplated division would inevita-
bly ruin said society, voted it by a bare majority; list of whole, only nine
thousand, exclusive of separate society; give a minister now but seventy
pounds a year which by no means supports him, and we are very much put to
collect that now in this distressing time; people behindhand on account of
great changes and scarcity of money, and to divide in the way proposed will
certainly ruin and break up the whole."

Residents near the centre of the town, viz., Thomas Bradford, Joseph Withe, Abijah Cady, Jacob Smith, John Wheeler, Jacob Green
and John Pellet also remonstrated, declaring:—

"That the society will be eight miles in length and two and a-half in width,
and that we live quite at the east part of new society, and have a good road
to the meeting-house, and if we are stated to the west society shall be as far
from their meeting house, if they ever build one, as we are now, with no road
to travel on, and the way so bad that it is *impossible* there will ever be a good
one made, and pray to be allowed to stay in the east society."

To forestall division it was now proposed that a new meeting-house
should be erected in the centre of the town, but no vote could be obtained for it. In May, 1769, the western inhabitants farther represented that their number had greatly multiplied and was constantly increasing, that the society would not allow them to be set off or build a
new meeting-house in the centre, and begged for relief. Their request
was continued till October, and thus answered:—

"Upon memorial of Stephen Frost, Robert Herrick, Ebenezer Goodell and
others, inhabitants of first society of town of Canterbury, situated in west

part of said society, showing to this Assembly their great distance from the established place of public worship in said society, whereby they and their numerous families are very unable to attend the same; also, showing to the Assembly the vote of said society signifying their consent to have the same equally divided into distinct ecclesiastic societies by a north and south line parallel with the line dividing between the towns of Windham and Canterbury, at the centre of said first society, ascertained by a late survey made by Seth Paine, county surveyor, approved by said society—praying this Assembly to make and constitute the men situate on the west side of said north and south line a distinct ecclesiastic society according to the form and extent of said vote, and to be invested with all the rights and privileges to such societies appertaining (except such inhabitants as by law are exempt from contributing to the support of the established ministry). It is resolved by this Assembly, that the inhabitants living within the limits aforesaid (excepting as before excepted) shall be, and they are hereby made, erected and constituted a distinct ecclesiastic society, endowed with all the powers, privileges and immunities usually belonging to ecclesiastic societies in this colony, and shall be known and called by the name of Westminster. October, 1769."

The organization of the new society was speedily effected. The reports of the first meetings have not been preserved, but there was evidently no lack of spirit and enthusiasm. Arrangements were soon made for building a meeting-house. There was no occasion here for quarrelling over its site. "Natural fitness" at once assigned it to a broad hill-summit near the centre of the society. About four acres of land at the crossing of the roads were given by John Parks for meeting-house spot, burial ground and common. The bushes were at once cleared off and ground made ready for building. Capt. Sherebiah Butts was employed as master builder, and served so efficiently that the house was made ready for occupation during the following summer, that same busy season in which the rival edifices of Brooklyn Parish were in progress. "At a convention of professing Christians belonging to Westminster society Nov. 2, 1770," arrangements were made for church organization. The neighboring ministers—Reverends Samuel Mosely, James Cogswell, Josiah Whitney—and Capt. John Howard, Dr. Jabez Fitch, Dea. Nathaniel Brown and Col. Israel Putnam, messengers, comprised the council. A number of brethren appeared before it, and after professing their belief in the articles of the Christian faith revealed in the Word of God, and engaging to walk together agreeably to the directions of his word, signed the following covenant and were acknowledged as a regular church of Christ:—

" 1. We do take the Holy Scriptures as the only ultimate rule of our faith and manners, and in subordination hereto, the confession of faith called the Westminster,* which we look upon to be agreeable to the Word of God. . . . . .

3. We submit ourselves to the watch and discipline of Christ's church, according to Cambridge platform.

Stephen Frost.	Thomas Bradford.	Amos Woodward.
Robert Herrick.	William Bond.	Ebenezer Davis.
John Lewis.	Jacob Foster.	Anthony Glass.
Isaac Woodward	Enos Woodward.	John Herrick.
Daniel Davis.	Peter Woodward.	

Westminster, Nov. 20, 1770."

---

*It is not improbable that the society adopted its stately name in honor of this venerable confession which held so high a place in their esteem.

Within a few months John Staples of Taunton, Mass., was called to the pastorate and ordained April 17, 1772. Stephen Frost, John Herrick and Jonas Bond were chosen to serve as deacons; many were added to the church, and the society pursued its way in much peace and prosperity.

Although the First society in Canterbury managed to maintain its existence after the division of its territory, it did not escape many of the evils so dismally foreboded. During the preceding controversy ani mosities had been engendered, and it was found impossible to effect a peaceable settlement. Dea. Frost, for some unassigned reason, chose to retain the society records and papers, and also the school-fund money previously entrusted to him. John Felch was now society clerk and treasurer; Jabez Fitch, Jun., Eliashib Adams and Joseph Woodward were the committee. At a society meeting Feb. 7, 1770, Capt. Dyer was appointed "agent, to go immediately in the name of society and demand the record books and other papers belonging to the society now in the hands of Dea. Stephen Frost, and in case of refusal, prosecute." Asa Bacon was also empowered "to recover loan school money in the hands of Dea. Frost." These efforts proving unsuccessful, the society committee was instructed to sue for school money. An agent was afterwards appointed to lay the case before the Assembly. Finally, April 22, 1771, the leading men in the society, viz., John Felch, Capt. Elijah Dyer, Dea. Eliashib Adams and Captains Elkanah Cobb and Aaron Cleveland, were chosen "to treat with Westminster society about an amicable settlement of the dispute between said societies respecting loan school money, and also to make a final settlement and full conclusion of all other matters of controversy subsisting between said societies respecting a part of Mr. Cogswell's salary for the year in which said society was divided." Through their mediation the various difficulties were in some measure surmounted.

The most serious evil resulting from society division was the loss of Mr. Cogswell. The First society was unable to raise what he deemed needful for his support, or even to pay arrearages in full, and consented "to his quiet and peaceable dismission." The church, "taking into consideration our difficult circumstances, with much reluctance consent that our pastor be dismissed; testify our sincerest regards and part with him not because we are dissatisfied with him as to anything relating to his ministerial conduct, but think it may be for the good and peace of the society, and most cordially recommend him." Mr. Cogswell preached for a short time at East Haddam, where his good friend and adherent, Deacon Samuel Huntington, had lately removed, and then returned to Scotland Parish. The Canterbury church remained for many years without a settled pastor to its great detriment. Nathaniel

Niles of Norwich, preached for a season but declined a call to settlement. Samuel Spring, Job Swift and Ephraim Judson also served as supplies during this unsettled period. Eliashib Adams succeeded to the deacon's office on the removal of Dea. Huntington in 1769. Jabez Fitch, Jun., was elected deacon two years later. William Bingham, William Darbe and Benjamin Bacon were made choristers. Though destitute of a settled pastor, public worship was maintained with considerable regularity. Jabez Fitch, Esq., Timothy Baldwin, Jabez Ensworth, John Bacon and Elijah Dyer looked after the proper seating of the meeting-house, and ordered needful repairs, and "if swept twelve times a year" paid twenty shillings for it. Tixhall Ensworth held the responsible position of key-keeper. In 1773 the resources of the society were somewhat enlarged by the annexation of Black Hill, the lands in possession of Timothy Backus, Isaac Allerton, William Underwood, Joab Johnson, Curtis and Ezekiel Spalding, Jabez Fitch, Jun., William Bingham, John Hough, Elkanah Cobb and Obadiah Johnson being joined by act of Assembly "with the First Society of Canterbury for society and ecclesiastic privileges, but not for schooling, military and other purposes."

Schools in Canterbury up to this date were receiving little attention, and the old system of "squadrons" was still maintained. In 1770, Ezekiel Park, Captain Elijah Dyer, Nathan Waldo, Joseph Clark, Joseph Woodward, Asa and Joseph Stevens were ordered, "To take care of the schools in their respective squadrons, and to hire suitable persons to keep the schools." A division into twenty-three districts was soon after effected and the number of schools increased. Private schools were often supported in different neighborhoods. A "night school" was kept at one time by Joseph Carter in "the school-house nighest to Westminster meeting-house." After his mercantile experiment in Pomfret this young man returned to Canterbury, keeping store or school as occasion offered, and, like a true-born Yankee, turning his hand to anything. Succeeding in time to the office of deputy-sheriff, he combined with it a carrying trade, conveying letters and packages back and forth with his prisoners, and serving his neighbors with household supplies as well as warrants. With all his Yankee facility one duty came hard to him. He did not mind applying the lash to the bare back of a male culprit, but he hated to *whip a woman*, and unfortunately for him the number of female offenders was very large. Stealing, vagrancy and worse offences brought many a hapless victim to the public whipping-post. The compassionate sympathy of the tender-hearted sheriff led him on one occasion to employ a substitute, but the neophyte in his zeal for justice inflicted the blows with so much more spirit and cogency that he was fain to submit thereafter to do his own whipping. One petty pilferer escaped with a lighter punishment. A very respectable citizen living north of the Green was led to suspect that one of his neighbors was helping himself to his hay, and keeping a sharp look-out at last espied the offender creeping up to his barn one evening and coming out with a large bundle tied up with a rope. The good man might have roused the neighborhood with a hue-and-cry, but with sudden impulse he hurried into his house, snatched a blazing fire-brand, and managed unseen to.overtake the thief, and thrust the brand into the bundle. Crackling flames suddenly bursting over his head terrified the poor fellow almost out of his senses, and thinking that the Lord had sent fire from Heaven to consume him, he dropped the blazing hay and ran home as fast as his trembling limbs could carry him. The next day he sought his neighbor in great distress and penitence, confessing all his misdeeds and the punishment that the Lord had sent upon him, and promising never to do the like again. This promise it is believed was faithfully kept, and the story was never told till after the decease of the penitent offender.

John Felch usually served as town clerk during this period. John Bacon, Jun., was graduated from the College of New Jersey in 1765, and after essaying ministerial settlement in various fields removed to Stockbridge, Mass., and distinguished himself in secular service. Aaron, youngest son of Josiah Cleveland, Elijah, son of Colonel Dyer, John, son of John Adams, were among Canterbury's rising young men at this date. Obadiah Johnson was colonel of the regiment which comprised the militia of Plainfield and Canterbury. Mr. Cogswell reports a public library founded by the citizens in 1771.

IV.

TOWN AFFAIRS IN WINDHAM. WYOMING SETTLEMENT. SOCIAL LIFE. SCOTLAND PARISH.

WINDHAM as head and shire town of the county was now exceedingly prosperous and prominent, surpassing, according to cotemporary judgment, " every inland town in the Colony in trade and merchandize." It had four well-trained military companies, four meeting-houses, a court-house, prison and jail, numberless stores and taverns, and many handsome private residences. The officers requisite for the proper management of public affairs in 1760 were five selectmen, five constables and rate collectors, seven grand-jurors, ten tithing-men, seven listers, twenty-three surveyors, four branders and tollers, three pound-keepers, three packers, one weight-sealer, one measure-sealer, two to take care of provisions paid for colony tax, one excise collector, two surveyors and packers of tobacco.* The Rev. Stephen White remained in pastoral charge of the First Church and society. Samuel Gray served efficiently as town clerk. Nathaniel Wales, with his son Nathaniel, filled many public offices to great acceptance. Eliphalet Dyer and Jedidiah Elderkin were actively engaged in the practice of law, and ranked among the prominent public men of Connecticut. The excellent Jonathan Huntington retained his eminence and popularity as a medical practitioner, and while exhibiting "marvelous skill" in the art of healing, served as judge of the County Court and member of the Governor's council. His cotemporary in years, Dr. Ebenezer Gray of Boston, probably brother to Samuel Gray, Esquire, also "practiced physick" in Windham and its vicinity. Dr. Joshua Elderkin, the somewhat erratic brother of Jedidiah, practiced medicine, engaged in trade and experimented in manufactures. In that revival of business and commercial enterprise following the close of the French war, Windham actively participated. James Flint, Ebenezer Backus and Ebenezer Devotion, Jun., of Scotland Parish, engaged extensively in mercantile traffic, buying up domestic produce to exchange for West India goods and articles of taste and luxury. Under this stimulus, the products of the town were very largely increased. Much attention was given to wool-growing, the culture of hemp, flax and tobacco, and the making of cheese and butter. Great flocks of sheep and herds of cattle ranged over Windham pastures and commons. Wheat and other cereals were extensively grown and exported, and so brisk was trade in

---

*List of Officers: Dr. Joshua Elderkin, moderator; Samuel Gray, town clerk (chosen first in 1755, "in room of Eliphalet Dyer, gone in ye army," and retained in office more than thirty years); Captain Samuel Murdock, George Martin, Capt. Henry Silsby, Mr. Samuel Webb, Lieut. Prince Tracy, selectmen; Hezekiah Manning, Paul Hebard, Abiel Abbott, constables and collectors of town rates; Joshua Reed, Hezekiah Huntington, Nathaniel Lord, John Manning, grand-jurymen; William Warner, Nathaniel Wales, 2d, Nathaniel Warren, John Clark, Joseph Burnham, Nathan Luce, Joseph Manning, tithing-men; Benjamin Lathrop, Jonathan Babcock, James Flint, Jonathan Burnap, Nathaniel Mosely, Andrew Burnham, Joseph Woodward, listers; Edward Brown, Ebenezer Fitch, Ebenezer Bingham, John Bass, Isaac Andrus, Gideon Hebard, Thomas Tracy, Samuel Murdock, Nathaniel Huntington, Daniel Martin, Jeremiah Clark, Zebadiah Coburn, Stephen Park, Jeremiah Utley, William Holt, Josiah Hammond, Simon Wood, Joshua Farnham, John Manning, Joseph Woodward, Richard Kimball, Jonathan Luce, Joseph Ginnings, highway surveyors; Samuel Webb, Edward Brown, William Durkee, Isaac Ringe, John Webb, David Ripley, fence-viewers; Hez. Huntington, John Fuller, Elisha Palmer, Jun., Eleazer Palmer, branders and tollers; Edward Brown, Isaac Ringe, Reuben Robinson, leather-sealers; Joseph Huntington, Joseph Sessions, Elisha Palmer, Jun., pound-keepers; Joseph Huntington, Jeremiah Durkee, Joseph Manning, packers; Samuel Gray, town treasurer; Elijah Bingham and Thomas Tracy, to take care of the town bridge; James Flint, receiver of provision paid for discharge of colony tax; John Abbe, collector of excise; Hezekiah Manning and Shubael Palmer, surveyors and packers of tobacco.

all parts of the town that it was proposed to petition the Assembly " for a free fair or market." When compelled by English exactions to relinquish her foreign trade, Windham turned her energies to manufactures. John Brown, a highly respected and useful citizen, then occupying the home farm on the Willimantic laid out to his grandfather, Capt. John Brown, in 1706, not only entertained travelers according to the fashion of the day, but cultivated his farm, manufactured potash and refined saltpetre. Ezekiel Cary carried on his trade as a tanner and currier in this vicinity. Colonel Elderkin, among his other avocations, interested himself in silk culture ; and set out a fine orchard of mulberry trees in the south part of Windham. In 1773, he wrote to Clement Biddle of Philadelphia, "that he had a large number of trees fit for improvement, had made considerable growth of silk, spun and improved some, but failed for want of proper reels and experienced workmen, and desired a reel or caldron, and a young woman to teach them." With this aid he succeeded in making a strong, coarse silk, used for handkerchiefs and vestings.

Travel and trade, and the increased and cheapened supply of liquors, made many taverns needful. License was granted in 1760 to James Lasell, Paul Hebard, Ann Warner, Elias Frink, Ebenezer Bingham, David Ripley, Jacob Simmons, Ebenezer Griffin, Stephen Fitch, Jabez Kingsley, John Parish, Samuel Silsby. Mercy Fitch of Windham Green was also allowed to retail strong drink to whomsoever asked for it. Licenses were granted in following years to Abner Flint, Eleazer Cary, John Howard, Nehemiah Tinker, Edward Badger and Nathaniel Linkon. These numerous taverns were all well patronized, especially during the Court sessions. Jonathan Trumbull of Lebanon, was now judge of the County Court ; Shubael Conant, John Dyer, Jabez Fitch and Joshua West, associates ; Samuel Gray, clerk ; Eleazer Fitch, high sheriff ; Paul Hebard, sheriff deputy. Due care was taken of the court house and jail, and certain limits assigned to such as were imprisoned for debt. Debtors unable to pay were made to work out their debts in various service. In 1762, the prison-yard was reported in a decaying state, and the sheriff ordered to take the same down. Twelve years later, assistants and justices met at the court house " to take into consideration the state of the county jail." A large number of prominent men from all the towns were present. It was judged that repairs were needful, and a farthing tax ordered upon polls and ratable estates. Samuel Gray, Nathaniel Wales and Capt. James Stedman were appointed to make repairs. A collector was appointed for each town, viz.: Jabez Huntington, Windham ; Samuel Eaton, Ashford ; Nathaniel Marcy, Woodstock ; John Hough, Canterbury ; Seth Grosvenor, Pomfret ; Joshua Dunlap, Plainfield ; James Gordon, Voluntown ; Ephraim Warren, Killingly.

Windham's alertness in promoting home interests was surpassed, if possible, by her activity in all public affairs. Her citizens were fully imbued with the spirit of those stirring times, and were ready not only to participate but to lead on "all emergent occasions." The grand colonization scheme, so happily inaugurated within her borders, still enlisted her warmest sympathies, and after the return of peace, renewed efforts were made to carry it into execution. After a lapse of five years, the Susquehanna company resumed active operations. At a meeting in Hartford, March 12, 1760, Col. Tolcott was chosen moderator ; Samuel Gray, clerk. It was recommended that the committee previously appointed, "with all expedition carry into execution the several betrustments reposed in them ;" also, that this committee should join with the committee of the Delaware Purchase in sending home to England. In the following year, it was voted to send an agent for both companies, and add two hundred more shares to pay expenses. Eliphalet Dyer was chosen as this agent with a salary of £150. The object of this mission was to procure confirmation of the Wyoming territory from the Crown. Jonathan Trumbull, Hezekiah Huntington, David Edwards, Samuel Gray, Jedidiah Elderkin and George Wyllis were appointed to collect materials and make all necessary preparations to help said agent. A committee was also empowered to treat with Indian Chiefs, and liberty given to settle two townships. This liberty was improved by several Connecticut families, who effected a settlement in the Wyoming valley in 1762–3, but were soon attacked and butchered by the hostile savages. The Promised Land was not to be possessed without an arduous conflict. The government of Pennsylvania, holding the territory by formal treaty and purchase, scouted the claim of Connecticut and prepared to resist her every effort at settlement. Powerful Indian tribes contesting the land were also arrayed against her. Dyer's mission though urged with great eloquence and persistency was unsuccessful. The King forbade the settlement of the disputed territory. Both companies were summoned to Windham Court-house, Jan. 16, 1765, to hear the report of their agent, returned from Great Britain with many things of importance to communicate. Jabez Fitch, John Curtis, Isaac and Elisha Tracy and Ebenezer Backus served as committee for the Delaware company ; Eliphalet Dyer, Jedidiah Elderkin and Samuel Gray, for the Susquehanna. Undeterred by rebuff and threatened opposition, the latter company continued its efforts. Renewed attempts were made to gain the sanction of Connecticut. Colonel Dyer in particular so warmly pleaded its cause, and so

7

glowingly depicted the charms of the Wyoming valley, as to call out from one of the wits of the day a poetic impromptu:—

> " Canaan of old, as we are told,
>   Where it did rain down Manna,
> Wa'n't half so good for heavenly food
>   As Dyer makes Susqu'hanna."

But though greatly favoring the colonization scheme, and most anxious to establish its claim to all the land prescribed by its Charter the government of Connecticut was too wise and wary to expose itself to collision with Pennsylvania, and discreetly withheld its formal endorsement of the enterprise. The Susquehanna company was, however, too powerful an organization and too strongly entrenched in popular favor, to be repressed by lack of official aid or recognition. At a meeting in Hartford, 1768, it was voted, that five townships, five miles square, should be surveyed and granted each to forty settlers, being proprietors, on condition that these settlers should remain upon the ground and defend themselves and each other from the intrusion of all rival claimants. As further encouragement—the sum of two hundred pounds was appropriated to provide implements of husbandry and provisions. Great as was the risk many were ready to meet it. The chance of gaining a home in the beautiful valley, was worth a contest, and indeed to some who had shared in the exciting service of the French war, the prospect of a brush with the " Pennymites " may have furnished an additional incentive. Early in 1769, forty adventurous Yankees descended upon Wyoming. Foremost among them were old French war campaigners, Captain Zebulon Butler of Lyme, and Captain John Durkee of Windham, now removed to Norwich. Thomas Dyer, Vine Elderkin, Nathaniel Wales, Nathan Denison of Windham, and Timothy Pierce of Plainfield, were among this heroic " forty." They found the " Pennymites " already in possession, and after a sharp and spirited contest were obliged to quit the field, leaving Durkee and other leading men in the hands of the enemy. Colonel Dyer and Major Elderkin were equally unsuccessful in attempting to negotiate an amicable settlement with the Proprietary Government of Pennsylvania. Ebenezer Backus, Captains Joseph Eaton and Robert Durkee acted with gentlemen from other parts of the Colony in raising funds for the relief and support of the prisoners. In 1770, a still larger force of Yankees returned to the charge and after a yet more serious contest was also compelled to retire with loss of life and great destruction of property. After taking and losing Fort Durkee in the course of the following winter, the Yankees opened the siege in the spring of 1771, with fresh forces and leaders, resolved to carry on the war to the last extremity. The "Pennymites" met them with their usual spirit and gallantry, though greatly crippled in resources. The Proprietary Government, unpopular at home and unsupported by Great Britain, was unable to meet the demand, and declined to continue so costly and fruitless a struggle. After gallantly defending Fort Durkee for several months, Captain Ogden was forced to accept articles of capitulation, and with all the Pennsylvania troops withdrew from Wyoming, leaving the rejoicing Yankees in possession of the land so valiantly contested.

Organization was now speedily effected. The towns already laid out were divided into farms and distributed. Those who had fought for the prize were rewarded by bountiful homesteads, and many other families from all parts of Connecticut eagerly sought a share. Windham County, so active in proposing and promoting the settlement of the Susquehanna valley, was equally ready to take possession, and scores of valuable families removed thither in the course of a few years. Stephen Fuller, John and Stephen Abbott, John Carey, Elisha Babcock, Robert Durkee of Windham; Simon Spalding, Ezekiel Pierce, John Perkins of Plainfield; Captain Samuel Ransom, Captain James Bidlack and Elisha Williams of Canterbury; George and John Dorrance, Robert Jameson, Cyrus Kinne of Voluntown; Anderson Dana, Joseph Biles, Stephen Whiton of Ashford, were among the many who emigrated to Wyoming valley. Many of these were men in the prime of life with large families, accustomed to the management of public affairs, and eminently fitted to aid in laying the foundation of social order, and moulding the new State after the pattern of Connecticut. The fertility of the soil, the mildness of the climate, the beauty of the country and the abundance of its resources far exceeded expectations, and such glowing reports came back to the rocky farms of Windham County, that emigration raged for a time like an epidemic and seemed likely to sweep away a great part of the population.

The burthen of bridge-making, always heavy in Windham, was so augmented by the increase of travel consequent to the great emigration to Wyoming and other new countries, as to be quite insupportable. An "extraordinary flood" and great accumulation of ice in 1771, demolished and carried away nearly every bridge in Windham County, making a clean sweep of the Nachaug, Willimantic and Shetucket. As these bridges were upon public highways, "abundantly used" by great numbers of families with cattle and teams from Plainfield, Voluntown and the south part of Rhode Island, "traveling to the great part of Massachusetts Bay, New Hampshire and north part of New York," the authorities of Windham refused to reconstruct them without aid from other quarters. Several roads were thus rendered impassable, travelers were forced to travel many miles out of their way to find suitable fording-places, and then were flung from their horses and exposed to drowning. Complaints were laid before the General Assembly that Windham refused to rebuild her bridges, or do anything about the same, so that people were likely to be subjected to great hardships. Dyer, Elderkin and Nathaniel Wales, Jun., were deputized by the town to represent " that these bridges were on the edge of the town; that *five* large bridges had been built within a few years at the expense of £800; all carried off by extraordinary floods which seemed to be much increasing; that this expense was heavy and intolerable, as several of these bridges were more to accommodate other towns and the public, and beg relief." Their request was refused and a bill passed, " That Windham should build and maintain a good and sufficient cart-bridge over each of said rivers at the places designated by petitioners, viz., one over the Shetucket, on the road from Windham to Hartford, known as Old Town Bridge, and one over the Willimantic, called the Iron Works Bridge. Mansfield was directed to rebridge the Nachaug. In 1774, the town of Windham was ordered to build and maintain a bridge across the Shetucket upon a road lately laid out to New Hampshire, to accommodate the travel to the new college in Hanover. The selectmen of Windham were now required, "To provide suitable houses for the poor, and persons to take care of them, rates for the same to be paid in provisions."

Social life in Windham was still characterized by exuberant hilarity. "Jaunting and junketing," feasting and merry-making were more and more in vogue. A very free and generous style of living had been adopted by the upper circle, rivaling that of the leading families in the larger towns. Windham's relations with Norwich were especially close and cordial, and were marked by continual interchange of hospitalities and festivities. Entertainment was made easy by the great number of negroes. Nearly every household owned its servants, generally a man and wife, with a great brood of children. They were a careless, happy set, fond of joking and fiddling, and added much to the general jollity. Colonel Dyer's body-servant Jack, the son of an African prince, was chief among these negroes. He accompanied his master upon many public missions, and was distinguished for gentlemanly demeanor. Colonel Dyer had a houseful of negroes, great and small, and entertained much company in fine style. Pictures and rarities brought from abroad adorned his handsome residence. A very prominent and popular household at this time was that of Colonel Eleazer Fitch, son of Joseph Fitch of Lebanon. Remarkably distinguished in person, being six feet four inches in height, and three hundred pounds in weight, and called "the best-looking officer in the American army," he was still more noted for social attractions and elegant accomplishments. Inheriting an ample estate, he had enjoyed superior educational and social advantages, and was especially distinguished for musical taste and acquirements, and appreciation of art and literature. Entering early into public life he had served as an officer in the French war, aided in negotiating the Delaware purchase, and secured the position of high sheriff of Windham County. His stately mansion, built in 1769 on Zion's Hill, was one of the most tasteful residences in Eastern Connecticut. Here many daughters were growing up and taking their place in society, distinguished like their father by beauty, grace and musical culture. The daughters of Mr. James Flint were ranked among the Windham belles of this date.

In schools Windham was still deficient. The grammar school enjoined by law upon towns of her standing and population was not maintained with any degree of efficiency. These brilliant young ladies were indebted for their training to "a dame's school" on the Green, and a few months "finishing" in Hartford or New London. Moses Cook Welch of Mansfield, opened a grammar school on Windham Green after his graduation from Yale in 1772, but soon relinquished it to study law with Colonel Dyer. The young men of the wealthier families were usually sent to college after preparatory study with Mr. White, or Dr. Wheelock in Lebanon. Windham was deeply interested in the various educational movements initiated by the latter. One of his early Windham neighbors and playmates, Joshua More, gave a house and land in Mansfield to be appropriated to the training up of Indian youth for ministerial and missionary service, and a good Windham lady left a legacy in behalf of this Christian enterprise. Windham made earnest but unsuccessful efforts to retain this school. Her ministers, Rev. Messrs. White and Mosely, were members of the convention for considering its removal, and Windham students accompanied President Wheelock on his migration to the wilderness, and were among the first graduates of Dartmouth College. Samuel Gray, Jun., was graduated with the first class in 1771, and Augustine Hebard the following year. The latter soon went out to Canada on a mission to the Indians. Hezekiah Bissell, Joseph Huntington, Vine Elderkin, Ebenezer Gray, Hezekiah Ripley and Shubael Abbe were also graduated from Yale College during this period. Most of these young men remained in Windham, filling the places left vacant by death and emigration. Dr. Ebenezer Gray died in 1773; Dr. Jonathan Huntington in 1777. After a life marked by "piety to God and benevolence to mankind," this distinguished and beloved physician endured the most intense sufferings without a murmur or complaint, exhibiting to its close "a striking picture of that fortitude and patience which christianity alone can inspire." They were succeeded in practice by Dr. Samuel Lee of Goshen, a young man of "herculean strength and agility" and ardent patriotism, who had enjoyed the professional training of Dr. Ezekiel Porter of Wethersfield.

Windham's First Church was less prosperous than in previous periods. Its numbers were lessening, and its stated worship was losing its hold upon the public mind. The mild and gentle character of Mr. White's preaching and influence was little fitted to cope with increasing worldliness and many opposing elements. Deacon Nathaniel Skiff died in 1761. Nathaniel Wales, Sen., and Joseph Huntington still served in the deacon's office. Jonathan Martin and Elijah Bingham were chosen junior deacons in 1765. The numerous "sectaries" continued their opposition to the standing order. Those in the first society had now become very much imbued with Baptist sentiments. Mr. Benjamin Lathrop, a worthy and respected citizen, obtained "ordination in that line," and had a small number of followers to whom he administered religious ordinances, but had no fixed place of worship. Elijah Bibbins served as its deacon.

Scotland Parish shared in the secular prosperity of the town. Rev. Ebenezer Devotion was held in high reputation throughout the colony as "a great divine, a pious man, an able politician, eminent for every kind of merit." So great was the public confidence in his judgment and wisdom that after the passage of the Stamp Act he was sent by Windham to represent her in the General Assembly, as the man most competent to advise in that great crisis, "a very singular instance," according to President Stiles. While strongly favoring the popular side in politics, and encouraging his fellow-citizens in their resistance to arbitrary enactments, he never forgot the respect due to constituted authorities, nor omitted his public prayer for the King and Royal Family. Still less did he waver in his hostility to religious sectaries, or favor any dissent from the ecclesiastic constitution of Connecticut, or fail to send his negro every Sabbath morning with a written order for Rev. John Palmer, forbidding him to preach within his territorial limits. Although this Separate Brunswick Church had been for many years organized, and maintained its regular worship, its members were still forced to pay rates for Mr. Devotion, or suffer the loss of cattle and goods, or imprisonment in Windham jail. In 1765, Deacon Edward Waldo made confession for unlawful separation, and was restored to his former standing in the First Church. Deacons Cary and Kingsley continued many years in active service. Mr. Devotion died while yet in the prime of life to the great grief of church and community. An elaborate epitaph on the monument in Scotland's burying-ground testified to the high character and reputation of the deceased pastor, and is pronounced by most competent authority* "not beyond the truth :"—

" To the memory of the great and good man—the Rev. Ebenezer Devotion, first Pastor of the Congregational church in Windham. He was born in Suffield, May 8, 1714, ordained, Oct. 22, 1735, and died July, 1771. Descended from venerable ancestors, he increased the honor of the family. His genius was universal, which being cultivated with diligence rendered him eminent in the various branches of science and most peculiarly as a Politician and Divine. He was an example of benevolence, gravity, fortitude, sobriety, cheerfulness, prudence and hospitality ; an unshaken friend, a kind husband, a tender parent, a sincere Christian, a wise and faithful minister of Christ. Greatly esteemed by all good judges of his acquaintance and beloved by his flock.

<blockquote>
Death wounds to cure; we fall;
We rise; we reign.
We spring from our fetters,
We fasten in the skies."
</blockquote>

Mr. Devotion was succeeded in the pastoral office by Rev. James Cogswell, then recently dismissed from Canterbury, who received a unanimous call from church and society, with the offer of £60 settlement, £80 salary, and "the liberty of getting his firewood on the lot the society had of James Manning." Notwithstanding many doubts and qualms as to his ability to fill the place of so distinguished a personage, Mr. Cogswell personally appeared and accepted, and with the countenance and aid of his most valued ministerial brethren, was happily installed Feb. 19, 1772. The Reverends Throop, White, Whitney, Ripley and Lee were present, together with Joseph Huntington, a son of the Scotland church, John Devotion, brother of the former pastor, and an honored deacon or leading brother from each church represented in the council. Ebenezer Devotion, Experience Robinson, Nathaniel Hebard, Jeremiah Bingham, Joseph Ginnings and James Gager served as providing committee. With far less strength and decision of character than his predecessor, Mr. Cogswell was probably not his inferior in culture, or in pulpit ministrations, and his kindliness of temper and genial manners soon won popular favor. Scarcely had he removed to Scotland when he was called to severe affliction, in the loss of his wife, Mrs. Alice Fitch Cogswell, and their only daughter, Alice, who, in the twenty-third year of her age, May 11, 1772, "departed this vain transitory life in firm hope of a glorious immortality." Her funeral sermon was preached by Rev. Mr. Hart, who touchingly bemoaned this only daughter of her dear mother now no more, who had grown up from infancy with great promise, making most uncommon progress in the useful as well as

*Professor James L. Kingsley, Yale College, 1851.

ornamental parts of female learning. Following the example of many of his ministerial associates Mr. Cogswell in due time married the widow of his predecessor—Mrs. Martha Lathrup Devotion—and occupied her pleasant homestead. Her children were now mostly settled in life. Ebenezer, the only son, had married a daughter of Dr. Jonathan Huntington, engaged in trade and held many public offices. One daughter was married to Samuel Huntington of Norwich, another to Rev. Joseph Huntington, and a third to John M. Breed of Norwich. Two bright young daughters still cheered the family mansion. The uncommon social accomplishments of Mr. Cogswell and his three promising sons made them a welcome acquisition to this large family circle, and the Scotland parsonage with its agreeable inmates and throngs of distinguished visitants became one of the most attractive of Windham's many famous social centres.

With a new minister, Scotland aspired to a new meeting-house. After having been compelled "to mend the glass when much broken, by taking from other windows and boarding them up where least useful"—it was voted, Nov. 9, 1772, to build a meeting-house for the public worship of God, and there were ninety-eight yeas and twenty nays. Elisha Lillie, Captain Joseph Ginnings, Seth Palmer, Experience and Reuben Robinson, were chosen "to draw a plan of bigness of meeting-house." It was agreed to give Mr. Elisha Lillie £750, for building the house, walls clapboarded with rived pine clapboards, and colored with a decent color; but it was not till June, 1774, that a committee was chosen to procure the necessary rigging and help, together with suitable provisions for raising the frame. The opposition of the Separates was one cause of this delay. Finding that they were about to be taxed heavily for this new house of worship, they appealed to the General Assembly, showing:—

"That in 1749, believing in good conscience that the principles and articles and some of the doctrines adhered to by the Scotland church and people, were not agreeable to the gospel, and as they or most of them hoped they were enlightened by the light of God's countenance, and found by repeated trials that they could not profit by the ministrations of Mr. Devotion, and in 1749, confederated together separate from said minister and people, and set up a religious worship according to the dictates of their own consciences, and called Mr. John Palmer as elder or teacher, who was ordained over them and has continued preaching the gospel and administering the sacraments to your memorialists, and they have freely contributed to his support, and built a comfortable house to accommodate those who join with them in divine service, and all this time have been forced to pay for the support of Mr. Devotion and Mr. Cogswell, and repairing the meeting-house, and other society charges, although they have earnestly requested relief in vain,— wherein they beg you to consider if it is agreeable to the laws of Christ or consonant to the rules of equity for your memorialists and their children, to have their effects by force of law taken from them to support a minister with whom they never did nor can join in worship, and support their own

minister too, and pray you to take their distressing case into your consideration and enact that they be made a distinct society.

Zacheus Waldo.	John Walden.	John Silsbury.
Zebulon Hebard.	Stephen Webb.	Timothy Allen.
Lemuel Bingham.	Israel Hale.	Samuel Baker, Jun.
Ebenezer Webb.	William Perkins.	Jedidiah Bingham.
John Palmer.	Joseph Allen, Jun.	Henry Bass.
Benjamin Cleveland.	Jonathan Brewster.	Moses Cleveland.
Joseph Allen.	Ebenezer Bass.	

Windham, April 5, 1773."

This reasonable request obtained a favorable hearing, and Brunswick church was at last released from its heavy burden The standing society was greatly aggrieved at this curtailment of their powers
and privileges, and bitterly bemoaned this "act of Assembly, taking
a number of inhabitants, and discharging them from paying taxes."
At a society meeting called to consider how to make up the deficit,
it was voted to lay a tax for that purpose. "All inhabitants over
ten years old" were ordered to be listed, and a rate of twelve-pence
of the pound found needful. The school-house seeming likely to
endanger the meeting-house by fire, was moved a suitable distance.
Pews were built as ordered, and the meeting-house seated by a competent committee in December, 1778, and in the succeeding May, it
was formally accepted "as built by Elisha Lillie." The old house
then "put upon sail," brought back seventeen pounds.

V.

WINDHAM'S SECOND SOCIETY. PEW DISPUTE. SCHOOL DIS-
TRICTS SET OUT. CONTROVERSY WITH REV. SAMUEL
MOSELY. VOLUNTOWN.

CANADA Parish continued to increase and prosper though subjected to the usual secular and ministerial controversies. The
venerable Deacon Thomas Stedman generally presided at society meetings; Stephen Durkee served as clerk; Captain John Howard of Howard's Valley, David Fuller and Joseph Burnham as society committee;
Jeremiah Durkee and Jacob Simmons, collectors; Ichabod Downing,
Capt. William Durkee and Lieut. Jonathan Kingsbury, school committee. Ten pounds were added in 1762 to the salary of Rev. Samuel
Mosely. The congregation and community were much disturbed at
this date by a difficulty in seating the new and elegant meeting-house.
The persons entrusted with this delicate office had not exercised due
judgment. Not only did they seat six grown persons in one pew—
and persons grown in this goodly neighborhood attained capacious

8

dimensions—but they allowed "men of little or no estate to sit very forward and in high pews," while others of good estate and high in public esteem were compelled with shame to take a lower seat. Galleries and body-seats were left very thin compared to these coveted pews, and the galleries were so given over to light-minded youth that the tithing-men were obliged to leave their seats below to keep them in order. This state of things created much talk and uneasiness especially among the foremost men, that they should be so crowded and misplaced in order to get men into the pews that never paid enough for the meeting-house to build one pew, and after enduring this grievance several years a meeting was called, Dec. 9, 1762, to rectify it. William Bennett was chosen moderator, and it was voted by a great majority, "To sell the pews at public vendue, no man to buy no more than one, and no man out of the society to buy one ; Capt. Robert Durkee to serve as vendue master." This action greatly increased the public excitement. The older members of the society were at once aroused to the inexpediency and danger of allowing private individuals to select their own seats in the house of worship, and become proprietors of a part of the sacred edifice. In spite of remonstrance and opposition the vote was carried out, and the valiant Captain who had served so bravely in the French and Indian war, now sold the pews in the face of the opposing enemy. Twenty-five pews on the floor of the house were assigned to the following purchasers, at prices ranging from fourteen pounds to three, viz.: Jeremiah Utley, John Fuller, Hezekiah Hammond, Stephen Durkee, Timothy Pearl, Zebediah Farnham, Ebenezer Hovey, Capt. John Howard, Dea. Ebenezer Griffin, Henry Durkee, Daniel Farnham, Thomas Stedman, Jun., Isaac Bennett, Jephthah Utley, William Farnham, Joseph Burnham, John Hammond, Benjamin Cheddle, Stephen Arnold, John Sessions, Jonathan Clark, Samuel Fuller, John Smith, Gideon Martin, Isaac Clark. Although many of these purchasers were the leading, solid men of the society, the clamor was not in the least abated. Some with no families, but single persons— "bachelors, who had never paid rates for more than one head and a horse," and some not qualified voters had presumed to bid off pews and gain possession of an uppermost seat in the synagogue, "whereby the society was thrown into the most unhappy contention." Another meeting was called, and Lieut. Kingsbury appointed agent, "to take advice concerning the difficulty concerning pews," who straightway laid the case before Colonel Dyer, Major Elderkin and Major Griswold. By their advice another society meeting was held April 21, 1763, the vote for selling the pews was set aside by a large majority, and Jacob Simmons deputized to represent the affair to the General Assembly and secure confirmation of their proceedings. The purchasers of the pews attempted to show that the vote to sell the pews was not suddenly passed; that no open objections were made till after the sale; that only five of them were young men without families, and that nine societies in Windham County already held pews as private property. These representations were ineffectual, and the famous pew vote of December 9, and proceedings thereupon, were made null and void by Act of Assembly. The society resumed possession of its much valued pews, appointing Abiel Abbott, Joseph Marsh and Ebenezer Hovey to seat the congregation therein with the requisite order and formality. Sundry residents of Canterbury, viz. : Jethro Rogers, James Bidlack, Aaron Fuller and Zebediah Farnham were now admitted to society privileges in Canada. Captain William Durkee was directed " to search after the right (if any we have) to the lot of land called the Ministerial Lot in Windham ;" the society committee " to distribute the books called Saybrook Platform sent to the society by Government ;" and Robert Holt " to bring and take care of the christening basin as occasion shall require."

In 1763, Captain William Durkee, Lieut. Kingsbury, Nathaniel Ford, Zebediah Farnham, Abiel Abbott, John Sessions and Joseph Burnham were appointed a committee to set out school districts, which was accomplished within two years. The First or Central district began very properly by " taking in the Rev. Mr. Mosely and ranging so as to take in Mr. Joseph Sessions, and from thence west to Burnt Cedar Swamp, and then following the main stream of Cedar Swamp Brook till it comes to the road below Benjamin Burgess', and from thence to said Mosely's." Number Two extended " from old Mr. John Perkins' to Mr. Joseph Burnham's, and all east and south of Cedar Swamp Brook." Number Three ran " from Jonathan Holt's, taking in Holt's house, and north, taking in all the inhabitants situated on the road to Mr. Joseph Marsh's, taking in said Marsh's house, and from thence taking in Mr. William Alworth's and James Alworth's house, and ranging north to the easternmost extent of the society." Number Four took in " Mr. Stephen Clark's house, and then south all the inhabitants west of Cedar Swamp, and so far as to take in Mr. Jonathan Fish's and Mr. David Canada's houses, and so south and west to the extent of the society." School-house sites were affixed by William Osgood and Seth Paine of Pomfret, and Benajah Cary of Windham, viz. : one in the northeast district near Deacon Griffin's house, and two in the northwest or fourth district, one nine rods south of William Holt's ; another eight rods west of John Fuller's. " Eleven months schooling by a master, to be kept in each district according to its list," was thought sufficient for the whole society in the winter, and school-dames were engaged for the little ones in the summer. Upon the humble petition of Joseph Durkee, Jonathan and David Fish, Benjamin Flint, Edward and Samuel Coburn, Jonathan Holt, William Neff and Joseph Utley, a fifth district was set off in 1774, in the northeast section, known as Appaquage.

Efforts were now made to secure greater local privileges. Connection with Windham was in many respects burdensome and inconvenient. The distance was great, and town and parish had few interests in common. In 1767 it was voted, "That this society is desirous to be made into a district, to be allowed all the powers and privileges of a town, except choosing our own deputies and other business of freemen's meeting." Jacob Simmons, Ebenezer Hovey and Abiel Abbott were chosen to apply to the selectmen of Windham, and to endeavor to obtain consent of town, and to consult with counsel and procure necessary preparations in order to obtain our request. Captain John Howard was also empowered to aid them in preparing a petition. This proving fruitless in the following year it was further voted, "That this society is desirous to be made into an entire and distinct town, and will apply to the General Assembly." Captain Jonathan Kingsbury was appointed agent in their behalf, but his pleas though repeatedly urged were unsuccessful.

In 1768 the society voted to repair and new color the meeting-house. Captain Kingsbury, Abiel Abbott and Thomas Fuller were appointed a committee to color said meeting-house as aforesaid, and—in order to be in the highest style of fashion—they were farther ordered, "To color the same something like the color of Pomfret meeting-house." Captain John Howard was added to this committee in 1771, in place of Capt. Kingsbury, deceased.

The prosperity of Canada Parish was somewhat checked during these years, by a very unpleasant controversy with Mr. Mosely. Possessing a strong will and very positive opinions, he had assumed with advancing years more and more authority over his people, and by excessive use of the negative power allowed by Saybrook Platform was able to exercise supreme control in all church affairs. A large majority of the church were opposed to Saybrook Platform, and especially the ministerial negative derived from it, but, esteeming their pastor an eminently holy and godly minister, silently acquiesced in his administration. A few of the leading men, warmly imbued with the revolutionary spirit of the times, resented this infringement of their religious rights and resolved to resist it. The original covenant of the church by which they simply took the Scriptures for their guide, allowed, they thought, too great latitude to the pastor. A more explicit covenant and plan of discipline were suggested, and also "a body of ruling elders" to balance the power of "the teaching elder," but as Mr. Mosely was much opposed to any innovation and would only warn church meetings at his own pleasure they found it very difficult to bring the matter before the church. They therefore requested Mr. Mosely to call a church meeting, " to learn the mind of the church about dealing with baptized persons, and about choosing some of the fathers to assist therein." At this meeting, Feb. 9, 1769, the church unanimously voted, to proceed to deal with baptized; *i. e.*, " Half-covenant " members, but when the second article was proposed " one and another went off from it and spoke for a Platform and ruling elders," to which Mr. Mosely replied, that they were settled on the Word of God for their Platform, that with their different sentiments they should not agree on any Platform of human composure, that if agreed in the great essential things to bear down sin and promote holiness they must exercise mutual forbearance in their different sentiments about lesser matters; that he was thankful to God they were so well agreed in said important articles and thought he should sin if he indulged in debate about Platforms,—and " being much overcome with cold," straightway dismissed the church. Thus debarred from discussion or opportunity of further action, the indignant brethren appointed five prominent church members, viz.: William Durkee, Jonathan Kingsbury, Jonathan Burnap, George Martin and William Foster, to remonstrate the matter with their pastor, who entreated him as a father to look into the subject, and consider the expediency of having an explicit model or Platform of church discipline deduced from Scripture and introduced peaceably as soon as might be into their church, according to the commendable example of the best Reformed churches in Christendom. They also entreated him to satisfy them and the church they represented, by what authority, divine or human, his claim and exercise of a supreme and sole power over the church of Christ met in his name was warranted. "This exertion of the teaching elder's power and authority, in opposition to almost every other church in New England, abundantly convinced them of the necessity of having other office bearers in the church, viz.: *ruling elders*—joined in ruling and governing the church with the elder that labors in word and doctrine. The brethren of the church had usurped no authority, nor encroached in the least upon the prerogative, office or dignity of the pastor, but in a modest and peaceable manner moved to confer upon the duty and expediency of a Platform without pretending to say upon what model it should be formed; whereupon the pastor did dissolve the meeting, contrary to the duty of a moderator in all meetings civil or religious, contrary to the law of the Colony which prohibits their *adjournment* without consent of the majority; much less to *dissolve* the meeting without such consent."

"We entreat you," continued the remonstrants, "to consider whether this alarming exertion of authority doth not carry in it some appearance of lording it over God's heritage, so detested by our fathers that it drove New England out of Old, to avoid a yoke that neither we nor our fathers could bear. . . . We entreat you, timely to consider, that if after such an unprecedented dissolution of the church meeting, you are pleased to take advantage thereof, and refuse to be entreated by us because you have disabled the church to appear by a legal representation, and will no more warn a church meeting to treat with them upon the premises. Sir. your triumph upon a victory so gained will be short. Can you think, sir, in this day of struggle in defence of civil liberties and rights in America, this church will tamely submit to be deprived of their divine and sacred privileges, so preferable to all our inheritance besides, and give such an example of slavery and dependency as to submit to such a supreme authority in the ministry over the church. Was the church made for ministers or ministers for the church ? Think you there are none who will appear on the Lord's side in this case, and all other sidings we detest and hold in contempt. Are not all the constitutional clergy and churches and cloud of witnesses in New England and throughout the Reformed Protestant churches listed under this banner, whose footsteps we are essaying to trace out. Would you have us stand still and be robbed of those sacred liberties and privileges that have flowed to the church in the blood of Christ, the Supreme Head thereof. Sir, the Lord forbid that we should give the inheritance of our fathers unto thee. Shall not we possess what the Lord our God hath given us to possess. Finally, sir, we entreat you to let us, and the church by us know, what we are to expect from you for the future in this matter, and if upon cool reflection you find . . . you have unadvisedly dissolved said church meeting, you would be pleased without loss of time upon better advisement to warn another meeting for the purpose and end aforesaid, wherein we desire you to go before us in the good work aforesaid, according to the duty set forth by the prophet Ezekiel. 'Thou son of man, shew the house to the house of Israel, and shew them the form of the house.'   *Windham, Feb. 20, 1769.*"

Mr. Mosely thereupon called and held a church meeting, March 3, to consider these matters, and so. "terrified" the weaker brethren by representing to them that they would have to support their ruling as well as teaching elder, and might have to settle a new minister and pay damages to the old one by insisting upon a church Platform, that a majority voted against the proposed changes. The minority thereupon drew up a paper far more inflammatory and bitter than the previous "remonstrance," in which they alleged various specific charges against the pastor, as follows :—

"1. The power and right you claim in negativing the church we deny, and say the key of discipline was given to the church by Christ . . . and can find no rule in Scripture for your prerogative power except you take it from Diotrephes, who loved to have preëminence . . . and the apostle saith he wrote to the church there, and that his evil example ant to be followed.
    2. Your dissolving church meetings in the midst of business without the consent of the church we say is an error, and there is no scripture warrant for such a prerogative power.
    3. We think you exert unreasonable and unscriptural power in confining the church in their meetings to what you have put in the warning, and your taking the power of putting in what you pleased, in this you are more arbitrary than any of our civil powers . . . Sir, we do think the church ought to enjoy as great a privilege in their meetings as towns and societies do, for if we may believe Christ and the apostles, no men on earth have greater liberty than the church of Christ.
    4. We think, Sir, that you err much as moderator in our church meetings, for you will have the chief of the talk, and so lay your plan and scheme and

pursue the same in the church that we think such plans and schemes laid and pursued in the church resemble deceit more than honesty. . . . . .

9. We think you very much err in opening the door so wide into the church as to admit members without some satisfying account of a work of grace on their hearts, and without the consent of the church, merely because they say they are a mind to come. We think, sir, it is the right way to let Anti-Christ into the church full breast, for certain unclean persons and hypocrites have no right in Christ's church.

10. Sir, your taking the key of the meeting-house and holding it, we say is contrary to God's word, and you have no right to it, and not content with that, you rob us of the key of the whole society. Sir, we are bold to say Christ never gave you them keys nor no other man on earth, for he knew how full the world always was and would be of false prophets and teachers that would turn the key against his disciples. Pray, sir, to what purpose had it a ben for our Saviour to have sent out the apostles as he did to preach the gospel to every creature, if these keys had been given to the ministers? Why they must truly have turned back without preaching to *any* creature, with this complaint, Lord, thou sent us out to preach the gospel to every creature but had given the keys of every city, town and house to the *ministers*, and they forbid us. Sir, are you wiser than Christ? Do you know how to manage the keys better than Christ? He never gave them to you. For God's sake give them up, for thou hast nothing to do with them. Can you think, sir, that such a power as you claim is from Christ? No, assuredly you can't unless you make this addition—ANTI—for darkness and light are as near alike as your power and the spirit of Christ—and do consider, Sir, your ingratitude to a people that maintains and supports you; that you should chastize us with scorpions and rule us with a rod of iron and put such chains and bonds on us that we nor our fathers were not able to bear. ! Tell it not in Gath!'

11. Sir, we take it hard that the case of Mrs. Keyes was not brought before the church when so many requested it.

12. Sir, we should be glad to know the reason of your parting Cuff and his wife, and as she was a sister in ye church and in regular standing as far as we know, yet we understand that you did deny her partaking with us.

13. And there are others who have withdrawn from the church these many years and hant been called to no account, and we know not the cause of such a separation. Pray, sir, if you think the key of discipline belongs to you we think you have much neglected your duty. Sir, for you to rob us of ye keys and *not use* them can't be right.

14. We think you are much to blame in denying people copies of the church record when the church has been a dealing with them . . . . and unless you reform we think it duty for this church to appoint some other man to hold the records. . . . .

16. We think, sir, you are very partial in your visits for some houses you visit not for years, others you visit much. Pray remember Christ and his Apostles' commands, and do nothing by partiality, for God is not a respecter of persons.

17. Sir, we desire the church records may be read in this church, even as far back as your ordination, that we may search after the Achan that troubles us, and who can tell but that God will discover it to us, and save us, as he did Israel by Phinehas, or as he did the nation of the Jews by means of the King's hearing the Book read . . . . On that night could not the King sleep, and he commanded to bring the book of the Chronicles, and they were read before the King.' "

This paper, embodying the principal charges against Mr. Mosely, was read before a number of brethren of the church, but as some thought the charges laid too high it was not formally adopted, but kept to aid in preparing something that might be suitable to lay before church and minister in due season. The report of its existence and private circulation greatly exasperated Mr. Mosely, who attempted " to deal " with the chief offenders both publicly and privately. As usual in such affairs many hard things were said on both sides, and charges of misrepresentation and lying were freely interchanged. Each party accused the other of promising copies of votes and documents, and then withholding them. William Foster, who was especially zealous in defending the church against ministerial usurpation, not only affirmed openly, "that Mr. Mosely had lied and he could prove it," but, when reproved by him, replied, "That he saw the Pope's horns begin to bud some years ago, and now they were grown out." Mr. Mosely's method of dealing with these offending brethren was certainly not un- papal. After bickering through the summer, they called a council of ministers and delegates in October, which agreed "That the aggrieved brethren might rationally expect from an undoubted right founded on reason and the Word of God, and agreeable to the general sense and practice of churches in New England, a church meeting for a full, free and open conversation respecting the introduction of some platform of ecclesiastical discipline and government into the church in which it had been too long deficient." But when in accordance with the advice of this council, the aggrieved brethren in a decent and becoming man- ner, without heat or bitterness, earnestly and unitedly besought and entreated their pastor to call a church meeting for a conference upon this important subject, they were answered by a summons to appear before the church for trial :—

"I. For publishing a defamatory paper containing divers misrepresenta- tions and railing words and expressions against the pastor.
II. For taking God's name in vain in said paper, against the third com- mandment.
III. For abominable deceit in asking their pastor to warn a church meet- ing to consider dealing with baptized persons, when their true object was to introduce this question of a Platform."

These charges were tried before the church, Mr. Mosely himself act- ing as moderator in spite of the protestations of the accused brethren. About forty members of the church were present. Seven voted in favor of censure and seven against it. Again the pastor asked if they should proceed to censure, and adding his vote to the seven, pro- nounced the question carried, refusing to call the negative. Eight votes, including those of the pastor, his brother, and nephew, decided the case in a male membership of over fifty denied the liberty of ex- pressing their non-concurrence, an act of ministerial domination rarely surpassed in audacity. The negative power, according to Mr. Mosely, was solely intrusted to *ministers*. In accordance with this vote, Ebene- zer Hovey, Dea. Ebenezer Griffin, Jonathan Burnap, Capt. William Durkee, Jonathan Kingsbury, George Martin, John Clark, Jun., and William Foster were pronounced "guilty of scandalous violation of the third commandment, of publishing a false and scandalous paper, of abominable deceit, contemptuous abuse of the divine institution of discipline, scandalous violations of gospel injunctions," &c., and it was adjudged that these offenders ought to make a public acknowledgment of their sins, or otherwise be proceeded with in a way of censure, and this charge and sentence were publicly read on the Lord's day before church and congregation.

Nothing but the sterling virtues and high Christian character of Mr. Mosely saved him from the storm that followed. The outraged brethren refused to submit to the censure, and insisted upon its retraction. Public opinion and ministerial counsel sustained them in this demand, and in almost any church a rupture and separation would have been inevitable. But in spite of his wilfulness and arbitrary government, Mr. Mosely was greatly beloved and respected by the majority of his people. Many who disapproved of his conduct chose to retain him as their pastor, and by their conciliatory efforts both parties were brought to intrust decision to a council. The Reverends Solomon Williams, David Hall, Benj. Throup, Aaron Hutchinson, Aaron Putnam and Levi Flint, with delegates from their respective churches, were convened in Windham Village, May 22, 1770, " to hear, judge and advise between the pastor and major part of the church and a number of aggrieved brethren," and decided, " That the charges against the aforesaid brethren were not sustained; that they ought to be acquitted from censure; and that the church should accordingly release them from the censure they had laid them under and restore them unto their charity." This advice was followed, and the brethren restored to fellowship. Still, the breach was far from healed. Violent recriminations had been interchanged between the combatants. William Foster persisted in reiterating that " Mr. Mosely had lied," whereupon he was again arraigned before the church to account for his false and scandalous language. Foster offered to submit to trial under an impartial moderator unsubjected to the pastor's negative. The church voted to go on with their pastor for moderator according to their custom, upon which Foster " left the meeting, refusing trial." Mr. Mosely immediately led the church to vote him guilty of contempt of that authority which Christ had placed in the church, and proceeded to excommunicate him. The aggrieved brethren called another council, i. e., Dr. Hopkins and Dr. Stiles of Newport, Leonard of Woodstock and Fuller of Plainfield. These gentlemen " might have cleared them " on the same ground that the previous council had done, but disapproved of the severe and bitter expressions against the pastor, and deferred decision. A second attempt was more successful, and a general concession and forgiveness on both sides agreed to, William Foster, the chief offender and sufferer, declaring:—

9

"That although in the time I did think I had occasion to think Mr. Mosely did in some measure evade the truth, yet upon a more mature deliberation I am sensible I preferred my charge against him with an undue temper of mind, and unnecessarily published the same, and especially in telling him, 'He knew he lied,' in his own house, but on a further consideration of the matter I would charitably hope and believe that Mr. Mosely was not guilty of wilfully departing from the truth, and therefore ask forgiveness of Mr. Mosely and my offended brethren, and pray them to receive me into their charity. *Windham Society, Oct.* 31, 1771."

In spite of these concessions and retractions the controversy soon broke out afresh. The root of the difficulty had not been reached. An explicit church covenant had not been secured nor Mr. Mosely's power restricted. A majority of the aggrieved brethren accepted the decision and walked in harmony with the church, but Capt. Durkee, Jonathan Burnap and William Foster still resisted and remonstrated. Each side accused the other of violating the agreement. The old charges were interchanged, civil suits instituted. After some years of strife and violence, the following complaint against Mr. Mosely was laid before the Windham County Association:—

"Whereas, I, the said William Foster, do esteem myself to have been grievously.oppressed and injured for a number of years past by the *arbitrary and unscriptural proceedings* of the said Rev. Mr. Mosely in his church administrations and otherwise; in particular, *in his repeatedly entering processes against me in his own name, and judging in his own cause,* as also in troubling me and other peaceable members of said church *with unscriptural processes* to the vexation of the church, and the disturbance of its peace and edification; *in his withholding copies of church votes* that I had right to, and adding thereto such prevarications relative to the same, and such shifts and evasions *as I cannot but esteem a breach of the ninth command;* in leading the church to pass votes concerning me in church meeting without notifying me to be present, *and refusing to let me see the votes afterwards or to allow me copies of the same;* in *his refusing* a christian conference on matters of grievance, *or to join in a council* to hear and settle all matters of controversy; *in his refusing to lay matters of church concern before the church; in his wantonly dissolving church meetings in the midst of business of great concern to the church;* in his neglect of discipline to scandalous members in the church, and preventing the exercise thereof in the church by other members, and opposing all means used in the church for a reformation; *in his refusing to administer baptism to my children* for no justifiable reason, and while they have an indisputable right thereto; and it is a matter of grievance to me *and I take it to be the spring* of all the arbitrary proceedings above said; that said Mr. Mosely *challenges a power* over the church unknown in the Holy Scriptures; it is also a matter of grievance, that said Mr. Mosely has *needlessly troubled me in the civil law* when I was always ready to have all matters of controversy heard and decided in an ecclesiastic way according to the rules of the gospel, and whereas I have used every method in my power for the redress of the aforesaid grievances and the removal of offences but to no purpose, the honor of God, the interest of religion, the peace and edification of said church, and my own as well as the good of the said Rev. Mr. Mosely, unitedly and most strongly oblige as well as necessitate me to lay this information and complaint and represent my grievances before this Reverend Association, that such order may be taken and measures may be directed to and pursued as may tend to the removal of the aforesaid grievances and offences according to gospel rule.   WILLIAM FOSTER.
Sept. 23, 1778."

These charges were considered, first, by a council, and afterwards, by the consociated churches of the County, Jan. 4, 1779. It was adjudged that neither party was guilty in manner and form as alleged. The Reverend pastor was entreated as a venerable and much beloved father to examine himself and labor after greater perfection of gentleness and circumspection ; the offending brother admonished to search his own heart and ways, and strive and pray that in future he might possess and discover a more meek and peaceable spirit, and show a more decent regard to the sacred ordinances of Christ, giving no just offence to his ministers or churches ; and the people of God earnestly advised and exhorted, " never more to revive, nor suffer to be revived any of those matters of difficulty which had been under the consideration of the council, but to bury this long unhappy con tention in everlasting oblivion."

This excellent advice was apparently followed. No change in the administration of church affairs was effected during the life-time of Mr. Mosely, and with advancing years he became less arbitrary and exacting. That his people were not inclined to submit to over-exactions may be inferred from their choosing a committee to wait upon him to learn his reasons " why he took sixty pounds for his salary, when by computing silver at six and eight-pence per ounce it would be but fifty-nine pounds, two shillings and five-pence." Whether he was compelled to refund the surplus shillings and pennies is not recorded.

In thrift and activity Canada Parish kept pace with other sections of the town, and " Windham Village " on its fair hill-top was hardly less a power than Windham Green in the southwest corner. The bountiful harvests gathering in Apaquage's beautiful valley incited the farmers to unusual efforts during the revival of commercial prosperity. Captain James Stedman owned much land and carried on extensive farming operations, and was greatly respected as a man of substance and business capacity. His brother Thomas, the skillful builder of meeting-houses, was equally respected. Deacon Ebenezer Griffin, Captain John Howard, Jacob Simmons and many other men of weight and influence were actively engaged in business and public affairs. Jeremiah, fifth son of John Clark, was trader as well as farmer, buying up such produce as he could take to Newport or Providence on horseback. John Brewster of Scotland Parish, after studying medicine with Dr. Barker of Franklin, married a daughter of Captain William Durkee, and settled in Windham village, and gained an extensive practice as the first and only physician in the vicinity. The women of this parish were especially thrifty and notable, true help-meets to their husbands. Mrs. Jeremiah Clark and Mrs. Wil-

liam Holt were skilled in the art of making fine lace, as well as all
needful domestic fabrics. The emigration to Wyoming carried away
many of these energetic and valuable families. Captain Robert
Durkee, cousin of John Durkee of Norwich, Stephen Fuller and John
Holt were among these emigrants. Captain Durkee was a man of
great courage and distinguished himself in many daring exploits, while
Mr. Stephen Fuller was equally useful in attending to the ordinary
routine of town affairs.

Other sons of Canada Parish went out into the world upon more peace
ful missions. Ebenezer Martin, a Yale graduate of 1756, after preaching for a time among the wilds of Berkshire, returned to labor in the
new parish of Westford, in his native county. Ebenezer, son of
Rev. Samuel Mosely, was graduated in 1763, and after preparatory
studies was licensed to preach by the Brookfield Association, Massachusetts, June 19, 1765. Two years later he was ordained and sent
out by that body to labor in the Indian Mission, established in 1762,
among The Six Nations, at Onohoquaga on the Susquehanna. "The
mortification he must endure in a situation so remote from any English settlements" was deeply commiserated by the missionary society
which had charge of the enterprise, but perhaps the most serious
danger which threatened the young missionary while among the
savages was a matrimonial proposition from the principal sachem,
"who offered and urged his daughter upon him for his wife." As a
direct refusal of this flattering overture would give great offence and
might endanger the lives of the missionaries, Mr. Mosely could only
plead the necessity of gaining consent of his father, a plea whose
validity was fortunately recognized by the Indian code of etiquette.

Voluntown was still in an unsettled and unhappy condition, the
greater part of its inhabitants averse to the established church, and
yet compelled to pay rates for the support of the aged minister. Attempts were made by residents of each end of the town to procure
distinct society privileges. A petition signed by Ebenezer Dow, town
clerk and one of the principal inhabitants, together with John James,
Joshua and Moses Campbell, Jeremiah, James and Moses Kinne, Hugh
and John Wylie, Jonathan Minor, David Kennedy, Moses Fish and
others, represented to the Assembly, September, 1762:—

"That there was but one society in Voluntown, twenty miles long and four
or five wide; list in 1761, £10,786; inhabitants settled at each end and dispersed in almost every part, about one hundred and eighty families, some
dwelling seven, some nine and ten miles from meeting-house; trouble of
transporting ourselves and families very great and heavy; town conveniently
situated for division; such burden of travel hardly to be found in any other
town—and prayed for division."

In 1764, Roger Billings and others asked for a new society, "beginning where Pachaug River runs out of Pawcamuck Pond," and taking in the north parts of Stonington and Preston. A committee was appointed and reported against petition, as the Preston people were already well accommodated. Voluntown they found more than sixteen miles long and three or four in width, occupied by two hundred families; inhabitants much scattered; many six and eight miles from any place of public worship; roads bad; yet inasmuch as a majority of them were against division, and were less able to bear great charges than usual by reason of drought and uncommon public charges, they would not recommend it.

As Mr. Dorrance increased in years and infirmities, the town became more and more reluctant to pay for his support. A committee was sent to him in 1769, "to see whether he did not think there was a proper vacancy in the town, and that it was high time he should lay down his pastoral charge over the town in order that they may take some proper way more effectually to accommodate themselves on account of the Gospel," but Mr. Dorrance declined to listen to their proposals, whereupon the town withheld the stipulated salary. After two years wrangling Mr. Dorrance agreed "to join with the town and church in the most easy manner, call a council and be dismissed from the pastoral charge, provided the town paid him the judgment obtained in Court for his salary in 1769, and £44, 6s. 6d. for 1770, and £25 per annum every year so long as he lives." A council was accordingly held March 5, 1771. Mr. Cogswell reports "that the affair was conducted amicably; that Mr. Dorrance seemed to bear his age wonderfully and was dismissed in peace." He survived his dismissal a few years, and died Nov. 12, 1775, aged ninety years. The Providence *Gazette* eulogizes him as "a zealous contender for the faith once delivered to the saints, and an ornament to the religion he professed." His son Lemuel remained upon the homestead; Samuel removed to Coventry, R. I.; James to Brooklyn Parish; John and George emigrated to Wyoming. His daughter, Susanna, married to Robert Dixon, resided in the north part of Voluntown.

Various changes followed the dismissal of Mr. Dorrance. Isaac Gallup, Thomas Douglas, John Keigwin, Joseph Parke, Israel Babcock and others—"very desirous to enjoy public worship as we think right which is according to the Congregational platform"—now received liberty from the town and General Assembly to join in a society by themselves without being interrupted by any other society. A society called Nazareth was thereupon organized in the south part of Voluntown, and a church gathered there. Feb. 13, 1772, Mr. Levi Hart of Preston, preached a sermon and gave advice, and Jeremiah, James,

Moses and Ira Kinne, William Hewson, Thomas Stewart and Moses Fish were embodied into church orders according to the "Congregational Independent platform." They agreed :—

"That no coercive measures be used for supporting the minister.

That it is the duty of every one to contribute of his worldly substance for the maintenance of the ministry, and every one of this church who neglects and refuses to do so shall be deemed an offender in the sin of covetousness.

That our minister shall have liberty to preach among the Separates.

That private brethren may exhort in public, provided they do not interrupt other parts of duty, and speak to the edification of the church."

April 18, Solomon Morgan of Groton, was ordained pastor of the Nazareth Church. It gained in membership and influence, but did not succeed for some years in building a house of worship.

In 1772, fifty-four persons north of Moosup River, including John James and George Dorrance, Robert, Thomas and James Dixon, Robert Montgomery, John Coles, John Gaston, Mark and David Eames, some of them six, seven, eight and nine miles from Voluntown meeting-house, and greatly impeded by bad roads and traveling, received liberty from the Assembly to organize as a distinct society or join in worship with Killingly. A number of these northern residents consequently united with the church in South Killingly, and after some years organized as a distinct society.

The mother church in Voluntown centre, weakened and crippled by these repeated losses, was unable to settle a pastor and could scarcely maintain regular worship. Its numbers and strength were still farther diminished by the large emigration to Wyoming. Many of the descendants of the Scotch Presbyterians joined in this exodus, and the character of the church was so changed that after a few years it was thought expedient to reorganize upon the Congregational basis. June 30, 1779, a meeting was called for this purpose. The Reverends Solomon Morgan, Levi Hart and Eliphalet Wright were present. Those wishing to unite in the new organization related their experiences. A covenant was read agreeable to the Cambridge Platform under the Congregational form of discipline, and signed by ten males and sixteen females, the remnant then representing the ancient First Church of Voluntown. The services of the Rev. Mr. Gilmore were then secured, and regular religious worship stately maintained.

In town affairs there was gradual improvement. In 1762, John Gordon was chosen grand school committee, "to take into his hands the school bonds belonging to the town, and to collect the interest on bonds, and to receive the proportion of money granted by Government to the town out of the Colony's rate, and to dispose of the same, and all other money coming from Plainfield, &c., and town's proportion of the sale of Norfolk." In 1766, David Eames, John Cole, Joseph Parke, Thomas

Douglas, John Gaston, John Gordon and John Wylie were appointed to set out school districts throughout the town. Thirteen districts were specified, each of which thenceforward managed its own school under the supervision of a "grand school committee man," appointed by the town.

The financial affairs of the town were greatly embarrassed. The poverty of the soil exposed it to frequent losses by drought, so that many of the inabitants were unable to pay their proportion of public charges. The payment of the minister's salary, and legal expenses incurred in prior resistance, added to their debt and burden. In consequence of this remissness, a heavy debt accrued to the Government for which the town treasurer, Mr. Robert Jameson, was held responsible. Having no funds to meet this demand, Mr. Jameson was arrested and confined in Windham jail. In 1771 a committee was appointed "to go to Windham in term of the Superior Court, and get the best advice concerning a trouble for which Robert Jameson is now confined in Windham jail." Isaac Gallup was ordered to take and have secured all said Jameson's estate for the use of the town in settling the debt for which he was imprisoned. This imprisonment lasted for two years, when Mr. James Gordon was appointed agent to settle with Robert Jameson, "now confined in Windham County jail for the colony tax due for said town," and soon effected his liberation. Mr. Jameson soon after his release removed to Wyoming, with his sons Robert, William, John, Alexander and Joseph, who gained a permanent home in that beautiful valley, and were numbered among its most respectable and influential citizens.

VI.

RELIGIOUS SETTLEMENT IN PLAINFIELD.   GENERAL TOWN AFFAIRS.

PLAINFIELD though still harassed by religious dissension was regaining her secular prosperity, having the good fortune to number among her citizens many strong and enterprising men willing to devote time and energies to public service. Captain John Douglas was now one of the fathers of the town, and had sons of great promise. Major Ezekiel Pierce filled the place of his honored father, serving many years as clerk of the town and of the Probate office. Isaac, son of Rev. Joseph Coit was held in high esteem. Dr. Elisha Perkins, now married to the daughter of Captain Douglas, was continually gaining public confidence and popularity. Elisha Paine of Canterbury, son of the distinguished Separate minister, had removed

his residence to Plainfield, engaging in the practice of law, and marry-
ing Elizabeth Spalding. Andrew Backus of Norwich, and Daniel
Clark of Preston, were new and helpful citizens. At the town meet-
ing, December, 1765, Elisha Paine, Esq., served as moderator; Isaac
Coit, James Bradford, James Howe, Joseph Eaton and Elisha Paine,
were chosen selectmen; Major Ezekiel Pierce, town clerk; John
Pierce, Elisha Paine, Lieut. John Douglas, Dr. Robinson, Azariah and
Jedidiah Spalding, Ebenezer Kingsbury, Stephen Warren, William
Cady and Timothy Parkhurst, highway surveyors; Reuben and David
Shepard, D. Perkins, Nathaniel Deane and Simeon Burgess, listers;
Captains Eaton and Coit, fence-viewers; William Park and Azariah
Spalding, leather-sealers; William Robinson and Joshua Dunlap,
grand-jurors; Samuel Hall, Joseph and Philip Spalding and Simon
Shepard, tithing-men; Hezekiah Spalding, sealer of weights and
measures; Captain Cady, toller and brander of horses. Little was
done at this meeting but to make provision for the support of schools,
and a needy fellow-citizen. A subject far more important than
schools or town's poor was under consideration. The religious status
of the town was most unhappy. More than two-thirds of its inhabitants were avowed Separates attending upon the ministry of the Rev.
Alexander Miller, but were still obliged to pay taxes for the benefit
of a small minority, holding possession of the ancient town meeting-
house. By earnest and persistent appeals they had wrung from the
Assembly the exemption of one-third of the population from this rate-
payment as a second society, but this still left upon them an "unreasonable burden." The remnant of the First church receiving this
compulsory tribute had not sufficient vitality to supply their meeting-
house with a minister. The Plainfield Separate church was a respectable and orderly body, differing little from the orthodox churches of
the day, except in opposing the support of the ministry by taxation.
The ancient bitterness and party feeling had greatly subsided, and it
was now proposed "that the inhabitants should try to come together
and have but one meeting, or else be made into two distinct, independent societies." A town meeting was called early in 1766, to consider this proposition, which appointed Benjamin Wheeler, William
Bradford, Isaac Coit and others—

"To take into consideration the difficulties subsisting in town, so as to
unite in their principles, so as to all join together in the public worship of
God in one meeting, or any other way."

This committee reported in favor of all joining together in one
church, and worshiping in one meeting-house. The voters were again
convened "to see which church they would join, and were almost
universally inclined to join with the Separates." The Separate

meeting-house was however, small, shabby and quite out of the main route of travel, while the old town meeting-house was ample and accessible, and it was thereupon voted that Mr. Miller should preach in the latter house until the pulpit should be otherwise supplied. Reinstated after so many years in this ancient house of worship, the town majority willingly voted its shingling, glazing and general repairing. Great pains were taken to bring back the whole congregation but it was found impracticable. Members of the old church objected to Mr. Miller, "because they did not deem the Separate mode of ordination valid." Others were unwilling to sacrifice their standing as an independent society and laid their grievances before the Assembly, Oct., 1767:—

"Showing that Plainfield was made two societies; that the First society was in a deplorable condition and had been for several years destitute of a minister; that the Second society worshipped in their meeting-house, had not allowed the two-thirds rate and tried to break them up."

Hezekiah and Jabez Huntington and Zebulon West were thereupon appointed a committee to repair to Plainfield, investigate and advise, who decided that the people had better unite and agree in calling some learned and orthodox preacher—thereby intending to exclude Mr. Miller. Notwithstanding this judgment the town still clung to its old pastor. Messrs. Paine, Wheeler and Coit, Captain Bradford and Doctor Wells, after earnest conference with him and his church "to see how far they would condescend in regard to having the gospel preached, so that the whole of the town may unite and attend it," were unable to agree upon a satisfactory basis. Mr. Miller and his followers kept possession of the meeting-house according to the town vote, and thus the remnant of Plainfield's first church was shut out from its ancient house of worship and deprived of religious privileges. Again the first society laid "its deplorable state" before the Assembly. "Second society would not pay rates according to agreement; town had voted that the Separate preacher should preach in the meeting-house, and they were obliged to go to other towns on Sunday, and therefore prayed that the old agreement might be maintained, and liberty still allowed them to lay taxes on two thirds of the inhabitants." Captain John Douglas, agent of the town to oppose this memorial, alleged the following "reasons" for its dismissal:—

"1. This town has been unhappily divided for more than twenty years, to their great hurt and damage in their civil and religious interests, owing to the rigid exertion of the civil power in religious matters which has tended to divide and separate very friends and brothers, and we apprehend the granting of said memorial would tend to augment and carry them to a greater hight; did not consider the agreement just or equable but it was the best they could do at the time; should say that more than two-thirds of the inhabitants upon a serious inquiry and deliberate consideration and con-

10

ference with each other upon the subject of religion, and the way and manner of worship, were unanimously agreed and united in the same; that but fifty-four appear on the memorial, representing £2.030, and against it were fifty-nine from the first and sixty-three from the second society, representing £7,123.

Whereupon we say, that it would be most unreasonable and unprecedented to grant the prayer of said memorialists, and instead of promoting religion and peace, throw us into the greatest confusion and most unhappy contentions. But as there seems to be a number who cannot join with us, we are fully willing they should be released from paying anything for minister or meeting-house, and be made a distinct society, and have such proportion of the old meeting-house on equitable terms, each person to belong to that society he chooses, but to join any person by coercive measures we are persuaded will directly tend to stir up contentions and dissensions. *May* 18, 1768."

The Assembly thereupon appointed Jonathan Trumbull, Hezekiah Huntington and Zebulon West to be a committee to endeavor to consummate a union, and by their judicious efforts union was at last happily consummated. Few difficulties could withstand the conciliatory mediation of Jonathan Trumbull. Concessions were made on both sides. The odious two-thirds tax was forever abolished. As the church party a few years previous dismissed an honored minister for the sake of peace, the Separates now reluctantly resigned Mr. Miller. Certain modifications were admitted in the church covenant, bringing it nearer the pattern of the Cambridge Platform, and both churches united in choice of Mr. John Fuller for their pastor, provided he would publicly eschew certain Separate errors, and obtain a regular ministerial ordination. Mr. Fuller was a native of Lebanon, an earnest Christian laborer, then preaching acceptably to the Separate church of Bean Hill, Norwich. Willing to assist in healing the breach, Mr. Fuller accepted the call upon those terms and signed the following declaration :—

"I believe that some separations if they had been conducted in a regular manner might have been justified, but the separations in general are not justifiable, especially in the manner of them, as they have been attended by many spurious notions which excel in them and party spirit, as well as many irregular practices. And notwithstanding I have borne a public testimony against their rash and uncharitable dispositions and conduct; yet I am fully sensible that I have in several instances countenanced and encouraged them in their precipitant way and manner of separating—the which I ought not to have done; for which I hope Heaven's pardon and forgiveness, and the forgiveness of all God's people whom I have offended, and desire their prayers that I may have wisdom. And it is my desire to unite with the regular ministers and churches of Christ in anything wherein we are agreed, and to forbear one another in love in circumstantial matters wherein we cannot be perfectly united.   JOHN FULLER.
Plainfield, Feb. 2, 1769."

A council of ministers chiefly from Massachusetts called by the uniting brethren accepted this declaration, and aided in the installment of Mr. Fuller. Its proceedings were thus reported by the New London *Gazette :*—

"On the 3d instant, Rev. John Fuller was ordained over the church in Plainfield. Rev. Mr. Hart of Preston, preached from Psalm cxxxiii., showing,

1, Nature of Christian union; 2, Wherein this union doth consist; 3, Fruit and effects of this union—all conducted in a decent and most solemn manner.
N. B.—Occasion of Mr. Hart's preaching from this text was on account of the happy *Union* come into by the two churches of this town, and the names *Old* and *New* swallowed up in most amicable union."

Peace was thus happily restored after more than thirty years of conflict. While all parties were satisfied the Separates had especial cause for rejoicing. They had achieved the object for which they had separated. A minister of their own choice and persuasion preached to the town in the town meeting-house, and assessment for his support was positively prohibited. Far in advance of her generation Plainfield had soon the privilege of religious freedom, and her inhabitants were free to attend service where they pleased and support minister and meeting-house without legal coercion or interference. Among the many who welcomed this joyful reunion was our old friend, Mercy Wheeler, now Mrs. Case, reported from time to time by friendly visitors as "the same pious, thankful, humble woman," as in the days of her distressing infirmity and wonderful deliverance. Mr. Miller, when released from his charge, returned, it is believed, to his former home in the north part of Voluntown, and lived to a good old age in peace and happiness, respected by all who knew him.

As religious animosities and difficulties subsided the town resumed its efforts for secular improvement. The education of its youth had always enlisted the especial sympathy of its citizens. In 1766 a committee was appointed to lay out school districts, which thus reported:—

"1, Flat Rock district, bounded south on Preston, east on Voluntown; 2, Stone Hill district, north of Flat Rock; 3, Goshen, bounded north by Moosup River, south by Stone Hill; 4, South, bordering south on Preston, west on Canterbury; 5, Middle, extending from Mill Brook up Main street, butting east on Stone Hill; 6, Black Hill; 7, Moosup Pond, northeast corner; 8, Moosup River; 9, Shepard Hill; 10, Green Hollow, beginning at Snake Meadow Brook or Killingly line."

Dr. Perkins, Daniel Clark, Stephen Kingsbury, Andrew Backus, John Howe, Jonathan Woodward, Philip Spalding, Samuel Warren, Samuel Hall and Isaac Allerton were appointed a committee, one for each district, to see that the schools were kept. Although the number of teachers and schools was increased by this arrangement, the leading men of the town were not yet satisfied with their attainments, and in 1770 proceeded to form an association "for the purpose of providing improved facilities for the more complete education of the youth of the vicinity." They erected a brick school-house of respectable size, procured teachers of a higher grade, and established a more thorough system of instruction in common English branches, but were unable to organize a classical department.

Roads and bridges required much attention. The "tedious" Quinebaug was still fractious and turbulent, necessitating continual bridge-building and repairing. In 1763, a project was set on foot for enlarging the bed of this stream so as to make it passable for boats. A convention was held in Plainfield to consider this scheme, which was attended by most of the leading men of the county, who expressed their views and wishes in the subjoined memorial :—

"That the Quinebaug River from Danielson's Falls until the Thames empties itself into the cove at Norwich, thirty miles, is so flat and level that it may easily be made passable for boats to pass up and down at the expense of some four hundred pounds to be laid out in cleaning, and pray for a lottery.

Ebenezer Grosvenor.	William Robinson.	Nicholas Parker.
Willard Spalding.	Isaac Shepard.	Benjamin Wheeler.
Silas Hutchins.	Mason Cleveland.	John Smith.
Benj. Spalding.	John Tyler.	John Dyer.
Jabez Fitch, Jun.	Samuel Stewart.	Ezekiel Pierce.
John Fitch.	Jonathan Parkhurst.	Isaac Coit.
Samuel Adams, Jun.	Benjamin Coit.	Hezekiah Lord.
Joseph Woodward.	Elisha Paine.	James Bradford.
Andrew Spalding.	Ebenezer Cady.	Joseph Eaton.
Jonas Shepard.	Ebenezer Robinson.	Benjamin Backus.
Nathan Waldo.	Jeremiah Cady.	John Larrabe.
Daniel Kee.	Theophilus Clark.	James Cleveland.
Jabez Fitch.	Benjamin Spalding.	Robert Jameson.
Edward Wheeler.	Samuel Danielson.	Samuel Huntington.
William Danielson.	John Grosvenor.	
May 9, 1763."		

Though urged by men of such position and influence this request was denied. In 1767, the bridge over the Quinebaug was again swept away by a freshet, when the town voted a reward to the Widow Williams for heroically saving twenty planks of the same. Captain Eaton, Robert Kinne and Isaac Coit were appointed to oversee its rebuilding, and others were employed after its completion " to take care of the new bridge, and cut away ice round the anchor." The constant travel over this bridge made its preservation very important. The great country road passing through Voluntown and Plainfield connected Providence and the north part of Rhode Island with Hartford and the opening regions westward, and many emigrants were now toiling over it *en route* for the new countries. Special orders relative to the renewal and maintenance of " the Plainfield road " were issued from time to time by the Governments of Connecticut and Rhode Island. A road laid out from this highway to Butts Bridge now accommodated Norwich travel. In the summer of 1768 a weekly stage-coach was run over it from Providence to Norwich, exciting much wonder and admiration and greatly promoting the business interests of Plainfield. A spacious tavern house for the accommodation of the great throng of travelers was now built and opened in Plainfield Village by Captain Eaton, which became a very noted and popular resort. Taverns were also kept in other parts of the town by Thomas Stevens, Israel Underwood, and others. In 1771, the town voted to provide a house for the poor and a proper overseer. The few Indians still left in town were properly cared for by town authorities or benevolent individuals.*

The great exodus to the new countries took from Plainfield some valued citizens. A number of respectable families joined the first emigrants to Oblong and Nine Partners. Major Ezekiel Pierce and Captain Simon Spalding were prominent among the bold men who took possession of Wyoming. Elisha Paine, so active in professional and public affairs, removed in 1767 to Lebanon, New Hampshire. The township of Sharon, Vermont, was purchased and settled by a Plainfield colony. Isaac Marsh, Willard Shepard and others went on in advance, selected land, built huts, sowed grass and prepared for the main body of emigrants. William, son of Captain John Douglas, though but a lad of sixteen, served valiantly in the French war, and after the return of peace took command of a merchant ship sailing between New Haven and the West Indies, making his residence in Northford. These losses were in some degree made up by occasional new settlers. Timothy Lester of Shepard Hill, Isaac Knight of Black Hill, were among its acquisitions. John Aplin, an Englishman, a man of much learning and address, who had gained a handsome estate by the practice of law in Providence, became involved in political and personal controversies, and removed to Plainfield about 1766. John Pierce succeeded to the position of town clerk for a few years, and was in turn succeeded by William Robinson in 1772.

VII.

TOWN AFFAIRS IN KILLINGLY. THOMPSON PARISH. PROGRESS
IN FIRST SOCIETY. SOUTH KILLINGLY CHURCH. BAP-
TIST CHURCHES IN THOMPSON AND
CHESTNUT HILL.

KILLINGLY during this period was in the main peaceful and prosperous. Despite the size of the town and its various society divisions its general affairs were carried on without apparent jealousy or collision. Town offices were equitably distributed; general town

---

*The provision made by Mr. Joshua Whitney for his negro servants at his decease in 1761 shows the conscientious scrupulousness with which some good men of that day fulfilled the responsibility of ownership. Not only did he make Sandy, Cæsar, Judith with their children *absolutely free,* but bequeathed to each household six acres of land, stock and farming tools, gave to one his "oldest little Bible," and to the other several good books; enjoined Sandy to take care of Bess, his wife, and give her decent burial, and directed Cæsar and Judith " to see that their children were in no ways left to perish."

meetings were held in the great meeting-house on Killingly Hill. At the annual meeting in 1760, Samuel Danielson was chosen moderator; Thomas Moffat, town clerk and treasurer; Pain Converse, Deacon Daniel Davis, Ebenezer Larned, Lieut. Benjamin Leavens, James Dike, selectmen; Hezekiah Cutler, collector of country rates; Benjamin Merriam and Lieut. William Danielson, constables; John Jacobs, John Whitmore, Phinehas Lee, Benjamin Joslin, Daniel Alton, John Corbin, Francis Carroll, Nathaniel Daniels, Ensign Benjamin Cady, Nell Alexander, Joseph Hutchins, Jaazaniah Whitmore, John Sprague, highway surveyors; Enoch Leonard, Ephraim Cady, fence-viewers; Hezekiah Cutler, Benjamin Merriam, William Danielson, collectors of town rates; Zebediah Sabin, Moses Winter, Eliezer Warren, Joseph Bateman, key-keepers of the several meeting-houses; Enoch Leonard, leather-sealer; David Barrett, Ensign Joseph Cutler, Wyman Hutchins, grand-jurors; Jacob Bixby, Ensign Benj. Cady, Daniel Winter, Ezekiel Little, Joseph Newell, tithing-men; Samuel Watson, Richard Child, John Johnson, Benjamin Joy, Daniel Winter, Abijah Adams, listers; Joseph Cady, sealer of weights and measures; Ensign Edward Converse, Joseph Leavens, Jun., James Day, horse-branders; Captain Michael Adams, collector of excise. Ezekiel Little, Richard Bloss and Benajah Spalding were admitted inhabitants. John Sprague and Simeon Spalding, residents of the south parish, had liberty granted to build a town pound to accommodate themselves, and also keep the same in repair at their own cost. Money for "doctoring Charite Priest" was granted Dr. Freeman.

The charge of its poor was always a heavy burden upon this township. Parts of its territory afforded but a scanty support for its inhabitants, and its border position exposed it to incursions of vagrants and foreigners. In addition to its own poor it was obliged to support its quota of Acadian refugees, paying sundry sums for services and supplies to the French people. In 1765, it was voted, "To raise one penny a pound for the support of the poor of said town; also, that the persons supporting the poor take their pay in specy, i. e., Indian corn, at two and sixpence per bushel; rye at three and sixpence; wheat, four and sixpence; beans, the same; salt pork without bone, one shilling per pound; flax, eightpence. These poor people were then scattered about the town in the charge of the lowest bidder. In 1770, a movement was made for improving their condition by providing a permanent habitation under the care of responsible persons. It was voted by the town, "That Samuel Watson and James Dike provide a work-house for the parish of Thompson, and be masters of the same; also, Capt. Warren to provide a work-house and be master of the same in like manner in Killingly."

Bridges and highways also required much care and legislation. In 1767, Briant and Nathaniel Brown and Benjamin Leavens were appointed "to join with Pomfret gentlemen in repairing the bridge called Danielson's." However well repaired it was soon carried away by a freshet, and a new committee appointed in 1770, "to rebuild our part of the bridge at Cargill's Mills, and view the Quinebaug above and below where Danielson's bridge stood, and see where they could set a bridge." William Danielson was allowed twenty-nine pounds for building half the latter bridge, and a new road was laid out from it to Voluntown. In 1774, the Quinebaug was bridged between Cargill's and Danielson's, near the residence of Deacon Simon Cotton. Various new roads were granted from time to time in Thompson Parish, and so much space in the town book was occupied by returns of highway surveyors that after an unsuccessful attempt in 1759 to procure a new record-book these returns were left on file, and were finally scattered or destroyed so that the laying out of many important roads cannot now be determined. The travel upon these numerous ways was accommodated in various noted taverns kept by John Jacobs, Benjamin Wilkinson, Edward Converse, Zebediah Sabin, John Felshaw, Ebenezer Larned, William Danielson, Nathaniel Stone and others. Medical practitioners at this date were Doctors Freeman, Gleason and Cheney in the centre and south parishes, and Dr. Joseph Coit in Thompson. Four hundred families were reported in the town in 1767.

The north parish of the town was prospering. In 1760, Jacob Dresser, Esq., served as clerk; Deacon Lusher Gay, collector; Jacob Dresser, Deacon Simon Larned and Ephraim Guile, committee. The school committee were Jacob Dresser, Joseph Averill, Captain Henry Green, Daniel Russel, Solomon Bixby, Deacon Gay, Squier Hascall and James Fuller. The Rev. Mr. Russel was allowed four pounds ten shillings for getting his own wood for the year; Josiah Converse, eight shillings for sweeping the meeting-house. Additional pew accommodations were still found needful—Stephen Crosby, Nehemiah Merrill, John Ellithorpe, Solomon Ormsbee, Obadiah Clough, Asa Converse, Benjamin Joslin, Thomas Ormsbee, William Whittemore, Jun., William Richards, Eleazer Child and Francis Elliott receiving liberty to build a pew "where the hind seat is in the men's side gallery," provided it "be built no higher than the hind seat is now." A number of young women appeared at a subsequent meeting, viz.: Bathsheba Converse, Betta Town, Margaret Town, Dorothy Bixby, Susannah Bixby, Mary Hascall, Jane Crosby, Mary, Zerziah and Sarah Joslin, Sarah Porton, Elizabeth Knap and Susannah Hascall, desiring the privilege of building a pew upon the women's side gallery, which was at first granted, but upon reconsideration made over to Joseph Averill, "pro-

vided he let so many young women have it for their seat as can conveniently set in it." In response to a petition from Theophilus and
Samuel Chandler, Moses Marcy, William Nelson, Edward Bugbee
and Benjamin Wilkinson, residents west of the Quinebaug, in the northwest corner of the society, these petitioners with their lands were annexed to the north society of Woodstock.

The renovation of the school districts next agitated the society.
Stephen and Joseph Brown, Joseph Town, Samuel Fuller, Robert and
Ebenezer Prince, Joseph and Francis Elliott were leaders in this movement, entering their dissent against the society's proceedings in regard
to schools. Michael Adams, Pain Converse, Squier Hascall, James
Dike and William Alton were appointed a committee to "vewe the
districts" and see if they thought best to make any alterations. They
recommended the setting off of ten school districts, and selected a suitable site in each for a school-house. Each district was designated by
the name of some central or prominent inhabitant. The first district
—Landlord Converse's—included Thompson Hill and vicinity ; school-
house "to stand betwixt Landlord Converse's and the Widow Flint's,
at the end of the lane where Samuel Converse comes out into the country rhoad." The south neighborhood was designated "Capt. Adams'
district." Captain Green's district embraced Quaddie and its vicinity ;
school-house betwixt the houses of Ebenezer and Amos Green. Nathan
Bixby's included Brandy Hill ; school-house near by Sergeant Timothy
Cooper's ; Samuel Stone's occupied the northeast corner of the society,
extending from Joseph Munyan's to Rhode Island line ; thence to and
upon the Bay line to Captain Cutler's ; thence south to John Jacobs' ;
school-house upon Isaac Burril's land near the river. Joseph Brown's
district lay west of Stone's, including Porter's farm ; "school-house
near the little Pond upon the rhoad." Squier Hascall's was still farther west upon the Bay line, with school-house "near where said Hascall crosses the mill-rhoad in coming to meeting." Nathaniel Crosby's
embraced both sides of French River, from Nathaniel Mills' to Ebenezer Prince's ; school-house about half-way between old Mr. Elliott's
and Joseph Elliott's. John Hewlet's extended from John Younglove's
north to the Bay line, thence west to the Quinebaug, embracing a strip
four or five miles in length east of that river ; school-house "to stand
where it is." Lastly, Esq. Dresser's district was "bounded as follows : All
upon the west side of Quinebaug River, and including Joseph Nichols,
Henry Merrill, John Russel, Jonathan Eaton, Marston Eaton, all upon
the side of the said river, "and it was the opinion of the committee, "that to have the school-house in the senter will not accommodate
this district well, it lays so ilconveniant," but that it would be best to
keep the school at two places ; one at the Widow Hibbard's, or there-

abouts; and the other at the house where the Widow Commins did live, or thereabouts—two months at each place, and draw one-quarter more money than other districts."

This report was accepted, Sept. 23, 1762, and the lines established as soon as practicable, though some difficulty was found in carrying out the designs of the committee. Several of the designated sites were unsatisfactory. A pitiful petition was presented from "inhabitants in the northwest part of the district called Hewlet's," showing "that they have been overlooked by the committee, who supposed that no one lived northwest of a certain great hill but Clement Corbin, whereas there were *twelve* families there so remote from that school-house that they could not send their children there to school and had but little or no benefit (the most none at all) of the school kept there, and never had any of the loan money, and not so much of the tax money as they did pay." Captain Clement Corbin and his son Clement, Samuel Palmer, Elijah and Ezra Corbin, Benjamin Morris, John Whitmore, Joseph Winter, Mark Clawell, John Webster and Benjamin Fairbanks, inhabitants living northwest from the aforesaid "great hill," were accordingly set off as "Captain Corbin's district." School-house sites were changed to accommodate other districts and in time the new system was satisfactorily established. Esquire Dresser's district was divided in 1772, the south part retaining the old name; the north to be known as Perrin's district.

The enlargement of the meeting-house next claimed the attention of the society. After some ineffectual attempts to procure a vote for a new one, it was voted, Feb. 16, 1769 :—

"1. To put in a piece of fourteen feet in the middle of the meeting-house, cutting the same in two, and tilling up the same by lengthening the seats.

2. To finish the meeting-house by clapboarding the same.

3. That the money in Collector Hascall's hands should be forthwith collected and laid out for stuff for the meeting-house.

4. Likewise the money in the old collector's hands to be forthwith collected, and laid out upon the meeting-house.

5. Also voted and chose Jacob Dresser, Benjamin Wilkinson and Samuel Watson, a committee to take the money and do the meeting-house."

The committee proceeded to bisect the house as ordered, move one of the severed halves and insert the fourteen-foot strip. This feat being accomplished after some delay and difficulty, it was next decided "to culler our meeting-house," and, having perhaps seen the folly of following their own architectural devices, they resumed their ancient practice of copying their neighbors, and further voted, "that the cullering of the body of our meeting house should be like Pomfret, and the Roff should be cullered Read." The previous committee were empowered to accomplish the coloring, and also to sell the refuse stuff that

11

should be left and the old glass. The filling up the inserted strip with suitable seats was a work of great difficulty. Votes for pew-spots were passed and revoked. June 4, 1770, four pew-spots were granted; one east side the pulpit to Nathaniel and Stephen Crosby, west side to Ephraim Guile; a spot west side the great or south doors to Deacon Jonathan Clough and his son Obadiah, east side to Samuel Watson— the grantees to build the pews, finish the meeting-house up to the gallery, maintain the glass and pay the parish ten pounds. Francis Elliott, William Whittemore, Jun., Asa Converse, Daniel Davis, Jonathan Firman, Calvin Gay, Davis Flint and Briant Brown, Jun., were also allowed to lengthen out the front pew in the men's gallery at their own charge for their own seat. Other pew-spots were obtained the following year by taking up "the two hind seats in the men's and women's side," and this process of demolition and reconstruction went on until the old "body of seats" was replaced by capacious pews, handsomely finished and surmounted by balustrades, the balusters of which were so wide apart that an investigating child could thrust its head between them. A broad alley extended from the great double south door to the pulpit, with cross alleys to the "men's and women's doors," on the east and west sides of the house, and little twenty-inch alleys meandered among the pews "for the people to go into the seats." In 1771, it was voted "to plaister the inside of said meeting-house and pint the under-pinning;" Samuel Watson appointed to keep the key, and ten shillings allowed for sweeping. Two years later a special committee was chosen, "to take care of said meeting house, and to prosecute any person or persons that shall hurt or damage said meeting-house, or open the same without leave or consent from said committee or the key-keeper." Jacob and Benjamin Converse and Ebenezer Gay were now appointed choristers, and Joel Converse and Thaddeus Larned—son of Simon—requested to assist the above "in tuning the psalm." The large meeting-house was ever well-filled with hearers. The various rough "ways" leading to Thompson Hill were thronged on Sunday with the multitudes coming up to worship—the older men mostly on horseback with their wives and daughters on a pillion behind them, and troops of young people on foot. Mr. Russel continued to preach to the acceptance of the church and people, and was greatly beloved and respected by all. In proof of this affectionate regard it is told of one good sister of the church that in treating her pastor to the rare luxury of a cup of tea she attempted to highten the favor by half filling the teacup with *molasses*. "Stop, stop, my good lady!" besought the alarmed divine. "Plenty, plenty, I assure you." "Ah," replied the worthy dame with another douse into the teacup,

"*Clear molasses an't too good for Mr. Russel*,"*—a saying greatly commended and handed down to succeeding generations as expressing the proper sentiment of a native Thompsonian towards his minister. Regard for this dignitary was indeed one of the fundamental articles of his creed at that period. He took him for life, for better or worse, and would as soon have thought of *changing* his religion. Jacob Dresser, Esq., Lusher Gay and Simon Larned, still served as deacons.

Other improvements followed the renovation of the meeting-house. Sabin's "old red tavern" had passed to Benjamin Wilkinson, who after some ten years occupation of the Morris farm on the Quinebaug, had been induced to make sale of it to Mr. John Holbrook of Woodstock. Making preliminary reconnoissance in the guise of "a shabby old traveler," Holbrook carelessly asked the price of the farm, and to the great astonishment of Mr. Wilkinson, appeared a few days afterwards "with a bag full of gold and silver," ready to bargain and take possession. Amused at his promptness and ever eager for trade and change, Wilkinson yielded the farm and purchased the Sabin Tavern on Thompson Hill, where his energy and public spirit found ample exercise. Under his auspices the open broken land about the meeting house was transformed into a comfortable common and training-field. He cut down the brush, dragged off stones and dug out the relics of aboriginal tree-stumps. The dilapidated pound was "rectified" and an extensive peach orchard set out east of the common. Mr. Wilkinson was accustomed to plant a peach stone by every rock upon his premises, and also along the roadside, that boys, travelers and church-comers might have a free supply. Under his skillful administration the old tavern-stand became more popular than ever, and was a place of great resort for public meetings and merry-makings. In winter time it served as a "Sabba-day-house" for the shivering congregation, glad to find warmth by its glowing hearth, and perhaps something more stimulating. On one occasion only its proprietor incurred censure. As a native of Rhode Island, his views of Sabbath-keeping were less strict than those of his neighbors, but he had never been detected in any overt transgression till one particular Sunday, when all through the service the congregation was disturbed by what seemed the creaking

---

* It should be said that this story is not peculiar to Thompson. Other old ladies in other Windham County towns boast a like lavishment of superfluous sweetness. A good story often finds so many claimants that it is difficult to decide upon the true author, but in this instance the credit clearly accrues to Thompson. Not only is the name and service of "old Miss Cluff" still held in grateful remembrance, but it receives farther corroboration from the acknowledged proclivity of the Thompsonians for both *ministers* and *molasses*. The arrival of the first hogshead of this favorite luxury was celebrated with public rejoicings, and all the boys of the vicinity were allowed a free treat in honor of the occasion.

of a very rusty-handled grindstone upon his premises. Even Mr. Wilkinson could not be indulged in such an outrage, and proper officials waited upon him at intermission and solemnly called him to account for it. The suspected culprit promptly denied the charge. "Why, we hear it now," retorted his accusers, as the long-drawn creak became more distinctly audible. "Come and see for yourselves," replied the smiling landlord, leading them into his dooryard and formally presenting to them *a pair of Guinea hens*, (the first brought to Thompson), whose doleful cries aggravated by homesickness had subjected their owner to so serious an imputation.

While so useful and active in the standing society Mr. Wilkinson was equally ready to extend his aid to other orders. The Six-Principle Baptist Church, so early established in Thompson, after many struggles and trials became extinct about 1770, upon the removal of its pastor and some leading brethren to Royalston. Most of the Baptists that remained were connected with the church of Leicester, Mass. Attendance upon worship at such a distance was found very burdensome ; Baptist sentiments were becoming more popular, the heavy tax levied for repairing the meeting-house on Thompson Hill excited much dissatisfaction, and many persons declared their willingness to support a different worship. A number of persons accordingly came together, Nov. 17, 1772, and, "in consideration of the love and unity" they had for the Baptist constitution and way of worship," declared their purpose by the help of God to make it their general practice of public worship, and their willingness to be helpful in building the cause of God in that way either by building a house for public worship or in settling a minister, and any other necessary charge according as they were able, and found in their minds to be duty according to Scripture record, not believing that there ought to be any compulsion in such cases or carnal sword used." This agreement was signed by about seventy-five subscribers, many of them men of established character and comfortable circumstances. Mr. John Martin of Rehoboth, was then chosen to preach to them on trial, an earnest and "gifted" preacher, of such repute at this period that he had the honor of preaching the funeral sermon of Elder Thomas Green of Leicester, one of the fathers in the Baptist ministry.

Service was maintained through the winter in private houses, and in June a meeting was called, and it was found that they were ready "to settle into church state." It was agreed to meet in forenoon, June 17, "for public worship, and in the afternoon to tell of our experience of God's grace which he hath wrought in our souls to each other," and so much had they to tell that it occupied another summer afternoon. August 26, they agreed to send a petition to the church in Leicester to get leave to embody as a distinct church. James Dike was appointed to write the petition, and with Ebenezer Green carry it to the Leicester church. Their request was granted, and on Sept. 9, the petitioners, *i. e.*, Widow Deborah Torry, Mary Green, Elizabeth Atwell, Sarah White, Widow Deborah Davis, Lydia Hall, Hannah Jones, James Dike, Ebenezer Green, Jonathan Munyan, Levi White, Thaddeus Allen, John White, together with John Martin, John Atwell, John Pratt, James Coats and Levisa Martin, "firstly gave ourselves to the Lord, and to each other, and signed a written covenant." The progressive and liberal spirit of these brethren is shown in the position accorded to the female members, who were given precedence in signature to petition and covenant instead of coming in at a later date as was then customary among the standing churches, and also in their leniency towards those who still held to the practices of the Six-Principle Baptists, as manifested in the last article of their Confession of Faith, viz :—

"And since singing of Psalms, and the laying on of hands, and the washing of feet is practiced in some of the churches of the saints, and some there are that doth not practice two of these, to wit, the laying on of hands and washing of feet, which makes a separation between each party since some brethren are tender on these points and don't see so clearly through that practice, we do unanimously consent and agree to bear with each other's judgments on that account, so that there may be free and full liberty without offence to each other to practice or forbear the same."

On the day of organization the church invited Mr. Martin to assume its pastoral care. On Sept. 21, the society concurred in the call with "not one vote to the contrary." After ascertaining that all previous difficulties were settled, and agreeing that if any church member should ever bring up these buried difficulties "he should be dealt with as a transgressor," Mr. Martin "gave his answer in the positive." James Dike and Ebenezer Green were chosen to serve the church in the office of deacon, and in case enough should not be brought in to supply the wants of the ordaining council were to provide for the lack at the expense of the church. Ordination services were held Nov. 3, 1773, under a large apple-tree near the Jacobs Tavern. Preparatory examination of the candidate at the house of Deacon Dike was satisfactory. Elder Ledoit began the public service with prayer. "A sermon suitable to the occasion was preached from Phil. 1 : 18, by Elder [Isaac] Backus ; Elder Green [of Charlton] gave the charge, and Elder Winsor [of Gloucester] the right hand of fellowship. The whole was conducted with decency and order." A brother was soon baptized into the fellowship of the church. Dec. 9, the deacons were formally inducted into office with appropriate solemnities. It had been previously decided that each of these worthy church officers had a gift of prayer and exhortation that ought to be improved for the benefit of the church, but

they were "not to rise up of their own head and open a meeting by
prayer without invitation from the elder, and though they might without offence after sermon if they saw any point that they could advance
any further upon agreeable to what had been said improve such oppor-
unity, yet if the church in general should judge that they did not advance anything forward or give some further light they should be
gently reproved, and if after repeated attempts and reproofs they failed
to give light, they were to be silenced." In the face of such judicial
scrutiny and requisitions Deacon Dike managed to exhort to such general enlightenment and satisfaction that in the following year he was
formally licensed to preach, and still later the vote was "crost out"—
the church expressing its willingness that they or any other brethren
"should improve according to the ability that God shall give at proper
times and seasons as the church shall judge."

The society meantime had carried out its purpose of building a house
for public worship, having first voted "to allow the Baptist Church the
decisive vote in choosing her gifts to improve in the meeting-house," or
in other words granting its occupancy and control to the church. Half
an acre of land "in the fork of the roads where Oxford and Boston
roads meet" was given to the society by Mr. Benjamin Wilkinson,
"for the love and friendship he has to the Baptist people of Killingly,
. . . . so long as they do use the same for a meeting-house lot." The
society committee, Ezekiel Smith, Ebenezer Starr and Jonathan Munyan, had charge of building the house which was ready for occupation
in the summer of 1774. Many were added to the church in this and
subsequent years.

Though Thompson was now sending men and families "to the new
countries" her population was increasing. The influx was yet more than
the outflow. Jonathan Aldrich, Abraham Tourtellotte and Josiah
Perry removed to the northwest part of the parish soon after 1770.
John Holbrook, Jun., and Jason Phipps occupied parts of the old Mor-
ris farm on the Quinebaug. James Wilson, James Rhodes, Thomas
Davis, Simon Howard and Jeremiah Barstow settled in the vicinity of
Brandy Hill. Andrew Waterman, Stephen Blackmar and Stephen
Bates of Scituate, took up land on or near Rhode Island colony line.
Issachar Bates of Leicester, in 1772, purchased a farm northwest of
Thompson Hill, land first laid out under grant to Humphrey Davy.
Jonathan Nichols of Sutton had now taken possession of the Sampson
Howe farm, near what is now West Thompson Village. Stephen
Keith had bought land on the Quinebaug. The mill privilege at the
upper falls of this river, first improved by Deacon Jonathan Eaton,
had now passed to his sons, John and Marson, whose business enter-
prise rivalled that of Captain Cargill at the lower fall, half a mile

below. By their efforts a bridge was after a time constructed upon the site of the subsequent Rhodesville bridge, and a new road laid out to Thompson meeting-house. The old road winding about Park's Hill had hitherto answered all purposes, but with increasing business a more direct route was demanded. In response to petitions from Paine and Edward Converse and John Eaton, Jacob Dresser, Esq. and Daniel Russel were appointed a committee, who laid out "a road from Captain Daniels' land to another highway between Landlord Converse's and Martha Flint's" in 1763.*

The brief interval of peace following the French and Indian War was marked by a general revival of business and commercial enterprise. Trading vessels again traversed the seas bringing back foreign goods in exchange for colonial products. A great variety of useful and fancy articles were thus brought into market, and a *furor* for trade broke out in all the colonies. Even remote inland settlements like Thompson caught the infection and engaged in various business operations. Its first achievement was a perambulating vehicle called the Butter Cart that roamed all over the parish picking up butter, eggs and all sorts of domestic products to be repaid in goods from Boston. Good housewives, hitherto restricted to a scant supply of absolute necessities, could now indulge in a whole row of pins or a paper of needles, and even in beads, ribbons and finery for their blooming daughters, and many were the ventures sent out by the freighted Butter Cart whose return was welcomed as if it bore the treasures of the Indies. Daniel, oldest son of Samuel Larned, followed in the same line, merely picking up at first all the surplus produce of the South Neighborhood, but in a few years he was joined by Mr. John Mason of Swanzey, and the business was greatly extended.

*As roads have usually some definite terminus it is to be inferred that this road as laid out *ran into* and joined *another road* passing *through* "Captain Daniels' land," to Cargill's Mills, at the Great Falls of the Quinebaug. There is no evidence of the *laying out* of this valley road, but many hints at its existence, and it was probably "trodden out" at a very early date to meet the wants of travelers and incoming settlers. The absence of early town records in Killingly makes it impossible to determine the original laying out of many important roads. A way through Killingly from Plainfield to Boston must have existed as early as 1690, but when or how it was constructed has not been ascertained, but subsequent alterations in it prove that it was nearly identical with the present road over Putnam Heights and Thompson Hill. Allusions in old deeds show that there was a road from "Hartford to Mendon," *west* of the Quinebaug, extending north from the Great Falls in 1703, but this seems to have been superseded by another road east of the river, and also east of French River, which it followed closely, connecting with the Connecticut Path in the north part of Thompson. That this road to Boston, "abundantly used," by many travelers, did not cross Thompson Hill is evident from the necessity of having special roads made to that locality. The south part of the road of 1763 has been discontinued, but the greater part of it is still intact and traversed as the "old," middle, or "mountain road," between Putnam and Thompson.

Agents were sent far and wide, even up to the new settlements in
northern Massachusetts and Vermont, buying up meat, grain, ashes
and any marketable product to be exchanged for rum, sugar, molasses
and other articles in Providence.   Foreign goods and luxuries became
comparatively cheap and abundant in consequence.   Tea, once so
rare that nobody knew how to use it, and after general consultation
over the first sample, decided to serve it up as "greens" for dinner,
now took its place as a grateful beverage on festive occasions.   Ginger,
allspice and cinnamon came into common use.   West India rum flowed
as freely as cider or water, and as for molasses—it became so cheap
and plentiful that a poor old woman could treat her minister according to his deserts, and little boys indulge unstinted in the favorite
juvenile dainty of the neighborhood,—hot roasted potatoes hastily
soused therein, and crammed all sizzling and dripping down the
throats of the happy urchins.   The candy of later generations could
scarcely furnish so toothsome and enjoyable a banquet.

This thriving business gave a new impulse to the south part of the
town.   New families were drawn there, farms rose in value, wild land
was taken up and fine house serected.   Daniel Larned purchased land
west of the country road, building under the Great Elm set out by
Edmond Hughes, the former proprietor.   Mr. Mason's residence was
southward on the line between the parishes.   The homestead farm
long occupied by Joseph Cady, Esq., was purchased by Darius Sessions,
deputy-governor of Rhode Island, who made his summer residence
here, and brought it under high cultivation.   The farm adjoining owned
by the first William Larned, was sold by his heirs with dwelling-house
and farm to Isaac Park of Pomfret, in 1761.   Land on Park's Hill as
it was now called, and in other localities, was purchased by Daniel
and Simon Davis of Killingly, who both removed to Thompson Parish.
This increase of business and population made the parish restive.   At
its first organization it had asked for town privileges, and after forty
years suspension the petition was renewed.   At a general town meeting called "to see if it be the mind of said town to be divided, viz.:
the middle and south parishes to be made into one town, and Thompson Parish to be made into one town," it was voted "that Thompson
Parish be set off as a town, and that Jacob Dresser, Esq., be agent to
prefer a memorial to the General Assembly that Thompson be made a
town."   This memorial represented:—

"That the town of Killingly was nearly sixteen miles long . . . . and
divided into three societies.   Thompson Parish not so large in dimensions
but more on the list than the other two.   Place for holding town meetings at
the middle society—many have to travel ten and eleven miles, making their
situation extremely burthensome.   Petitioners knowing their burthens by
experience at a legal town meeting voted to have the north society made a
town by the name of Watertown, two south societies remaining Killingly."

Although a majority of the voters favored division and were represented in this memorial their request was denied. The petitioners were residents of the north and south extremities of the town. The inhabitants of Killingly Hill and Thompson's South Neighborhood, including many leading citizens, opposed division, and in the threatening condition of public affairs changes were deemed inexpedient. The Assembly deferred decision, and the town voted to delay farther action till times were more propitious.

Killingly's First or Central Society was influential and prosperous though not exempt from losses and annoyances. Its records having the misfortune to be "much damnified by fire," John Leavens, Barachiah Cady and Hezekiah Cutler, were appointed to consider the situation, who advised to buy a book for society records and transcribe the same, which was done at the cost of ten shillings. In 1760, Joseph Leavens, Jun., served as society clerk; Thomas Moffat, collector; Ebenezer Larned, Benjamin Leavens, Hezekiah Cutler, committee. The great meeting-house demanded much attention. One brother was allowed to cut a window in his pew; others to take up seats and build themselves pews. Competent committees were chosen, in 1762, to consider what was needful for repairing and finishing the house; the former found it needful to re-shingle the roof and stop the cracks with lime or bark; "a burying cloth and cushing for ye desk" were suggested by the latter. School affairs also claimed the consideration of the society. "Squadrons" were out of date, and Deacon Larned, Benjamin Cady and Nathaniel Brown were appointed to divide the parish "into proper districts." Their report was accepted, five districts promptly set off, and ten men chosen for school committees, viz.: Benjamin Leavens, Ichabod Turner, northwest district; Benjamin Joy, Moses Winter, middle district; Joseph Torrey, Ebenezer Larned, northeast district; Josiah Brown, Philip Whitaker, southeast district; Nell Saunders, John Brooks, southwest district. Among other improvements Landlord Felshaw was allowed the privilege of building a pound on his own land, thirty feet on the outside and six and a half feet high.

Church affairs were wisely ordered by Rev. Aaron Brown. In compliance with that article of the church covenant which required two or more of the principal brethren to help the pastor in the management of prudential affairs, Ebenezer Larned was invested with advisory power and dignified by the title of Elder. Lieut. Benjamin Leavens succeeded Samuel Buck in the office of deacon, in 1765. Watts' version of the Psalms was now used in the afternoon service. Church and society were strengthened by the accession of new inhabitants. In 1763, Joseph Torrey, son of Dr. Joseph Torrey, South Kings-

12

ton, R. I., settled on part of the College Farm, east of Killingly Hill, marrying a daughter of Rev. John Fisk. He was soon followed by his brother, Dr. Samuel H. Torrey, a young man of much more thorough medical training than was common at that period, who soon gained an extensive practice. His young wife, Anna Gould of Branford, brought with her four slaves as part of her marriage portion. These brothers identified themselves with church and town, and were active and influential. The sons of Rev. Perley Howe were now entering upon the stage and taking part in various affairs. Hezekiah Cutler,* who had removed from his farm on the eastern line of the town to the vicinity of the meeting-house, was prominent in town and church. His nephew, Benoni Cutler, son of Timothy, was an active young man, much interested in military matters. Sons of Justice Joseph Leavens, Joseph Cady and Captain Isaac Cutler, were now in active life.

The mill privilege on the Five-Mile River, afterwards occupied by "the Howe Factory," was now improved by Jared Talbot and David Perry, who accommodated the neighborhood with sawing and grinding. Noah Elliott purchased land of Nehemiah Clark, "removed from town."

The rage for emigration had not yet seriously affected Killingly, though some of her most gifted and promising young men were going out into the world. Manasseh, son of Hezekiah Cutler, and Joseph, youngest son of Rev. Perley Howe, were fitted for College by Rev. Aaron Brown and entered Yale in 1761. Although then but fourteen years old, Howe manifested uncommon force and maturity of mind, and was graduated " the first scholar in a class which had its full share of distinguished names." After teaching for a time with great success in Hartford, he accepted a tutorship at Yale College, "where his literary accomplishments, especially his remarkable powers of elocution, not less than his fine social and moral qualities, rendered him a general favorite. It is said to have been owing in no small degree to his influence that the standard of polite literature and especially of public speaking in Yale College about this time was very considerably elevated." Preaching during this interval at Norwich, Hartford and Wethersfield, he was everywhere welcomed, caressed and urged to settlement. Visiting Boston for the benefit of his health, the New South church, after twice hearing, invited him to become the successor of Rev. Penuel Bowen of Woodstock, " the character which Mr.

---

* Not the son of Isaac Cutler as erroneously stated in Volume I., but of John Cutler of Lexington, who purchased land on the Rhode Island line at a very early date but did not occupy it till about 1713. Mr. Cutler died in a few years after his removal to Killingly, leaving a widow and many children.

Howe had received from the voice of mankind," explaining such unwonted precipitancy. After a year's delay Mr. Howe accepted this call and was ordained in Boston, May 19, 1773. It is not a little remarkable that this most honored position should have been filled successively by young men from Windham County.

Cutler was also "distinguished for diligence and proficiency, and graduated with high honor from college" to attain distinction in various departments. After practicing law for a time in Edgartown, he studied theology and was ordained pastor of the church at Ipswich Hamlet, Mass., Sept. 11, 1771. While performing his pastoral duties with great fidelity and acceptance, Mr. Cutler gave much time and thought to political and scientific investigations, fitting him to bear a most prominent and useful part in the development of the future Republic.

Another Yale student fitted for college by Mr. Brown was Amasa, son of Deacon Ebenezer Larned, who after first studying and serving in the ministry turned his attention to the law and entered into political life, representing his adopted home, New London, in state and national councils.*

Justice Joseph Leavens, a founder and father of the town, the last survivor of the first settlers of Killingly, after having faithfully served God and his fellow-citizens for successive generations, "departed this life Nov. 5, 1773, aged ninety years." His cotemporary and first pastor, Rev. John Fisk, died the same year. Deacon Ebenezer Larned, in 1779. His brother, James Larned, had now settled on Killingly Hill, near Felshaw's residence. Thomas Moffat and Capt. John Felshaw, though far advanced in years, were able to attend to public affairs. Tavern patronage increased with political agitation and disturbance, and Felshaw's tavern was one of the most noted. The growing military activity, the more frequent trainings and parades, demanded larger accommodation. In January, 1775, a number of public-spirited citizens secured from Rev. Aaron Brown and Sampson Howe a deed of about three acres of land adjoining the meeting-house lot, "To have and hold the above-granted premises with all the profits and privileges thereof

---

*These brilliant young men were probably not so unlike other collegians. It is related of Amasa Larned that in the first flush of Freshman dignity he composed a very elaborate and ornate *Latin epistle* which he sent home to a younger brother destined to dig roots only from the parental homestead, with this condescending *post-scriptum:* "If you can't read this show it to Mr. Brown"—his revered and reverend preceptor. The young farmer was not as much overcome as may have been expected. In former boyish rencontres he had managed to hold his own. His brother's extremely dark complexion was a common subject for banter, and now he hastened to concoct a medley of Hog Latin and nonsensical lingo, which he dispatched to the Yale student with his vernacular postscript: "If you can't read this show it to some *other Indian.*"

for the use and benefit of a common forever, and to be by them faithfully appropriated to said use; to use, occupy and improve the said
premises for the good of the public as a common forever." The amount
requisite for this public benefit which secured a beautiful common for
future generations was given by the subjoined subscribers, in sums
ranging from £2, 8s. to six shillings:—

Aaron Brown, Perley Howe, Benjamin Joy, Benjamin Leavens, Asa Lawrence, Nathan Day, Hezekiah and Benoni Cutler, Benjamin, Jonathan, Nede-
biah, Joseph, David and Isaac Cady, Penuel, John. Jacob and Charles Leavens,
Resolved Johnson, Stoughton Ricard, Eleazer Mighill, John Adams, David
Perry, Joseph Wilder, Jonathan Buck, Thomas Smith, Samuel H. Torrey,
Noah Elliott, Ebenezer, Asa and James Larned, Sampson Howe, Jared Talbot, Simeon Lee.

The South Society of Killingly, though not inferior in size and
natural advantages, was far less prosperous than the north and central
societies. The "irreconcilable religious differences" that led to its
erection increased in bitterness. Three churches widely opposed in
sentiment struggled for life and ascendency. The established church
centering on Breakneck Hill battled bravely for a few years. Under
the faithful ministry of Rev. Eden Burroughs, it was somewhat
strengthened for a time, and received some important accessions. Daniel Davis of Oxford, who settled in 1752 on a valley farm north of
Whetstone Brook, and John Sprague, who removed to the south of
Killingly at about the same date, united with this church and served
usefully as deacons. Samuel Danielson, Boaz Stearns and Ephraim
Warren were still its earnest supporters. Mr. Burroughs was an able
and active pastor, highly esteemed by his ministerial brethren. Yet
with all their efforts they were unable to maintain their footing. As
the older members passed away and neighboring churches increased it
was found very difficult to provide for the support of the minister, and
after many struggles and trials he was reluctantly dismissed in 1771.
Mr. Burroughs then removed to East Hanover, Mass., was one of the
first trustees of Dartmouth College, and served as pastor of the college
church. The Breakneck Church did not succeed in settling another
pastor, and gradually wasted and dissolved. Its few surviving members united with other churches; its records were burnt up, its meeting-house moved off the hill and devoted to secular purposes, and
nothing left to tell the story of the vanished church and its battles but
a few mouldering gravestones on the rugged summit of Breakneck.

Substantial settlers from time to time purchased homesteads in Killingly Centre. A valuable farm adjoining James Day's was purchased
from Deacon Daniel Davis by William and Jonathan Dexter of Smithfield, R. I., in 1769. John Coller bought land eastward of Ephraim
Warren; George Corliss of Providence purchased of Michael Hewlett.

Barzillai Fisher of Preston secured the farm and residence left vacant by Mr. Burroughs. These new-comers with the numerous Hutchins families and other descendants of first settlers were obliged to attend worship in the south part of the town, even if not in sympathy with those who conducted that worship. This Separate Church gained in strength and numbers, though still greatly burdened with questions of discipline, " dealing " even with its pastor " for ronging some of his nabors in putting off to them that which was not marchantable." A brother was publicly admonished for stripping a greatcoat from a dead soldier, and re-admonished " in that he held there was no wrong in the act, only that it grieved the brethren." Two sensitive sisters were unable to travel with the church " because it held as a principill that it was a censorable eavill for a member of the church to marry with an onbeliever." A former act of the church in suspending a most exemplary deacon upon this charge had probably subjected it to the imputation of holding a principle, so inimical to the matrimonial aspirations of its sisterhood. Finding upon investigation that this distasteful " principill " had indeed been very much imbibed, the church " exploded it on conviction," confessed its fault and graciously welcomed back the pacified sisters. Rate-paying being utterly tabooed the Gospel was supported by what was denominated " free contribution," viz. : " the church met together by legal warning at an appointed time and place to *show their liberality*, and those who wilfully or carelessly neglected their duty in that respect were to be looked upon as covenant breakers."

After the death of Rev. Samuel Wadsworth in 1762, the church, according to the practice of its order, proceeded to select a pastor from its own membership. The gifts of Deacon Stephen Spalding and brother Thomas Denison were found useful to the church. Mr. Denison had been prominent in the early days of the Separate movement, and, after embracing and renouncing " Anabaptism," had assisted in ordaining most of the Separate ministers, but had lost the confidence of his friends through weakness and infirmity of temper, and after many trials and difficulties had recently removed to Killingly. His fluent prayers and exhortations were so acceptable to his hearers that without inquiring into his character and antecedents the church proceeded to call him to the vacant pastorate, but soon found cause to regret their hasty action. Mr. Denison's principles were far less satisfactory than his preaching, and were in many respects " contrary to the travel of the church and brought a great division among them." A majority of the church went back from their call and declined to proceed to installation, but a number persisted in holding him for their pastor, and he in holding himself to be sent of God to be the pastor of

the South Killingly Church. Great confusion and embroilment followed. Seven prominent members of the church brought specific, sus-
tainable charges against Mr. Denison, whereupon they were sharply
admonished and suspended from church privileges ; and they in turn
admonished and suspended their admonishers. Mr. Denison, as clerk
of the church, took possession of its records and refused copies of votes
to his opponents, who had no resource but to "send their distressed
cries" to other Separate churches to look into their deplorable case
and give counsel and assistance!! John Fuller, Paul Parke, John Palmer, Joseph Marshall and Alexander Miller, ministers of Separate
churches, and a brother from each church, accordingly met in council
in the South Killingly meeting-house, May 2, 1764, and after due examination gave in their judgment with refreshing plainness and im-
partiality. That Mr. Denison had "intruded" in voting for himself
with the minor part and opposing the major vote was evident, but " as
to his being accused with crowding," it appeared that the church had
never regularly dismissed him from the call it gave him, and were
presently divided among themselves. On the whole, they found the
whole affair from first to last very imprudent. The hasty proceedings
of the church in receiving Mr. Denison into membership without further acquaintance with him or recommendation from some other
church seeing he was a stranger, and being in such haste to call him
for their minister was very censurable ; and they could not but think
Mr. Denison entirely out of the way of his duty in insisting upon his
being chosen by said church when he could not but see the irregularity
of the whole affair and the lamentable divisions consequent upon the
same; and as for their admonishing one another, could they do it in a
brotherly way it might in some instances be commendable and their
duty, but for either side to assume the power of the church, they could
not expect the same to have any good effect at all, and for Mr. Denison and those with him to admonish as reported was entirely wrong
both as to matter and manner.

Whereupon the council proceeded to advise Mr. Denison—

"To desist his improvement entirely amongst them under the notion of
his being their pastor, seeing the division is so grate and the consequencis só
contrary to the very designs of the Gosple of Peace, and although the said
Mr. Denison did not send for our advice in particular yet as well-wishers to
himself and the interest of religion we cannot avoid advising him as he ten-
ders the glory of God his own comfort and peace, and the welfare of this
people, and we cannot but hope and expect that he will comply with our
advice, especially when it appears that none from no quarter abroad can join
in said affair, and also seeing his ministry in other places hath been attended
with difficulties of the same nature.

We likewise advise those brethren that appear so forward for settling Mr.
Denison after all, to come to a deliberate consideration of the evil consequences which hath already attended said affair, and when this is done we
shall hardly need to advise them to desist for we think they will do so of

themselves, unless they design their own ruin with their brethren as to their church state. And as for those brethren that sent for us we advise you to lay aside all contention, and as new born babes desire the sincere milk of the Word that ye may grow thereby, and let the whole affair cease as to any more debate about the same."

The church by formal vote now dismissed Mr. Denison from his call, and with solemn prayer and fasting invited Eliphalet Wright of Mansfield, to become their pastor, whose ordination was speedily effected, May 16, 1764,—the most noted Separate ministers of the day assisting in the services. Mr. Wright was a man of good sense as well as of fervent piety, and soon restored good order and harmony. Working with his own hands at his trade of saddle and harness-making, he required so little pecuniary aid, that his church was released from compulsory contributions, and enabled to give more care to its spiritual edification. Having suffered much for lack of some definite form, it now adopted the 'Articles of Faith and Covenant used by the Separate church of Plainfield, " as a good and wholesome system of faith and practice by which it would walk in future, still looking for more light." John Eaton and Jonathan Day were chosen deacons. Oct. 4, 1765, Abraham and Hannah Spafford, Nathaniel Bennet and Hannah Wright—the only remaining members of the once flourishing Separate church in Mansfield—were received into church fellowship. A powerful work of grace began ere long which brought some fifty persons into the church and greatly strengthened and refreshed it. In 1768, Abraham Carpenter was ordained into the office of deacon by the laying on of hands, and dismissed after five years service, to become the pastor of the church of Plainfield, New Hampshire.

As years passed on this church lost some of its distinctive Separate features. In 1774, Wyman Hutchins and Joseph Bennet were chosen to assist the pastor in the government of the church, to inspect into the conduct of the church both with respect to their attendance on public worship and their daily walk. Greater secular privileges had now been obtained. Exemption from paying rates to the south society had been restricted solely to those who first petitioned the Assembly, so that their children and later members of the church were still compelled to pay tribute, but as public opinion became more enlightened, " the said society were themselves convinced that this was a hardship and injustice," and agreed unanimously "that something ought to be done about it." Samuel Danielson, Boaz Stearns and Deacon Sprague were accordingly appointed a committee on behalf of the south society to meet in conference with Deacons Stephen Spalding, Wyman Hutchins and Jonathan Day, and consented that the Separates should be incorporated into a distinct ecclesiastical society—"division to begin at the Quinebaug River, run east to Joshua Whitney's dwelling-house, and so to Rhode Island line." A petition to this effect was thereupon preferred to the General Assembly and society privileges granted, October, 1770.

The "Separate brothers and sisters" at Chestnut Hill, received liberty from the main body to meet occasionally by themselves on the Sabbath for public worship, and had the sacrament administered to them once in three months. Mr. Denison remained in Killingly after "being dismissed from his call," and there is some evidence that he served as pastor to this diminishing "branch." The Baptists of this vicinity had no church organization at this period, but remained faithful to their principles and even gained adherents, laying the foundation for the future establishment of their order. As the Revolutionary troubles came on many residents of the seaboard sought security in Windham County. Among these emigrants were several earnest Baptists, filled with missionary zeal, who went about preaching the word, and building up and strengthening Baptist churches. The scattered Baptists in Chestnut Hill and its vicinity gladly welcomed the call to unite as a distinct body. Agreeable to a request from a number of baptized believers, desiring to unite in a visible church state, Elder Joseph Winsor of Gloucester, Elder James Manning of Providence and Elder Job Seamans of Attleborough, with delegates from their respective churches and from the Baptist church in Thompson Parish, convened in East Killingly, May 22, 1776. President Manning was chosen moderator. Articles expressing the sentiments of those desiring to embody touching both doctrine and practice received the approbation of the council, and were signed by nearly sixty baptized believers, male and female, mutually covenanting and agreeing to unite together as a church. Others were soon added both by letter and profession. Eber Moffat was chosen clerk. July 26, the church unanimously agreed to give Mr. George Robinson, of Attleborough, a call to settle with them as their elder. On the same day a Baptist society was organized—its members voluntarily agreeing "to attend on divine service on every first day of the week, Extrodinarys being excepted, and also to contribute to the support of the Gospiil ministery with our Christian friends, the breatheren of the church in this place, as necessity my require." Eber Moffat was elected clerk of the society, and the call to Mr. Robinson confirmed. Mr. Robinson desiring time for consideration, in October church and society renewed their request and he gave answer in the affirmative. Robert Baxter, David Law, Joseph Smith, William Givens, Ezekiel Blackmar and Ephraim Fisk, were chosen by both bodies, To buy a settlement and take a deed of the same for a ministerial lot for the use of the Elders.

William Givens was chosen treasurer for the church. Ordination services were held at the house of Mr. David Law, Nov. 12. Elders Isaac Backus, Abiel Ledoit, John Martin, Joseph Winsor and Charles Thompson were present. Elder Backus was chosen moderator, and Elder Thompson, clerk. Inquiring first into the constitution and articles of the church, they found them so consistent with the rules of the gospel, that they gave them fellowship as a sister church. The relation of the candidate's "call out of Nature into Grace and also his special call to the great work of the ministry," gave "such full satisfaction that we heartily agreed to answer the church's request in ordaining of him," and on the following day "the Elders met and separated Brother Robinson to the work whereunto God had called him by laying on of hands and prayers." Thus happily established the church went on its way rejoicing, as is shown by its records :—

"First day, January ye 5th, 1777. We had the sacrament administered to us by our Elder—a comfortable day it was.
First day, January ye 26. Mary Aldreig offered herself to this church and was received, and was baptized with decency by our Elder."

A building was soon built or procured which served for a place of worship. There is no evidence that the appointed committee succeeded in buying a ministerial lot for Elder Robinson, but he himself for two hundred pounds purchased a hundred acres of land of Robert Baxter, who had recently removed from Scituate. Ephraim Fisk of Swanzey, and David Law, were newly arrived residents. A committee was now appointed by the First society "to assist in examining the certificates of people called Baptist," which reported "that such as produce proper certificates ought to be exempt."

VIII.

WOODSTOCK'S THREE PARISHES. BAPTIST CHURCH. TOWN AFFAIRS. TROUBLES WITH MASSACHUSETTS.

WOODSTOCK in 1760 had just emerged from a bitter and protracted controversy, resulting in church and society division. A new society had been erected in the north part of the first society. Three religious societies with each a distinct church organization were thus comprised within the township. The Rev. Stephen Williams was still the stated pastor of the New Roxbury or West Society. Rev. Abel Stiles was claimed by the North Society. The First or South Society was without a pastor. It had saved its meeting-house, but lost its minister, and some years passed before this loss was supplied. Much time and money were expended in "going after ministers." The young licentiates from Pomfret recently graduated from

13

Yale College—Chandler, Craft, Grosvenor and Weld—were heard successively and unsuccessfully. Worthy neighboring ministers labored with appropriate prayer and fasting to bring them to a decision. True to their Massachusetts proclivities, church and society at length united in choice of Abiel Leonard of Plymouth, a graduate from Harvard College in 1759. His fine personal appearance, agreeable manners and marked ability in the pulpit, won universal favor, and on June 23, 1763, he was inducted into the vacant pastorate. Eleven Massachusetts churches were invited to participate in the installation services. The only Connecticut church thus honored was the First of Killingly, Rev. Aaron Brown, pastor. The sermon preached by Rev. Mr. Barnes of Scituate was so satisfactory that the brethren of the church manifested their desire to have it printed. Liquors, lemons and sugar provided for this joyful occasion gave equal satisfaction. William Skinner and Jedidiah Morse were soon after installed in the office of deacons. It was also voted, " That a chapter in the Bible should be read publicly every Lord's day if agreeable to the congregation." Thus provided with an acceptable pastor after so many years of strife and destitution, the church on Woodstock Hill enjoyed a season of unwonted harmony and prosperity. At peace with itself it was ready to make peace with its neighbors, and passed the following act of amnesty : " Dec. 8, 1766, pastor and brethren of ye church in ye first society vote to overlook and forgive all that has been offensive to us in ye church in North Woodstock, engaging to conduct towards them as becomes a church in Christian fellowship." The question of singing was next brought under consideration. Hitherto the whole congregation had been accustomed to join promiscuously in this part of divine worship, but in 1769, the psalm-tuner formally petitioned, " That some convenient place in the gallery be appropriated to the use of the singers." The society responded, " That it would be exceedingly glad that the three forward seats in the front gallery might be sequestered to the use of the singers ; and also that the three seats on the women's side might be sequestered for the same use ; and further that those women both elder and younger that are favored with agreeable voices would occupy said seats is the society's desire." This proposition to limit the privilege of joining in sacred song to such as could sing agreeably met much opposition, and was not carried into execution for several years.

Woodstock's north society was formally incorporated by Act of Assembly in 1761. Though inferior in extent and numbers to the previous societies it had the advantage of compactness and unity. Its chief supporters were numerous families of Child and May, long resident in this northeast section of the town. The long and arduous conflict by which they had gained their independence had strengthened the ties of blood, and their appreciation of distinct religious privileges, and led them to engage with much harmony and spirit in establishing stated worship. Families in neighboring parishes were eager to join with them in this effort. A petition from Theophilus and Samuel Chandler, Moses and William Marcy, and Edward Bugbee, residents of Thompson Parish, represented:—

"That the extent and quantity of the land in said society of North Woodstock is but small for a parish and its list only £4709; that they were five and even six miles from the meeting-house in Thompson, and separated by the Quinebaug which for the greater part of the year was not passable unless by bridges, which necessitated a longer journey; that they were much nearer the centre of North Woodstock, and should be much better accommodated, to be made a part thereof; while the remaining part of Thompson would have numbers, estate and extent quite sufficient."

Henry and Peter Child of New Roxbury also begged for annexation to the north society on the plea that the west society contained half the land in the whole town, and that in the north was small compared with the other. Both requests were granted, and the several petitioners formally annexed to the north society. With these additions it now embraced some fifty-five families, and was able to provide a place of worship and support its minister in a creditable manner. A meeting-house was soon erected on the site of the present church edifice in East Woodstock. Land for this purpose was probably given by members of the Child family, but the absence of records makes it impossible to gain authentic details. It is traditionally asserted that some opposed this site as not in the centre of the society, and that when one party gathered to raise the frame another appeared to push it down, but this too is doubtful. Land adjoining the meeting-house was purchased of Elisha Child by Rev. Abel Stiles in 1763, and on this pleasant spot the much-tried minister found an agreeable retreat from the storms by which he had been so long beset. He reports to his nephew, Dr. Ezra Stiles, that their "domestic circumstances are comfortable. The long uproar has ceased since the disruption of the society. I am in peace with my people." His experience had left him a very unfavorable opinion of ecclesiastic councils and judgments. Dr. Stiles, requesting him to collect results of councils in Windham County for the last fifty years to be compiled "in a brief history of New England councils," his uncle replies:—

"Why Woodstock alone would furnish and suggest matter for a volume equal to Father Cowper's Anatomy! . . . . As to the results in Woodstock since I have been here, they appear to me as contrary as the good and bad figs in Jeremiah's vision; some very good, others very bad; nor do I think it in the power of mortals to prevent erroneous and injurious results. In a word, were I half so sure that a history of New England councils would prevent future mischief, as I am of having been repeatedly injured by past results, I would cheerfully send you all the results I am able to collect."

Dr. Stiles was himself a frequent visitant at the North Woodstock parsonage, attending meetings of association and consciation, preaching for the different ministers and noting with keen eye whatever came within his cognizance. His minutes give no hint of any unpleasantness or lack of harmony in the new society. The church was somewhat annoyed by the difficulty of obtaining recognition as the *First Church* of Woodstock, a dignity tenaciously claimed by the standing church on Woodstock Hill. It consented nevertheless to consider the conciliatory overtures made by that body, and after first distinctly voting Dec. 16, 1766, "That this church has full right to consider themselves the first church of Woodstock," it agreed "To overlook and forgive all that has been offensive to us in the South Church." So far as can be ascertained both churches were correct in their assumption. Neither one or other had organized anew or made such change as to forfeit its standing under the original covenant. Both had sprung from the same root and as north and south branches now represented the original Woodstock church. Loss or absence of records makes it impossible to trace the course of the North Church for many years.

The church and society of West Woodstock pursued their way peacefully and prosperously under the guidance of Mr. Williams, till their tranquillity was disturbed by the development of a new religious interest. It had been a time of great spiritual dearth and declension; church members had become cold and formal; social religious meetings were unknown; the young people were much absorbed in frolic and merry-making. A chance sermon preached by an earnest Baptist minister, Rev. Noah Alden, while passing through the town in December, 1763, was a means of fixing conviction of sin in the conscience of the chief leader in fun and levity—Biel Ledoyt—and after arduous conflict, his soul was brought into gospel liberty. "A world lying in wickedness and the necessity of men being made new creatures fell with such weight upon his mind," that he felt constrained to speak to them about it, and that with such earnestness and power, that those young companions who came to laugh him out of these new notions, "stood like men amazed" and were themselves convicted and converted. A meeting was appointed in a school-house, and though it was a dark lowery night people flocked to it from all parts of the parish till the house was full. Ledoyt and two of his young friends carried on the meeting, and so impressive were their exhortations that about forty young persons were "struck under conviction." The meetings were continued. Convictions increased greatly. Parents were surprised to see their giddy children distressed for their souls. All frolicking came to a stop. The Bible and other good books were much in use. The groves rang with the bitter outcries of the distressed youth. Professing Christians were led to lament their previous coldness and backsliding, and join with these young disciples in labors for the conversion of others. So powerful was the work that none dared at first to say a word against it, but after a time opposition was manifested. Some older church members looked with suspicion upon a religious movement begun and carried on outside the church, and feared it would result in excesses and irregularities. They cautioned the converts about spending so much time in meetings and staying out so late at night, and advised them to refrain from exhorting, but finding their advice unheeded, "fell to crying Error and Delusion." The flaming zeal of the young disciples was only hightened by this opposition. The regular meetings of the church and the ordinary services of the Sabbath conducted by Mr. Williams, seemed to them cold and lifeless. Disparaging remarks were made upon both sides and ere long a bitter antagonism was developed between the friends and enemies of the revival. The church, alarmed at the condition of affairs, proclaimed a fast and called in the neighboring ministers, who saw in this great religious awakening a new outburst of the spirit of Separatism, and "fell to reading about false spirits and Satan transforming himself into an angel of light . . . . . intimating, that the work was from Satan, and such ministers as were instruments of it, the servants of Satan," and "plainly warning them against the first instruments of their awakening, as being the *deceivers* which should come in at the last times." This injudicious action and uncharitable surmising, "grieved the hearts of the tender lambs," and plainly taught them that edification, the great end of Christian society, was not to be enjoyed in the church of their fathers. Other Baptist ministers had probably followed Mr. Alden. A remnant of the old Six Principle Baptists still existed, and now a large proportion of the young converts turned in sympathy to the Baptists and embraced their peculiar principles. Unable to walk in harmony with the standing church, they felt compelled to separate from it, and in the autumn of 1764 agreed to meet together as a society, improving the gifts which God had given them. At the first favorable opportunity several were baptized by immersion and in February, 1766, fifteen of these baptized converts embodied in church estate, and soon others were added. Their meetings, conducted by several gifted brethren, were well sustained and attended, so that it was apparent to all that God's work went on amongst them. One of the most earnest and active of these brethren was Biel Ledoyt, who felt called of God publicly to preach his word, which he did in a manner so satisfactory to the church, that May 20, 1708, he was ordained as its pastor. The growth and prosperity of this Baptist church awakened much jealousy and opposition. As the only church of this order then within Windham County limits its position was prominent, and a bitter and persecuting spirit was manifested by its opposers. Attempts were made to waylay and assault its pastor, and rates for the support of Mr. Williams were extorted from its members. Embittered by the loss of so many of their congregation, the established society of West Woodstock denied the validity of the Baptist church and society organization. Jan. 29, 1770, Daniel Perrin, Samuel Harding and Samuel Chase were appointed by this society, " to examine the records of those people among us that call themselves Baptists ; also, to hear the pleas of those persons in regard to their principles and the reason of their conduct towards us, and consider how far they are freed from paying rates." These gentlemen reported, that we have been to Mr. Elnathan Walker's, whom our Separate neighbors call their clerk, to look into their records to see what regulations they were under and could find no record at all, neither at Mr. Walker's, nor with him they call their elder, that the good and wholesome laws of this Colony know anything of. In view of this report the society voted, "That the Ana-baptist people in this society are *not* freed from paying minister's rates amongst us ; and to leave the affair with the society committee." The committee thus empowered attempted to levy the rates but met such determined opposition and argument from the indignant Baptists, who were at this time greatly encouraged and strengthened by the frequent visits and counsels of Deacon Bolles of Ashford, that they were fain to relinquish the futile effort, and after a year of wrangling the society again voted :—

" To take the advice of Hon. Jonathan Trumbull in the affair between the society and those people among us calling themselves Baptists and Ana-baptists, and his advice should determine the matter how said society should proceed with and towards said Baptists, and for his Honor to take the rules of law for his guide in his advice to the society."

Ebenezer Paine, Daniel Perrin, Samuel Harding, Samuel Child, and Nathaniel Marcy were instructed to draw up some suitable instrument to lay before Governor Trumbull, and Deacon Corbin, to present the affair to him. The honored governor duly considered the matter and replied with that candor and fairness which gave such weight to his counsels :—

" Inhabitants of New Roxbury, Woodstock. Gentlemen: I received by hand of Deacon Ebenezer Corbin, a request from your committee, showing, that there has been and still is a number of people in your society who profess themselves to be Ana-baptists, and did some time in the month of Feb., 1766, form themselves into a church state, and under the conduct and direction of three churches of the same denomination, have settled a teacher or elder among them, do steadily attend the worship of God and his ordinances among themselves according to their way and manner, and say they have taken all those steps and measures the law requires, and are under the patronage and toleration of the laws of this Colony; that some of your society suppose that they have not; that those Baptists have been every year put into the tax bill made for the support of your minister, except the last year they were left out by the committee that they have paid no such tax nor any distraint made therefor; that by reason of different sentiments in religious affairs and different minds in the society respecting those who differ from them with regard to taxing them, a great difficulty has arisen; and therefore asking my opinion and advice in the following particulars :—

1. How is a Baptist to be known in law, whereby he is to be exempted from paying taxes to the support of the established worship or ministry in this Colony?

2. Whether the Baptist churches in general in this Colony, are otherwise known in law than those in your society, and if so, in what manner?

3. In order that a Baptist may be known in law by his certificate, by whom it must be signed and to whom directed?

That, at your late society meeting it was voted to take my advice in the affair, to determine how the society should proceed with and towards the Baptist people among you.

Whereupon, it is my opinion, that a Baptist is known in law so as to be excused from paying any tax levied for the support of the established ministry in the society where he dwells, when he dissents from the same, attends the worship of God in such way as is practiced by the Baptists and joins himself to them, whereby he becomes one of their society; that the Baptist churches in this Colony are no otherwise known in law than that church of Baptists in your society is, that those people having formed themselves into a Baptist church and society, they, and the particular persons who hereafter do attend their meeting for the worship of God and join with them in this profession, are excused from paying any part in your society tax for the support of your minister. The certificate mentioned in the law is to be produced from such Baptist church, signed by the elder or other known proper officer, and directed to your society committee or clerk. The law doth not oblige those people to make application to the General Assembly or County Court to be qualified for such exemption, which was formerly the case and is probably the occasion of your present difference in sentiments.

That you may be of one mind, live in unity and peace under the Divine protection and blessing, is the sincere desire of your most obedient humble servant,   JONATHAN TRUMBULL.

Lebanon, March 21, 1771."

The standing society accepted this decision as final, and directed its committee to examine reports of Baptist people, and see who are exempt. About forty persons were then released from ratepaying. Recognized as a lawful body, the Woodstock Baptist Church increased in numbers and influence, united with the Warren Baptist Association, and gained a respectable standing among its sister churches. The West Woodstock Congregational Society, extending over a large and opening territory, gradually recovered its losses. Like its sister churches in town it was now greatly exercised by the question of singing. Four "queristers" were chosen in 1776, and it was voted, "That the singers should sit in the front gallery in any seat (except the fore seat in front) according to their age and common usage in sitting; that the several queristers should be seated, and sit in the fore seat in the front gallery, men's side." But the new arrangement did not work well, and after a few months trial it was again voted, "To come into some cordial agreement that each one may enjoy his right and property, so that we may all celebrate the praises of God together, both heart and voice, in every part of the meeting-house."

All parts of the town united in care for its public interests. "Notifications" for town meetings were set up in four places that all might receive due warning. Town meetings were still held in the meeting-house on Woodstock Hill. As the disturbances with England came on their meetings were conducted with increasing spirit and solemnity. The Reverends Stiles, Leonard and Williams now took the freeman's oath, and each in turn opened the April town meeting "with a religious service of prayer and a sermon." At the annual meeting in 1760, Isaac Johnson was chosen moderator; Thomas Chandler, town clerk and treasurer; Isaac Johnson, Thomas Chandler, Nathaniel Johnson, Ebenezer Smith, Jun., Nathaniel Child, selectmen; Moses Chandler, constable and collector of colony tax; Moses Child, collector of excise; Samuel McClellan, George Hodge, Elijah Lyon, Abner Harris, John Chamberlain, Amos Paine, Matthew Hammond, Jonathan, Henry and Ebenezer Child, Ebenezer Corbin, Jonathan Morris, Hezekiah Smith, Captain Joseph Hayward, Joshua Chandler, highway surveyors; Silas Bowen, Hezekiah Smith, grand-jurors; Silas Bowen, Moses Child, Moses Chandler, Stephen May, Ebenezer Child, Jun., Samuel Child, Jun., listers; Nathaniel and Abijah Child, Samuel Bowen, collectors of rates; George Hodge, Josiah Hammond, Stephen Marcy, Asa Morris, Caleb May, Elisha Child, tithing-men; Benjamin Bugbee, William Chapman, fence-viewers; Darius Ainsworth, Zebediah Marcy, Joseph Manning, Ezra May, Isaac Bowen, Nathan Child, haywards; Moses Child, receiver of stores; Jedidiah Morse, packer; Joseph Peake, guager; Richard Flynn, Daniel Bugbee, branders. Town bounds demanded much attention. The report of a committee relating to the line between Woodstock and Union was accepted. Thomas Chandler was appointed agent to oppose Union's petition, and with John Payson, Jabez Lyon, Samuel Chandler, Edward Morris and John May—the fathers of the town—wait upon the committee sent by the General Court. Nathaniel Child and Joseph Peake were chosen to meet with Jacob Dresser and Jaazaniah Horsmor to renew the line between Woodstock and Killingly, and all the remaining bounds were perambulated and renewed. The renovation of the town pound excited some discussion. It was voted "to build a new pound in the centre of the town," but this was revoked, and in 1765 it was ordered, "To build one pound near the old pound in the first society of the same bigness as the first with stones, selectmen to have charge of the same." Again, the question was reconsidered, and it was finally decided that the new pound should be built with oak posts and chestnut rails, six rails high and four lengths of ten-feet rails square. Manasseh Horsmor also received the privilege of using his barn-yard for a public pound. Swine were allowed the liberty of the highways and commons if sufficiently "yoked and ringed." A bounty of twelve shillings was offered in 1771 to any person who should kill a wildcat. Captain William Lyon, Samuel Chandler, Nathaniel Child, Captain Daniel Paine and Ebenezer Child, appointed at about this day to examine the financial status of the town, reported " That the town's money for a number of years had been prudently handled," and that its treasury was in good condition. It was now ordered that a workhouse should be provided to accommodate the town's poor, and also that idle and dissolute persons might be put therein and employed. In 1773, highway districts were set out, viz.: in the First society, five districts, under the care of Thomas Baker, Jonathan Allen, Jonathan Lyon, Jedidiah Bugbee, Matthew Bowen; New Roxbury society, four districts, Daniel Paine, southeast overseer; Benjamin Haywood or Howard, southwest; John Perrin, 2d, northwest; Samuel Narramore, northeast; North society, Caleb May, southeast overseer; Ephraim Carpenter, northeast; Eliakim May, northwest; Stephen Tucker, southwest. A communication relating to Colonel Putnam's petition for a public highway to New Haven leading through Windham County was favorably received by the town, and referred to the consideration of the selectmen. New roads were laid out from time to time in different parts of the town, connecting with or replacing the old range-ways originally laid out. Schools were managed by the religious societies. A proposition to sell the old cedar swamp and appropriate avails to the support of the gospel, "provided said gospel be carried on according to the Congregational or Presbyterial Scheem," failed of accomplishment. In 1765, it was voted to sell the same and apply the proceeds to schooling. Four years later sale of certain portions of proprietors' land was reported and accepted, and £115 allowed for schools. The remainder of the cedar swamp was left for private sale. Committees were still chosen to take care of the hearthstone lot and prosecute trespassers.

Woodstock was now losing many of its citizens by emigration. Thomas, youngest son of Captain John Chandler, removed with his family of sons and daughters in 1761, and after a brief sojourn in Walpole, New Hampshire, decided to lay the foundations of a new settlement westward. Jabez Sergeant, Edward and Isaiah Johnson, Charles May, William Warner and others from Woodstock joined with him in building up the township of Chester, Vermont. John and Noah Payson, William Bartholomew, Seth Hodges, Benjamin Bugbee, John Chamberlain were among the many Woodstock emigrants who went out into the wilderness and aided in settling towns in New Hampshire, Vermont and New York. This outflow was perhaps made needful by

14

the great natural increase of population—Rev. Abel Stiles baptizing
in his society in twenty-five years no less than 367 boys and 415 girls—
while at the same time it was favored with remarkable exemption from
sickness and epidemic disease, so that in some 210 families the yearly
average of death was only twelve persons. Many lived to great age
and quietly dropped away.

An elaborately carved slate-stone in the graveyard at New Roxbury
commemorated the decease of Joshua, third son of Honorable John
Chandler, April 15, 1768 :—

> " In his last days he in
> Hopes of another world
> Saying by and by Glory,
> Glory, Glory.
> Blessed are ye dead
> That die in the Lord."

Other honored and lamented citizens left still more enduring monuments. Deacon William Lyon bequeathed to the town for the instruction and spiritual edification of its citizens his copy of Willard's Body
of Divinity, a most elaborate and exhaustive theological compendium.
The town signified its acceptance and appreciation of this gift by
voting, "That it be annually removed from one parish in town to
another, to be kept at the meeting-houses of the respective societies."
Captain Benjamin Lyon's bequest of fifty pounds was restricted to the
north society, to be applied towards procuring a library. The United
Lyon Library, comprising some two hundred and fifty volumes, mostly
divinity books, and including the remains of the ancient Union Library
of Woodstock and Pomfret, resulted from this thoughtful and wise bequest. About ninety proprietors had rights in this library.

Captain Samuel Chandler, last surviving son of Honorable John
Chandler, occupied for many years the original Chandler homestead in
South Woodstock. His son, Charles Church Chandler, was graduated
from Harvard College in 1763, studied law, married Marian Griswold
of Lyme, and entered upon the practice of his profession at the old
homestead in his native village. He was a young man of marked
ability and promise, and soon became very prominent in town and public affairs. This village of South Woodstock was now noted for public
spirit and patriotism. Dr. David Holmes, its well-known physician,
and Samuel McClellan, trader, were both very active in military and
political affairs. The mercantile traffic carried on by the latter participated in the revival of business enjoyed for a season, and large quantities of English and West India goods were distributed throughout the
town. No men in Woodstock were more respected and useful at this
period than the deacons of the south church—William Skinner and
Jedidiah Morse—who, with their popular pastor, are also reported as

"the largest and finest looking men in the parish." Nor were the wives of these excellent men less respected and honored, but were rather regarded "as models of domestic virtues and Christian graces." The "excellent character and noble bearing" of Mrs. Temperance ———, wife of Dr. Holmes, impressed all who knew her. Mrs. Jemima Bradbury, widow of Hon. William Chandler, also occupied a high place among Woodstock's notable and honorable women. "Endowed with superior natural and acquired abilities," kind, courteous, benevolent, religious, she was especially noted for her interest in natural sciences, geography, history and all kindred investigations, and for skill in imparting to others "most valuable instructions." Certain bright little boys then growing up in the families of Deacon Morse and Doctor Holmes may have received their first impulse to geographical and scientific studies from the teachings of this gifted and intelligent woman. Bright little girls as well as boys were also growing up in Woodstock. Alathea Stiles studied Latin with her accomplished father, and reports her progress in this and other studies to her learned cousin. Other young ladies excelled in housewife accomplishments, and some of their exploits even found their way into the newspapers. The Hartford *Courant*, January 9, 1766, reports that Miss Levina, daughter of Capt. Nehemiah Lyon of Woodstock, and Miss Molly Ledoit of the same town, in one day carded and spun twenty-two skeins of good tow yarn, and that a few days after, Martha, sister of Levina, spun 194 knots of good linen yarn in one day. The same paper records an unfortunate casualty occurring at an October training. Elisha Lyon, oldest brother of these young ladies, a most promising young man, twenty-four years of age, was shot through the head by the accidental discharge of a musket and immediately expired.

The tranquillity of Woodstock during this period was somewhat disturbed by renewed demonstrations from the Government of Massachusetts. That Colony had never yielded her claim to the Indented townships. Proclamations of Fast and Thanksgiving had ever been sent to them and assessments for taxes, and now she resolved to compel them to return to their allegiance. At the meeting of her General Assembly, Feb. 25, 1768, the following resolution was presented:—

" *To the House of Representatives :—*
Whereas the inhabitants of Somers, Enfield, Suffield and Woodstock, did in 1749, revolt from their subjection to this Government under which they were at first settled, and by which they had been protected at great charge in several wars, and did apply to Connecticut to receive them as being within said Colony, and said Government did at first disclaim any share in said revolt, but afterwards, by an act or law artfully established a new form of words expressive of the bounds of Hartford and Windham counties, in order to give color to the officers of said counties to exercise jurisdiction over said revolting inhabitants, and whereas after various attempts to persuade and compel said inhabitants to return to subjection, war began and for many years con-

tinued, during which Massachusetts Government desisted from all compulsory measures lest damage should accrue to his Majesty's service, and whereas by restoration of peace reasons for such forbearance cease and inhabitants still continue in revolt.

Resolved and ordered, That these inhabitants ought to have been, and from henceforth to all intents and purposes shall be considered within the limits of this Province, and under the jurisdiction of this Government, and civil and military officers are required to govern themselves accordingly, but in case of their return no arrears of taxes required of them; notified to forbear payment of future taxes to Connecticut; selectmen required to give in a list of polls and estates, and if they don't, assessment to be made in lawful manner; sheriffs desired to deliver copies of this resolve, to give notice to the inhabitants."

This resolution was adopted by both Houses and attempts made to carry it into execution. A copy was left by Sheriff Gardner Chandler with Jedidiah Morse, selectman of Woodstock, but it received no attention. The inhabitants of Woodstock had no desire to return to Massachusetts government, but rather manifested undue, undutiful eagerness to take another slice of her territory. The committee appointed in 1753 by Rhode Island and Connecticut to examine the boundary line between Massachusetts and Connecticut, had reported, "That the dividend line was wrong from the outset; that the point selected by Woodward and Saffery for the head of Charles River was *four miles* south of the true head, and the stake on Wrentham Plain more than *seven miles* south of the most southerly part of Charles River, instead of *three*, as prescribed by Massachusetts' charter." Nehemiah Lyon, Jedidiah Morse, Silas Bowen, Samuel McClellan and Charles Church Chandler were now appointed by Woodstock to invite Rhode Island to appear in person before the General Assembly of Connecticut, and unite in asking to have the boundary line settled. Rhode Island so far complied with this invitation as to appoint a committee to apply to Connecticut to ascertain the result of the joint petition of 1753, "and if they can't tell, write to Mr. Partridge [her agent in England] and request him to examine the papers and inform us of the circumstances the affair was under at the commencement of the late war." Woodstock, meanwhile, appealed herself to the Assembly for the redress of this and other grievances. Its distance from Windham Court-house was a great inconvenience and trial to this township, and it eagerly joined with other northern towns of the county in devising a remedy. At a meeting held in Pomfret, Feb. 11, 1771, at the house of Colonel Israel Putnam, Samuel Chandler, Nehemiah Lyon, Nathaniel Child, Daniel and Ebenezer Paine appeared on behalf of Woodstock, consulting with gentlemen from Killingly, Thompson Parish, Ashford and Union, in regard "to some new bound for the county." This conference had no immediate result. Pomfret wished the county seat transferred to her own borders. Woodstock had her own views upon the matter, thus embodied in petition, after careful consideration and amendment, May 2, 1771 :—

"Whereas your memorialists, upon a mature consideration of the excellency of the form of Government in Connecticut, and of the wise, equitable and righteous administration of the same, did in 1749, place themselves under the jurisdiction and patronage of the Gen. Assembly, with raised expectations of a plenary protection being granted them against the claims and demands of Massachusetts, but had been exposed to some peculiar inconveniences, suffering greatly in their time, in their estates by seizures and distraints from the Province of Massachusetts, and to this day not exempt, and Massachusetts continuing its claims, and from year to year they have been assessed for their proportion of that Province tax, and by a resolve passed in its General Assembly, Feb. 25, 1768, your memorialists were warned to forbear payment of any future taxes to the Government of Connecticut, and the selectmen of the indented towns required to give in a list of estates before next session, and in case of refusal to be assessed in such proportion as the other inhabitants of Massachusetts and payment enforced by law; and, 2, your memorialists being more than twenty-five miles distant from the court-house in Windham, are put to great cost in attending the same and the multiplicity of business necessary to be transacted, whereby the time of the court to a great degree lengthened and frequent adjournments takes place, causing much needless travel and long absence from their respective families and occupations in life, enhanceth their burdens, increases their charges and greatly tends to their impoverishment; all which grievances we have patiently borne for twenty-two years from the hope that they would be redressed; and whereas it is the prevailing sentiment in Windham County that said county should be divided, on account of the multiplicity of business whereby parties are with their witnesses obliged to be on charge frequently week after week and cases deferred from time to time, and the inconvenience of other towns by being situate at a great distance, particularly Pomfret, Killingly, Ashford and Union, and whereas Woodstock is most conveniently situated for a shire-town, as the boundary line between Massachusetts and Connecticut now runs seven miles north from the centre of its first society upon a strait line, and the northeast corner of said boundary line at Killingly's northeast corner being about eleven miles distant, and the northwest of Union about fourteen miles, southeast corner of Killingly fourteen miles, southeast corner of Ashford fourteen miles from centre of first society, and upon supposition that the boundary line be run agreeable to the manifest intent of the Province Charter, three miles south of any part of Charles River, it would be about four and a half miles farther north; and as the court-house in Windham, by being placed about two and a half miles from the south line of the county, puts the inhabitants of these north towns—some twenty and even thirty miles distant—to very great inconvenience and charge, beg for a committee to unite with Rhode Island in fixing boundary line with Massachusetts, and also to take a just survey of Windham County, the situation of Woodstock, and its conveniency for a shire-town.

ELISHA CHILD,
JEDIDIAH MORSE,
Agents."

William Williams and Joseph Trumbull were appointed by the Upper House to consider this memorial, but the Lower House dissented. The question of removing the court-house was not yet to be considered, and as for the boundary line, so long as Connecticut *had the towns*, agitation was unadvisable. In attempting to gain four miles, she might lose the whole disputed territory, and so both questions were left for future generations to grapple.

BOOK VI.

WINDHAM IN THE REVOLUTION, 1764–83.

I.

OPPOSITION TO STAMP ACT. NON-IMPORTATION. HELP FOR
BOSTON. RESOLVES AND ONSETS. A GREAT UPRISING.

DURING the period of time embraced in the preceding section
events were occurring that demand a separate record, and
careful review and consideration. The Revolution by which the
American Colonies were forever released from the dominion of Great
Britain was in progress. Windham County so alert and active in
administering its domestic affairs was equally awake to the great
public questions of the day. Its citizens had been reared to an intelligent participation in the government of Connecticut. As soon as a
town was able to pay its part of public expenses it had sent representatives to the General Assembly, and the proceedings and reports of
those representatives were closely scrutinized and debated at home.
The management of their towns, churches and schools had developed
a spirit of self-reliance and independent judgment, and wise leaders
and administrators were found in every community. The unusual
privileges conferred by the charter of Connecticut gave her citizens
for many years no pretext for murmuring, and they had been noted
for attachment and loyalty to the British government in contrast with
their rebellious neighbors in Massachusetts. Restrictions upon trade
and manufactures, though burdensome and prejudicial to development,
were viewed as perhaps needful commercial regulations, and excited
no general distrust or disaffection. It was not till Great Britain
claimed the right to impose a direct tax upon her American Colonies
that her Connecticut subjects were roused to resistance. Taxation for
the support of civil government had been hitherto associated with a
voice in its administration. No town presumed to send deputies till
it could pay public charges. Ministers exempted by law from rate-
paying were expected to refrain from voting. The vital connection
between taxation and representation had thus infused itself into the

popular mind, and was held as a primal axiom not to be disputed or dislodged. The report that the House of Commons had resolved, that it was proper to charge certain stamp duties in the Colonies and plantations, awoke Connecticut to a sense of her danger. The great mass of her citizens united with those of other Colonies in expressing their determination to resist this arbitrary imposition. Admit the right to levy this tax, and no security was left to them. In the great conflict that followed, Windham County was deeply implicated. Her position on the main thoroughfares of travel brought her into very close and constant communication with the leading towns in the Northern Colonies. Filial and fraternal relations connected her with the flaming patriots of Boston and Providence. The earnest words and warnings of Colonel Dyer, then in London with opportunity of judging the aims and temper of the British Government, made a deep impression upon the citizens of Windham. "If the Colonists," he wrote, "do not now unite, they may bid farewell to liberty, burn their charters, and make their boast of thraldom." A still more potent stimulus was found in the pervading influence of Putnam, Durkee, and other popular military leaders, men of mettle and experience, quick to apprehend the exigency and most effective in appeal to popular sympathy. Windham County's appreciation of the importance and solemnity of the crisis was shown in the character of the men sent to share in the deliberations of the General Assembly. Her shire-town sent its senior minister, Rev. Ebenezer Devotion, together with the venerable Nathaniel Wales, and in the following session, Hezekiah Manning, and men of years and approved judgment were selected by all the towns, viz. :—

Pomfret—Samuel Dresser, Samuel Craft.

Canterbury—Captain Jabez Fitch, Captain Daniel Tyler.

Plainfield—James Bradford, Isaac Coit.

Killingly—Briant Brown, Ebenezer Larned.

Woodstock—Nehemiah Lyon, Ebenezer Smith.

Voluntown—John Gordon, Moses Kinney.

Ashford—Amos Babcock, Jedidiah Fay.

Lebanon—Captain Joshua West, William Williams.

In spite of petitions and remonstrances from America, and earnest protestations from her friends in Parliament, the British government persisted in its purpose, and on March 22, 1765, the famous Stamp Act received the sanction of the King. The news of its enactment was received in America with the most violent demonstrations of indignation and defiance. Virginia's House of Burgesses then in session, at once resolved, "That the inhabitants of that Colony were not bound to yield obedience to this law, and that any person who should maintain that any persons other than the General Assembly had any right or power to impose taxation upon the people should be deemed an enemy to the Colony." Its resolutions in their first unmodified draft were eagerly caught up, printed on broadsides, and sent throughout the land, were copied into the public journals of New England, and everywhere accepted as a true expression of public sentiment. Simultaneously and spontaneously as it seemed, inhabitants of hundreds of towns and villages banded together as Sons of Liberty, pledging themselves to use their utmost endeavor to resist the execution of the Stamp Act. As intelligence arrived that certain individuals had been designated to receive and distribute the obnoxious paper, which after the first of November was to be used in all business transactions, the excitement increased, and public indignation vented itself upon these prospective officials. In the larger towns there were violent uprisings and tumults, stamp officers burned in effigy and their offices and dwellings sacked and demolished, while rural communities manifested their spirit and sympathy by uproarious gatherings and effigetic hanging and burning. The newspapers of the day applauded and incited these proceedings.

> " What greater pleasure can there be
> Than to see a stamp-man hanging on a tree,"—

was the general cry.

Windham, the most effervescent of Windham County towns, was the first to act upon this suggestion. Intelligence that one of her own citizens had been appointed deputy stamp-master under Ingersoll, threw her into great excitement. A self-appointed vigilance committee instantly waited upon this gentleman, compelled him to give up the letter announcing his appointment and solemnly promise to decline the office. On the morning of August 26—famed for many similar outbreaks in other towns—this " ever memorable and respectable gentleman made his appearance in effigy, suspended between Heaven and Earth," on some conspicuous elevation upon Windham Green. People came in crowds from all the surrounding country to witness the show and join in the demonstrations. Effigies of other suspected and unpopular individuals were successively brought forward and hung up amid the jeers and opprobriums of the excited spectators. After hanging till evening the several figures were taken down and paraded all about the village and then consumed upon a bonfire with great rejoicing The staid and decorous Lebanon observed the day with more dignity and solemnity, draping her public buildings with black, and subjecting her effigies to a formal trial and sentence before proceeding to hang and burn them.

15

These noisy demonstrations were but the prelude to more serious action. The citizens of Windham and New London Counties were fully determined to prevent the distribution of the stamps. When it was found that Governor Fitch was preparing to carry out the instructions of the King, that the colony agent, Jared Ingersoll, after faithfully opposing the passage of the bill had accepted the position of stamp-master, and that the western counties were less awake to the crisis than their own, they sallied out in great force to end the matter at once and forever. Five hundred horsemen armed with clubs and other weapons and provided with eight days' provision, marched deliberately across the country under the leadership of Captain John Durkee, intercepted Ingersoll on his way to Hartford and compelled him to write his name to the formal resignation prepared for him. Putnam, accredited with a prominent share in the instigation of this irruption, was detained from personal participation by illness. As soon as possible he waited upon Governor Fitch in behalf of the Sons of Liberty, to ensure that no other stamp-master should be appointed, and no farther attempt made to enforce the Act, and with his usual directness assured him that if he should refuse to relinquish the control of the stamped paper his house would be "leveled with the dust in five minutes." Nathan Frink, King's attorney in Pomfret, was appointed deputy stamp-master for the north part of Windham County, and went so far as to build an office for their reception, but was most positively assured by his fellow-citizens that he would never be allowed to use it for that purpose. So great was the public excitement and interest that the very stones were made to cry out. "LIBERTY & EQUALITY," "DOWN with the STAMP ACT," inscribed on a stone tablet, and hoisted in a conspicuous position above the door of Mr. Manning's dwelling, met the eyes and stimulated the zeal of the many passers over Manning's bridge in the south part of Windham town.

In the various public convocations of this eventful epoch Windham bore a conspicuous part. Colonel Dyer was sent as delegate to the first general Congress, held in New York, in October. At a meeting of the Sons of Liberty in Hartford, March 25, 1766, "much more generally attended by the two eastern counties of Connecticut"—Colonel Putnam, Major Durkee and Captain Ledlie were appointed a committee to arrange a correspondence with the loyal Sons of Liberty in other colonies, and Ledlie, then resident in Windham, was sent as representative to a general convention of that order in Annapolis. Stamps destined for Connecticut were forcibly taken from the sloop *Minerva* and destroyed by the Sons of Liberty in New York harbor. By this vigorous combination and resistance the Stamp Act was made inoperative. When the first of November came not a sheet of the stamped paper was to be procured. It had been destroyed or sent back to England, or stowed away for safe keeping. Nearly all the business of the Colony was thus suspended. Courts and ports were closed and thousands of public offices. Land could not be legally conveyed nor debts collected, nor wills made, nor marriage licenses procured. Relief could only be obtained by a special dispensation or permit from such governors as ventured to exercise this power in cases of extreme urgency. The consequent business derangement affected England almost as seriously as America. No debts could be collected nor goods sold in the Colonies. At the re-opening of Parliament, London merchants most earnestly urged the repeal of the odious Act. Pitt, and other friends of America, exerted their utmost eloquence and energies in this behalf and after a violent and protracted contest its repeal was effected. The Colonies received the tidings with many manifestations of joy and gratitude, commercial intercourse was renewed and trade and business speedily revived.

Peace and prosperity had but a brief continuance. The spirit that had evoked the Stamp Act manifested itself in other aggressions. In 1767, a bill was passed in Parliament imposing duties on tea, glass and paints, from which a public fund should be formed to be expended in defraying the expenses of its government in America. Her Colonists resented both the tax and disposition, as thus their governors, judges and other public officers were made entirely independent of themselves and their Assemblies, and were confirmed in their suspicion that the British Government was bent upon their subjugation. Her previous policy in restricting Colonial trade and manufactures in order to leave the market open for her own productions, appeared to them another evidence of this design and showed them the necessity of more vigorous resistance and effective combination. Great Britain had schemed and legislated to compel America to purchase her productions; it behoved America to thwart those schemes and evade that legislation by devising some method for supplying themselves with needful articles. A meeting was called in Boston, October, 1767, to consider what effectual methods could be agreed upon to promote industry, economy and manufactures, and prevent the unnecessary importation of European commodities. A committee was appointed which suggested and prepared an explicit "form" in which the signers pledged themselves to encourage the use of American productions, and refrain from purchasing articles of European manufacture. A copy of this agreement was sent to every town in Massachusetts, and many in the adjacent colonies, requesting their consideration and signature. Windham town with its usual promptness held a meeting, December 7,

1767, "to consider the letter and matters from the selectmen of Boston," appointed a number of leading citizens in each of its three parishes to prepare a suitable response, and met again a month later to receive this report:—

" Being sensible that this Colony in its situation and soil and the commodities which it is naturally adapted to produce by a proper exertion of labor and industry, will not only afford the inhabitants much the greater part of the necessities and conveniences of life but a considerable surplus for exportation, but the surprising fondness of its inhabitants for the use and consumption of foreign and British manufactures and superfluities, even to a great degree of luxury and extravagance, which has so far increased beyond our ability to pay as has proved detrimental to our Mother Country, and has such pernicious influence upon the inhabitants of this Colony as, if persisted in, must involve the great part in irretrievable distress and ruin; at present plunged in debt, the balance of trade greatly against us, our small commerce declining, and poverty with all its melancholy attendants threatening, which loudly calls upon every friend to his country to exert every patriotic virtue in its full force to extricate the inhabitants from their perplexed and embarrassed circumstances, the consequences of which are so far felt as fully to be dreaded, and being of opinion that frugality and industry with a fixed attention and application to American manufactures are the most direct and obvious measures to answer these salutary purposes and are absolutely necessary to extricate ourselves from our present load of debt, as well as for the future prosperity of the community, do engage with and promise each other that we will not from and after the first day of March next, by land or water, transport into this Colony either for sale or our own family's use, nor purchase of any other person, any of the following articles produced or manufactured out of North America, viz.: Loaf-sugar, cordage, coaches, chaises, and all sorts of carriages and harnesses for the same, men's and women's saddles, and bridles and whips, all sorts of men's hats, men's and women's apparel ready-made, men's gloves, women's hats, men's and women's shoes, sole-leather, shoe and knee buckles, iron ware, clocks, nails, gold, silver and thread lace, gold and silver buttons, diamond stone and paste ware, snuff, tobacco, mustard, clocks and watches, silversmith and jeweller's ware, broad-cloth that costs above 9s. pr. yard, muffs, tippets and all sorts of head-dress for women, women's and children's stays, starch, silk and cotton velvet, linseed oil, lawn and cambric that costs above 4s. pr. yard, malt liquors, cheese, chairs and tables, and all kinds of cabinet ware, horse combs, linen exceeding 2s. per yard, silks of any kind in garments, men's and women's stockings, and wove patterns for breeches and vests.

And we do farther engage to each other that we will discourage and discountenance to the utmost of our power the excessive use of all foreign teas, china ware, spices and black pepper, all British and foreign superfluities and manufactures not herein enumerated as by due encouragement are or may be fabricated in North America, and also the present excessive use of rum, brandy and other spirituous liquors in all house-holders, families, taverns and laborers. And all extravagant, unnecessary and expensive *treats*, as have by custom been introduced by military officers, holding such in reputation who shall for the future neglect the same—and whereas wool and flax are the natural produce and staple of this Colony, the increase of which must prove beneficial; it is farther agreed not to drive out of this Colony to market any wethers of more than two years old, or ewes of more than six years old, for the space of three years next coming, and would recommend the raising of flax, hemp, and barley for the making of good beer which would have the greatest tendency to discourage the pernicious use of distilled spirits; also would recommend to families to save and preserve all refuge linen rags to promote the manufacture of paper in this Colony; also recommend an inquiry into the method and expediency of manufacturing glass—and furthermore, to the end that this union be not violated and the good effects be frustrated, if any inhabitant does not sign and conform to these regulations but still continues to import and introduce any of the above-mentioned restricted articles, such persons shall be by us discountenanced in the most effectual but decent and lawful manner, and that a committee be appointed to correspond with committees from the several towns in the County in order to render the fore-going proposals as extensive and effectual as may be.

JEDIDIAH ELDERKIN.	DAVID ADAMS.
SAMUEL GRAY.	JOSEPH GINNINGS.
NATHANIEL WALES, Jun.	JONATHAN KINGSLEY.
JACOB SIMMONS.	JOSHUA ELDERKIN.
HEZEKIAH MANNING.	ELISHA HURLBUT.
WILLIAM DURKEE.	EBENEZER HOVERY.

EBENEZER DEVOTION, Jun."

The foregoing report being publicly read three times was accepted in a very full meeting of the inhabitants of the town, *nemine contradicente ! !*

It was farther voted, " That the form of subscription be the same as come into by the town of Grafton, and that the previous committee with Joshua Reed, Thomas Tracy and Nathaniel Linkon should take care and see subscription filled up by the inhabitants of the town, and when completed lodge the same with the town clerk." In compliance with the suggestion of the report, " Nathaniel Wales, Jun., Esq., Samuel Gray, Esq., and Dr. Joshua Elderkin were appointed a committee to correspond with committees from the several towns of the county to render the foregoing proposals as extensive and effectual as may be." The honor of " inventing " the system of corresponding committees which proved so effective in promoting the Revolution has been ascribed to Samuel Adams and other notable persons, but we find it at this early date proposed and carried into execution by Windham. The stringent agreement was signed by nearly every inhabitant and faithfully observed though at great loss and self-sacrifice. The foreign traffic that had so enriched them was given up. The foreign luxuries so freely used were all abandoned. The enthusiastic Windhamites rejoiced in this signal opportunity of testing their patriotism and devotion. Home-raised food and home-spun clothes came at once into use and fashion. A decoction of the common red-root " of very salutary nature," under the dignified appellation of Hyperion or Labrador tea, replaced the prohibited Hyson and Bohea. Ribbons, laces and all foreign finery were vociferously eschewed by the ardent " Daughters of Liberty." The wedding of Miss Dora Flint during this December was made a grand patriotic demonstration. The numerous guests from Norwich and Windham were all arrayed in home-spun. The bountiful refreshments were of colonial production, their flavor heightened by patriotic fervor. Any infringement of the agreement was quickly observed, and reported to the town authorities. " Joshua Elderkin, one of the committee, not keeping the same but importing felt hats and worsted patterns, the town agrees to look upon him as a person not fit to sustain any office of trust or profit till he properly manifests his repentance."

The spirit and self-sacrifice of Windham were emulated by the other towns of the county, and all were ready to pledge themselves to total abstinence from foreign luxuries. Ashford held a meeting Dec. 14, and appointed Captains Elisha Wales, Benjamin Clark and Benjamin Russel, Elijah Whiton, Esq., and Benjamin Sumner, Esq., "to be a committee to correspond with other committees in the county and elsewhere, to encourage and help forward manufactures and a spirit of industry in this government." Canterbury citizens met Dec. 21; Joseph Woodward, moderator. Jabez Fitch, John Curtis, Samuel Huntington, Captain Benjamin Pierce, Lieutenants Aaron Cleveland and Stephen Frost, Ensign Benjamin Smith and Mr. Solomon Paine were chosen committee to consider the premises and make report. Their report was accepted and provision made for procuring subscriptions to the agreement. Plainfield made haste to express her concurrence with the other towns, and agreed to draw up subscriptions in pursuance of their wise and happy measures for the encouragement of frugality, economy and our own manufactures. The formal Non-Importation Agreement of 1769, as promulgated by ardent patriots in Virginia and adopted by the several colonies, was most heartily endorsed by the citizens of Windham County. When it was found that interested individuals connived at the evasion of the Agreement by the illicit introduction of contraband goods, such persons were publicly denounced as covenant-breakers and enemies of their country. The withdrawal of New York from the Non-Importation league excited general indignation and reprobation. Many spirited meetings were held in Connecticut in 1770, to devise more effectual means for the enforcement of the Agreement. "Merchants and traders" met at Middletown, Hartford and New Haven, condemned the conduct of merchants in Newport and denounced the insolent behavior of New Yorkers. The names of the New York importers were printed and hung up in every public house in Connecticut for public execration. "What is the difference," asks a Connecticut journal, "between an Importer and an Indian? An Indian drinks cyder; an Importer drinks the blood of his country; an Indian is enemy only to himself, an Importer is an enemy to America." A meeting of the several committees of correspondence at Hartford Statehouse, August 9, recommended a general convention at New Haven the day after Commencement, every town to send delegates. Windham County responded with delegates from every town and implicit instructions. One or two specimens will show the temper and spirit of its inhabitants. Canterbury agrees:—

"1. That Jabez Fitch and Benjamin Bacon be chosen to represent the town at the meeting of the Mercantile and Landed Interest of this Colony, to be convened at New Haven on the day next after the ensuing Commencement.

2.   That if any person, whether an inhabitant of this town or not, shall at any time before a general importation takes place bring into this town either for their own use or for sale any British manufactures which have been imported contrary to the Non-Importation Agreement, or any goods whatever which have been purchased by those persons who have violated said agreement, they will incur the displeasure and resentments of the inhabitants of this town.

3.   That whereas the Parliament of Great Britain have continued the duty on all *Tea* imported into and consumed in any of the American Colonies as a Test and Proof of their right to tax America, which we think very unreasonable and unconstitutional; therefore, voted, That all persons who will at this critical time persist in using tea until the duty is taken off show a great disregard for the rights and liberties of America, and deserve to be treated with contempt."

Ashford was especially earnest and emphatic in resolving :—

" 1.   That we will not give up our native and loyal rights.

2.   That in the patriotic Agreement of the merchants, the interests and rights of America were thoroughly considered.

3.   That to break in upon the Non-importation Agreement strikes at the life of America and is a multiplied evil.

4.   That as the faith and virtue of sundry of the merchants have notoriously failed it is high time for the people to step forward in earnest to support the tottering cause and afford their united assistance to those merchants who still abide by the patriotic Agreement; and, therefore,

5.   Our utmost effort shall be put forth in vindication of the Non-importation Agreement, as a measure without which the safety and prosperity of the Colonies cannot be supported.

6.   That peddlers who without law or license go about the country selling wares are a nuisance to the public, and, if in our power, shall be picked up and put to hard labor and compelled to earn their bread in the house of correction.

7.   We highly resent every breach of the Non-importation Agreement, and are always ready to let our resentment fall upon those who are so hardy and abandoned as to violate the same.

8.   It is our earnest desire that every town in this Colony and in every Colony in America would explicitly and publicly disclose their sentiments relating to the Non-importation Agreement and the violations thereof.

9.   That the infamous conduct of the Yorkers in violating the patriotic engagement of the merchants is a daring insult upon the spirit and understanding of the country, an open contempt of every benevolent and patriotic sentiment, and an instance of treachery and wickedness sufficient to excite astonishment in every witnessing mind, and we doubt not but their actions will appear infamous till the ideas of virtue are obliterated in the human mind, and the advocates of liberty and patriotism are persecuted out of the world.

10.   That if the people of America properly attend to the concern of salvation and (unitedly) resolve upon an unshaken perseverance in the affair of non-importation till there is a total repeal of the revenue acts and an ample redress of American grievances, we shall be a free and flourishing people !

In consequence of the above resolutions we have chosen Capt. Benjamin Clark to attend the general meeting of the mercantile and landed interests at New Haven—the sense of the town as above—and to use his utmost influence to establish in the most solid and durable form the Non-importation Agreement."

Elisha Wales, Benjamin Clark and Samuel Snow were at the same meeting chosen a committee " To see that no merchants, shop-keepers nor peddlers import, put off, or traffick in Ashford, any goods, wares or merchandize that are imported contrary to the Non-Importation Agreement."

This important gathering was attended by representatives of a great majority of the towns in the Colony. Gurdon Saltonstall presided. Silas Deane served as clerk. After full and large discussion it was unanimously resolved:—

"That the Non-Importation Agreement come into by the Colonies in general, and by this in particular by their formal agreement, and the more general one entered into at Middletown, Feb. 20, was founded on patriotic principles and must be most effective, that we find no reason for relaxing said agreement now, to which we do agree and resolve that until Acts of Parliament be repealed, or until a general importation be agreed to we will not by ourselves or others, directly or indirectly [purchase] any goods except those mentioned in Agreement. The late defection in New York we highly reprobate, and judge it needful to break off commercial intercourse with New York."

These various convocations and combinations fired the zeal of the people and strengthened their determination to resist British exactions. Events successively occurring—the massacre at Boston, the burning of the *Gaspee* at Newport, the destruction of the tea in Boston Harbor —heightened the flame. Reports of every new aggression and collision flew at once over the land and were discussed in every town and hamlet, and when at length the news came that Boston was to be punished for her contumacy by having her harbor shut up, the Colonies rose as one to express their indignation and abhorrence. "The ancient destruction of Sodom and Gomorrah by fire and brimstone from the Lord out of Heaven was a just, righteous and merciful dispensation of the Most High God compared with the late Boston Port Bill!"

Connecticut's General Assembly, having recommended and observed a day of public fasting and prayer, expressed their sentiments in the following resolves:—

"1. We do most expressly declare, recognize and acknowledge his Majesty King George the Third, to be the lawful and rightful king of Great Britain, and all other his dominions and countries; and that it is the indispensable duty of the people of this colony as being part of his Majesty's dominion, always to bear faithful and true allegiance to his Majesty, and him to defend to the utmost of their power against all attempts upon his person, crown and dignity.

2. That the subjects of his Majesty in this Colony ever have had, and of right ought to have and enjoy all the liberties, immunities and privileges of free and natural-born subjects within any of the dominions of our said King, his heirs and successors, to all intents, constructions and purposes whatsoever, as fully and amply as if they and every one of them were born within the realm of England; that they have a property in their own estates, and are to be taxed by their own consent only, given in person or by their representatives, and are not to be disseized of their liberties or free customs, sentenced or condemned, but by lawful judgment of their peers, and that the said rights and immunities are recognized and confirmed to the inhabitants of this Colony by the royal grant and charter aforesaid, and are their undoubted right to all intents, construction and purposes whatsoever.

3. That the only lawful representatives of the freemen of this colony are the persons they elect to serve as members of the General Assembly thereof.

4. That it is the just right and privilege of his Majesty's liege subjects of this colony to be governed by their General Assembly in the article of taxing

and internal policy, agreeable to the powers and privilege recognized and confirmed in the royal charter aforesaid, which they have enjoyed for more than a century past, and have neither forfeited nor surrendered, but the same have been constantly recognized by the King and Parliament of Great Britain.

. . . .

7. That any harbor or port duly opened and constituted cannot be shut up and discharged but by an Act of the Legislature of the province or colony in which such port or harbor is situated, without subverting the rights and liberties, and destroying the property of his Majesty's subjects.

8. That the late act of Parliament inflicting pains and penalties on the town of Boston, by blocking up their harbor, is a precedent justly alarming to the British colonies in America, and wholly inconsistent with, and subversive of their constitutional rights and liberties.

9. That whenever his Majesty's service shall require the aid of the inhabitants of this Colony, the same fixed principles of loyalty, as well as self-preservation, which have hitherto induced us fully to comply with his Majesty's requisitions, together with the deep sense we have of its being our indespensable duty, in the opinion of this House, will ever hold us under the strongest obligations which can be given or desired, most cheerfully to grant his Majesty from time to time our further proportion of men and money for the defence, protection, security and other services of the British American dominions.

. . . .

11. That it is an indespensable duty which we owe to our King, our country, ourselves and our posterity, by all lawful ways and means in our power, to maintain, defend and preserve these our rights and liberties, and to transmit them entire and inviolate to the latest generation; and that it is our fixed determination and unalterable resolution faithfully to discharge this our duty."

This calm and lucid exposition of Connecticut's position, her claims and purposes, was accepted by the Lower House with great unanimity, but the more cautious Council deferred action till the following October. Meanwhile these resolutions were circulated throughout the Colony and ratified by the several towns. The inhabitants of every town were called together to discuss the situation and act for the relief of Boston. The Windham County towns hastened to obey the summons and embodied their views in many spirited declarations. A very full meeting was held in Woodstock, June 21. Nathaniel Child was chosen moderator. The resolves of the General Assembly were then read, and the following declaration adopted:—

" 1. That the thanks of this town be given to Capt. Elisha Child and Jedidiah Morse, Esq., the representatives of this corporate body, for their consenting to, and voting the above resolves in conjunction with the other representatives of this Colony, in General Court assembled, as said resolves do honor to the worthy representatives of a free, loyal and virtuous people, are very expressive of the sentiments of the inhabitants of this town, and by them judged necessary in such a day as this, when we have the most convincing proofs of a fixed and determined plan of the British administration to overthrow the liberties of America, and subject these colonies to a bondage that our fathers did not, would not—fled into the wilderness that they might not, and God grant that we, their posterity, never may—bear.

2. Being animated from the consideration of the absolute importance of adopting every rational and probable means in our power for the political salvation of our country, we engage to contribute our utmost exertions in defence of our American liberties and privileges, and stand ready to join our brethren in this and the other American colonies in every probable measure that may influence Great Britain to withdraw her oppressive hand. At the same time,

16

we apprehend that a General Congress consisting of delegates from each colony on the continent, is necessary speedily to be formed that the sentiments of the whole may be known, and such an unity in measures established as may constitute a strength invincible by tyranny, and break out in one general burst against the attempts that are made, and making, to destroy the constitution of their governments.

3.   And inasmuch as the promotion of industry, frugality, economy, arts and manufactures among ourselves, is of great importance to the good of a community, we determine, from this very day, to live as much within ourselves, and purchase as few British goods, wares and merchandizes as possible, and give all due. encouragement to every useful art among us.

4.   It having been judged needful at this alarming crisis, and generally come into, that committtees of correspondence be appointed—Voted,

That Capt. Elisha Child, Charles C. Chandler, Jedidiah Morse, Esqs., Capt. Samuel McClellan and Nathaniel Child, Esq., be a committee for maintaining a correspondence with the towns of this and the neighboring colonies.

5.   *Voted*, That a copy of these votes be printed in the New London *Gazette*, to manifest the deep sense we have of the Parliamentary invasion of the constitutional rights of the British Americans."

Pomfret, June 23, thus expressed her sentiments :—

" The present situation of the American colonies and plantations on account of the measures pursued by the Parliament of Great Britain respecting them, has become of so much importance and of so serious a nature, that it calls aloud for the sentiments of every town and even every individual to be known and communicated.   We therefore hereby assure our brethren, that we will to the utmost of our abilities, contribute to the maintaining and supporting of our just rights and privileges, and to the removal of those evils already come upon us, and more particularly felt by the town of Boston, viewing them as the more immediate sufferers, yet that our liberties and privileges are all thereby threatened and endangered.

We do therefore Resolve to this important end, we will unite in the necessary measures that may be adopted and more particularly pointed out at the proposed General Congress, which, we pray may be hastened—the several dissolutions of the House of Assemblies by their Governors, to prevent the same, notwithstanding.   And in the meantime we cannot refrain from adding, we will exert ourselves in promoting and encouraging useful and necessary manufactures, and such a spirit of economy and frugality among ourselves, as may prevent much of our present demands for British manufactures.

And we do resolve, that every person who shall hereafter send for, and import any British manufactures from Great Britain, or trade or deal with any who shall do so, until the loyal subjects of America are restored to, and can enjoy their just rights and privileges, shall be deemed and treated by us an ungrateful enemy to America, and with such person or persons we will have no commerce or deal."

Colonel Ebenezer Williams, Thomas Williams and Samuel Crafts were then chosen a committee to correspond with other Committees of Correspondence in Connecticut and other colonies.   On the same day, Windham thus declared herself with her accustomed vehement volubility :—

" This meeting being impressed with a deep sense of the present alarming aspects of Divine Providence over the British colonies in North America, arising from the present depressed situation and condition of the capital of a neighboring province, in having their harbor and port blocked up by ships-of-war in hostile array to the terror of the people, totally and actually obstructing all commerce by sea into or from said port, thereby forcibly preventing the due performance of all private maritime contracts, rendering useless their whole navigation, stores and wharves, built and erected at a vast expense by the inhabitants; a principle which threatens ruin and destruction both to the liberties and properties of every subject throughout the British empire.

And being further alarmed by a bill late depending before the Parliament of Great Britain, for regulating the the government of the Massachusetts Bay, too long to be here recited, though replete with arbitrary threatening resolutions, threatening destruction to all corporations in Great Britain, and all chartered rights in America. In view of these, as well as many other impending dangers and calamities, and from a firm belief and persuasion that there is a supreme almighty, infinitely good and merciful Being, who sits at the helm of universal nature by whom kings reign and princes decree justice, and who has the hearts of all princes and potentates of the earth in his hands, and under his almighty control; and however faulty the instruments and procurers of those calamities may be, yet considering our sins and impieties, they are just on coming from the hand of God, and are to be averted by humiliation, deep repentance and reformation. We therefore sincerely wish and hope a day may be set apart for solemn fasting and prayer as recommended by our late General Assembly; and beg further to intimate to our brethren in the several towns in this colony, to render the observation of that day more agreeable to the divine direction (viz.: to undo the heavy burdens, and let the oppressed go free, to distribute to the necessities of the distressed), that on that day we be united in opening our hearts in contributing to the relief of the injured and oppressed indigent inhabitants of the town of Boston, especially those who are now more immediately so by means of the late iron hand of oppression on that worthy metropolis.

But fully to express our sense of the late attempts upon the town and port of Boston, the arbitrary attacks on the most sacred rights of communities, the violent depredations on private property and liberty, and those more virulent efforts to break down the great barriers of civil society, founded on the solemn compact of kings, a principle proclaiming sudden destruction upon all corporations throughout the British dominions at the will and pleasure of a vengeful British ministry, even without complaint, notice, trial, or constitutional adjudication or forfeiture—words fail and the English language is deficient. But this is in part executed, and much more than threatened, only under the pretence at most, that some of the inhabitants of Boston or the neighboring towns have committed a trespass on the property of the East India Company, a company (horrendum dictu!) who have spread destruction over the eastern world! Behold the tragic scenes in that eastern clime! the murders of millions by sword and baleful famine; depriving those innocents of the necessaries of life, who by the favor of Heaven and their own industry, were overflowing with the wealth and profusion of the Indias, and all to satisfy the insatiable lust of gain and oppression! Let the Spanish barbarities in Mexico, and the name of Cortez sink in everlasting oblivion, while such more recent superior cruelties bear away the palm in the late annals of their rapine and cruelty; though many worthy individuals of that body ought no doubt to be excused from the general imputation. We applaud the solemnity of the noble Virginians and Philadelphians in their religious observations of that memorable first day of June; we approve their opinions and sentiments as to the threatened calamities and dangers impending America; as also the Maryland resolves, with the others by many worthy towns and bodies of people in this and neighboring provinces. We only wish there may be no delay in appointing time and place for a General Congress, which only can give union, firmness and stability to the whole. We impatiently wait for injured Boston to give the lead in that appointment. Providence no doubt has put into our hands the means to work out our temporal salvation, which has been repeatedly suggested. Let us, dear fellow Americans, for a few years at least, abandon that narrow, contracted principle of self-love, which is the source of every vice: let us once feel for our country and posterity; let our hearts expand and dilate with the noble and generous sentiments of benevolence, though attended with the severer virtue of self denial. The blessings of Heaven attending, America is saved; children yet unborn will rise and call you blessed; the present generation will, by future—to the latest period of American glory—be extolled and celebrated as the happy instruments, under

God, of delivering millions from thraldom and slavery, and secure permanent freedom and liberty to America.

We cannot close this meeting without expressing our utmost abhorrence and detestation of those few in a devoted province, styling themselves ministers, merchants, barristers and attorneys, who have against the sense and opinion of the rest of that respectable government, as also of the vast extended continent, distinguished themselves in their late fawning, adulating address to Governor Hutchinson, the scourge of the province which gave him birth, and the pest of America. His principle and conduct (evidenced by his letters, and those under his approbation), are so replete with treason against his country and the meanness of self-exaltation, as cannot be palliated by art nor disguised by subtilty In general, we esteem those addresses a high-handed insult on the town of Boston, and the province of Massachusetts Bay in particular, and on all the American colonies in general. Those styled merchants may plead their profound ignorance of the constitutional rights of Englishmen as an excuse in some degree; but for those who style themselves *barristers* and *attorneys*, they have either assumed a false character, or they must in some manner be acquainted with the constitutional rights of Englishmen and those of their own province—for them to present such an address is a daring affront to common sense, a high insult on all others of their profession, and treason against law; and from that learned profession, (who are supposed to be well acquainted with the English constitution, and have the best means, and are under the greatest advantages to defend the rights of the subject, and who have been famed as the great supporters of English liberty), for any of these to make a sacrifice of ALL to their pagod of vanity and fulsome adulation, is mean, vile and unpardonable, and cannot be accounted for upon any other principles but those of their master, who would sacrifice his country to become the independent head of a respectable province; and the few leaders of this infamous law-band would, it seems, give their aid and support therein to obtain the first places in his new kingdom. The addressing clergy we leave to the reproaches of their own consciences, but lament to find that they are the first in the ignominious homage of their idol."

These resolutions were unanimously adopted, and measures taken for carrying them into immediate execution. Nine of their most respected citizens in the several parishes of the town were appointed a committee to proceed at once to procure subscriptions for the relief of Boston. Their appeal was most effectual. Windham's fields abounded with sheep, and her hearts with generous sympathy. The poor sent of their poverty and the rich of their abundance, and within five days a bountiful offering was on the road to Boston with the following letter addressed to its selectmen:—

"WINDHAM, June 28, 1774.
Gentlemen:
'Tis with pity mixed with indignation that we have beheld the cruel and unmanly attacks made by the British Parliament on the loyal and patriotic town of Boston, who seem destined to feel the force of ministerial wrath, the whole weight of parliamentary vengeance leveled at them in a manner so replete with cruelty and injustice as must strike every heart with horror, and fill every breast with rage that is not entirely void of every sentiment of honor and justice and callous to all the common failings of humanity. But when we consider the cause of all these calamities—that is nothing less on your part than a strict adherence to the fundamental principles of the constitution, which when attacked you dared openly to assert and vindicate and stand foremost in the glorious cause of Liberty, in which you are contending not only for your own but ours, and the common rights of every American; when we reflect that it is this for which you are suffering such horrid cruelties, for which your streets have been stained with blood, and for which you now feel

the horrors of a military government—we are overwhelmed with a conflict of tumultuous passions, and filled with that manly ardor which bids us join you hand in hand and suffer with you in the common cause; nay, even if the sad exigencies of affairs should ever require it, to determine in defence of everything for which life is worth enjoying, to meet that death which will be glorious and infinitely preferable to a life dragged on in that low, servile state which is evidently planned for us, and which nothing less than the most heroic fortitude, and the highest exertion of every civil and Christian virtue can prevent. Give us leave therefore, to entreat, to beg, to conjure you, by everything that is dear, by everything that is sacred, by the venerable names of our pious forefathers who suffered, who bled in the defence of Liberty—not to desert the cause in this trying crisis, but to use your utmost influence in pursuing and persevering in every measure which may have a tendency to produce the desired effect.

Gentlemen, we hereby assure you, that to the utmost of our power we will assist you in every measure necessary for the common safety, not regarding our own private views and interests when in competition with the public good.

This town is very sensible of the obligations we, and with us all British America, are under to the town of Boston, who have been and still are the generous defenders of our common rights and liberties. We know you suffer, and feel for you. As a testimony of our commiseration of your misfortunes, this Town on the 23d instant, at a legal and very full meeting unanimously chose a committee to procure subscriptions for your present relief. Accordingly we have procured a small flock of sheep, which at this season are not as good as we could wish but are the best we have, and the people of this town are almost unanimous in contributing to this purpose.

This small present, gentlemen, we beg you would accept, and apply to the relief of those honest, industrious poor who are most distressed by the late arbitrary and oppressive Acts. And rest assured that if Parliament does not soon afford you relief and there should in future be any need of our assistance we shall with the utmost cheerfulness exert our influence to that purpose.

We are, gentlemen, with great respect your most obedient and humble servants.

> SAMUEL GRAY,
> NATHANIEL WALES,
> EBENEZER DEVOTION,
> EBENEZER MOSELY,
> HEZEKIAH BISSEL,
> JOSEPH GINNINGS,
> WILLIAM DURKEE,
> JOHN HOWARD,
> HEZEKIAH MANNING,
> *Committee of Correspondence.*"

This opportune gift, coming from so great a distance, and apparently the first arriving in Boston, was received with much delight and gratitude. The Boston *Gazette*, of July 4, reported: "Last week were driven to Roxbury two hundred and fifty-eight sheep—a generous contribution from Windham." On the same day the town voted:—

"That the thanks of this town be and hereby are given to our worthy friends, the inhabitants of the town of Windham, Connecticut Colony, for the kind and generous assistance they have granted this town under its present distress and calamity in voluntarily sending two hundred and fifty-eight sheep as a present for the relief of the poor, distressed inhabitants of this place, who by a late oppressive and cruel act of Parliament for blocking up the harbor of Boston are prevented getting subsistence for themselves and families."

So greatly were the people cheered and comforted by this prompt expression of sympathy from inhabitants of another colony that British sympathizers attempted to detract from its value by slanderous insinuations, giving out that the present of sheep sent from Windham "came only in consequence of *money sent to buy them*." The Boston *Gazette* could only express its sentiments thereupon by exclaiming:—

"How weak, how false, how little and how low!" Indeed, considering the scarcity of money, the insinuation was sufficiently absurd.

Pomfret's gift to Boston soon followed Windham's. A hundred and five sheep were promptly dispatched, and their reception thus acknowledged:—

"JULY 8, 1774.

Gentlemen:
By the hand of Mr. Elias Wells we received your generous and kind benefaction for the poor of this distressed town. We cannot enough express our gratitude for this instance of your bounty, in which you have liberally contributed to the relief of many. What you have thus lent to the Lord, we trust and pray that he will pay you again. It gives us great consolation amidst our complicated and unparalleled sufferings, that our brethren in the other colonies show such Christian sympathy and true benevolence towards us. That we are greatly distressed, needs no comment. Our harbor blockaded by a fleet of ship; our foreign trade actually annihilated; thousands of poor reduced to extreme want; troops continually pouring in upon us, to insult us in this our distress, is a consideration that must excite pity in the most obdurate. However, although we thus suffer, we are willing to suffer still more, rather than give up our birth-right privileges. With great regard, we are your brethren and most humble servants.

JOHN SEELY,
TIMOTHY NEWELL,
SAMUEL AUSTIN,
JOHN PITTS,
Selectmen of Boston."

The remaining towns in Windham County were equally earnest in their resolutions and benefactions. At a meeting in Canterbury, June 17, 1774, the following declaration was unanimously adopted:—

"This town, taking into consideration the alarming situation of the British colonies in North America, respecting sundry late acts of the British Parliament, and especially that for shutting up the port of Boston, which we look upon to be an abridgment of Charter rights and privileges. And considering the inhabitants of Boston as suffering under said Act in the common cause of the Liberties of all America, therefore voted:—

1. That we are willing and desirous to come into any reasonable measures that shall be adopted by the towns in this Colony for obtaining redress of our grievances.

2. That we esteem a general congress of the Colonies the most proper method to adopt an uniform plan for the preservation of the whole; and we recommend it to the Committee of Correspondence in this Colony to choose a committee to attend said Congress as soon as may be.

3. That if it shall be thought best by said Congress to stop all trade with Great Britain and the West Indies, we will most cheerfully acquiesce in this determination.

4. That Solomon Paine, John Felch, Daniel Paine, Dea. Eliashib Adams, Dea. John Herrick, Capt. Ebenezer Spalding and Asa Witter be a committee to correspond with the committees of the several towns in this and the neighboring colonies, and that they transmit a copy of their votes to the Committee of Correspondence in this Colony.

5. That the above committee are hereby particularly instructed to make diligent inquiry into the distress of the poor in Boston, so far as they appear to be brought upon them by the above Act of Parliament, and to take such

steps for collecting something for their relief as said committee shall judge the most effective for that purpose."

Killingly, June 29, expressed herself with unusual fervor :—

"At a meeting of the inhabitants of Killingly, having taken into consideration the dark and gloomy clouds which hang over and threaten the liberties of this, our native country, in general; the distressing circumstances of Boston, in particular—their harbors blocked up, cut off from all commercial trade and dealing on which they depended for a supply of bread, principles adopted for its government unconstitutional and oppressive imposed by military power; charters, which we once doted upon as unalterable as the laws of the Medes and Persians, and gloried in as the power and bulwark of these Colonies, we now see failing to protect the liberty of the subject and altered at pleasure; taxes, revenues, imposed without our consent attained or even asked for; and, in short, SLAVERY itself, protected by *Tyranny*, advancing with hasty steps towards this land of Freedom and Liberty. With the attention such a subject demands, and, at the same time we hope, with the candor and calmness so horrid a scene will admit of—we have thought proper to pass the following resolves :—

"1.   That we will choose a Committee of Correspondence to meet with the committees chosen by the neighboring towns, that they may agree upon some universal plan that may have the tendency under divine blessing to secure our just rights and privileges.

2.   That we will not purchase any goods of linen or woolen manufacture imported from Great Britain, and will break off all trade and commerce with the Indies if it be thought best by the committees in general Congress.

3.   That we will to the utmost of our power encourage manufactures amongst ourselves.

4.   That we will not sell any flax-seed to any person, except to be sold in the country or ground into oil.

5.   That we will religiously abide by these resolves, till the port of Boston is opened and the liberties of the people restored.

Also, voted, That these resolves with the preamble be published in the Providence *Gazette*.

Voted and chose a committee to take in subscriptions of the inhabitants of this town for the benefit of the poor of Boston, in sheep or otherwise, to be transmitted to the poor in Boston.

Voted to choose Joseph Torrey and Daniel Davis for this committee."

The less effusive Plainfield simply voted:—

"That the resolves of the General Assembly of Connecticut, May last, respecting the liberties and privileges of the English colonies are most salutary, and very heartily adopted by this meeting, and that it is the earnest desire of this meeting that deputies from the respective colonies meet as soon as possible in General Congress.

That we are willing to contribute our mite to the poor of Boston, and that Captain Joseph Eaton, James Bradford, Robert Kinsman, Andrew Backus, Abraham Shepard, Ebenezer Robinson, Joshua Dunlap, Perry Clark and Curtis Spalding be a committee to receive subscriptions for that purpose."

James Bradford, Isaac Coit, Major John Douglas, Dr. Elisha Perkins and William Robinson were also appointed Committee of Correspondence. Voluntown concurred with the resolves of the Assembly, and sent a contribution to the relief of Boston. John Dorrance, Thomas Douglas, Samuel Stewart, James Campbell, James Crary received and forwarded her gift ; Isaac Gallup and James Gordon served as Committee of Correspondence. Jedidiah Fay, Captain Ichabod Ward, Captain Elisha Wales, Benjamin Sumner, Esq., Amos Babcock and Ingoldsby Work were chosen Corresponding Committee for Ashford.

As the season advanced the several towns sent on their promised relief. Briant Brown, Ebenezer Larned, Benjamin Leavens and Perley Howe, committee for Killingly, sent a few sheep as a token of gratitude, and reported their town "to be well united, and determined to maintain its privileges at the risk of lives and fortunes, and ready to contribute to the necessities of those called to suffer." "Taking into serious consideration the present distressed and suffering circumstances of Boston," the citizens of Woodstock voted unanimously "to contribute to their relief." Captain Benjamin Lyon, Samuel McClellan, William Skinner, Timothy Perrin, Samuel Harding, Jonathan Morris, Nehemiah Lyon, Thomas May, Asa Child and Nathaniel Marcy—chosen to receive and transmit donations—had soon the privilege of forwarding sixty-five fat sheep, which were received by the authorities of Boston as an appropriate peace-offering from their revolted subjects. The selectmen of that town took especial pains to express their " unfeigned thankfulness that Woodstock had expressed such favorable sentiments of their town as laid them under particular obligations to persevere in a firm opposition to the attempts of arbitrary power."

Brooklyn Parish in August forwarded a hundred and twenty-five fine sheep through the hands of Israel Putnam, Joseph Holland and Daniel Tyler, Jun.—meaning therewith "in the first place to attempt to appease the fire (raised by your committing the Indian Tea to the watery element as a merited oblation to Neptune) of an ambitious and vindictive minister by the blood of rams and of lambs; if that do not answer the cure we are ready to march in the van, and to sprinkle the American altars with our heart's blood if occasion should be." Putnam remained some days in Boston and was received with high honors. Bancroft reports him " Warren's guest and everyone's favorite." The Boston *Gazette* informs its readers that "the town has had the satisfaction to be visited by the renowned Colonel Putnam so well known throughout North America that no words are necessary to inform the public any further concerning him than that his generosity led him to Boston to cherish his oppressed brethren and support them by every means in his power. A fine drove of sheep was one article of comfort he was commissioned to present us with." Another newspaper correspondent reports Plainfield as "preparing to send a flock of sheep," and similar offerings were sent from Ashford, Voluntown and Canterbury. Captain Aaron Cleveland transmitted in the autumn "a fatted cow," accompanied by the following letter :—

" *Gentlemen :*
Being affected with a sense of the righteousness of the cause that the people of Boston are suffering under, as it concerns all the people of America to be

roused to support them that they may not faint under their distress, it took hold on my covetous heart and made me willing to contribute my little mite, which I have sent by Mr. Green of Malden—a beef cow for the distressed— and ordered him to deliver it to the committee for that purpose; and may the Lord deliver the people of America out of the hands of a wicked and despotic power, who are exerting all the subtilty and malice of hell to enslave us. O! may Almighty God still rouse and farther unite the people of America as one man to a sense of their liberties, and never give them up as long as sun, moon and stars shall endure; and never submit to be slaves, but be willing to sacrifice life and all things to the defence and preservation of them; which is the earnest desire of your humble servant,

AARON CLEVELAND.

Canterbury, Nov. 27, 1774."

Windham's patriotic zeal during this fervid summer was shown in overt acts as well as " resolutions," by deeds of violence as well as those of beneficence. Mr. Francis Green of Boston, one of the "addressers" and adherents of Governor Hutchinson, having ventured into Connecticut to collect debts and transact private business, was forcibly expelled from Windham town and Norwich. Upon returning to Boston Mr. Green issued a proclamation offering the reward of one hundred dollars for the apprehension "of five *ruffians*, calling themselves by the names of Hezekiah Bissell, Benjamin Lathrop, Timothy Larrabee, Ebenezer Backus and Nathaniel Warren," all of Windham, who, aided by a great number of others, "did assault the subscriber, surround the house in which he was stopping, forcibly enter the same, and with threats and intimidations insist upon his immediate departure; also, of Simon Huntington of Norwich, and other villains and ruffians, who (it was supposed by the instigation of the above) did threaten, assault and lay violent hands upon the subscriber, and by force compel him to quit his lawful business and depart from their town." This proclamation, and the complimentary epithets applied to such men as Bissell, Backus and Huntington, excited much laughter and derision in both towns, and was reprinted in handbills and hawked about the streets with appropriate comments. Mr. Green's ejection was characterized by the patriot journals as "the cool, deliberate remonstrance of the Sons of Freedom." An eye-witness reports that in Windham " he was treated with great humanity and courtesy, allowed to stay all night, and reluctantly constrained to do by command what he would not do by courtesy." Colonel Eleazer Fitch, a French war veteran, high-sheriff of the County, who loved his royal master and hated violent demonstrations, had the temerity to assert "that the Norwich and Windham people had acted like scoundrels in treating Mr. Green as they did." The people thus stigmatized came together in great wrath, and, though they did not choose to lay violent hands upon one so honored and beloved, showed their displeasure by resolving that they would administer tar and feathers to any blacksmith, barber, miller, or common laborer,

17

"who should aid said Fitch in any way," and so his wheat and grass were left standing, and "the whole of a considerable trade withdrawn from him."

The speech and conduct of Mr. John Stevens, the proprietor of extensive plantations in Ashford, subjected him to an inquisitorial visitation, resulting in the subjoined declaration:—

"Whereas a number of the loyal people of the towns of Ashford and Mansfield, have convened together on suspicion that Mr. John Stevens of Ashford was an enemy to the constitutional rights of American liberty, and that we chose a committee to which he gave the following satisfactory account, that he never wrote any letters against the rights of American liberty to any person, and that he never received one from any person on that occasion. And furthermore as I, the subscriber, have talked at sundry times against the chartered rights of American Colonists, I do humbly ask their forgiveness, and I further declare that I never will talk or act anything against the Sons of Liberty—but do solemnly declare that I am a true Son of Liberty, and will remain so during my natural life. In witness whereof I set my hand.
Aug. 5, 1774.   JOHN STEVENS.
In presence of Stephen Johnson, Jeremiah Howe, Aaron Whitmore, Richard Felch, John Keyes, Ashford and Mansfield committee."

The zeal of Windham patriots was far too ardent and effusive to be restricted to county limits. Their intense enthusiasm in the popular cause led them to take an active part in all aggressive demonstrations. Inspectory committees were constantly on the alert, and "Windham boys" were ever ready to aid in forays upon suspected Tories. Colonel Abijah Willard of Lancaster, Mass., a man of large wealth and high character, had made himself obnoxious to the people by accepting the office of Mandamus Councilor to Governor Gage. He had business interests in Connecticut which were intrusted to two attorneys in Windham, whom he invited to meet with him for consultation in the town of Union. A report of his intended visit took wing, and when Colonel Willard arrived in Union he was met by hundreds of ardent patriots from Windham and adjoining towns, who took him into their keeping, guarded him through the night, conveyed him next morning over the line into Brimfield, where they formally delivered him over to a body of Massachusetts citizens. A trial was held and the prisoner convicted and sentenced to the Simsbury mines. Finding that his judges were bent upon carrying out this decree, and actually proceeding to carry him thither, Colonel Willard succumbed, "asked forgiveness of all honest men for having taken the oath of office, and promised not to sit or act in council."

In the dealings with Rev. Samuel Peters, the well-known church missionary at Hebron, Windham was also implicated. This sturdy churchman and Tory not only openly avowed his loyalty to the King and government, but stigmatized the Sons of Liberty as rebels and traitors, and presumed to ridicule their fervent resolutions and declarations. He was also suspected of sending information abroad and carrying on clandestine correspondence with the agents of government in several Colonies. "A formidable multitude" of some three hundred men from different towns with vengeance lowering on their brows accordingly waited upon Peters, Monday morning, Aug. 15, and extorted from him various concessions and pledges, together with a copy of certain satirical "Resolves* of Hebron," which he had prepared for the press—treating him, however, according to the report of his friends "with as much civility as might be expected."

In September, the report of various disturbances in Boston aroused the whole country. Powder stored in Cambridge by the patriots was removed to Boston by a detachment of troops under orders from Governor Gage. The people immediately rushed out in great excitement, loudly denouncing the act and demanding the restitution of the powder. In the clamor and confusion a report was somehow started that the British fleet and garrison had commenced hostilities. Swift-footed messengers caught this rumor and hurried off with it in various directions. It was afterwards asserted that this story was sent out by the patriot leaders for the express purpose of showing the British government the temper and spirit of the Colonies. If this were so they gained their end. The rumor flew on three great traveled routes, gaining in flight. Southward, it came to Esquire Wolcott of Oxford, who forthwith posted his son off to Boston, "to learn the certainty," but receiving farther confirmation of the great news at Grafton, the young man turned back, and took it straightway on to Curtis's tavern in Dudley. One Clark, a trader, caught it up and hurried it on to his

---

* " 1. All charters are sacred to serve the end for which they were given and no farther. 2. No charter from the King can be found by which the grantees have a right to the seas, as all our charters bound us upon sea-coast as that runs. 3. The duty laid on teas is not a tax upon America because it grows not within the limits of America. 4. Since they have not placed a tax upon ours but their own specie which they certainly have a right to do, it is our duty not to purchase their teas unless we have a mind to do it. . . . . 11. Bostonians would be able to support their own poor after Windham and other towns have paid them their legal demands. 12. We cannot find any good reasons why the good people of Windham undertook to arraign and condemn Governor Hutchinson and others for ignorance, insult and treason against law and common sense only for differing in sentiment with some of their neighbors—since there ' were a few names in Sardis.' 13. Farmington burnt the Act of Parliament in great contempt by their common hangman, &c. We sincerely wish and hope a day may be set apart by his Honor very soon for fasting and prayer throughout the Colony, that the sins of those haughty people may not be laid to our charge as a government, and we recommend a due observation of said day to all our neighbors, by giving food and raiment to the indigent poor in every town in Connecticut; and also to draw up resolutions that for the future we will pay the poor their wages and every man his due."

father in Woodstock. Captain Clark in hot haste bore it on to Captain Keyes of Pomfret, and he—at 11 a. m., Saturday, Sept. 3—brought it to Colonel Israel Putnam. Hitherto the news had gone from mouth to mouth like the Highland war-cry :—

> Boston, our Boston is in need!
> Speed forth the signal! Patriots, speed!—

But now Putnam gave it a more tangible form by scrawling off the following lines to Captain Aaron Cleveland of Canterbury :—

"POMFRET, Sept. 3, 1774.

Captain Cleveland :

Mr. Keyes has this a. m. bro't us the news that the Men of War and troops began to fire on the people of Boston last night at sunset, when a post was sent immediately off to inform the Country. He informs that the artillery played all night, that the people are universally [rallying] from Boston as far as here in arms and desires all the assistance possible. It [alarm] was occasioned by the country people's being robbed of their powder [from Boston] as far as Framingham, and when found out people went to take the soldiers and six of our people were killed on the spot and several were wounded. Beg you will rally all the forces you can and be on the march immediately for the relief of Boston and the people that way.

I. P."

"Fast as hoof could fly" this was conveyed to Cleveland, countersigned by him, and sent by express "along to Norwich and elsewhere." Reaching Norwich at 4 P. M., it was forwarded by Captain John Durkee. At New London, it was endorsed by Richard Law, Nathaniel Shaw and Samuel Parsons, and hurried on to New Haven and New York. Gaining credence and fresh signatures at every stopping place it speeded southward, and at nine o'clock Tuesday morning—just seventy hours from Pomfret—it was laid before the Continental Congress, just assembling in Philadelphia. Thus from Boston to Pennsylvania, the whole country had been aroused. From the great centres the news had spread in every quarter. The hour of conflict had come; Boston was attacked and all were summoned to her relief. Never was rallying cry more effective. Coming from Putnam and endorsed by prominent and responsible men it was everywhere received and obeyed. "To arms!" was the quick response, and thousands hurried to the rescue. A thousand men took up arms in the three lower counties of Delaware. *Twenty* thousand were reported *en route* in Connecticut. The summons coming on Sunday it had the effect of putting that Puritanic colony "into alarm and motion on the Lord's Day." Colonel Putnam's missive was read publicly in most of the congregations, and furnished the text for many a stirring exhortation. In many of the more distant towns the messenger brought the tidings to the meeting-house in the midst of divine service, and worthy members of the church militant left the sanctuary for the battlefield. Even ministers were said " to have left their pulpits for the gun and drum, and set off for Boston." In Norwich, Putnam's letter was " printed off, and circulated through the town in handbills," and on Sunday morning over four hundred men, well-armed and mostly mounted upon good horses, started for Boston under command of Major John Durkee. Two hundred ardent volunteers, well-armed and mounted, left Windham town at sunrise, and bodies of men were dispatched from all the other towns of Windham County.

Putnam, having sent the dispatch, set out himself with four comrades for the scene of action, and had proceeded as far northward as Douglas, when he heard " that the alarm was false and Massachusetts' forces returning." He immediately turned back and after a sixty miles ride reached home at sunrise, and " sent the contradiction along to stop the forces marching or rallying." The Norwich troops were met seven miles from their town, with the intelligence *via.* Providence, that the report was without foundation. The Windham men marched on to Massachusetts line before receiving counter-tidings. This revelation that the great mass of the people was ready to take up arms whenever occasion called them greatly cheered the patriot leaders and stimulated them to farther resistance. The report of this uprising excited much interest at home and abroad. " Words cannot express," wrote Putnam and his committee in behalf of five hundred men under arms at Pomfret, " the gladness discovered by every one at the appearance of a door being opened to avenge the many abuses and insults which those foes to liberty have offered to our brethren in your town and province. But for counter intelligence we should have had forty thousand well-equipped and ready to march this morning. Send a written express to the foreman of this committee when you have occasion for our martial assistance." The rapid transmission of the news was considered very remarkable. On Nov. 12, it reached England, and the report of its reception there came back to New York on January 20. A few affected to treat the whole affair with ridicule. Colonel Malbone of Pomfret received the news from Putnam. Though so opposed in character and political sentiment there existed a certain personal sympathy and good fellowship between these neighbors, and many verbal skirmishes were interchanged between them. Before taking the field Putnam sent this missive :—

" SAT., 12 P. M.

To COLONEL MALBONE:
    Dear Sir—I have this minute had an express from Boston that the fight between Boston and the Regulars [began] last night at sunset, and the *cannon*

began to [   ] and continned all night and *they beg* for help—and dont you think *it is time to go?*

I am, sir, your most obedient servant,

I. PUTNAM."

"*Go to the Devil,*" was the prompt and emphatic answer. [These doughty church members and church builders were equally expert in *swearing.*]

The opposition of Rev. Samuel Peters was more pronounced and bit-ter. On that memorable Sabbath when all Connecticut was in motion, Peters forbade his flock to take up arms in behalf of High Treason, and insulted "the public grand cause of Liberty by calling it rebellion." This offence filled the measure of his political iniquities. The patriots of the neighboring towns, roused to fever heat by the late alarm and uprising, felt that they could bear with him no longer. Yet as usual at this period nothing was done without some show of official authority. Timothy Larrabee, Hezekiah Huntington, Vine Elderkin, Ebenezer Gray and John Ripley of Windham—men of high character and posi-tion—together with Captain Seth Wright, Captain Asahel Clark and Mr. Hill of other towns, were appointed a committee by the Sons of Liberty in their respective towns "to visit and deal with Rev. Samuel Peters of Hebron," and on Tuesday, Sept. 6, proceeded to his house accompanied by some hundreds of their fellow-citizens from all the surrounding country. They found the house barricaded and filled with people said to be armed, and sent in a deputation of their principal men to make known to Mr. Peters "their determination to obtain re-traction and satisfaction" for his late conduct. A parley was held through the window. Mr. Peters attempted to justify himself and argue with the gentlemen, assuring them that he had no arms but two old guns out of repair. They replied that they did not care to dispute with him, and advised him to address the people who thronged about the house, assuring him at the same time "that it was not for his religious sentiments, or because he was a churchman" that they de-manded this satisfaction, "for some of the people were of that denomi-nation, and they were so far from hurting or injuring anyone that did profess it that they were ready to defend and protect them with all their strength, but for the things and matters before mentioned."

Assuming his white priestly robe, Peters now came out to the people with all his official dignity, and with his usual address and facility pro-ceeded to plead his cause till the discharge of a gun within the house startled his hearers. The indignant patriots tore down the barricades, rushed in and searched the house, finding loaded guns and pistols, swords and heavy clubs. In spite of this discovery he was allowed to finish his harangue and retire unmolested with the understanding that he should draw up and sign a satisfactory declaration. Peters delayed, equivocated and quibbled till the waiting crowd weary and hungry lost all patience, and proceeded " to deal" with him in more summary fashion, forced their way again into the house, seized the struggling divine, tearing his clothes and sacred Episcopal gown, put him upon a cart and hauled him by his own oxen to the meeting-house green, where they sat him upon the public horse-block, and compelled him to sign a declaration and humble confession framed by the committee to the intent that he repented his past misdeeds and would give them no farther cause of complaint. He was then made to read this paper aloud, sentence by sentence, to the great crowd surrounding the horse-block, which thereupon gave three triumphal cheers and quietly dispersed. Peters in reporting the affair declares that the Sons of Liberty not only " destroyed his windows and rent his clothes even his gown, but almost killed one of his church people, tarred and feathered two and abused others, but his word cannot be taken without corroborative evidence." In response to his appeal to Governor Trumbull for protection, the civil authority of Hebron were directed "to preserve peace and good order, and put the laws in execution." Notwithstanding this charge Mr. Peters thought best in a few days to retire to Boston, and sailed for England in November. The rancor of his subsequent letters is the best apology for his assailants. To his mother he writes that " six regiments were now coming from England and sundry men-of-war, and as soon as they come hanging work will go on ; destruction will first attend the seaport towns—lintel sprinkled on the side-ports will preserve the faithful ; " to Dr. Auchmuty, New York,—" the clergy of Connecticut must fall a sacrifice with the several churches very soon to the rage of the Puritan mob-ility, if the old Serpent, that Dragon is not bound. . . . Spiritual iniquity rides in high places, halberds, pistols and swords. . . . Their rebellion is obvious, and treason is common and robbery their daily devotion. The bounds of New York may directly extend to Connecticut River. Boston must then . . . and Rhode Island be swallowed up as Dothan."

" The means of making the contents " of these very letters known furnished another striking example of " Puritan mob-ility " and spirit. According to authentic published report these letters were brought back by two friends of Peters who had accompanied him to Boston, and were intercepted on their return by a suspecting party of patriots who met them at a tavern, questioned them and suffered them to depart, but as they went on their way they were overheard by a man behind a fence to say " that they might yet be searched before they got home, might be brought into trouble and therefore had better hide the letters." From his hiding-place this man saw them alight near a

136

HISTORY OF WINDHAM COUNTY.

stone-fence, remount and hurry onward. Help was called, letters found in the wall, the men followed, brought back and again questioned. They denied having any letters, even offering to declare upon oath that they had none, but upon these being produced were forced to own the bringing and hiding. Tradition gives the town in which this incident occurred and other attendant circumstances. *Windham Village*, the home of famous military veterans, the seat of most flaming and aggressive patriotism, claims the credit of search and seizure. Her account ignores the intervention of non-resident parties. Her own vigilant citizens were the sole detectives and judges. The story of the capture of *Peters's spies* was quickly borne through the neighborhood and brought all its inhabitants, young and old, men, women and children, to the scene of action. The convicted tale-bearers, beset by the angry throng, begged in vain for release and mercy. Public sentiment demanded their instant and effectual punishment but differed as to its nature. Ordinary delinquencies might be satisfied by a public whipping at the townpost, but so flagrant an offence seemed to demand a more signal and characteristic penalty. "Running the gauntlet," suggested probably by the experience of some French war captive, met the views of the populace but the victims were allowed their choice. Between two evils they chose the least familiar, greatly to the delight of the great crowd of people who could all take part in its infliction. Men, boys, perhaps women and girls, every body that fancied, were straightway formed in two opposing lines, stretching from the tavern across the great street and green to the meeting-house, and Peters' unfortunate emissaries were made to run between them, receiving from each in turn a cuff, kick or poke, with every insulting epithet that could be devised by the ingenuity or malice of their tormentors.

[An additional item, showing the position of Windham County leaders towards the Stamp Act, deserves notice and preservation. When Governor Fitch called his Council together to decide what to do with the king's law, there was difference of opinion and warm discussion. After a day of fierce debate Governor Fitch avowed his determination to enforce the Act, and called upon Trumbull to administer the needful oath. "No," said Trumbull, "I will take no part in, nor witness such a scene as this"—and with Colonel Dyer, Shubael Conant and four other members of the Council, withdrew from the chamber; thus emphasizing their belief "that the Stamp Act contravened the chartered rights of the Colonies," and their determination to give no countenance to its execution.]

II.

PREPARATION FOR THE CONFLICT. ONWARD TO CAMBRIDGE.
BUNKER HILL. HOME AFFAIRS. DEATH OF
REVEREND JOSEPH HOME.

THE revelation that the great mass of the people were ready to take up arms whenever occasion demanded, greatly encouraged the patriot leaders, and also showed them the necessity of making all possible provision for the inevitable conflict before them. A convention of delegates from New London and Windham Counties was held at Norwich, September 9, a few days after the alarm, wherein the greatest harmony and unanimity of sentiment appeared, and "the cheek of every member glowed with resentment and martial fire," and "not a man among them but was willing with the utmost alacrity to fly to the relief" of oppressed patriots in any Colony. In preparation for future emergency the convention recommended,

"1. That the Selectmen of every town in these counties should as speedily as possible supply their town stock with a full complement of ammunition and military stores as by law required. 2. That every particular troop and military company within said counties, both officers and soldiers, should as speedily as possible arm and equip themselves, agreeable to the direction of the laws of the Colony. 3. It was seriously recommended to such, as a matter of very great importance, that as expeditiously as might be they should improve in and learn the use and design of their arms by artillery exercises or otherwise, that so they may answer the important purpose of their instruction when occasion shall require. And as very great and special advantage must arise from regimental reviews and exercises in the militia of this Colony, as the law requires, and the same having been neglected and omitted, it was earnestly recommended to the officers of the regiments that during the present Autumn they should call together their respective regiments for this purpose, and also that these officers should issue orders to the captains of the several companies in their regiments that their companies should immediately comply with legal requisitions, both as to their equipment and ammunition, and a due attention to the cultivation of military skill and the art of war; and that said chief officers should exert themselves in every proper and legal way for a general improvement in, and cultivation of, the noble and important art of military skill and discipline."

The General Assembly, at its October session, enacted that each military company in the Colony shall be called out twelve half-days and exercised in the use of their arms, between this time and the first of May. It was also resolved, "That the several towns in this Colony be and are hereby ordered to provide as soon as may be, double the quantity of powder, balls and flints that they were heretofore by law obliged to provide." Four additional regiments were now organized. A convention of delegates from Hartford, New London, Windham and Litchfield Counties was held in Hartford, September 15, which most earnestly supported the Non-Importation Agreement, and denounced "such mercenary wretches" as purposed to evade it, declaring its determination to defeat their designs if possible. Yet while entering upon

18

these "aggressive methods" for resistance to oppression, they declared it "the warmest wish of our hearts that the wisdom and equity of the British Parliament may relieve us from our fears and dangers, and that we may once more and forever look up to our parent country with confidence and pleasure, and, secure in our own rights, contribute all in our power to promote the honor, interest and happiness of our elder brethren in Great Britain." The General Congress at Philadelphia, of which Col. Dyer was a member, while also expressing its loyalty and attachment to the king, published an elaborate declaration of the rights of the Colonists, agreed "that all America ought to support the inhabitants of Massachusetts," requested the merchants to suspend all importation of merchandize from Great Britain, and further stipulated that all *exportation* of merchandize to Great Britain, Ireland and the West Indies should cease after September 10, 1775, unless the wrongs that called out these agreements should be redressed prior to that period.

The report of the proceedings of this Congress was accepted by the several towns. Windham, December 5, voted, "That this town does accept, approve and adopt the doings of the Continental Congress held at Philadelphia in September last, and agree and oblige ourselves religiously to keep and observe the same." Joshua Elderkin having now manifested a proper repentance for his violation of the Agreement, it was voted, "That the vote passed June 26, 1768, respecting said Elderkin, be repealed and made null and void," and he was again held amenable "to office of trust or profit." Plainfield approved of the methods proposed, and pledged herself to strict adherence thereto. She also voted with but *one* dissenting vote, "That we will not in future purchase for ourselves or families any *East India tea*, until the Port of Boston is opened, and until the unreasonable Acts of the British Parliament are repealed." "Agreeable to the eleventh Resolve of the General Congress," Canterbury elected David Paine, John Herrick, Thomas Adams, Jabez Fitch, Jr., Joseph Burgess, and Captains Obadiah Johnson and Joseph Cleveland, a committee of inspection. Captain Asa Bacon, Thomas Bacon and Samuel Ensworth were added to the committee of correspondence. Woodstock, at an adjourned town meeting, December 26, 1774, Captain Lyon, moderator, expressed her views with greater fullness, viz:—

"Being sensible and deeply impressed with the late cruel and oppressive measures taken by the British Parliament, and as cruelly attempted to be executed upon the most loyal and affectionate subjects any prince could ever boast of, by which cruel measures to enslave millions of free-born subjects and their numberless posterity, in opposition to which the tongues, the pens, the hearts and hands of every true Briton, both in Great Britain and America, we trust are engaged, and especially the grand Continental Congress convened at Philadelphia on September 5th, as appears by the number of their resolves, for which and to whom, we, the inhabitants of Woodstock, as a part of their constiuents, return to them our warmest thanks; and that we, the inhabitants of Woodstock, may give the strongest proof of our zeal and attachment and in defence of the great and common cause :—

Resolved, nem. con., That we do approve of and oblige ourselves to the utmost of our power, and all persons for and under us shall comply with association of the aforesaid Congress in every part and paragraph thereof, and more especially in Non-Consumption Agreement by them recommended. Nehemiah Lyon, David Holmes, Ephraim Manning, Elias Mason, Silas Bowen, Amos Paine, Timothy Perrin, Nathaniel Marcy, David Perry, Samuel Harding, Shubael Child, Daniel Lyon, Stephen May, Samuel Corbin and Thomas May were appointed a Committee of Inspection, who were attentively to observe the conduct of all persons, and conduct towards them agreeable to the advice contained in said association agreement."

A penny-rate to purchase arms and other warlike stores for the use of the town, was also ordered.

The suggestions with regard to military preparations were carried out with promptness and alacrity by all the towns. The military ardor of the citizens needed little stimulus, but there was great lack of drill and discipline. Company trainings had been statedly observed in every neighborhood, but the prescribed regimental reviews had been to a great degree omitted. A grand military parade had indeed been held in Plainfield some time in 1773, especially memorable for inciting the first stirrings of military enthusiasm in the heart of a young Rhode Island Quaker, Nathaniel Greene, who rode many miles, with hundreds of other spectators, to witness the scene. A review of the eleventh regiment had also been held at Woodstock the following May, very notable for the large numbers present and patriotic enthusiasm. The troop of horse under Captain Samuel McClellan figured largely on this occasion. A mock fight was carried on under the direction of Capt. McClellan. A party dressed up like Indians appeared upon the Common and caught and carried away some of the children present, but were pursued by the troops and the frightened children rescued and brought back. The success of these gatherings and the increasing interest in military affairs encouraged the officers to meet the recommendation of the Norwich convention by a more general and elaborate review than anything yet seen in Connecticut. Field officers and commissioners from New London and Windham counties elaborated a plan for a great regimental meeting to be held at Windham town in the latter end of April, or first of May. Details of the proposed plan were completed January 20, when ten colonels, representing as many regiments, "appeared and signed it." The military companies in Plainfield, Canterbury, Voluntown, and the south part of Killingly now formed the twenty-first regiment. The other regiments remained as before, viz: companies of Windham, Mansfield, Coventry and Ashford formed the fifth regiment—Jedidiah Elderkin, Colonel, Experience Storrs, Lieut.-Colonel; Thomas Brown, Major. Pomfret, Wood-

stock and the north and central companies of Killingly were included
in the eleventh regiment—Ebenezer Williams, Colonel ; William Dan
ielson, Major. Lebanon was included in the twelfth regiment, and
Union in the twenty-second. A troop of horse was attached to each
regiment. Company trainings were held at least once a month during
the winter, and special preparation made for the projected parade in
April. Liberty-poles were set up in many of the towns with appropriate exercises. A great crowd assembled on Killingly hill and
hoisted two long sticks of timber united by a couple of cross-ties.
From the top of this high pole a flag was flung to the breeze, deco-
rated with a rising sun and other suggestive devices. A stray Englishman who had settled in the neighborhood smiled scornfully at the
demonstrations. "Ah," said he, "you know nothing of Old England ;
she will come and *cut down* your liberty pole for you."

No event of especial significance occurred during the winter. The
colonists waited for the session of Parliament to learn the effect of
appeals and statements made by Congress to the king and people of
Great Britain. That body when convened showed little spirit of conciliation, and it was soon manifest that no redress of grievances could
be expected. Yet unless such redress was guaranteed farther collision
was unavoidable. The colonists saw no course but persistent and more
effective resistance. Such preparation was made as circumstances per
mitted ; ammunition was gathered up, the prescribed military exer
cises faithfully performed, the rights and principles for which they
were contending more earnestly examined and discussed. It was no
light matter to rise up against the government of Great Britain, the
lawful government to which they owed allegiance, and could only be
justified by supreme necessity. This winter of 1774–75 was one of
"sober second thought" to the citizens of Windham County. Resting from their summer toils and raids, they now had time to ask themselves on what grounds are we preparing to take up arms against our
rightful sovereign. A little book opportunely brought to public notice answered this query in a most comprehensive, conclusive and
satisfactory manner:—"English Liberties, or the Freeborn Subject's
Inheritance"—a compendium of the laws and rights "bought and
vindicated by Englishmen at the expense of much blood and treasure,"
comprising Magna Charta, the Habeas Corpus Act, a Declaration of
the Liberty of the Subject, and much other kindred matter—was published in England in 1691, and so favorably received that in thirty
years it had reached a fifth edition. An edition of this priceless work
was issued by John Carter, of Providence, in 1774, and extensively circulated as "a campaign document." No better evidence could be given
of Windham's intense interest in the pending struggle than her de-

mand, when money was so scarce and books so rarely purchased, for more than a hundred and twenty copies of this compilation.* These plain, rough-spoken country farmers meant to know for what they were fighting. They took their stand upon their right as British subjects to the privileges won by their fathers, and were ready to sacrifice their lives and fortunes to secure their confirmation. Fortified with arguments and equipped with arms and ammunition, they were well prepared for the contest that awaited them. Many circumstances gave Windham County unusual prominence at this juncture, and enabled her to render most effective aid to the patriot cause. The towns of Lebanon, Mansfield, Coventry and Union were then included in her territory. Among her citizens were JONATHAN TRUMBULL and ISRAEL PUTNAM, Connecticut's honored governor and the most popular military officer in America. And in addition to these great leaders she was favored with men in every town who seemed to have been raised up expressly to meet this exigency, brave soldiers and wise civilians, men of valor and men of judgment, alike endued with ardent self-sacrificing patriotism. She had a stalwart, sturdy body of yeomanry, united as one man in devotion to the patriot cause. She had a learned, able and faithful ministry, in full sympathy with the people, and ready to encourage, strengthen and sustain them. She had women with strong hands and resolute hearts, urging the men to action, and willing to bear all the additional burdens that might be brought upon them. Her geographical position was favorable, remote from sea board alarms and revenue entanglements, yet on the main thoroughfares of travel between the larger towns—posts from Boston to Hartford and

---

Names of Windham County subscribers :—

Joseph Allen, Ebenezer Backus, Edmund Badger, Hezekiah Bissell, Benjamin Dyer, Joshua Elderkin, Royal Flint, Andrew French, Ebenezer Gray, Esq., Stephen Greenleaf, Capt. Jabez Huntington, John Ripley, Jacob Simons, John Walden, Jun., Nath. Wales, Jun. Esq., Nath. Wales 3d, Nath. Warren, *Windham.* John B. Adams, Peleg Brewster, Elijah Bennet, Nathaniel Clark, Gideon Carver, Capt. Aaron Cleveland, William Foster, Jabez Fitch, Jun., Abel Lyon, Rev. Nathaniel Niles, Nath. Satterlee, Joshua Tracey, Nathan Waldo, Asa Witter, Elijah Williams, *Canterbury.* Capt. James Bradford, Lieut. Andrew Backus, Isaac Coit, William Dixon, Esq., Robert Kinsman, Rev. Alexander Miller, Elisha Paine, Esq., Elisha Perkins, *Plainfield.* Ebenezer Dow, John Dixon, *Voluntown.* Benjamin Converse, David Day, Noah Elliott, Perley Howe, Ebenezer Knight, Rev. Noadiah Russel, 6, George Robinson, James Thurber, Joseph Torrey, Capt. Benj. Wilkinson, *Killingly.* Samuel Craft, Thomas Cotton, 6, Thomas Grosvenor, Esq., Caleb Grosvenor, Ebenezer Holbrook, Esq., John Jefferd, 6, William Osgood, Esq., John Parkhurst, Jun., Rev. Aaron Putnam, Amasa Sessions, Alexander Sessions, Daniel Tyler, Ebenezer Williams, Esq., Thomas Williams, Esq., Rev. Josiah Whitney, *Pomfret.* Nathaniel Clark, Nath. Child, Esq., 6, John Goodell, Jun., Capt. David Holmes, Asa Lyon, Jedidiah Morse, 6, Nath. Marcy 6, Hadlock Marcy, Hugh 6, Ebenezer Paine, Joseph Peake, Jun., 6, Rev. Stephen Williams, *Woodstock.* Elijah Whiton, Esq., *Ashford.*

New York, and from Providence to Norwich and New London, pass
ing over her highways. Her resources* had largely increased since
the war of 1756. Trade and enterprise had been lively. Food and
clothing were far more abundant. She had sheep enough for home
use and consumption, and to spare great flocks to the needy. Despite
the large emigration, she had added more than eight thousand to her
population as shown by Connecticut's second census, taken in 1774.†

Practically this population was a unit at this juncture, and in this
unity lay, perhaps, Windham's greatest strength. Opposition if it
existed, dared not or cared not to show itself openly. The few tories
within her towns were mostly recent emigrants, like Malbone and
Stevens, with little sympathy or influence with the people, and taking
no part in the administration of town affairs. A notable and most
unhappy exception, was the high-sheriff of the county, Colonel
Eleazer Fitch of Windham. Having served in the French war
under the commission of King George, a sense of honor and loyalty
forbade him to turn against his master and former comrades. Friendly
ties attached him to the British army. The roughness and bluntness
of the ardent patriots shocked his fine taste; their vehement denunciations and violent onslaughts outraged his sense of justice; yet his
official position, his business and family connections, his true regard for
his own countrymen, made open opposition impossible. He therefore
held himself aloof from public affairs, voiceless in the general hubbub,
unable to affiliate with patriots or loyalists. His high position and
great personal popularity saved him as yet from violence and inspectorial
visitation. "Everybody loved Colonel Fitch," and hoped he might be
brought to share in the popular sympathies, and most earnest efforts
were made by Governor Trumbull, his former partner in business, and

---

* *Grand List of Windham County towns in* 1775:—

Ashford,	£17,273 11 3	Voluntown,	13,801 4
Canterbury,	20,730	Windham,	32,222 10 7
Killingly,	27,907 12 4	Woodstock,	20,800
Plainfield,	14,216 16		
Pomfret,	27,711 12 4		£174,665 6 6

†TOWNS.	WHITES.	BLACKS.	TOWNS.	WHITES.	BLACKS.
Ashford,	2,228	13	Voluntown,	1,476	35
Canterbury,	2,392	52	Coventry,	2,032	24
Killingly,	3,439	47	Lebanon,	3,841	119
Plainfield,	1,479	83	Mansfield,	2,443	23
Pomfret,	2,241	65	Union,	512	2
Windham,	3,437	91			
Woodstock,	1,974	80		27,494	634

Taking from this list the towns afterward affixed to other counties, the
population of the towns now embraced in Windham County was 18,666
whites, 466 blacks.

other patriot leaders, to overcome his scruples and induce him to espouse their cause.

Windham's forbearance towards Colonel Fitch was quite exceptional. It was scarcely safe for a resident or visitant of this belligerent township to be suspected of the slightest proclivity towards toryism. Any deviation from the Non-Importation Agreement, or from the popular standard of patriotic duty, might subject one to a visit from official inspectors, the publishment of his name in the *New London Gazette* as an enemy to his country, or even to some outrageous personal infliction. The use of *tea* was especially offensive to the public. All the indignation that justly belonged to the concocters of the impost was wreaked upon the innocent herb that seemed to be looked upon as the root of all evil, a more baleful gift to mankind than Eve's original apple. "Another great cargo of tea," writes Putnam to Trumbull, "so that we are to be plagued with that detested weed —nothing but a *Non-Consumption Agreement* can save America." Windham village, so fierce against suspected spies, was equally severe upon her own children. Jeremiah Clark, a most useful and industrious citizen, had opened a little trade with Newport, exchanging butter and domestic commodities for sugar, molasses or other articles, by means of two deep boxes put in a bag and laid across the back of his horse. Whether with or without cause, suspicion was aroused that he was *smuggling tea* into the town, whereupon the neighbors assembled with tar and feathers, intercepted him on his way homeward, and only released him after they had made sure by thorough search that no contraband goods were included in his budget. Even the sacred office and avowed patriotism of the reverend minister of Scotland Parish did not save him from very serious annoyance for a very trifling indulgence. His household was visited by severe affliction—the distressing sickness of Mrs. Cogswell's youngest daughter, Betsey Devotion, a very beautiful and interesting young woman, greatly admired and beloved, who in March, 1775, was seized suddenly with malignant fever and died in a few days. The bereaved parents, greatly overcome by the loss and shock, were persuaded by sympathizing friends to indulge in the soothing stimulus of a cup of tea. Their delinquency was soon made public. Mr. Cogswell was informed that they would be reported to the Committee of Inspection. He immediately waited upon that body, and by certificates from the attendant physicians, that the tea had been taken as a medical prescription, was able to satisfy them; but the general public was not so easily appeased. Aggrieved patriots continued to express their resentment by staying at home from church and upon remonstrance, doughty old foreman rode away from Pudding Hill with rebuke and grumble, and sharp-tongued goodwives did not hesitate to assure their minister that the public would not be satisfied without a public confession and apology from the pulpit. Some insisted that his name and offence should be published in the *Norwich Packet* and *New London Gazette.* Poor Mr. Cogswell, always nervously sensitive to public opinion, was greatly annoyed and distressed by these manifestations of displeasure, which continued till the great news from Lexington swept away all minor excitements.

The rencontre between the king's troops and the provincials occurred on Wednesday morning, April 19. A post was dispatched from Watertown at 10 A. M., charged to alarm the people as far as the Connecticut line, "that the British have landed two brigades, have already killed six men and wounded four others, and are on their march into the country." A copy of this dispatch was forwarded by the town clerk of Worcester to Daniel Tyler, Jun., Brooklyn, who received it about 8 o'clock on Thursday morning, and sent it on by post to Norwich, while messengers on horseback, with beating drums, carried the news in all directions about the county. Putnam, plowing in the pleasant April morning, heard the joyful summons, and "loitered not" but left his young son, Daniel, "the driver of his team, to unyoke it in the furrow," and hurried off for consultation with town committees and military officers. A second express, *via.* Woodstock, was brought to Colonel Ebenezer Williams, Pomfret, at 3 P. M., and forwarded at once to Colonel Obadiah Johnson of Canterbury, with a postscript stating that a merchant "just returned from Boston, *via.* Providence, informs that a thousand of our troops had surrounded the first brigade—50 of our men killed and 100 regulars. It would be expedient for every man to go who is fit and willing."

This summons was swiftly borne to every part of Windham County, and found thousands ready to meet it. Nearly all its male population were not only "fit and willing," but most eager to hurry to the rescue; yet there was no headlong rush, no undue precipitation. Putnam, on returning from his consultory tour, found hundreds of men already assembled on Brooklyn Green, awaiting his orders. He bade them wait till regularly called out as militia, and march with their respective regiments as had already been arranged with the military officers of the County, and without rest or special refreshment started at sunset on his memorable night ride to Cambridge. There is some evidence that Killingly received the news at a still earlier hour on Thursday morning by a direct express from Boston, brought to the house of Mr. Hezekiah Cutler. He arose from his bed and fired his gun three times to give the alarm, and before sunrise, with fifteen men, had started for the battle-field.

Friday was spent in active preparation throughout the county. The

Fifth Regiment was to rendezvous in Pomfret; companies from the other regiments to hasten on as soon as they could be properly mustered. Officers were riding rapidly around in every direction with their warnings, bullets were run, accoutrements and rations provided. Many, especially in the northern towns, snatched their guns and marched off without waiting formal orders. Killingly's stock of powder was stored in the meeting-house, under the charge of Hezekiah Cutler, who had left orders that each volunteer should be furnished with half a pound, and the house was thronged all day with squads of men coming from all parts of the town to claim their portion and march onward to Cambridge. Early on Saturday, April 22, Lieutenant-Colonel Storrs led "sundry of ye troop" to Windham Green, and "had a further conference with Colonel Elderkin with respect to our disposition of the regiment." Selected companies from Coventry, Mansfield and Windham were already on the ground, ready to march, and hundreds of joyful spectators were coming in to see the men and cheer them on their way. Officers and companies "attended prayers in the meeting-house," led by the reverend ministers of the town. It was nearly sunset before they set off for Pomfret. They were passed on the road by Colonel Parsons of Lyme, hurrying on to Boston; found the companies from Canada Parish and Ashford awaiting them —the former led by Captain James Stedman. Ashford's picked company of seventy-eight had chosen Thomas Knowlton for its Captain. Late as it was, the regiment paraded before dismissal. The officers were entertained by Mr. Ebenezer Grosvenor, the men bivouacked wherever it was convenient. It was a night much to be remembered in Pomfret throughout all generations. News of the military rendezvous had been widely circulated, and men were thronging in from all parts of Windham County. That sacred Sabbath morning witnessed a strange spectacle—more than a thousand men offering themselves in sacrifice. There were veterans from the old French war, filled with martial and patriotic enthusiasm, and young men yet untried, equally eager to show their zeal for the cause of liberty. Many, as they looked upon this great company so full of spirit and self-sacrificing devotion, could exclaim with Adams and Hancock—"O, what a glorious morning is this!"

The officers of the regiment were embarrassed by the great numbers that presented themselves, and doubtful about maintaining their regimental exclusiveness. They sent for the Rev. Mr. Putnam to pray with the companies, and "after prayer formed a hollow square and communicated to the regiment orders from Colonel Elderkin." The

19

following letter received the day previous may have been also communicated :—

"CONCORD, April 21.

To Colonel Ebenezer Williams:

Sir,—I have waited on the committee of the Provincial Congress, and it is their Determination to have a standing Army of 22,000 men from the New England Colonies, of which, it is supposed, the Colony of Connecticut must raise 6,000, and begs they would be at *Cambridge* as speedily as possible, with Conveniences; together with Provisions, and a Sufficiency of Ammunition for their own Use.

The Battle here is much as has been represented at Pomfret, except that there is more killed and a Number more taken Prisoners.

The Accounts at present are so confused that it is impossible to ascertain the number exact, but shall inform you of the proceedings, from Time to Time, as we have new occurrences; mean time I am, Sir, your humble servant,   ISRAEL PUTNAM.

N. B.—The Troops of Horse are not expected to come until further notice."

The regiment was then dismissed till 1 P. M., while the officers held a council. During this interval religious services were doubtless held in the great meeting-house, thronged we may well suppose with eager, anxious listeners. It was agreed by the council "to take out *one-fifth* of the companies, and order the overplus (of ten present) to return home. Divided the remainder into three companies and their officers."* How this selection and division were accomplished is not apparent. The whole Ashford company and a larger number from Pomfret, under Captain Ingalls—Eleventh Regiment—appear to have been chosen, which would leave but a small proportion from the other companies. The greater part of the volunteers were thus sent home. The elect *fifth*, selected probably like Gideon's three hundred, in consideration of their special fitness for military service, set out on the march at about 5 P. M. Mounted officers led the little band and some twelve or fifteen men with pack horses followed. Lieut.-Colonel Storrs accompanied them to Moulton's tavern at Woodstock, where they passed the night, and on to Dudley the next morning, when feeling that Providence called more loudly to duties in Connecticut, he left them to pursue their way under charge of Major Brown and Captain Knowlton. Their orderly and soldierly bearing attracted great attention on their march, and they were received at Cambridge with special distinction as the first trained companies that had come from abroad to the aid of Massachusetts.

Detached companies and squads of men from various towns had preceded this body. The "troops of horse" under Captain McClellan, had gone in advance of Putnam's message. Lieut. Keyes, Corporal Seth Grosvenor, and Albigence Waldo, clerk, were all from Pomfret. Perley Howe, Killingly, served as cornet, John Flynn, Woodstock,

---

* Colonel Storrs' manuscript.

trumpeter. Each town furnished its due portion of troopers. Other men and companies followed on as rapidly as possible till more than a thousand men were accredited to Windham County.* The great regimental muster planned for April, was transferred from Windham Green to Cambridge. In some towns every able-bodied man obeyed the call. Killingly was left so destitute as to subject those who remained at home to a serious fright and panic. Colonel Malbone's sharp tongue and open toryism had made him a terror in the north part of the county. It had been currently reported and believed that he had privately drilled and equipped his negroes, and intended to take up arms for the King when the hour of conflict came, and amid all the agitation and anxieties of the first alarm, word came to Killingly Hill that "Malbone's niggers" were close at hand, burning and butchering everything before them. " Our house," says an eye witness,† " was filled with trembling, frightened women and children. There was not a fire-arm or weapon in the place, and only a few aged men. I remember they prepared kettles of heated water, and the boys were stationed as sentinels to give timely notice of their approach. My place was the top of my grandfather [Cutler's] gambrel-roofed house, but we saw no negroes, nor indeed anybody else, for the place seemed deserted." Other women in Windham County passed the day in very different fashion. There was exultant joy and thanksgiving in many a household. Rachel Abbe of Windham, now Mrs. Samuel McClellan, shared in the patriotic fervor which so characterized the women of her native town, and after fitting out her husband and his horsemen, she set out memorial trees in honor of the joyful occasion. Four sapling elms brought up on horseback from the old Windham homestead, were carefully transplanted into the soil of Woodstock—two in front of her dwelling and two on the slope of the adjoining common. Nurtured with care and pains they soon took root and flourished and for more than an hundred years have told the story of Lexington. True trees of Liberty, they have grown up with the Nation, and still

---

* Woodstock, 140 men under Captains Benjamin and Daniel Lyon, Ephraim Manning, Nathaniel Marcy and Lieut. Mark Elwell, together with her proportion of the troops of horse; Captain McClellan. Windham, 159 men; Captains William Warner, James Stedman, John Kingsley, Lieut. Melatiah Bingham. Canterbury, 70 men; Captains Aaron Cleveland, Joseph Burgess and Sherebiah Butts. Union, 26 men; Captain Thomas Lamson. Ashford, 78 men; Captain Thomas Knowlton. Pomfret, 89 men; Captain Zebulon Ingalls. Plainfield, 54 men; Captain Andrew Backus. Killingly, 146 men; Major William Danielson, Captains Joseph Cady and Joseph Elliott. Coventry, more than a hundred men; Major Thomas Brown, Lieut. Joseph Talcott. Lebanon, Captain Daniel Tilden, men not given. Mansfield, Lieut.-Col. Experience Storrs, Capt. Jonathan Nichols, men not given. Brooklyn Parish; Colonel Putnam. Canterbury; Lieut.-Colonel Obediah Johnson.

† Manuscript of Judge Ephraim Cutler, Marietta, Ohio, 1820.

stand in majestic beauty, living witnesses to the patriotism and devo
tion of the women of Windham County.

Wednesday, April 26, the General Assembly of Connecticut met in
adjourned session at Hartford. After securing and storing a quantity
of powder for Mansfield, and "fitting off a wagon load of provisions
after our people" in camp, Lieut.-Col. Storrs was ready to aid in
public deliberations. A committee had been already sent to New
York to learn the disposition of the people there. With characteristic
caution the Assembly avoided for a time any direct recognition of the
revolutionary proceedings in Massachusetts, but appointed Capt.
Joseph Trumbull and Amasa Keyes a committee "to procure provisions for the families of those who had gone to the relief of the people at the Bay, and to superintend the delivery and apportioning the
same among them." As the transmission of correct reports was a
matter of great importance, Thaddeus Burr, of Fairfield, and Charles
Church Chandler, of Woodstock, were authorized at the expense of
the Colony, to employ two news-carriers to perform regular stages
from Fairfield to Woodstock, and from Woodstock to Fairfield, so as
to arrive in Hartford each Saturday, and forward all proper intelligence through the country with all convenient speed. Gurdon Saltonstall, of New London, was also authorized to engage two news-carriers
to perform regular stages from Woodstock to New Haven, in such
manner that they should severally arrive in New London on each
Saturday, and forward all their intelligence every Monday morning to
Woodstock and New Haven. These gentlemen were also authorized
to forward at the public expense all such extraordinary and important
intelligence as should appear proper and necessary. Colonel Storrs
reports:—"*Bad weather for Tories in the House; yet we have some.*
April 27. Resolved on ye Grand question of making preparation in
ye Colony for our defence, appointed a large committee, two from each
County, to prepare a bill for our guide. Was appointed one of a
committee to direct the commissaries in their duty at present. We
are rejoiced to hear that the Yorkers are united with us in the cause,
as we find they have secured the arms of that city."

Putnam left his duties at Cambridge for a brief season, to advise
with the Government upon military affairs. It was agreed that one-
fourth part of the Colony militia should be immediately enlisted and
equipped for the safety and defence of the Colony, and be distributed
into companies of one hundred men each, formed into six regiments.
David Wooster was appointed major-general of this force; Joseph
Spencer, brigadier-general; Israel Putnam, second brigadier-general.
Under this regulation, the Windham County soldiers were mostly
enrolled in the Third Regiment. Israel Putnam, colonel; Experience

Storrs, lieutenant-colonel; John Durkee, Norwich, major. The companies were thus constituted:—

1. Israel Putnam, captain; Jonathan Kingsley, Scotland, first lieutenant; Thomas Grosvenor, Pomfret, second lieutenant; Elijah Loomis, ensign.
2. Experience Storrs, captain; James Dana, Ashford, first lieutenant; Ebenezer Gray, Windham, second lieutenant; Isaac Farwell, ensign.
3. John Durkee, captain; Joshua Huntington, first lieutenant; Jacobus Delbret, second lieutenant; Samuel Bingham, ensign—all of Norwich.
4. Obediah Johnson, captain; Ephraim Lyon, first lieutenant; Wells Clift, second lieutenant; Isaac Hide, Jr., ensign; Lieut. Clift, of Windham; others of Canterbury.
5. Thomas Knowlton, captain; Reuben Marcy, first lieutenant; John Keyes, second lieutenant; Daniel Allen, Jr., ensign—all of Ashford.
6. James Clark, captain; Daniel Tilden, first lieutenant; Andrew Fitch, second lieutenant, Thomas Bell, ensign—all of Lebanon.
7. Ephraim Manning, captain; Stephen Lyon, first lieutenant; Asa Morris, second lieutenant; William Frizzell, ensign—all of Woodstock.
8. Joseph Elliott, captain; Benoni Cutler, first lieutenant; Daniel Waters, second lieutenant; Comfort Day, ensign—all of Killingly.
9. Ebenezer Mosely, captain; Stephen Brown, first lieutenant; Melatiah Bingham, second lieutenant; Nathaniel Wales, ensign—Brown of Pomfret, the other officers and men from Windham.
10. Israel Putnam, Jr., captain; Samuel Robinson, Jr., first lieutenant; Amos Avery, second lieutenant; Caleb Stanley, ensign—all of Brooklyn.

Daniel Tyler, Jr., who had married a daughter of General Putnam, served as his adjutant. Dr. John Spalding of Canterbury, was appointed surgeon of this regiment, taking the place of Dr. Huntington of Ashford, who had followed the company to camp. Penuel Cheney and Elijah Adams served as surgeon's mates. Its commissary was Captain Stephen Keyes of Pomfret. Its chaplain, Abiel Leonard, the eloquent and patriotic pastor of Woodstock's First Church. The society could not bring itself to vote consent to such a sacrifice "but by its silence manifested its *resignation* to said appointment." Many who had gone out at the first alarm were mustered into this regiment without returning home. Lieut.-Colonel Storrs was "put out," after the usual military fashion, by the appointment of Commissary Keyes, and sighed for Major Durkee's promotion, but was none the less eager in forwarding regimental equipment when released from Legislative duties. At the opening of the May session of the Assembly he was again present, though many of its elected members were with the army at Cambridge. Windham County had sent the following deputies:—

Windham.—Colonel Jedidiah Elderkin, Ebenezer Devotion.
Lebanon.—Colonel William Williams, Jonathan Trumbull, Jr.
Mansfield.—Lieutenant-Colonel Experience Storrs, Nathaniel Atwood.
Woodstock.—Captains Elisha Child, Samuel McClellan.
Coventry.—Captain Ebenezer Kingsbury, Jeremiah Ripley.
Canterbury.—David Paine, Eliashib Adams.
Killingly.—Stephen Crosby, Eleazer Warren.
Pomfret.—General Israel Putnam, Dr. Elisha Lord.
Ashford.—Captains Benjamin Sumner, Ichabod Ward.
Plainfield.—Captain James Bradford, William Robinson.
Voluntown.—Major James Gordon, Robert Hunter.

An Act for regulating and ordering the troops that were or should be raised for defence of the Colony was now considered and adopted —its preamble setting forth the causes compelling such action. A number of gentlemen were appointed to assist the governor when the Assembly was not in session, direct the marches and actions of the soldiers enlisted for the defence of the Colony, and supply them with everything needful, as a committee of safety. Eliphalet Dyer, Nathaniel Wales, Jr., William Williams and Joshua Elderkin were active and prominent members of this committee. Hezekiah Bissell, also of Windham, was one of the commissaries appointed by the Assembly to supply necessary public stores and provisions. The Embargo forbidding the transportation of sundry vital necessities out of the Colony was continued until August. Bounties were offered for the manufacture of fire-arms and saltpetre, now greatly needed. Captain Jabez Huntington of Windham, was given charge of all the powder belonging to Windham County.

Lieut.-Colonel Storrs having orders for the captains of his regiment to be in readiness to march as fast as possible returned to Mansfield, May 15, and devoted himself with great energy to enlisting men, and procuring their outfit. Blankets and arms were impressed for the use of the soldiers. Saturday, 27th, "the company met and received their ammunition to be ready for their march on Monday next, May 29. Met this morning at 9 o'clock, attended prayers and sermon delivered by [Rev.] Mr. Salter. After sermon the company marched off for Cambridge. 30th. Set out this morning and overtook ye company at Kendall's, at Ashford. They appeared to be in high spirits. Tarried at Dudley." The Norwich company and others from Windham County were in advance of Colonel Storrs. June 2, he left all under care of Lieut. Gray and proceeded with Lieut. Dana to report at headquarters (at Inman's Farm, now Cambridgeport) to General Putnam, and on the following day marched in with probably the greater part of the regiment. "Met General Putnam on ye road, came to ye house of Mr. Fairweather where we make our quarters. After dinner went up to headquarters to show ourselves to ye General. He recommended our being immediately provided for action. 4. Lord's day. Heard Mr. Leonard, our chaplain, on ye Common." A few other Windham County soldiers may have enlisted in the Sixth Regiment, Samuel H. Parsons, colonel; John Tyler, lieutenant-colonel ; but the great majority of her men were in this Third Regiment under Putnam's immediate care and authority, occupying a most responsible and prominent position as part of the central division of the gathering army.

While these absent ones were busily occupied with drill, discipline and preparations for expected service, friends at home were equally alert and active.   Farms and domestic labors were to be carried on as usual and an army to be raised and supported.   Scarce a household that had not some concern with fitting out men and sending supplies to them.   All private interests seemed to be laid aside and every thought and energy devoted to the great popular cause.   Large bodies of men passing over the great thoroughfares of travel needed care and accommodation.   Many new taverns were opened in the different towns. Pomfret citizens joined with Abel Clarke in representing to the Assembly,

"That the present marching of troops and increase of travel by his house, and the necessity he is under of providing for them excites him to pray for leave to keep a tavern in said Pomfret, where he dwells on the country road from Windham to Boston, in the parish of Abington, directly opposite the dwelling-house of Ephraim Ingalls, who keeps a tavern thereat, and for many years has done to the good acceptance of people, yet in this day he cannot provide for the great numbers passing and repassing on said road, and judges it necessary that he [the petitioner] should, too.   *May* 15, 1775."

This petition was promptly granted and leave given also to Moses Branch, of Plainfield, and petitioners from other towns to offer every possible accommodation to these countless travelers.   Efforts were also made in Windham County to supply the lack of military munitions.   Hezekiah Huntington of Windham, had arranged to enter the army as major, but seeing the miserable condition of the guns and muskets supplied to the soldiers he threw up his commission, and with the permission and encouragement of the Government, opened a shop at Willimantic for their repair and manufacture.   In the same vicinity John Brown was successfully carrying on the preparation of saltpetre.   Nathan Frink was projecting a similar establishment in Pomfret.   Even predestined divines like Samuel Nott and Moses C. Welch, preparing to promulgate the Gospel of peace, were experimenting in saltpetre and destructive ingredients.   Colonel Elderkin and Nathaniel Wales, Jr., with all their civil and military engrossments, were arranging for the construction of a powder-mill.   All these busy brains and hands were working for the army.   Constant communication was kept up with the camp at Cambridge.   Aged Jesses and fresh young Davids were going down every week to take things to their sons and brethren and see how they fared.   As yet all was bright, cheerful and hopeful.   The visitors marveled at the number of soldiers collected, their parades and manœuvers, and were too unused to war to discern their lack of discipline and equipments.   Windham County was in high favor at headquarters.   Putnam was "the hero of the day," assigned by popular verdict to the first place among American officers ; Knowlton's courage and military aptitude were already recognized, and his company esteemed one of the best in the service, and the eloquent and patriotic "performances" of Chaplain Leonard excited general admiration.

Reports of successful skirmishes and demonstrations, followed by that of the battle of Bunker Hill, incited the Windham patriots to stronger hope and more ardent enthusiasm, and their grief for their slain was almost swallowed up in their exultation that their own sons and brethren, plain farmers and civilians, could withstand and put to flight the trained and tried soldiers of Great Britain. Of the two hundred Connecticut men detailed under Captain Knowlton for special service, on Bunker Hill, on the evening of June 16, 1775, Putnam's regiment furnished one hundred and twenty, drafted from the first, second, fourth and fifth companies, under Lieutenants Dana, Grosvenor, Keyes, and probably Hyde.* "One subaltern, one sergeant and thirty privates" were also drafted from Captain Chester's company, second regiment, and probably a similar number from Captain Coit's company. These were the men who toiled all night and early morn upon Prescott's redoubt, banked with wet grass the famous rail fence, and, aided by "Hampshire boys" under Stark, and Connecticut reinforcements led by Captains Chester, Clark, Coit and Major Durkee, drove back from it again and again with great slaughter the serried columns of the advancing British, and saved the retreating garrison from capture or annihilation—"all efforts insufficient to compel them to retreat till the main body had left the hill." A most honorable share in the glory of this most momentous battle was won by Windham County. Her Putnam, the chief projector of the movement, chief in command upon the hill during the day, labored with all his heart and energies against unsurmountable obstacles to reinforce Prescott and maintain their perilous position, and even those who would rob *him* of his laurels allow that "no service was more brilliant than that of the Connecticut troops whom he was authorized to command." Many incidents of the fight were carried home to Windham County. Josiah Cleveland of Canterbury kept guard through the night while the men were digging entrenchments, and heard the unsuspicious sentinels on the opposite shore sing out their illusory "All's well." Tough old "'Bijah Fuller," from Windham, Dana's orderly sergeant, helped Gridley draw the lines of the fortification on Breed's Hill, and wrought with equal skill and strength in fitting up the impromptu line of fence and wall devised to complete the line of defence, and repel an unexpected flank movement. Knowlton, with coat off, walked to and fro before this

* There is some doubt as to the leader of the men in Company Four. Canterbury men are known to have been engaged throughout the action. Ephraim Lyon declined to serve as first lieutenant, and it is probable that Isaac Hyde had been promoted second lieutenant and led the detachment.

unique and ingenious breastwork, as much at ease as if in his own
hay-field, cheering his men, loading and discharging his own faithful
musket till it was bent double by a stroke from a cannon ball.
Lieutenant Dana, second in command, was the first to detect and give
notice of the enemy's flank movement, and the first to fire upon the
advancing army, "death" being threatened to any man who fired
before him. Lieutenant Grosvenor fired with the same precision and
deliberation that he was accustomed to exercise in shooting a fox, and
saw a man fall at each discharge of his rifle. Lieut. Keyes, Sergeant
Abijah Fuller, Corporal Joel Webb, and other old campaigners were
equally cool, deliberate and effective. "Boys," said Putnam to these
old friends, as he rode past them, "Do you remember my orders at
Ticonderoga?" "You told us not to fire till we could see the whites
of the enemy's eyes." "Well, I give the same order now," and most
literally was it obeyed. Fresh companies coming up at the close of
the fight were amazed at the audacity of these fire-hardened veterans. Timothy Cleveland of Canterbury had the breech of his gun-
stock shot off when in full retreat, and exclaiming "the darned British
shall have *no part of my gun,*" ran back in face of the advancing foe,
and bore it off in triumph. Regardless of balls whistling around him,
Putnam stood by a deserted field-piece urging the retreating troops to
make one more stand, until the enemy's bayonets were almost upon
him. Robert Hale, a saucy Ashford boy, discharged an artillery-piece
in the very teeth of the foe, and escaped unscathed. Abiel Bugbee,
also of Ashford, was one who held his ground to the very last of the
fight, throwing *stones* when his ammunition was expended. A raw
Killingly recruit met a Windham friend immediately after the action,
—"You look tired, Mr. Pettingill," he exclaimed. "Just hold my gun
while I take a chaw of tobacco," was the reply. The smoking gun-
stock and begrimed face told the rest of the story. Daniel Strong,
of Lebanon, sent to the hill with Surgeon Spaulding's medical chest,
finding officers and men in great need of drink, with no means of
obtaining any, took meat casks and filled them with water, and dealt it
out to such as were almost famished with thirst, till his wagon was
struck by a cannon ball. Colonel Storrs relates in his diary his own
experience :—

"*June 17th.* At sunrise this morning a fire began from ye ships, but moderate. About 10, went down to General Putnam's post, who has the command.
Some shot whistled around us. Tarried a spell, and returned to have my
company in readiness to relieve them. One killed and one wounded when I
came away. About 2 o'clock there was a brisk cannonade from ye ships, on
ye batteries or entrenchment. At —— orders came to turn out immediately,
and that the regulars were landing at sundry places. Went to headquarters for
our regimental ——. Received orders to repair with our regiment to No. 1
and defend it. No enemy appearing, orders soon came that our people at ye

20

intrenchment were retreating, and for us to *secure ye retreat.* Immediately
marched for their relief. The regulars did not come off from Bunker's Hill,
but have taken possession of the intrenchment, and our people make a stand
on Winter Hill, and we immediately went to entrenching. Flung up by
morning an intrenchment about 100 feet square, done principally by our regiment under Putnam's direction."

And there Putnam was found on the next morning, Sunday, June
18, by his young son, Daniel, "dashing about among the workmen,
throwing up intrenchments, and often placing a sod with his own
hands. He wore the same clothes he had on when I left him, thirty-
eight hours before, and affirmed he had never put them off or washed
himself since." Colonel Storrs reports the loss of two of his men,
Matthew Cummins and Phillip Johnston, killed at the breastwork, and
seven wounded, none he hoped mortally. Ichabod Sabin, William
Cheney, Pomfret, Benjamin Rush, Samuel Mosely,* Ashford, were
reported among the slain or missing, and five or six other men from
Putnam's regiment were killed or taken prisoners. Lieutenant Grosvenor was wounded in the hand and obliged to retire from the field.
Dana was struck down by a blow on the breast from a hit rail, which
disabled him for several days. Many of the privates were wounded
slightly, but the loss was very slight in comparison with that suffered
by Massachusetts. The gratitude with which waiting friends at home
received the tidings of the escape of those exposed to such great
peril, and the anxious solicitude which followed the men in camp and
battle are best shown in a mother's letter, written by the sister of
Colonel Dyer to her son, Lieut. Ebenezer Gray, in Camp at
Cambridge :—

"JULY 31, A. D. 1775.

Dear Child :—I, this morning heard by Mr. Trumbull, who passed through
town in haste last evening, that you are preparing to meet the enemy, or to
drive them from their new intrenchments. I could not hear it without some
emotion of soul, although I firmly believe God is able to deliver and will
deliver us out of the hands of these unnatural enemies in his own time. Our
cause is just I don't doubt, and God in his holy and righteous providence has
called you there to defend our just rights and privileges. I would commit
you into the hands of a just and merciful God, who alone is able to defend
you. Confessing my utter unworthiness of the least mercy, would trust in
unmerited mercy through Jesus Christ for all that strength, courage and
fortitude that you stand in need of in the business he is calling you to. Trust
in the Lord and be of good courage; the eye of the Lord is upon them that
fear him; upon them that hope in his mercy. Confess your sins daily
before the Lord, and forsake every evil way; walk in all the commandments
of the Lord. Be careful to set a good example before those that are under
you, especially in observing the Sabbath. The surest way of conquering our
enemies is to turn from every evil way, and seek the Lord with all our hearts
with confession of our sins. I am more afraid of our sins than of all the
forces of our enemy. As to profane swearing, which is very common in
camps, I always thought you were not inclined to, and I trust you will take
all possible care to prevent it in those that fall under your care.

---

* Son of Rev. Samuel Mosely, Canada Parish.

I think we have abundant reason to praise the name of the Lord for his wonderful assistance and deliverances our people have experienced at one time and another, especially at Bunker's Hill. Well, may we say, 'Had it not been the Lord who was on our side when such a number of troops rose up and surrounded our people, then they had swallowed us up quick when their wrath was kindled against us.' These merciful assurances of God for us ought to encourage us to call upon God, and strengthen our faith in Him. That you may put your trust in God, and go on with courage and fortitude to whatever work or business you may be called to, is the sincere prayer of your Loving Mother, LYDIA GRAY."

The signal valor displayed by the few provincials who confronted the dreaded Regulars at Bunker Hill, excited the most rapturous admiration and enthusiasm throughout the Colonies. Putnam's distinguished services in the whole affair were warmly recognized and applauded, and rewarded by immediate promotion to the position of Fourth Major-General of the American Army. This appointment though naturally distasteful to senior officers in Connecticut, gave great satisfaction to the general public. Silas Deane writes from Philadelphia—"The cry is here, Connecticut forever, universally applauded conduct of our Governor, and the brave intrepidity of old General Putnam and his troops . . . His appointment gave universal satisfaction. . . . Better lose four Spencers than half a Putnam, on whom by every account the whole army has depended since the Lexington battle. Putnam's merit rung through the continent; his fame still increases. Every day justifies the unaminous applause of the continent. Let it be remembered he had every vote of the Congress, and his health has been the second or third at almost all our tables." The General Assembly of Connecticut testified their sense of the superior merit of General Putnam. The public press echoed his praises. "A friend to Truth," writing from Watertown, declares :—

"It is needless to expatiate on the character and bravery of Major-General Putnam, whose capacity to form and execute great designs is known through Europe, and whose undaunted courage and martial abilities strike terror through all the hosts of Midianites, and have raised him to an incredible height in the esteem and friendship of his American brethren. It is sufficient to say that he seems to be inspired by God Almighty with a military genius, and formed to work wonders in the sight of those uncircumcised Philistines at Boston and Bunker Hill, who attempted to defy the armies of the living God."

The services of Knowlton and Dana were also highly commended, and rewarded as soon as practicable by promotion, the former becoming major, the latter captain. A gold-laced hat, a sash and gold breast-plate were presented to Major Knowlton by a Boston admirer in recognition of "his behavior in the battle."

After Washington assumed command, July 3, Putnam had charge of the central division of the army with headquarters at the Inman house, Cambridge. The reading of the manifesto issued by Congress, setting forth the reasons for taking up arms was made the occasion of a grand patriotic demonstration, July 18. Putnam's division was paraded in full force upon Prospect Hill, and after hearing the declaration read with great pathos and solemnity by Chaplain Leonard, each soldier responded thrice with deep and fervent "Amen." At the instant a signal was fired, and General Washington stepped forward from headquarters, holding in his hand a new and beautiful standard sent by Connecticut to Putnam's regiment. Captain Dana was ordered to receive and display the flag but warned that in so doing he must not let the colors fall, as that would be deemed ominous of the fall of America. The great six-foot captain, who could face a hostile army without flinching, shrank like a child from this display and fain would have declined the honor, but Putnam cheered him on by a friendly clap on the shoulder, and " Cuth it, Dana! You look like a white man ; take the colors and clear away ; " whereupon Captain Dana advanced and received the flag from Washington's aide, and carried it three times around the interior circle of the parade, amid the rapturous applause of the delighted soldiers. It was one of six flags ordered by Connecticut for her first six regiments. The ground of this was scarlet. "An appeal to Heaven" was inscribed in golden letters on one side ; Connecticut's armorial seal upon the other—three detached vines and the trustful legend, *Qui transtulit sustinet*. The presentation and display were followed by an animated, pathetic and highly patriotic address by Mr. Leonard, closing with a pertinent prayer. " The whole was conducted with the utmost decency, good order and regularity and to universal acceptance of all present."

No noteworthy event occurred for several succeeding months. The Continental Army maintained its position, and gradually extended its lines about Boston, but was unable to indulge in offensive operations. Men, money and munitions were lacking. Commissary Trumbull writes to Colonel Dyer, Sept. 23, "that no one has power to draw on Philadelphia, and begs him to procure him a hundred pounds, lawful money, to pay Mr. Tracy, who has advanced money for Arnold's expedition, and to relieve him of the additional trouble of having his heart dunned out of him, and be for weeks unable to pay for a bushel of potatoes." Putnam cried in vain for powder. Knowlton brought his stalwart soldiers into more rigid military discipline, serving as " a sort of voluntary body-guard to the Commander-in-chief," with whom he was an especial favorite. Leonard was not only ready to officiate on all public occasions but labored effectually to promote the moral and religious interests of his soldiers. " A prayer composed for the benefit of the soldiers in the American Army, to assist them in their private devotions," prepared by Mr. Leonard, is believed to have been the first attempt to supply the camp with religious literature. It was published by S. E. Hall, Cambridge, in a tract of nine pages, and pronounced "a highly creditable performance." Windham County sent more men to the field in Connecticut's eighth regiment, Jedidiah Huntington of Norwich, colonel, John Douglas of Plainfield, lieutenant-colonel. This regiment* was the best equipped of any in the Colony, sporting for uniform "a quantity of English red coats taken in a prize vessel." Plainfield's honored pastor, Rev. John Fuller, became its chaplain, and her most beloved physician, Dr. Elisha Perkins, served as surgeon, Albigence Waldo of Pomfret, assistant. A company of Canterbury militia under Captain Ephraim Lyon, was sent to Norwich, in August, upon an alarm occasioned "by vessels prowling about the Sound," and were retained to build a battery or redoubt at Waterman's Point—the Government allowing them the needful "spirits when in said service." Ephraim Squier of Ashford, together with Simeon Tyler and Asa Davison, probably of Brooklyn, left their companies at Cambridge, in September, to join in the Northern expedition of Colonel Benedict Arnold, but after suffering incredible hardships on their journey up the Kennebec and through the wilderness of Maine, carrying their batteaux and provision, wading through mudholes in persistent rains, the rear detachment was ordered home again, and after ten weeks absence they arrived in Cambridge, Thanksgiving day, November 23, "abundantly satisfied."

At home all thoughts and energies were absorbed in the war. Not a town meeting was reported through all these busy months. It was a time of action—not of talk and resolutions. The County Court met in June, licensed some fifty taverns, granted execution in a few cases, and adjourned. Everybody was occupied doing double duty in farm work, gathering up supplies or manufacturing military munitions. Hezekiah Huntington had wrought to such good purpose as to receive from the State treasury in the autumn, a bounty of thirteen pounds "for fifty-two guns well made and wrought," besides repairing and refitting great numbers of old guns. Timothy Larrabee assures the Assembly "that since the alarming circumstances of the present time, he had applied himself to making saltpetre, and had become master of the same in all its branches, and was confident that when said art was known powder could be manufactured in the Colonies or in any part of the world, and although at this time we are able to collect some small quantities from abroad, yet when the question is asked, why business that was expected to be done failed—answer: '*army not furnished with warlike stores.*'" Petitioner proposed to erect works in Hartford

---

* Calkins' History of Norwich.

or New Haven, open to all inspectors, every branch of the manufacturing open to the public, *if* the General Assembly would grant him £150; but the sanguine experimenter did not gain the confidence of the cautious government. The general tone and spirit of the towns was still healthy and hopeful. Constant communication was maintained with friends in the army. Posts, carriers and special messengers were daily passing to and fro, and every citizen that could leave his home took a peep at Cambridge. "Father and I went down to camp," and "Yankee Doodle" was heard on every side. Among the throng of visitants was our old friend, Rev. Mr. Cogswell, with his brother minister, Andrew Lee, who reports the army in health and spirits, and in general orderly, with good men at the head. The works appeared formidable on both sides; preparations for war terrible yet animating—but what gave him most confidence was "men of sense and religion."

Amid the many engrossments and excitements of this eventful summer, Windham paused to lament a great and irreparable loss. While scores of young men, full of life and hope, were going out to win laurels on the battle-field, and make for themselves names that would never die, one more gifted and excellent than all had passed away—Rev. Joseph Howe of Killingly, the beloved pastor of the New South Church of Boston. Never has Windham sent out into the world a son of greater or perhaps equal promise. "The world expected much from his eminent abilities, great attainments, and uncommon goodness of heart." Influential churches in Boston, Hartford and Norwich had sought his services. "Though of a frail, weak, and crazy constitution, enfeebled by hard study and labor," Mr. Howe had exercised "his ministerial functions at Boston to great and universal acceptance," till the breaking out of the conflict and the dispersion of his church and congregation. The exciting scenes through which he passed, and anxiety for his church and country, prostrated his strength, and after vainly seeking rest and recuperation among his old haunts in Connecticut, he succumbed to an attack of "complicated disease," and died at Hartford, August 25, ere he had reached his thirtieth year. A large circle of devoted friends bemoaned his loss; his scattered church was overwhelmed with sorrow. A writer in the *Hartford Courant*, though sensible that the critical situation of America engrossed every thought, was sure that not one who had ever heard of Mr. Howe—a description that designates almost all the inhabitants of New England, and not a few of other countries—could be inattentive to an account of his excellencies, and eulogized him as a light and benefactor to the world, the beauty of whose mind was without a parallel, whose life was a treatise of ethics and theology, recommending the whole duty of

man more powerfully than libraries of moralists and divines. The
early death of one so gifted with genius and graces, made a deep
and lasting impression upon the public. His memory was fondly
cherished through all the generation that had known him, and years
later, when many of his cotemporaries had passed into oblivion, his
character was portrayed in that of the model hero in one of the first
original popular tales published in America.* In Windham County
the impression made by the death of Mr. Howe was deepened by
attendant bereavements. His step-father, Rev. Aaron Brown, of Killingly, died suddenly on the way home from his funeral, and the
bereaved wife and mother survived but a few months.

III.

CAMPAIGN OF 1776.   STRUGGLES AND DISASTERS.   DEATH OF
    KNOWLTON.   TOWN RESOLUTIONS.   CAMPAIGNS
          OF 1777-78.   DISCOURAGEMENTS.

THE long period of inaction following the battle of Bunker Hill,
    was a sore trial to the Windham County soldiery. The mechani-
cal routine, the restraints, privations and discomforts of camp-life,
unrelieved by the rush and stir of actual encounter with the enemy,
became very irksome to men accustomed to the freedom of country
life and a voice in town meetings. Bad fare, scant pay, misapprehen-
sion of the plans of their leaders and the true condition of affairs so
exasperated the Connecticut soldiers, that many who rushed so eagerly
into service at the Lexington alarm declined re-enlistment in the proposed Continental Army, subjecting General Washington and his
associates to the most serious anxiety and peril. Even men in Putnam's own Windham County regiment were infected with this spirit of
disaffection and mutiny, and thirty of the ardent volunteers from
Captain Mosely's company, Canada Parish, seven from Knowlton's
Ashford Company, and three from Elliott's, Killingly, marched off
home when their time of enlistment had expired without waiting a
formal discharge, unwittingly incurring the opprobrium of *deserting*.
It is said that the wives of these men were so outraged by their conduct
that they gave them a hearty scolding, and threatened to drive them
back to camp, and that " the people in the towns where they belonged
were so affected by their unreasonable conduct that they would readily

* The Coquette, or the History of Eliza Wharton.

march to supply their places." Washington's sense of military discipline was greatly shocked by this unceremonious leave-taking, and he sent after them, wishing to make examples of them. Governor Trumbull and his Council, with better understanding of the character and grievances of the men, did not think best to comply with this requisition, but stigmatized their conduct as "very reprehensible, and considered them deserters though their time had nearly expired; considered it a critical time to form a new army, and doubted their power to act upon the subject." It appearing upon inquiry that the men had lapsed mainly from ignorance and inadvertence, and were ready to re-enlist upon the first favorable opportunity, the offence was passed over, and these same deserting soldiers served in many subsequent campaigns with honor and fidelity.

A majority of Putnam's Regiment are believed to have remained upon the field, re-enlisting in the Twentieth Regiment of Washington's Continental Army. Benedict Arnold, whose brilliant services in the Northern expedition were then attracting great admiration, was appointed its colonel; John Durkee of Norwich, lieutenant-colonel; Thomas Knowlton, major. Company 1, Ephraim Manning, captain; Nath. Webb, lieutenant; ——— Brown, ensign. Company 2, Jedidiah Waterman, captain; John Waterman, lieutenant; Walter Clark, ensign. Company 3, Thomas Dyer, captain; Daniel Tilden, first lieutenant; Nehemiah Holt, second lieutenant; Joseph Durkee, ensign. Company 4, Wells Clift, captain. Company 5, Thomas Grosvenor, captain; Josiah Cleveland, ensign. Company 6, Stephen Brown, captain. Company 7, John Keyes, captain. Company 8, John Robinson, captain. Other subalterns, whose companies cannot now be determined, were—Lieutenants Melatiah Bingham, William Adams, Beriah Bill, Robert Hallam, Samuel Brown, Seth Phelps, Josiah Fuller, Nathaniel Bishop, James Holt, Daniel Putnam, and Ensigns Briant Brown, Silas Goodell, John Buell. Its chaplain was Rev. Abiel Leonard. Lieutenant Ebenezer Gray served as quartermaster. Dr. John Spaulding retained his position as surgeon; Luther Waterman served as surgeon's assistant. Forming a part of the central division of the army, this regiment came under the more immediate control and supervision of Washington, "serving as a sort of voluntary body-guard to the Commander-in-chief." The continued absence of Arnold left it in charge of Durkee and Knowlton, under whose efficient training it attained "the same enviable position as to discipline and soldierly deportment that Knowlton's own company had previously held." Other Windham County soldiers re-enlisted in Huntington's and Patterson's regiments, and a still larger number in a militia regiment sent to Boston early in January, to take the place of those whose term of service had expired. John Douglas of Plainfield was its colonel; Dr. Elisha Perkins, surgeon; Thomas Gray of Windham, surgeon's mate. Plainfield's excellent minister, Rev. John Fuller, served as its chaplain. Woodstock would gladly have recalled her ministerial favorite at the close of the winter's campaign, but yielded to the wishes of the Commander-in-chief and their own honored leader, as expressed in the following letter:—

" *To the Church and Congregation of Woodstock :—*
Mr. Leonard is a man whose exemplary life and conversation must make him highly esteemed by every person who has the pleasure of being acquainted with him. It therefore can be no surprise to us to hear they are loth to part with him. His influence in the army is great. He is employed in the glorious work of attending to the morals of a brave people who are fighting for their liberties—the liberties of the people of Woodstock—the liberty of all America. We therefore hope that, knowing how nobly he is employed, the congregation of Woodstock will cheerfully give up to the public, a gentleman so very useful. And when, by the blessing of a kind Providence, this glorious and unparalleled struggle for our liberties is at an end, we have not the least doubt but Mr. Leonard will, with redoubled joy, be received in the open arms of a congregation so very dear to him as the good people of Woodstock are.
This is what is hoped for—this is what is expected, by the congregation of Woodstock's sincere well-wishers and very humble servants,
GEORGE WASHINGTON.
ISRAEL PUTNAM.
HEADQUARTERS, *Cambridge, 24th of March,* 1776."

The prayers and preaching of Mr. Leonard were often commended by the patriot journals. On the Sabbath after evacuation of Boston by the British, and its occupation by the Americans, he is reported to have preached an excellent sermon in the audience of his Excellency, the General, and others of distinction. . . . . from Exodus iv. 25 : "And took off their chariot wheels, that they drove them heavily ; so that the Egyptians said, 'Let us flee from the face of Israel, for the Lord fighteth for them against the Egyptains.'"

Renewed operations in the spring, followed by the withdrawal of the British troops from Boston, inspired the Windham patriots with new courage and enthusiasm, and stimulated them to intense activity in preparations for the summer campaign. The powder mill at Willimantic was now under full headway, sending out large supplies to the Continental Army. All the saltpetre which could by any method be fabricated was quickly swallowed up by this important establishment, which was guarded day and night at the expense of the Government. Black lead for its consumption was taken from the hills of Union. So great was the throng of people and teams resorting thither, that David Young was ordered to open a house of public entertainment in its vicinity. With the transference of the seat of war to New York, travel was greatly increased on all the public highways. Regiment after regiment was marched through Windham County, and endless trains of military stores. Five battalions of the Continental Army, and the whole body of riflemen under Brigadier-General Heath, and six battalions under General Sullivan, set out March 29, 1776, *via.* Norwich, passing through several towns in Windham County. Brooklyn and Ashford were gladdened by a brief glimpse of their favorite heroes, Putnam and Knowlton, as they hurried on their way. Farm work began early. Demands for supplies called out the utmost energies of the people. Commissaries and jobbers were scouring the towns for provisions, taking off all the pork, beef and sheep that could be spared from home consumption. Selectmen were now making requisitions for scales, clock-weights, anything that could be wrought into ammunition. Orders for knit stockings, tow cloth for tents, and home-made shirtings and vestings kept thousands of nimble fingers in motion. Great quantities of military stores were lodged in Plainfield, Windham and Canterbury. Depots were constructed for their reception and carefully guarded, and teams were constantly occupied hauling them to and fro. A large number of prisoners, dangerous Tories, captured seamen and soldiers, confined in Windham jail and neighboring towns, required much care and attention. Dyer, Elderkin and Wales, as members of the Committee of Safety, were intensely active in providing for these various demands, and spent many days at Governor Trumbull's war office in Lebanon, where many an important interprise was devised and set in motion, and the committees of the different towns were almost equally occupied in schemes for the public welfare. One-fourth of the men in each militia regiment, perfectly equipped with arms, balls, flints and other needful articles, were ordered to hold themselves ready to march on the shortest notice, while recruiting for the various new regiments ordered by Connecticut, was pushed forward with the greatest activity. As the summer came on it was evident that the most urgent efforts were demanded. Great Britain was sending over strong fleets and hordes of hired soldiers, hoping to crush out the rebellion by one vigorous campaign. A special circular, issued by Trumbull, August 1, begging for more recruits at the earliest moment, was sent to the civil authority of every town, and also to many of the ministers, with the request that it should be read at the close of public worship. Windham County met the demand with her usual spirit and promptitude. She sent her men to Canada, to New York and to New London. Charles C. Chandler replies to Governor Trumbull that "Woodstock had already sent seventy men under the new requisition for the departments in Canada, New York and Boston, which was near one-half of the militia of the town and a much greater number than their proportion, but were still ready to do everything in their power to advantage the public cause at this critical day." Other towns were equally ready to do more than their proportion. Many Windham County men were enlisted in the First regiment, Andrew Ward, colonel; Obadiah Johnson of Canterbury, lieutenant colonel; William Douglas, major. James Stedman, Nathaniel Wales, 3rd, Waterman Clift, Daniel Allen, Jonathan Nichols, Jr., James Dana, Elijah Sharp, James Arnold, Benoni Cutler, William Manning, Joseph Durkee, Obadiah Child, were officers in this regiment. Its chaplain was Rev. Benjamin Trumbull, the historian of Connecticut; its paymaster, Royal Flint of Windham. The seventh company of the first battalion sent to the relief of the northern department was from Windham County—Vine Elderkin, captain; William Frizzell, first lieutenant; Abner Robinson, second lieutenant, Lemuel Grosvenor, ensign. In the third battalion raised for service in New York, Comfort Sage, colonel; Company 1, was from Lebanon, James Clark, captain; Company 3, Voluntown, John Dixon, captain; Company 5, Killingly, Stephen Crosby, captain, Josiah Robbins, first lieutenant, Jonathan Buck, second lieutenant, Sylvanus Perry, ensign. The sixth battalion, Colonel John Chester, comprised at least three Windham County companies, Company 4, Ashford, Reuben Marcy, captain; John Holmes, first and Samuel Marcy, second lieutenants; Daniel Knowlton, ensign, and 79 privates. Company 5, Woodstock, Stephen Lyon, captain; Josiah Child, first lieutenant. Company 6, Canterbury, Asa Bacon, captain; Abner Bacon, first lieutenant; Aaron Cleveland, ensign. "Sabbath morning, June 30, 1776," Brigadier-General Wadsworth writes thus to Colonel Chester.

"Last evening, by express, I received another letter from General Washington, requesting in the most pressing manner, not to lose one moment time in sending forward the regiments destined for New York. Must therefore, direct, that you give all possible attention to the raising, equipping and sending forward immediately your regiment in manner before directed, as the safety of our army under Heaven, depends much on the seasonable arrival of the Connecticut regiments."

This order was forwarded as soon as possible to Captains Marcy, Lyon and Bacon, with instructions to march the companies under their command by land or water to New York on the following Thursday, July 4. If the whole company was not in readiness, they were to march with twenty-five men, forwarding the remainder as fast as they became ready with all convenient speed. They were to see that the men were "well furnished with good arms, bayonets and cartouch boxes, blankets and knapsacks." The order from headquarters expressly enjoined "that the men be furnished with arms, and that none be suffered to go without, as it will be impossible to procure them here, and their service will consequently be rendered useless."

These needed arms could doubtless be procured at the establishment of Hezekiah Huntington, who kept busily at work making and repairing.

As fast as possible the recruits were fitted out and sent to the field. No time was spent in speech-making now ; all energies were absorbed in preparation for the approaching struggle. The County Court met for two days only in June. Judge William Williams, Justices Jabez Fitch, Ebenezer Williams and Ebenezer Devotion were present. Jedidiah Elderkin was dismissed from being *King's Attorney*, and appointed attorney of the *Governor and Colony of Connecticut.* The select-men of Ashford complained of John Stevens and wife, who had succored themselves under the Ministerial army, and of Adam Knox, who was serving "as pilot in the Ministerial navy." The Court ordered Captain Elisha Wales to improve the lands of Captain Stevens, re-licensed the usual number of tavern-keepers, and adjourned.

News from New York became more and more alarming. Fleets, armies and munitions of war were concentrating in its vicinity. Skirmishing with skulking Tories in New York and Long Island was to give place to a hand-to-hand grapple with the British foe. With all the men and means that could by any possibility be mustered, Washington prepared for the encounter. Very heavy requisitions were made upon Connecticut. In addition to the veterans previously in service, and the ten regiments enlisted during the summer, fourteen regiments of militia from the western part of the State were ordered, August 11th, "to march forthwith to New York, and place themselves under General Washington until the present exigency should be over." Windham County was already strongly represented in Durkee's, Huntington's, Ward's and other regiments. Her officers and soldiers under Major-General Putnam, had rendered effective aid throughout the campaign in New York, and were among those upon whose valor and fidelity Washington most confidently relied at this dark hour. Most of the men who had been connected with military movements since the breaking out of the war were probably with the army at this time. Some who had gone out from the county were there with their brethren—Colonel William Douglas of Northford, and John Chandler of Newton, lieutenant-colonel of Gold Silliman's brigade. A hundred picked men from Col. Durkee's regiment, led by Lieut.-Colonel Knowlton, were conspicuous for courage and devotion, and had already signalized themselves by valorous exploits. Changes and promotions were made in the other regiments, defences maintained and strength-ened as far as practicable, and every means tried to make the American force as effective as possible.

These preparations were all insufficient. The raw Continental army, made up of incongruous elements, imperfectly drilled and equipped, lacking in experience and resources, was wholly unable to compete with the vastly superior force arrayed against it. Tidings of the disastrous defeat at Brooklyn and the withdrawal of the American army from Long Island, sent dismay to every patriot heart. The Windham County soldiers in the Connecticut Line suffered severely. More than a hundred and fifty officers and privates were "missing" from Huntington's regiment alone.* Several men from Pomfret were killed; Surgeon David Holmes and others from Woodstock and adjoining towns were taken prisoners. Durkee's and Chandler's regiments were detailed by Washington to cover the retreat from Long Island, keeping guard with intense vigilance until the perilous transit was accomplished. Word was then sent to them "to get off as they could, in order or not." "Where are we going?" asked a bewildered soldier as they stole off through the darkness over the black river. "To Heaven, I hope," answered a cheery Windham captain, prepared for any result. With report of these events Windham County received immediate summons to the field. The militia in Eastern Connecticut, including the Fifth, Eleventh, Twelfth and Twenty-first regiments, together with the regiment of horse, were ordered to march at once to New York, "to be ready to co-operate with the Continental army, and defeat the designs of the enemy." Already preparing to march for the defence of New London, these regiments were soon under way, led by their respective officers. The troops of horse under Major Ebenezer Backus speeded on in advance and were soon reported at Westchester.

They found affairs in the greatest confusion, the enemy threatening on every side, and distrust and disaffection pervading the American ranks. Disheartened by sickness and defeat, hundreds of men were stealing off to their homes, but the Windham County militia not unused to war, and having full confidence in their leaders and in the justice of their cause, gladly took the places assigned them in Putnam's division, and bravely stood their ground with the older regiments. Scarcely, however, had they reached the field when they were called to leave it. Beset on every side by hostile force, the Americans had with great difficulty maintained their position in New York. Washington's headquarters were already removed to Harlem. September

---

* John Waldo of Scotland, a private in Huntington's regiment, thus reports to his parents:—"The loss our regiment met you have no doubt heard of. Two hundred and twenty is the number missing, lost in that action in our regiment, among which is our lieut.-colonel, surgeon's mate, adjutant, six captains, twelve subalterns, and almost all the sergeants of the regiment. We are now left without any field officer that is well but one captain; however, we hope that almost all that are missing are taken captive. We expect an attack from the enemy every day or hour. Our fortitude yet remains and we hope with a common blessing to be able to make a noble stand, and be a means of saving our country yet—a righteous God grant that we may prosper.   *Camp at New York, Sept. 9, 1776.*"

15th was a day of sore battle. "The regulars landed on the Island of York both on the North and East Rivers on Sabbath day morning," and Putnam's division was forced to make a hasty retreat. Many Windham County men were slain, taken prisoners, disabled by wounds, and cut down by indulgence or exposure. Captain Stephen Crosby of Thompson, Conn., Third battalion, Company 5, "being over hot went into a house and drank cold water, and died immediately. Lieut. Buck was either killed or taken, and other Killingly men."* Artillery and military stores were left in the hands of the enemy. Nothing but the extraordinary exertions of Putnam and the beguiling courtesies of a quick-witted patriot lady who detained the pursuit, saved his division from far greater loss, if not annihilation or capture.

Exhausted by their hurried flight, chilled by a severe shower and sudden change of temperature, "their hearts sunk within them by the loss of baggage, artillery and works in which they had been taught to put great confidence," the escaped soldiers "lay upon their arms, covered only by the clouds of an uncomfortable sky." Before daylight Knowlton was out with his Rangers, endeavoring to ascertain the exact position of the British. This distinguished corps had been formally organized since the retreat from Long Island, and now embraced volunteer officers and men from several of the New England regiments, ready to engage in scouting or any special service at a moment's warning. Captains Nathan Hale, Stephen Brown, Thomas Grosvenor, and many other gallant and faithful men made up this heroic band. On this very night or a few hours previous, Hale had manifested his patriotic devotion by volunteering to go out alone within the enemy's lines to learn something more definite of their position and movements. Knowlton soon came upon the enemy's pickets about a mile below the American lines, and engaged in a brisk little fight with their advanced guard, "gave them nine rounds and retreated" in good order, though with a loss of ten of his Rangers.

The good conduct of the handful of men engaged in this brief rencontre, the insolence of their pursuers who now appeared in open sight blowing their bugle-horns as if on a fox chase, and the opportunity of redeeming the disgrace of the previous day, led Washington to attempt to effect their capture. A detachment of volunteers made a demonstration in the front of the enemy, while Knowlton with his Rangers, and three Virginia companies under Major Andrew Leitch, "stole around to the rear of the enemy." The movement was successful. The Americans behaved with great spirit and steadiness, "charging the enemy with great intrepidity, beating them in open fight and

* Letter from Thomas Dike to his parents.

driving them everywhere before them, and at last making an orderly retreat when a large body of British was put in motion. This unexpected success, which greatly inspirited the troops and restored the confidence of the officers, was purchased by the sacrifice of two most valued leaders—Leitch and Knowlton. Hurrying after the flying enemy in the first eagerness of pursuit, Leitch was severely wounded, and " a bullet pierced Knowlton's body." "My poor Colonel," wrote Captain Brown, "was shot just by my side. The ball entered the small of his back. I took hold of him, asked him if he was badly wounded. He told me he was; but says he, 'I do not value my life if we do but get the day.' He desired me by all means to keep up this flank. He seemed as unconcerned and calm as though nothing had happened to him." He was carried from the field by Sergeant Nehemiah Holt, assisted by General Joseph Reed. "Gasping in the agonies of death, all his enquiry was if we had drove the enemy," and his dying charge to his young son—"You can do me no good ; go, fight for your country." His death was a great loss to the army. All felt with Washington, that a gallant and brave officer, "who would have been an honor to any country," had fallen. Gifted with uncommon military genius and many noble and attractive qualities, he had given his whole heart and energies to the patriot cause. "The favorite of superior officers, the idol of his soldiers and fellow-townsmen, he fell universally lamented." Washington and Putnam regarded him with peculiar fondness, and even the fastidious and world-experienced Aaron Burr was tenderly drawn to him, and pronounced him one whom it was impossible to promote too rapidly. He was buried on the following day, September 17, near the spot where he fell, on Harlem Heights, with firing of artillery and customary military honors, his beloved chaplain, Abiel Leonard, officiating in the religious service. A brother colonel present expressed his sympathy in impromptu verse :—

> "Here Knowlton lies—the great, the good, the brave;
> Slain on the field, now triumphs in the grave.
> Thus falls the valiant in the martial strife—
> The coward lives, his punishment is life."

Another noble son of Connecticut, and Windham County,* sent out by Knowlton on the night preceding his own decease, met his untimely fate a few days later with equal heroism, regretting only that he "had but one life to give for his country." One in service and devotion, death did not long divide them, and they left behind them names that shall never perish.

---

* Captain Nathan Hale.

These losses and disasters carried mourning and consternation to every household in Windham County. Ashford was stricken to the heart at the loss of its honored Knowlton, even the man called his only enemy weeping over him as for a brother. Many other homes had been bereaved and desolated; many children left orphans. Most of the slain were men in the prime of life with wives and children dependent on them. Colonel Knowlton left eight living children; Captain Crosby of Thompson, six. Widows lost their only sons; fathers those on whom they had hoped to lean. There was wailing for the dead and intense anxiety for the living. Some were "missing," their fate left to harrowing conjecture; some were prisoners, incarcerated in the sugar-house or prison-ship; many were sick and wounded, suffering every imaginable discomfort. Disease was raging in the crowded camps and devastating the retreating army. Every post and messenger brought tidings of fresh calamity. Thomas Dike of Thompson, writes to his parents, that his brother Samuel is missing :—

" The last account I had of him he was sick and in the hospital . . . and came that day up to the regiment, but being weak could not travel any farther, and several of the company told me that there were carriages provided to carry the sick that could not travel over to the Jersey side, among which was Sergeant Jesse Larned, who is since dead, Samuel Dike, Amos Green and many others. . . . .
Colonel Williams' regiment [Eleventh militia] is ordered off to the Jersey side, and we expect to go from here to-day. It is very sickly among the militia. William Smith and Ebenezer Nichols we left behind. Solomon Smith and John Barret must stop here or return back. The Lord be merciful to us all for we have got where the inhabitants show no pity. I beg your prayers for me that I may be preserved from sin, sickness and sword, and be soon returned to my family and friends. . . . . Remember me to Mr. Howard and his wife. Tell them that I have not heard from their brothers. Tell my little children I long to see them, but when I shall I cannot tell. It is all confusion here.
Westchester, September 20, 1776."

Simon Larned writes of the death of his brother Jesse —.

" I saw him at Saturday noon, September 14, and he said he thought he could stand it to be moved, as he did, but being so very weak it must worry him much. He died Sabbath-day night and had his senses perfectly well till he died, and seemed to leave the world very well composed. While he was in York, I never failed of going to see him once and twice a day, and spared no pains to get him everything in my power to make him comfortable. . . . I am something poorly myself but not so but I keep about, and I hope it is nothing more than a bad cold. I saw Killingly company and they seemed to be in good spirits."

Fears for the patriot cause aggravated their personal anxieties. Pressed on every side, there was little hope that the army could maintain its position. From Oliver Grosvenor, commissary of Colonel Williams' regiment, came vivid pictures of the situation :—

" BERGEN, Monday, 2 P. M., September 23.
This minute the men-of-war landed on Paulus' Hook where I was yesterday at this time, which was immediately after our arrival here, which was within

ten minutes after I got off my horse, There was an alarm and our companies not all got in. Those that had immediately marched down to Paulus' Hook, which is about one mile and a half from our encampments which we made last night about sundown; and now this minute the cannon begin to roar like thunder, and the drums beating to arms, thereupon you'll excuse me from adding more, for how can I write when I expect immediately to be called to action? for fight we must or else retreat six or eight miles up North River, as this is a neck of land something like New York, and we expect they will try to land above us to cut off our retreat and the Lord only knows how it will fare with us. We have no fort now to retreat to near us. Colonel Durkee's regiment left the fort at Paulus' Hook on the approach of the men-of-war, having brought their cannon and baggage. The greatest confusion here. I have not had time to sit down one minute to-day, and much fatigued with yesterday's alarm, riding from this place to Paulus' Hook to and from in the utmost haste to get a little bread and liquor to our people that were called for before they sat down to rest one minute. . . . God's name be praised that I am so well as to contribute my assistance to our friends fatigued in their march and numbers unwell. Our tents are their hospitals on the ground with blankets, not having time last night to get straw for them or ourselves. Payson Grosvenor is very sick, not like to live by what I hear. Young Dr. Lord is quite poorly to-day. My kind regards to all. As to my affairs at home I think nothing of them. I hope, God willing, to return home safe after some time. From your loving, tender husband, OLIVER GROSVENOR."

" —————, October 3, 1776.

Beloved Wife.—As I have opportunity by Post Morris this day (tho' but a day or two since I wrote), It gives me some ease tho' I am unwell, taken last evening with the common and almost universal disorder, camp-ail—had a very uncomfortable night, being obliged to be abroad several time in the night, occasioned by the sick of the regiment crowding into my room, not being able to get in anywhere except into the church which has no fireplace, and the soldiers choose rather to be in their tents than to go into it, let the consequences be what it will, and I must either forbid everyone or admit the whole, which consisted last night of more than twenty sick and nurses. Six of them took vomits and continued to vomit all night long without any intermission, it being in the room where I slept. I never saw such a night before and is like to be worse; the sick daily increases in numbers; some companies not more than two or three in their returns fit for duty; the rest sick and taking care of the sick. We have carried a number out of the church to Newark . . . also have sent a number up to the skirts of the town two or three miles back; also we have a number now in the church, several of them very dangerous.

I expect to be worse before I am better . . . but am not at all discouraged, hoping in a few days to inform you of my better state of health through the goodness of God, who wounds and heals again, and demands the praise due to his name for common mercies, more especially for signal deliverances.

The above wrote in the morning when better able to write than now. I am exercised at present with hard pain in my head as well as elsewhere and feel the symptoms of a fever coming on which I fear more, and renders more difficult and discouraging, as there is no conveniency or care for those sick. The concern for each other here appears far less than what we commonly exercise for the brute beasts at home. It is not in my power to paint to you the doleful scenes I behold every hour; neither did I believe that rational creatures could be divested of that humanity that I find they are subject to in the camps, where sickness and sin so much prevails. Alas for our land which now mourns beneath the horrors and distress of the present war. This I write Friday evening. I have been much to-day as I was yesterday as to the headache, but otherwise better; so well that I was obliged to make provision for the whole regiment since dark, as the General gave out orders this afternoon to have each one provided for three days provision immediately and to have it cooked. But where designed or for what purpose is yet a secret. Six of our regiment have died since the day before yesterday, and now there are a number I expect to hear are dead in the morning."

"FORT CONSTITUTION, October 19.

Through the still preserving and upholding power and goodness of God, I am in that degree of health that renders me in some measure comfortable. . . . I have not eat two pounds of meat this fortnight. I have no relish for it. I get some milk, make some chocolate and coffee, but nothing suits me so well as roasted potatoes and apples. Cheese I want and cheese I can get, but the bread that we have baked here is so high-seasoned with leaven I cannot eat it, I have such an aversion to it. I often think of and long for a crust of brown bread, but not one morsel have I eat since I left West Haven, but thus much for my hankerings after those things I have not. . . . It appears quite uncertain whether we shall be dismissed soon; rather think now that the fate or salvation of our land is near at hand; or, in other words, that there will be a sore battle fought before this comes to hand, and very like to me within 48 hours. You'll hear before I write you of the enemy's landing yesterday at New Rochelle, and of the skirmish that followed. Our people, I think, intend to evacuate the whole island of New York entirely, as they have already carried off the heft of the artillery. Some of our people have been haleing up the cannon and mortars brought over this side this evening.

Brother Ezra is well, tho' those that are their duty is very hard. Every other day, and some days when they go on fatigue in the forenoon, they are taken to go on guard in the afternoon perhaps for two or three days. I wrote Lemuel a letter this week by Corbin, who lives at Albany. He told me Captain Elderkin was sick at his home, but heard nothing of Brother Lemuel. I wrote this in my tent on my knee when others are asleep. Embrace Charle for me. Yours with the tenderest sympathy.   OLIVER GROSVENOR."

These letters were most welcome even though telling of sickness and disaster. Communication with the absent had become very difficult and infrequent. The pleasant intercourse of the year before, the running back and forth from camp, had all gone by. Now anxious friends must depend upon tardy "posts" and chance messengers. The distant post-office at New London, was practically of no account. A daily mail and hourly telegram were beyond their utmost conception. Postmen Morris and Craft rode to and fro between Woodstock and headquarters as fast as the rough ways and weather would permit, and passing travelers brought news, not always the most reliable. The situation was indeed most critical and alarming. Should the army be defeated in the general action that seemed inevitable, the whole country was in peril. The victorious British could sweep through Connecticut as well as through New York and the Jerseys. New London and Rhode Island were already threatened by naval forces. And in this time of peril and extremity Windham was left almost without protection. Every able-bodied man between sixteen and sixty had gone with the militia, and only aged men, invalids, and here and there a needful official, were left with the women and children. What marvel that every item of news should be seized and hurried all over the county, and the most exaggerated and distorted rumors obtained credence. New London and Providence were burned, or "Connecticut was taken," or armies were marching directly to Windham County. Anxious eyes turned many times by night and day to the various high places where bonfires were built up to be lighted at the first alarm of approaching peril. A kettle of burning tar on the cross-ties of the liberty pole at Killingly Hill served as a danger signal for the surrounding country. The south neighborhood of Thompson suffered a very serious panic during these anxious days. A saucy Dudley boy was knocked down by a suspected Tory. At about the same time a courier with special dispatches from Boston galloped through the towns, too much in haste to pause to answer curious questions. Report of these incidents magnified by excited imaginations flew all over the country. "Four men shot down dead in Dudley street," was a popular version. The fearful inhabitants of this remote neighborhood, waiting in suspense to hear from absent friends and the expected engagement, were horrified by the tidings that their own homes were in danger, that the Tories of Dudley and Oxford and the remnant of the old Indian Paygan tribolet had risen to prepare the way for the expected British army, and that "Malbone's niggers" were coming on to meet them, burning and slaughtering everything before them. "The Tor-ies are coming! The Tor-ies are coming!" was the cry, sent to every house. What was to be done? How could they meet this onset? British and even Hessians might give quarter but only downright butchery could be expected from heathen negroes and savage Indians. Not a man left at home but decrepit grandfathers and paralytics, no arms, no ammunition. Flight seemed the only resource, and a dismal, miry swamp was selected as the place of refuge. A boy was sent to rally all the neighbors. He ran to Larned's store, then a well-known business centre. Lieut. Larned had gone to the front with his regiment, leaving business and family in charge of his wife. She was not one to run from the face of danger. A rousing fire was blazing in the huge kitchen fire-place, filled with kettles of water and every iron implement that could be mustered, with which she intended to make a stand against the invaders. "Old Granny Leavens"—the aged widow of the first William Larned of Thompson—was equally resolute. She had survived several Indian wars and two husbands, and now sinking back into her chimney corner exclaimed with Calvinistic resignation—"If I *am* to be killed by the Tor-ies to-night, why then I *shall be*, so I'll e'en stay with Becky." Their heroic example had no effect upon their weaker sisters, already in full flight. "Tell Becky" they retorted, "that hot irons will *never do* for the British." They hurried off to the swamp, a most forlorn and panic-stricken company. Poor old lame "Uncle Asa," suffering from a disease incident upon excessive flip-drinking, was greatly exercised. "Thither," he pleaded, as he hobbled along; "Thither, I've forgot my plathter." "Hurry up, Asa, you'll never dress your knees again in *this* world," replied the comforting sister. The swamp when reached was so "damp, moist and unpleasant," that all could join with Aunt Nabby in her heart-felt ejaculation, "I'd give a wedge of goold as big as my foot for *one good dram.*" The unfortunate old people too feeble for flight were in a still more pitiable condition. One bed-ridden old woman who had not stood on her feet for years, and was *forgotten* in the flurry and left at home alone, managed to crawl out of bed and stow herself away into a cupboard, and a disabled old captain trembling with palsy barricaded the door and valiantly held it with a pitch-fork.

One other family remained tranquilly at home through all the panic. Good Deacon Gay had gone with four of his sons to the army. Farm and family were in the charge of the fifth son, a lad of seventeen. He was a stout young fellow and could handle a musket deftly, but his trust was not in carnal weapons. Hot irons and cold swamps he thought "but vain things for safety." Young Joseph went calmly on with his harvesting through the day, "did the nightly chores," and then gathering the family around him in the great kitchen for their usual evening worship, read comforting words in the old Bible brought from Dedham, and " led in prayer." Thus stayed and strength-ened they passed the night in peace. Nothing was heard of Malbone, or other marauders. The morning sun dispelled all phantoms of terror. The wearied fugitives stole back from the swamp to encoun-ter volleys and shafts of ridicule. Their fright and flight and ridicu-lous sayings were told all over the town and even carried to camp, giving the men a hearty laugh amid all their sorrowful surroundings and forebodings.

Even the darkest day has gleams of light. Windham Green had her fun even in this gloomy autumn. In her eagerness to answer every requisition of Government she left her prison doors too slightly guarded. Four British seamen captured the June preceding in H. M. S. *Bom-brig,* effected their escape. There was an alarm, a rush, search and pursuit, but all in vain. The prisoners had gone beyond recovery, but left behind them a unique and lasting memorial—the image of their favorite Divinity, Bacchus, the God of mirth, wine and good cheer, carved with their jack-knives from a block of pine during the idle hours of their captivity. That their choice of a subject was suggested by what they saw going on around them, as well as by their own pecu-liar regard and devotion, is very probable. "Excessive drinking," denounced ten years before, was none the less common after the break-ing out of war. "Military treats," even then too much the fashion, had become more and more in vogue. Those hard-headed old fighters were also hard drinkers, and we may be sure that every company that marched out from Windham Green had its parting *drams* as well as prayers. Prisoners were allowed the liberty of the yard and certain public resorts, and no taverns were more popular than those kept by Mistress Warner and the Widow Carey. This good widow must have looked upon the English sailors with especial favor and sympathy, for to her was bequeathed the work of art which had occupied their leisure. The comical Bacchus, with his dimpled cheeks and luscious fruits, bestriding a wine cask, was straightway hoisted above the tavern for a sign and figure-head, to the intense admiration and delight of all beholders. Returning soldiers hailed his jolly figure with cheers and shouts of laughter, and were only too ready to offer up libations at his shrine, and the tavern of the sympathetic widow received a far greater share of public patronage.

This *escapade* excited much comment and led Windham citizens to consider "their situation with regard to a sheriff." Colonel Fitch had still been allowed to retain this office in the hope that he might experience a change of sentiment, but the remonstrance of friends, the forbearance of opponents, and the promise of high position in the patriot army, had failed to overcome his scruples. Even now his fellow-townsmen were loth to proceed against him, but citizens of other towns unbiased by personal affection took the matter in hand, and represented to the General Assembly that this office of High Sheriff was "in their opinion very badly supplied (by reasons we apprehend well-known to your Honors), and hoped that the place might be filled with a man whose principles are agreeable to the public, and at no time suspected by the candid ; would recommend Captain Jabez Huntington, who had long served with good acceptance. Experience, ability and good conduct speak in his favor, as well as the remotest consideration of his being the son of an excellent sheriff of this county, whose service was eminently acceptable. A grateful remembrance of the deceased prompt our regard to the only surviving son, as well as the good of the County, and the public in general." This suggestion was quickly carried out, and the sheriffship transferred from the faint-hearted loyalist to one whose heart and energies were devoted to the popular cause, and who could thus administer this important office with far more zeal and efficiency. Nathaniel Hebard of Windham now served as jailor, guarding and providing the numerous prisoners with great care and watchfulness.

The general engagement so justly dreaded by the patriots was evaded by the wise policy of Washington, and the Windham County militia were allowed to return to their homes, but were soon called to further action. A great fleet of men-of-war and transports was hovering about the Sound, and after greatly alarming New London, pushed on to Narraganset Bay, and threatened Newport and Providence. The eastern regiments previously summoned to New London, were now ordered to march with all speed to Rhode Island. Colonel Elderkin and Lieut.-Colonel Storrs being occupied with other public duties, the command of the Fifth Regiment was given to Major Thomas Brown. Major Samuel McClellan led the Eleventh, and the troops of horse hurried on under Major Backus. Ere these arrived Rhode Island was seized and fortified by a strong body of British troops, supported by the naval armament, and fears were entertained of their invasion upon other parts of New England. Eliphalet Dyer and Nathaniel Wales were appointed a committee with other gentlemen from Connecticut, to meet committees from the other New England states, in Providence, December 23, to consult upon their mutual and immediate defence and safety, and other important matters. It was recommended that Connecticut should send as its quota of the army proposed for the defence of Providence against the army then in possession of New port, 1092 troops. Captain Ebenezer Mosely of Windham Village, was chosen by Governor Trumbull to enlist this body of men from Windham and New London counties. Many other Windham soldiers re-enlisted during this autumn for continental service in various battalions and regiments. During this autumn of 1776, the militia of Connecticut was organized in six brigades—David Wooster, major-general ; Hon. Jabez Huntington, second major-general. The Windham County regiments were included in the fifth brigade, Eliphalet Dyer, general. William Danielson, Killingly, was now appointed colonel of the Eleventh Regiment in place of Col. Williams, whose failing health compelled him to relinquish service; Samuel McClellan, lieutenant-colonel. Company 1, Daniel Lyon, captain; Benjamin Ruggles, lieutenant ; Nathaniel Brown, ensign. Company 2, Caleb Clark, captain ; John Wells, lieutenant ; Stephen Griggs, ensign. Company 3, Amos Paine, captain ; Thomas Baker, lieutenant ; William Lyon, ensign. Company 4, Joseph Cady, captain; Jonathan Cady, lieutenant ; Elisha Lawrence, ensign. Company 5, Ephraim Warren, captain ; Daniel Waters, lieutenant. Company 6, Stephen Tucker, lieutenant ; Phinehas Walker, ensign. Company 7, Paine Converse, lieutenant. Company 8, Zebulon Ingalls, captain ; William Osgood, lieutenant ; Robert Sharpe, ensign. Company 9, John Green, captain ; Obadiah Clough, lieutenant ; Daniel Larned, ensign. Company 10, Jonathan Morris, lieutenant ; Richard Peabody, ensign. Company 11, Samuel Chandler, captain ; John Holbrook, lieutenant ; John Whitmore, ensign. No special changes were made in the other regiments. Colonel Elderkin and Lieut.-Colonel Storrs retained their positions. John Douglas of Plainfield, was appointed general of the fifth brigade in place of Colonel Dyer, who declined the appointment.

Among her other engrossments Windham interested herself this autumn in fitting out in Norwich, the schooner *Oliver Cromwell*, for privateer service. Phinehas Cary, Solomon Lord, Eleazer Welsh, Eleazer Spofford, Lemuel Stoddard, Hezekiah Abbe, Arad Simmons, all of Windham, and Thomas Holbrook of Lebanon, formed its crew; its captain was William Coit of Norwich. Dr. Samuel Lee of Windham, was appointed its surgeon, and his two students second and third mates under him at £3 per month each. Dr. Albigence Waldo succeeded Dr. Lee as chief surgeon in a few months. Dr. Lee with Doctors John Clark, Elisha Lord and James Cogswell, and other physicians from different parts of the State, were made a committee for examining all persons in the State that offered to serve in the army.

The spring of 1777 found Windham County preparing for further action. Its citizens for two years had been so engrossed in carrying on the war that their own internal affairs had received but little attention, and even the ordinary town meetings had been greatly neglected, but the prospect of a long continuance of the war and the heavy demands upon their resources called for public deliberation and action. Their share of soldiers were to be raised, bounties given, families cared for. Many important questions were under discussion. The depreciation of currency, and the increased price of the necessaries of life, the scarcity of breadstuffs and salt, caused much anxiety and alarm. The General Assembly in December, attempted to meet these evils by regulating the price of labor and provision, instructing the selectmen of the towns to distribute salt, and forbidding the distillation of liquor from wheat, rye or Indian corn. The change in their political status, the severance of the tie that bound Connecticut to the Mother Country and her assumption of authority as a free and independent State, necessitated some action and endorsement from the several towns, and it became necessary again to assemble in town meetings, provide for these various public matters, and take the oath of allegiance to the State. Pomfret voted to use her utmost endeavor to support the credit of the continental currency. Committees were chosen to procure clothing for the soldiers:—Joshua Sabin, John Jeffards, Lemuel Grosvenor for the first society; Dr. Baker, Capt. Daniel Tyler and Samuel Scarborough for Brooklyn; Daniel Trowbridge, William Osgood and Stephen Utley for Abington; John Grosvenor, Esq., Capt. Amasa Sessions and Capt. Ebenezer Holbrook were also chosen to meet committees from other towns in the county to consult such measures as should appear most salutary for the common good, and most conducive to stop the growing evil of the depreciation of our currency.

Windham, March 24, 1777, voted, "That the inhabitants of this town will with one consent join with, and support to the utmost of their power in carrying into execution the laws made for regulating and affixing the prices of certain articles. 2. That a committee be appointed and directed to engage in behalf of the town to provide necessaries for the families of soldiers belonging to this town who shall go into any of the continental armies." Plainfield voted, "That the families of those who shall enlist into the continental service for three years, or during the war, shall be supplied with the common necessaries of life at the price stated by the General Assembly. 2. To give to effective men $30 above the bounty affixed by the state. Canterbury chose a committee to provide for the families of soldiers and use their endeavors to encourage men to enlist." Killingly agreed April 14, that in case a hundred and nineteen able-bodied men shall enlist themselves into the continental army within ten days from this time for the term of three years or during the present war for the town of Killingly, for their further encouragement shall be entitled to and paid by the town aforesaid, the sum of six pounds each man for every six months they shall continue in said service—but shrewdly provided, that if the General Assembly of the State should make any additional grant to those soldiers, it should be considered as a part of the extraordinary encouragement promised by the town. On the same day she further voted :—

" That this town do freely comply with the acts of the General Assembly passed in December last, stating the prices of the necessaries of life, and do resolve with cheerfulness to exert our best endeavors within our sphere to support the honor of that good and salutary law, and will hold such as willingly violate the same in any point as designing, mischievous enemies to this and the rest of the Independent States of America, and will refrain from all commercial commerce with them until they shall give satisfaction to the public for every offence they shall commit against the law, and this town do hereby recommend it to all informing officers as they value their oath or the good of their country strictly to enquire into and make due presentment of all breaches of said act, and it is farther recommended to all friends of mankind without reserve to give evidence of any breach of said law to such informing officer."

Voluntown voted to provide for the families of soldiers, and abate the colony and town taxes of non-commissioned officers and soldiers. Laws respecting engrossers and monopolizers to be strictly enforced. The selectmen of the several towns were directed to apportion and distribute the salt to each district. Killingly with great particularity, ordered, that the salt that belongs to the town shall be divided according to the number in each family, and each family that buys the salt shall pay four shillings per bushel ; also, that the selectmen divide the above salt to each parish according to the number of families, and the selectmen in each parish to deliver the salt in each parish to the families. Woodstock not only provided for her soldiers and complied with the Assembly's recommendation, but again consented to part with her beloved pastor, and having found voice with the other towns thus formally expressed herself:—

"*Feb.* 20, 1777. Whereas all public bodies of men as well as individuals belonging to the United States of America, at such a time as this, when their sacred as well as civil rights are in danger of being subverted by unnatural, brutal, merciless and unreasonable enemies; ought from principles of religion and virtue, and from a sacred regard to the good of their country and posterity, to manifest the most vigorous and persevering exertions to prevent so fatal a calamity, and to deny themselves every [indulgence] that stands in competition with the public good;—We, an Ecclesiastic Body, First church of Christ in Woodstock, have once and again given our consent that our Reverend pastor should absent himself from this church, and engage in the public service, and assure him that we shall consider his pastoral relation to us by no means violated by his absence, and wish him God speed."

The Windham County Association of Ministers, now felt it their duty to express their views, and offer rebuke and counsel "Considering the peculiar circumstances of our land during the present calamities of war, wherewith the holy and righteous God is pleased to exercise us; the decline of religion and prevalence of iniquity; think it our duty to stir up ourselves and the people of our charge to additional attention to our duties, and propose to General Association to recommend professors of religion to renew their covenant with God that family religion and order might be maintained." A committee was appointed to prepare a suitable address which was published, and a thousand copies distributed among the twenty parishes of Windham County.

Encouraged and strengthened by these manifestations of public sentiment, Windham County entered upon the campaign of 1777 with renewed spirit and confidence, filling her quotas for home and Continental service with her usual readiness. Veterans whose times had expired usually reënlisted. Ebenezer Gray was now Major in Colonel Douglas's regiment. Dana and Keyes were recommissioned as captains, probably in Durkee's regiment. John Ripley of Windham was appointed major of four companies under Captains Ebenezer Mosely, Kinne, Leffingwell and Kingsbury, stationed at Rhode Island, and as when their term of enlistment had expired there was "a great appearance of British ships and troops off New London," companies from the Eleventh and Twenty-first regiments were immediately accoutred and marched to Providence under command of Major Ripley, although "the more eastern regiments in the State had been frequently called into service." Dr. Waldo was now appointed surgeon in Huntington's regiment; Dr. David Holmes in Chandler's regiment, Dr. Thomas Gray of Windham, surgeon's mate in Durkee's regiment. The Second company of the Fourth regiment of Light Horse were reorganized, Perley Howe of Killingly, captain; Asaph Wilder, lieutenant; Ste-

23

178   HISTORY OF WINDHAM COUNTY.

phen Tucker, cornet; Davis Flint, quartermaster. Spirited gentlemen in Brooklyn having liberally agreed to furnish " three or four light constructed field-pieces and equip them fit for service," Daniel Tyler, Jr., and thirty-five petitioners obtained leave to form an independent matross company, subject only to be commanded by the commander in-chief or either of the major or brigadier generals of the State of Connecticut. Ammunition was now more plentiful. In the three months preceding February, 1777, 42,666 pounds of saltpetre made in Windham County were received at the Willimantic powder-mill. Private individuals in every town were engaged in this manufacture. Abel Clark of Pomfret, reports 364 pounds made at his works, "out of home material, pure, clear and dry;" the Elderkin brothers furnished about 900 pounds; Thomas Stedman, 381; Andrew Durkee, 308; while others send less than twenty pounds. The selectmen meanwhile report 881 pounds in scale and clock weights, shot and bar lead, delivered at the powder-mill. As in preceding years every possible effort was made to raise and equip recruits, and maintain the patriot cause, and yet again they were doomed to disappointment and calamity. Captain Elderkin's company suffered severely at Ticonderoga, and after helping to maintain that fortress for many months, rejoicing even over raw pork in their extremity of hunger, were forced to an ignominious retreat before Burgoyne's advancing army. Putnam's division at Peekskill, weakened by sending its best men to the aid of Gates and Washington, was humiliated by the irruption of Sir Henry Clinton, the seizure of important forts, and great destruction of property, and Washington, after a laborious and painful campaign, chequered by alternate success and defeat, was compelled to leave Philadelphia in the hands of the British, and yield those forts upon the Delaware which had been so valiantly manned and defended. A regiment of Windham County militia under Colonel Samuel McClellan, fitted out in September to serve in the northern department, was detailed instead upon an expedition for the recovery of Newport under General Spencer, which for various reasons proved a complete failure. And while thus called to defeat and disaster, it so chanced that but few of the Windham soldiers participated in the victory of Saratoga,—a part of a regiment drafted from Peekskill, and straggling volunteers* in Lattimer's militia.

With these failures and disasters were bereavements that caused peculiar sorrow. Captain Stephen Brown of Pomfret, a most brave and faithful officer, who had succeeded Knowlton in immediate com-

* Among these volunteers was Ephraim Squier of Ashford, whose regiment lost some eight or nine killed, and thirty wounded, and who had the pleasure of seeing " the prisoners march by towards Head-Quarters, a very agreeable sight."

mand, was killed instantly by a shot from a ship while defending Fort Mifflin, with unparalleled bravery. Among the slain at Saratoga was Captain Daniel Clark of Plainfield, "who departed this life in the field of battle at Stillwater, September 19, 1777, leaving a distressed widow and six orphaned children to bemoan his unhappy fate, and their own most gloomy prospects." Plainfield mourned also the death of her faithful minister, Rev. John Fuller, chaplain in the army, and Woodstock's beloved Leonard passed beyond human judgment. His brilliant career closed in great darkness and sorrow. Overstaying a furlough in consequence of the dangerous sickness of one of his children, he was met on his journey back to camp by the tidings that he had been censured and superseded. Keenly sensitive to public opinion, he felt unable to endure the disgrace, and in the first shock of mortification took his life with his own hand. Putnam's affectionate heart was deeply moved by this distressing calamity. Other personal afflictions were weighing heavily upon him. His step-son, Septimus Gardiner, a young man of great promise, who had served as his aid, died during this autumn, and was soon followed by Mrs. Putnam. These losses brought much sorrow and mourning to Windham County. Mrs. Putnam, so long known and beloved, was greatly lamented by her old friends in Pomfret, their grief being heightened by the accompanying report that she "had died in prison in the enemy's hands." Colonel William Douglas died during this year of disease produced by exposure on the battle-field ; Commissary Joseph Trumbull, and Dr. David Holmes of Woodstock, were compelled by ill health to retire from active service. The closing misfortune of the year was the blowing up of the Willimantic powdermill, December 13, with the loss of one life, valuable machinery and material, mournfully chronicled by patriot journals, "amongst other obstacles to impede our success."

Public affairs looked more and more discouraging and gloomy. The winter of 1777–78 was one of great hardship and suffering, abroad and at home, in the camp and by the fireside. The incessant drain was depleting the resources of the towns. The farms were suffering for the lack of suitable tillage, and production had lessened. There was scarcity of grain, meat, salt and clothing. Currency was rapidly depreciating in value, and financial affairs becoming hopelessly entangled. Terrible stories came to Windham County homes, of the sickness and destitution of sons and brethren at Valley Forge—soldiers even freezing to death in their tents—and stories of sickness, death and even destitution went back in return. Mothers asked tearfully how they should carry their little ones through the winter, and "God answered them by taking them to himself." The officers with their slender pay, constantly diminishing in value, were even more embarrassed than the soldiers, whose families were cared for by the selectmen of the towns, and many were forced to resign to keep their families from starvation.

Yet still, in spite of disaster and discouragement, the towns went bravely on, upholding the Government and providing food and clothing for the soldiers—not only meeting their quotas, but sending donations and contributions. The Articles of Confederation recommended by Congress were received, discussed and formally adopted. Pomfret instructed her representatives to use their endeavors that the Articles of Confederation be come into and established. Windham "accords to the same in every article and case," but insists "that the Delegates to the Continental Congress should be chosen by the freemen of the State and not by the Assembly." Canterbury expressed her views with great fullness. At a town-meeting January 12, 1778, Mr. John Felch, moderator, it was voted :—

"That we have carefully examined the Articles of Confederation agreed on by Congress, and think them well calculated for the proposed design, and cannot be altered with any emendation better to accommodate us in this State, and therefore voted to accept and approve them, and that the representatives of the town be instructed to give their vote for them in General Assembly; also, to procure an alteration in the mode of taxation; also, to have the delegation in Congress chosen in the same manner as for Governor; also, to have the debates in the Assembly as public as may be, and that the yeas and nays in every important measure be noted in the Journal, and published, that the towns may have them; also, to procure an act to be passed to punish *profane swearing and cursing* by disability to sustain any office or place of trust and profit in any civil department, at least for the second offence."

The scarcity of salt was a very serious grievance, and "threatened at times to disturb the public peace and safety of the State." A permission had been given to Ebenezer Griffin, Jr., of Canada Parish, the preceding summer, to transport cattle, butter and cheese to Massachusetts or Providence, to purchase salt and other West India goods. A number of the citizens of Pomfret associated in the autumn of 1777, "for the purpose of chartering or purchasing a good sea-vessel, and loading the same to send immediately to the West Indies for salt and other necessaries." Twenty-four gentlemen* contributed about seventy pounds for this object, and agreed to meet at Major Ripley's in Windham, October 15, to make choice of captain and supercargo, and contrive such measures as were needful to accommodate and accomplish the voyage. The "brig *Litchfield*, 130 tons burthen," was proposed and examined, but whether the project was carried through is extremely doubtful, as measures were taken from time to time to pro-

* Ebenezer Stoddard, Ebenezer Holbrook, John and Samuel Dresser, William Osgood, Jr., Appleton and Zach. Osgood, Seth Stowell, Calvin Holbrook, Josiah Chandler, Jr., John, Daniel, James and Caleb Trowbridge, Amasa Sessions, Jr., Joseph Ingalls, Edward and Benjamin Ruggles, John and Isaac Williams, Joseph Whitney, Elijah Dana, Israel Putnam, Jr.

cure this vital necessity from other quarters. Plainfield ordered thirty-six bushels carted from Boston, Messrs. Dunlap and Pierce to distribute the same according to polls. Joseph Torrey of Killingly, was allowed to exchange six firkins of butter for salt, while limited supplies were secured with much labor and difficulty by home manufacture.

Prompt and liberal provision was made by all the towns in the spring of 1778, for the raising of their respective quotas. Thirty-seven men were demanded from Windham. She offered to each man who would enlist for a year's service, six pounds bounty, in addition to the same sum paid by the State; twelve pounds at the end of the year, and his wages of forty shillings a month, all in lawful money. A rate of sixpence on all the polls and ratable estates, to be paid in beef, pork, flour, &c., was levied to meet this outlay. Similar offers from other towns met with ready acceptance. Favorable news from France revived public cheerfulness and courage. Recognition, alliance and aid were offered to the struggling States. Soldiers went out again with hopeful hearts and patriots labored on at home, hoping that brighter days were at hand; but just as the French fleet was nearing the American coast came rumors more appalling than anything yet heard during the war — rumors of Indian descent and massacre in Wyoming's lovely valley. These terrible rumors were but too literally confirmed. Robert Durkee, Robert Jameson, Anderson Dana, George Dorrance, James Bidlack, Thomas and Stephen Fuller, Stephen Whiton, John Abbot, Samuel Ransom, Elisha Williams, Timothy Pierce, John Perkins, and many other honored sons of Connecticut and Windham County, had been most barbarously tortured and butchered, their homes burned, their farms ravaged, their families taken prisoners, or driven out naked and starving into the wilderness. Aged fathers and mothers in Windham County waited in harrowing suspense to hear from their lost children, and after many anxious days received these stricken families, as one by one they found their way to the old hearthstone. Mrs. John Abbot and Mrs. Thomas Fuller, each with nine children, and utterly destitute, begged their way back as best they could to their Windham homes. Mrs. Stephen Fuller came on horseback with her little Polly. Mrs. Anderson Dana, with her widowed daughter, Mrs. Whiton, the bride of a few weeks, and six younger children, toiled back to Ashford, having first the presence of mind to save and bring with her most valuable public and personal papers belonging to her husband. Mrs. Elisha Williams left on that bloody battle-field her husband, two promising sons, and a daughter's husband, and with her five surviving children sought refuge at her father's house in Canterbury. And after many months had passed, and all hope of seeing them again had perished, Mrs. Esther Minor Yorke, with twelve children, barefoot and starving, reached her old home in

Voluntown, having with great difficulty escaped from their Indian captors and accomplished the perilous journey, the baby dying on the way from cold and exposure. Another hunted fugitive arriving at about the same date, was Rufus Baldwin, an emigrant to Newport, New York, who had killed an Indian, and was obliged to flee for his life, and traveled through the wilderness to Canterbury "with only a chunk of raw salt pork in his pocket."

Meantime another calamity had befallen the patriots. Their hope of aid from France had proved illusive. The fleet, so warmly greeted, had only brought them fresh disappointment. Another effort had been made to regain possession of Newport. A large force under General Sullivan was to coöperate with the French fleet. Again Windham County militia and troops of horse hurried down to Rhode Island. Young Joseph Joslin, one of three brothers sent from Thompson, gives a graphic picture of his share in the campaign :—

"*August* 6. Did march to town and barrack in the Court House. 7. As soon as light, got up and see the Continentals march for Tivertown; got some breakfast, and then I went to the New Light meeting-house and got a canteen, and about 12 we set out for Tivertown, marched through Pawtuxet into Sekonk or Rehoboth, and did lie in the meadow on the side of a fence. 8. Mustered about 2 or 3 o'clock and marched into Swanzea, and then over States Ferry into Freetown, and then over Fall River to Tiverton, and I encamped by side of a hay stack. 9. Had bowl of chocolate and went to Parade, and fixed our guns for business; then rode over the ferry and landed upon Rhode Island; formed and marched up to the fort, and lay down in the great chamber. 10. French did engage the English batteries with their ships, and cannonaded very smart for three hours, and brothers Jesse and John went to the lines scouting at night. I went upon guard to the bridge, and did sleep in the road. 11. Jesse and John fixed a little wall to break the wind, and we have nothing to eat hardly. 12. Knocked about and built us a stone house and covered it with hay, and it rained very hard, and the house leaked and we thought we could not stand it, went about a mile and got wet to the skin, and found a hay stack, and almost chilled to death we rolled off some hay and did lie by the stack, and were almost dead in the morning. 13. Crept out, and came to stone house; found John alive, and after a while I got dry, and had a boil on my eye, and did feel very poorly. Our folks fixed up all our barracks, and got a little green corn to eat."

This terrible storm was the chief cause of the failure of the enterprise. The fleet was scattered and disabled, and the land force greatly worn down and dispirited. Several soldiers died that night, and many were made ill. Provision and ammunition were greatly damaged. Governor Trumbull had already made requisition upon Ebenezer Devotion of Scotland Parish for a hundred barrels of musket powder, and all the cartridges in his hands, to be forwarded with all speed to General Greene at Providence—needful teams to be impressed if necessary—and now sends swift express, stating that the storm had wet most of the cartridges in General Sullivan's army, and begs him to hurry on stores with the utmost dispatch, as powder sufficient for supply was not to be had in Providence. In face of this great disaster, Sullivan continued his operations. Joslin reports:—

"*Aug.* 14. Got up and paraded and marched to the water and fired by platoons. 15. Not well, nor John either, and all the brigades marched to the lines and we got our packs brought down and encamped in a huckleberry plain, and I had a clean shirt and trousers come and felt very poorly; blind with one eye, and not any tents nor ha'n't had but the heavens to cover us. Huckleberries very thick. We built a house of bushes. John and I drawn out to entrench and made a fort and almost finished it. 17. Very poorly; ate nothing. 18. Still very poorly. The enemy keep a constant firing at our men while they are building the fort. John and I go upon guard. Two or three wounded to-day. Many guns broke, some the breeches off, some the barrels struck asunder. 19. A little firing on both sides. 20. They fire a little; are all the time entrenching and building forts. I washed my knapsack and feel some better. 21. Set out upon fatigue down the lines, had to dig in plain sight of the enemy. The ground was but just broke and we got to work when they began to fire upon us very fast, but we received no damage. I got home alive to my tent. 22d. One man killed, one wounded. 23d. Enemy firing hot shells and we begun the breastwork for the great mortar. Two of our men were taken. Jesse, John and I worked till noon and placed the great mortar. 24. Constant firing. 25. All paraded and went to headquarters; went three miles for rum. A great gun ball took a board off the store and struck here and there. 26. Paraded; six or seven men killed; an eighteen-pounder split all to pieces and a brass mortar. Aug. 27. Paraded and took our cooking utensils and went to headquarters and delivered them up, and marched through Portsmouth to Bristol Ferry and went on board a vessel to go to Providence. There was but little wind and that was wrong, and at two the men came jumping down into the hold and said we were all prisoners, for there was an English privateer just by, but it proved to be one of our own, and we got along slowly and beat along almost to Conanicut Point and cast anchor and lay till light and then struck for Warwick Rock and landed and came along . . . and got some victuals and I feel very poorly. Camp Middletown, Aug. 28. Hear that they had a smart fight."

Deserted by the French fleet, and alarmed by rumors of large accession to the forces of the enemy, Sullivan was compelled to abandon his enterprise, and instead of the brilliant victory so confidently anticipated the patriots could only rejoice that the army had safely retreated. Several Windham County soldiers were slain or wounded in the "smart fight" with the pursuing British. Theodore, son of Deacon Lusher Gay, of Thompson Point, a most promising and engaging young man of nineteen years, died of sickness at Tiverton.

IV.

DISCOURAGEMENTS. ENDURANCE. HOME AFFAIRS.
BRIGHTENING PROSPECTS. VICTORY.

WITH such reiterated defeat, disaster and disappointment the war dragged on. The succeeding year brought no improvement. Little was attempted or accomplished. Financial embarrassment, internal dissension and insufficient supplies, compelled inaction. Never were affairs more gloomy and discouraging. The best that could be said was that the army was not annihilated, that the States and

General Government still maintained their integrity, that after all the efforts and expenditures of Great Britain, rebellion was not crushed out, the Colonies were not subdued. The people all over the land were weary, depressed and discouraged. Their property was becoming worthless, the comforts and even necessaries of life almost unattainable. Thousands of their brethren had been sent out to die in camp, prison and battle, and to little apparent purpose. And there were things harder to bear than discomforts, loss of property and even friends. There was demoralization, degeneration and defection. Young men came back wrecked in health and character, dissolute in habit and infidel in principle. Even Windham County had its ARNOLD. Poor Colonel Fitch, with all his chivalrous devotion to the royal cause, could never openly take ground against his countrymen; but Pomfret's dashing attorney was less scrupulous. Nathan Frink, a shrewd and successful lawyer, who had gained an extensive legal practice and wide reputation, seeing no hope for success on the patriot side, left home and friends and offered himself and his services to the British commander in New York! His aged father most piteously bemoaned "that he had lost his son, lost his education, lost everything in him that was dear to him," and soon went down into the grave mourning. His sister, the wife of Schuyler Putnam, a large circle of family connections, and all the earnest patriots of Pomfret and its vicinity, were overwhelmed with grief, shame and resentment at this " mournful defection."

And even among those who claimed to be patriots there were things that caused sorrow and discouragement. There were murmurings, and bitter wranglings, and selfish speculation and extortion. Men kept back their goods for a price, though they knew their soldiers were starving and naked. The brief sessions of the County Court were chiefly occupied with hearing complaints against various people for selling cattle and swine at foreign markets and for unauthorized prices, and for other breaches of wholesome laws made to encourage fair dealing and restrain and punish sharpers and oppressors. Ebenezer Gray, now Lieutenant-Colonel, thus writes of the sufferings of the soldiers :—

"CAMP, Jan. 7, 1779.

Dear Brother—I wrote several times to my father and Dr. Elderkin to procure me some butter and cheese, and if they should not do it pray procure me some, and forward by the first State or Continental teams that come to the army, for I am in great need of them as there is nothing to be bought here and our allowance very short, only fourteen ounces of meat for seven days, or three gills of rice and three-fourths of a pound of corn bread of buckwheat and corn not sifted, and sometimes neither. I am credibly informed that some officers have been so hard pressed by hunger as to kill and eat *their dogs*. We certainly fare very hard. My own hunger and the cries of a distressed regiment for victuals as well as for clothes gives me sensible pain, and in such a manner as I never felt before. I hope I shall be able to get well through it. I have no news only our present difficulties for want of supplies. The patience and submission of our men under such difficulties and trying scenes are incredible. The avarice of the people, which depreciates the currency, is, I believe, the grand source of our present troubles. Your affectionate brother."

Doctor Waldo of Pomfret, returning home during this winter upon a furlough, "found his family on the point of famishing with mere want of food and every other necessary." Money received from sale of a small possession and such wages as had been paid him, reduced to a trifle in value, were now wholly gone, and he was compelled by sheer necessity to resign his place as surgeon to protect them "from the insolence of pressing want."

Yet in the face of all these difficulties and discouragements, Windham County continued steadfast, trusting in the justice of the patriot cause and in that Providence which had so wonderfully led and sustained the people of America. The high position assumed by her at the breaking out of the Revolution was steadily maintained. Those vehement and somewhat over-confident "resolutions" had been followed by abundant performance. In darkest days she stood firm and unwavering, striving with unceasing diligence to strengthen the hands of government and carry forward the war. Though in the increasing poverty and scarceness these demands were very burthensome, the several towns never failed to meet them. Year after year they taxed themselves heavily to pay bounties, furnish clothing, and provide for the families of the soldiers. Those sturdy fathers and patriots who had taken so bold a stand in the beginning of the great struggle carried the towns onward. Solid as their own granite rocks they stood in unbroken phalanx, manfully bearing the heavy financial burden, and faithfully fulfilling social and political obligations. Ebenezer Smith of Woodstock, called to attend a special session of the General Assembly in winter when the roads were snow-blocked, walked the whole distance to Hartford on snow-shoes rather than fail of attendance, and there were scores of men in that and other towns equally ready to perform any patriotic service in the same self-sacrificing and conscientious spirit— men who had pledged their lives, their fortunes and their sacred honor to the patriot cause, who sent their sons to the front and went themselves in any extremity, who held up the hands of Trumbull, and made Connecticut a tower of strength throughout the war. Washington never called in vain upon "Brother Jonathan," and Trumbull was sure of instant response from his own County. Again and again those patriot fathers stepped into the breach and led the people onward ; went forth themselves into the field or furnished vital aid to those engaged in battle. General Douglas of Plainfield, Colonels Williams, Danielson and Johnson, though now advanced in years, led the militia many times on alarm of danger, and Major Backus time after

24

time hurried his troops of horse to the relief of New London and Rhode Island. McClellan not only served almost continuously in the field, but paid his regiment out of his own pocket when the public treasury was empty. General Douglas, Colonel Johnson, Major Ripley, Commissary Waldo, and, indeed, very many of those leading men who had money at command, advanced it repeatedly to pay out bounties or fit off expeditions.

Col. Dyer, when not representing Connecticut in Congress, devoted his time and energies to deliberations with the Council and Committee of Safety. Elderkin and Wales maintained their place on this Committee. Samuel Gray served as assistant-commissary to Col. Joseph Trumbull, and after his decease was appointed by Congress, deputy commissary-general of the Eastern Department, comprising New England and New York, a most laborious and responsible office. Very many men were employed by him in Windham County, securing and forwarding for the use of the suffering army all provisions that could possibly be spared. Elderkin and Gray repaired their powder-mill and were able to send out fresh supplies of ammunition, under the supervision of their efficient and ingenious superintendent, Henry De Witt; and Hezekiah Huntington continued to repair and manufacture arms at his State Armory at Willimantic, while others with equal diligence and efficiency labored to fulfill varying demands. Town acts and votes were still unanimous. No attempt was made to evade military or civil requisitions. The leaders kept their post and the people faithfully upheld them. That spirit of detraction and suspicion which wrought such mischief within the patriot ranks was denounced and held in abeyance. Judge Ebenezer Devotion of Scotland thus writes to Dr. Waldo:—

"We have many loud declaimers against the times, the very worst that ever were known; the Americans have in three years lost all their virtue, their honor, their patriotism; but what is the foundation of this outcry? The principal thing is the depreciation of our currency, by which so many worthy men have suffered, which has highly disgusted and soured them. They cry out, Public virtue is at an end. Congress hath promised and not performed. I confess I am unable to see wherein Congress has been to blame, except that it did not *tax more* and *higher*. This might have lessened but not prevented the difficulty and might have excited in the minds of the people a most fatal uneasiness. Congress has been obliged, as there was no other possible way to carry on the war, to emit vast sums. It is a certain known maxim that the prices of commodities will be proportionate to the plenty or scarcity of cash, taking into due consideration the quantity of and demand for such commodities. It is, I believe, an undoubted fact, that the quantity of necessaries of life usually produced in this country have since the war diminished, while for obvious reasons the demand has greatly increased. These two causes, co-operating with the first, viz.: the amazing superabundant quantity of money, have produced the effect they never failed to produce in one instance since the siege of Samaria. The honest merchant and farmer have acted on the same principle as ever before—in open market to sell their merchandize or produce at as high a price as the purchaser was willing to give. Rogues and knaves we have now as before, but God forbid that the State should take its complexion from them. It is on this principle and not on the total decay of virtue and public spirit, I have to account for the depreciation of currency. A people never lost their virtue in a day."

Colonel Dyer was particularly sensitive and scrupulous with regard to the fulfillment of every pledge and promise, and thus writes Governor Trumbull in reference to the Burgoyne contract which some thought of evading:—

"It concerns us inviolably to keep our faith and maintain our honor, pledged for the punctual fulfillment on our part of all treaties, contracts or conventions, made even with our enemies; as we would not offend Heaven by our perfidy, nor forfeit our honor and reputation in the eyes of this or the European world, which are and will be most attentively watchful over every part of our public conduct, and will fix their opinion and form their estimation of these American States on no part more than that which concerns our public faith and honor. In the beginning of this infant Empire the greater care is to be taken to establish a fair and reputable character which if once lost is hardly to be regained."

Public calls found Windham town ever ready for speech or action. An address from Congress, May 26, 1779, requesting "the immediate, strenuous and united effort of all friends to the United States of America for preventing the mischiefs that have arisen from the depreciation of their currency," was met by a prompt assemblage of the inhabitants of this town who unanimously voted to unite with other towns of the State in all proper Constitutional measures. The published report of the proceedings of the meeting failing to incite other towns to action, the Committee of Correspondence, viz.: Eliphalet Dyer, Nathaniel Wales, Jr., Samuel Kingsbury, Ebenezer Mosely and Hezekiah Bissell, fearing that by a long delay in so important a crisis the whole should prove abortive, issued a circular, urging the "vast importance of supporting our public and national faith, especially in time of war," and the necessity of having the whole State agreed in any plan proper to be pursued. But as no method had been proposed for calling a State meeting, a meeting of the several towns in Windham County was deemed "expedient and necessary to give spring to the whole," and though they did not by any means claim a right to dictate, yet since one must needs be first in a matter of this kind they therefore requested the several towns in the County by their committees or selectmen to meet "at the Court house in Windham on the first Monday of September to take the matters aforesaid into their consideration and agree on such measures as they may judge necessary to accomplish the end designed."

With such unfailing spirit, resolution and persistence Windham carried on the war. The substratum of strength underlying the early effervescence was more and more apparent as the years went on. All were ready to do their part and share in the sufferings and sacrifices.

Men went out to battle and council and provided for public demands, and women labored as efficiently in their own especial fields of usefulness. The burdens and distresses of the war fell very heavily upon these women. They sent out husbands, brothers, sons, and labored to fill their places. Farm work was added to their ordinary domestic duties. They had to take care of their *stock* as well as their children, to plant and reap as well as spin and weave, to cure herbs for their own tea, and manufacture their molasses out of corn-stalks. These various demands stimulated ingenuity so that whatever the call they were ready to meet it. Mrs. Philemon Adams of Brooklyn, left by her husband ere their house was finished, laid the floor herself and made it ready for the occupation of her family. Somebody in Windham Village had the enterprise to begin to build a house during this period, but when the timbers were ready there was not a man to help about the raising. The spirited and capable women of the district came to the rescue, and under the lead of an old lame carpenter set up the frame of a large two story dwelling in so satisfactory and workman-like a manner that after more than a hundred years it stands as a memorial of their achievement. Many marvelous feats of handiwork were accomplished. A good lady in Thompson hears of a chance to send a package to her husband and in one day and night knits a pair of long woolen stockings. Shubael Dimmock of Mansfield comes home in rags for a brief furlough in midwinter. There was no cloth in the house, but there was a web of warp drawn into the loom and an old black sheep nibbling round the dooryard. Instantly the sheep was caught, sheared, and bundled down cellar in a blanket, and in forty-eight hours its black fleece was transmuted into a golden suit of clothes wending its way to the army. Mother, sisters, and neighbors, working with skill and dexterity, had woven the wool into cloth, cut and made the garments. Children as they grew up caught the pervading spirit. Lads hurried off to camp or worked like men at home; young girls devoted all their overflowing energies to useful labors. The only daughter of Captain James Stedman, of Canada Parish, often worked in the fields with the hired woman, while her father and workmen were on militia service, and before she had completed her eleventh year had achieved by the sole labor of her own hands—carding, spinning and weaving—a *web* of *tow cloth* which she took down herself on horseback to Windham Green and exchanged for six silver teaspoons, to be treasured as priceless heirlooms by appreciative descendants. And while thus burthened with business and family cares they were ready for any patriotic and neighborhood service. Trumbull, with his neighbor, Jonathan J. Hazard of Rhode Island, "stumped" New London and Washington Counties in the hard winter of 1777-78, urging all the women "to com-

mence making yarn and knitting stockings for the suffering army"—
but a single telegraphic dispatch from headquarters was enough to elec-
trify the knitting needles of Windham County. Thousands of cartridges
were made by Plainfield women to keep up the supply of military
stores at their depot. Sick and weary soldiers passing along the public
highways were nursed and tended. A widow in Thompson, who had
spared her only grown-up son to the service, found time with all her
other labors to brew every day in summer a barrel of beer to stand by
her door step for the especial refreshment of these way-worn soldiers.

With such support and sympathy from town and fireside the soldiers
sent out by Windham County could hardly fail to do her honor. Their
early reputation for courage and good conduct was abundantly sustained. Many who had sallied out at the first cry from Lexington remained in service throughout the war. The officers of Putnam's first
regiment—the CONNECTICUT THIRD of 1775—thus served with but few
exceptions. Lieutenant Thomas Grosvenor went on from rank to rank,
succeeding Durkee in command when that valiant leader was compelled
by ill-health to retire from active service. Lieutenant Ebenezer Gray
served the whole seven years, attaining the rank of Lieutenant-Colonel.
Captain Mosely was often called to command the militia in special service at Rhode Island or New London. Captains Dana, Clark, Cleft,
Manning; Lieutenants Daniel Marcy, John Keyes, Daniel Allen, John
Adams, Melatiah Bingham, Benoni Cutler, Josiah Cleveland, Nathaniel
Webb, William and Stephen Lyon served with distinction through
successive campaigns and were honored by various promotions. Nor
less faithful and devoted were many of the subalterns and privates of
that first regiment and hundreds of subsequent recruits. Their beloved
leader and general, under whom they had first enlisted, was taken from
them in 1779, paralyzed and disabled, but they were able to fight on to
the last, supporting Washington and his immediate command through
all their privations and disappointments. Even when roused by poor
food, insufficient clothing and worse pay to the very verge of mutiny,
and preparing with other Connecticut soldiers to march to Hartford
and demand redress from the General Assembly, they yielded at once
to this characteristic appeal from General Putnam :—

"My brave lads, whither are you going? Do you intend to desert your officers and to invite the enemy to follow you into the country? Whose cause
have you been fighting and suffering so long in? Is it not your own? Have
you no property, no parents, wives or children? You have behaved like men
so far. All the world is full of your praises, and posterity will stand astonished at your deeds, but not if you spoil it all at last. Don't you consider
how much the country is distressed by the war and that your officers have not
been any better paid than yourselves? But we all expect better times and
that the country will do us ample justice. Let us all stand by one another,
then, and fight it out like brave soldiers. Think what a shame it would be for
Connecticut men to run away from their officers!"

Many of these old Windham heroes were noted in the army. Diah Farnham was the bully among Connecticut soldiers; Ralph Farnham, the heaviest man in the Connecticut line, but a wiry little Killingly expert managed to bring down both those mighty champions. It was said that Sergeant 'Bijah Fuller could throw any man in the army but Ralph Farnham, and carried this big fellow off on his back when he was wounded at the battle of White Plains, the enemy close upon them and "bullets falling like hail around them." He would turn round upon his pursuers, "pick his man," bring him down, and hurry on with his wounded comrade. Captain Abner Robinson of Scotland, Josiah Cleveland of Canterbury, Daniel Knowlton of Ashford, Joel Webb, Joseph Ashley, John Burnap and John Bingham of Windham, and many from other towns, were valiant veterans serving throughout the war, returning to the field at the first opportunity, if wounded or taken captive. Daniel Knowlton was twenty-three months in the enemy's hands, suffering from bad air, bad food and every possible discomfort and annoyance. When first taken he was confined in an old meeting-house without a particle of food or drink for four days. A compassionate woman, hearing of the condition of these prisoners, concealed food and a bottle of water under her clothing and prevailed upon the guard to allow her to visit them. She found them almost in a dying state, the feeling of hunger had passed, their only suffering was from faintness, and but for her timely relief they would soon have perished. But while those hardy veterans withstood for so many years danger, disease and imprisonment, thousands had perished on the way—some slain in battle, the greater number dying from sickness or imprisonment. Unnumbered sons of Windham County homes were sleeping in unknown graves in distant States. No tongue or pen can do justice to the service and sufferings of these men. Their names cannot be sought out; their deeds cannot be recorded. The system of enrollment at that date was so confused and imperfect that it would be impossible to obtain the whole number sent out from any section, and very difficult to form even an approximate estimate. This much we know, that the several towns of Windham County fulfilled every requisition for Continental or militia service. The burden of the war was borne by the whole population, and a complete muster-roll of Windham's Revolutionary soldiers would probably include the name of nearly every family in the County, while many families sent very large representations. It is said that *seventeen* cousins named Fuller in Windham's second society were in the service, and Adams's and Cleveland's almost without number. Peter Adams of Brooklyn, and Ephraim Fisk of Killingly, had each six sons in the army; Barzillai Fisher and Lusher Gay, each four; and larger numbers from many other families. The following list, taken from the church records of Plainfield, could probably have been paralleled in every other town had they taken care to inscribe the names of those who had fallen :—

"List of men killed and died in ye Army and Navy after April 1, 1775 :— Samuel Gary, Roxbury; Roswell Spaulding, Asa Chapman, 1775; William Dunlap, 1776; John Kingsbury, New York-ward, 1777; Samuel Cole, Zerniah Shurtleff, New York-ward, 1776; four negroes by sickness; William Farnham, captivity; Captain Daniel Clark, Paul Adams, killed at Stillwater, Sept. 19, 1777; Asa Kingsbury's son killed at Fort Mifflin, nigh Philadelphia; Dr. Nathaniel Spalding died at Halifax a prisoner, last of 1777; Dr. Phinehas Parkhurst, surgeon of brig *Resistance*, died at Portland, May, 1778; Daniel Parish died at Newport a prisoner; Simon Spalding at Martinique after being wounded; Enos Tew, New York, captivity, Dr. Ebenezer Robinson, Jr., at New York, prisoner, July, 1779."

And still despite these many losses the quota was kept up from year to year. The spirit evoked in "'76" outlived the sufferings and struggles of succeeding years. As fathers and older brothers were stricken down or disabled, younger sons, full of the same fire and enthusiasm, were only too ready to follow in their footsteps. A notable feature of the later years of the war was the number of very young men, lads of fourteen and onwards, who enlisted when permitted, or attached themselves to some popular officer. Samuel Calvin Adams of Canterbury, not then quite fourteen years of age, waited upon Capt. Aaron Cleveland at the time of Governor Tryon's assault upon Horse Neck, and saw General Putnam plunge down the steep bluff, the bullets of the baffled dragoons whizzing around him and even passing through his hat. William Eaton of Woodstock, at sixteen ran away from home to join the army and prevailed upon Captain Dana to receive him as his servant. John Pettengill of Windham, enlisted at fourteen, and served till the close of the war under the same popular leader. Levi Bingham of Windham, entered the service at fifteen. Daniel Waldo, at seventeen served a month under Capt. William Howard, at New London, and then enlisted under Capt. Nathaniel Wales, for continental service. Many a household was forced reluctantly to part with even its Benjamin. Laban, the youngest son of Barzillai Fisher, appears at dawn of day with gun upon his shoulder. "O Laban, you are not going!" besought his distressed aunt. "Yes," he cheerily answered, "but don't tell father," and so he went to his fate in the Jersey prison-ship. Undeterred by the hard experience of those who had gone before, young men were still eager to brave the perils and share the honors of military life. The surgeons' places vacated by the death or withdrawal of Spalding, Holmes, Lee, Gray, Waldo and others, were filled by Dr. Lord, Dr. David Adams, and Dr. Walter Hough of Canterbury, who had just completed his studies. The hearts of older veterans in the field were cheered by this continued infusion of new blood and muscle into the army. The patience and fortitude of these men, young and old alike, amid such depth of destitution and discomfort, excited the wondering admiration of Washington and sympathetic officers. Turning their very wants and woes into sportive song,* they faithfully kept their posts and did their duty, trusting that their labors and sacrifices would at length meet fitting reward and help work out the freedom and prosperity of their country.

Though the carrying on of the war was the first and chief object during the Revolutionary period, Windham was not wholly absorbed by it. Amid all the distractions and perplexities of the time the daily routine of life flowed on—eating and sleeping, sowing and reaping, buying and selling, birth, marriage and death. Public worship was statedly maintained, children taught in intermittent fashion, town affairs faithfully administered. In some respects there was decided growth and progress. Experience was widened; ingenuity and invention stimulated. Among the gains of the time were substantial families from sea-board settlements. These new comers interested themselves in town affairs and engaged in various business operations. James Thurber and Lemuel Chandler opened a store in Pomfret, selling groceries and liquors. Hannah Miller of Boston, obliged "to flee from the merciless troops of that town as from a nest of hornets," sought refuge in the happy and peaceful State of Connecticut with a hogshead of rum and a tierce of coffee which she "had brought to live upon," selling and bartering the same with the neighbors, in Pomfret. Jonathan Hale of Concord, engaged in the manufacture of hand-cards to great public convenience. The home production of salt, saltpetre and potash was very largely increased.

The religious interests of the county suffered severely by loss of men, diminished means, public distractions and increasing skepticism.

---

* A lady in Chaplin sends this fragment, sung to her in childhood by Mr. Joseph Martin, a fine singer and prominent person in the community and church, who used to take her on his knee and sing to her many of the old Revolutionary songs, sung in camp by the soldiers :—

> " O once I could eat of that bread, that bread,
>   That was made of the finest of wheat;
> But now I am glad of an Indian cake,
>   And glad if I can get it to eat.
>
> O once I could lie on that bed, that bed,
>   That was made of the softest of down;
> But now I glad of a bundle of straw
>   To keep my head off from the ground.
>
> O once I could drink of that beer, that beer,
>   That was made of the berry so brown;
> But now I am glad of a cup of cold water
>   That runs through an Indian town."

The Baptists alone gained ground. Their bold and earnest championship of civil and religious freedom was in unison with the spirit of the
age, and brought them into public favor. Their growth in Windham
County was greatly aided by the influence of President Manning of
Brown University, who after the shutting up of the college devoted
himself to missionary labors. Many of the new comers to the county
were earnest Baptists. A Baptist Church was organized in the eastern part of Killingly in May, 1776. In June, Baptists in Canada and
Abington parishes united in church fellowship, electing one of their
number, William Grow, for their pastor. Mr. Manning was present,
and preached the ordination sermon. During this busy summer of
1776, a Baptist society was also organized in Pomfret. Public religious
services were held by Mr. Manning at the houses of the Thurbers and
other friends, which excited much interest. The Rev. Mr. Putnam
was considerably annoyed by this invasion upon his parochial bounds
and the increasing predilection for Baptist principles and preaching,
and attempted to meet it by inviting Mr. Manning to a public discussion of the the points at issue between them. The result was precisely contrary to what was intended. Mr. Manning had greatly the
advantage of his opponent in vigor and eloquence if not in argument,
public interest was heightened, and Baptist sentiments far more widely
disseminated and embraced. The Baptist residents of the Quinebaug
Valley in Pomfret and Killingly organized as a distinct religious
society, and instituted regular worship. The Rev. Mr. Kelly labored
with them for a time, holding services at convenient residences, which
were "attended by a large gathering of people, and the prospect was
encouraging of great good to be done." After his departure Mr.
Manning very earnestly urged Mr. Thomas Ustick of Ashford, to
enter upon this field, with the view of settling in it for life. Hitherto
the Baptists of Windham County had been mostly of the lower classes
of society, and their ministers had been men of little or no education.
Now, men of higher standing were entering the Baptist ranks and
a different ministry was demanded. Mr. Manning besought Mr.
Ustick to visit Pomfret and help the people under their disappointment, and should he decide to settle there he wished him immediately
"to engage in a Latin school as a nursery for the college," and "endeavor to influence his people to educate their children, as the present
state of the Baptist society must convince all of the importance of
having men of education in all parts of the country." Mr. Ustick did
not think best to occupy this field, and no permanent pastor was
secured, nor church organization effected at that date. President
Manning looked after its interests as long as he was at liberty, and
often visited his friends in Windham County, confirming and encourag-

25

ing the churches, and preaching "to crowded audiences, very attentive and affected."

The only Congregational churches formed during this period was that of Eastford, and one in the north part of Windham. Several of the churches were weakened by the loss of their pastors. The church on Woodstock Hill was very seriously affected by the long absence and sorrowful death of Rev. Abiel Leonard. The services of Eliphalet Lyman of Lebanon, proved acceptable to church society, but their hereditary dread of Saybrook Platform and Connecticut derelictions obliged them to make a searching inquiry into his views and principles respecting church government and discipline before venturing to invite him to settlement. The investigating committee reported his doctrinal sentiments to be Calvinistic; as to government, he thought a minister ought ever to call church meetings when desired by a majority; that the voice of the majority ought to be decisive, and denied the right of the moderator to a negative vote. This giving satisfaction, a "call" was given and accepted, and Mr. Lyman ordained September 2, 1779. He proved himself "worthy of the high and important office," and aided in restoring the church to its former standing. Upon his reiterated assertion "that he desired not the name of holding to a negative in the church," that body "made no objection" to his joining the Windham County Association.

The church in East Woodstock was greatly afflicted by the increasing infirmities and disabilities of Mr. Stiles. This good minister, once so full of life and controversial zeal, had fallen into deep religious depression, "his soul wading in clouds and temptations," aggravated by family afflictions and public anxieties. Unable to perform the duties of his office, Mr. Joshua Johnson, a graduate of Yale College, was ordained colleague pastor, December 27, 1780. The West Woodstock Church was chiefly exercised by the difficulty of keeping up the credit of the minister's salary, which so depreciated in value that Mr. Williams was obliged to ask for help. This deficiency labored much in the minds of his people, but after suitable discussion it was thought prudent not to make any further grant. Mr. Williams meekly acquiescing and expressing a hope that they would not see him suffer, each member present in society meeting voluntarily promised to do something for their pastor's support, as in duty they found themselves inclined.

Plainfield was unable to fill the place of her lamented Fuller. That excellent minister had wrought a great work, binding up old wounds and healing animosities. The terse and touching inscription on a gravestone on Burial Hill, best tells the story of his life and ministerial service:—"John Fuller, after watching for the souls of his people as those who must give account, fell asleep, October 3, 1777, Æ 55."

In attempting to supply the loss of Rev. Aaron Brown, the First Church of Killingly was involved in great difficulties, unhappily making choice of Emerson Foster, son of the somewhat notorious Isaac Foster of West Stafford. In face of an earnest remonstrance from Deacon Ebenezer Larned and other prominent brethren who mistrusted the doctrinal soundness of the candidate, the council of reverend ministers and delegates meeting at Capt. Felshaw's tavern, January 21, 1778, thought it their duty to proceed to his ordination. The County Association represented by its Eastern committee, concurred in this judgment, and Mr. Foster was ordained with the usual formalities. The result was most unhappy. Mr. Foster's aberrations became more pronounced and manifest, and so many withdrew from church and society, that it was found very difficult to fulfill pecuniary obligations. In the fervor of their eagerness to secure Mr. Foster, the society had offered him two hundred pounds settlement, and twenty pounds salary, —the latter to be made as good as the same sum in 1776, and the former to be paid within six months after his settling. The friends of Mr. Foster labored vainly to collect this sum. Times were now very hard, public demands urgent, and currency so depreciated that the former salary of a minister would scarcely suffice " for keeping the key and sweeping the meeting-house." People refused to pay and took certificates from the new Baptist Society. A committee was appointed to assist the society committee "to examine certificates of people called Baptists," and reported that "such as produce proper certificates ought to be exempt from taxes." Disaffection rapidly increased. Captain Howe resigned the office of clerk, J. Cady Howe, B. H. Torrey and Jacob Leavens refused to serve as collectors. Mr. Foster remonstrated with the society respecting encouragement for support prior to ordination. A committee was appointed to treat with him " about depreciation of currency, and what will make him easy." Mr. Foster not only insisted upon all that was his due " but wished the society to amend or rectify the vote passed previous to ordination." The society most positively declined to alter the vote, but strictly adhere to the same and regard it as the foundation on which the superstructure was reared. Church, society and pastor agreed to submit all matters of difficulty to a council, July 27, 1779. That body dismissed Mr. Foster from his pastorate, but did not adjudicate the pecuniary question. Amasa Learned, now entering upon the practice of law in New London, was deputized to treat with Mr. Foster " but was unable to come to terms," whereupon the ex-pastor resorted to legal process, bringing a suit against the society for lawful arrearage and damage. Eleazer Moffat, Capt. Cady and Sampson Howe were chosen to carry on a correspondence with the plaintiff, and after much delay and bickering it was agreed to submit all matters of difficulty between them to the arbitration of Esquire Wales of Windham, Capt. Nehemiah Lyon of Woodstock, and Capt. Carpenter of Lebanon, meeting to be held at Felshaw's tavern ; the previous committee to attend on behalf of the society and employ an attorney to plead. The result of the arbitration was less favorable than had been hoped, and the society was obliged to make good its promise. No baptisms or observance of communion were reported during this unhappy controversy. Public worship was maintained with some degree of regularity, Russell Cook and others supplying the pulpit. An unsuccessful attempt was made to unite with some of the inhabitants of the middle society in supporting the gospel.

Abington Society was obliged to seek the dismissal of its honored pastor, Rev. David Ripley, in consequence of a distressing and incurable disease brought on, he averred, by close application to ministerial labors, by which he was every year confined to his bed for weeks with excruciating pains, and disabled from efficient service, whereby many became uneasy that his salary and support should be continued. "For the sake of peace and to avoid contention," Mr. Ripley consented to be dismissed from his office, March, 1778. The question of arrearages and equivalent was referred to "four judicious and distinguished gentlemen, viz., Reverends James Cogswell and Josiah Whitney, Col. Levi Nott and Hon. Charles Church Chandler," and satisfactorily settled by the payment of three hundred pounds. This dismission in no wise effected Mr. Ripley's ministerial standing, and he officiated in the pulpit at home and abroad whenever his health permitted, and supposed himself still entitled to all the privileges and immunities of his office. The "listers" of Pomfret were, however, of a contrary opinion, and being greatly burdened with public demands, they made out a list of his real and personal estate and came upon him for town and state taxes, nor would the town authorities consent to any release or abatement. Having neither "ways, means, ability or income," to discharge the same, Mr. Ripley was compelled to carry his "distresses" to the Assembly, and fight it out with his fellow-citizens before that body. Pomfret insisted that the petitioner was much better able than the major part of the inhabitants to pay his proportion of taxes, "considering the profits of his farm and having a grammar school, together with sums of money in the loan office and other sums at interest," supporting her position by specific enumeration of acres of land and heads of cattle. Dr. Lord of Abington, the church committee, and influential members of the society, testified on the other hand to the past usefulness of their superannuated pastor, his excruciating sufferings by which he was made incapable of bodily labor ; that his circumstances were never affluent, and that he had a family of children, young and unsettled, to educate and support from the profits of his farm. It appeared upon cross-examination that the grammar school consisted of one pupil, and the three hundred pounds in the loan office had been paid in paper money at the nominal sum. An attempt to show that Mr. Ripley's disease had been aggravated by "taking the bark" was equally unsuccessful. The Assembly ordered the collection of the taxes to be suspended and deferred decision from session to session, and thus the matter ended. Mr. Ripley was able to preach occasionally to his former charge, and no other minister was settled for several years.

The Episcopal worship so prosperously established in Brooklyn Parish fell into great disfavor after the breaking out of the war. The King's headship in the church could no longer be recognized by revolted subjects. All good patriots fell away and only avowed royalists remained in the church connection. Prayers for the king and royal family were no longer in order, and, as Mr. Fogg like other churchmen thought it inconsistent with his ordination vows to omit them, public service was suspended. Trinity church was closed and its congregation scattered. Mr. Fogg remained quietly at his post of duty, ministering to his few faithful followers, conducting himself "in so peaceable and quiet a manner," as to retain the confidence and respect of the community. Col. Malbone was also allowed to pursue his way unmolested. Though open and outspoken in his attachment to the royal cause, he did nothing to promote it, and by his ready wit and cool assurance managed to evade demands and disarm opposition. A pert little official once called to warn him to a "training," or some such public service. Malbone—a cultured gentleman of much presence and dignity—scanned scornfully his insignificant figure, and taking him by the coat collar to a mirror, glanced at the images so strikingly contrasted and quenched him with the query:— "Do you think God Almighty made *you* to give *me* orders?" The negro force that caused so much alarm in Thompson and distant neighborhoods, gave no great uneasiness to the people of Pomfret, who had better means of judging its efficiency. The church service held in Col. Malbone's dwelling-house excited some dissatisfaction but it was not thought best to interfere with it. Dr. Walton continued faithful in his adherence to the Church and King, and as a renegade and pervert was far more obnoxious than Malbone. His son was an officer in the British army, and wounded fellow-officers were said to have been secreted by him in Dr. Walton's dwelling-house.

One of the most remarkable of Windham County achievements during the war was the opening of the Plainfield Academy.

Stimulated doubtless by a legacy left by Isaac Coit, Esq., at his decease in 1776—"the annual interest of which was to be applied to the maintenance of a Latin or Grammar school in the new brick house in Plainfield; and more especially for the benefit of poor children of good genius, whose parents are not able to give them suitable learning,"—the associated friends of education proceeded in 1778, to organize a classical department, securing for rector Mr. Ebenezer Pemberton of Newport, a gentleman of high scholarship and accomplishments, and unusual aptitude for teaching. His reputation and the favorable location of the school attracted at once a large number of pupils. Colleges and academies had been generally suspended. Seaboard towns were exposed to invasion, but this remote inland village offered a safe and pleasant refuge. Gentlemen in Providence, New London, and even New York, gladly availed themselves of its advantages, and many promising lads from the best families in the States were sent to Plainfield Academy. The good people of the town welcomed these students to their homes and firesides. More teachers were demanded and the popularity of the school increased until it numbered more than a hundred foreign pupils, besides a large number from Plainfield and neighboring towns.

After the transference of the seat of war to the Southern States Windham was less actively participant, though still called to raise her quota of men and supplies for State protection and Continental service. The large number of men already sent out made it more difficult to secure recruits. Windham's proportion of fifteen hundred men, raised by Connecticut for six months' Continental service in May, 1780, was thus distributed among the townships:—Ashford, 17; Canterbury, 9; Coventry, 18; Killingly, 37; Lebanon, 36; Mansfield, 20; Plainfield, 16; Pomfret, 25; Union, 6; Voluntown, 17; Windham, 34; Woodstock, 20. The towns at once made provision for enlisting these men, but before it was accomplished a thousand men were called for three years' service. Colonel McClellan thus instructs the officers of two Woodstock companies:—

"In consequence of orders received from General Douglas, I am authorized to acquaint you that you are appointed recruiting officers for your companies, and to be rewarded therefor—you, and each of you, are hereby directed to enlist out of your said companies, Capt. Bowen, two, and Capt. Paine, four, able-bodied effective men to serve during the war three years, or until the last day of December next, unless sooner discharged . . . If said men are not enlisted on or before the 26th of June, instant, you are hereby directed to make a peremptory draft to make up your complement as above directed, to serve until the last day of December next, unless sooner discharged; and you will apply to the selectmen of your town for blankets, if need be, in case the recruits or detached men should not furnish themselves—and see them marched to the house of Capt. Natha'l Clarke in Woodstock, on Monday, the third day of July next, by nine o'clock in the morning, in order to be mustered, receive their bounty and march on emeaditly to the army without returning to their respective homes. You will use your utmost endeavors to get the men by enlistment, taking the Act of Assembly for your direction. Make due return of your doings.

Given at Woodstock, June 19, 1780.

SAM'L MCCLELLAN, Col."

A town meeting was held June 26, when it was agreed to offer a bounty of forty shillings per month. Colonel McClellan, Captain Daniel Lyon, and Mr. Ebenezer Smith were appointed a committee to confer with the several militia companies then convened and had no difficulty in procuring the requisite number of soldiers ; and even at the succeeding call it was reported that they could get their men and double the number wanted at the price voted. Windham offered £20 money, equal to wheat at five shillings a bushel. In December, she offered £12 in silver money as a bounty for the first year and £9 silver for each succeeding year. Plainfield offered £100 to any five men who would enlist for three years ; and generous bounties promised by other towns procured recruits without resort to drafting. Requisitions for corn, wheat, beef and clothing were promptly met by all the towns. The raids upon New Haven, Fairfield and Danbury, the frequent alarms of invasion upon New London and Rhode Island, exposed the militia to continual call and repeated service, and even while gathering these quotas for the general army, a sudden summons hurried a large force to Rhode Island. " Captain Timothy Backus with his troop of veterans from Canterbury," Captain Daniel Tyler's matross company from Brooklyn, the militia companies, under Captain Abner Adams and Captain William Frizzel, of Pomfret and Woodstock, were ordered to rendezvous in Greenwich, and the selectmen of the several towns to furnish the provisions to support them on their march.

And yet, notwithstanding the increasing demand for men, money and supplies, and the little apparent progress made by the Continental arms, the prospects were brightening. It became more and more evident even to the fearful and despondent that whatever might be in store for them the States could not be conquered. Amid disasters, defeat, and defection, there were favorable gleams and omens. La Fayette had returned full of hope and courage. France was taking their side more boldly and heartily. Marion, Sumter and Green were winning laurels and occasional victories in the Carolinas. The marching of Gates and his division through Plainfield, Canterbury and Windham on their withdrawal from Newport, the quartering of the French Huzzars at Windham for a week and at Lebanon through the winter of 1780-1, gave new life and stimulus, and encouraged the people to hope for better days. The Marquis De Chastellux dined at Windham with the Duke De Lauzern. The gay young French officers were very fond of society and cordially accepted hospitalities extended to them, and the blooming belles of Windham, Lebanon and Norwich had the good fortune to participate in many brilliant entertainments, while the silver freely lavished by these young men found its way to many a farmer's pocket. Supplies of every kind were now becoming more plentiful, brought into Norwich by lucky privateer or secret smuggler. Molasses, spirits, and many kinds of foreign goods, were cheap and abundant during the latter years of the war, and the young ladies attending balls with French officers were not compelled to wear *homespun*. Muslins, laces, and even silk and jewelry were now attainable. A fair young fiancée in Pomfret, who had been much troubled in reference to her wedding dress, was gladdened by the sight of a traveling merchant with the loveliest pattern of *pink satin* that ever met the eyes of a young maiden. But the cost was so enormous! The young girl knew very well what heavy burdens had been borne by her father, how much he had paid out for taxes and bounties, and clothing for the soldiers; how good money advanced by him had been repaid by worthless scrip; how strongly he and other patriots denounced these skulking mischievous peddlers who traded with their enemies—but how could she resist this exquisite piece of goods, which more than realized her highest aspirations. Woman's tact won the day and dress. She did not dare to *ask* the favor, but stealing into the room where the rough old father sat brooding in his armchair, she knelt before him and with pleading glance held up the shimmering satin. Revolutionary fathers, rough and gruff though they might be, were still not adamant nor unappreciative. The mute appeal, the graceful tableau, melted the father's heart and opened his money chest. Without a word he unlocked his treasures and placed in his daughter's hand *forty silver dollars*, and the ten yards of satin was made up into the tastefullest of wedding dresses and also furnished a frontispiece for the wedding waistcoat of the bridegroom.

Home patriots were also encouraged by more cheering words from those in the field. Ebenezer Gray writes of improved prospects:—

"*Aug.* 13, 1780. The army is again formed and encamped at this place (Tappin or Dobbs' Ferry). Two brigades of Light Infantry, under the Marquis De La Fayette, are in front about four miles. General Green commands the right wing, consisting of two divisions. . . . . . We now form a very beautiful and extensive camp, with a large park of heavy artillery. We are all daily expecting some general maneuver."

" CAMP, Dec. 7, 1780.
Dr. Brother—I know not where to date my letter. I believe it is *nowhere*—that is a place, if you can conceive of such a thing, at a great distance from every other place. We are building hutts in a central place in a direct line from West Point to Fishkill, a place to and from which there never was, or will be, a road—by land. At this place I am now building a hutt on Thanksgiving Day, which I shall keep with a little beef and half an allowance of bread, without any drink but the pure stream, with a thankful and grateful heart to the Bountiful Giver of all things, and in heart and soul rejoice with

all those who have all the outward comforts and dainties of life to manifest it with. May you, parents, brothers, sisters and little ones solemnly and seriously rejoice and be glad on this day for the great and many blessings of a public and family way which hath been bestowed upon us.

My best wishes attend my cousins and acquaintances, and should be happy in joining in the usual festivity, etc.

EBENR. GRAY."

" CAMP HIGHLAND, Dec. 22, 1780.

Dr. Brother—I have one moment to write you by Calf, who tells me he is going to Windham. I am hearty and well and have got thro' the greatest difficulty (as I hope) of the winter. Our huts are built where there is plenty of wood and water. We have had our starvation season—I hope the whole of it. It seems as if 'twas decreed in the Book of the *Fates* that whenever we hut we should have short allowance; and when Congress order us to keep a day of thanksgiving and rejoicing in the success and plenty wherewith Providence hath blessed us, that the army have nothing to make the heart glad and a dismal and dark prospect before us.

This hath been the case for three years past; but I hope and pray and believe that the scene is changed and better days and times are coming. May the happy day of pease and plenty soon come and with grateful hearts may we be prepared to receive and injoy the blessing.

We are now fed with beef and bread at the usual rate, with a small deduction of bread, and no money.

I am your dear brother,

EBENR. GRAY."

With fresh requisitions for men, beef, pork, grain and powder in 1781, came also renewed hopes of coming success and triumph. Windham patriots watching eagerly the signs of the times, heard dim rumors of more fleets and troops on the way from France, and " fifteen tons of silver in French hornpipes ; " and in June they were treated to the sight and entertainment of Rochambeau's grand army as it marched from Newport to Hartford. "Magnificent in appearance, superb in discipline," with banner and music, and all the pride and pomp of war, it passed in four divisions* over the great highway through Voluntown, Plainfield, Canterbury and Windham. All the country people from far and wide flocked to the Providence road to see the brave array. Barrack-masters appointed by the Governor and his council met them at every stopping-place, and provided suitable accommodations. A hundred eager school-boys in Plainfield village gave

---

* It is quite probable that one of these divisions took the more northerly route to Hartford through Killingly, Pomfret and Ashford. Tradition confidently asserts the passing of the French army through these towns, and points out the very place of their encampment in Abington. The accompanying tradition that Washington and LaFayette were with the army makes it difficult to fix the date of their passage, as LaFayette was with the southern forces in June, 1781. It is most probable that the army passed at this date, and the visit of the two generals occurred at some other period—perhaps after the cessation of hostilities. They are reported to have passed a night at Grosvenor's in Pomfret, waited for breakfast at the hearth-stone of the Randall House in Abington, and spent another night at Clark's tavern in Ashford, where their names are still to be seen upon an antique window pane.

26

them vociferous welcome. Encamping for a day or two in Windham, they were visited by all the leading patriots. Mr. Cogswell* reports them "a fine body of troops, under the best discipline; not the least disorder committed or damage done by them." Dr. Joshua Elderkin and other public officers accompany them all the way on to West Point, with great satisfaction to Count De Rochambeau. They are followed day after day by long lines of baggage-wagons and stout carts bearing chests of silver money, guarded by French soldiers. The combined armies "marched for the southward," the French fleet, reported off Sandy Hook, steers for the south. Mr. Cogswell hopes that "a telling blow is about to be struck in that quarter," but just as hope is dawning in his heart he is appalled by a sight more terrific than anything yet witnessed during the war—the lurid flames of consuming New London. Pastors and people gathered in the meeting-house for a peaceful "Thursday afternoon lecture" hear the booming cannon and see the red light in the southern sky. Men snatch their arms and hurry to the scene of carnage. Their report on return confirms the preceding rumors—"the biggest part of the town laid in ashes, the misery of the people great beyond description, the cruelty shown to the garrison shocking to humanity, many butchered in cold blood, begging for quarter; Arnold, abandoned of all good and to all evil, threatening to do to Norwich as he had done to New London. And Nathan Frink, a son of Windham County, now aid-de-camp to Arnold, most active and efficient in this terrible butchery and destruction. The situation of the New England States, destitute of fleet and army, seemed more critical and alarming than ever before, yet again in a few days their anxieties are relieved. "News from Europe and East

---

* While Mr. Cogswell's diary allows us a peep at the French troops *en route* for the Hudson, a journal kept by Claude Blanchard, commissary of the French auxiliary army, enables us to look at Windham through the eyes of its foreign visitants :—

"At night I lay at Plainfield, fifteen miles from Waterman's tavern. The country is a little more cleared especially in the environs of Plainfield, where nevertheless there are only five or six houses. I saw some farms sown with rye and wheat but especially with maize (what we call Turkish corn in Anjou) and also potatoes. I also passed through many woods mostly of oak and chestnut trees, my lodging cost me fifteen livres.

On the 17th June, 1781, I set out at half after six for Windham, where I arrived at ten o'clock, after a journey of fifteen miles. The country is very similar to the environs of Plainfield; yet we see more pasture lands there which are in the valleys, so we have to ascend and descend continually on this road. Windham seemed to have sixty houses, all pretty; there is also a very handsome *temple*, called in this country a meeting-house. . . . There is another village between Plainfield and Windham called Strickland [Scotland] which seemed to me to be pretty, and where we also saw a temple. . . . . . It is eighteen miles from Windham to Boston [Bolton], and we had to ascend and descend. . . . On the 18th I arrived at Hartford, the capital of Connecticut, fourteen miles from Boston [Bolton]; the road is fine."

Indies much against Great Britain ; " " the French fleet has certainly
arrived at Chesapeake ; " " Washington and his army are there in high
spirits ;" and on training day, November 6, comes the great news of
Cornwallis's surrender, and thousands exclaim with Trumbull :—
" Praised be the Lord of Hosts for our deliverance ! "

More specific details only increased the general joy and thankfulness,
and made the glorious results more apparent.   Durkee's old regiment
under Grosvenor had been present, and Windham veterans released for
a time from service brought back full reports of the successful siege
and surrender.   All felt that the war was virtually ended ; that Great
Britain would be forced to relinquish her vain attempts to conquer the
sovereign States of America.   There were still alarms from time to
time and hostile demonstrations ; the army had to be maintained ;
troops and supplies provided.   The inhabitants of the several towns
were now divided into classes according to their rate list, each class to
furnish a recruit and take charge of his family.   Negotiations with
Great Britain made slow progress.   Mr. Cogswell in his despondency
declares more than once " that he sees no prospect of peace."   In
September, 1782, a hostile fleet again threatens New London, and
the militia of Windham and New London Counties are called out
by Colonel McClellan, but after two days of intense anxiety the
intruder withdraws without inflicting damage.   A flag telegraphing
" P. E. A. C. E." is reported the following March.   April 19, 1783,
Washington announces the cessation of hostilities.   Of festivities and
rejoicings upon the reception of this announcement we hear little.
The joy of the citizens of Windham County was perhaps too deep for
noisy demonstration.   It had been a long, hard, deadly struggle.
Many precious lives had been sacrificed.   There had been great
expenditure of money and forces ; there were hard problems still to
face ; and so the rejoicings were mostly expressed by religious
solemnities.   Public services were held in the meeting-house on
Windham Green, and our friend Mr. Cogswell preached a celebration
sermon which received much commendation.   Joseph Joslin of
Thompson, shared with the last returning troopers their bountiful
treat of cake and egg rum at Esquire Dresser's tavern, and marched
with them into " Priest Russel's meeting-house " for religious service.
The first soldiers were sent out from the public sanctuary with prayer
and supplication, and the last were taken to the same sacred spot for
appropriate thanksgiving, and yet it may have been difficult upon that
Sabbath morning " to discern the noise of the shout of joy from the
noise of the weeping of the people."   For in the galleries and great
pews there were many places vacant.   The aged deacons who sat
beneath the pulpit had laid their precious sons upon the altar.   There

were other parents there whose sons had been stricken ; there were
widows bowed with grief ; there were children who were fatherless ;
there were fair young girls whose hearts still yearned for missing lover
and brother—and thanks for the great blessings of peace and Independence were hallowed by a deep consciousness of the great price
that had been paid for them.

BOOK VII. 1783-1807.

I.

DISPOSITION OF TORIES. SUFFERINGS OF SOLDIERS. WAR SET
TLEMENTS. ADOPTION OF FEDERAL CONSTITUTION.

A NEW era had opened. Windham County was now a part of a
free State, a confederated Republic. The Independence of the
United States was secured and acknowledged. Old things had passed
away, many things had become new. New systems, new politics were
to be devised; a NATION to be evolved and established. Little did
the people of the several States in the first fervor of jubilant exultation realize the greatness of the work before them. Their thoughts
and energies were rather mainly occupied with the work already
wrought. War claims and questions pressed heavily upon them.
Two classes of inhabitants demanded instant consideration—the men
who had fought for freedom and those who had opposed it. In the
long controversy great bitterness had been engendered. The cruel
treatment of the patriot prisoners, the brutal massacres at Wyoming
and New London had excited intense resentments. Tories had shown
greater barbarity than British or Hessians, and were regarded with
peculiar hatred. The few avowed Tories in Windham County were
straightway driven out of it. No formal process of ejection was
served upon them, but they were given to understand that they would
be no longer tolerated. Dr. Walton of Killingly, had made himself
especially obnoxious, concealing British officers in his house, and
boasting of his influence with British commanders. Upon the news
of the surrender of Cornwallis, he was visited by a large number of
citizens who wished to send him off at once, but, through the intercession of Col. Danielson, he was allowed to wait for that great company
of refugees which sought shelter in Nova Scotia. Col. Fitch and his
family, Nathan Frink, and descendants of Captain John Chandler
of Woodstock, were as far as can be ascertained the only other
representatives of Windham County among that dishonored band of
exiles which left New York, in September, 1783. Though not absolutely forced from Windham, Col. Fitch could no longer remain in his

old home with any degree of comfort. The personal prestige that had so long shielded him from ill-treatment passed away with the lapse of years. The new generation growing up forgot his past services and position, and only thought of him as an enemy to his country and the patriot cause. It was difficult for him to obtain needful supplies for his family. Ardent Sons of Liberty had decreed "that no mills should grind for, no merchant sell goods to, a Tory." He was insulted, watched, guarded, subjected to vexatious and ruinous prosecution. His son complains to the General Assembly, that having been "prosecuted, tried and acquitted for inimical words, an execution had been levied against him for cost, as though it was not sufficient for an innocent man to suffer the disgrace of a criminal prosecution but he must be subjected to such enormous costs." Broken in health and spirit and ruined in fortune, nothing was left for him but to withdraw from Windham and spend the remainder of his days in hopeless exile, the unhappy victim of misplaced loyalty and a too chivalrous devotion to an unworthy sovereign. Windham took care to prevent his return by voting in town meeting, 1785, that "there be a committee of inspection appointed to observe and take care that those refugees and inimical persons who have gone from us since the commencement of the war be not allowed to come in among us."

Still more unhappy was the fate of Joshua, son of Joshua Chandler of West Woodstock, one of those bright young men so hopefully graduated from Yale College before 1760. Settling in New Haven he had won wealth and a high position, all sacrificed by his adherence to the king, yet the loss of property and home weighed less heavily upon him than his subsequent conviction that his sacrifice had been for naught. Visiting England to represent his claims and losses, he thus writes to a friend in New Haven :—

"I found the nation in great tumults and commotions—myself perfectly lost in politics as well as in compass . . . The kingdom, without a miracle in its favor, must be lost. You can have no idea of their corruption, their debauchery and luxury; their pride, their riches, their luxury has ruined them. It is not in the power of human nature to save them. I like not the country, neither their manners nor even their soil. Give America the chance and in one half the time she will rise superior to anything in this country.

My own prospects in life are dahsed. My only care is for my children. The idea of a compensation is very faint. . . . Thus this unhappy controversy has ruined thousands. The sacrifices, the prospects of my family, are not the only thing that fills my mind with distress. I yet have a very strong affection to and predilection for my native country; their happiness would in some measure alleviate my great distress, but cannot suppose my country can be happy in its present state. I wish Dr. Stiles would admit into the library Dr. Holmes' History of the British Constitution to aid his country in forming a new Constitution, for one she must have sometime.

For customs, this nation has copied after and imported the luxuries, the follies and vices of France. But whatever may be the fate of kingdoms and powers of Europe or my own, I sincerely wish happiness, honor and glory to the country that gave me birth. In the hour of contest I thought, and even yet think, my country wrong, but I never wished its ruin. I wish her to support a dignified character, that can be done only by great and dignified actions, one of which is a sacred and punctual adherence to public faith and virtue. My first and last prayer will be to meet where no political dispute can ever separate from near and dear friends."

Colonel Chandler returned to Annapolis unsuccessful in his mission and after further delay started, March, 1787, for St. John, New Brunswick, with his son and daughter, and all the books, papers and evidence of his colonial property, to meet commissioners appointed to adjust his claims. A violent storm arose and the vessel was driven among rocks. Hoping to secure it, William Chandler fastened a rope around his body and jumped overboard to swim to land, but was instantly crushed between the vessel and rocks. With great difficulty Colonel Chandler managed to reach the shore with his daughter and climbed upon a high point of rocks to look out and find where they were, but benumbed with cold he fell from it and soon died. The daughter and a friend, Mrs. Alexander Grant, wandered in the woods for two terrible days and perished from cold and hunger. The story of their sad fate made a deep impression upon surviving relatives and friends in Woodstock, and was handed down from generation to generation as the most thrilling tragedy of the revolutionary drama.

Colonel Malbone was suffered to remain unmolested, but lost much of his property. A seven-thousand dollar mortgage upon his farm in the hands of Charles Paxton, a refugee, was forfeited to government. Lands in Ashford belonging to Apthorpe, land in Plainfield owned by Bayard, two acres in Windham in payment of execution against Eleazer Fitch, " the real and personal estate of Nathan Frink of Pomfret," were also forfeited to the State. An attempt was made to confiscate land in Thompson : (seven tenements of land and houses, belonging to the heirs of Robert Thompson, England), but after the first heat and bitterness of conflict had subsided, this old established claim, purchased by one of the most faithful friends of the early Colonists, was allowed to remain with his descendants. Mrs. Martha Stevens, heir of Anthony Stoddard, making declaratien before the County Court " that she was always a hearty friend to the rights and privileges of America," was allowed to resume possession of her land in Ashford.

Those unfortunate Royalists who received such slight and tardy compensation for all their sacrifices and devotion were not alone in their complaint of ingratitude and ill-usage. The soldiers who had conquered independence by their arms had met but a poor return for all their sufferings and sacrifices. Some had returned without pay ; some with scrip that proved a worthless mockery ; some were disabled by wounds or disease, and incapacitated from active labor. The later recruits were mostly young men, without farms or trades or means of earning a livelihood. The Windham towns, already heavily burdened with debt incurred in carrying on the war, were unable to make suitable provision for these returned soldiers. Canterbury, after debating the expediency " of allowing anything to the soldiers on account of the failure of the public in making their wages good," voted at first to do nothing, but upon reconsideration appointed a committee to act with the selectmen in settling with the same according to their best judgment. Windham voted ten pounds "to Elijah Linkon, a Continental soldier, enlisted during the war, for his past good services and present necessities." Relief was obtained in other cases from private sources and employment furnished whenever possible. As the Windham County recruits had received a generous bounty in silver and provision for their families during their absence, they probably suffered less than their officers, who had their families to support upon their nominal pay, the artizans who had furnished them with arms, and the town officers who had advanced money for their bounty and support. Three months' wages due to Dr. Waldo when he left service barely paid a trifling debt due to an attorney. Colonel Ebenezer Gray, after seven years' faithful service, which had ruined his health and incapacitated him from resuming his legal practice, received no compensation but the certificates of Congress for five years' commutation pay, which immediately depreciated to ten cents on a dollar. Hundreds of other officers were paid in the same way and reduced to still greater necessities. Among those who suffered most severely in Windham were Hezekiah Huntington and Henry DeWitt, who had devoted all their time and energies for many years to manufacturing arms and ammunition for the Continental soldiers. After exhausting his own means in this work, Mr. Huntington "effected a settlement with the Government at Philadelphia, receiving as his pay seventy-four thousand dollars in Continental paper," which so depreciated in a short time "that a hundred dollars of it would not buy a breakfast," and he was forced to struggle the remainder of his days with poverty. Still harder was the fate of DeWitt, who took the Government paper in payment till it became valueless, " and his Boston creditors put him in Windham jail and he lived within the jail limits for many years." Many who had advanced good money to buy stores for Government were paid with bills which made them bankrupt. The case of Nehemiah Tinker of Windham, who " had laid out his whole property and pledged his credit in purchasing supplies for the army," was one of peculiar hardship. Dying suddenly just before the declaration of peace, the thousand-dollar paper in his hands " would hardly pay for his winding sheet and coffin." With heavy debts pressing upon her, and *eleven* children to maintain, the bereaved widow attempted to gain relief by prosecuting one " who had reaped the benefit of her husband's transaction as contractor," but only lost the little that was left to her. With one bed and the remains of her furniture she took her children to her husband's workshop and tried to support them by needle-work ; but even here the merciless creditors pursued her. She held her two youngest children by the hand while the constable sold at the door her andirons, chairs, bed, table, bedding, everything but the barest minimum prescribed by law. The children gathered chips out of the street, and with stones for andirons, and a spoke of a broken wheel for poker, they managed to keep a fire and preserve existence, though often reduced to extremity of destitution. But the strong faith and piety of Mrs. Tinker supported her in the darkest hour, and her earnest prayers were often followed by relief from unexpected sources. One Saturday night when she had nothing to eat Deacon Samuel Gray brought a sacred offering, "the crusts of several loaves of bread prepared for sacrament" on the morrow, together with wood and other supplies. Other good people interested themselves in her behalf and found homes for the children, and Benjamin Lathrop, the sturdy old Baptist who would take no hire for his preaching, then took the widow to his own house, and with his excellent wife became to her "mother, brother, sister, friend and physician ;" providing for her necessities, till her children were able to assist her. Eliashib Adams of Canterbury, Capt. Daniel Davis of Killingly, were among the scores of sterling men "who sacrificed all for their country during the Revolution." And when their own estate could not satisfy demands, others, like Joshua Elderkin, were "thrown into Windham jail and there spent many months." Many affluent families, once enjoying all the comforts of life, were reduced to poverty and destitution by the inability of the government to redeem its pledges.

Despite these remaining shadows there was great hope and buoyancy ; pride in the past and confidence in the future. A new spring and impulse was felt throughout the States, and while settling up their accounts and storing their military munitions the Windham towns were already preparing for development and expansion. Brooklyn, Canada and Thompson Parishes asked for local independence and town privileges, and Pomfret renewed its efforts for a removal of the county seat. At a town meeting in Killingly, May 1, 1782, it was voted :—

" 1. That said town be divided.
2. That Thompson Parish be a distinct town.
3. That Col. William Danielson and Mr. Daniel Larned be agents to prefer a memorial."

27

Their petition was opposed by a strong minority, showing that division would be very detrimental both to State and town, increasing taxes already so large that the inhabitants groaned under the burden— and division was consequently deferred for three years. Brooklyn and Canada were also compelled to wait till affairs were more settled. An application to the General Assembly in 1786, for a new county "with Pomfret for shire-town," met with positive rejection, while Coventry and Union were incorporated into the newly-formed County of Tolland. Hezekiah Ripley, Shubael Abbe, Samuel Gray, Jr., and Hezekiah Manning, appointed by Windham for the examination and settlement of war accounts, had meanwhile agreed to pay the balance due by the town ; Ashford's selectmen adjusted the accounts of Kendall, Knox and Russ, for going to Boston for salt ; Killingly appointed a committee " to examine affairs of soldiers that did a tour of duty at Horse-Neck," while Seth Paine, Major Israel Putnam and Nathan Witter of Brooklyn, staked out a piece of ground by the side of the common for the purpose of keeping their much prized field-piece, and Canterbury's firearms, " properly scoured, cleaned and oiled," were stowed away in a chest, and its "wooden bowls sold, and taken care of." Its selectmen were also empowered to sell as much of the stock of powder as they should think would be for the benefit of the town— the avails of such sale to discharge town debts.

The Courts of the County now resumed their wonted functions. Shubael Abbe was appointed sheriff after the death of Sheriff Huntington. Large numbers of tavern-keepers were appointed and a number of impost collectors, viz. : Windham, Ebenezer Gray ; Pomfret, Thomas Grosvenor ; Woodstock, Jedidiah Morse ; Voluntown, Benjamin Dow. Benjamin Howard, John Parish, Moses Cleveland, David Young and others, were admitted attorneys. In 1782, it was ordered that a yard be erected around the jail twelve feet high, as soon as the money can be procured from the County. The limits assigned to certain classes of prisoners included " Capt. Tinker's house, Samuel Gray's trading shop, Thomas Reed's workshop, Major Huntington's blacksmith shop, then a straight line to the tavern sign-post belonging to the heirs of John Fitch, next to an elm tree in front of John Stamford's dwelling-house, and thence back to the jail." In 1785, a special meeting of associates and justices was held—Col. Dyer, Jeremiah Mason, Isaac Perkins, General James Gordon, present—who agreed to lay a tax of three farthings for repairing prison and administration of justice. Ebenezer Gray, collector.

In the various important questions claiming the consideration of all good patriots during these experimental years, Windham was keenly interested. With her usual alertness she watched the signs of the times, and was ever ready to speak her mind upon all needful occasions. Immediately upon the close of the war, October 3, 1783, Ashford commissioned Dr. Thomas Huntington to draft these formal " instructions " to her representatives :—

" To Captain Simeon Smith and Isaac Perkins.
  Gentlemen :—Although we repose the utmost confidence in your ability and integrity, yet at this critical conjuncture of our affairs, we conceive it will not be disagreeable to you to be informed of our sentiments with regard to several important matters.
  1. Oppose all encroachments of Congress upon the sovereignty and jurisdiction of separate States, and the assumption of power not expressly vested in them by Articles of Confederation.
  2. Inquire into the very interesting question whether Congress was authorized by the Federal Constitution to grant half-pay for life, and five years full pay to officers—and if the measure be ill-founded, attempt every constitutional method for its removal.
  3. Promote a strict inquiry into public and private expenditures, and bring to a speedy account delinquents and defaulters.
  4. Use your endeavors that vacant lands be appropriated for the general benefit of the United States.
  5. Pay particular attention to the regulation and encouragement of commerce, agriculture, arts and manufactures.
  6. We instruct you to use your influence for the suppression of placemen, pensioners and all unnecessary officers.
  7. Also, to use your influence to promote the passing an act in the Assembly to enable Congress to lay an impost on the importation of foreign articles.
  And, finally, we instruct you to move in the Assembly that the laws for the promotion of virtue and good manners and the suppression of vice, may be attended to, and enforced, and any other means tending to promote a general reformation of manners."

The deputies from Windham town were requested to urge "that effectual methods be adopted, that the yeas and nays upon every important political question taken in future in the General Assembly be published." Also, to oppose the resolve of Congress recommending five years pay to officers. As it became increasingly evident that the existing confederation was inadequate, and that farther consolidation and centralization were essential to the peace and permanence of the United States, the situation was discussed with greater earnestness. Committees were chosen in several towns to correspond with committees of other towns in Connecticut, "on the subject of public grievances." The proceedings of the convention called to remedy their grievances by revising the Articles of Confederation, and strengthening the executive powers of the central government, were anxiously debated. The Federal Constitution when submitted for consideration and acceptance, was most carefully scrutinized. Canterbury, November 12, 1787, selected ten of her most competent citizens "to examine the new form of government made by the Convention at Philadelphia, and show to this meeting their arguments and opinions thereon." Dyer and Elderkin were chosen delegates the same day by Windham to attend a State Convention at Hartford, "to take into

consideration the new Constitution proposed by general convention."
Public opinion was at first greatly divided. Many looked with sus-
picion upon the new form of government as calculated to rob their
State of its rights, and give too much power to the General Government. At Woodstock when called to the choice of delegates, the new
Constitution was heard on motion, and "largely and warmly debated
until the dusk of the evening," when the meeting was adjourned after
much debate and opposition. A very full attendance but no choice.
The Canterbury committee declared itself unprepared to report.
Windham appointed a day for especial consideration, and, "after a
very able and lengthy discussion, the town resolved by a large
majority, that as the proposed Constitution was to be determined on
by State Convention, it was not proper for the town to pass any vote
on the subject." The young town of Hampton called a special meeting and appointed a large number of its leading citizens, viz.: Thomas
Fuller, Elijah Wolcott, Philip Pearl, Ebenezer Hovey, Abner Ashley,
James Stedman, James Howard, David Martin, Andrew and Benjamin
Durkee, Thomas Stedman and John Brewster,—a committee to consult on matters concerning the country, reported by delegates assembled in Philadelphia, and draw up instructions for our delegates."
These instructions were accepted a month later, December 17, and
formally communicated to the delegate, Amos Utley, but for some
unassigned cause Hampton is reported "unrepresented," by a State
historian. Woodstock managed in adjourned meeting to elect representatives though "it was said, sundry voted not legal voters." At
the State Convention assembled in Hartford, January 3, 1788, the
following delegates appeared from Windham County:—

Windham.—Eliphalet Dyer, Jedidiah Elderkin.
Canterbury.—Asa Witter, Moses Cleveland.
Ashford.—Simeon Smith, Hendrick Dow.
Woodstock.—Stephen Paine, Timothy Perrin.
Thompson.—Daniel Larned.
Killingly.—Sampson Howe, William Danielson.
Pomfret.—Jonathan Randall, Simon Cotton.
Brooklyn.—Seth Paine.
Plainfield.—James Bradford, Joshua Dunlap.
Voluntown.—Moses Campbell, Benjamin Dow.
Lebanon.—William Williams, Ephraim Carpenter.
Mansfield.—Constant Southworth, Nathaniel Atwood.

The strong arguments urged in behalf of the Federal Constitution
by those great men, Ellsworth, Sherman and Johnson, who had borne
so prominent a part in its construction, allayed the doubts and fears of
many distrustful delegates. Windham's Samuel Huntington, now
governor of the State, and Lieutenant-Governor Wolcott, addressed
the convention in favor of ratifying the Constitution. Nine of the

Windham County towns voted in favor of ratification. Pomfret, Woodstock, Mansfield and one of the Lebanon delegates were unable to consent to it. The great majority of the inhabitants of Windham County accepted the result with approval and rejoicings, and with great unanimity and heartiness proceeded to cast their votes for Washington as president, and assume their various responsibilities as citizens of the United States of America.

II.

WINDHAM'S PROSPERITY. THE *WINDHAM PHENIX*. RELIGIOUS DECLENSION. POLITICAL AGITATION. GENERAL TOWN AFFAIRS.

WINDHAM County's energetic shire town entered upon the new *régime* with great spirit and animation. Having borne so prominent a part in carrying forward the REVOLUTION she was equally ready to lead in building up and pushing onward the NATION. Those public men who had served State and country so faithfully in the long struggle were growing old, cautious and conservative, but young men full of life and courage were hurrying up to fill their places. Foremost among the prominent men of the new generation was Zephaniah Swift of Tolland, now established in Windham town, and winning immediate success as a lawyer. Jabez Clark and Samuel Gray, Jr., had married daughters of Col. Elderkin, and engaged in legal practice. Col. Ebenezer Gray resumed the practice of his profession, and engaged in public affairs as far as his enfeebled health would permit. Timothy Larrabee and the older lawyers still continued in practice. Both old and new generations appear among town officers. Hezekiah Ripley succeeded Samuel Gray, Sen., as town clerk and treasurer in 1786. Shubael Abbe, William Rudd, Capt. Eliphalet Murdock, Ebenezer Bass, Capt. Zephaniah Swift, Majors Backus and Clift, were chosen selectmen; Henry Hewett, Thomas Tileson, Jonathan Kingsley, Melatiah Bingham, William Robinson, John Walden, listers; Jedidiah Bingham, Gideon Martin, Manasseh Palmer, Col. Thomas Dyer, Joshua Maxwell, collectors of town taxes; Elisha Abbe, constable and collector of State taxes; Josiah Babcock, Elisha White, Samuel Kingsbury, Elijah Robinson, Nathaniel Huntington, Ashael Allen, William Cary, tithingmen; Gideon Hebard, Jonathan Badger, Josiah Linkon, Jr., Dr. Penuel Cheney, William Robinson, grand-jurors; Jacob Robinson, sealer of weights and measures.

Sixteen highway-surveyors, four fence-viewers, two pound-keepers, and two leather-sealers, were also elected. Zenas Howes was appointed to take care of the Iron Works bridge, near his residence on the Willimantic; Capt. Murdock had charge of the old bridge; James Flint, Jr., the Island bridge. Town affairs required little attention. The several societies ordered their schools; the poor were let out to the lowest bidder. As there were many returned soldiers about town destitute of employment, and many idlers hanging about the village without regular business, depending upon jobs at Court sessions, the town enjoined upon its selectmen, "To attend vigilantly to the laws respecting idleness, bad husbandry and tavern-haunting, and see that the same be carried into effectual execution against such of the inhabitants of the town as shall in future be guilty of a breach of said law."

As business revived under the new ordering of public affairs this charge was less needful. With debt funded, credit restored, and a government to aid and protect them, the people of the United States began to reap the fruit of their hard struggle. Selfish laws no longer shackled their teeming energies. The world was all before them to feed and clothe, and no man willing to work was forced to remain idle. The various industries initiated in Windham before the war were now resumed with redoubled spirit. Agricultural operations were greatly extended. All kinds of farming produce were demanded, for home consumption or exportation. Shubael, Phinehas and Elisha Abbe and other solid men engaged in various "branches of husbandry." Grass on many farms had now taken the place of wheat, and great attention was given to stock raising and dairy manufactures. A large surplus of beef and pork was barreled on the farms for market, and cheese became so plentiful "that a speculator could sometimes buy a hundred thousand pounds in a neighborhood." The superabundance of wool developed a home industry—"the knitting of woolen stockings and mittens for New York market"—by which many women found pleasant and profitable employment and several thousand dollars were yearly brought into the town. Peter Webb, Henry Stanley, Jonathan Jennings, the Taintor brothers, Clark and Dorrance, Timothy Warren, and many other business firms successively established, were busily occupied in buying up these various products, and retailing West India goods and great variety of merchandise. Commercial enterprise was by no means restricted to these mercantile houses. Elisha Abbe was one who claimed the privilege of shipping his own products without the intervention of "middle men," and built for his own accommodation "THE WINDHAM," a brisk little craft, with a huge frog cut in its bow for a figure-head.

Manufactures were also progressing. Col. Elderkin trimmed and enlarged his mulberry orchard, and resumed work in his silk factory, turning out annually some ten or twelve thousand pounds of hosiery-silk to meet the demand for fashionable long stockings. Handkerchief and vest patterns were also manufactured there "in considerable numbers." He procured a loom and weaver from Europe and succeeded in fabricating sundry pieces of silk which furnished dresses* for his daughters. Col. Dyer expended much money and labor in constructing a dam and flouring works upon the Shetucket in South Windham. He also carried on a grist-mill at the Frog Pond brook, and gave his son Benjamin a thousand pounds to start the drug business at Windham Green. Dr. Benjamin, as he was called, went to New York and expended his whole capital in one purchase, buying it is said a hundred and fifty pounds of *wafers*, and other things in proportion. The Windham people made much sport of it after their fashion, but his immense variety gave him the custom of all the physicians in the surrounding country, and his advertisements claimed for him "the largest assortment of drugs, dye-stuffs, paints, spices, &c., to be found in Eastern Connecticut." He was accustomed for a time to import directly from London. The practising physicians of Windham at this date were Dr. Samuel Lee, Dr. Thomas Gray and Dr. John Clark. John Staniford followed the art of working in silver. An industry deserving notice was devised by Henry DeWitt while confined within the jail limits. From hoops and refuse iron picked up in the streets by his boys he managed to fabricate headed tacks that supplied a need in the community, and by their sale was able to provide sustenance for his family. Mills for grinding and sawing; establishments for fulling and dressing cloth, tanning leather, malting and distilling liquors, were in active operation in all parts of the town. John and Stephen Brown continued the manufacture of saltpetre and potash at their home farm on the Willimantic. The neighborhood of the Old State Armory had made no great advances. The fine privilege offered by the Falls was but scantily improved, running only a single grist-mill and saw-mill and supplying water for Ezekiel Cary's tannery. John Bingham "tended the grist-mill," and occupied an old house opposite built by Amos Dodge, an early resident of this vicinity. The red house built by Deacon Nathaniel Skiff, was occupied by his son Joseph, a bachelor with three maiden sisters. Bela Elderkin for a time kept tavern in the Howes House. These with the families of Stephen Fitch, Zenas Howes, David Young, and one or two others,

---

* Letter from William W. Campbell, Cherry Valley, New York, December 25, 1857.

made up the population of the "Old State." Yet notwithstanding the comparative insignificance of this part of the town, one of its residents, little old Uncle Amos Dodge, "was impressed with the conviction that Willimantic Falls was destined to become a great place," and by his faith and eloquence so wrought upon the minds of his neighbors that they actually consented to go out in the woods with him and prepare timber for a *meeting-house* which he insisted should be made ready for the prospective inhabitants, but after raising a frame their faith failed them, and many years passed before Willimantic was favored with a house of worship. That the Falls should ever become a great business centre and the head of the town seemed as improbable to that generation as that Windham Green should ever lose its leadership. The efforts made by the northern towns of Windham County to effect a change of county seat excited for a time only derision, but the boldness and persistency of the leaders of the movement at last compelled attention. In 1797, Timothy Larrabee, Jabez Clark and Shubael Abbe, were appointed agents of the town to meet with gentlemen of other towns opposed to removal of county seat. So alarming was the prospect that these agents were authorized to consent, "that if a court-house and accommodations should be completed in any other town without expense to the public, courts might be held half the time in them."

Business enterprises were stimulated by new facilities for advertising. In 1790, John Byrne of Norwich, set up a printing-press in the lower room of the Court-house, and early in the following year began the publication of Windham County's first newspaper.

THE   PHENIX;
Or, WINDHAM   HERALD.

Vol. I.]   SATURDAY,   MARCH 12, 1791. [Numb. 1.

Windham: Printed by *John Byrne,*   CONABIMUR.   North of the Court House.

The journal launched upon the world under this portentous figure-head was a modest little sheet of coarse bluish-gray paper, bearing little resemblance to its illustrious prototype save in the progeny of county newspapers destined to spring from its ashes. Striving for success in conformity to his motto, Mr. Byrne achieved a very creditable country newspaper, fully equal to its cotemporaries. Like them, it lacked "leaders" and "locals." Its editor made no attempt to lead or form public opinion. Windham's rampant politicians cared little for such guidance but only asked for facts from which they could draw their own conclusions. General and foreign news was furnished with all possible dispatch, viz.: foreign news of three months date; congressional reports ten or twelve days old; full reports from Connecticut election in three weeks. These, with advertisements, short moral essays, humorous anecdotes, and occasional casualties, made up the table of contents. Meagre as it was it satisfied the public. The *Phenix* was accepted as the organ of Windham County, and in a few years numbered some twelve hundred subscribers, and was carried about in all directions by post-riders. Jonathan Ashley of Hampton, was one of the first of these riders. Another was Samuel Farnham, who gave place in 1797, to Benjamin Hutchins, Jr., who would "take the usual route through Hampton, Pomfret, Woodstock, Ashford, and Mansfield." The eastern towns were visited by their own post-man. All other mail accommodations were supplied by Norwich till January 1, 1795, when a post-office was opened at Windham Green—John Byrne, postmaster. Residents of all the neighboring towns now repaired to this office. Letters for Ashford, Brooklyn, Canterbury, Hampton, Mansfield, Killingly, and even distant Thompson, were advertised in the *Windham Herald*.

Newspaper and post-office added to Windham's importance and influence. Its superiority "to every inland town in the State in trade and merchandise," was reiterated with greater confidence. Its numerous stores, warehouses, taverns, and all places of public resort, were well filled and patronized on ordinary occasions, and on festive days its streets were thronged with visitors from all the surrounding country. There were the usual Training and Election days and mighty regimental musters. Most of the county convocations and public gatherings were held in Windham, meetings of the Western Land Company, of the Windham Medical Society, and of other embryo associations. The sessions of the Court brought a train of judges, lawyers and witnesses. Soon after the close of the war an academy was opened, securing for a time the services of Dr. Pemberton, and though for lack of permanent funds it was unable to retain so popular a teacher, it maintained a respectable standing, and was well sustained by Windham and its vicinity. Public schools were yet poor, but efforts were made for their improvement. In 1794, thirteen school districts were set off, designated according to the fashion of the day by some prominent resident, viz.: 1, Frederick Stanley's; 2, Solomon Huntington's; 3, Jabez Wolcott's; 4, Timothy Wales'; 5, Eliphalet Murdock's; 6, William Preston's; 7, Zebediah Tracy's; 8, Josiah Palmer's; 9, James Cary's; 10, Joseph Palmer's; 11, William Cary's; 12, John Walden's; 13, Zenas Howe's. Private schools were often sustained in different neighborhoods.

Much consideration was now given to the improvement of high-

28

ways. Highway districts were instituted identical with the school districts, and liberty procured to levy a tax to keep them in order. Projected turnpikes called out much discussion.   Jeremiah Ripley, Timothy Larrabee, Moses Cleveland, Luther Payne, James Gordon, and such others as should associate with them, were incorporated as The Windham Turnpike Company, in 1799, constructing a turnpike from Plainfield to Coventry, past Windham Court-house, which became the great thoroughfare of travel between Hartford and Providence.   Very great efforts were made by the town to compel this company to lay its road over the Shetucket, where the bridge was already standing.   Elijah Selden, Capt. Abner Robinson and Dr. Penuel Cheney, were appointed in 1801, to negotiate for alterations in the new turnpike so as to avoid re-bridging the Shetucket, but were obliged to submit to the unwelcome necessity.   After several attempts to keep up new and old town bridges, the latter was abandoned in 1806.   Timothy Larrabee, Charles Taintor, Eleazer Huntington and Roger Waldo, were constituted a corporation in 1800, "by the name of The Windham and Mansfield Society, for the establishing a turnpike road from Joshua Hide's dwelling-house in Franklin to the meeting-house in Stafford," connecting with a turnpike leading from New London and Norwich.   The laying out a projected turnpike from Woodstock's north bound to the south bound of Connecticut at New London, passing through Scotland Parish, was very vigorously and persistently opposed by Windham, and the road was finally laid out farther eastward.   She also successfully opposed a road from Woodstock through Ashford and Mansfield to Windham Court-house, not only keeping the Courts but refusing to shorten the road to them. In her own roads and bridges she manifested due enterprise and liberality, assuming the charge of the Horse Shoe bridge at the request of Joseph Skiff and others, and advancing two hundred dollars for reducing hills and mending the road from Scotland meeting-house to Jared Webb's.

With such a rush of business and travel Windham's taverns might well flourish. Nathaniel Linkon, John Flint, David Young, John Keyes, John Parish entertained the public in different parts of the town ; Nathaniel Hebard, John Staniford, John Fitch, received on Windham Green. The "Widow Cary," now the wife of John Fitch, had brought to her new home the jolly image of Bacchus, occupying a conspicuous perch on the sign-post of the "old Fitch Tavern." Travelers, court attendants and fellow-townspeople found agreeable entertainment beneath his beaming countenance, and in the other village taverns, famed as they were for the flow of wit and liquor, as well as more substantial fare.   Windham's old-time reputation for jokes and jollity was abundantly sustained in this day of prosperity and universal liquor-drinking. The many Revolutionary veterans resident in the vicinity were habitual frequenters of these attractive resorts, fighting over their battles and telling marvelous tales of hair-breadth escape and harrowing adventure. Quaint old characters abounded whose odd sayings and doings furnished exhaustless merriment. There was one "jolly boy" of whom it was said "he could not go by Hebard's tavern without stopping to get a drink of rum." A friend remonstrated with him and finally made a bet that he could not do so. The old man went down town and marched triumphantly past the tavern. "Now," said he, "I'll go back and *treat Resolution*." Once when somewhat obfuscated by drink he wandered off into the fields and went to sleep but forgot on rising to put on his old cocked hat. Some boys found it and brought it back to him, thinking to cover him with confusion. "In which lot did you find it?" he inquired blandly. "In Mr. White's pasture, near the bars." "Well, boy, *go take it right back, that is my place to keep it*."

One comical old wag had a turn for rhyming. Meeting one day a rough-looking countryman with tawny hair and beard, and butternut-colored coat, riding on a sorry sorrel nag, he flung up his hat at the uncouth figure and exclaimed:—

> "Man and mare, beard and hair
> All compare, I swear!"

Another, calling at one of the taverns when it chanced to run low, suggested as inscription for the sign:—

> "Nothing on one side—nothing on t'other,
> Nothing in the house, nor in the barn nuther."

Among Windham's merchants and leading men were some who delighted greatly in jokes and story-telling. Staniford's house was a great place of resort for these worthies, an exchange-place for all manner of quips, pranks and witticisms, where each would strive to catch or outvie the other. X had a cow which gave two full pails of milk morning and evening, and finally he had her milked *at noon*, and she gave two full pails and just as much at the other milkings as before, but Z's cow gave milk so continuously "that he had an aqueduct built from barn to house to bring it, and the milk was so rich that every quart made a pound of butter." One man had killed nearly a cart-load of pigeons at one shot. Another shot "a great lot of crows in a pitch dark night." X was obliged to hoe beans once, while his brothers were permitted to go fox-hunting. He "heard the dogs coming, looked up and saw the fox which jumped over the fence into a snowbank, and he killed him with his hoe before he could get onto his feet." "But," says Z, "it was a queer time to have a heavy snowbank in a lot where you were *hoeing beans!*" "The climate has changed in fifty years," responds the unabashed Munchausen. Reminiscences of the cold winter of 1779-80, called out some marvellous statements. "The snow was already three feet deep on a level, and the day of the great snow it began snowing early very hard, but about 11 o'clock it snowed as large flakes *as chipping-birds*—it snowed *an inch deep every minute* for an hour and a half, and continued to snow as hard as in common storms all day. Whereupon X relates that on the cold Sunday of that famous winter his family went to meeting about two miles away. The big dinner-pot was put on before leaving, with pork and beef, turnips, cabbage and potatoes, all to boil together for dinner, and a big fire of logs made under it in the old-fashioned fireplace. When they returned they found the kitchen door blown open "and it was so cold that the *steam had frozen in a solid cone* on the top of the pot, and the pot was boiling furiously below it!" That story, all agreed, could never be matched. X announced one night that he had discovered what salmon lived on. He had found two *flying squirrels* in the maw of one just purchased, but the rogue who had *crammed them down the salmon's throat* had the best of the joke that evening. These lively jokers were not addicted to drinking and as they did not patronize the bar they were accustomed to send each a cord or two of wood a season to help keep up the sparkling fire that added zest to their stories. Their host was noted for his exploits in eating. Three large shad for thirty consecutive days, with plenty of accompaniments, and a whole fresh tripe at a dinner, were among these feats. When melting silver one hot summer day he was known to drink *two gallons* of West India rum without feeling the least intoxicated.

A large number of waiters, hostlers, drivers, purveyors, occupied at Court time, but with little to do but lounge and tell stories the remainder of the year, hung about the taverns and stores, and added to the general merriment. Negro men and boys were still very numerous and made much sport for all classes with their droll mimicry and endless tricks and capers. Change of status made little difference to this class. A few went out into the world as freedmen, but the larger number even though freed clung to their old masters and were always supported and cared for. The most intelligent among them was General Job, brigadier of the colored brigade that met for parade on the Norwich Line every year. He married Rose, a very handsome negress, belonging to Elisha Abbe, and they owned a house on the back road.

With all Windham's advancement in one respect there was retrogression. Her secular affairs were most flourishing, but religion had sadly declined. It was a transition period—a day of upheaval, over-turning, uprootal. Infidelity and Universalism had come in with the Revolution and drawn multitudes from the religious faith of their fathers. Free-thinking and free-drinking were alike in vogue. Great looseness of manners and morals had replaced the ancient Puritanic strictness. In former golden days Windham could proudly sing :—

" That her great men were good and her good men were great,
    And the props of her Church were the pillars of the State."

Now, sons of those honored fathers and the great majority of those in active life, were sceptics and scoffers, and men were placed in office who never entered the House of God except for town meetings and secular occasions. In a sermon preached upon the fiftieth anniversary of his settlement, December, 1790, Mr. White strikingly portrayed the contrast :—

" In those days there were scarce any that were not professors of religion, and but few infants not baptized. *No families that were prayerless.* Profane swearing was but little known, and open violations of the Sabbath not prac-ticed as is common now. And there were no *Deists* among us. The people as a body were fearers of the Lord and observers of the Sabbath and its duties. But the present day is peculiar for men's throwing off the fear of the Lord. Declensions in religion have been increasing for about thirty years past, such as profaneness, disregard of the Sabbath, neglect of family religion, unright-eousness, intemperance, imbibing of modern errors and heresies and the cry-ing prevalence of infidelity against the clearest light."

The standing church had to contend with the FRIENDS as well as the foes of religion. About one-third of the inhabitants of Windham were now "certificate people or Sectaries," bitterly opposed to the ecclesiastic constitution of Connecticut, and the churches founded upon that basis. The Baptists were steadily gaining in numbers, strength, and influence under the charge of their worthy elder, Benjamin Lathrop. In the north part of Windham, which was now becoming a populous neighborhood, a remarkable worship was conducted by Joshua Abbe. Rev. Moses Cook Welch of Mansfield represented " these Abbe-ites as a sect of Baptists, differing from any and all of that denomination that had ever risen in any age, having no communication even with other Baptist churches. Their meetings were characterized by jargon, disorder and great confusion ; all were allowed to speak at pleasure, women as well as men, three, four or six sometimes speaking at once, while groans, sobs and sighs were reiterated by others." Doubtless this report is colored by orthodox prejudice, but whether dis-orderly or not these meetings were permitted. Any sect or church within the State of Connecticut had now the privilege of worshipping according to its own dictates. The State only insisted that every man should worship *somewhere,* or, at least, bear his part in maintaining some religious worship. The Saybrook Platform had been dropped from the statute book in the revision of 1784, but the old society organization was retained. Every man within the limits of a stated society was taxed for the support of its religious worship, until he lodged with the clerk of the society a certificate of membership of some other society. The old Separates and Baptists were not in the least satisfied with these concessions and were still forced to submit to what they deemed a degrading vassalage, while the opposition of the free-thinkers to the established churches was greatly heightened by being obliged to help support preaching which they disbelieved and hated. After forty years of conflict the agitators had won the privilege of worshipping as they pleased and paying ministers after their own fashion. Now they claimed the right of *not* worshipping if they pleased, and neither hearing or paying ministers except at their own fancy. The "movement" began by the early Separates was destined to go onward till every legal restriction was removed, and all religious questions and worship left to the settlement of the individual conscience.

The political status of Windham was greatly affected by these religious dissensions and complications. A large majority of her population were Federalists for a time, staunchly supporting the Federal Constitution, and Washington's administration, but on State and local questions they were greatly divided. Connecticut's ecclesiastical constitution and parish system, and those ministers and public men who upheld it, were very obnoxious to the Sectaries. There was also a strong radical element in the town, a feeling of hostility to the aristocratic pretensions and style of the upper classes, the college-bred Grays, Elderkins, Dyers, who had been so prominent in public affairs. Far back in 1775 " a miserable junto " * had contrived to defeat Colonel Dyer's renomination to Congress, and this opposition was constantly increasing. Samuel Webb, a man of strong common sense and much native force of character, was deeply imbued with radical and revolutionary ideas, and had much influence among the masses. The few " Grumbletonians," or anti-Federalists, joined with the Sectaries, and in 1786 sent Benjamin Lathrop and Samuel Webb to the General Assembly. In the following year Zephaniah Swift was sent as deputy. Federal in politics, he was yet a friend to progress and religious freedom, and an open and earnest opponent to the existing church establishment. Sectaries of every shade gladly welcomed him as their leader and sought to place him in office, while members of the standing church were outraged that a *free-thinker* should be sent to represent them. The ministers of these churches, Messrs. White and Cogswell, " were grieved and displeased

---

* Letters of Silas Deane.

that men should have so little regard for religion as to choose a man for deputy who has none," and marvelled at the inconsistency of "those Separates, Baptists and enthusiasts who pretend to so much more religion than we, yet vote for a profane, irreligious man, who scarce ever attends public worship." Rev. Moses Cook Welch, now settled in Mansfield Centre, was loud in condemnation of their conduct. In spite of strong opposition Swift carried the two succeeding elections. Judge Devotion of Scotland won the day in October, 1788. The contest went on year after year with the vigor and bitterness characteristic of religious warfare. Charges of extortion and imprisonment hurled against the standing churches were met by accusations of excesses and immoralities. The ministers carried the questions into their several pulpits. Mr. Cogswell reports, April 12, 1790: "Went to Freeman's meeting and voted according to the dictates of my conscience, but could not succeed to keep Capt. Swift from being chosen deputy . . Believe, nevertheless, that *my preaching* did good yesterday, for Judge Devotion had almost as many votes as Swift." In 1793, Swift was sent to Congress, the first representative from northeast Connecticut.

As inherent differences of opinion became more defined and outspoken, and opposition to Federalism assumed political organism, Windham was ready for the conflict. Swift indeed kept his place in the Federal ranks, but a great majority of the opponents to the standing order accepted Jefferson as their leader, and united with the anti-Federal Republicans. The sons of Samuel Webb were among the foremost leaders of this new party, which gained a strong hold in the town but was not able for several years to control its elections. The ability and audacity of its advocates, and their ruthless onslaught upon the Federal Government and established institutions, excited great opposition and alarm. The staunch old Federalists of the town, Col. Dyer, Judge Devotion, the Grays, Jabez Clark, Shubael Abbe, the standing clergy, with their organ, the *Windham Herald*, endeavored by every means in their power to stay the progress of these pernicious principles and check the growth of this insurrectionary party. When in addition to their assaults upon the General Government, they proceeded to attack the *Constitution of Connecticut*, and propose a substitute for that sacred Charter under which its inhabitants had enjoyed such freedom and privileges, words were inadequate to express their indignation. Peter Webb, a successful merchant in Windham town, was one of the first to discover and proclaim that Connecticut "had no government." When Pierpont Edwards in 1804, issued a circular calling upon Republicans "to meet in convention at New Haven upon the subject of forming a constitution," a correspondent of the *Windham Herald* thus describes its reception in Windham County :—

"In the town of Sterling, a meeting was convened by Mr. Lemuel Dorrance, to whom the circular letter of Mr. Edwards was addressed. Mr. Dorrance was chosen chairman of the meeting. It was composed of twenty-nine or thirty persons, and on discussion of the subject of the circular letter, it was voted that no delegate should be chosen. Whether Mr. Dorrance obeyed the *direction* of the letter, to *come on himself*, if none was chosen, we are not fully assured.

The circular was submitted to a meeting of those who call themselves republicans (exclusively), on the 13th of August, inst., at Plainfield. The meeting was attended by more members than any other meeting of the kind ever held in that town, and on full deliberation it was (we mention it to their honor) voted not to choose any delegate to the proposed convention. It is, however, understood, that after the return to that town, of a gentleman *from Court*, on Saturday last, a few, very few persons met on Monday, and made choice of Mr. Elias Woodward. How the republicans in general, by whom the proposition was rejected, will receive this we cannot tell.

From the town of Voluntown we only learn that Mr. Nicholas Randall has gone on to New Haven.

From Thompson we learn nothing, but presume no person attends from that town.

In the town of Woodstock a meeting was publicly warned, and notice given, that it would be open to all parties, but when the democrats met, they called for a private room and refused admission to any but their own sect. They consisted of *twenty-three* persons, five of whom were not freemen, one is a pauper maintained by the town, and ten persons who have come to reside in Woodstock from other towns, mostly from Rhode Island. Mr. William Bowen chosen.

In the town of Pomfret a meeting was held and composed of twenty persons, six of whom declined voting affirmatively on the question, and Mr. John Chandler was chosen by fourteen votes.

Mr. Benjamin Arnold has gone from the town of Killingly; whether the democrats in that town held a meeting for his election, we have not learned.

From Brooklyn, we understand, that Master Harry Stanley, is the representative, and took a seat in the stage for New Haven, on Monday evening; but have heard of no meeting for his election—some run before they are sent.

In the town of Canterbury, in pursuance of the circular, a private meeting of a small number of persons was holden, and elected Mr. Ephraim Lyon.

In the towns of Windham and Lebanon, we understand they are in favor of a large representation, and elected four persons in each town; of whom Messrs. Baldwin and Manning attend from Windham, and Mr. Andrew Metcalf, from Lebanon.

At Ashford, Messrs. D. Bolles, and Jason Woodward.

At Hampton, Mr. Roger Taintor.

At Mansfield, Mr. Edmond Freeman.

At Columbia, Mr. Stephen Buckingham.

We are fully assured, that whenever meetings of democrats have been holden in this county, in pursuance of the circular letters, they have excluded all persons, not avowedly democrats, from acting in their meetings. With what pretentions these friends of the people can claim the right of manufacturing new forms of government for the good citizens of this state, against their consent, and without their advice, we know not. We only ask, do these proceedings furnish evidence that the party are actuated by a spirit of equal liberty, or a spirit of usurpation and tyranny ?"

The *Herald* also reports that so far as it can learn " the proposition was received with coldness mingled with alarm even by those who have hitherto favored the democratic party. Less *alarm* would probably have been excited if these Constitution-makers had admitted that Connecticut now has a *Constitution*, but that it is a bad one and requires renovation. But when the bold ground is assumed that Connecticut has *no Constitution*, and that all the acts of the Legislature for many years past have been acts of usurpation and tyranny, most reflecting men startled at the consequences which may flow from admitting this proposition." Yet notwithstanding this alarm, and the earnest efforts and solemn warnings of the Federalists, their opponents succeeded this same year in electing Mr. Peter Webb as deputy to the General Assembly, and thenceforward the republicans were often able to carry the elections, the Sectaries holding the balance of power. The earnestness and eloquence of the Windham republicans, and the prominent position of their town, gave them great political influence during the Jeffersonian conflict and administration.

The third settled pastor of Windham's First Church, Rev. Stephen White, died January 9, 1793, in the seventy-fifth year of his age and fifty-third of his ministry. His gentle and lovely character, consistent Christian life, and faithful ministerial service, had won the regard of all "whose approbation was worth possessing." His funeral sermon was attended by a great concourse of people—his former pupil, Rev. M. C. Welch, preaching the sermon, and all the neighboring ministers participating in the exercises, which were prolonged till the dusk of the evening. His excellent wife, sister of Col. Dyer, survived her husband ten years. The *Windham Herald* in announcing her decease asserts, "that the life of this old lady furnished a pattern worthy to be imitated by the most pious and most exemplary. From a very early period of her life she was a professor of the Christian religion and ever adorned her profession by the most distinguished piety and godliness. Rectitude was uniformly her object, and love and esteem were the affections which she uniformly inspired." Of her thirteen children, three daughters, greatly esteemed for piety and excellence of character, long occupied the modest homestead. Mr. White was succeeded in the ministerial office by Elijah Waterman of Bozrah, who was ordained in Windham, October 1, 1794. The unusual energy and zeal of the young pastor found ample exercise in his new field. His church was cold, backward and almost without influence in the community. Irreligion was rampant and aggressive. Infidel books and doctrines were widely disseminated. Books demonstrating Universal salvation were advertised in the *Herald*, and subscriptions received for them in its office. Good-fellowship and jollity were degenerating into revelry and dissipation. Intemperance had become alarmingly prevalent. Card-playing and other questionable amusements were much in vogue. A social club, comprising all the

29

"good fellows" about town, afforded opportunity for free indulgence in such pastimes. And while the forces of evil were thus united and strong, the few church members and christians were expending all their energies in battling and beating one another. Mr. Waterman devoted himself to his work with great earnestness, and by his faithful labors and pungent exhortations soon aroused a new religious interest in his church, and received encouraging accessions to its membership. Like his predecessors he found a wife among his own people—Lucy, daughter of Shubael Abbe—and it was hoped that like them he would remain for life in Windham. Wide in sympathy as well as fervent in spirit, Mr. Waterman interested himself in all the reformatory movements then in progress at home and abroad. He was an active member of the Windham County Association and prominent in effecting the formal Consociation of the churches. At home he labored for improvement of public schools and the formation of a school library in place of the former Social Library which with other good things had been suffered to decline and fall to pieces. He transcribed the records of the church and provided for their better preservation, and prepared a faithful historical discourse for the commemoration of its hundredth anniversary. He also collected materials " for a complete history of Windham County," which in subsequent years were unfortunately scattered.

Yet notwithstanding Mr. Waterman's acknowledged ability and excellence, his pastorate was stormy. His open and uncompromising hostility to vice and irreligion aroused strong opposition and made him many personal enemies. Finding that in spite of his earnest remonstrances the club of jolly fellows persisted in hunting rabbits and playing ball on Fast and Thanksgiving days in defiance of law, he made complaint to the magistrate and secured the exaction of fines. These victims and other aggrieved parties united their forces against the zealous minister and proceeded to organize as an Episcopal society, under the auspices of Rev. John Tyler of Norwich, who held church service with them as often as practicable. By this device they evaded the payment of rates and made it very difficult for the society to provide for the support of Mr. Waterman. The church, however, clung faithfully to its pastor and would probably have succeeded in retaining him in spite of the pecuniary difficulties but for the removal of one of its strongest pillars and supports, Mr. Sheriff Abbe, who was stricken down with apoplexy, April 16, 1804. His worth and labors were thus portrayed by mourning friends:—

" He graduated at Yale College, 1764. He was several years in the business of merchandize and by his own exertions became largely engaged in husbandry. In 1783 he was appointed sheriff of the County of Windham and continued in the most punctual and unexceptionable manner to discharge the duties of that office till his death. He was often chosen representative of the town. In 1798 he was appointed by the President one of the commissioners of the Land tax, and by the Assembly one of the committee to manage the School Funds. In domestic life he was indulgent and decisive. In public business, active, punctual and correct. In his attachment to civil and religious institutions he was exemplary, and to the poor and afflicted humane and generous. His ability and integrity secured to him the esteem and confidence of his fellow-citizens. And his death was extensively and deeply regretted. He left a widow, three sons and five daughters to mourn an irreparable loss.

> Tears flow nor cease where Abbe's ashes sleep,
> For him a wife and tenderest children weep,
> And justly—for few shall ever transcend
> As husband, parent and a faithful friend."

In view of this great loss and the combined opposition, Mr. Waterman thought it unwise to remain in Windham and was dismissed by council, Feb. 12, 1805, the church still attesting its regard. Of eighty-nine admitted to the church during his pastorate only twelve were males. The venerable deacons—Nathaniel Wales, Sen., Joseph Huntington and Nathaniel Skiff—had now been dead many years. Deacon Samuel Gray died in 1787, Deacon Jonathan Martin in 1795, Deacon Elijah Bingham in 1798. Samuel Perkins, Esq., and Capt. Eliphalet Murdock were elected deacons during the ministry of Mr. Waterman.

Many of Windham's honored citizens were now passing away. Colonel Ebenezer Gray, after suffering greatly from disease contracted in Revolutionary service, died in 1795, greatly respected and beloved. It was said that his extreme generosity to the poor lost him his position as selectman. With other Windham officers he was an honored member of the Society of the Cincinnati, established to perpetuate Revolutionary friendships and associations, and relieve the widows and orphans of those who had fallen. His widow survived him many years. His brother Thomas, physician and merchant, died in 1792. Colonel Jedidiah Elderkin died in 1794, Deacon Eleazer Fitch in 1800, Elder Benjamin Lathrop in 1804, Samuel Linkon in 1794, after entering upon the second year of his second century. Windham's "oldest inhabitant," Arthur Bibbins,* had preceded him several years and also exceeded him in length of life. Colonel Dyer, now far advanced in years, was still hale and hearty, and though no longer participant in public affairs was still keenly interested in all that was passing. A gentleman of the old school, punctilious in dress and manners, his familiar form was often seen on Windham street, and his voice often heard in earnest deprecation of the alarming growth of radicalism, Jacobinism, infidelity and immorality. Swift had now completed that famous "Digest of the Laws of Connecticut," which brought him so much honor, served as secretary on an important foreign mission, and in

---

* This venerable patriarch, according to Windham Church records, attained 108 years, but a more careful investigation reduces his years to 102. " He is represented to have been a man of great vigor and health, never sick a day until after he was one hundred, when he was thrown from a horse and injured, after which he was confined until his death."

1805 was appointed a judge of the Superior Court. Samuel Perkins, after studying for the ministry, had decided to enter the legal profession, and engaged in practice in Windham. John Baldwin and David W. Young also settled as lawyers in their native town. Henry Webb now served as high sheriff, Charles Abbe, deputy-sheriff; Phinehas Abbe, jailer. Thomas Grosvenor of Pomfret succeeded William Williams as chief judge of the County Court in 1806, Ebenezer Devotion, Hezekiah Ripley, James Gordon, Lemuel Ingalls, associates. Samuel Gray was clerk of the Superior and County Courts. Windham enjoyed during this decade the excitement of two public executions—that of Caleb Adams of Pomfret, Nov. 19, 1803, and of Samuel Farnham of Ashford, two years later. The lamented death of Sheriff Abbe was thought to have been hastened by his official duties at the execution of the former.

Colonel Elderkin's silk factory passed, after his decease, into the hands of "Clark and Gray," who were initiating many business enterprises, but it was soon bought by Mansfield experimenters who were making great efforts to increase and improve silk manufacture. Capitalists were buying up land and attempting to establish various manufactures at Willimantic, but after the death of Amos Dodge the residents of this vicinity lost faith in its immediate up-building, and suffered the meeting-house frame to be carried to Windham Green where it did good service on Zion's Hill as a public school-house. Willimantic was a place of much resort in the spring for its fisheries of shad and salmon, and the new turnpike brought throngs of travelers and customers to David Young's tavern, but the great rush of business and enterprise still sought the Green. Mr. DeWitt's tack business had been ruined by the invention of nail-making machinery, and his shop had passed into the hands of Jedidiah Story, where might be found "*Hats* of the newest fashion, warranted to be as good and cheap as at any factory in the State." John Burgess offered for sale "excellent soal-leather" and as good morocco and calf-skin shoes as could be found in market, and also a new fashioned four-wheel vehicle, called a wagon, which had somehow come into his possession and which most people thought a very impracticable invention. Business and trade were as brisk and lively as ever. The columns of the *Windham Herald* teemed with solicitations and demands. Brown, white and striped tow cloth of home manufacture, blue and white striped mittens, stockings of all textures and colors, good shoe thread, cheese, butter, geese feathers, rags, old pewter, brass and copper, rabbit skins and other furs, were taken by all the merchants and manufacturers who offered in return the usual variety of household and fancy articles. All dealers were urgent and profuse in offering rum, gin, brandy and wines at the lowest figure. "Good sweet rum at five and sixpence per gallon;" "the best of Jamaica rum at the moderate price of one dollar and six cents per gallon;" hogsheads, barrels and kegs of good rum for farmers and housekeepers who wished to supply themselves by the quantity and provide for their help in haying, were temptingly paraded. The increasing use of liquor in public and private and the great number of idlers who hung about the stores and taverns, was, perhaps, the reason that Windham with all its business and bustle seemed to have lost something of its thriftiness, and to the keen eye of Doctor Dwight, as reported in one of his inspectorial tours, exhibited "marks of decay." Both churches in its first society were now destitute of a pastor, Mr. Daniel C. Banks declining a call to the First Church. Many valued families were lost to churches and town by the rage for emigration. The children of Wyoming emigrants returned to the Susquehanna Valley, and gained possession of the lands claimed by their fathers. Thomas Dyer, Jr., grandson of Col. Dyer, settled in Wilkesbarre, where he was greatly esteemed. The sons of Col. Elderkin removed from Windham after the death of their father. Major Ebenezer Backus and Dr. John Clark followed their children to Central New York. Representatives of the old Windham families were scattered abroad in all parts of the opening Republic. Dr. Samuel Lee died in 1804. His son Samuel, associated with him in practice, had already distinguished himself by the composition of "Lee's Windham Bilious Pills"—one of the first patent medicines that came before the public. So great was their reputation that the lawyers at Court maintained that even to carry a box of Lee's pills in their pockets would ward off disease. Windham with its usual vivacity interested itself in experiments for the amelioration of that much dreaded disease—Small-pox. William Robinson and Samuel Bleight offered to inoculate its inhabitants in 1800, for Kine or Cow-pox, which they declared to be a perfect security against the small-pox, and only to be communicated by inoculation. Dr. Vine Utley and Mr. Jonathan Woodward went about the County in the following year, inoculating scores of people in every town with very satisfactory results.

Windham's loss of population—a hundred and twenty, between 1790 and 1800—made little apparent difference in its animation and activity. Taverns and stores were as well patronized as ever. Public meetings were held in increasing number and variety. In 1801, the Masons of Windham and Lebanon were gathered into the Eastern Star Lodge with appropriate ceremonies. The Festival of St. John the Evangelist was celebrated in Windham the following Christmas day with much rejoicing. The first Republican or Democratic celebration of which we have report was held July 4, 1806, at the house of Mr. John Staniford, innholder. A large attendance was expected and doubtless secured.

III.

SCOTLAND'S FIRST BELL. THE SCOTLAND PARSONAGE. SOCIAL
LIFE. CHANGES. CONTROVERSY BETWEEN PASTOR
AND PEOPLE.

SCOTLAND Parish shared in the general growth and prosperity of
the town, raising its due proportion of sheep, swine and cattle, and
sending butter and cheese, beef, pork and wool to market. Ebenezer
Devotion, though now judge of the County Court and employed in
many public affairs, was still engaged in trade. Zebediah Tracy's shop
accommodated the public with many useful articles. A new firm,
French and Allyn, offered choice New York goods to purchasers,
together with groceries and a few hogsheads of St. Croix rum very
cheap in exchange for stockings, mittens, tow cloth, etc. Returned
veterans—Captains John Baker, Abner Robinson and others—engaged
with renewed zest in the arts of peace. Samuel, Jeremiah and
Jedidiah Bingham, John and Jacob Burnap, William and James Cary,
Jonathan Kingsley, Eliphalet Huntington and various other descendants of the early settlers, were now in active life, attending to their
farms and other industries. Major John Keyes of Ashford, appointed
in 1786, adjutant-general of the militia of Connecticut, had now
removed his residence to Scotland village, and his comfortable tavern
had become a famous place of resort for the many old soldiers residing in this part of the town. Its physician, Dr. Penuel Cheney, was
very active and useful in society and town affairs. The parish bore
its part in civil administration, and was allowed the privilege of
holding one-third of the allotted town meetings in its convenient
meeting-house. Having fortunately erected a new house just before
the breaking-out of the war, it had no special home demands during
this period, and was able to do its part with great care and efficiency,
furnishing many men of tried fidelity and valor. One of its first
achievements after the return of peace was to procure a bell for its
meeting-house steeple which involved it in a series of misadventures.
According to popular tradition the bell was cracked upon its first
journey; returned as unsound, and re-cracked upon its hanging;
re-mended and re-cracked in celebrating its successful return and suspension—the whole population venting their joy by ringing it—and
by farther mischance was twice disabled, sent back and returned
before its final exaltation and installment into office. Probably these
reports were exaggerated by their jolly neighbors of Windham, only
too glad to retaliate the banterings upon their own frog panic, but the
records show that they were not unfounded. Dr. Cheney was

appointed to procure subscriptions for a bell in 1790. In June the following year, Dr. Cogswell reports that the subscribers for a bell voted not to have the bell which is now in use here, nor any other of Davison's but to apply to Dolittles, (New Haven). In November, the society voted to accept the bell provided by the committee for that purpose, and to provide some suitable person to ring and toll it. In 1793, it enjoins upon its committee, to take care of the bell, get the tongue mended, make fixture for deck and keep the wet out. Two years later it is ordered to get the bell repaired, and again, 1796, to get the wheel repaired and make it more convenient to ring the bell. A singing school had been instituted during this time through the efforts of Captain Robinson. Young people were prompt and eager in attendance and the singing so much improved that young Mason Cogswell affirmed that they sang better in Scotland than in Hartford. A social library for the benefit of the east part of the town was formed about 1790.

Mr. Cogswell's ministrations were still acceptable to church and society. In 1790 he received a doctor's degree from Yale College—the first Windham County minister thus honored. His church shared in the prevailing religious declension, receiving few accessions and meeting many losses. Deacon John Cary died in 1788; Deacon John Baker in 1791. Some members were lost by emigration, some by secession to other churches. Religious feeling was at a low ebb; social conferences and prayer meetings were not encouraged, and the "gifts of the church" were so little exercised that when its pastor was kept at home by sickness and sent his son to read a sermon to the congregation there was not a brother in the church willing to offer a public prayer. Whatever spiritual life existed was drawn to the Sectaries. Zealous Baptist itinerants, Lyon of Canterbury, Dyer Hebard and Jordan Dodge, held meetings on Pudding Hill and remoter neighborhoods, and through their instrumentality "a religious stir," or revival, was incited at which many professed conversion and received baptism by immersion, uniting with the Baptists in Windham and Hampton. The Brunswick Church, under its aged minister, was greatly weakened by this new element, but still maintained regular worship. Unlike many Separates, Elder Palmer had a respect for education, his son David graduating at Dartmouth College in 1797. Schools in Scotland were maintained and catechized as the law required. The central school flourished for two seasons under the charge of a teacher who afterwards became very famous—William Eaton, the conqueror of Tripoli.

In politics Scotland parish was more conservative than the western part of the town, standing squarely by its favorite candidate, Judge

Devotion, and when it came out in full force sure to carry the election. This result may have been due in great measure to the influence of its honored son, Samuel Huntington, who, after serving as president of the Continental Congress, and chief justice of the Superior Court of Connecticut, was elected governor of the State in 1786. Public cares and high position did not lessen his interest in his early home, but with increasing years he seemed to find it more attractive. Every few weeks Dr. Cogswell's journal reports a visit from the Governor, and instructive discussion of national and scientific questions. Mingling thus freely with old friends and townsmen a man of such weight and elevation of character could hardly fail to become a power for good to the community.

Governor Huntington's brilliant brothers were also frequent visitors at that pleasant parsonage as well as many other celebrities. It was a day of universal visiting and social intercourse, not only between the residents of particular towns but between different towns and neighborhoods. The mode of traveling was eminently conducive to sociability. One-horse chaises and rough roads compelled short stages. Travelers were accustomed to stop at every friend's house for rest and refreshment. In these slow old days everybody seemed to have time to drive about and chat with their friends and neighbors, and the Scotland parsonage was a place of especial resort and popularity. Its family circle was large and lively. Children, grandchildren and hosts of relatives were continually coming and going. Neighbors and parishioners were dropping in at all hours of the day, bringing news and asking counsel. Scarce a day passed without a call from some neighboring townsman— Dr. Baker of Brooklyn, Esquire Perkins of Newent, Dr. Adams of Westminster, Colonel Mosely and Mr. Stewart from Hampton, Colonels Dyer and Danielson, and even "old General Putnam." Nightfall often brought with it some traveling minister—poor broken-down Mr. Rowland with his budget of troubles; Mr. Williams of Woodstock, "a serious, pious man and good divine," or Dr. Huntington with "metaphysical paradox that seemed to favor Universalism." These visits, with other family affairs, the general news of the day and appropriate moral reflections, were duly recorded in the Doctor's voluminous diary. Not only did he entertain these constant visitors, prepare sermons and lectures, visit the sick, catechize the schools, attend numberless associations and ordinations, manage farm, orchard and garden, but he contrived to read all the newspapers and new books that came in his way, and make a daily record of all these doings. He also maintained a very close and friendly intercourse with his brethren in the ministry, soothing the declining years of Messrs. White and Mosely; extending aid and counsel to perplexed Mr. Staples, and interchanging weekly visits and confidences with his dear friends Lee and Whitney. To young men just launching into the ministry he was especially helpful and considerate, and kindly encouraged them to test their powers in his pulpit. Men now remembered as hoary dignitaries in church and state were among these trembling neophytes. Daniel Waldo, the centennial chaplain of Congress, was then " a sensible, serious, growing youth, no orator, but likely to do good in the world." Ebenezer Fitch, the future president of Williams College, " preached and prayed exceedingly well ;" but the young man destined to important home mission work in Connecticut had unfortunately " been praised too much and made self-important." Dr. Cogswell was much pleased with Samuel Perkins of Windham, " a judicious, prudent, pious young man and fine scholar," who, against his advice and much to the regret of all, left " preaching for law." He also rejoiced in the promise shown by the grandson of Voluntown's much tried minister, Gershom Dorrance, and thanked God who raised up children in room of their parents. Young Hendrick Dow was much liked in Hampton. Parish and Tyler of Brooklyn were promising young men whom he rejoiced to see in the ministry. " Jonathan Kingsley's son James "—Yale's erudite professor—was pronounced " a very forward, likely boy."

The Scotland parsonage had its shady side as well as its sunny. The genial pastor had his own trials. One of them was a frequent headache, accompanied by inexplicable "luminous flashes " and loss of temper and patience. He was troubled by his own "airiness," a perverse tendency to exceed in jokes and stories and neglect opportunities for personal religious conversation ; and still more by the flirting and frolicking of the young people under his roof and the painful necessity of administering reproof to them. Even some of his young ministers were found to be dangling after his wife's granddaughters. He was harassed in money matters, receiving his small salary in driblets and seldom settling with any one without throwing off a few shillings, "if it seemed to come hardly." His yearly supply of wood, cut and drawn from the ministerial wood lot by the voluntary labor of his parishioners on a day set apart for that purpose, gave him much anxiety, the varying height of the wood-pile in successive years marking his rise or fall in the affections of his people, while his mind was always exercised in regard to the " treat " befitting the occasion, lest the women should lay themselves out too much or the hungry swarm of volunteers fail of a full supply. Then his sensitiveness was sometimes wounded by the jokes and banters of the rough wood-choppers, especially when they turned upon the seating of the meeting-house, and he was obliged to remind them "that it was too serious a subject to be merry about." But though so troubled in collecting his legal rates and dues, Dr. Cogs-

well was aghast at the proposal to abolish them. If people would not
half pay their ministers under legal compulsion what would they do
without it? If ministers could hardly live *with rates* they would certainly starve without them. The talk of setting aside the religious
constitution of the State and depriving the government of any jurisdiction in religious worship and affairs, filled the Doctor with consternation
and he believed that such action would " tend to the great injury if not
to the total overthrow of religion." The increasing laxity of the times,
the growth of Universalism, infidelity, French Jacobinism, and anti-
Federalism also alarmed him greatly, but hardly gave him so much
personal annoyance as the high Calvinism and Hopkinsianism then
coming into fashion. With such ministerial brethren as professed
themselves " willing to be damned if it were for the glory of God,"
Dr. Cogswell had no sympathy. Such depths of self-abnegation were
wholly beyond his attainment. He preferred the half-way Covenant
and Calvinism very much diluted, and thought it a great mistake " to
debar the unregenerate from so potent a means of grace as partaking
of the sacrament."

But by far the greatest of all Dr. Cogswell's ministerial trials was
the prevalence of "Sectaries." Separates and Ana-baptists were
thorns in his flesh throughout his long ministry. Natural amiability
and engrafted charity and philosophy failed to reconcile him to their
existence, or to enable him to see the least good in them. *Avoidance*
of *rate-paying* was the secret spring of all schism and separation. The
ruling passion of the Separates was *avarice.* His contemporary, John
Palmer, pronounced by candid, competent testimony a most excellent
man and devoted christian laborer, figures in Dr. Cogswell's journal as a
mischief-maker and *liar*, and a sensational young Baptist exhorter of
great popularity he reports as " an Universalist, a Socinian and probably a Deist." These " Ana-baptists " were in his estimation as bad
as the Separates and acted the same part, breaking up churches and
drawing off church members. The " religious stir " in the north part
of the town, in which large numbers were awakened and professed
conversion, he regarded with great suspicion and anxiety, and records
in his journal with apparent endorsement the remark of a zealous
adherent of the standing order—" That such teachers as come into a
neighborhood, and take off from the standing and stated worship, and
endeavor to seduce opinion, deserve *to be whipped out of town.*"

The happy family circle met with many bereavements. A second
Elizabeth Devotion, daughter of Judge Devotion, " a lovely, charming
girl, blooming as the rose of June," was suddenly smitten with mysterious disease, a loathing for food and drink which baffled the utmost
skill of the physicians, and after four months languishing ended her

life, "aged eleven years, eleven months and twice eleven days." The
bereaved father never recovered from this loss but went down into the
grave in a few years, mourning.   Dr. Cogswell's oldest son, James, died
while yet in the prime of life, in New York city, where he had become
eminent for professional skill, and unobtrusive but effective piety.
His second son, Samuel, died September, 1790, from the accidental
discharge of a gun.

The pastor and his family were also called to sympathize in many
neighborhood afflictions and calamities.   Within one week they
attended the funerals of Mrs. William Cary and her three daughters,
all dying of throat distemper.   One Sabbath spring morning the
people flocking to church discovered a strange object dangling from a
beam in a carriage house, and find the lifeless body of one of the
village young men, a promising youth of cheerful temper with a good
home and happy prospects, and no known losses or crosses that could
give the least clue to his self-destruction.   This "tragical event"
deeply affected the whole community.   The aged mother of the
deceased was bowed to the earth but did not murmur.   Dr. Cogswell
with his usual self-distrust was troubled to know what to say with
propriety upon so delicate an occasion, but succeeded in satisfying both
friends and public by a most impressive and appropriate discourse
upon the words of the Saviour—"Suppose ye that these Galileans
were sinners above all the Galileans because they suffered such
things?"   Still more distressing was the sudden death of one of the
prominent men of Windham, a son of one of her most honored
families, who had fallen into evil courses, amassed property dishonora-
bly, officiated "as head to a drinking club—a striking instance to
warn mankind against profligacy of manners and irreligion."   A few
months later three fast young men of most respectable families
"drank Geneva rum on a wager at Dorrance's tavern till all were
drunk," and then started off "for a Voluntown frolic."   One of them,
suffering from effects of the Presidential influenza, was much overcome and unable to proceed beyond Scotland village.   His companions
becoming alarmed carried him into Tracy's shop, called in medical assistance but were unable to arouse him, and the unhappy young man died
in a short time.   Dr. Cogswell, called up "to pray with the corpse,"
was at no loss for expressions on this occasion, but was carried out of
himself in awe and horror at such an end of such a life—"relatives
sad and serious; spectators solemn; the father most deeply affected."
Such were some of the fruits of the prevailing levity and license.

The declining years of Dr. Cogswell's life were embittered by other
domestic bereavements and sorer trials and perplexities.   His burdens were "more heavy as he was less able to bear them."   Mrs.

Cogswell died in December, 1795, broken down by the death of her beloved daughter, Mrs. Governor Huntington,* whose honored husband† soon followed them. His brother Joseph had died a year preceding, and that gay and brilliant circle that had so long gathered around the family hearthstone passed suddenly away. Dr. Cogswell married in time one of his parishioners, Mrs. Irena Hebard, and amid increasing opposition endeavored to discharge his pastoral duties. He was annoyed by the irrepressible activity of his neighbor, Mr. Waterman, who insisted upon preaching within the Scotland lines without asking permission, and the alarming prevalence of " Hopkinsianism " among the younger members of the County Association. This latter grievance was abated by the formation of the Windham Eastern Association, representing a milder type of theology, which was joined by Dr. Cogswell, and the Reverends Whitney, Lee, Staples, Putnam and Atkins. The great trial and affliction of Dr. Cogswell's later years was however a controversy with his people, one of those unhappy difficulties which often occurred when a minister's life was prolonged

---

* "Mrs. Huntington died June 4, 1794, in the 56th year of her age. She was a daughter of the Rev. Ebenezer Devotion of Windham, of an amiable disposition and condescending manners, she had many to lament her death—among other excellent parts of christian character her benefactions to the poor ought not to be forgotten. The number is not small of those who on such ground, ' rise up and call her blessed.' "—Norwich paper.

† " GOVERNOR HUNTINGTON was descended from an ancient and respectable family in this State. He was son of Nathaniel Huntington, Esq., of Windham; his childhood and youth were distinguished by indications of an excellent understanding and a taste for mental improvement. Without the advantage of a collegiate education or that assistance in professional studies which modern times have wisely encouraged, he acquired a competent knowledge of law and was early admitted to the bar, soon after which he settled in this town and in a few years became eminent in his profession. . . . In the year 1774, he was made an assistant judge in the Superior Court. In 1775, he was chosen into the Council, and in the same year elected a delegate to Congress. In 1779, he was made president of that honorable body and in 1780, re-chosen. In 1783, he was again a member of Congress. In 1784, he was chosen lieutenant-governor and appointed chief justice of the State. In 1786, he was elected governor, and was annually re-elected by the freemen with singular unanimity till his death.

The public need not be informed of the usefulness of GOVERNOR HUNTINGTON, or the manner in which he discharged the duties of his various and important offices, especially the last; the prosperity of the State during his administration and the present flourishing condition of its civil and military interests, are unequivocal testimonies of the wisdom and fidelity with which he presided. . . . .

As a professor of christianity, and an attendant on its institutions, he was exemplary and devout; he manifested an unvarying faith in its doctrines and joyful hope in its promises amid the distresses of declining life till debility of mind and body produced by his last sickness rendered him incapable of social intercourse.

Under the influence of a charitable belief that he is removed to scenes of greater felicity in the world of light, every good citizen will devoutly wish that others not less eminent and useful may succeed; and that Connecticut may never want a man of equal worth to preside in her councils, guard her interests and diffuse prosperity through her towns."—Norwich paper.

Engraved by J. C. Buttre, New York.

Sam^{el} Huntington

SAMUEL HUNTINGTON, LL.D.

GOVERNOR OF CONNECTICUT AND PRESIDENT OF CONGRESS.

to unreasonable limits. " Length of days " was not desirable when a minister was *settled for life.* "A very ancient man, worn out with the infirmities and decays of nature,"—he could not preach to the acceptance of the congregation. The people refused to pay for what they did not like and the pastor declined to renounce his legal dues. In many similar cases a compromise was effected, but in Scotland this painful controversy went on for many years. The meetings of the Windham Eastern Association were mainly occupied with attempts to arrange matters between their venerable father and his rebellious parishioners. Doubtless there was obstinacy and ill-temper on both sides. The people were very willing to release their poor old pastor from his official duties, but declined to make provision for his support in that case, or to procure an assistant, and so with failing voice and faculties he continued to preach to a remnant of the congregation till his ministerial friends, "in their concern and tenderness for their aged and much loved father in the Gospel," addressed a letter to Dr. Mason F. Cogswell of Hartford, recommending him " to gratify his father's desire of spending his last days with his only surviving child, taking such measures to obtain compensation from his people as he might judge expedient." Dr. Cogswell complied with this suggestion and removed his father to a comfortable home in Hartford, and, "as the Scotland society was clearly under obligation to support the minister who had worn himself out in their service," he brought a suit for the recovery of damages. The society, greatly weakened by defection and dissension, was hard pressed to carry this onward, but authorized Captain Rudd and Jacob Burnap to apply to Mr. Calvin Goddard for advice, and decided to stand trial. Meanwhile an acceptable minister had been called, June 13, 1805, Mr. Cornelius Adams of Canterbury, with the promise of a hundred pounds annually and the use of parsonage so long as he should *actually perform* the duties of his office. In view of their troublesome contest with Dr. Cogswell, to make assurance doubly sure, they farther voted, Sept. 12, "That if Mr. Adams accepts the call and be settled, it shall be on these terms : that said Adams shall have right at any time, on giving society six months' notice, to be honorably dismissed, and the society giving six months' notice should be no further holden for his support." This important point being thoroughly settled, Mr. Adams was ordained Dec. 5, Reverends Andrew Lee, Abel Abbot, Elisha Atkins, Erastus Learned, William Ripley and Abiel Williams conducting the services. The church at the same time took a new departure from the practice of its aged incumbent by voting : "That for the future none should be required to own the covenant or permitted to do it, without having a right to come into fellowship, and being under

the watch and discipline of the church as members in full communion."
The troublesome bell had again called for repairs.   In 1804 the society
authorized its committee to secure the deck of the steeple, and if there
was not money enough on hand, to take the remainder of the money
raised to procure preaching with.   Now it was voted to repair, *i. e.*, recast, the bell.   James Gray, James Carey, John Baker, Zeb. Tracy and
Ebenezer Devotion were appointed a committee to get subscriptions to
add to weight of bell and see that it was repaired.   A land tax was
voted for this purpose, but sufficient money being raised by subscription
the tax was remitted.   The new bell was not suspended without the
customary casualties ; a plank falling from the bell-deck broke the arm
of Mr. Eleazer Huntington and struck the head of Mr. Jeduthan
Spencer so that he died within a short time from the effects of the blow.
Harassed by the protracted contest with Dr. Cogswell and repeated
losses, the Scotland church and community were called to a great disappointment and affliction in the rapid decline of the young minister
in whom they had so happily united, who died in less than a year from
the day of his ordination, while the life of his venerable predecessor
was still prolonged.   Notwithstanding its embarrassments, lawsuits and
heavy burdens, the society maintained its footing.   Its farms and workshops were prospering.   Stephen Webb carried on an extensive shoe
manufactory in the north part of the parish.   Thomas Coit of Norwich
succeeded to the mercantile traffic carried on by Messrs. Ebenezer and
Jonathan Devotion, offering the usual " variety of well-chosen goods,"
and receiving most kinds of country produce in payment.   The *parish*
found far greater favor in the eyes of Dr. Dwight than the mother
town, everything therein wearing "the aspect of festivity, thrift,
industry, sobriety and good order."

IV.

HAMPTON TOWNSHIP.   DEATH OF REVEREND SAMUEL MOSELY.
SETTLEMENT OF MR. WELD.   PROSPERITY AND PRO-
GRESS.   GRENADIER COMPANY.   GROW CHURCH.
DEACON BENJAMIN CHAPLIN.

THE Second Society of Windham, Canada Parish, long burthened by
" its remoteness from the place of public convention " for negotiating town affairs, resumed its efforts for independence soon after the close
of the war, but was checked by opposition from Canterbury and Pomfret.
In 1785 the society again voted to petition for town privileges, Colonel
Mosely, as agent, represented to the Assembly " their remote and difficult circumstances—ten and even fourteen miles from the seat of busi-

ness, amounting at times to a total deprivation of those rights and privileges which God and nature have given them," and prayed that the extreme parts of Mansfield, Pomfret and Canterbury might be united with them in a distinct township, inhabitants of these sections joining in the request. The Assembly thereupon resolved "That the memorialists be made a distinct corporation, with power to transact their own prudential affairs, yet be and remain a part of Windham for the purpose of choosing representatives—first precinct meeting to be held first Monday in December, Captain James Stedman and Isaac Bennet giving warning of the same—but as this expedient did not abate the principal grievance and called out strong opposition, consideration of the matter was deferred till another session. The inhabitants of Canada Parish thereupon redoubled their efforts, procured the signatures of interested parties in the several towns, and by a happy chance managed at the autumn town meeting to secure a vote by one majority "not to oppose the memorial for said town." Upon news of this vote the Assembly speedily enacted :—

"That the inhabitants of the Second Society of Windham, and those of Pomfret, Brooklyn, Canterbury, Mansfield and First Society in Windham be constituted a town by the name of Hampton . . . . . entitled to receive from the respective towns their share of school and other public monies, and should pay their part of the debts of said towns, and take upon them the charge and support of their part of the town poor. *Oct. 2, 1786.*"

The bounds prescribed are identical with the present north, east and south bounds of the town, but on the west it extended to the Nachauge River, taking in a section now included in the town of Chaplin. Brooklyn yielded twelve hundred acres, a generous slice was taken from Mansfield and narrow strips from Canterbury and Pomfret.

The rejoicing inhabitants hastened to exercise their new privileges. Their first town meeting was held Nov. 13, 1786, Captain James Stedman serving as moderator. Thomas Stedman was chosen town clerk; Captain Stedman, Deacon Bennet, Jeduthan Rogers, selectmen; Andrew Durkee, Joseph Fuller, William Martin, Jun., constables; Philip Pearl, Ebenezer Hovey, Josiah Kingsley, Silas Cleveland, Andrew Durkee, Amos Utley, Thomas Fuller, Colonel Mosely, committee to act in conjunction with that appointed by the General Assembly to view the situation of the bridges in the old and new townships. This committee had been called out by a forcible remonstrance from Windham. The parent town, like Pharoah of old, had already repented that she "had let the people go." A second town meeting had been held, Colonel Dyer in the chair. Dyer, Larrabee, Hezekiah Bissel, Captain Swift and Jabez Clark had been directed to prepare a remonstrance, which was presented to the Assembly by Dyer and Larrabee, showing that "the vote had been obtained by divers accidents and want of suitable warning and did not represent the wishes of the inhabitants; that the proposed division was unequal and unjust, and that certainly these inhabitants should not be set off without taking with them a suitable proportion of bridges and other burdens." Elisha Lathrop, Samuel Chapman and Colonel William Danielson were accordingly commissioned to attend to the latter grievance, and in May, 1787, repaired to the Widow Carey's tavern and listened to statements laid before them by agents of both towns. They found "that three large bridges across the Shetucket had been affixt on Windham," at an annual expense of about £36, of which they decided Hampton should pay £10. Possibly the good cheer enjoyed under Bacchus' beaming countenance influenced the decision of the commissioners, which was exceedingly offensive to the inhabitants of the younger town, who straightway dispatched Isaac Bennet to inform the Assembly, "That the gentlemen did not *view* the bridges, but trusted reports, and did not consider that Hampton had to maintain two long bridges over the Nachauge." Upon this consideration their annual payment was reduced one half.

A dispute concerning the division of the poor was happily settled by a committee from each town, nominated by their respective selectmen. Hampton then voted, "That the poor be kept by those persons who will keep them cheapest." A single man was accordingly "bid off" by Jonathan Hovey at five and nine-pence a week; an aged couple by Amos Utley for five shillings, and a poor widow woman taken by another bidder at two shillings.

Highways and schools received immediate attention. Philip Pearl, Thomas Fuller and Ebenezer Hovey were appointed a committee "to procure a deed of the trodden path that leads from Hampton to Scotland where it crosseth individual lands." Nineteen highway districts were laid out, and arrangements made for building a new bridge over the Nachauge on the road from Hampton to Ashford. Eight school districts were reported containing 189 houses. The eighth district in the northwestern part of the town contained but ten houses, "and the lots known as Philips' and Chaplin's." The census return of 1790, ascribed to Hampton 1,332 whites, one slave—an excess of eight over the population of its new sister, Brooklyn. The greater part of its inhabitants were engaged in agriculture. Col. Mosely after the close of the war opened a store and engaged successfully in various business enterprises and public affairs. Capt. James Howard was early interested in manufactures, running grist, saw and fulling-mills in the valley that bore his name. Dr. John Brewster was widely known as a medical practitioner. Thomas, son of Capt. James Stedman, opened a law office on Hampton Hill about 1790, occupying a house north of the meeting-house built for him by his uncle, and greatly distinguished himself in his profession. His honored father so prominent in town and military affairs died in 1788.

Society bounds were unaffected by the conferrence of town privileges. Canada ecclesiastic society had no jurisdiction over the territory annexed to it, but its inhabitants were left in their former society relations. A number of these citizens, *i. e.*, Phinehas, Timothy and John Clark, Ebenezer Hovey, Josiah Hammond, Jonathan Kingsbury, Aaron Goodell, Paul Holt, Lemuel Sparks, Uriah Mosely, Phinehas Ford, William Durkee and others—now represented that though connected with the First ecclesiastic society of Mansfield, they lived within four miles of Hampton meeting-house, and that it was much more agreeable and convenient to attend meetings there than in Mansfield, and Hampton inhabitants were willing they should be annexed to them, and therefore prayed that all their persons and lands might be annexed to said society of Canada, and receive their proportion of school and other society money. Residents of Hampton still affixed to Windham's first society, *i. e.*, Benjamin Flint, Judah Buck, John Clark, Asa and Moses Wolcott, Roswell Bill, Hezekiah and Elijah Coburn, William Martin, William Marsh, Aaron, Jeremiah and Ebenezer Clark, John Richardson, Luke Flint, John Ginnings—asked a similar privilege—being much nearer to Hampton meeting-house " with a better road to it, and as many of our families are numerous, it makes it difficult, and in some cases impossible, to get them to meeting on the Lord's day." These reasonable requests were promptly granted, and Hampton church and society strengthened by the addition of these worthy families.

The Rev. Samuel Mosely still retained his pastoral charge over the church of Hampton, though now incapacitated from public service by increasing age and distressing bodily infirmities. He was confined to his bed many years with acute rheumatism and paralysis, suffering severe and often excruciating pain, and becoming almost wholly helpless. His christian principle and native force of character enabled him to bear this long confinement and suffering with remarkable patience and submission. He was cheered and sustained by the restored affection of his people, the friendly sympathy of ministerial brethren and the tender ministrations of dutiful children. His youngest daughter, Sarah, with her husband, Rev. Joseph Steward, a graduate of Dartmouth, " who had been unwell for several years and could not preach," was his constant attendant. His old friend and neighbor, Dr. Cogswell, reports him from time to time as " bearing his affliction with christian fortitude and heavenly mindedness," or " in much pain, longing to depart but not impatient," retaining his

31

faculties and "supporting the christian character well to the last." He died somewhat unexpectedly, July 26, 1791, in the eighty-third year of his age and fifty-eighth of his pastorate. His funeral was attended with the usual formalities, all the neighboring ministers assisting in the services, and Dr. Cogswell preaching the sermon as the deceased had requested. Mr. Mosely left two sons and six daughters. Col. Mosely was now deacon of the church and much employed in public affairs. William Mosely had graduated from Yale College, and was established in legal practice at Hartford. Mary had married Rev. Joshua Paine now of Sturbridge. Hannah, Elizabeth, Ann and Abigail Mosely were married to respectable citizens of neighboring towns. Mrs. Steward and her husband remained for a time in Hampton. Mr. Steward had frequently supplied the pulpit during Mr. Mosely's long confinement, and some efforts had been made to settle him as colleague pastor but his health would not admit. Meanwhile he had practiced in portrait-painting with very considerable success. A portrait of Capt. James Stedman executed after his decease was very satisfactory. He also painted likenesses of Mr. and Mrs. Ebenezer Grosvenor of Pomfret, and other notable persons. Under his example and instruction, a deaf and dumb son of Dr. Brewster acquired very creditable proficiency in this art and followed it through life as his profession.

Various young ministers had officiated during Mr. Mosely's illness. Hendrick Dow of Ashford, had been much liked but was unprepared for settlement. Ebenezer Fitch of Canterbury, gained many suffrages but was engaged in opening an academy at Williamstown. Now that the pastorate was vacant, all happily united in choice of Ludovicus Wells of Braintree. The question of church platform was raised again after long suspension, and the following Rules of Discipline propounded :—

" 1. That general rules for discipline are contained in the Word of God.

2. That the Scriptures should be considered as the platform by which the proceedings of a church should be regulated.

3. That there is a rule in Matthew, XVIII, 15, 16, 17, by which to proceed with an offender whether he be pastor or a private brother.

4. That there is no positive precept in Scripture against a council in case of difficulty.

5. As there are cases sometimes occur in which the church and pastor do not unite in sentiment, we view it expedient that the difficulties be referred to a council mutually chosen. We will mention, however, an exception to which we believe a pastor might with propriety conform, viz. : When a church judge a man innocent whom the pastor supposeth deserves censure; we believe in this case he may not insist upon a council but consider the vote of the church decisive; and we believe it on this principle, that two guilty persons had better go with impunity than that one innocent person suffer.

The above articles were handed to the church by Mr. Weld, as containing in short his ideas of church discipline, and were agreed to and voted by the church with this addendum :

That we will not be confined either to Cambridge or Saybrook Platform for our rule of church discipline."

Two hundred pounds having been accepted by Mr. Weld in lieu of a parsonage, and a suitable salary provided, he was ordained, October 17, 1792, and was ranked among the foremost of the Windham County ministry, "being especially noted for his skill in composing sermons." In 1796, a bell was procured through the instrumentality of Col. Mosely, and was ordered "to be rung at nine o'clock at night, at noon, and at eight o'clock Saturday nights; to be tolled for evening meetings and lectures, and to give the day of the month every evening." The office of deacon was now worthily filled by Isaac Bennet, and our Revolutionary friend, Sergeant Abijah Fuller, one of those stalwart members of the church militant who could pray as zealously as he could fight.

With new minister, church platform, and local independence, Hampton pursued its way in much peace and prosperity. Its leading citizens were men of intelligence and public spirit, abreast with the times and ready to facilitate improvements. Farms were well tilled and good breeds of cattle imported. Large and commodious dwelling-houses were built upon Hampton Hill, and in other parts of the town. New bridges were built, and roads opened and improved. One of the first achievements of the town was a pound, ordered to be built with a stone wall for foundation, six feet high, four feet thick at the bottom and two feet at the top. Three feet from the ground it was bound by a tier of flat stones, and a similar tier upon the top, and finished with four sticks of hewed timber ten inches thick, linked together, with a good gate four feet wide. The erection of this structure was awarded to Amos Utley, who accomplished it in the most workmanlike and satisfactory manner. Philip Pearl was appointed an agent to prosecute those who harbor transient persons. The care of the town's poor required much consideration. It was voted in 1788, that the poor be bid off to be kept in sickness and health, those who keep them to have the benefit of all their labor; also, that the idea of the town is, that they who bid off the poor are to furnish them with *all necessary spirits*. As these poor people were mostly aged and ailing, the small sum bid for them was found inadequate to pay their doctor's bills, and so a special sum was allowed for this purpose. Abraham Ford, Royal Brewster, Samuel Spalding, Thomas Stedman, Jr., James Utley and others, bid off the doctoring of the poor for sums ranging from £2 16s. to $22. The bidder in some cases was to employ what doctor he pleased; in others, "the poor were to be gratified with their choice of a physician." A kindly spirit was manifested towards these unfortunates. Amos Ford was allowed five shillings at this late date "for fixing out his son in the time of the war." Clothing and use of cow left by London Derry was generously "given to

Ginne." The unexpected return of Clement Neff after long captivity
in Algiers excited much interest, and the immediate query " whether
he was an inhabitant of Windham or Hampton." A notice appearing
in the *Windham Herald* affixed him to the latter town and must
have heightened the sensation caused by his re-appearance :—

" MARRIED, last week, in the Episcopalian form by Timothy Larrabee, Esq.,
Mr. CLEMENT NEFF of Hampton, to Miss PATIENCE DEAN of this town.
N. B.—Mr. Neff has been a prisoner in Algiers 24 years, in 12 of which he
never saw the sun. He is now in the youthful bloom of 65, and has lost an
eye—his bride a blushing maid of 28."

Hampton's forebodings of future charges were justified by the event.
Within four years of the reported wedding, Mrs. Patience Neff was
under care of her selectmen.

In all public questions the town was ready to express its interest.
Col. Mosely as representative was directed in 1792, "to use his influence to prevent the western lands being sold." Philip Pearl, Thomas
Stedman, Jr., and James Howard, attended a meeting at John Jefferd's
tavern, "to have the Courts at a more central place." Delegates were
sent to Mansfield, in 1797, to confer upon county matters, the town
voting thereafter that the inhabitants of this town are desirous and
wish to have the Courts of the County of Windham, moved to this
town. A committee for this purpose was kept up year after year, and
any effort to procure a half-shire town vigorously opposed. Rules for
the better regulation of town meetings were adopted, September 15,
1800, viz. :—

" 1. Choose a moderator. 2. Annual meeting be opened by prayer. 3. Every
member be seated with his hat on, and no member to leave his seat unnecessarily, and if necessary do it with as little noise as possible. 5. Members
while speaking shall address the moderator and him only, and speak with the
hat off. 6. No member to speak more than twice upon one subject without
leave of the meeting, and but once until each member has had opportunity to
speak. 7. As soon as a member has done speaking he will take his seat and
not speak after he is seated. 8. Every member must speak directly to the
question before the meeting. 10. No persons have any right to do private
business in any part of the house."

Upon the reception of Pierpont Edwards' circular, calling for a
convention to discuss Connecticut's constitution, the question was put
in town meeting :—" Is this town satisfied with the present constitution of Connecticut ? " Eighty-three answered in the affirmative;
thirty-eight in the negative.

The military spirit that had so characterized the residents of this
vicinity was not suffered to decline with occasion for its exercise.
Hampton took especial pride in her company of grenadiers, formed
soon after the close of the war, and sustained with great spirit for
many years. Thomas Stedman, Jr., Thomas Williams (removed from
Plainfield to Hampton), Roger Clark and Philip Pearl, Jr., were

successively captains of this famous company which inscribed on its roll the names of many noted Revolutionary veterans. Strength and size were indispensable qualifications for admission to this honored band, and many of the Hampton Grenadiers were worthy of a place in Friedrich Williams' Tall Regiment. It played an important part on many public occasions and took the first and highest places in the great regimental musterings for which Hampton Hill was especially famous. Its spacious common afforded convenient space for military exercise and display, and ample accommodations for the great throngs who came to witness it. The militia companies of the town were also well sustained. Ebenezer Mosely was appointed colonel of the Fifth Regiment in 1789; Elijah Simons served several years as its lieutenant colonel, and Lemuel Dorrance, one of Hampton's young physicians, as its surgeon.

In all parts of the town there was life and business enterprise. Shubael Simons received liberty to erect a dam on Little River for the benefit of his grist-mill, and potash-works were carried on in the same vicinity. Edmond Hughes made and repaired clocks and watches. Col. Simons engaged in trade. Roger and Solomon Taintor, who removed to Hampton about 1804, carried on an extensive traffic, exchanging domestic produce for the foreign goods that were becoming so cheap and plentiful. With these gains there were many losses of useful citizens emigrating to new countries Capt. John Howard who removed to Western New York, was drowned in Lake Otsego. Hampton's first practicing lawyer, Thomas Stedman, Jr., "one of the most urbane, genteel, intelligent and obliging men of the day," already mentioned as a candidate for public honors and even the governorship of the State, was induced to remove to Massena, New York, where he quickly won public confidence and respect, and acquired a large landed property. Younger men from Hampton were also going out into the world. Ebenezer Mosely, Jr., was graduated from Yale College in 1802, studied law and secured an extensive practice in Newburyport. Elisha, son of Nathaniel Mosely, was graduated from Dartmouth at an earlier date, and studied for the ministry. Thomas Ashley, a Dartmouth graduate of 1791, studied law and settled among the wilds of Michigan.

Col. Ebenezer Mosely had succeeded Thomas Stedman, as town clerk, in 1797, and retained the office many years. He was often sent as deputy to the General Assembly, and agent for many important affairs. Other deputies during these years were Deacon Isaac Bennett, Philip Pearl, Jonathan Kingsbury, Dr. John Brewster and William Huntington. Col. Mosely, Deacon Bennett, James Burnett and Philip Pearl, also served as justices. In postal facilities Hampton was still deficient, depending upon its established post-riders. The first of these useful officials was Ebenezer Hovey, who brought papers and letters from New London and Norwich. After the opening of the post-office in Windham, Thomas and Samuel Farnham came into office, taking the *Windham Herald* to its numerous subscribers. A public library was instituted in 1807, which soon numbered over a hundred volumes.

The Baptist church organized in the eastern part of Hampton in 1776, gained in numbers and influence including some forty families among its resident attendants. A great scandal was occasioned by the immoral conduct of its first pastor, who was forced to resign his office and remove to Vermont. Jordan Dodge, Dyer Hebard, and other zealous exhorters were accustomed to preach to this flock in their own house of worship and adjoining neighborhoods, to the great annoyance of the old ministers, Messrs. Cogswell and Mosely, but they undoubtedly reached a class which would have been impervious to more formal and orthodox ministrations. Mr. Abel Palmer of Colchester, a brilliant young Baptist, supplied the pulpit for a time to great satisfaction. In 1794, Peter Rogers was called and settled as pastor, and remained in charge for a number of years. The patriarch of this church was its worthy deacon, Thomas Grow, whose name was affixed to the meeting-house on Grow Hill, built mainly by his efforts. He was a man of strong faith and large heart, whose fatherly care embraced the whole church as well as his own fourteen children. It is said that he was accustomed to furnish dinner at intermission hour to all who came to worship.

The northwest part of Hampton was very sparsely settled, having remained for many years in the hands of non-residents. Its first permanent settler was Benjamin, son of Deacon Benjamin Chaplin of southwest Pomfret, who upon coming of age went out into the wilderness, took up land on the Nachauge and cleared himself a homestead. He lived some time single and having little money supported himself by making baskets and wooden trays. In 1747, he married the Widow Mary Ross, daughter of Seth Paine, Esq., of Brooklyn, and ere long built a large and handsome mansion still known as the old Chaplin House, where he reared a numerous family. Mrs. Chaplin equalled her husband in thrift and economy and they soon accumulated property. Like his father-in-law, Mr. Chaplin was a skillful surveyor and became very familiar with all the land in his vicinity, buying large tracts at a low figure. Tradition represents him as taking advantage of the ignorance of non-resident owners, maligning the land as swampy, overgrown with alders and deficient in water, and paying for it with prospective wheat, a bushel for an acre, or in wooden shovels to be made from its timber. In 1756, Mr. Chaplin purchased of William and Martha Brattle of Cambridge, in consideration of £1,647, seventeen hundred and sixty-five acres of land mostly east of the Nachauge and crossing it in nine places—which with other acquisitions gave him a princely domain. Some eligible sites were sold to settlers from Windham and adjoining towns but the greater part was retained in his own possession. He laid out farms, built houses and barns, and ruled as lord of the manor. He was a man of marked character, shrewd and far-sighted, a friend of mankind, the church and the State, and was very much respected throughout his section of country. He was very fond of reading and delighted greatly in books of divinity and religion. He attended church in South Mansfield, a Sabbath-day journey of six miles, riding on horseback over the rough path, with saddle-bags full of bread and cheese for luncheon, and a daughter on the pillion behind him to jump down and open the bars and gateways. In 1765, he united with the First Church of Mansfield, and ten years afterward was chosen one of its deacons. Though his residence was in Mansfield he owned much land in Hampton, and was actively interested in all its affairs. His daughter Sarah had married James Howard; Eunice was the wife of Zebediah Tracy, Esq., of Scotland Parish; Tamasin, of Isaac Perkins, Esq., of Ashford; Hannah, of Rev. David Avery. In 1789, Deacon Chaplin was greatly afflicted in the loss of his only son, Benjamin, a young man of much promise. Dr. Cogswell laments him as "a growing character, heir to a great estate," and reports the father "very tender about his son's death," but he hopes resigned. He was married to a granddaughter of President Edwards, and left three sons, Benjamin, Timothy and Jonathan Edwards. Deacon Chaplin died March 25, 1795, in the 76th year of his age. His funeral was conducted with all the ceremony befitting his means and position—a great assemblage of people with dinner and liquor for all, and so much time was needed for these preliminary exercises that it was nearly night before entering upon the ordinary services. The funeral sermon delivered by Rev. Moses C. Welch was highly eulogistic according to the fashion of the period. An elaborate epitaph also testified to the virtues of the deceased, as follows:—

" Deacon Benjamin Chaplin, that Friend of Man, that supporter of the State, that ornament of the Church, who, having witnessed a good Confession for the doctrines of grace, for the purity and prosperity of public worship, a faithful steward of his Lord's goods, provided liberally in his last will and testament towards a permanent fund for the maintenance of the Gospel ministry, and after he had served his own generation, by the will of God, fell on sleep, March 25, 1795, in the 76th year of his age."

Deacon Chaplin's estate was valued at nearly £8,500, including over two thousand acres of land, four houses and eight barns. After providing liberally for his wife, daughters and the education of his son's children, he gave three hundred pounds for a permanent fund, the interest of which was to be applied to the support of a minister professing and preaching the doctrines of the Gospel, according as they are explained in the Westminster Confession of Faith, in a society to be formed before January 1, 1812, within a mile and a quarter of his dwelling-house. A number of families had now gathered in this vicinity, very "desirous of bettering their circumstances for attending the public worship of God." In their remoteness from the meeting-houses of Windham, Mansfield and Hampton, some of these families had hitherto worshipped with the church in North Windham formed during the Revolutionary war. One of its members, Mr. Ames, had given land for a house of worship on Chewink Plain, about two and a half miles southeast from the present Chaplin Village, and the Rev. John Storrs of Mansfield acted as its pastor. The small number of worshippers and the failing strength of its pastor made its continuance doubtful, and a movement was made in 1796, for taking advantage of Deacon Chaplin's bequest. "A number of subscribers in the eastern part of Mansfield and parts adjacent," i. e., Ames, Abbe, Hovey, Barton, Balch, Sessions, Hunt, Stowell, Ward, Clark, Cary, Russ, Ross, Wales, Geer, agreed to give a certain amount for a fund, provided that enough could be guaranteed to add fifty pounds yearly to the interest of Deacon Chaplin's legacy, but did not succeed in carrying out their object. Organization was deferred for some years and the Nachauge residents attended worship where it best suited their convenience. The church in North Windham became extinct—thirteen of its members returning to the First Church of that town. Its only pastor, Rev. John Storrs, died in 1799. A feeble church, scarce gaining name or footing, it is memorable for its connection with a distinguished ministerial succession. Its pastor was the father of Rev. Richard S. Storrs, D. D., of Braintree, and he the father of the present Rev. Richard S. Storrs, D. D., of Brooklyn, L. I. "An old burying ground long unused, grown up to brush and trees, the gravestones well nigh illegible," now marks the site of the extinct church and "Ames meeting-house."

V.

ORGANIZATION OF BROOKLYN TOWNSHIP. GENERAL TOWN AFFAIRS. ADAMS' DISTRICT. CLOSING YEARS OF GEN. PUTNAM. COL. MALBONE. CAPT. TYLER. GROWTH AND PROSPERITY.

BROOKLYN, like its youthful neighbor, was wide awake and stirring. Erected the same year, they seemed inclined to healthful emulation in enterprise and public spirit. Brooklyn's first town meeting, warned by Joseph Baker, Esq., was held in its much-esteemed meeting-house, June 26, 1786. Colonel Israel Putnam was called to the chair. Seth Paine was chosen town clerk, treasurer, and first selectman; Andrew Murdock, Asa Pike, Daniel Tyler, Jr. and Joseph Scarborough, selectmen; Peter Pike, constable; Ebenezer Scarborough, Abner Adams, Joshua Miles, Jedidiah Ashcraft, Jun., Salter Searls, Nathan Witter, Joseph Davison, Samuel Williams, Stephen Frost, James Dorrance, Elisha Brown, Reuben Harris, surveyors; John Jefferds, Eleazer Gilbert, fence-viewers; Abijah Goodell, Isaac Cushman, tithing-men. The bounds of the town were at first identical with those of the previous society, but twenty-four hundred acres were soon released to Hampton. Seth Paine was appointed to agree with the agents of Canada Parish on a straight line between Brooklyn and the new town, and consent that they may have as much land as prayed for if they will maintain the poor. The Quinebaug formed the eastern bound. North and south lines remained as previously settled. Pomfret was allowed to retain a projection on the southwest, now Jericho, on the supposition that it would never be able to pay its own expenses. It was voted that the town line should be also the society line, and the pound already built near Dr. Baker's be a town pound.

Appropriation bills were next in order. It was voted to raise a tax of a penny a pound to defray the expenses till the time of annual meeting, and two-pence for next year; also, to mend highways by a tax. Highway districts were speedily laid out, the town agreeing that each man and team have three shillings for a day's work in the spring and two in the fall. An amendment allowed two-and-sixpence a day in September. A half-penny rate was voted for the support of schools. The committee for settling with Pomfret was ordered to make a tax on the inhabitants of Brooklyn, originally of Pomfret (provided Pomfret will not do it), for the purpose of paying up the arrearage

32

due to Pomfret. The latter town apparently *not* doing it, a list* was made out and tax levied. This list includes some 237 rate payers with estates valued at £9,338, 10s. 2d. Jabez Allen, John Malbone, Andrew Murdock, William Smith, Daniel Tyler, Jun., the Putnams, Scarboroughs and Williams's, paid the heaviest assessments. Special taxes were levied upon John Jefferds, Eleazer Gilbert, as "Taverners and traders;" Peter Schuyler Putnam, Reuben Harris, taverners; Erastus Baker, trader; Joseph Baker, physician; William Baker, as proprietor of a grist-mill; Stephen Baker, of a saw-mill; Daniel Clark,

---

* A true list of the Polls and Ratable Estate of the Town of Brooklyn for August the 20th, A. D. 1788:

Adams, Samuel, William, Asaph, Lewis, Ephraim, Philemon, Shubael, Abner, Noah, Willard, Peter, Ephraim, Jun.; Allyn, Jabez, John, Joseph; Allen, Parker; Ashcraft, Jedidiah, John, Jedidiah, Jun.; Alworth, James, William; Aborn, James; Baker, William, Doct. Joseph, Joel, Stephen, John, Erastus, Joseph, Jun.; Brindley, Nathaniel; Butt, Samuel; Brown, Shubael, Alpheus, Jedidiah, John; Bowman, Elisha, Walter; Barrett, William; Bacon, Joseph, Asa, Nehemiah; Benjamin, Barzillai; Cushman, William, William, Jun., Isaac; Clark, Moses, Daniel, Caleb; Cleveland, Davis, Joseph, Elijah, Phillips, Phinehas; Cady, Gideon, Ezra, Jonathan, Uriah, John, Phinehas, Ebenezer, Benjamin, Asahel, Nahum, Nathan, Daniel, Widow Lydia, Eliakim; Copeland, William, Asa, Joseph, Jonathan, James; Chaffee, Ebenezer; Coller, Jonathan, Asa; Cogswell, Nathaniel; Cloud, Norman; Chapman, Amaziah; Darbe, Ashael, William, Alpheus; Downing, Jedidiah, David, Ichabod, James; Denison, David; Davison, Joseph, Joseph, Jun., Peter; Dorrance, James; Davis, Samuel; Davidson, William; Eldredge, James, Gurdon; Eaton, Ezekiel; Fasset, Elijah, Josiah, Joab, John; Foster, Daniel; Fling, Lemuel; Frost, Stephen; Fuller, John, Josiah; Fillmore, William; Goodell, Abijah, Alvan; Gilbert, Rachel, Joseph, Eleazer, Benjamin, Jedidiah, John; Geer, John; Herrick, Benjamin, Rufus; Howard, Charles; Hubbard, Ebenezer, William, Benjamin, Jun.; Hutchins, Isaac; Hewitt, Stephen, Increase; Harris, Samuel, Reuben, Paul, Amos, Ebenezer; Hancock, John; Hide, Jabesh; Holmes, Nathaniel; Jefferds, John; Joslin, David; Ingalls, Samuel; Kendall, Peter, John, David; Litchfield, Eleazer, John, Israel, Uriah; Mumford, Thomas; Miles, Jesse, Joshua, Thomas; Murdock, Andrew; Malbone, John; Merrett, Charles, Thomas; Morgan, Roswell; Mason, Shubael; Medcalf, Hannah; More, Daniel; Putnam, Daniel, Peter Schuyler, Israel, Jun., Reuben; Pike, John, Joseph, Peter, Jonathan, Asa, Willard; Paine, Simeon, Seth, Jun., Delano, Seth, Daniel, Benjamin; Prince, Timothy, Timothy, Jun., Abel; Pierce, Benjamin; Preston, Jacob; Palmer, Elihu, Thaddeus; Pettis, Joseph; Pellet, Jonathan; Pooles, Amasa; Rowe, Isaac; Smith, William, Thomas; Stanton, Thomas; Stevens, John; Storrs, Dinah; Scott, William; Searls, Daniel, Salter; Scarborough, Ebenezer, Jeremiah, Joseph, Samuel; Stowel, Calvin; Shepard, Josiah, Benjamin; Spalding, Abel, Ebenezer, Caleb, Rufus, Ebenezer, Jun.; Shumway, Ebenezer; Staples, Abel; Tracy, Zebediah; Tilley, James; Tyler, Asa, Daniel, Daniel, Jun., Oliver; Thayer, Elijah; Wheeler, Timothy, Job; White, Joseph; Weaver, Remington, John; Wilson, Samuel, Ignatius; Williams, Stephen, Samuel, Jun., Roger Wolcot, Asa, Martha, Marian, Job, Joseph, Samuel, Samuel, 2d; Witter, Nathan, Jun., Nathan, Josiah; Withy, James, Hazael, Eunice; Weeks, Ebenezer, Anna; Wood, Benjamin; Woodward, Ward, Peter.

DANIEL TYLER, JUN.,
ANDREW MURDOCK,
JAMES ELDREDGE,
NATHAN WITTER,
ISAAC CUSHMAN,
Listers.

of saw and grist-mills. The multiplication of taverns was a sore annoyance to sober men, and had called out a vigorous remonstrance from Gen. Putnam to the Honorable County Court in session at Windham, viz.:—

"GENTLEMEN:

Being an enemy to Idleness, Dissipation and Intemperance, I would object against any measures which may be conducive thereto; and, the multiplying of public houses, when the public good does not require it, has a direct tendency to ruin the morals of youth, and promote idleness and intemperance among all ranks of people, especially as the grand object of the candidates for licenses is money; and, when that is the case, men are not over apt to be tender of people's morals or purses. The authorities of this town, I think, have run into a great error. in approbating an additional number of public houses, especially in this parish. They have approbated two houses in the centre, where there was never custom (I mean traveling custom) enough for one. The other custom (the domestic) I have been informed, has of late years increased; and the licensing another house I fear would increase it more. As I kept a public house here myself a number of years before the war, I had an opportunity of knowing, and certainly do know, that the traveling custom is too trifling for a man to lay himself out so as to keep such a house as travelers have a right to expect. Therefore, I hope your Honors will consult the good of this parish, so as to license only one of the two houses. I shall not undertake to say which ought to be lecensed. Your Honors will act according to your best information.
    I am, with esteem,
          Your Honors' humble servant,
                    ISRAEL PUTNAM.
Brooklyn, Feb. 18, 1782."

Public schools received immediate attention. In emulation of Plainfield, Brooklyn had already attempted to establish an academy. The *Providence Gazette* of 1783 informs its patrons that " for the promotion of Literature a number of inhabitence in the parish of Brooklyn have procured a gentleman to begin a Grammar school. The public may be assured that the character of the teacher both in regard to his scholarship and disposition comes vouched in the best manner from the Governors of Cambridge College, where he had his education. He will teach the Greek and Latin tongues and any other branch of literature taught at any private school in the State. Daniel Tyler, Jun., John Jefferds, Joseph Baker, Eleazer Gilbert, Jabez Allen, committee." Failing to succeed in this effort the town gave more care to public education. Andrew Murdock, Daniel Tyler and James Eldredge were appointed to take charge of the school money; Daniel Putnam, David Denison, John Brown, Roger Williams, Joseph Scarborough, Salter Searls, Nathan Witter, James Dorrance, to hire schoolmasters each for the district in which he lives; Delano and Timeus Pierce, Jonathan Copeland, James Dorrance, Samuel Butt, Jonathan Pike, Daniel, Peter and Jonathan Kendall, were made a separate district for schooling. Captain Ebenezer Spalding and other neighbors were allowed their part of the money, if they lay out the same in schooling. Town and society in 1795 expressed their approval of the proposed act of the General Assembly respecting the Western lands with these alterations—that the avails of the land be paid into the town treasury of the respective towns of the State, and the interest be appropriated solely to the support of religion of all denominations, and schools.

Brooklyn was much interested in agricultural affairs, and its dairies were reported as "not exceeded in the State." Putnam's example and precept had a beneficial and stimulating influence in this direction. His various farms were now in charge of his sons. Daniel Tyler, Jun., the Williams's, Scarboroughs, Litchfields and other leading families, had fine farms under good cultivation. Population was very generally diffused throughout the town—the village as yet boasting but seven dwelling-houses. Captain Andrew Murdock, who had married a daughter of Major Holland, and added to her patrimony land purchased of Widow Isaac Allyn, was a very enterprising and successful farmer. His "farms and accommodations were truly curious and wonderful—all the product of his own industry and economy." Allyn's grist-mill was carried on successfully till the dam was carried off by a freshet and public opposition delayed its rebuilding. Allen Hill, though owned and occupied by descendants of Richard Adams, received its name from vicinity to this much frequented grist-mill. Four sons of Peter Adams after fighting through the Revolutionary war removed to new countries. The oldest son, Philemon, with younger brothers, engaged in various industries, running a linseed oil mill and manufacturing pottery and potash. One son acquired the art of working in silver and fabricated family teaspoons, while a daughter gifted with æsthetic taste transformed rude homespun into a thing of beauty. With wooden stamps cut out by her brothers and dyes extracted from native plants, she achieved a most successful imitation of the rich flowered brocades then in fashion, making dress patterns, vests and furniture coverings that were the admiration of all beholders. Living remote from neighbors on so large a tract of land, this family long retained primitive characteristics and habits, a patriarchal community almost independent of the busy world beyond them. A few Indian families still occupied their wigwams in the depths of the uncleared woodland, and while gradually acquiring the arts of civilized life imparted forest secrets in return, teaching the children the nature and use of herbs, the best methods of hunting and snaring, with many an aboriginal tradition. Peter Adams, the patriarch of this little community, was still hale and hearty. A mighty hunter from his youth he pursued the practice even down to old age and had the honor of killing the last *bear* reported in

Windham County. As so much has been said of the last wolf it is but fair to chronicle the last of the Bruins, especially as it was an animal of most exemplary morals, never suspected of purloining so much as a chicken, and instead of routing out a whole town for its destruction was so accommodating as to set itself up for a target. Even his presence had been unsuspected until one pleasant spring morning, when Mr. Adams espied him on a knoll not far from his residence. Approaching unperceived he managed to get a shot at him when the bear fell backward, uttering such terrible and unearthly cries as to be heard even across the distant Quinebaug. Another shot stilled the cries and sent the last bear to his fathers. The size and weight of the defunct representative of a departed race were very remarkable and it was conjectured that he had long outlived the ordinary limits of bearish existence. The year of his demise cannot be settled but it was probably about 1780.

General Putnam, now resting from his arduous labors and conflicts, must have been greatly interested in hearing of this exploit, recalling as it would the much more famous adventure of his early days.* The later years of Putnam's life were eminently peaceful and happy. Disabled as he was with right arm paralyzed and useless, he was still able to share in the pleasures and duties of life; could ride about his farms and attend public meetings and social gatherings. Released from the burden of keeping up an establishment, he made his home with his sons, Colonel Israel, Peter Schuyler and Daniel Putnam, and frequently visited his daughters, Mrs. Tyler, Mrs. Waldo and Mrs. Lemuel Grosvenor. We catch pleasant glimpses of him in these restful years, enforcing with admonitory staff prompt obedience upon his numerous grandchildren, encouraging young girls with hearty applause upon their first essay in a public ball-room, or making a friendly call upon his neighbor, Dr. Cogswell, to the detriment of the Sunday sermon of the ungrateful minister. He was frequently seen at "a raising" and other social gatherings and merry-makings, "surrounded by a crowd of children and grandchildren, friends and neighbors, relating abundant anecdotes of the olden time, while his happy audience greeted with loud laughter the outflowing of his ready wit and his kindly and genial humor." He was the oracle in tree-culture, stock-raising and other practical matters, ever ready to advise with his quick eye and clear head, ripening and mellowing as the years passed on. He was cheered by visits and letters from his military friends and comrades, and many tributes of respect and gratitude from fellow-

---

* See Appendix.

citizens at home and far and wide over the land. He rejoiced with his whole great heart in the achievement of American Independence, the adoption of the Federal Constitution, the new impulse it brought to the Nation; and in the various projects for growth and development. Always a respecter of religion, long a member of the church, he was drawn with advancing years to a deeper appreciation of spiritual things. He studied the Scriptures carefully, he abjured the use of profane language, he expressed "a great regard for God, and the things of God." To his dear friend and pastor, Mr. Whitney, he freely disclosed the workings of his mind. Good old Elder Benjamin Lathrop of Windham had also "a free and friendly talk with the old General," and reported him "much engaged in getting ready to leave the world"—and so a sudden summons found him calmly waiting his discharge. "Death, whom he had so often braved on the field of battle, had no terrors to him on his dying bed, but he longed to depart and be with Christ." He died May 19, 1790, after two days' illness. His funeral as befitting his character, rank, and distinguished public services, was the most imposing ceremonial that Windham County had then witnessed. The grenadiers of the Eleventh Regiment, the Matross Company of Brooklyn, and military companies from other parts of the State, the brethren of the Masonic order, together with a large number of strangers and a great concourse of friends and neighbors, accompanied the remains "to the Congregational meeting-house in Brooklyn; and after divine service performed by the Rev. Dr. Whitney, all that was earthly of the patriot and hero was laid in the silent tomb under the discharge of vollies from the infantry and minute guns from the artillery." An eulogium was pronounced at the grave by Dr. Waldo in behalf of the Masonic brethren. An inscription prepared by President Dwight of Yale College most faithfully portrayed the character of the great leader, who held to Windham County the relation of Washington to the Republic—"first in war, first in peace, first in the hearts of his countrymen."

Sacred be this Monument
to the memory
of
ISRAEL PUTNAM, Esquire,
senior Major General in the armies
of
the United States of America;
who
was born at Salem,
in the Province of Massachusetts,
on the 7th day of January,
A. D. 1718,
and died
on the 19th day of May,
A. D. 1790.
Passenger,
if thou art a Soldier,
drop a tear over the dust of a Hero,
who,
ever attentive
to the lives and happiness of his men,
dared to lead
where any dared to follow;
if a Patriot,
remember the distinguished and gallant services
rendered thy country
by the Patriot who sleeps beneath this marble;
if thou art honest, generous and worthy,
render a cheerful tribute of respect
to a man,
whose generosity was singular,
whose honesty was proverbial;
who
raised himself to universal esteem,
and offices of eminent distinction,
by personal worth
and a
useful life.

[It would be pleasant to leave General Putnam in his last resting place with a grateful remembrance of his life, character and services, but subsequent developments and modern theories compel a brief notice. For Windham County readers, indeed, no word is needed. They have not cared to look at their old friend through modern eye-glasses, fashioned in New York and Boston. Insinuations as to his military capacity and standing, his courage and loyalty, have failed to make the least impression upon the minds of those who look upon General Putnam through the eyes of their fathers and grandfathers, men of sense and judgment, who saw him face to face, and knew just what he was and what he had done. The words with which General Lemuel Grosvenor of Pomfret, sent back a pamphlet concocted by one of the early propounders of the modern theory are here given, as expressing the involuntary sentiment and impulse of every Windham County citizen :—

"Sir, your letter enclosing a pamphlet was duly received, but I do not thank you for a publication which is intended to slander a character of one now deceased with whom I had the honor of a personal acquaintance as a townsman of mine, and so distinguished a friend to his country—and whose whole life was devoted to their service in the French War, but more especially in the Revolution and especially at the Noted Battle of Bunker Hill, where he was a distinguished commanding officer, and not an idle carrier of the intrenching tools as you represent. I therefore return the pamphlet as I do not wish it to disgrace my library.   Yours, etc.,
                                             LEMUEL GROSVENOR.
Pomfret, January, 1832."

But while accepting the testimony and verdict of cotemporary associates, we would not shrink from candid, critical investigation, and would deprecate indiscriminate eulogy as well as vindictive censure. Rather with scriptural plainness and fidelity would we record the errors and failures as well as the virtues and triumphs, remembering that the best of men are still but human. That Putnam's military career during the Revolution fulfilled the extravagant expectations of enthusiastic admirers cannot be maintained. His age, his lack of early military training, the character of his previous military experience, were all against him. Yet the service that he rendered, especially at the breaking out of the war, was most vital, and it may be doubted if without his prestige and popularity the army would have cohered or Bunker Hill Battle have been fought. He held the helm till it was taken by Washington, and like John the Baptist prepared the way for his master. The world is indebted to Dr. Tarbox, for his chivalrous championship and successful vindication of Putnam's claim to leadership at Bunker Hill. Johnson's late "Campaign of 1776," relieves Putnam from reputed responsibility for the mischances and defeat at Long Island, and closer investigation in other cases where he has been blamed, prove that he did the best possible under the circumstances, and justify the words of President Sparks:—"That he never made mistakes I would not say, for it cannot be said of a single officer in the Revolution, but I am sure it may be safely affirmed that there was not among all the patriots of the Revolution a braver man, or one more true to the interests of his country, or of more generous and noble spirit." John Adams declares, "That he never heard the least insinuation of dissatisfaction with the conduct of General Putnam through his whole life." Colonel Thomas Grosvenor, his townsman and military associate, reports him "ever the first in public life at the post of honor and danger," and in his private conduct "excelled by none." The honored friend and associate of Washington and Trumbull, the faithful counsellor and supporter of Connecticut's sturdy patriots throughout the Revolution, he lived and died " respected and beloved ; " " his word an ample security for everything it pledged ; "* his uprightness commanding "absolute confidence." Against such overwhelming testimony from those who knew him, charges brought many years after his decease can have little weight, based as they are upon professional and sectional jealousies, and that captious spirit of criticism which would blacken the purest character and belittle the most heroic deeds. Leading as they have to a more careful and critical examination, they will give to the world a more correct understanding of his services, and a higher estimate of the worth and weight of his character.

A contemporary report† lately come to light we leave to its own merits, premising that the writer was like Peters a banished Tory, who compiled his "History" between 1780 and 1790.

Note on General Putnam [extract]. "He is resolute, bold, enterprising and intrepid, has no notion of fear, and is at the same time, generous, kind and humane ; was fond of doing good acts, and ever treated loyal prisoners with the same attention and hospitality as he treated his own soldiers. In 1775, he offered his services to General Gage, the commander-in-chief of America, if he could have a provincial regiment, which he offered to raise at his own expense. The proposal was rejected with scorn and indignity."

How widely this report was circulated we have no means of knowing, but it might very easily have arisen from the subjoined incident recorded in Humphrey's Life of General Putnam :—

"Not long after this period [May, 1775], the British commander-in-chief found the means to convey a proposal privately to General Putnam, that if he would relinquish the rebel party, he might rely upon being made a Major-General on the British Establishment, and receiving a great pecuniary compensation for his services. General Putnam spurned at the offer, which, however, he thought prudent at that time to conceal from public notice."

From the nature of the case it is not probable that direct proof of either offer can ever be obtained, and we are left to choose between the assertion of the Tory historian and that of Putnam's authorized biographer ; which of the two is most worthy of credit, it is not for us to decide, but it is easy to see which is the most in accordance with common sense, and the facts and probabilities of history. Knowing what we do of Putnam's sentiments and conduct during the summer of 1775, we could as soon believe that streams could run up hill, or the sun go back in its course, as that he could have made such an extraordinary proposition.]

Putnam's antagonistic neighbor, Colonel Malbone, accepted defeat and change of government with becoming philosophy, and by his

---

* President Dwight of Yale College.

† History of New York during the Revolutionary War, by Thomas Jones, 1879.

kindness and open generosity, his scorn for anything like pretension or hypocrisy, gained the respect and admiration of those most opposed in sentiment. The later years of his life were harassed by pecuniary embarrassment. His experiment in slave labor* brought him poor returns. His negroes were idle and wasteful, costing more than their profit. Thirty pairs of shoes a year, their price paid in gold, was one item of outlay. They were a happy, jolly set, fond of fiddling and frolicking. Once a year they held a grand jubilee, electing a *king*, and installing him in office. Pero, the most intelligent of their number, son of an African king, usually obtained their suffrages and received royal homage. Some of these negroes left their master during the Revolution. Others in time obtained their freedom under the Emancipation Act. A few adhered faithfully to their master and mistress, and clung to the Malbone estate even after their decease. Notwithstanding his losses and embarrassments, Colonel Malbone was ever ready to go beyond his means in sustaining his church, or befriending a needy neighbor. Some one in his presence expressed a great deal of sympathy for a poor man who had lost his cow, the main support of his family. "How much are you sorry?" was the sharp query. The informant hesitated. "Well! I'm sorry twenty dollars," he replied, taking that amount from his pocket-book. Another characteristic retort merits preservation. An aristocratic kinswoman expressed her desire that there might be "*a place fenced off in Heaven* for servants and common people." "It would be so disagreeable to be mixed up with everybody." "And I," roared the angry colonel, "hope there'll be a place fenced off in Hell for d—d fools."

Colonel Malbone's death preceded that of Putnam by several years. The epitaph, written by John Bowers of Newport, gives a truthful impress of his character :—

"Sacred be this marble to the memory of Godfrey Malbone, who was born at Newport, R. I., September 3, 1724, and died at his Seat in this town, November 12th, 1785. Uncommon natural Abilities, improved and embellished by an Education at the University of Oxford, a truly amiable disposition, an inflexible integrity of Heart, the most frank Sincerity in Conversation, a Disdain of every Species of Hypocrisy and Dissimulation, joined to manners perfectly easy and engaging, nobly marked his character and rendered him a real Blessing to all around him. That he was a friend of Religion this Church of which he was the Founder testifies; as do all indeed who knew him that he practiced every virtue requisite to adorn and dignify Human Life."

* Inventory of stock appraised by Godfrey Malbone, sen., when conveyed to his sons, Godfrey and John, October 16, 1764 : 80 cows, 45 oxen, 30 steers, 40 two-year-olds, 20 yearlings, 39 calves, 6 horses, 600 sheep, 150 goats, 150 hogs, 27 negroes, viz., Prince, Harry, Pero, little Pero, Dick, Tom, Peter, Peter Virginia, Domino, Caddy, Adam, Christopher, Dinah, Venus, Rose, Miriam, Jesse, Primus, and others, negro boys, etc.

Trinity Church was greatly weakened by the loss of its chief patron, so that Mr. Fogg for a time even meditated upon withdrawing from the pastorate. The stipend from the Missionary Society had ceased, Dr. Walton had removed, patriotic adherents had withdrawn their countenance, dreading the imputation of disloyalty. Trial by fire had, however, left a grain of pure metal. A faithful few still clung to the church of the Mother Country, and for their sake Mr. Fogg decided to remain and continue the Episcopal worship. Thirty acres of land intended by Colonel Malbone for a glebe were confirmed to the parish in 1787, by his brother, John Malbone. Captain Evan Malbone, a relative of Godfrey and John, had now removed to Pomfret, and aided in supporting the church. Another acquisition was Dr. John Fuller, successor of Dr. Walton, who had made a large fortune by privateering, and was accustomed to treat the whole congregation to cake and wine during the intermission of service. With great assiduity and fidelity, Mr. Fogg resumed his ministerial labors, "submitting himself to every ordinance of man for the Lord's sake;" "Giving none offence that the ministry might not be blamed," and gaining the respect and confidence of the whole community.

The Congregational Society, as it was now called, was in a prosperous condition, and though its members had paid heavy taxes for war expenditures and town organization, they proceeded in 1788, to repair their elegant meeting-house. A hundred dollars, to be paid in flax seed, or any other material that could be used about the work, was appropriated for painting and repairs. Thirty dollars were allowed to Mr. Whitney to supply himself with wood at a dollar a cord. Liberty was granted in 1793, to repair the meeting-house clock or put up a new one. In the following year it was voted to raise a small tax for the purpose of paying a singing-master to teach the art of singing—society committee to hire, *direct* and pay said singing master. Singing thus dignified into an "art," received more and more attention, and after a few years the society chose a committee of *eight* "to set up a singing school, viz., one out of each school district to look up and collect the singers therein, and a sub-committee of three to look up and hire a singing-master, and to raise such sum as the committee shall see fit to lay out for the purpose of recruiting the singing." Accustomed to the management of general secular affairs, the society still acted in matters that would seem without its province, choosing delegates to represent it at the great meeting held at Jefferds' tavern in 1794, for the purpose of securing the transferring of the Court-house, and voting "to persevere" in effort when the petition was rejected. Its own especial functions were discharged with much efficiency. Dilatory rate-payers were brought to time by the enactment, " That the names of the persons that have not paid their society taxes shall be publicly read for the future at the opening of the annual society meeting," but this was quickly set aside as too stringent a remedy. Twenty-five pounds were added to Mr. Whitney's salary in 1796, " on account of the present high price of provisions."

Mr. Whitney held his place in the affection of his people and the esteem of all. Though moderate in his doctrinal views and opposed to the High Calvinism then coming into fashion, he enjoyed the respect and confidence of his brethren in the ministry, and maintained strict church and family discipline. Deacons Baker, Scarborough, Witter and Davison, together with Esquire Frost, were constituted a committee to inquire into matters of scandal and reclaim offenders. Neglect of family prayer was pronounced a censurable evil. In 1799, Mr. Whitney with Dr. Cogswell, Rev. Andrew Lee, Rev. Elisha Atkins, and one or two other ministers of congenial sentiment, united as the Eastern Association of the County of Windham, representing a milder type of theology than the larger body. That his church favored this step, and sympathized with him in his regard for the old Half-way Covenant now eschewed by the more rigid churches, was manifested by the following discussion and decision, occurring as late as 1805 :—

" *Query.* Whether children of age or above twenty-one years, still living with their parents, members of the church, might be baptized on their parents' account.
Church generally of opinion that if such children's character was good, and they desired to receive baptism on their parents' account, they might be allowed. Accordingly Lucy and Joseph Prince, children of Major Timothy Prince, were baptized with their brothers and sisters, minors."

In 1802, Mr. Whitney was honored by the conferring of a doctor's degree from Harvard College, upon which accession of dignity the society appointed a committee to confer with Dr. Whitney relative to the settlement of a colleague, " but ten years passed before an assistant was procured." During this interval the church had commemorated the fiftieth anniversary of its pastor's settlement—February 2, 1806—Dr. Whitney preaching from Job x. 12, an historical discourse suitable to the occasion. Only three of the membership of 1756 survived to witness this anniversary, 447 had been added to the church during his ministry and 718 received the ordinance of baptism. The long pastorate had " commenced with the affectionate regard of the fathers, and their continued friendship, their cordial, candid acceptance of his labors, and repeated kindnesses, had continued to make the relation happy." The affection between pastor and people became even more cordial and tender as time went on, the ready sympathy and playful humor of the venerable divine, endearing him to old and young. He was noted for his skill in administering reproof or instruction through the medium of "a little story," and his quick retorts and keen hits elicited much amusement and admiration. His roguish son attempted to frighten him once while performing perfunctory service one dark night as bell-ringer, and draped in white with deep sepulchral voice announced "I have come for you." "Well, if you have come, take hold and ring the bell," was the cool reply. "Do you make a p—int of this thing?" asked a slurring brother when the flowing bowl was passed at a minister's meeting. "A *quart* when ministers are present," returned the smiling Doctor. But when upon another occasion a brother minister urged that they might partake of some superfluous beverage on the ground that they were *military men*—he was answered by the coachman's retort to the English church dignitary, who swore in his private capacity—"When the devil comes for John De Lancy, what will become of the Archbishop?" A flaming Universalist bored him with interminable discussion of his favorite doctrine till silenced by being told that he reminded him of Betty, the cook, who was troubled by chickens coming into the kitchen and kept driving them out with her broom, each time with increasing clatter, till losing all patience she at last burst out—"You are like the Universals that don't know when their heads *are* taken off."

Mrs. Lois (Breck) Whitney, Dr. Whitney's first wife, died in 1789. Their two oldest sons died during the Revolution, being seized with small-pox on their return from a privateering expedition. Another son, Robert Breck, a teacher and composer of music, very highly esteemed, died of consumption at the age of twenty-one. Six daughters survived their mother. Dr. Whitney married for his second wife the widow* of Samuel Chandler of Woodstock.

Daniel Tyler, Esq., senior member of the church, and oldest inhabitant of the town, died February 20, 1802, having nearly completed the first year of his second century. Throughout his long life he had been an active and useful member of society, closely identified with the growth of church and town. The church edifice of 1770-1, constructed under his oversight, still testifies to his skill and public spirit. Of his many sons only Daniel, the youngest, remained in Brooklyn. Having married soon after his graduation from Harvard College, a daughter of General Putnam, Captain Tyler was very prominent during the Revolutionary era, serving as adjutant to his distinguished father-in-

---

* Dr. Cogswell lets us into the secret that Dr. Whitney in his widowerhood "speculated" concerning sundry eligible spinsters of his acquaintance, but none who look upon the stately figure of Mrs. Anna Paine Chandler, as represented by her relative, Mr. Winthrop Chandler, can marvel that such *solid charms* should outweigh any fanciful *speculations*. The superior attractions of *widows* were recognized before the days of Mr. Weller.

law in many campaigns. He also raised and equipped the Brooklyn Matross Company, which rendered such efficient aid when New London and Rhode Island were threatened with invasion. Like his father-in-law, Captain Tyler was favored in matrimonial connections, his second wife, widow of the lamented Benjamin Chaplin, Jun., daughter of Judge Timothy Edwards, and granddaughter of President Jonathan Edwards, inheriting many of the traits of her distinguished ancestry. Captain Tyler was now actively engaged in business, receiving and disbursing large quantities of produce. He advertises in 1784, in *The Norwich Packet*, "for five hundred bushels of FLAX SEED, for which he will pay in ROCKSALT, West India or European GOODS at the lowest advance." He also offers the highest price for good butter and cheese, and requires a large quantity of good pork. In 1799, he reports in *The Windham Herald*, that "he will pay cash for 3 or 4,000 wt. of good tallow; he also wants to purchase a few good lots of pork, about 20 fat oxen, 1,000 wt. of clover seed and 500 bushels of barley; for which a generous price will be given and good pay made." Captain Tyler's sons entered early into active life. Paschal P. Tyler engaged in business with his father. Daniel Putnam was graduated from Yale College in 1794, and died of fever soon after his settlement in Whitesborough, New York. Septimus, also a Yale graduate, engaged in teaching in the South. Dr. James Tyler, nephew and ward of Captain Tyler, shared for a time the Brooklyn medical practice with Dr. Baker. Mabel, sister of Capt. Tyler, married Seth Paine, Jun., like his father a skillful surveyor and prominent citizen of the town. Both died in February, 1792, and were buried within the same week, "Honored and lamented."

Of General Putnam's sons only Daniel remained in Brooklyn, Colonel Israel removing to Ohio, and Peter Schuyler to Williamstown, Mass. Colonel Israel Putnam's farm was purchased in 1795, by Joseph Matthewson of Coventry, R. I., the successful competitor for a gold medal offered in Philadelphia "for producing in market five hundred pounds of *cheese* to beat the English." Major Daniel Putnam, now proprietor of much of the Malbone estate, is reported by Dr. Dwight as having the largest dairy in town, "cheese not excelled by any this side the Atlantic." It probably found a rival in that of Mr. Darius Matthewson, who after a few years carried on the Putnam farm, and, having married one of the notable daughters of Ebenezer Smith of Woodstock, may have managed "to beat" all other Brooklyn cheese as well as English. Other incoming citizens brought new blood and energy to town. Captain Elisha Lord of Abington, Captain John Smith and Samuel Dorrance of Voluntown, John Parish and the Cleveland brothers of Canterbury, William Cundall and

Daniel Kies of Killingly, Vine Robinson of Scotland, were among these acquisitions. Great variety of elegant and useful articles were offered by Frederic Stanley, in his new and fashionable store in 1801. Gallup and Clark, and George Abbe and Co., also engaged in merchandise at Brooklyn village. Captain Eleazer Mather engaged extensively in the manufacture of hats. Dan Rowe informs the public through the columns of *The Windham Herald*, "that he has set up the clothier's business, where in addition to the usual business done by clothiers, he carries on blue dyeing either in wool, yarn or cloth, of all shades from sky-blue to navy-blue." Vine Robinson carried on a cooperage, and served in many public capacities. A distillery was kept in active operation by Dr. John Cleveland and his successor, George Abbe, transforming many thousand barrels of comparatively harmless cider into a far more potent and dangerous beverage. Brooklyn's first lawyer was Miles Merwin, who soon removed to Philadelphia. He was succeeded by John Parish, who gained a permanent footing, teaching a select school until his business was established. William P. Cleveland left the field after a few months trial. Kies, his successor, held his ground and received his share of patronage. Dr. Joseph Baker, Joseph Scarborough, James Eldredge, John Parish, Roger W. Williams and Daniel Putnam served as justices. Joseph Scarborough, Roger W. Williams, John Parish and Daniel Putnam were sent successively to represent the town. Notwithstanding the gain of so many valuable citizens they were outbalanced in number by emigrants to new countries, so that the census report of 1800 showed a loss of over a hundred.

With increasing business and influence, Brooklyn sought with greater earnestness to gain those administrative prerogatives which she believed due to her central position in Windham County. The petition preferred in 1786, to obtain a new county, comprising the towns of Ashford, Pomfret, Killingly, Thompson, Woodstock, with Pomfret for shire-town ; court-house in first society, near the dwelling-house of Landlord Ebenezer Grosvenor—the town to build a handsome and suitable court-house and jail by a voluntary subscription free from taxation, received no attention. Believing that removal was more feasible than division, and that her own village offered the most central and commodious site for a court-house, Brooklyn took the lead in 1794 in inviting all the towns interested in the movement to meet at Jefferds' tavern for farther discussion and renewed action. Delegates from all the invited towns were present and unanimously agreed "that the northeast part of Windham County was greatly aggrieved at being obliged to go so far to attend Courts and obtain justice." A forcible representation of the views and wishes of these delegates, presented to the Assembly by a competent committee, produced such an impression that a large majority of the Lower House voted to consider the premises, but were overruled by a vote of the Council. Brooklyn called an especial meeting to consider this result, Major Daniel Putnam, moderator, and after premising that justice to a very considerable part of the County absolutely requires a removal of the Courts, unanimously voted, "That this town will persevere in a measure so just and necessary, and they earnestly request the several towns most interested to coöperate with them and to persevere until the object is finally accomplished." Messrs. James Eldredge, Daniel Putnam and John Parish were directed to remain agents for said purpose until the same be accomplished. In 1800, Mr. Joseph Scarborough and Captain Daniel Tyler were chosen to coöperate with agents in petitioning for the removal of the Courts—agents to draw a hundred dollars from the town treasury for needful expenses. In May, 1803, Brooklyn, Plainfield, Sterling, Voluntown and Canterbury petitioned the Assembly—that Windham County ought to be divided into two shires, and that the sessions of the County and Superior Courts be holden alternately at Windham and Brooklyn, as soon as a convenient court-house and gaol should be erected at Brooklyn, free from expense to the County. Thomas Y. Seymour and Nathaniel Terry were thereupon appointed to examine and report. Captain Tyler, John Parish, Esq., Roger W. Williams and Vine Robinson were at once appointed a committee to wait upon these gentlemen, but with all their arguments they failed to secure further action, and were forced to abide the inevitable issue with prolonged patience.

. Other public improvements were attained at less cost and labor. A new road through Plainfield to Providence, greatly accommodating the south part of the town, was accomplished about 1790. Samuel Butt, Ebenezer Scarborough and Daniel Putnam were commissioned to confer with Plainfield gentlemen and construct a suitable bridge at Pierce's fordway, where it crossed the Quinebaug. The projected turnpike from Norwich to Woodstock excited much discussion. Parish, Putnam and Joseph Scarborough were delegated " to meet the state committee sent to view said road, and show them the minds of said town respecting said business." Public sentiment apparently favored the project as the town afterward voted to oppose report of Daniel Putnam to oppose Norwich highway. Ebenezer Scarborough, Captain Roger W. Williams and Capt. Andrew Murdock assisted the committee to lay out Norwich turnpike in 1799, the town again declining to oppose it. It also declined to oppose a highway from Brooklyn meeting-house to Windham, but appointed an agent to oppose a highway petition brought by Asa Bacon of Canterbury.

Thᵒˢ Grosvenor

Highway districts were remodeled in 1803. Bridges over Blackwell's Brook as well as the Quinebaug Bridge were maintained at the expense of the town. The question relative to the town's poor was promptly met by directing the selectmen to vendue them to the lowest bidder.

Village improvements were not neglected. The burial-ground so early given to the society had received more than customary attention. Propositions were made from time to time to enlarge and improve it. In 1802, it was voted that a committee be appointed to find the bounds of the burying-ground, and agree with the adjoining proprietors for an enlargement of the same. Two years later it was voted to purchase land as an addition to the same and wall it in. Captain Tyler at the same date leased the society land for a pass-way, a row of Lombardy poplars, one rod apart, to be set out on each line.

VI.

PROGRESS IN POMFRET. THE DODGE CONTROVERSY. RE-FORMED CHURCH. METHODISTS. BAPTISTS. TURNPIKE OPPOSITION. TRIAL AND EXECUTION OF CALEB ADAMS.

POMFRET'S prosperity and standing were unaffected by the loss of its southern section. Its central position and influential public men gave it increasing prominence in the County. Its Probate office brought it business from Ashford, Woodstock, Thompson and parts of Killingly and Brooklyn. Its post-office, established January 1, 1795, accommodated all the neighboring towns. Lemuel Grosvenor presided as Probate judge and post-master, and was also prominent in military affairs. Colonel Thomas Grosvenor had resumed his legal profession, served in the Governor's Council, and was held in high repute throughout the State,—his office a place of constant resort for soldiers, Indians, and all who needed help and counsel. Older men, once prominent in the town, had passed away. Colonel Ebenezer Williams died in 1783; Captain Stephen Keyes in 1788; Samuel Craft, Samuel Carpenter, Daniel Trowbridge, Isaac Sabin, Isaac Sharpe and Dr. John Weld, all prior to 1790. Benjamin Thurber and other refugees returned to Providence after the close of the war. Lemuel Chandler, young Dr. Weld and many other sons of the first settlers, removed to Vermont and the distant Genesee Country. These vacant places were quickly filled by new comers from abroad or rising

34

young men at home. Daniel Dwight of Thompson engaged in mercantile business in Abington. Major Hale continued his card manufacture. John Wilkes Chandler, son of Peter, married Mary Stedman of Hampton in 1792, and, after a year of tavern-keeping, devoted himself with great energy to farming in the old Chandler homestead on the Mashamoquet line. A beautiful farm near the centre of the town, inherited by Elisha, son of Ebenezer Williams, was purchased and improved by Captain Evan Malbone, who stocked it with negroes as well as with cattle and sheep, his southern propinquities making their help more congenial than that of the blunt yeoman who claimed an equality of race and privileges. Malbone land in Wiltshire sold under mortgage was purchased by Aaron Cleveland of Canterbury, Thomas Mumford of Newport and John Hancock of Boston. Several families had now settled in the extreme west of the town, Alexander Sessions, Jonathan Randall, James Wheaton, Seth Chase, Jeremiah Brown and others. Colonel Nightingale, who removed to Pomfret with many of these families during the war, "had a grand farm; lived most elegantly and entertained hospitably." Ithamar, son of Eleazer May, took possession of a fine farm east of Prospect Hill. Business was lively in all parts of the town. Capt. Cargill built a new mill house in 1787, and set up "three complete sets of grist-mills and a bolting-mill," together with a blacksmith's shop and two trip-hammers, a fulling-mill, "a mill to grind scythes, and a mill to *churn butter*." The Sessions's ran saw-mills upon the Mashamoquet, and an oil-mill and potash works were carried on by Ebenezer Holbrook and Sons. Business was also developing in the southeast section near Cotton's bridge. Mills were running merrily, and a barter store opened by the Gilberts, where so much produce and merchandize were *landed* that the cluster of mills and dwellings came to be known as "Pomfret Landing." Stores were opened in Pomfret street and Abington village, and shoe-manufacturing carried on by Capt. Joseph Griggs and Mr. Seth Williams of Raynham, who removed to Pomfret about 1791. Among other business projects a *mining* company was attempted, Gillem Philips, the proprietor of a reputed lead-mine, making over his right of mining lead in 1784 to Evan Malbone, Benjamin Cargill, Elisha Lord, Jonathan Hall, Edward Knight, David Brayton, Jonathan Randall, Jr., Benjamin Durkee, Ephraim Tucker, Thomas Angell, Penuel Cady, Jeremiah Fields, Stephen Williams, Pardon Kingsley and Thomas Grosvenor—the grantor receiving one thirty-second part of the profits; also Pardon Kingsley, one-sixteenth. Henry Chandler of Woodstock, opened shop near the north school-house as a tailor, hoisting for sign the painted likeness of a full grown cabbage head.

Many public matters claimed the attention of the town. At the annual town-meeting, December 3, 1787, Samuel Crafts was chosen moderator ; Ebenezer Kingsbury, Lemuel Ingalls, Joseph Chandler, selectmen ; Captain Josiah Sabin, town clerk and treasurer ; Elijah Williams and Elisha Lord, collectors; Samuel Perrin, Oliver Grosvenor, Aaron Cleveland, John H. Payson, Elijah Philips, Elisha Harrington, Captain Edward Knight, Richard Goodell, Ithamer May, Silas Chandler, Joshua Sabin, Peter Cunningham, Amasa Goodell, James Trowbridge, Samuel Keyes, Eliphalet Sharpe, Daniel Goodell, surveyors; Nathan Dresser, Stephen Averill, Peter Chandler, Nehemiah Dodge, Daniel Goodell, Amasa Kinne, a committee to divide the town into highway districts. Peter Chandler having fenced out a new road near his house was allowed to fence *in* the old one. Highways continuing refractory, the selectmen were ordered "to divide and point out to each surveyor his district of ways to be repaired, and apportion to each the inhabitants he is to employ and collect tax from, and call all surveyors to account for labor done and money collected." Particular inhabitants not accommodated by a public highway to their houses were allowed to expend part of their highway tax on their own private ways at the discretion of the select-men. The laying out a public highway from Pomfret street to Cargill's Mills gave the town a great deal of trouble. John Williams, Esq., Peter Cunningham, Caleb Fuller, Ithamer May, Lemuel Ingalls, Captain Fields, Zech. Osgood, William Sharpe, were appointed a com-mittee, September 29, 1794, to join the selectmen in examining the old road to this locality, the new road from Abraham Perrin's house, and the road leading from Eleazer and Ithamer May's, and " say on which of the above roads Colonel Lemuel Grosvenor shall lay out the public money now in his hands." The town refused to accept their report, or to alter the road leading from Perrin's house, or to lay out a new road, strongly urged by some parties, running an east course from the Gary school-house south of Mr. Samuel Perrin's house to the Quinebaug, where it was proposed that a new bridge should be erected. In the spring a committee of nine, viz., Benjamin Cargill, Peter Chandler, Ebenezer Kingsbury, Benjamin Durkee, Joshua Sabin, Squire Sessions, Lemuel Ingalls, James Wheaton, William Field, were appointed to examine the several roads and Cargill's bridge, and fully empowered to carry into execution the contract of the selectmen with Messrs. Abraham, Noah and Jedidiah Perrin, or continue the old road if they thought best, and " their determination should bind the town therein and be a sufficient warrant for the laying out the turnpike money so called." The "road from Little Bridge that crosses Mill River, leading to nigh the dwelling-house of Mr.

Abraham Perrin," was accordingly established and recorded, May 14, 1798. It was also voted, to rebuild Mill River bridge and repair Cargill's bridge.

The poor were carefully maintained. Bidding them off at vendue was little practiced in Pomfret. In 1788, a house was hired for their accommodation, and Dr. Jared Warner appointed their physician in all cases, his services to offset his taxes of every kind. The selectmen were ordered the following year to make the best disposition of the poor for their comfort and the least expense to the town, by putting them to one man or otherwise as they should think proper, and to be vigilant in putting out all vagrants and idle persons that were found residing in the town and not legal inhabitants. In 1794, it was voted to build a house for the poor, and Deacon Robert Baxter and Mr. Joseph Chandler chosen to superintend the care of the poor. The house was not accomplished for two years when it was further ordered to be built on land belonging to the town, to be sixty feet long and fourteen wide, one story high with two stacks of chimneys, two cellars and four rooms. Selectmen were required to take care of the poor after their removal to the townhouse.

Two pounds were ordered in 1795, one in Abington on the old ground, and one in the First Society on the common. This vote was revoked the following year and it was decided "to build one good and substantial pound of stone, anywhere adjoining a road running east and west through the south part of Captain Amasa Sessions' farm, procuring from him a right to improve the same forever." A by-law was passed in 1797, restraining horses, asses, mules and sheep from going at large on the commons. Swine, well-yoked and rung, and geese were allowed to rove till 1806, when they were restricted under certain penalties. Cows were left apparently to their own discretion. A bounty of seventeen cents was offered for every crow's head.

In the county-seat movement Pomfret was deeply interested, and its agents—Sylvanus Backus, Evan Malbone and Lemuel Ingalls—instructed "to continue in office till the business is completed one way or the other—under this restriction, not to put the town to any expense." Again and again they joined in memorial for relief in the place of holding courts. The project for a half-shire had a few advocates. In 1802, Captain Seth Grosvenor, Peter Chandler and General Lemuel Grosvenor, were appointed agents to petition, with or without others, for a half-shire. When in response to a vigorous effort a committee was actually sent by General Court to inquire into the expediency of erecting a Court-house at *Brooklyn*, Pomfret indignantly withdrew from the field and declined to send a committee to wait upon the state committee, and the matter was allowed to rest for several years.

Pomfret was famed during this period for the excellence of its physicians. Doctors Elisha Lord and Jared Warner were well established in Abington. Dr. Jonathan Hall, younger brother of Dr. David Hall, was now settled in the First Society, and giving promise of future eminence. The leading physician in the northern part of Windham County at this date was undoubtedly Dr. Albigence Waldo, who had returned from the Army with a greatly increased reputation, especially for surgical skill. He was a man of much breadth and energy, devoted to his profession, greatly interested in scientific questions and discoveries. The following note from a name famous in modern medical practice will show something of Dr. Waldo's position among his cotemporaries :—

"LEICESTER, *February* 7, 1793.

DR. ALBIGENCE WALDO, *Dear Sir :*—About sunset this day, my eldest son received a kick from a horse, which has fractured his cranium. This is therefore, in the name of your devoted friend, desiring you to make no delay in making us a visit. For God's sake, fail not! but let dispatch and dexterity hasten you. I am in confusion and know not what to say further. Only fail not. In haste, 8 o'clock, P. M. Yours, etc., AUSTIN FLINT."

Dr. Waldo was greatly interested in the association of medical men for the advancement of their profession, and through his efforts the leading physicians of Windham County and its vicinity instituted a monthly meeting some years previous to the formation of the Connecticut Medical Society. In June, 1786, Dr. Waldo reports a meeting at Dudley; August, at Stafford; September, at Cargill's; "October, at Canterbury. Present: Doctors Coit, Thompson; Palmer, Ashford; Gleason, Killingly; Lord and Warner, Abington; Clark, Hampton; Spalding, Mansfield; Huntington, Westford Parish." These meetings were continued with increasing numbers and interest till 1791, when "Proposals, together with Rules and Regulations for a Windham County Society," were issued, and a more formal organization effected —Dr. Albigence Waldo, clerk. He also assisted at the organization of the State Society in 1792. Dr. Waldo was famed for literary accomplishments and wrote much upon scientific and political questions. He excelled in public speaking, especially upon funeral occasions. His eulogies at the burial of Putnam and other prominent persons were greatly admired, as were also the eulogies and epitaphs composed by him upon various occasions. Mrs. Lucy Waldo, daughter of Captain Cargill, sympathized with her husband in literary pursuits, and enjoyed local celebrity as a writer in prose and verse, being especially proficient "in the art of letter-writing."

Society in Pomfret was very brilliant during this period, but had the reputation of exclusiveness. Some of the new families affected a superior style of living. The old established families had also fine houses and furniture, and were thought by their plainer neighbors to live in great magnificence. Many distinguished visitors from abroad were entertained at these fine mansion-houses. Fashionable belles and beaux came up from Providence and Newport. John Hancock improved his purchase for a summer country-seat and brought thither many distinguished strangers from Boston. Visits were exchanged between these notabilities; balls and dancing parties were given. Pomfret Assemblies became very famous and fashionable, and drew together all the *élite* of the vicinity. The airs and graces of the assembled gentry, and the aristocratic assumption of some families, excited the ridicule of the country people and led some local wit to affix to the fashionable quarter the derisive sobriquet of "*Pucker Street*," by which it was long distinguished. Several fine houses had been built on this beautiful street, and the elm trees set out by Oliver Grosvenor and the banished Frink were already its pride and ornament. The present "Eldredge house" was completed by Colonel Thomas Grosvenor in 1792. Its raising was accompanied by great mirth and festivity—a young Indian delighting the crowd by *dancing* upon its *ridgepole*.

The United Library was reorganized at the close of the war. Captain Amasa Sessions, Deacon David Williams, Deacon Samuel Craft, Lieutenant Joshua Grosvenor, Messrs. John Payson, John Parkhurst, Samuel Waldo, Elijah Dana, John Grosvenor, Jun., Elijah Williams, William Sabin, Jun., Phinney Davison, Captain Josiah Sabin, Deacon Simon Cotton, and the Widow Coates, were admitted members. It was voted that the twelve dollars, continental money, belonging to the Library which had so greatly depreciated should be considered as the proprietors' loss, the clerk not answerable for or obliged to make it good; also, that Mrs. Sabin, Squire Abishai Sabin's widow, where the Library now is, should continue to keep the same. Miller's History, Dr. Mather's Christian Philosopher, Boyl on Seraphic Love and Dr. Owen on Justification, were added to the collection; Thomas Howard, Joshua Sabin, Ephraim Ingalls, Nehemiah Williams, Samuel Carpenter, Richard Goodale, Joseph Williams, Jonathan Sabin, Jun., Samuel Craft, Stephen Williams, Elisha Gleason, John Dresser, Samuel Perrin, Joseph Baker, Samuel Waldo, Daniel Goodale, Rev. Oliver Dodge, Deacon Joseph Davison, and Deacon Caleb Haywood, were afterwards admitted proprietors. The preponderance of theological and dogmatical works was very detrimental to the popularity of the library, and it was now losing ground in public favor. A Social

Library formed in 1793, brought in works of a lighter character, better adapted for general reading—but this too failed to meet the wants of the whole community, and in 1804, a Farmer's Library was instituted. The last recorded meeting of the "Proprietors of the United Library in Pomfret for Propagating Christian and Useful Knowledge," was held February 12, 1805, when the Librarian was directed "to call upon the Proprietors to return the books into the Library agreeably to the original Covenant."

Abington Society was now rejoicing in the ministrations of Rev. Walter Lyon, a native of Woodstock and graduate of Dartmouth College, who was ordained as pastor, January 1, 1783. The occasion was one of unusual interest. The three churches of Woodstock, with those of Pomfret, Brooklyn, Canterbury, Eastford, Thompson, Scotland, Sturbridge and Shrewsbury, were represented by pastor and delegates. The Reverends Joseph Sumner and Joshua Paine, sons of Pomfret churches, assisted in the service. The ordaining prayer was offered by Dr. Cogswell; charge to the pastor given by his former minister, Rev. Stephen Williams; right hand of fellowship by Mr. Whitney of Brooklyn. Robert Sharpe and Benjamin Ruggles were chosen deacons in 1785; Joshua Grosvenor and Samuel Craft in 1793. The first pastor of the church, Rev. Daniel Ripley, after long infirmity and suffering, died in 1785.

Mr. Putnam remained in charge of the First church of Pomfret, conducting pulpit services and also instructing young men as long as his health permitted. Among his pupils who became celebrated in after life, were Elisha, son of Ebenezer Williams, Samuel Dexter and William Prescott of Boston. While yet in the prime of life he was in great measure disabled by a failure of voice and physical weakness which obliged him to seek the aid of a colleague, a painful necessity which led to still more unhappy consequences. Hitherto this church had been remarkable for harmony and order. Alone among Windham County churches it had withstood the tide of Separate agitation, eschewing all fellowship with "New Light stuff," and stoutly defending the supremacy of the Saybrook Platform, but its day of trial and defection came. The period of Pomfret's highest secular prosperity was that of her deepest spiritual abasement, when brethren waged fierce war upon each other and her ancient church was rent asunder and almost annihilated. The young man invited to aid Mr. Putnam in the pulpit was Mr. Oliver Dodge of Ipswich, a recent graduate of Harvard. His lively and agreeable manners, and eloquent discourses, so strongly contrasting with Mr. Putnam's stiffness and solemnity, made a most favorable impression upon his hearers, and after a few months' probation he was called to settle as colleague pastor—Mr. Seth Grosvenor alone advising delay. In the brief interval preceding ordination others became dissatisfied. Mr. Dodge manifested at times an alarming license in speech and conduct, and unfavorable reports concerning him came from abroad, so that when the ordaining council was convened, April 19, 1792, a small number of "aggrieved brethren" appeared before it and objected to the ordination of the candidate, on charges of disregard to truth, neglect of duty, irreverent application of Scripture and unbecoming levity. The Council was greatly perplexed and troubled. The engaging manners of Mr. Dodge, and the warm attachment of a large majority of the church and congregation, pleaded strongly in his favor, and yet there was evident ground for distrust and apprehension. Decision was deferred till July, and then referred to a special Council of thirteen ministers and delegates, nine of whom were to be chosen by the friends of Mr. Dodge and four by the opposition. The Reverends Jos. Huntington, Joseph Sumner, Josiah Dana, Timothy Stone and Jabez Chickering were invited from abroad, together with several of the county ministers. The council assembled September 4, and after four days' session was satisfied that Mr. Dodge had been guilty of a culpable disregard to truth, irreverent application of Scripture and behavior unbecoming the gentleman and Christian minister," and, as it was of great importance that a minister should be of good repute, they were unanimously of opinion that they could not proceed to ordination. In cordial and paternal love they earnestly besought him to comply with this result in the true tenor of it, and by the grace of God endeavor to maintain that Christian spirit, and live that exemplary and holy life that every obstacle that might impede his usefulness might be removed, and that all the excellent and amiable talents and accomplishment with which God had been pleased to favor him might be improved in the future to eminent and most important purposes in his day and generation." Mr. Dodge demeaned himself through the trial with the utmost propriety, accepted the admonition with humility and thankfulness, reflecting upon himself in the various instances alleged, excepting that of *falsehood*, of which he was not consciously guilty. Dr. Huntington's sympathy and admiration were so aroused in his behalf that in the face of his recent vote he arose and offered, "That it was the opinion of the Council that as Mr. Dodge had accepted the Result, he now stood fair to be improved as a preacher of the Gospel, or as a candidate for the ministry, either here or elsewhere"—an opinion which the Council hastened to disavow, declaring, "That as Dr. Huntington was not desired nor directed to express what he did, the Council had nothing further to say upon it but referred to the Result."

This Result was but the signal for a "new departure." The friends of Mr. Dodge, encouraged by Dr. Huntington's imprudent suggestion, wholly declined to accept it. Opposition had but heightened their attachment and strengthened their determination. The society held a meeting on the very day the Result was published, and requested Mr. Dodge to continue preaching with them, "as they did not consider the Result of Council as dismissing him from the work of the ministry." The church was called to concur in this invitation, and make provision "in a regular constitutional manner" for another ordaining Council. The meeting was largely attended. Great excitement and strong partisan spirit were manifested. A large majority were eager to vote for Mr. Dodge and a new council. The "aggrieved brethren" in the flush of recent triumph saw the fruits of their victory about to be snatched from them. There was no time to be lost; the danger was imminent. They had but one resource—the *negative power* allowed to ministers by Saybrook Platform. Believing that Mr. Dodge was unfit for the ministerial office, Mr. Putnam exercised the power thus vested in him and dissolved the meeting without permitting a vote upon the question. This act, if legal, was little less than suicidal. The outraged majority, debarred from farther expression and action, indignantly repudiated all connection with the First church and society, and straightway organized as the Reformed Christian Church and Congregation in Pomfret. A satisfactory covenant was hastily drawn up and adopted, and divine service instituted in friendly private houses. The young minister thus released from previous restrictions, was more eloquent and fascinating than ever. Crowds flocked to the new places of worship, and the old meeting-house and minister were almost deserted. But twelve male members were left in the church, *i. e.* Rev. Aaron Putnam, pastor, Oliver, Asa, Seth, Ebenezer and John Grosvenor, John and John H. Payson, Caleb Hayward, Josiah Sabin, Simon Cotton and Jabez Denison. In their distress and perplexity these bereaved and aggrieved brethren could only resort to that unfailing balm for every wound—"the venerable Consociation of Windham County." Sixteen pastors with their delegates convened at the house of Mr. Putnam, December 21, "to hear, advise and determine upon the unhappy difficulties in the First church of Pomfret." The good ministers found their powers extremely limited. They could indeed "hear and advise," but "determine" nothing. The seceding church-members had wholly withdrawn from their jurisdiction. Mr. Dodge scouted their citation to appear before them and declared himself in no respect amenable to the Consociation of Windham County, and "no more

35

under their control and jurisdiction than under the control and jurisdiction of the Bishop of London." They could only express their
deep sympathy and concern, and solemnly enunciate what everybody
knew before—"that it was fully implied in the Result of the late
Council that they viewed it highly inexpedient for Mr. Dodge to
continue to officiate as a candidate in this place after the publication of
said Result."

These "results," and full accounts of the other proceedings in Pomfret, were speedily published in the Windham County *Herald*, and
serveral state newspapers, exciting much remark and interest. Their
bearing upon one of the vital questions of the day gave them especial
importance at this juncture. The Ecclesiastic Constitution of Connecticut, had become extremely unpopular. Zephaniah Swift of
Windham, the ablest lawyer in Eastern Connecticut, had attacked it
with great vehemence, incurring thereby the reprobation of the
orthodox clergy. Several of the Windham County ministers had
deemed it their duty to oppose his election to Congress upon this
ground, and had stigmatized him in their pulpits as a scoffer and free-
thinker. Swift was far too keen sighted to neglect such an opportunity
to repay them for this injury and expose the arbitrary assumptions of
Saybrook Platform. Having suffered severely himself from what he
deemed the injustice of the clergy, his personal sympathies were also
strongly called out in behalf of this new victim. Upon the publication of the result of the consociation in the Windham *Herald*, Swift
rushed at once to the defence of Mr. Dodge, pronouncing the charges
against him, "false, scandalous and malicious," and the power arrogated
by the consociation in its late inquiry "more unwarrantable and dangerous than that exercised by the pretended successors of St. Peter."
Explanations and defence in behalf of that body urged by Dr.
Cogswell, Rev. Thomas Brockway and Samuel Perkins, only called
out more vehement denunciations. The attempt of the consociation
thus to adjudicate was "an open attack upon religious liberty and the
rights of conscience." The act of Mr. Putnam in dissolving a lawful
assembly, and "nullifying the voice of the church by his *single voice*,
his *sovereign negative*, was a most conspicuous instance of the arbitrary power vested in ministers by that celebrated code of ecclesiastic
jurisprudence, known by the singular appellation of SAYBROOK PLAT-
FORM." Hard indeed was the situation of the people of Pomfret, to
have a minister, who could do nothing but defeat them from obtaining
another. Was it not time for people to look about and see whether
"such *despotism* was founded in *Scripture, in reason, in policy, or
on the rights of man!* A minister by his *vote*, by his *single voice*,

may negative the unanimous vote of the *church!* Are ministers composed of *finer clay* than the rest of mankind, that entitles them to this preëminence? Does a license to preach transform a man into a higher order of beings and endow him with a natural quality to govern? Are the laity an inferior order of beings fit only to be *slaves* and to be *governed?* Is it good policy for mankind to subject themselves to *such degrading vassalage and abject submission?* Is the exercise of such a power compatible with the equal rights—the unalienable birth-right of man? To these questions the answer is obvious to every capacity not hoodwinked by ecclesiastical influence. Reason, common sense, and the Bible with united voice proclaim to all mankind, that they are all born *free and equal;* that every member of a church or christian congregation must be on the same footing in respect of church government, and that the CONSTITUTION which delegates to *one* the power to negative the vote of all the rest, is SUBVERSIVE OF THE NATURAL RIGHT OF MANKIND AND REPUGNANT TO THE WORD OF GOD!"

The force of this powerful attack was greatly weakened by the accompanying abuse and personalities. Dr. Cogswell's meek expostulation was "a miserable and wretched performance," and his ejaculatory prayer for the forgiveness of his opponent, "an act of profanity and impiety." The Reverends Eliphalet Lyman and Moses C. Welch, who hurried to the defence of their disabled brethren and the *Results,* were impaled with greater force and fury. Both these ministers had distinguished themselves by active opposition to Swift, and most joyfully did he seize the opportunity to punish them. Every derisive and opprobrious epithet was heaped upon them. They were charged with deceit, fraud, suppression and destruction of evidence, slander and political intrigue. Mr. Lyman was the Don Quixote, Mr. Welch, the *Bully* of the consociation. Dodge was the innocent victim of clerical revenge and malice;" a young man of superior genius and merit suffering from the danger of the private assassin, "a shining ornament of the clerical profession, a *second Luther* battling against ecclesiastic despotism." The ministers in reply returned his compliments with interest. Swift was pronounced by Mr. Welch to be "destitute of delicacy, decency, good manners, sound judgment, honesty, manhood and humanity; a poltroon, a cat's paw, the infamous tool of a party, a partisan, a political weather-cock and a rag-a-muffin." His remarks "if brought into one view, would be the greatest piece of nonsense, inconsistency and boobyism ever thrown together." He was called a promoter of vice and a Deist, and not only dubbed a fool in their own words, "but had mustered and applied to him every text of Scripture wherein they could find that epithet." This disgraceful controversy was carried on for years in the columns of *The Windham Herald*, both sides indulging in the most unscrupulous abuse and vituperation. Every phase of the Dodge affair was paraded before the public. Depositions maintaining or disproving the charges alleged against him were sought out and published. Attacks and rejoinders were then gathered into pamphlets and carried all over the county.

While this newspaper war was waging Pomfret was given over to discord and confusion. The Catholic Reformed church and its pastor were indeed prospering beyond the most sanguine expectation of its supporters. Dodge was the hero of the day; the champion of popular rights and free religion; the representative and apostle of a new ministerial dispensation. "The reign of long faces had passed." Ministers were now to act and talk like other men, "and unite with them in mirth, festivity and amusement." The old Puritan blueness and austerity were to be superseded by good fellowship and universal jollity. "God was best served by merry hearts and cheerful voices." In that period of religious deadness these views and sentiments set forth by an eloquent and graceful speaker, were exceedingly attractive. The disciples of free religion could not have asked for a more eligible leader than this elegant and accomplished young minister, who could charm all hearts with religious rhapsodies, and dance, drink and joke with equal acceptance. A great congregation gathered around him. Many of the leading men in Pomfret united with the church. Its creed was simple and evangelical—its members taking the Scriptures of the Old and New Testaments as their sole and sufficient rule of faith and practice, and engaging to walk together as a christian society in the faith and order of the Gospel. Full liberty of interpretation was allowed. All knotty points of doctrine were discreetly ignored. No provision was made for administering discipline or for associating with other churches. Dr. Waldo gives these reasons for signing this agreement:—

"1. Having examined with carefulness, find it to be founded on that great Christian scale which unites mankind in the finely-polished golden chain of equality and brotherly love, and cannot make any material objection to the mode and principles which it is designed to inculcate.

2. My only brother has signed it after due consideration, and I wish to worship and get to Heaven with my brother."

The first public act of the new society, December 28, 1792, was to invite Mr. Oliver Dodge to settle as its minister, and in the following February he was ordained over it. So strong was the feeling against him that ministers of good standing shrank from the responsibility of introducing him into the ministry, and of many invited only the Rev. Isaac Foster, his sons, and son-in-law—all of doubtful orthodoxy— assisted in the ordaining services. This ministerial reprobation only increased the fervor of his adherents. His personal friends clung to him with unwavering fidelity. His levities and indiscretions, which all were forced to acknowledge, were but the irrepressible exuberance of a free and generous spirit and were more than compensated by his ingenuous confessions of wrong and great social attractions. The newspaper controversy and Swift's avowed championship gave him great notoriety, and attracted many hearers from abroad. The old Grosvenor House in which his church now worshipped, could hardly contain the congregation. No minister in the County had so wide a popularity. Some of the most respectable families in Brooklyn, Abington Parish, Woodstock, Thompson and Killingly, left the churches of their former attendance and united with the Reformed church of Pomfret. The young men of Canterbury attempted to organize a new society upon this attractive model. But while the masses were thus carried away by the fascinations of the popular preacher, a small but powerful minority were banded together against him. Deacons Oliver Grosvenor and Simon Cotton, old Esquire John Grosvenor, Captain Seth and Ebenezer Grosvenor, Esq., Josiah Sabin, town clerk, the Paysons and Caleb Hayward, were among the eleven faithful disciples who clung to their ancient church and minister. They were supported and encouraged by the ministry of the County, and sober men in the neighboring towns. The Windham County Association justified Mr. Putnam in opposing the measures of the majority of the church for ordaining Mr. Dodge, and declared that his dissolution of the church meeting amounted to nothing more than would neces sarily have followed had the church been allowed to vote, in which case he would have left them and they would have been incapable of any further proceedings. That the majority had any *rights* in the case was a matter that they did not even take into discussion. They also justified the aggrieved brethren in refusing to attend the ministrations of Mr. Dodge, and encouraged them in maintaining public worship by themselves, "manifesting great freedom in assisting Mr. Putnam to supply the pulpit and administer the sacrament." An attempt made by the Reformed Society to obtain possession of the house of worship was unsuccessful, the Windham Court deciding "that Mr. Putnam's adherents were the First Ecclesiastic Society and had a right to the society property." This legal action and decision only made the con- troversy more bitter. Friendly intercourse between the contending parties was wholly suspended. Brothers, relatives and life-long friends became as strangers and enemies. Even the children of these families joined in the quarrel, and mocked and jeered each other as "Dodge-ites" and "anti-Dodge-ites." The controversy was carried into town elections. Opponents of Mr. Dodge were excluded from office. A flaming Dodge-ite was elected town clerk in place of Josiah Sabin, who left this parting record on the town book :—

"Here ends the services of a faithful servant of the public, who was neglected for no other reason than because he could not DODGE ══════════ ."

Woodstock was also implicated in this famous controversy. Mr. Lyman was one of the most active opponents of Mr. Dodge, but many members of his society were carried away by the prevailing infatuation. Some of these admirers wished him to preach in their own meeting-house on Woodstock Hill, and made known their desire to Mr. Lyman. Mr. Russel of Thompson had complied with a similar intimation, and had himself attended the services to see that no harm came of it, but the Woodstock minister was made of "sterner stuff" and promptly referred the matter to the committee of the society, "after which he would be ready to signify his mind thereon." One member of this committee "did not object to the proposed lecture," and without waiting more formal permission, notice was given on the following Sabbath after the close of service by the singing leader, "that the next Thursday would be a singing meeting in the meeting-house, and that the Rev. Mr. Dodge would attend and preach there." Mr. David Holmes, one of the society committee, was thereupon dispatched to Pomfret to represent to Mr. Dodge the minds of the minister, and the majority of the church and committee, and request him "not to come." Mr. Dodge received him with his accustomed ease and urbanity ; listened to his "very lengthy and earnest expostulation" with the utmost politeness, but as he was "under some engagements believed he must go over, as he did not choose to disappoint his good friends at Woodstock. And whether he preached or not, he should get a *mug of flip*, and *a good dinner*." Accordingly upon the appointed Thursday, November 7, 1793, Mr. Dodge galloped over to Woodstock, and with four gentlemen of the society called upon Mr. Lyman and asked his presence and assistance at the lecture. Mr. Lyman expressed his willingness to conform to the wishes of any of his people when he could do so consistently with order and regularity, but in this instance was constrained to make objections, and further asked Mr. Dodge whether he thought upon such an invitation he had a right to preach in the meeting-house. Mr. Dodge replied with his usual smiling audacity, "that he *had* as good a right to preach in that meeting-house as Mr. Lyman had, and that

Mr. Lyman had no more right to the pulpit than he had to the common or any other place." Repairing to the meeting-house, he found a goodly number of hearers collected ; the singers with their leader in their accustomed place, Major Elijah Williams and many other prominent Woodstock gentlemen, and at once commenced the service. Captain Jonathan Morse, another of the society committee, was present with a written remonstrance from the pastor, and at the close of the first singing arose and attempted to read it to the congregation, but voice and courage failing, he broke down with the first sentence and hastily withdrew to report his ill success to Mr. Lyman. That gentleman instantly hastened with Captain Morse to the meeting-house, and finding Mr. Dodge at prayer, they quietly walked up the aisle and seated themselves in the ministerial pew till the close of that exercise, when Mr. Lyman arose, and, remarking that he had something to communicate to the society, read a formal remonstrance, stating his objections to the present procedure, after which both gentlemen "walked moderately out of the meeting-house," and Mr. Dodge completed his service without farther interruption. In punishment for this offense, Mr. Lyman and Captain Morse were both indicted for *high crime* and *misdemeanor* in disturbing a religious assembly, "by violently and repeatedly walking across said meeting-house," and "by impeaching and scandalizing the people so met and the Rev. Oliver Dodge then performing said public worship," and in spite of the efforts of their friends and of their counsel, Colonel Dyer, they were found guilty and sentenced to pay as high a fine as the law would allow. The case was appealed and carried on up to the Supreme Court, where, after a full investigation, the judgment of the Woodstock justice was set aside and Mr. Lyman and Captain Morse justified and acquitted. Every detail of this affair was published in the *Windham Herald*, together with a most ridiculous and exaggerated version of it by Captain Swift, who embraced the opportunity to cover Mr. Lyman with derision and invective, pronouncing his remonstrance "an infringement upon religious liberty, and the most consummate piece of folly."

This breach and controversy continued till near the close of the century. For more than six years Mr. Dodge maintained his ascendancy and his church grew and flourished, while the old mother church of Pomfret withered and wasted. Even some of the faithful eleven were lost to it. Captain Seth Grosvenor and his large and influential family removed to New York State, others were set aside by age and increasing infirmities, so that but a feeble remnant represented the church and supported the invalid pastor. Yet though "cast down" they were not quite "destroyed." Through all these weary years the faithful few maintained the stated Sabbath service in the great desolate meeting-house, the deacons praying and reading the sermons prepared by the speechless pastor, who cheered them by his presence and silent participation in their worship. The piety and faith of Mr. Putnam gave him great strength in this day of trial, and enabled him to impart courage and consolation to his followers. Deprived of his voice, he became more ready with his pen. "His written messages of love and faithfulness were passing daily to families and individuals of his parish." In the darkest hour he saw a light beyond the cloud and believed that all would yet be well. In compliance with the advice of the Assoication they made no attempt to censure or discipline those who had gone from them,—but endeavored to manifest "a mild, gentle and forbearing temper and deportment, hoping by such measures to effect their return and coalition,"—and their patience and forbearance were at last most signally rewarded. Satiate with success, the popular idol found his position irksome. With all "his excellent and amiable talents and accomplishments," he was in truth one of the most shameless profligates that ever disgraced the Christian pulpit and profession. Large as was the liberty allowed him by the laxity of the times and the blind partiality of his friends, it was all insufficient. Yielding to reckless impulse, he ceased to maintain the semblance of outward decency and gave himself up to dissipation. After a week's drunken revelry, driving round openly from one low tavern to another, and even delighting ribald auditors by offering blasphemous prayers for a glass of liquor, he had the effrontery to enter his pulpit and attempt to conduct the usual Sabbath worship,—but the end had come. The "innocent victim of clerical malice," the "second Luther," the brilliant young man, who had gained so high a position and wrought so much mischief, was slain by his own folly and wickedness. Attempting to speak he fell prostrate upon his pulpit, utterly overcome by the effect of his drunken orgies. The eyes of his infatuated followers were opened at once and forever. Never was fall more instant, more final. Of the crowds who had followed him, not one adhered to him or attempted to defend him. At a meeting of the Reformed Church of Pomfret, July 4, 1799, "upon complaint exhibited and notified to Mr. Oliver Dodge, that he had been guilty of repeated instances of intemperance in the use of spirituous liquor or strong drink, and of indecent if not profane language in the course of one month last past—

Voted, That Mr. Oliver Dodge be, and he is hereby excluded from the rites and privileges of this church till by his reformation and amendment of life he shall be again restored to our charity."

No restoration was effected. Whatever efforts were made were wholly ineffectual. The unhappy young man seemed given over to evil and died miserably after a few wretched years. The Reformed Church vanished with its founder. Like Jonah's gourd it perished in a night. Its grieved and mortified brethren had no desire to perpetuate it, and welcomed the first conciliatory advances from the church they had deserted. At their last meeting, November 4, 1799, a committee was chosen "to join with the committee of the church in the first society to call in the assistance of the Rev. Messrs. Whitney, Hart and Day, to advise in the method and on what ground the two churches may join and become one church." No difficulty was found in arranging a satisfactory basis. Both parties rejoiced to unite and become again "one church," and "a most amicable and Christian" union was speedily effected. So serious a rupture was never more thoroughly and happily healed. The social and family feuds that had grown out of it were also made up. This happy result is said to have been largely due to an opportune *dancing school*, that brought all the young people together upon a common footing, and had a most magical effect in restoring harmony and good fellow- ship—a not inappropriate *finale* to the famous Dodge episode, and very characteristic of the low tone of morality and religion evinced throughout the whole affair.

In view of the continued disability of Mr. Putnam, Mr. Asa King of Mansfield was engaged as his assistant, and after suitable probation invited to settle as colleague, but by the advice of the council called to ordain him in that capacity, a change of base was effected. Mr. Putnam was dismissed from the position he could no longer fill, and Mr. King duly installed as the pastor of the First Church of Pomfret, May 5, 1802. A great concourse of people filled the meeting-house on that occasion, and "the greatest regularity and decorum were observed throughout the day." The ordination ball in the evening was no doubt equally satisfactory. The anniversary of this auspicious event was observed, according to the *Windham Herald*, by a gathering of young ladies, who "met at the house of Rev. Mr. King, and presented his lady with more than two hundred double skeins of yarn, spun by their own skillful hands." The evening *dance* was doubtless not omitted. Winning the hearts of his young people by kindly sympathy and indulgence, Mr. King gradually led them to a higher sense of life and its responsibilities. Meetings for prayer and conference were cautiously introduced. The older people at first trembled at this innovation, and feared it would lead to confusion and disorder, but the meetings grew in favor and finally held their own with the dancing-school. Secular improvements were also accom-

36

plished. The meeting-house was repaired, its back seats replaced by fashionable pews, and an additional sounding-board suspended under the massive canopy.

While the First Pomfret church was passing through such vicissitudes, a new religious interest had developed in the eastern part of the town. That wonderfully efficient Methodist organization with its one clear head guiding thousands of willing feet, had gained a foothold in the Quinebaug valley. It was during the year of the great rupture and secession when Dodge was dazzling the multitude with his specious eloquence, that a young minister of very different stamp came to Cargill's Mills one evening and asked leave to hold a religious meeting. Kindly Captain Cargill granted the use of his press-room, and a few of his workmen and the neighboring young people went in to hear him. It was a very unpretentious gathering; very unlike the fashionable assemblies then crowding the old Grosvenor House, but the resulting influences were far more dissimilar. The plain and pungent preaching of John Allen struck conviction to the hearts of his hearers. Allen came again, and other preachers—famous lights of Methodism. A number of young women* professed conversion, and early in 1793 were gathered into a class. Soon they were joined by three young men, Elijah Bugbee, William Gary and Noah Perrin. The latter was appointed class-leader and opened the fine old Perrin House for public religious service. Pomfret was included in New London Circuit, and made a regular preaching station. Its presiding elder, George Roberts, watched and cherished this young flock, preaching himself at stated intervals, and sending other flaming messengers. In a day when Infidelity and Universalism were openly proclaimed in every corner, and an eloquent Dodge drew hundreds of adherents with "his finely polished golden chain of equality and brotherly love," and the power of the orthodox clergy was almost nullified by theological absolutism and ecclesiastical assumption, vivid pictures of man's guilt and danger and earnest offers of free, unlimited salvation, had very great effect. More converts were brought in. A number of respectable families united with the Methodists. The young converts were full of zeal and devotion, eager to work and speak for the good of souls and the spread of Methodism. Lively meetings, filled up with song, prayer and fervid exhortation, were held in the Perrin House and Cargill's press-room, and a new religious life and impulse pervaded the Quinebaug valley. The old churches upon the hill-tops looked with much suspicion upon this Methodist invasion. They had heard most unfavor-

---

* Sarah Bacon—afterwards the wife of Elijah Bugbee, Lucy Perrin—afterwards Mrs. William Gary, Lucy Marcy, Sally White, Mrs. Sarah Sabin.

able reports of that body. Representatives serving at Hartford and New Haven, had brought back alarming stories of their excesses and heresies. They were worse than Baptists, worse than the old-fashioned Separates, worse than anything that had yet afflicted Connecticut! Rev. Mr. Atkins of Killingly Hill, though but a moderate Calvinist, pronounced them a very dangerous people, and warned his congregation against attending their meetings. This prohibition and opposition but increased the activity of the Methodists and made people more anxious to hear them, and so they gained in influence and numbers. In 1795, Pomfret Circuit was formed, embracing the northeast section of Connecticut, and 169 professed Methodists. Jesse Lee was its presiding elder; Daniel Ostrander and Nathaniel Chapin, preachers. In 1801, this Circuit was included in New London District, and in the following year in New York Conference. Two years later it was joined to New England Conference—Daniel Ostrander, presiding elder; John Nichols and Samuel Garsline, preachers. Though meeting much opposition from the standing churches and drawing few adherents from families of old Puritan stock and careful religious training, the Pomfret Methodists increased slowly and steadily, and gained a strong foothold in different sections of the town, especially in neighborhoods aloof from other religious influences.

The Baptist society formed under the auspices of President Manning maintained its organization and held occasional services, but was much straitened by the loss of Benjamin Thurber and the lack of minister and house of worship. The "great religious stir" among the Baptists of Hampton in 1788–9, extended into Abington, and several residents of this society united with the new church. Others became connected with the Baptist church in South Woodstock. In 1803, brethren that lived in Pomfret and Killingly having asked the privilege of receiving communion in their own neighborhood, were "legally constituted a branch of the Woodstock church." Under the preaching and influence of Brother James Grow of Hampton, their numbers were multiplied. Regular services were held in the Gary school-house and at Pomfret Landing. The propriety of setting apart this young brother to the work of the ministry was considered and recognized, and on September 18, 1805, "a number of brethren from the following churches convened at the Gary school-house in Pomfret, and formed into a council," viz. :—

"Second church of Woodstock, Elder Amos Wells, Deacons Robert Baxter and William H. Manning; Brethren Henry Wells, James Wheaton, Elisha Sabin. First Woodstock, Elder Abiel Ledoyt, Deacon Samuel Crawford, Joel Gage. Hampton, Deacon William Elliott, Frederick Curtis, Jeremiah Field. Sturbridge, Elder Zenas S. Leonard, Stephen Haskel, Reuben Howe, Joseph Barret. Thompson, Elder Pearson Crosby, Deacons Samuel Knap and

Thomas Day, Joseph Town, Joseph Bates. 1. Chose Elder Crosby, moderator; Elder Leonard, clerk. 2. Deacons Thomas Grow of Hampton, and
Jonathan Harrington of Killingly churches, being providentially present,
were invited to sit with the council. 3. After prayer proceeded to hear
Brother James Grow's relation of the work of grace on his heart, his call to
the ministry and system of doctrine. 4. The council manifesting individually
their satisfaction in the candidate's relation on the points above-named, concluded to proceed to ordination. Accordingly appointed Elder A. Ledoyt to
preach the sermon, Elder P. Crosby to make the consecrating prayer, Elder
A. Wells to give the charge, and Elder Z. Leonard to give the right hand of
fellowship. 5. Met September 19, according to adjournment, and the several
parts were performed agreeably to appointment. 6. Brother James Grow,
being thus set apart by ordination according as we understand Apostolic
order, we recommend him to God, and the word of his grace to build him up
in the most holy faith, and make him faithful and successful till his death."

In the following April the branch became a distinct body and was
received into the fellowship of its sister churches as the Pomfret
Baptist church, Woodstock dismissing thereto the following mem-
bers :—Elisha Sabin, Artemas Bruce, James Grow, Pardon Kingsley,
Smith Johnson, Thomas Bowen, Charles Robbins, Guy Kingsley,
Stephen Chapman, Alvin Easting, Lucretia Cady, Mary Brown, Hannah Sabin, Patty Bruce, Phebe and Sarah Stone, Azubah Bowen,
Polly M. Spalding, Orpah Easting, Susanna Kingsley, Katharine
Ashcraft, Sabra Withey, Hannah Kent, Betsey Leavens, Hannah
Fling, Celinda Copp, Lucy Goodell. No meeting-house was erected
for several years, but services were still held in the Gary school-house
and other convenient centres. A few Quaker families were now
resident in the town, and a plain house of worship had been erected
for them by the Smithfield Conference.

Abington Society enjoyed much harmony and prosperity. Mr.
Lyon was a faithful and conscientious pastor, devoted to the work of
preaching the Gospel. Dignified in bearing, strict in discipline,
remarkably exact and methodical in all his affairs, he was also progressive and liberal in spirit, ready to engage in every enterprise for
the extension of Christianity or the development of the community.
Improvements in schools and house of worship, the libraries and
missionary efforts, enjoyed his countenance and support. A committee
was chosen in 1800 to estimate the expense of repairing the meeting-
house, and in the following year Joshua and Thomas Grosvenor, and
Lemuel Ingalls, were authorized to accomplish repairs. A bell was
promised by Mr. Samuel Sumner, and leave voted to certain individuals to build a steeple, leaving " it discretionary with the committee
as to repairing and painting." In 1802, the society voted to pay the
expense of hanging and raising the bell, and a rope to hang it. This
being procured and the bell successfully elevated, Daniel Goodell and
Thomas Grosvenor were appointed a committee to return thanks to
Mr. Samuel Sumner for his generous present. Farther repairs were

soon accomplished and the house brought into good condition. Improvements were also made in singing—Watts' Psalms taking the place of the earlier version, and singers ranged into a choir under the leadership of Mr. Ephraim Ingalls, a change "much against the feelings and prejudices of some of the old fathers." The government of the church was less absolute than that of Pomfret. It was voted in 1783, "that there be four of the brethren of this church chosen annually as a committee to join with the pastor in exercising discipline. The discipline of this church is that the negative power is lodged with the pastor and four brethren." An earlier vote prescribed, "that no offending member of said church should be dealt with in ye method of procedure against offending brethren till a regular and written complaint be exhibited against said member by some of ye brethren of ye church." The child of an irresponsible person was "admitted to baptism, on the account of its natural and religious relation to its grand-parents."

Schools were distributed about to suit the public convenience. In 1784, it was voted to divide the parish into four districts by an east and west line crossing the meeting-house, north and south parts to be equally divided thereafter, each district placing their own school-house and building the same, but several years passed before the district system was carried into execution. The ecclesiastic society continued its care of the schools, allowing sixteen months schooling a year for the whole society—schools kept at the usual places and voting that the schoolmasters have no more than forty shillings per month, they boarding themselves. Notwithstanding this scanty pay there was no lack of good teachers. No crop in Abington was more sure than its schoolmasters. Young men who toiled on farms through the summer were glad to recreate in a school-room for the winter. Samuel Craft was one of the early teachers. Mr. Samuel Sumner, the generous donor of Abington's first bell, taught school many winters, and was especially noted for the excellence of his penmanship. In 1795, a district school society was organized— Joshua Grosvenor, clerk. John Trowbridge, William Field and Squire Sessions were the first committee. In 1798, four school districts were formally set off and established, and suitable school-houses erected.

In 1793, a number of residents of Abington formed themselves into a *Propriety* for the purpose of establishing a library in their parish. It was agreed that this should be called The Social Library in Abington. At a meeting held March 14, at the house of Capt. Benjamin Ruggles, Rev. Walter Lyon was chosen moderator, Lemuel Ingalls, clerk. March 21, Rev. Walter Lyon was chosen librarian;

Joshua Grosvenor, Jun., Elisha Lord, Jun., Samuel Craft, standing committee; Rev. Walter Lyon, Lemuel Stowell, Lemuel Ingalls, Elisha Lord, Jun., Griggs Goffe, special committee to procure books; Captain Thomas Grosvenor, collector; Lemuel Ingalls, treasurer. The price of a share was stated at twelve shillings. Amasa Storrs, Daniel and Lemuel Goodell, William and Robert Sharpe, William Field, Samuel Sumner, Jun., Ebenezer Ashley, Amos Stoddard, Zechariah Osgood, John Holbrook, Philip Pearl, Edward Paine, Squire Sessions, Aaron Stevens, Nathl. Ayer, were early members of this association, which soon enrolled the prominent residents of the parish. Thomas Williams of Hampton was elected to the privilege of membership. A hundred volumes or more were soon procured, and a suitable case provided for them, together with "good, substantial wrapping paper or sheepskin sufficient to cover them." Still the public was not satisfied. Many excellent standard works had been brought into their families: histories, travels, poetry, scientific treatises; but there was still a great preponderance of the theological element. "Too much Stackhouse," was the verdict of one critical subscriber, and so a "Junior Library" was organized. "At a meeting holden at Amasa Goodell's, November, 1804, *Voted*, That John Holbrook be librarian, Solomon Gilbert clerk, John Holbrook collector and treasurer." Joshua Grosvenor, John Holbrook, Artemas Osgood, William Goodell, Darius Hutchins, committee. Some ninety volumes were soon collected, whose range must have satisfied the most progressive readers, enabling them to expatiate with Tom Jones, Humphrey Clinker, Gil Blas, Roderic Random and other popular favorites. The circulation of these volumes was apparently much more limited than those pertaining to the senior institution. The librarian of the Junior Library, John Holbrook, Esq., was now established in legal practice in his native parish, occupying the homestead built many years previous by his grandfather, Ebenezer Holbrook. Dr. Darius Hutchins had succeeded to the practice of Dr. Lord. Captain Lord, removed for a time to Brooklyn after marrying for his second wife a daughter of Dr. Whitney, but afterward returned to his old home. One of the most active and useful of Abington's citizens at this date was Lemuel Ingalls, Esq., who after filling many lesser offices with great credit was made county surveyor and associate judge in 1806.

Pomfret was greatly agitated at this date by the proposed construction of various turnpike roads through her territory. Progressive spirits favored these enterprises, but the heavy outlay and prospective imposts terrified a majority of the tax-payers. At the first proposal "to lay a road from Hartford towards Boston to the Massachusetts or

Rhode Island line," the town appointed Colonel Lemuel Grosvenor, Lemuel Ingalls, Esq., and Captain Josiah Sabin, to make such preparations for surveying as would be necessary for information, and to wait upon the committee sent by General Court. In December, the town deferred acting upon raising money to pay assessments to individuals for road laid out by State committee, and appointed Peter Chandler, Seth and Joshua Grosvenor to confer with neighboring towns respecting laying out road from Hartford to Douglas, and for preparing a memorial for alteration of road or repeal of Act. In the following year the town refused to raise money to pay assessments on the road laid out by the State committee, or allow accounts to the persons who waited upon them. When in spite of their grumbling and resistance the Boston and Hartford Turnpike was actually completed through the whole length of the town, Lemuel Ingalls and Seth Grosvenor were appointed to have it altered in certain points and the expense lessened. All efforts proving unsuccessful, the town was reluctantly compelled to levy a tax of three and a half cents to meet expenses and pay assessments, but declined to accept shares in the company or to allow Captain Sabin for attendance upon committee. Projects for a new road in the west part of the town through Joseph Sharpe's land to Brooklyn, and for two other turnpikes, increased the town's ill humor. It would not view the different routes through Killingly nor do anything about it, and appointed agents to oppose the memorial of Sampson Howe and others, and also acceptance of a road laid out through Pomfret from Norwich to Massachusetts line, but were again obliged "to raise money to pay assessments made by State committee for said road." The Pomfret and Killingly turnpike was also carried through after much opposition and refusing to pay the cost of the jury that laid it, and in 1803 it agreed to build a bridge in company with the town of Killingly over Quinebaug River, south of Noah Perrin's—Caleb Trowbridge, Benjamin Durkee and Freeman James, committee to build said bridge. It also voted, To build a bridge across the stream near the burying-ground, and also one on Mashamoquet "where the turnpike crosseth it where old road is discontinued." So great was the outlay caused by all these turnpikes and bridges that it was proposed to *sell* the newly constructed town house. Before accounts were settled another turnpike was demanded— a direct road from Providence to meet the Boston and Hartford Turnpike in Ashford. Oliver Grosvenor and Sylvanus Backus were at once empowered to oppose this farther imposition. Surveys were however made, and two routes offered for consideration. In 1806, the town voted, that the north route by Samuel White's to Cotton's bridge would best accommodate town and public, and to oppose the route from said White's to the Landing, but again as in previous cases they were forced to give up their way and submit to road and taxes.

Important changes were now going forward in the Quinebaug valley. The Cargill Mills had passed into other hands. Advertisements in the *Providence Gazette* had made known to the public the superior business advantages of this locality, as follows:—

"Being stricken in years and past labor, and having a desire to lead a more peaceable and retired life, is now to be sold and entered upon the ensuing spring, THE NOTED INHERITANCE OF BENJAMIN CARGILL of Pomfret, situated on Quinebaug River, containing five hundred acres of land, much of which is of the most valuable kind; sixty acres of it are mowing land, and watered by canals from said river, so that the drier the season the more hay will it produce; together with houses and barns; a smith shop, with two trip-hammers for scythe-making; a saw-mill, fulling-mill, malt-house and gin distillery; also a grist-mill having three pairs of stones under one roof, with water sufficient to grind three hundred bushels the driest day ever known, and has ground nearly five hundred bushels, nearly all by day-light, which now can be proved. The above works are all built in the best manner, almost all new, and go with great force and rapidity, and well situated for custom. Paper and oil mills would be of great advantage. It is and must be a place of great trade. Those inclined to purchase may chance to enquire of some people who perhaps may tell them that it is impossible that the Owner can have any real idea of selling such a situation: but they are cautioned to mind no such clamors until they really find it so by the activity of the Owner, who is fully determined to sell at a very low estimate, and fully convinced of meeting with success. Two gentlemen in company in the mercantile line might perhaps be suitable purchasers. One half of the money in hand would be agreeable. For further particulars, inquire of
BENJAMIN CARGILL.
Pomfret, September 26, 1793."

In spite of these inducements the Cargill "inheritance" remained in market till 1798, when it was purchased by Moses Arnold and John Harris of Rhode Island. The latter soon sold his right to the Messrs. Knight of Providence, and the various mills were run by "Knight and Harris" under the superintendence of Rhode Island's future governor, young Mr. Nehemiah Knight. The "churning-mill" had now given place to a popular distillery, made needful by the increased demand for spirituous and distilled liquors. A store was opened in one of the Cargill houses. Some local improvements were effected by Mr. Knight, who beguiled his lonely hours in this isolated valley by laying out a "solitary walk" on the tongue of land between the Quinebaug and Mill Rivers. The romantic beauty of this sequestered pathway was recognized by the few residents of the vicinity, and "Solitaire," as it was named, became a favorite place of resort for merry girls and youthful lovers, as well as for lovers of nature. Captain Cargill removed to Palmer, Mass., with his widowed daughter, Mrs. Waldo, and the remnant of their families, but his name was long associated with the mills and waterfall.

Pomfret's interest in military matters was quickened in 1804 by the promotion of Lemuel Grosvenor to the command of the Fifth Brigade, and of John Wilkes Chandler to that of the accompanying regiment of cavalry. Major Chandler was a very popular officer, entertaining military friends and his whole company at his own house. He was also a leader of the Republican party in Pomfret, and delegate to Pierpont Edwards' constitutional convention. A large majority of the town were still Federalists. Judge Grosvenor held his place in the Probate office and Governor's Council. The Representatives sent during this period were Ebenezer Kingsbury, Lemuel Grosvenor, Evan Malbone, Josiah Sabin, Sylvanus Backus, Benjamin Durkee and Lemuel Ingalls.

Dr. Waldo had passed away in the prime of life and height of professional eminence, and was greatly mourned "as a man endowed by the God of nature with the most brilliant and distinguished abilities, and with a heart susceptible of all those amiable and benevolent virtues which adorn the human breast." He was borne to the grave by his brethren of the medical profession, in the presence of his Masonic brethren and a great concourse of weeping friends and admirers. "A serious and sentimental discourse" was delivered by Mr. Dodge, and an "ingenious and pathetic eulogy" pronounced by General McClellan in behalf of the Masons.

The monument erected by his fellow Masons bore the following inscription :—

The master wardens and brethren
Of Moriah Lodge
In testimony of their esteem and respect
For the virtues, talents and usefulness
of their late worthy brother
Erect this monument
To the memory
of Albigence Waldo, surgeon.
Who attentively studying the works of God
In the admirable frame of man
Rose to eminent distinction
In the noble art of healing.
His name was charity;
His actions Humanity;
His intercourse with men benevolence and love.
Born in Pomfret, Feb. 27, 1750.
Died 29th Jan. 1794.

Dr. Waldo left many scientific and medical treatises which it was hoped "would afford great light and benefit to future ages." His bereaved widow made many fruitless efforts to publish a collection of his writings. He was succeeded in practice by one of his own pupils and townsmen—Thomas, son of Benjamin Hubbard—who though yet under age had made such proficiency in medical studies and had such natural aptitude for the profession as to fill the position with great credit and usefulness, and gain in time a reputation

37

surpassing that of his predecessor. Dr. Hall was also held in high repute abroad and at home, both professionally and socially, and his children as they came upon the stage were shining ornaments of that polite and refined society which so distinguished Pomfret at this day. To this brilliant society was now added Sylvanus Backus of Plainfield, who had opened a law office on Pomfret street and was already ranked among the leading lawyers of the County. His wife was the only surviving daughter of Dr. Waldo.

Among other notable events of this period Pomfret had the excitement of *two murders,* an extravagant allowance for a town of its size and calibre. The first was committed in November, 1795, by Ann, a negro girl twelve years old, belonging to Mr. Samuel Clark. " Not having the fear of God before her eyes but moved by the Devil," she turned against the little five-year-old Martha Clark who had offended her in their play, and with a sharp knife did so cut the throat of the child that she died almost instantly. With remarkable self-command and cunning, Ann herself rushed out and gave the alarm, calling to Mr. Clark that a straggler had killed little Martha. This story was at first believed by the distressed household, but suspicious circumstances appearing a skillful cross-examination elicited the truth. Ann was thereupon taken to Windham jail, tried, convicted and sentenced. Thirty-nine lashes were inflicted upon her naked body and the letter M stamped upon her hand for immediate punishment, and she was confined for life within the jail limits.

The second murder occurred in the south projection of Abington, a sunny little nook apparently far removed from the evils and temptations of the world, occupied by descendants of Mr. John Sharpe, and a few friendly neighbors. Among these residents were Reuben Sharpe and his wife Cynthia, a kindly elderly pair, uncle and aunt to the whole community. Childless themselves they loved to care for homeless children, and among the subjects of their beneficence was Caleb Adams, a motherless lad of weak intellect and morbid temper, who was apprenticed to Mr. Sharpe, and treated with great kindness. When Caleb was about seventeen years old, Oliver Woodworth, a nephew of Mr. Sharpe, came to reside with him, a most engaging little fellow, five or six years of age, who very naturally became the pet of the household. The caresses and attention bestowed upon the child excited the jealousy of Caleb, and his spleen was aggravated by the pranks and tricks of the little Oliver, who took a childish delight in teasing his surly comrade. One day when Caleb was pulling beans in the field, Oliver came out to him with his sled and besought him to go with him for grapes, and agreed at first to help and wait for him, but becoming weary of the work and wishing to leave, Caleb refused to let him have his sled and put it over the wall. Oliver got the sled and brought it back, when Caleb took it away and flung it up into an apple-tree, assuring the child that if he got it again he would be sorry for it, whereat the little fellow straightway pulled it down and doubtless looked defiance at the big boy who was trying to master him. Caleb instantly determined to kill the child, and warily carried out his purpose. Calmly and pleasantly he offered to go at once for the grapes, and also into the woods to cut a sled-tongue. The delighted boy went with him to the house, helped grind the butcher's knife and carry the cord and implements for his own destruction, and prattled along to the grapevines and into the deep woods, when a blow from the axe stunned and felled him.

> " A horrid gash with a hasty knife
> And then the deed was done."

As the little life ebbed away Caleb's senses came back to him. From the moment of " that first fierce impulse unto crime," he had thought of nothing but how he should accomplish it. " I did not think of the consequences to myself. The devil led me on till I had done it, and then left me." He could not even carry out his design of *dressing* his victim, and hanging him up like other butchered animals. His only impulse now was to shrink away from the sight of man, and he traveled off several miles to a distant uncle's residence. Night brought no boys to Uncle Reuben's hearthstone. The neighbors were aroused, search made, the pitiful remains discovered, Caleb traced out. At first denying the charge he was brought ere long to make confession. He was taken to Windham and committed to jail, September 15, 1803. The affair excited the greatest interest and many visited him in prison. The trial was held September 29. So great was the throng that the court adjourned to the meeting-house. There was little or no doubt as to the commission of the murder ; the only question at issue was the responsibility of the murderer. The boy had been tainted even before his birth. It was " confidently stated and supported by credible testimony," that six months before the birth of Caleb, his father had brought into his household a vile woman with an idiot child two years of age, and that he had persisted in keeping them there to the infinite distress of his neglected wife, who died with grief when her baby was about five months old. Within two months of her decease Mr. Adams married his paramour, and she had charge of the child until her own death, after which he was trundled about to any one who would keep him for a trifle. It was said that the form of his face and the motions of his body resembled those of the idiot child who had given such distress to his mother, and that he very early manifested great perversity and cruelty of temper, and an innate propensity to indulge in lying, stealing and various vicious practices, while the circumstances under which he had been placed had precluded any counteracting influences or suitable training. But all these facts and the alleged insanity of his father, which would seem to indicate the unsoundness of the prisoner and plead for a mitigation of sentence, only seemed to convince judge and jury of his unfitness to live, and the necessity of keeping him from further mischief, and the supreme penalty of the law was pronounced against him. A petition in his behalf was sent to the General Assembly but that body declined to interfere with the course of justice. As in the case of Elizabeth Shaw, very great tenderness and sympathy were manifested for the unhappy criminal, and most earnest efforts made to aid him in preparing for the great change. Mr. and Mrs. Sharpe visited him in prison; the latter in particular "was very tenderly affected towards him and treated him with christian compassion," freely forgiving him and hoping that God would also forgive him. His execution November 20, was made a grand scenic display, affording the highest satisfaction to many thousands of sympathetic spectators. Divine service was performed on the Green before the Court House. "Caleb walked to the place of public worship, accompanied by Sheriff Abbe and the attending clergy, exhibiting on a serene countenance signs of deep and solemn thought. A pathetic and well adapted prayer by Rev. Mr. Nott, opened the service," followed by a sermon from Rev. Elijah Waterman, upon words taken from Luke xi. 35:—*Take heed, there-fore, that the light that is in thee be not darkness*—a solemn and appropriate discourse upon the nature and power of conscience. The request of the prisoner to receive baptism and leave his dying testimony in favor of the religion which supported him, was then stated, and "after ascending the stage and making his confession of faith, the ordinance was administered by the Rev. Mr. Lyon, in the presence of thousands of solemn and deeply affected spectators. In walking thence to the place of execution, he conversed freely, and stated the ground of his hope, and the support it gave him that through Jesus Christ he should find mercy. When coming in full view of the gallows he observed it with a countenance unmoved," finding strength in prayer and passages of Scripture. Rev. Moses C. Welch thus opened his address, at the place of execution :—

"We are met, my friends, on one of the most interesting occasions. We are come together to see the sentence of law executed on one of our fellow-creatures, agreeably to the declaration of Jehovah:— *Who sheddeth man's blood by man shall his blood be shed.* Here we see the instruments of death prepared. Here we behold on the scaffold one bound for execution and going soon, even in a few moments, into the world of spirits, and to the bar of Jesus. While our minds are much affected with the awful spectacle it may be interesting to our feelings, it may be profitable to us, to hear a few facts concerning the prisoner's life with some reflections and remarks. This, at his request, I shall now attempt, not so much to gratify your curiosity as to do good to my fellow sinners."

Before and at the close of this address "Caleb kneeled and prayed with composure and in words well suited to convey his feelings and desires, that he might obtain mercy and find forgiveness of sins through Christ—that he might be supported in the trying moment— that all might be for the glory of God, and particularly that the people might take warning by his end and forsake the ways of sin." The Rev. Mr. Lyon, his pastor from Abington, "then addressed the Throne of Grace in language the most interesting and affectionate— at the close of which the criminal was launched into eternity." The tender-hearted sheriff burst into tears after performing his most painful office, and a most deep and solemn impression was left upon all who had witnessed the scene.

VII.

GENERAL AFFAIRS IN ASHFORD, VISIT FROM PRESIDENT WASHINGTON. TURNPIKE ENTERPRISE. DAVID BOLLES AND THE BAPTIST PETITION. CONGREGATIONAL AND BAPTIST CHURCHES.

ASHFORD was still prominent among Windham County townships, its citizens expressing their views upon all public questions and bearing their part of all public burdens. Captain Benjamin Sumner was still at the head of town affairs, and sometimes designated as *King* of Eastford Parish. Josias Biles in 1780 succeeded Isaac Perkins as town clerk and treasurer. Selectmen in 1783 were Esquire Perkins, Captain Reuben Marcy, Captain David Bolles, Lieut. John Warren, Edward Sumner; constables and collectors, David Brown, Jed. Ward, Ebenezer Bosworth, Captain Ebenezer Mason; highway surveyors, Ephraim Lyon, Joshua Kendall, Ephraim Spalding, Amasa Watkins, Jacob Chapman, Thomas Ewing, Jonathan Chaffee, Timothy Babcock, Isaac Kendall, Captain Samuel Smith, Medina Preston, John Loomis, Ephraim Walker, Stephen Snow; grand-jurors, Medina Preston, Samuel Spring, Abel Simmons, Deacon Chapman, Josias Biles. The selectmen were "desired and impowered to provide for the town a suitable house for the reception of idle, lazy and impotent persons, and the same employ at work in said house, and appoint an overseer, and the same supply with necessaries at the town's expense." Esquire Clark, Doctor Huntington and Ensign Lyon were directed to look after schools.

The *furor* for emigration that broke out so violently after the return of peace carried away many of Ashford's valued citizens. Captain James Dana removed with his family to Schoharie County, New York. Major John Keyes, his comrade in arms and many a gallant exploit—appointed in 1786 to the high position of adjutant-general of Connecticut militia,—stepped over the line into Scotland. The excellent Dr. Huntington, so useful in church and town, removed to Canaan, Conn., and many other sterling families sought Vermont, New York and opening regions westward. Among the gains of the town were Dr. Andrew Huntington of Griswold, who took the place of his relative in Westford, Jonathan Nichols of Thompson, Abner Richmond of Woodstock, James Trowbridge of Pomfret, Isaac Perkins of Mansfield, whose wife was daughter of Deacon Benjamin Chaplin. Lieut. Daniel Knowlton, Captain Marcy, and many other veterans who had served through the war, remained in Ashford, actively interested in military and public affairs. The former, who had suffered so severely in imprisonment, was especially noted for fervent affection for his own country and a corresponding hatred for all whom he deemed its enemies. He could never forget his sufferings in the old church and the *Jersey* prison ship, and was most inveterate in his resentments towards anything that bore the name of *Briton*. He was accustomed to attend worship with the Congregational church in Westford till one Sabbath when the minister read a hymn, having for its refrain, "Give Britain praise." Lieut. Knowlton immediately rose up in his seat and requested that this hymn should be omitted and some other sung in its stead, but the minister paid no attention to his request, and the choir beginning to sing, the old soldier marched deliberately out of the meeting-house, declaring he could not worship with a congregation that *gave Britain praise* in anything, and never entered it again.

These old soldiers must have been very especially interested in that most notable event of Ashford's history—a Sabbath-day's visit from General Washington and his suite on their return from the Presidential tour of 1789. Leaving Uxbridge before sunrise, Saturday, November 7, they breakfasted at a tavern kept by " one Jacobs," in Thompson—the well-known "half-way house" between Boston and Hartford—and thence proceeded on the road to Pomfret. Major Jackson and Private Secretary Lear occupied the state carriage with the President, and four servants followed on horseback, a goodly *cortege* indeed, and one that would have gladdened the eyes of hundreds of devoted adherents and admirers, but that unfortunately in that pre-telegraphic day none knew in advance of its coming, and only here and there a bewildered citizen caught an imperfect glimpse of his

Country's honored Father. At Grosvenor's, in Pomfret, they paused for rest and refreshment, and to inquire for General Putnam, whom Washington had hoped to see here and which indeed had been one of his inducements for coming this road, but finding that he lived five miles away and that he could not call upon him without deranging his plan and delaying his journey, he continued on the main road, up and down long hills some eight miles farther to " Perkins' tavern in Ashford," where he " rested on the Sabbath-day according to commandment." The host and hostess, taken unawares, doubtless did their best to accommodate their illustrious visitor, but to their lasting discredit the truth-telling President records that the tavern " *is not a good one.*" Tradition gives few details or incidents of this visit. Washington is said to have attended church, occupying the most honored seat in the house of worship, and Mr. Pond and the town officials doubtless paid their respects, but the Sabbath-keeping etiquette of the time did not permit any formal demonstration, and he was probably allowed to spend the day in peace and quiet after his own fashion. The citizens of Windham town were greatly mortified and annoyed that Washington instead of coming to their town, and giving them the opportunity to manifest their patriotic enthusiasm, should have " gone back and stole away from y[e] people, going by a by-road through Ashford to avoid pomp and parade." Dr. Cogswell also reports the accompanying visitation of a remarkable epidemic that followed the course of the President from New York to Boston, and all around the country, " even making many crazy "—a violent influenza which by curious coincidence has followed the footsteps of many less illustrious successors.

Ashford was greatly interested in the improvement of those public thoroughfares to which she owed so much of her prosperity and standing. William, son of Isaac Perkins, her first practicing attorney, was made in 1795, agent for the town in all road cases. A committee was appointed to treat with General Newell respecting the road by his mills in the north part of the town. Captain Ward, Lieut. Joseph Burnham, Major Smith and Asa Howe were also appointed to wait upon the committee sent by the Assembly " to lay out a highway from East Hartford to Massachusetts, or Rhode Island line." The Boston Turnpike Company was incorporated in 1797, and within two or three years the great Boston and Hartford Turnpike, running through Mansfield, Ashford, Pomfret and Thompson, was completed and opened to the public. James Gordon, Shubael Abbe and Ebenezer Devotion were appointed to oversee repairs, gates and collections upon this road. About half a mile east of Ashford village this road connected with another great turnpike leading to

Providence, constructed a few years later by the Connecticut and Rhode Island Turnpike Company. Unlike some other towns Ashford made no opposition to these improvements, but willingly paid the needful impost to gain better accommodations and increased travel. Daily stages passing to and fro over these roads made the town very lively. Chaises and other vehicles were coming into vogue. A large amount of freight was carried over the turnpikes. The numerous taverns needed to supply the wants of travelers and teamsters, were kept by Jed. Fay, Benjamin Clark, Isaac Perkins, Josiah Ward, William Snow, Josiah Converse, Stephen Snow, Samuel Spring.

In 1803, Ashford was accommodated with its first post-office, David Bolles, Jun., postmaster. Mr. Bolles after studying medicine for a time had turned his attention to law, and was now successfully competing with Esquire Perkins in legal practice. He was in high favor with what were called "the Sectaries" of Ashford and neighboring towns, by his open and uncompromising opposition to any taxation for support of public worship, and the religious Constitution of Connecticut. A little fellow of six years old, he had stood by his mother's side when her precious pewter was taken by the collector and carried to the town post to pay a "priest tax," and her tears and unavailing remonstrances had such an effect upon his childish mind that he then and there resolved that if he grew up to be a man he would fight those laws that had caused her such distress—a purpose which was still farther strengthened by surrounding influences and later developments. With tongue and pen he kept this childish vow and became one of the "foremost champions" of the Baptist cause, "defending them in pamphlets of his own, issued at the expense of himself or his friends." He was an earnest advocate for the celebrated "Baptist Petition for the Removal of Religious Restrictions," which was circulated throughout the State in 1802, obtaining many thousand signatures, and was one of the committee which laid it before the General Assembly. Much merriment was excited by the presentation of this petition. "Some called him fool; some mad," to think of overthrowing a system so thoroughly incorporated and so strongly intrenched. The Assembly, however, willing to examine its merits, referred the petition to a committee of eighteen members from the two Houses, to inquire and report. It was said that Oliver Ellsworth, chairman of the committee, "as he received the petition immediately threw it under the table, and putting his foot upon it, said, 'There is where it belongs.'" Several of the committee were suffered to be its advocates, and it was thoroughly canvassed and discussed until "every gentleman professed himself entirely satisfied that there was no ground of complaint which this Legislature could remove, except John T. Peters, Esq., who declared that nothing short of an entire repeal of the laws for the support of religion would accord with his views "—a declaration that was doubtless viewed as the height of presumptuous absurdity. Their report that the request was unnecessary, was accepted by both Houses without division and it was triumphantly believed that the troublesome question had been forever dismissed. A shrewd old Baptist Elder present told Mr. Bolles not to be discouraged:—" Let them talk as they will, you'll upset their dish yet."

David Bolles, Sen., though now advancing in years was still abundant in labors. In 1797, he was ordained as an Evangelist by the Stonington Baptist Association. In 1801, he accepted the call of the First Baptist Church in Hartford, and for two years officiated as its pastor, and was then dismissed at his own request, preferring to live in the country and preach without charge to destitute churches in the vicinity of his old home. His son Lucius was graduated from Brown University in 1801, and after studying three years with Dr. Stillman of Boston, was installed pastor of the newly formed Baptist Church in Salem. Among Dartmouth graduates of this date were Asa Carpenter of Eastford, who settled as a Congregational minister in Penfield, and Tower Whiton of Westford, who taught to good acceptance in Plainfield and other academies. Other sons of Elder Bolles engaged for a time in business in their own town. Mr. Richmond and his sons carried on shoe manufacture and other business enterprises in Westford. Mills for grinding and sawing, tanneries and distilleries, were active in various parts of the town. Dr. Nehemiah Howe attended to his patients and took a prominent part in town management, opening his office for public deliberations when the meeting-house was too cold for comfort. A second Dr. Palmer shared the practice of his father. The usual representatives of the town at this date were William Walker, Abel Simmons, Jun., Josias Biles and John Palmer. The election of Mr. Jason Woodward, who chanced to gain the vote in 1802, was contested upon the ground that he had obtained it " by distributing liquor; had treated the selectmen with four bowls of sling, and given to the people about his store four bottles of liquor," but fortunately for the honor of the town "the charges were not supported."

After the lamented death of Rev. James Messenger, the First church of Ashford remained for seven years without a stated pastor when it happily united in the choice of Enoch Pond of Wrentham, a graduate of Brown University, who, after a varied experience as a soldier and school-teacher, had turned his thoughts to the ministry, studied theology under the celebrated Dr. Emmons, and was ordained

38

and installed over the church in Ashford, September 16, 1789. Possessing unusual ability and cultivation, he gained great influence over his people and enjoyed an harmonious pastorate. Ebenezer Mason and Isaac Perkins, Esq., were chosen deacons the same year, and upon the death of the latter in 1795, were succeeded by Matthew Read and David Brown. The old meeting-house after seventy years' occupation was now enlarged and thoroughly repaired; the practice of admitting baptized persons to certain church privileges abolished by vote of the church. A revival of religious interest soon followed the settlement of Mr. Pond, and some sixty were added to the church. Two gifted young men were fitted by Mr. Pond for the ministry, Daniel and Hendrick Dow, though the latter, no less versatile than brilliant, left the pulpit for the bar.

The Eastford church maintained its high standing in doctrine and discipline. At a church meeting, November 22, 1782, voted:—

" I. That we will admit none to the privilege of baptism for themselves or seed but those who join in full communion.

II. That we esteem conversion necessary in order to right communion—therefore agree, that we will receive none to our holy fellowship, but those that make such a profession.

III. That those who belong to other churches and by letters dismissive and recommendatory offer themselves to join with us, shall prior to their admission submit themselves to examination, and make profession to our personal satisfaction.

IV. That those who remove from a distance and reside among us to whose faith and profession we are strangers, shall remove their relation with us when desired, or by letters recommendatory certify their good and regular standing elsewhere—otherwise be denied the privilege of communion."

Deacons Sumner and Perrin, and Captain John Works, were appointed a committee to assist in discipline. A very serious difficulty with a prominent church member was happily adjusted by an advisory council, but an erring sister was found guilty " of a breach of the eighth and ninth commandments," and debarred from church privileges.

After the close of the war the society was able to glaze the meeting-house, also to build the body of seats below, a breastwork and seats around the gallery, and provide hinges and bolts for the north door, and hang it. " Eight queristers " were installed in service with liberty to regulate the seating of the singers. An effort was made to do something for the more comfortable support of Mr. Judson. The prosperity of church and society was somewhat checked by the increasing infirmity of their pastor, who was afflicted with a hypochondriac melancholy, that at times incapacitated him for public service. In 1791, the society voted not to have preaching for the summer, and to petition the Honorable Association of the County to supply the pulpit for the year ensuing. Two years later, Mr. Pond was solicited to prepare a memorial to the Association for their assistance in preaching, and a committee appointed "to hire preaching eleven Sabbaths, if there be money enough." The malady increasing upon him, Mr. Judson mistrusted his ability to serve his people efficiently, and again and again asked their advice and dismission. Many councils were called but none thought best to dissolve the pastoral relation. Church and people exercised much kindness and patience under this heavy trial and labored in every way to aid and cheer their despondent pastor. In 1798, voted that their reverend pastor shall at his request have liberty to ride for his health, and be absent for the term of one year, he giving up his salary during his absence—or return sooner if convenient. Samuel Sumner was chosen deacon in the room of Deacon Sumner, Esq., and Noah Paine, Samuel Sumner and James Trowbridge, appointed in addition to the pastor "to attend and execute the watch and discipline of ye church." Noah Paine had been chosen deacon some years previous. Josiah Spalding, first clerk and treasurer of the society, was succeeded in 1795 by Alexander Work. Ezek Preston succeeded Abiel Simmons as collector of taxes. Mr. Judson with all his mental and bodily infirmities continued in charge till his death, November 15, 1804, and was aided in his later years by his son, John W. Judson, himself an invalid, and soon following his father. The society with its accustomed consideration voted "to continue Mr. Judson's salary to the bereaved widow." An effort was now made to raise a fund for the purpose of supporting the Gospel. The preaching of Mr. Allen was very satisfactory to the society but they were unable to retain him. Andrew T. Judson, youngest son of the deceased pastor, served as clerk of the society, while pursuing legal studies. He afterwards settled in Canterbury. One of the first young men who went out from Eastford Parish was Solomon, son of Josiah Spalding, who was graduated from Dartmouth in 1785. He read law for a time with Zephaniah Swift, but experienced a change in his religious views which led him to turn his thoughts to the ministry. He preached for a time in Cherry Valley, New York, and then removed to Ohio. Failing in health, he amused himself by writing an imaginary narrative of the wanderings of the Children of Israel across Behring's Straits to America, which, after his decease, was borrowed by Joseph Smith, and is said to have served as a foundation for the Mormon Bible.

Westford Society, in 1783, consented to the dismission of Rev. Elisha Huntington, in consideration of his low state of bodily health and insufficient salary. After the usual interim he was succeeded by Mr. William Storrs of Mansfield, who accepted a hundred pounds paid in building materials, neat stock, sheep fatted, pork, butter and cheese in lieu of the customary farm. Mr. Storrs was ordained and installed November 10, 1790, and continued for many years to administer the ministerial office in Westford to the great satisfaction of all—"a man of peace," piety and wisdom, much respected in the community and ministerial association.

A Baptist church was formed in this parish "in the glorious year 1780," through the instrumentality to a great degree of Mr. John Rathburn, who had removed from Stonington to this vicinity, and was ordained as its pastor, March 15, 1781. A membership of fifty-four was reported by Backus in 1795.

The Knowlton church, after some bickering with its pastor, Elder Ebenezer Lamson, with regard to the office work of deacon, and the manner of supporting ministers, (the Elder maintaining the strict Scriptural view that the deacons should literally supply the table of the minister), consented to his peaceable dismission in November, 1782, recommending him to the churches as a faithful gospel preacher. But upon review and reconsideration it decided that it _had_ contributed _well_ towards his support and fulfilled its agreement, and as Elder Lamson maintained the contrary, the church now confessed that it had _done wrong_ in giving him any recommendation and sent him and his wife "a gentle admonition." This affair led to mutual recriminations and councils, and doubtless hindered the church in securing another pastor. In 1786, both church and society united in choice of Mr. Robert Nesbet, and, as farther encouragement, made effort to finish their meeting-house and purchase a farm for the use of the minister. Zebulon Marcy, Samuel Brayton and Abraham Knowlton were appointed committee to lay out pew ground. "Glazing the windows," delayed by the difficulty of obtaining glass during the war, was now ordered. Ebenezer Walker, Thomas Knowlton and James Weston were ordered to look out for a ministerial lot, and Abraham and Daniel Knowlton and Samuel Johnson, "to draft subscription paper for the purpose of purchasing a farm and making assessments,"—subscribers agreeing "to purchase a farm for the use and improvement of a gospel minister for and under the control of the Baptist church and society of Ashford, said farm not to be disposed of for any other use—avails of farm to be restored to heirs of purchasers if not used for that purpose." Some fifty persons assisted in this purchase, in sums ranging from one shilling to over thirty pounds, Abraham Knowlton contributing the largest amount. While making these arrangements a formal call was extended to Mr. Nesbet, October 8, 1787—Elnathan Brigham, Deacon Hanks and Thomas Knowlton, committee—but just at this juncture the church was called to labor respecting the former difficulties with Elder Lamson, and possibly on this account he thus curtly declined:—

" *To the First Baptist Church of Christ at Ashford*, greeting. You was pleased to give me a call to the ministry, but upon serious serch, circumstances on my part forbid it. Farewell.

From your humble servant, ROBERT NESBET."

After some years' labor the church removed the admonition from their former pastor and proceeded, in 1791, "to take a deed of Mr. Benjamin Hanks of his farm in behalf of the church for the use of ministers." Elder Dyer Stark now manifested a freedom in administering special ordinances. September 12, 1793, Elder Stark was requested "to administer the ordinances of the gospel so long as he continues to reside amongst us." The society at the same time agreed to allow Elder Stark the improvement of the ministerial farm on which he then dwelt, so long as there was agreement between him and the church and society. It also voted, to admit new proprietors in the bettering the farm by fencing or walling. Elder Stark's ministry was blessed to the building up of the church which under previous broken administrations had made little advancement. A number of its members, viz. Deacons Knowlton and Hanks, and brethren Thomas Knowlton, Samuel Johnson, Elias Demick, Isaac Abbe, Moses Sibley, Azariah Hanks, John Utley, Jonathan and Abraham Weston and Chester Main, were allowed the improvement of their gifts in public prayer and exhortations. In 1798 the church was again destitute of a pastor and chiefly occupied in dealing with refractory members. In 1800, an effort was made to complete the unfinished meeting-house, a plat made and pew spots sold at auction, but ere the work was commenced the house was destroyed by fire, kindled it was suspected by a dissatisfied bidder. Elder Solomon Wheat had then been engaged to preach for a season, and stimulated by his presence the society promptly arranged to build a new house on the site of the old one, Stephen Eldridge agreeing to build and finish the same for the sum of $1,330. Previous bidders were allowed pews in similar locations in the new building, provided " they paid their bid." Failing to secure permission for a lottery, the lacking funds were made up by an assessment, and after so many years of delay and effort the "Knowlton meeting-house" was completed in 1802—a convenient and comfortable edifice for the times, with large, square pews and lofty, capacious pulpit. Provided with a satisfactory house for public worship, and a suitable home for its minister, the First Baptist Church in Ashford enjoyed a good degree of prosperity for many years, though its remote and inconvenient location was unfavorable to extended growth. Elder Wheat was succeeded in 1806, after a short interval of change and trial, by Frederic Wightman of Warwick, R. I. "The duty of all men to worship God," and distance from existing places of worship, led to the formation of other Baptist churches in Ashford during this period. A third Baptist church was organized within the limits of Eastford Parish, and Mr. Daniel Bolton ordained therein, June 27, 1792. Residents in Abington also united with this church, but owing to the rise of Methodism and the vicinity of other Baptist churches, it did not gain a permanent standing. A membership of thirty-eight was reported in 1795. In 1801, they had become so weakened as to unite with the Second Baptist church of Woodstock as a branch, reserving the privilege of resuming their former independency if it should be expedient.

In the northeast corner of Ashford, known appropriately as Northford, seven men organized as a Baptist society, November 11, 1793, and pledged themselves to build a house of worship and support a religious teacher. "In the winter following the Lord put it into the hearts of his people to set up conference meetings," and upon relating to each other the wonderful dealings of God with their souls, and discussing the rules, order and discipline of a church of Christ, they found such "a good measure of harmony and agreement, as to encourage them to organize as a church." A council consisting of pastors and delegates from the three Ashford churches and the First Baptist of Woodstock convened for this purpose, November 5, 1794, but upon examination it was found that those who had called the council had neglected to obtain letters of dismission from the churches to which they belonged. But the brethren were not to be frustrated in their design. Six new converts came forward asking church privileges, were baptized that day by Elder Daniel Bolton, and with one brother who was furnished with a letter, "were recognized as the Fourth Baptist church of Ashford." The good brethren who had instituted this worship were soon added to their number, and Elder Bolton, retained as their pastor, also brought a letter from the church in Wilbraham, Mass. The meeting-house was used for public services, though not completed for several years. A sufficient support was provided for the pastor, who also wrought with his own hands that he might be less chargeable to the brethren. Though few in numbers and far remote from the busy world, this church enjoyed uncommon grace and harmony and exercised a most beneficial influence upon the community. Pastor and delegates were present at the organization of the Sturbridge Association and faithfully retained relation with that body. Ephraim Howard and Joseph Burly served successively as clerks, and also as deacons. Elder Bolton administered the pastorate till 1806, to the great acceptance of all, and his name adhered to the meeting-house long after his removal to distant fields.

Methodism also gained adherents in Ashford.   Early itinerants passing over its convenient thoroughfares tarried to preach the word wherever they could find a hearing.   Elder David Bolles, ever ready to fraternize with all good christians outside *"the Standing Order,"* opened his house and heart to these zealous preachers.   Soon they were allowed to hold meetings in the village school-house.   Young Mr. Mumford, who had just started business in this vicinity, had his curiosity so excited by the stories brought back from Hartford by terrified town deputies of the disgraceful character and conduct of these Methodist invaders, that out of sport he dropped in to hear one, almost expecting to see a monster with hoof and horns.   He saw instead a most graceful and eloquent young man whose fire and pathos took his fancy by storm, and made him through life a devoted champion of Methodism.   In time he joined the society, helped build the first Methodist meeting-house, and by his zeal and influence proved a valuable acquisition to the Methodist ranks.   Many young people in the vicinity of Eastford were awakened and converted under Methodist preaching, and gathered into a class and society.   Stated preaching was held after a few years in a rough meeting-house built about 1800, it is believed, some two miles west of the village.   David Bolles, Esq., Captain Mumford, Leonard Deane, Nathan Palmer, Jun., were among the attendants upon this worship.

Ashford like several of its neighbors had the excitement of a *murder* during this period with the accompanying search, trial and execution.   Samuel Freeman, a dissolute colored man of mongrel blood, came up to Ashford from Rhode Island, and persuaded an Indian woman to live with him.   Returning with her one evening from a low drinking-house, he took her life in a fit of drunken rage, and threw her into a dank pool, still known as Squaw Hollow.   The crime was proved and Freeman hung at Windham Green, November 6, 1805, with all the usual formalities and more than the usual satisfaction, unalloyed as it was in this case by any disturbing doubts as to the justice of the penalty or by sentimental sympathy for the miserable criminal.

NOTE.   The "Ashford Whipping" reported *ante* page 28, was probably inflicted under Section 16, of the Act for the due Observation of the Sabbath, viz. :—" That whatsoever person shall be convicted of any profanation of the Lord's-day, or of any disturbance of any congregation allowed for the worship of God during the time of their assembling for or attending of such worship, and shall, being fined for such offence, neglect or refuse to pay the same, or to present estate for that purpose; the Court, Assistant or Justice before whom conviction is had, may sentence such offender to be whipt, not exceeding twenty stripes, respect being had to the nature and aggravation of the offence."

VIII.

CANTERBURY BRIDGES.   ENTERPRISING YOUNG MEN.   MASTER
ADAMS' SCHOOL.   GENERAL TOWN AND CHURCH
AFFAIRS.   WESTMINSTER SOCIETY.

EVEN amid the burdens and engrossments of the war, Canterbury
was compelled to expend money and labor upon her *bridges*,
which weighed so heavily upon her selectmen that they addressed a
letter to their neighbors in Norwich, in 1780, in which they lamented
"the great and unequal expense which they and several towns labor
under above other towns in the State, by being obliged to build and
maintain many great bridges over large rivers," and requested a committee of conference to consider some mode of relief. A committee
was appointed but found no practicable remedy for the evil, and the
town took its woes once more to the Assembly. Solomon Paine and
Daniel Frost in behalf of the inhabitants of Canterbury, October 10,
1782, averred, that they were obliged to maintain a large number of
bridges in said town, many of them across large and rapid streams,
viz.:—one and a half over the Quinebaug, four over Little River, six
over Rowland's brook; that the bridge over the Quinebaug known as
Butts' Bridge was in the southeast part of the town, where it was of
very little service to but few of the memorialists, but was of great
utility and service to the public traveling from Boston to Norwich,
and was now out of repair, and asked for a lottery of £250, to aid in
this new enterprise. The Assembly granting this request, John Fitch,
Daniel Frost, Dr. Welles, Deacon Asa Witter and Stephen Butts were
chosen managers of the lottery. Captains Sherebiah Butts, Jabez
Ensworth and John Adams were commissioned to have charge of the
building, and a stout bridge supported by stone pillars was speedily
constructed. The managers of the lottery were allowed to sell tickets
for town orders, and to transfer all that were left on their hands to the
selectmen. In 1788, the town was again called to join with Plainfield
in rebuilding Nevins' Bridge. Among other town expenses recorded
at about this date were payments for new sign-post and stocks, also
for "keeping Sibbel —— and dipping her sundry times," also for
"salivating" sundry persons.

The usual changes were occurring. John Dyer, Esq., colonel of the
Eleventh Regiment, judge of the Windham County Court, deputy at
the General Assembly at times for forty years, "all which parts he
sustained with unblemished correctness till impaired with age," departed this life February 25, 1779, in the eighty-seventh year of his
age. "A man of sound judgment and unbiased integrity." Dr.

Jabez Fitch, youngest son of Major James Fitch, having "for many years sustained with fidelity and honor the offices of justice of the Peace and Quorum, and judge of Probate," and also served as colonel of the Eleventh Regiment, died at an advanced age in 1784. Colonel Aaron Cleveland, so prominent in public affairs during the Revolution, was struck with palsy while yet in the prime of life, and after long and distressing sickness died in 1785. Deacon Asa Witter died suddenly in 1792, after being chosen town deputy and before the session of the Assembly. John Felch though advanced in years still served the town in many capacities. Captain Ephraim Lyon, Nathan Waldo, Eliashib Adams, Jabez Ensworth, David Baldwin, Benjamin and Asa Bacon, Captain John Adams, Daniel Frost, Captain Stephen Butts and other older men, were active and prominent in town affairs. Dr. Gideon Welles served acceptably as town clerk and treasurer. Dr. Jabez Fitch succeeded to the medical practice of his father. Dr. Walter Hough returned to Canterbury after the war, officiating as surgeon and sheriff. Dr. Jaireb Dyer engaged extensively in trade and medical practice.

Canterbury participated largely in that spirit of emulation and business enterprise that sprung into life with the Nation, and was especially distinguished by the great number of active and energetic young men, eager to make for themselves a career. Vicinity to Plainfield's excellent academy doubtless served as a stimulus to many of these young minds, furnishing them accessible facilities for fitting themselves for the higher walks of life. Many of the Canterbury youth availed themselves of this privilege, and of these a large proportion obtained a collegiate education. From Yale there were graduated in 1777, Ebenezer, son of Dr. Fitch, and Moses, son of Colonel Cleveland; in 1778, Asa Spalding; 1779, Elisha, grandson of Solomon Paine; 1793, Asa Bacon, Jun., William Pitt, son of Colonel Cleveland; 1794, Aaron, son of William Kinney; 1795, John, son of John Adams, and Rufus, son of Nathan Adams; 1797, Seth P., son of Rev. John Staples; 1803, John, son of Dr. Hough; Hezekiah, son of Deacon Frost; 1804, Parker, son of John Adams. Cornelius Adams, deacon of the old Separate church, sent four sons to Yale, viz.: Thomas, graduated in 1800; Stedman, 1801; Cornelius, 1803; Daniel, 1806. From Dartmouth were graduated, 1785, Moses Bradford; 1787, Eleazer Brown, Elihu Palmer; 1791, Ebenezer Woodward; 1795, Luther Jewett Hebard; 1794, James Brown, who died in Canterbury the following year. William and Ebenezer Bradford were also graduated from Princeton.

Many of these young men went out into the world to fill distinguished positions. Ebenezer Fitch was the first president of

39

Williams College, Asa Spalding one of Norwich's most brilliant and successful lawyers. Seth P. Staples won a high name among many legal competitors in New York city. Hough, professor in Middlebury College, was greatly admired for eloquence and varied accomplishments. His classmate, Frost, entered the legal profession and achieved a good position in Windham, Maine. Parker Adams served usefully in the Episcopal ministry, and most of the Dartmouth graduates were honored as Congregational ministers.*

Fortunately for Canterbury some of these energetic and brilliant young men remained in their native town. Moses Cleveland opened a law office on his paternal homestead, and engaged with much spirit in public and military affairs. Rising rapidly through the subordinate grades, he was made general of the Fifth Brigade in 1796. Previous to this date he had been appointed agent of the Western Reserve Land Company and was very efficient and active in the settlement of northeastern Ohio, and in other important business enterprises. He was also very prominent as a Mason, holding the position of grand marshal of the Grand Lodge of Connecticut. Though unable to give much attention to the practice of his profession he could direct others, and many young men studied law in his office. His brother, William Pitt Cleveland, Asa Bacon, Jun. and Rufus Adams were among those students, and all for a time practiced law in Canterbury. Elisha Paine also opened a law office in his own house in the south part of the town. John Adams after his graduation commenced a select school in his own neighborhood in the North Society, and at once exhibited such uncommon aptitude in instruction and management as to draw a large number of pupils. Plainfield Academy was at this time suffering a temporary depression, which gave Canterbury an opportunity to establish a rival institution. In the spring of 1796, Master Adams was induced to remove his school to Canterbury Green, where it achieved immediate success and popularity, attracting pupils from all the adjacent towns and even from distant Woodstock and Thompson. Mr. Adams had in large measure the true teacher's art of calling out the best that was in his pupils and awakening their enthusiasm for school, studies and master. Combining sympathy and kindness with authority he won their most affectionate regard. He was especially noted for his kindness to indigent young men seeking education. Among those thus aided and encouraged was Rinaldo Burleigh of Ashford, who, in the face of great poverty and hardship, having lost his father in early childhood,

---

*There is strong reason for believing that a still earlier celebrity—Jonathan Carver, the distinguished traveler and explorer of the Northwest wilderness—was born in Canterbury.

and his left arm a few years later, was struggling to fit himself for intellectual employment. Mr. Adams took him not only into his school but into his "very heart," enabling him to meet his expenses by assisting in teaching till he was qualified to enter college. No record of pupils has been preserved, but the number was evidently large. The sons of Cornelius Adams, Dr. Hough, Deacon Frost, and many other young men, were here fitted for college. Lemuel Grosvenor, afterward a successful merchant in Boston, Bela P. Spalding of Brooklyn, William Larned of Thompson, were among the students. Canterbury was never more flourishing than during the continuance of this school. The presence of so many energetic young men made everything lively. Business and trade were active. Many stores were opened on Canterbury Green. Farmers found a ready market for all their produce. Dr. Dyer carried on a brisk trade with the West Indies, dealing largely in horses and cattle, and maintained an extensive establishment in the south part of the town. John Clarke, an eccentric Englishman with ample means and a patriarchal family, reported to have been engaged in the tea-overthrow at Boston, also occupied a fine farm in that vicinity. Joseph Moore of Long Island, purchased land and settled in Canterbury. Thomas Coit, one of Norwich's sterling citizens, after a brief sojourn in Scotland removed to Canterbury Green, and engaged in mercantile traffic. John Francis of Boston, after trying Scotland long enough to find a wife there, followed on to Canterbury. Alexander Gordon of Plainfield opened trade in Westminster and won a high position among the solid men of the town. Luther, son of David Paine, engaged in trade. Jedidiah, grandson of Obadiah Johnson, "kept tavern," engaged in trade and was active in military affairs. Abel Brewster opened a jeweler's store. William Lord engaged in the manufacture of hats. Isaac and Consider Morgan entered into partnership in 1804, and opened a very large assortment of dry goods, drugs, hardware and groceries in the First Society of Canterbury. Many new buildings were erected at about this date, and a wing added to the tavern which accommodated four or five business establishments. William Moore built a large house on the northeast corner of the crossings in the village, and there opened Canterbury's first post-office in 1803. The hall in the upper part of the tavern building was celebrated for its many popular gatherings, and especially as the place for Masonic demonstrations. Generals Putnam and McClellan, Colonels Gray and Grosvenor, Moses Cleveland and other leading men in the County, were early connected with the Masonic Lodge at Hartford. Upon petition of Colonels Gray and Grosvenor, Moriah Lodge was instituted at

Canterbury, in 1790, and soon received into its brotherhood most of the active, leading men of the County. Its first grand master was Colonel Ebenezer Gray. Moses Cleveland, Evan Malbone, Thomas and Lemuel Grosvenor, Samuel and John McClellan, Daniel Larned, Daniel Putnam, William Danielson, Lemuel Ingalls, Albigence Waldo, John Brewster, Jared Warner, were among the many who were actively interested in this Lodge. Its annual commemoration of St. John's day in June was one of the great festivals of the year, exceeded only by Fourth of July and General Training. The Masonic brethren from all the surrounding towns in full regalia, marched through the street with banners, music and open Bible, to be entertained in hall or grove with a grand oration and fine dinner. The young men of Canterbury were enthusiastic in devotion to this order, and maintained its appointed services with much spirit and fidelity. An elaborate oration delivered by Asa Bacon, Jun., June 27, 1799, in which the youthful orator presumed to deviate "from the flowery field of friendship," into "the wilderness of politics," excited much attention and praise, and was deemed worthy of publication in *The Windham Herald.*

The "young blood" in the town was manifested in many public enterprises and improvements. An elaborate code of laws, adopted in 1796 for the better regulation of town meetings, shows the hand of the young lawyers, and hints at previous informalities, now to be remedied :—

"1. No motion shall be objected to, or considered within the possession of the meeting, except it be for reconsideration, without it be seconded by some other member than him who first made the same.

2. No member shall speak more than twice to one and the same question or motion before the meeting without leave of said meeting, nor more than once before each member desiring to speak has had his turn.

3. No motion shall be made for reconsideration of any choice, vote or act of said meeting, but by some member who acted the affirmative in passing the same, which shall all be done in the same meeting in which said vote was passed.

4. No member shall speak, or ask liberty to speak, when any other member is speaking, except to call the member speaking to order, and the member called to order shall sit down, and he may appeal to the meeting to decide the question of order, but if he refuse to make such appeal the moderator shall determine the same, and in either case it shall be done without debate, and the moderator shall, and any member of said meeting may call any person to order transgressing the foregoing rules.

5. That for the future we will choose our selectmen, listers and grand-jurors so as to place them in the different quarters of the town, and before we proceed to choose either of the above class of officers the moderator shall mention which quarter of the town to begin at. And the foregoing rules shall by the clerk or moderator be publicly read at the opening of our annual town meeting."

By-laws were passed the following year regulating the impounding of cattle, and geese were denied the liberty of the road unless "well

yoked and one wing cropt." The selectmen were authorized to purchase or hire a home for the poor, and Colonel Benjamin Bacon
offered to provide for them for one-fifth per week less than the year
preceding. Town meetings were held alternately in the meeting-
houses of the two societies. Schools were cared for by each society,
though "squadrons" had given place to modern districts. The central district of the First Society had liberty to erect a convenient
school-house on the green north of the meeting-house in 1795. In
the following year a school society was organized—Luther Paine,
clerk and treasurer. Colonel Benjamin Bacon, John Felch and Luther
Paine were authorized to take care of the loan money. Timothy
Backus, Rufus Baldwin, Walter Hough, Thomas Coit, Lot Morgan,
Waldo Brown, Daniel Frost, Jesse Ensworth, school committee.
Josiah Robinson, Elisha Paine, John Felch, Thomas Coit, Moses
Cleveland, John Adams, Daniel Frost and Jesse Ensworth, were
empowered to locate and bound school districts. Committees were
thenceforward appointed by the several districts, with nine overseers
to superintend them.

Turnpike projects called out the usual discussion and opposition.
The town wholly "disapproved of any turnpike gate being erected at
or near Mr. Samuel Barstow's blacksmith shop, on the great road from
Plainfield to Windham, judging it unjust and impolitic." The proposed "Norwich and Woodstock turnpike," excited much opposition.
General Cleveland at this date was usually moderator at town meetings, but now Colonel Benjamin Bacon was placed in the chair, and
with Elisha Paine and David Baldwin, made a committee to confer
with committees from other towns, and oppose the laying out of this
turnpike. John Francis and Nathan Adams, representatives to General
Assembly, were also instructed to oppose the same, and use their
influence to procure the rejection of the committee's report. As
usual in such cases their opposition was unavailing and in May, 1801,
Moses Cleveland, William Adams, Asa Bacon, Luther Paine and
Jedidiah Johnson of Canterbury, were incorporated with gentlemen
of other towns as "The Norwich and Woodstock Turnpike Company."
Its first meeting was held the following September at the tavern of
Jedidiah Johnson ; a committee was chosen to assess damages and
the road speedily constructed. The great road leading to Windham
was also made a turnpike in 1799, and a gate erected near the centre
of the town. Upon petition of the Windham Turnpike Company a
change was made in 1804, the central gate removed to near the
dividing line between Canterbury and Windham, and a new gate
placed near the line between Canterbury and Plainfield. The highway running north and south through Westminster Society was a

public thoroughfare from time immemorial, accommodating travel from Norwich town to the Massachusetts line. The earliest laying out of this road has not. been recovered, but it was improved from time to time and made more passable. Rough field stones were used to mark off the miles. It is said that in the original survey the road was marked out to run, a due north and south line over Westminster Plain, but that the occupant of the old Parks tavern nearly half a mile eastward, fearing to lose custom lay in wait for the engineers, and so plied-them with liquor and courtesies that they consented to lay out the road to accommodate the tavern, intersecting the original survey about one-and-a-fourth miles from the point of deviation. A highway was laid out in 1785, from Ephraim Lyon's Potash works to Parker Adams' mill, crossing the south part of the town. Stephen Butts and Phinehas Carter were also manufacturers of potash. Mr. Carter afterwards carried on coopering, on quite a large scale in Westminster village, employing from four to six hands in the winter season. Tanneries were now established in several parts of the town. The extreme west of Canterbury was first settled by one or more families of Downings, who gave their name to the brook in their vicinity, ran mills and set out orchards. A somewhat isolated com munity, they had little to do with the general affairs of the town; were fond of frolic and dancing and enjoyed the repute of having plenty of money. Saw and grist-mills were carried on successfully by the Morses and Bradfords in the North Society, a dam being allowed on Rowland's Brook in 1804.

President Dwight in his "Travels" reported Canterbury as suffering much from lack of clergymen, want of harmony and declension of morals. Standing and Separate churches were alike affected. Nathaniel Niles, Samuel Hopkins, Job Swift, supplied the pulpit in the First society at irregular intervals. The Separate church enjoyed the occasional ministrations of some wandering Separate or "Lyon, the Baptist." In 1784, attempts were made to unite both congregations under the ministry of Rev. Solomon Morgan, the standing church voting, "That there is a willingness and freedom that the members of the Separate church should meet with us in hearing the preaching of the Gospel, and have equal privileges with us if they desire it." Capt. Cobb, Asa Bacon, Dr. Gideon Welles, Samuel Adams, Jun. and Samuel Ensworth were appointed a committee to confer with one appointed by the Separates. A Confession of Faith, Heads of Agreement and Covenant, were accordingly drawn up and signed by a number of the members of both churches, and it seemed likely that they would unite and go on in peace and good agreement, but on calling a meeting to confer respecting the settlement of a

minister it appeared that the adopted articles were not understood
alike by both parties, and they were not disposed to practice alike
on them, "whereby the good ends and much-wished-for happy union
between the aforesaid churches were likely to prove abortive, and
come to an end." Each church was then requested to state in
writing the matter of dispute and difference between them. John
Bacon, David Kinne, Daniel Frost, John B. Adams and Esther Fish,
in behalf of the Standing church, therefore gave it as their opinion,
"That the real cause of disagreement was the question, 'Who shall be
the Council to ordain our minister in case we are happy enough to
agree in one, and who shall administer ordinances to us occasionally
when destitute of a settled minister?'"—to which they answered,
"That although they were willing that any of their brethren should
occasionally partake and commune with those churches and ministers
that are called Separate and practice lay ordination, and that those
ministers should preach amongst us occasionally, yet they did not
judge it proper or expedient that any of the above-mentioned ministers
should assist as council in the ordination of our minister, or administer ordinances to us as a body; and on their part, they did not
judge it expedient or proper to have those ministers officiate that
were offensive to their Separate brethren, especially those that practise
upon the Stodard-ean Plan, but did mean to have full fellowship with
such churches as are settled upon and practise according to what is
called the Edward can Plan."

The Separates apparently received this as a clear and satisfactory
statement of the cause of difference, but declined to accept the
situation. The Standing church and society proceeded to call Mr.
Morgan to settlement. Farther attempts were made to compound the
difference. The Reverends Paul Park, John Palmer, Levi Hunt and
Micaiah Porter, convened at their summons, tenderly urged their
Separate brethren to labor to agree on some churches and ministers
with whom they could all hold fellowship in gospel ordinances and
institutions, reserving to each individual the liberty of personal
communion with such churches and ministers as they might judge to
be for their edification. Before the installation of Mr. Morgan another
effort was made by both churches. The Reverends Joseph Snow of
Providence, John Cleveland of Ipswich (expelled from college forty
years before for attending worship with this same Separate church),
Timothy Stone of Lebanon, Paul Park of Preston, John Staples and
Micaiah Porter, met in council, and unanimously agreed:—

"1. As to the case of Capt. Shepherd and his wife, the church from which
they withdrew should take off the censure from those persons.
2. The Council was persuaded that there was a difference between the two
churches, which in their view appeared so important that they saw no

prospect of a happy union, and could only advise them for the present to maintain a spirit of Christian forbearance until God should open the way for them to be of one mind and one judgment.

3.   But whereas there was a prospect in the view of some that a door might by-and-by be opened for the removal of those things that made the difference between these churches and others under similar circumstances, the Council advised that both churches and congregations should unite together in the public worship of God, attending on the ministry of the Word as at present dispensed and cultivate harmony, if this may be consistent with their views and feelings—but, if they cannot thus agree, advised each church and congregation to set up and maintain that worship and order which appears to them most agreeable to the mind of God, without giving any disturbance or molestation to each other."

The Separates therefore called a meeting September 29, and with a gleam of their former spirit, voted :—

" 1. Respecting advice of Council, concerning Capt. Shepherd and his wife, as the Council has given no reasons why this church should take off their censure, nor offered any light upon the matter, they cannot consistently take off their censure till proper repentance is manifested to the church by the persons aforesaid.

2.   With respect to the advice of Council that both churches and congregations unite together in public worship, attending upon the Word as at present dispensed here, if this is understood to mean the ministry of Mr. Morgan, we can by no means comply therewith. Or if this advice should be construed to mean that we meet together as we have done for three months past by having equal privileges in carrying on the public worship, we cannot conscientiously comply with advice in this respect.

Therefore, in the third place, we are willing to comply, and do hereby comply with that part of the advice of Council, which advises each church and congregation to set up and maintain that worship and order which to them appears most agreeable to the mind of God. And we think it our duty at present to set up and maintain public worship as a distinct body from the people under the charge of Mr. Morgan."

On the following day, September 30, Mr. Morgan was installed over the Standing church. Eliashib Adams and Daniel Frost now served as its deacons; Joseph Moore was afterwards added. Walter Hough succeeded John Felch as clerk of the society. The Separates endeavored to carry out their resolutions but were unable to find a pastor, and became in time more reconciled to Mr. Morgan, who took great pains to conciliate them and unite the churches. He was so far successful that in 1788 about thirty of the more prominent Separates—including Moses, Timothy, Tracy and Eliphaz Cleveland, Benjamin, Jacob and Samuel Bacon, John and James Adams, William and Jacob Johnson, Luther Paine, Thomas Boswell and others—gave in their names and returned to the First Society. The remaining members of the Separate church persisted in separation, and now removed their meeting-house to the north part of the town, where they gathered a small congregation. William, son of William and Mary (Cleveland) Bradford, was graduated from New Jersey College in 1774 and ordained to the ministry, and after teaching and preaching in various fields, returned to his old home in the north part of Canterbury, and assumed the charge of this Separate flock. His brothers, Moses and Ebenezer Bradford, both entered the ministry, the latter settling in Rowley.

The few Baptists in Canterbury were extremely irregular in faith and practice, as well as in mode and place of worship. They held to what was called "mixed communion," and with a small number of similar churches, formed Groton Conference. Capt. Ephraim Lyon was one of the pillars of this clique, as ready to fight for religious as for civil freedom, but after a time he is reported to have become a Methodist, and his associates lost coherence and visibility. Some had been led away by the eloquence of Elhanan Winchester, baptized in Canterbury by Elder Ebenezer Lyon, who after a brilliant career as a Baptist popular preacher, had embraced the doctrine of Universal Salvation. Dr. Cogswell reports many Universalists in Canterbury, who despised and flouted Mr. Morgan and seemed likely to do much damage. Several united with the Universalist Society of Oxford, then under the pastoral charge of Rev. Thomas Barnes, who frequently held service in Canterbury and other Windham towns. So much interest was excited that meetings were advertised in school-houses, " to discuss whether the doctrine of universal salvation could be proved from Scripture."

So widely had free opinions leavened the town that in 1791, the First Society voted to admit occasionally to preach in the meeting-house on Lord's Day, preachers of the Gospel of different persuasions from the present established sentiments, provided those men should be persons of good moral character and professors of the christian religion, which shall be at the option of the present society committee, and their successors. This vote, opening the pulpit to "Friend Barnes," as he was called, and other heterodox preachers, occasioned much disturbance, and after some years of controversy the church prevailed upon the society to reconsider and revoke, and grant the control of the pulpit to the pastor. This decision gave great offence to Canterbury's spirited young men who were fully imbued with the revolutionary spirit of the day, averse to orthodox principles and preaching, and eager for a new meeting-house and minister, better music and other modern improvements. A movement was instantly set on foot to organize as an " Independent Catholic Christian society," after the pattern of one just formed in Pomfret, and met with great favor. Fifty of the leading men of Canterbury signified their dissent " from the doctrine preached and held by minister, church and society," and pledged their names to the new organization. This great defection filled church and society with consternation. A committee was at once appointed to confer with those who have lately separated from us, and also with Mr. Morgan, to see if they can devise

40

ways to accommodate matters and prevent division. The members of the Independent Catholic Society were most earnestly besought to unite themselves with the old society, "so that we may unitedly support the social and public worship in a more decent and respectable manner, and better promote our spiritual edification." In response to their entreaties, a council was held, viz.:—the Rev. Messrs. Hart, Benedict, Whitney, Staples, Lee and Porter, with Asa Bacon, John Felch and Thomas Coit to wait upon them. Through their mediation accommodation was effected. Mr. Morgan was dismissed from his charge, and old and new societies united—signing the following Articles of Agreement:—

"ARTICLE I. Charity, which is so strongly inculcated in Divine Revelation, and declared to be an essential christian duty, teaches us at all times to concede towards each other in our religious associations. We will therefore never withhold from each other a convenient and proper opportunity of receiving such different christian instructors as may be agreeable to their consciences—paying at all times a decent regard to engagements and priority of appointments.

ART. II. Whenever it shall be judged prudent and best to build a meeting-house, or procure instruments of music that will render the worship of God decent, orderly and graceful, the same shall be done by free and voluntary donations and used for the purposes assigned by the donors.

December 26, 1797."

This breach being healed, some improvements were effected. Five choristers were appointed, and a committee " to promote psalmody." A bell was procured by voluntary subscription, its ringing regulated by the society committee. In 1799, it was voted to build a meeting-house with a steeple. Asa Bacon, Jun., and Rufus Adams, committee to procure subscriptions, failed to secure sufficient encouragement. The proposal to unite with Westminster Society in building a new house of worship in the centre of the town was equally unsuccessful. The liberty granted by the Assembly of raising fifteen hundred dollars by a lottery encouraged the society to continue its efforts. Other sums were procured by private subscription, and in 1805 a new meeting-house was completed to the satisfaction of all parties. Daniel C. Banks and Thaddeus Fairbanks had supplied the pulpit during this interim.

The Westminster Society shared in the general growth and prosperity of the town, alloyed by occasional providential visitations and local differences. Dr. Cogswell in his diary, July 2, 1788, reports the devastations of a terrific thunder-storm—a black cloud seemed to settle down upon Westminster Parish; hail *nineteen inchés* deep; glass much fractured; grain and grass lodged; gardens destroyed, so that people in neighboring towns sent relief to the sufferers—and also irreconcilable feuds between prominent church members that seemed likely to lead to the dismissal of Mr. Staples, but which like the hailstorm left no lasting impress. To outward appearance there was more than usual harmony in the society. Deacon Eliashib Adams often presided in society meetings. Deacon Herrick and Captains William Hebard and Joseph Burgess served as committee; Stephen Butts, clerk; Nathaniel Butts, collector. Joseph Hebard and Elijah Herrick filled the useful office of chorister. Committees were appointed from time to time to seat the meeting-house. John Park had liberty in 1787, to take up four of the lower seats and replace them by four decent pews after the construction of those called pillar-pews, provided he gave up the same when built to the society. George Williamson, Captain Hebard, Sherebiah and Stephen Butt and Rufus Darbe, were authorized " to confer respecting the heavy tax that now lies on the society for the payment of the minister's salary." An abatement of thirty pounds was accepted by Mr. Staples. To prevent a recurrence of such difficulty a movement was instituted for " a perpetual fund for the purpose of supporting a preached Gospel, performed by men of zeal, practical piety, Calvinistic principles, and approved by Windham County Association," which resulted in the subscription of more than six hundred pounds.* Thus well established with fund and convenient house of worship, the society was little inclined to favor the proposed reunion with the First Society, but considered the question so far as to affix for a central site, a spot " within twenty rods of turnpike road, between the houses of Dr. Gideon Welles and Mr. Samuel Barstow." Mr. Staples continued to discharge his ministerial duties with fidelity and acceptance till " he died and rested from his labors, February 15, 1804, in the 61st year of his age and 32d of his ministry—ministers not being suffered to continue by reason of death." Called up in the night to pray with a dying mother of the church, he neglected to put on his accustomed *wig*, and either taking cold in consequence, or taking the fever from the aged lady, he followed her to the grave in a few days. His death made a great impression upon all his flock, and especially upon the young people who had ever regarded " Priest Staples " with the most reverential affection. The funeral was conducted with the usual elaborate formality. The bereaved church continued faithfully to observe the usual

---

* SUBSCRIBERS TO FUND : - Mary Davis, Joseph Safford, Thomas Jewett, Simeon Park, Reuben Park, David Munro, Joseph Butts, Phinehas Carter, Asa Burgess, Jonathan Kingsbury, Jonas Cary, Abner Robinson, William Howard, John Munro, David Munro, Rufus Darbe, John Barstow, James Howard, Gideon Butts, William Ripley, William D. Foster, Jabez Fox, Josiah, David, Asa, and John Butts, John Staples, Charles Justin, Samuel Barstow, John Smith, Sherebiah and Stephen Butts, Ebenezer Park, Jonas Bond, William Carew, Hezekiah Barstow, Peter Woodward, Robert Herrick, Ephraim Safford, Joseph Adams, Joshua Raymond, Joseph Raynsford, Rufus Johnson, James Burnap, Benjamin Raynsford, Bethuel Bond.
December 19, 1798.

seasons of worship, and also instituted a special meeting for religious exercises on the first Wednesday of every month. In November, a call was extended to Rev. Erastus Larned of Charlton, with a salary of $333.34. Mr. Larned accepting, Dr. Whitney, Messrs. Lee and Weld were invited to carry forward a preparatory service of fasting. A committee was then appointed to prepare the meeting-house for installation, and preserve order and regularity during the exercises. Mr. John Barstow's generous offer to make provision for the council was accepted with thankfulness. Eleven ministers and probably an equal number of delegates, partook of the proffered hospitality, and the installation was effected to general satisfaction. Mr. Larned won like his predecessor the affection of his people, and reared like him a large family of children who shared the friendly regard of the parish. A bequest from his father, Mr. James Larned of Killingly, enabled him to build a convenient house opposite the meeting-house. The widow of Mr. Staples occupied the house built by her husband, and her sons and daughters grew up to fill honorable positions in New York and New Haven. Seth P. Staples, long remembered in Westminster for boyish pranks and subsequent benefactions, attained to much eminence.

In care of its public schools Westminster vied with the older society. Alexander Gordon, Samuel Barstow and Asa Nowlen were appointed to oversee the schooling in 1787. Nine districts were set out, and Sherebiah Butts, John Barstow, Isaac Backus, Roswell Parish, Joseph Raynsford, Joshua Raymond, Daniel Downing, Robert Herrick and Nathaniel Smith, made each collector and committee-man for his respective district. With increasing travel brought by turnpike, and improved business facilities, Westminster village became a place of more importance. Its first resident physician was Dr. Rufus Johnson, brother of Col. Jedidiah Johnson, who purchased a strip of the meeting-house green in 1790, where after a time he built a dwelling-house. Captain Stephen Butts entertained travelers in an old house adjoining. The old "Ford house" on the Norwich road, and the Parks tavern-house, were said to be the oldest houses in the vicinity.

Lack of endowment and suitable building accommodations compelled Canterbury in 1801 to yield her honored "master" to the older institution in Plainfield. Asa Bacon, Jun., had now crossed over to Litchfield. William P. Cleveland after a brief practice in Brooklyn had settled in New London. The emigration movement had broken out with renewed vigor, and many "Canterbury pilgrims" were wending their way to distant States. Captain Josiah Cleveland, of Bunker Hill fame, removed to Owego, N. Y. Dr. Azel, son of

William Ensworth, settled southward in Palmyra, and was much respected "as an active, exemplary and influential citizen." A pleasant eminence in Rome called Canterbury Hill in honor of its first settlers, became the residence of Gideon, John, Elisha and Daniel Butts, Samuel and Asa Smith, Samuel Williams, Thomas Jewett, Daniel W. Knight, and other roving sons of Canterbury. Eliashib Adams, Jun., Elijah Herrick and William Bingham attempted settlement in Lewis County, near Lake Ontario, but Herrick was drowned in crossing Black River and Adams finally settled in Maine. Deacon Eliashib Adams, now far advanced in years, followed this son to a temporary home in Massachusetts. Alexander Gordon sought fortune in the far South; William Moore established himself in the snows of Canada. General Cleveland's connection with the Western Reserve Company may have led some emigrants to turn their thoughts to the Northwestern Territory, but no Canterbury names appear among the early settlers of New Connecticut. His own name already marked the site of the beautiful city that now adorns the southern shore of Lake Erie. In 1796, he had gone out as commander of an expedition sent by the Connecticut Land Company to survey and settle the Western Reserve. After a wearisome journey through the State of New York, and a successful conference with the chief of the Six Nations at Buffalo, they "arrived at the confines of New Connecticut and gave three cheers, precisely at 5 o'clock P. M., July 4." This auspicious arrival on the day memorable as the birthday of American Independence, and also "memorable as the day on which the settlement of this new country was commenced," seemed to demand "a just tribute" of respect. The men ranged themselves on the beach and fired a Federal salute of fifteen rounds, and then the sixteenth in honor of "New Connecticut." They gave three cheers and christened the place Fort Independence. Suitable toasts were drank:—

"4. May the Fort of Independence and the fifty sons and daughters who have entered it this day be successful and prosperous. 5. May their sons and daughters multiply in sixteen years, sixteen times fifty."

"Closed with three cheers. Drank severals pails of grog, supped and retired in remarkable good order."* July 7, General Cleveland held a council with the resident Indians, exchanged gifts and greetings, and smoked the pipe of peace and friendship. July 22, he coasted along Lake Erie and up the swampy banks of the Cuyahoga River till an Indian trail opened a path through the thicket, where he landed, and quickly mounting the bluff took possession of the site of Cleveland City. The "original plan of the

---

* Extracts from Journal of General Cleveland.

town and village of Cleveland, Ohio," was completed October 1, 1796. General Cleveland's energy, decision and buoyancy of spirit, admirably fitted him to command in this important enterprise, which he accomplished to the apparent satisfaction of all concerned. He was very popular with the Indians, whom in person he strongly resembled. His complexion was very dark; his figure square and strong, and the Indian dress which he wore upon this expedition so completed the likeness that the Indians themselves were ready to claim him as a brother. His connection with the Ohio settlement brought him honor, but little pecuniary profit. He continued through life very prominent in public affairs. His popularity at home was shown by the length of time he was retained in his military command when scarce a year was allowed to ordinary incumbents. He was sent as representative of the town whenever at liberty to accept the office, and intrusted with many important services. Under his direction the lamented death of General Washington was properly observed by the Masonic brethren and other citizens of Windham County. The *Windham Herald* reports:—

"*Feb.* 27, 1800.

On Saturday last, in compliance with the recommendation enjoined in the Proclamation of the President of the United States, the inhabitants of this, and many from adjoining towns, together with a number of the brethren of Moriah and Eastern Star Lodges, met at Mr. Staniford's, according to previous notice; from whence they walk'd in procession to the meeting-house, preceded by a military escort in uniform, and a band of music, where they united to offer their undissembled tribute of respect to the memory of General GEORGE WASHINGTON, the Father, Friend, and Protector of his country. The solemn services were appropriate, well performed, and very much contributed to awaken the feelings of a great assemblage of mourners. The Address of Gen. WASHINGTON, to the people of the United States, on his retiring from office, and declining their future suffrages, was read; the estimation of its worth and excellence by the people present, could not have been better expressed, than by the decorum and silence observed while it was reading; after which, an oration, by Gen. Cleveland, Master of Moriah Lodge, called to mind the great sacrifice of blood and treasure which the struggle for independence cost us, and impressed the mind with gratitude for the invaluable gift of Providence, in the Man, who finally led us thro' the perils of war, to the Ark of Safety.

After the exercises were over, the procession returned, and soon after dispersed, leaving, we believe, not a single trait of indecorum, to cast a shade on the good order which had been observed thro' the day."

General Cleveland's death in 1806, at the age of fifty-two, was greatly lamented at home and throughout the State, and his obsequies surpassed in dignified ceremony anything ever before seen in Canterbury.

IX.

PLAINFIELD CHURCH IN PURSUIT OF A PASTOR. NEW MEETING-
HOUSE. DR. BENEDICT. FLOURISHING ACADEMY.
DISTINGUISHED CITIZENS. TOWN AFFAIRS.

THE united church of Plainfield met with many trials and disappointments in re-settling the ministry after the loss of Mr.
Fuller. Having voted "to proceed upon principles of Christianity
without being directed by rules of civil law," they appointed a
committee to supply the pulpit and agreed to raise money for its
support by subscription. But to raise money by free contributions
at a time of so much scarceness proved so arduous an enterprise
that they decided to resort to the expedient of a fund, and appointed
General John Douglass, James Bradford, Esq., William Robinson,
Dr. Perkins, Captain Joseph Eaton, Perry Clark, John Cady, Ephraim
Wheeler, Capt. Samuel Hall, Elias Woodward, committee to draw up
subscriptions for that purpose. Several subscriptions had been
attained, and the project seemed likely to be successful, when it was
discovered "that the people had proceeded in a manner that the law
would not own." The world was not sufficiently advanced to allow
Christians to carry on business affairs without recognition of "rules
of civil law," and the church was obliged to retrace its steps and
appoint "Stephen Kingsbury, who had been a legal society clerk, to
assist and direct to warn a legal society meeting." This being
accomplished, and legal requirements satisfied, the subscription went
forward and a few hundred dollars were secured for the foundation
of a fund. To this was added in 1782, the sum of two hundred
pounds procured by the lease for 999 years of the old cedar swamp.
No stated minister was yet procured. Mr. Upson preached five
months; Mr. Alexander five weeks. The congregation met during
the winter seasons at the Brick school-house, "read sermons and
prayed." A conference was held on the first Monday of every month
in the meeting-house. The eyes of the church were very much upon
Mr. Job Swift, who had made himself very popular while preaching
at Canterbury, and Captain Eaton took a journey across the State to
Nine Partners to confer with this favorite, and had a "prospect of
getting him, but a remarkable unanimity in the church where he was
prevented his coming." Joshua Spalding of Killingly preached to
public acceptance. Ephraim Judson was invited to preach but
preferred to settle in Taunton; Micaiah Porter declined overtures in
favor of Voluntown. Again Mr. Swift appeared on the scene, but
after a long interval of suspense decided against them. Conferences

and deacon's meetings became at length so thinly attended that
the church closed the dilapidated meeting-house for a season and
let the people go where they fancied. Mr. Morgan was then
secured for a time, but yielded to more urgent appeals from
Canterbury. David Avery was next invited to settlement, "answer
long delayed and dubious at last." Wearied and discouraged, the
church remitted its efforts to procure a pastor, and joined with the
town in attempts to secure a more eligible and attractive house of
worship. May 10, 1784, a large number of prominent citizens, viz. :—
Captain Joshua Dunlap, Joseph Shepard, Timothy Lester, Dr. Ebenezer Robinson, Major Andrew Backus, Captain Abraham Shepard,
James Bradford, General John Douglas, William Dixon, Esq., Stephen
Clark, Dr. Elisha-Perkins, Nathaniel Parks, Elias Woodward, Jabez
Tracy, Samuel Fox and Ephraim Wheeler, were appointed committee
by the town to deliberate upon the very important question "of a
proper place for erecting a new meeting-house about to be built in this
town." Population was now gravitating towards the Academy
and turnpike, and it was decided to build in this vicinity
upon land purchased of Messrs. Jesse and Ezekiel Fox. Upon
memorial of William Dixon the County Court confirmed this
decision, and affixed the site of Plainfield meeting-house "on a lot
of land belonging to Esquire Fox, west side of country road that
leads north and south through the town, and west of Proprietor's
Hall." According to previous agreement no tax could be levied for
religious purposes, and the meeting-house was built by subscription
and contribution. In October, Rev. Joel Benedict, already favorably
known as pastor at Newent, came to preach on probation. At a
church meeting held at Mr. William Robinson's, Deacon Samuel
Warren served as moderator, Dr. Elisha Perkins, clerk ; — voted without one dissenting vote to call Mr. Benedict " if it be agreeable to the
society and support be obtained in a gospel way." This call was
accepted, and December 22, 1784— "having examined his orthodoxy
in sentiment, spiritual acquaintance with divine things, his ability to
teach and defend the doctrines of Christianity," and being fully satisfied therewith—Mr. Benedict was happily installed into office by a
proper ministerial council. The new meeting-house was ready for
the reception of the new pastor, and public religious worship so long
interrupted was established to general satisfaction.

Plainfield Academy so prosperously opened during the war continued to flourish "beyond the most sanguine expectation," of its
projectors, numbering "one hundred and upwards of youth from
abroad," together with a large number from their own town. A
petition laid before the General Assembly, January 13, 1783, repre-

scnted that the petitioners had erected suitable buildings for the reception and accommodation of youth, namely, one good and convenient brick house, and an elegant new hall or house, and were preparing to erect another house, for the use and benefit of said academy, and begged to be made a body corporate and politic. After a year's delay the request was granted, and Ebenezer Pemberton, Hon. Samuel Huntington, Hon. Eliphalet Dyer, Rev. Levi Hart, Preston; Rev. Joseph Huntington, Coventry; and General John Douglas, Major Andrew Backus, Dr. Elisha Perkins, Captain Joseph Dunlap, William Robinson, Samuel Fox, Ebenezer Eaton and Hezekiah Spalding of Plainfield, with such others as the proprietors shall elect (not exceeding thirteen in the whole), were made a body corporate and politic by the name of "The Trustees of the Academic School in Plainfield," and invested with ample powers for managing the affairs of the school. Only two schools had then been incorporated in Connecticut—the Union School, New London, and Staples School, Weston—and Plainfield Academy held a high position in popular favor. Its rector was one of the most accomplished teachers of the day, and its patrons and directors were among the leading men of the State. The village was pleasant and healthful, and its most respectable residents were proud of the school, and ready to open their homes and hearts to the stranger students. Dr. Perkins though now so much engrossed with the duties of his profession was alive to the interests of the Academy, receiving even scores of lads into his own family when boarding places were scanty. A prudential committee of three was chosen annually from the directors, who had charge of the buildings and supervision of the financial department, while a stringent code of by-laws regulated the department of the pupils. These laws provided :—

"That no scholar shall go to the tavern for purpose of entertainment without leave from his father, guardian or rector.

No scholar from abroad and boarding in any family shall remove to any other family unless so directed by his or her parents or guardian, or liberty from the rector.

No scholar shall keep a gun, or go on a shooting party, or ride out, or leave the town, or absent himself at any time from the school without leave from the rector.

No scholar shall purchase anything at any store on credit without a written order from his parent or guardian, or leave from the rector.

No scholar shall appear in the Academy or in public in extravagant, slovenly or indecent dress.

No immoral, indecent or profane language, or improper conduct shall be allowed in any scholar at any time, but all such breaches of good morals shall be exemplarily punished.

No scholar shall be allowed to stroll the street or fields on Sunday, but it shall be required of every one to attend on public worship, and to behave with becoming decency and propriety."

It was voted that the Regulations of the Academy should be read in open school at the commencement of each quarter, and an official inspector was maintained to note and report infractions.

The third Academic building known as "The White Hall," about a mile south of the others, was soon completed and occupied by the English department under the charge of Mr. Alpheus Hatch, a faithful and competent instructor. The Mathematical department in the brick school-house was assigned to Mr. Nathan Daboll, the author of the "Schoolmaster's Assistant, being a plain, practical System of Arithmetic"—a work highly commended by competent authority and recommended to public patronage. The principal academic building, known as "The New Hall," was devoted to classical instruction under the immediate charge of Dr. Pemberton. Many aspiring youth were here fitted for a longer residence in wider and more famous halls of learning. Calvin Goddard, who came on foot from Shrewsbury, seeking a chance to gain an education, Nicholas Brown of Providence, James Lanman of Norwich, Elijah and Ariel Parish of Lebanon, James L. Kingsley of Scotland, Ebenezer Fitch of Canterbury, William Danielson of Killingly, Alfred Johnson, Simon and Sylvanus Backus of Plainfield, were among the distinguished pupils of Dr. Pemberton. Kingsley of Scotland, already noticed at home as "a very forward, likely lad," won fresh laurels in this new field, surpassing older competitors in the translation of an elaborate Latin epitaph composed by Dr. Benedict. So excellent was the translation that it was inscribed upon the tombstone—a lasting monument to Yale's distinguished professor as well as to Plainfield's honored citizen:—

"In memory of Captain John Cady of Plainfield. He was of an engaging aspect and deportment; his genius naturally elevated was cultivated by reading and intercourse with mankind. He had a happy faculty in the dispatch of business; was exemplary in the discharge of every social duty, civil or domestic. A professor of the Christian faith, a blessing to mankind. He rests not here; he was drowned returning from New York, November 23, 1783, in the 40th year of his age. The glory of man is as the flower of the field."

After making an effort to secure Dr. Pemberton as "rector for life," the trustees were forced to resign him in the fall of 1784, and after a short sojourn in Windham, he became the principal of Phillips Academy at Andover. Mr. Miles Merwin filled his place in Plainfield, to great acceptance, but gave way for another college graduate as soon as he had completed his legal studies. The most serious obstacle to the prosperity of the Academy was the constant change of teachers. The rectorship was administered by a series of young graduates, who only engaged in teaching while fitting for other professions. Timothy Pitkin, Calvin Goddard, Sylvanus Backus, Lynde Huntington, Eliphalet Nott and Tower Whiton, followed Mr. Merwin, each averaging less than two years of service. John and Daniel Shepard, John D. Perkins, Joseph Eaton, James Gordon, Nathan F. Dixon, David Bolles of Ashford, Jedidiah Johnson of Canterbury, were students during this period. The death of Mr. Hatch, who had very ably sustained the English department for many years, was followed by a temporary depression when the main building was closed for a season, but with the advent of Mr. Benjamin Allen in 1798, the Academy quickly regained its standing and popularity, and "students came from the Carolinas, the Indies and the neighboring States." Mr. Allen employed for assistants Virgil Maxcy, afterwards *Chargé d'Affaires* at Belgium, and Levi Tower, the author of a system of penmanship that was ornamental and useful. His successors, Zachariah Eddy and Master John Adams, were equally successful in the management of the school, attracting pupils from some of the best families in the country. The annual public exhibition held in the meeting-house excited hardly less interest than a College "commencement." Mr. Eddy's exhibition in 1800 was especially remarkable for the large number of "good speakers, well drilled, with good parts. Among the speakers were Henry R. Storrs, George Perkins, George Hall, William and Thomas Williams (afterward of Norwich and New London), Samuel and Alexander H. Stevens, John Reed, Epaphroditus Champion, Wilkins Updike." Storrs, afterward member of Congress, was called the best debater. These exhibitions so agreeable to speakers and hearers, and adding such eclat to the Academy, were not a little burdensome to the trustees who paid the bills and had charge of fitting up the meeting-house. A committee was chosen each year to build the stage and a tax levied to meet expenses. A trusteeship in Plainfield Academy was not a merely honorary office, but involved a good deal of responsibility and outlay. Buildings were to be kept in repair; a bell and belfry, a set of globes, fences, &c. to be provided, and any deficiency in funds was to be made up by this honorable body. The place of older patrons from abroad was gradually filled by Plainfield's own citizens, viz.: Roger Olmstead, Phinehas Pierce, John Douglas, Jun., Doctors Daniel Gordon, Josiah and Jared Fuller, Calvin Goddard, Luther Smith, ——— Farlan and others—who administered Academic affairs with great wisdom and liberality. That their onerous duties were alleviated by good-humored fun and banter is manifested in the following vote, called out by some long-forgotten conjuncture :—

"At a meeting of the Trustees of Plainfield Academy at Capt. Elkanah Eaton's, in the eve, October 9, Voted, That each Trustee shall appear with his *broom* at the meeting-house, 15th instant, at 2 P. M., to sweep the meeting-house, and should he or they not appear, he or they should pay twenty-five cents."

A dollar each was also levied for the expense of the forthcoming exhibition.

The cordial interest manifested in the students by the residents of the town and their intimate association with many hospitable homes, left an abiding impression upon many who enjoyed these privileges. Gen. Williams of Norwich gives pleasant reminiscences of his school days:—

"I recall the remembrance of many of the students of Plainfield Academy that have been distinguished in professional life, and others who have been practical business men. Among the former, Hon. Henry Wheaton, distinguished as a scholar and editor, but more as the American Minister at the Court of Berlin; Samuel Hubbard, LL.D., judge of the Supreme Court of Massachusetts; James Hamilton, governor of South Carolina; Henry R. Storrs, member of Congress from the State of New York; John P. Cushman, at one time United States District judge of New York; Wilkins Updyke, late attorney-general of Rhode Island; Walter Wheaton, M. D., surgeon of the U. S. Army; Samuel and Alexander Stevens, sons of Gen. Ebenezer Stevens of Revolutionary memory—the former associated with DeWitt Clinton in political life, and the other eminent as a practitioner in the medical department. In the mercantile profession (of which Gen Williams was himself an honored example) was my brother, Hon. Thomas W. Williams of New London, who has also been a member of Congress, besides many who became practical business men. Among these were Col. Increase I. Wilson, Francis Allen, Henry Perkins, George Starr and Adam Frink, Esqrs., of New London. Capt. Allen resided for a long time in New London. His course as a ship-master and a merchant was distinguished. The honor of escorting as a guest and passenger the Marquis de LaFayette, in his memorable visit to this country in 1824, belongs to him. There were also at the Academy, the Messrs. Denison and Messrs. Palmer of Stonington. The school was organized for both sexes, and the arrangement was quite like the division in our evening conference meetings. It may not be irrelevant to notice among the young ladies, Miss Catherine Putnam, granddaughter of General Putnam of the Revolution, who married Francis Brinley, Esq., of Boston; the Misses Lester of Preston—one of whom married Hon. Lemuel Pomeroy of Pittsfield, Mass.; Miss Betsey Sheldon, who married N. Howland, Esq., of Brooklyn, New York; Miss Harriet Bowen of Providence, who married Commodore Charles Morris of the U. S. Navy; Miss Nancy Allen, who married Thomas W. Williams of New London, with many others who have adorned society by their example and their influence.

In calling up these reminiscences of Plainfield, my remembrance has been revived of the many respectable families then living in Plainfield in many of which the scholars were received as boarders; namely: Rev. Joel Benedict, D.D., Gen. Gordon, Gen. Douglas, Dr. Perkins, Hon. Calvin Goddard, Messrs. Eaton, Bradford, Dixon, Shepard, Smith, &c. I cherish the memory of Dr. Benedict's family, with whom I boarded a part of the time, and I love to contemplate the goodness of Providence to that humble, pious and learned minister—in the allotments of the members of the family in their marriage and connections in life. The impressions received at Plainfield abide with me still, and never do I pass up those valleys or over those hills without recalling a period of life, as free from its ills, and marked by as even, happy and progressive a tenor as any part of it. I believe others share in the same feelings for rarely have I met in after life any of those early acquaintances without mutual gratification in speaking of those by-gone years."

Master Adams continued in charge of the Academy from the spring of 1801 to the fall of 1803. During this period he reports "about two hundred different pupils, principally from the neighboring towns, but quite a number from Providence, New London, New York, &c."

The Academy was prosperous; as appears from the fact that the tuition money was abundantly sufficient to meet all expenses without absorbing any part of the income of the small, original donation. Among his pupils who entered Yale College were Rinaldo Burleigh, Parker Adams, William Kinne, John Pellet, Jason Allen, David Bacon, Rufus Chandler, Hezekiah Rudd, Ebenezer Young, James Howard, Daniel Huntington. The social attractions of Plainfield at this date called out another by-law, viz. :—

"That no member of the Academy shall attend a dancing school in the town during the time he is a member of the Academy."

Mr. Rinaldo Burleigh succeeded his honored preceptor immediately after his own graduation from college. His early struggles and varied experiences proved a valuable preparation for effective service and enabled him to sustain the reputation of the Academy. Though similar institutions were multiplying in all parts of the land, Plainfield retained its place in popular favor and sent out every year a goodly number of graduates fitted to pursue collegiate studies, or engage in business and the various duties of life.

Society in Plainfield was quickened and elevated by Academic influence. The brilliant young graduates who served as teachers found in this rural town a select circle of accomplished and attractive young women and usually carried away a wife, or left their hearts behind them. Miles Merwin married a daughter of Dr. Perkins; Preceptors Nott, Allen and Phinney won each the hand of a daughter of Dr. Benedict. Seven daughters graced the modest home of this good minister, conspicuous alike for good looks, sense and breeding. Attractive young ladies were to be found in the household of Mr. Luther Smith and other village residents. Plainfield was also favored with many intelligent and public spirited gentlemen. Its first lawyer was Mr. William Dixon of Voluntown, who engaged in practice about 1790. Calvin Goddard after his brief rectorship also engaged in legal practice and rose at once to eminence in professional and public service. James Gordon, judge of Probate and general of the Fifth Brigade, was promoted to the major-generalship of the Third Division of Connecticut militia. John Douglas, clerk of the Probate office, was also brigade-general.

Plainfield's most noted citizen at this date was unquestionably her much esteemed physician, Dr. Perkins, whose "Metallic Tractors" had won a world-wide reputation. Experiments in magnetic and electric currents had convinced him of the practicability of applying these forces for the relief of pain through the agency of pointed metallic instruments of opposite electrical condition. After having himself successfully tested these tractors, Dr. Perkins obtained a patent for his invention, and they soon came into notice. The professors of three universities in America gave attestations in their favor. Abroad, their success was much more signal. In Copenhagen, twelve physicians and surgeons instituted a series of experiments and decided that "Perkinism" was "of great importance to the physician." A Perkinian Institution was established in London, principally with the view of gratuitously in-tractorating the poor. "Disinterested and intelligent characters from almost every quarter of Great Britain, including professors, regular physicians, surgeons and clergymen," testified to benefit received from the application of Tractors. It was claimed that the extraordinary number of *one-and-a-half millions* of cures had been actually effected. But while so eminent in his profession, no man was more active and useful as a citizen, more ready to serve town and church in any capacity. "Few men in the world," reports Calvin Goddard, "were more public spirited, more hospitable, more free from all guile." The ailing poor were always cared for; the needy student found in him aid and sympathy. If boarding-places were lacking for importunate school-boys, his hospitable doors were opened. Distinguished in personal appearance, he was still more noted for a "winning cordiality of manner," and "in address and colloquial powers, few of his profession excelled him." The fate of his daughter, Mrs. Merwin, who, with her husband and two children, died of yellow fever in Philadelphia, 1793, turned his experiments in a new direction, and he concocted an antiseptic preparation which he used as a preventive for the disease but fell a victim to his own theories, dying of yellow fever in New York city, 1799, after four weeks unremitting assiduity in attending the sick. Mrs. Sarah (Douglas) Perkins died three years before her husband. The Tractors after their brief "run" fell into disuse, and were ranked with the innumerable delusions that have obtained transient notoriety. A volume called "Terrible Tractorations" covered them with ridicule, but the principle on which they were founded came again and again into notice, and his experiments in this and other fields entitled Dr. Perkins to a high place in the medical annals of his country.

Plainfield was also greatly favored during this period in the ministry of Mr. Benedict. Eminent alike for piety, learning and practical wisdom, he was one of the distinguished men of his generation, a pillar and a power in church and community. He was an accomplished Biblical scholar and critic, and especially noted for his fondness for the Hebrew tongue, which he was wont to call "the language of the angels." His preaching though mostly extemporaneous was very weighty and impressive, characterized rather by strength of thought and force of argument than by elegance of language or delivery. In the performance of pastoral duties he had few equals. Frail in constitution, and suffering much from bodily infirmities, he knew how to sympathize in the sorrows and pains of others. He was ever mindful of the wants of the poor, and assiduous in attention to the sick and dying. Though so feeble in health he was remarkably cheerful and happy, and had the rare gift of making all happy around him. Decided in his own religious convictions, he allowed the same liberty to others, and exercised a most enlightened and liberal charity towards those of differing opinions. Under his influence and instructions the party lines that had so long existed in the church were gradually obliterated. The radical element was drawn to the Baptists and Methodists, and the First church of Plainfield resumed its old position among the churches of the County, though not accepting Consociation. It had so far conceded to the ecclesiastic Constitution of the State as to consent in 1799 to the formal organization of a religious society, Messrs. Bradford, Douglas and Gordon giving warning of the same.

The Baptist interest in Plainfield was greatly strengthened by a remarkable religious awakening accompanying the labors of Elder Nathaniel Cole of Swanzey. A Baptist church was organized October 16, 1792, and in December following Elder Cole was installed as its pastor. Residents within the new town of Sterling and the south of Killingly joined with this church, so that its membership was increased in two years to eighty seven. Religious services were held in the Pond Hill school-house till 1800, when a meeting-house was built in the north part of the town. Methodist preachers had ere this found their way to the town, preaching in different neighborhoods, and organized a class and society, which in time held regular service in the old Separate meeting-house.

In 1784, the town ordered its sign-post removed to the new meeting-house lot, and appointed its meetings to be held, half the time at the new meeting-house near Rev. Joel Benedict's dwelling-house, and half the time at the meeting-house in the north part of the town near Joseph Prior's (the old Separate house). Public deliberations were mainly occupied with roads and bridges. In 1784, the town voted to join with equal proportions as Brooklyn in building a bridge over the Quinebaug at Parkhurst's fordway, but this needed accommodation was delayed for several years. In 1788, it joined with Canterbury in rebuilding Nevins' Bridge, "with three stone pillars in the river and suitable timber and planks for the upper works"—David Kinne, William Cutler and Ebenezer Eaton, committee. In 1790, aided by Brooklyn, it accomplished the new Quinebaug bridge. A requisition from the County Court the following year, ordered new attention to the "post road through Plainfield." Colonel Swift, Shubael Abbe and Captain Ezra Bishop, sent as committee, reported the necessity of an alteration between the house of Samuel Dow in Sterling and the mills owned by Elisha Perkins. The highway surveyors of the town made new arrangements and distribution, and labored zealously to satisfy the traveling public but were soon called to further outlay. William Dixon was appointed agent to defend the town against petitions brought from the County Court by Ebenezer Gray and others, praying for an alteration in the stage road from Norwich to Providence through Plainfield, and also to oppose a petition of John Jefferds and Andrew Murdock praying for an alteration in the road leading from Brooklyn to Providence. As usual opposition availed nothing, and "the New London and Windham County Society for establishing a turnpike road from Norwich to Rhode Island line, direct through Norwich, Lisbon, Preston, Plainfield and Sterling," was incorporated in 1795. A turnpike gate was allowed in Sterling, and another "within half a mile of Plainfield meeting-house." The old traveled country road from Plainfield meeting-house westward to Hartford, was turned over to the Windham Turnpike Company in 1799, and liberty granted to erect a turnpike gate near the dividing line between Plainfield and Canterbury. General James Gordon was a member of the several turnpike companies, and served as turnpike commissioner in behalf of the State. A committee was chosen in 1797, to attend the Turnpike Conference held by the Windham County towns, and also to examine the town's property in roads. Bridges were built over Moosup River to accommodate Captain William Cutler, and Mr. John Lester, and also to accommodate mills on other streams in various localities. William Robinson now served as town clerk, Ebenezer Eaton, treasurer; Squire Cady, constable. The selectmen in 1796, were Joshua Dunlap, Jonathan Gallup, Caleb Hill, Jun., Benjamin Gallup; surveyors, Moses Branch, General James Gordon, Captain Simon Shepard, Aaron Wheeler, Dr. Thomas Backus, David Kinne, Caleb Hall, Jun., William Clark, Thomas Smith, John French, Anthony Bradford, Esq., Joseph Whipple, David Knight; fence-viewers, Thomas Pierce, Robert Dunlap. Elijah Fox, Thomas Wheeler, Abijah Deane, Jeremiah Shepard, Nathaniel Parke, Colonel Abel Andrews, Nathan Kinne, Zebulon Whipple, John Avery, Hezekiah Spalding, Levi Robinson, John Burgess, Stephen Hall, Anthony Bradford, John Pierce, as grand school committee, had charge of the public schools. Fees for taking up and punishing strollers were willingly allowed. The selectmen were enjoined in 1801 to provide a suitable and convenient house for the reception of the poor. A pall, hearse and building for the same were also ordered. Military matters excited the usual interest. In 1799, it was voted that non-commissioned officers, musicians and privates, who should equip themselves as to arms, clothing and accoutrements and do military duty, should be exempt from all but highway taxes. Abel Andrus was now lieutentant-colonel of the Twenty-first Regiment; Shubael Hutchins, first major; Rev. Joel Benedict, chaplain; Sessions Lester, quartermaster; George Middleton, paymaster; Dr. Johnson of Westminster, surgeon; Daniel Gordon, surgeon's mate; Frederick Andrus, Aaron Crary, Samuel Douglas, Asa Burgess, captains of companies in the light infantry; Thomas and Daniel Wheeler, John Gordon, lieutenants and ensigns; Dr. Josiah Fuller, surgeon's mate of the cavalry regiment.

The fine water privileges of Plainfield afforded accommodations for an unusual number of mills and manufacturing establishments. Nathan Angell of Providence, purchased of Dr. Welles in 1777, a fine farm on the Moosup, with large mansion house, storehouse, cheese house, milk house, young orchard and various conveniences. Much other land was purchased by Mr. Angell, who ran saw and grist-mills and carried on extensive farming operations. The easy communication with Providence and Norwich, the stages daily running to and fro, stimulated traffic and agricultural enterprise. Captains Lester, Dunlap and others gave much attention to wool-growing and stock raising. Luther Smith, John and William Douglas and William Olmstead engaged in trade. George Middleton opened a harness shop, making a specialty of leather pocket-books and portmanteaus. Dr. Daniel Gordon kept an apothecary's shop. Potash works, tanning and hat-making were carried on in the valleys east and south of the village. Plainfield's first post-office—the third in Windham County—was opened in 1797, by Captain Ebenezer Eaton, whose popular stage-tavern maintained its ancient reputation. The justices in 1806, were William Dixon, Anthony Bradford, Calvin Goddard, Ephraim Wheeler, Joshua Dunlap, John Douglas. Calvin Goddard, Joshua Dunlap, Joseph Eaton, Anthony Bradford, Ephraim Wheeler, Joseph Shepard, Jonathan Hammet, William Pierce, Luther Smith, John Lester, Jeremiah Kinsman, were sent as representatives during this period.

42

X.

KILLINGLY'S RE-SETTLEMENT. AFFAIRS IN NORTH SOCIETY.
TRIALS IN BAPTIST CHURCH. SOUTH KILLINGLY CHURCH
AND TRAININGS. WEST KILLINGLY CHURCH.
EMIGRATION TO OHIO.

KILLINGLY, after the loss of her northern parish, hastened to
reorganize upon a new basis, voting that the three remaining
societies "shall be called by these names as following, North, Middle
and South," and "that all town meetings shall be held in the meeting-
house in the middle society." At the annual town meeting, December
12, 1785, Dr. Joseph Torrey was chosen moderator; James Larned,
Samuel Danielson, Jacob Spalding, Capt. Ephraim Warren and Zadoc
Spalding, selectmen; Sampson Howe, town clerk and treasurer; Silas
Hutchins, constable to collect State taxes; Elihu Lawrence and John
Day, constables; Edward Babbett, Col. Joseph Cady, Nell Alexander,
Obed Spalding, Sampson Howe, John Barret, Andrew Brown,
Benjamin Simmons, Elias Stearns, John Hutchins, Captain David
Cady, highway surveyors and collectors of highway taxes; James
Larned, Captain David Buck, Captain Ephraim Warren, Zadoc
Spalding, fence-viewers; Sampson Howe, Captain Jonathan Cady,
Andrew Brown, Jonas Danielson, Ezra Hutchins, Siloam Short,
listers; Captain John Felshaw, Captain Ephraim Warren and Deacon
Jacob Spalding, key-keepers. It was voted that Captain Warren's old
house be made a workhouse for the accommodation of the town's
poor and he master of the same. Accounts with Thompson were
amicably settled by their respective committees. The restriction of
the old town to a single representative excited great indignation and
called out a memorial, showing:—

"That such restriction deprived the town of one half their rights of
representatives which they conceive they have a right to enjoy agreeable to
the Constitution of this State—restriction laid on town without the consent
or knowledge or even the most distant thought of the inhabitants of
Killingly, and notwithstanding this restriction the freemen have continued
to choose two deputies who have had a seat in the General Assembly until
last October session, when it was judged to be inadmissible till the Act was
repealed, and therefore pray for such repeal which they conceived an
infringement on their constitutional rights and privileges so long as they
remain peaceful subjects of the State, and are considered in the common
burdens of the same, as they look upon the right of representation as one of
their most essential ones.

JAMES LARNED,
DAVID BUCK,
ELEAZER MOFFAT,
WILLIAM CUNDALL,
ZADOC SPALDING,
EZRA HUTCHINS,
EPHRAIM WARREN,
Committee.

Killingly, October 8, 1787."

This request was granted by both Houses, and Killingly confirmed in her constitutional rights and privileges. The executions brought against the town by the State treasurer for balance of taxes laid during the war were satisfied by an especial rate after much difficulty. The dividend line run between the old and new towns was accepted after some debate; the old Breakneck meeting-house converted into a suitable town-house, and all affairs arranged in a satisfactory manner. The charge of the numerous poor people continued a heavy burden. The services of Doctors Jonathan Bishop, Comfort Foster and Penuel Hutchins were often called in requisition, as well as constables to convey them out of town and lawyers to contest doubtful cases, while guardians were appointed to keep in watchful oversight such as by bad husbandry and mismanagement seemed likely to need public aid.

The North Society was reduced to such indigent circumstances by some of their most valuable settlements falling into the hands "of those who style themselves Baptists," and also by what is called "the maneuvres" of Mr. Emerson Foster, "whereby many were waxen cold towards the established religion," that it would gladly have resorted to the fashionable expedient of a lottery, the avails to be used in purchasing a small parsonage. Failing in this device, it had the good fortune to procure an excellent minister who so bound up old wounds and conciliated the disaffected that it was able to "re-settle the Gospel" without questionable assistance. Elisha Atkins of Middletown, a gentleman of culture and experience, was happily ordained and installed in the pastoral office, June 3, 1787, the society granting two hundred pounds settlement, fifty-five pounds salary, and the cutting and drawing the ministerial fire-wood. Not only was this done without serious difficulty, but it also took measures for repairing the meeting-house, though ten years elapsed before these repairs were fully accomplished. The old body of seats was in time removed. Pew spots were granted to Roland Leavens, Jedediah Sabin, Aaron Buck, Josiah Deane, John Lawrence, John E. Dorrance, Eleazer Leavens. In 1796, liberty was given to erect a belfry and procure a bell. James Larned, Sampson Howe, David Buck, Captain Jonathan Cady, William Kelly, Joseph Torrey, Willard Cady, Jesse Whipple, Hobart Torrey and David Copp were appointed a committee to see on what terms a belfry could be built. This was speedily erected and the bell procured the same year,—the people showing their satisfaction in this achievement by the many directions given for its right regulation:—

"Bell to be rung on week days at twelve o'clock at noon, and nine at night; Sundays, Thanksgivings and Fast days, an hour before meetings; and at noon on Sundays, half way between the intermissions, and fifteen minutes before meeting begins; at all said meetings to be rung not less than five minutes nor more than ten at any one time."

Sampson Howe was to have twenty dollars a year for ringing the bell, and sweeping the meeting-house. A subsequent vote ordained that the bell should be rung at noon the whole year, but from April 15 to August 15 be rung at sunrise instead of nine at night. The minister's salary of two hundred and fifty dollars was raised with much difficulty, and efforts were made to provide a permanent fund. William and Simon Copp, John Kelly and Welcome Whipple were appointed choristers in 1805.

Mr. Atkins proved a most excellent pastor and citizen, interested in all plans for the improvement of the town. He was particularly successful as a teacher, and many of the young people of his congregation received the benefit of his instruction. He not only received pupils into his own charge, but endeavored to further improvements in public education and took great interest in visiting the schools of the town. A committee was appointed in 1791, to ascertain the bounds of school districts, and two years later the bounds were changed and seven districts set off, viz.:—1. Northeast; 2, Chestnut Hill; 3. Talbot's mills; 4. South; 5. Pond; 6. Northwest; 7. North. Joseph Torrey, Eleazer Moffat, Sylvanus Perry, Isaac Cady Howe, Ebenezer Leach, Obed Spalding, Reuben Leavens, Azariah Cutler, Hobart Torrey, Nell Alexander, William Basto, Joseph Adams, committee. School money drawn from the State was distributed to the several districts in 1795, and school affairs thenceforward were left to the management of the districts.

Captain John Felshaw, so long prominent in town and public affairs, died at an advanced age in 1782. His large landed estate was divided between his sons, by Edward Paul, surveyor, under the direction of Deacon Lusher Gay and James Larned. The tavern stand on the corner was held for a time by Samuel Felshaw and sold in 1797 to Captain Aaron Arnold of Rhode Island, an energetic business man, interested in public affairs. Luther and Calvin Warren removed to Killingly Hill about 1794, settling on land purchased of Isaac C. Howe. Dr. Robert Grosvenor of Pomfret succeeded to the practice of Dr. Moffat. Dr. Josiah Deane also practiced medicine in this vicinity. A store was opened on the hill by Sampson Howe. William Basto engaged in the manufacture of hats. Stout chairs and excellent willow baskets were made by Jonathan and Joseph Buck.

Roads received much attention. A new road was laid out about 1795, from the country road near Dr. Hutchins' dwelling-house running east to Mr. Day's meeting-house, through lands of Penuel and Zadoc

Hutchins, Samuel Stearns, Wilson Kies, James Danielson, and the sons of Deacon Jacob Spalding. The petition for an open highway through lands of William Torrey, heirs of Rev. John Fisk, and others, was opposed for a time, but finally granted. A new road was also allowed from Jonathan and Philip Dexter's to Cutler's bridge in the east of the town. An act of the County Court obliged the selectmen to lay out a road from the road near Edward Babbitt's on Chestnut Hill to the meeting-house in the north parish. A jury met at Sampson Howe's, December, 1799, and laid out a road from Captain John Day's through lands of Carpenter, Alexander, Kelly, Leavens, Howe, Whipple and Warren—after which the town resolutely declined to do anything more in that line. It was soon however called to consider the question of turnpikes; refused to listen to Ashford's request for a turnpike to Providence, but negotiated with Pomfret, Woodstock and Thompson. After much discussion it was decided in 1801, "to lay out a turnpike from the Norwich Turnpike in Pomfret to the turnpike in Gloucester." This Pomfret and Killingly turnpike passing over Killingly Hill by the meeting-house, was accomplished in 1803, but the exhausted town declined to build half the new bridge needed for its accommodation till cited before the Court to answer for its negligence. Hobart Torrey, Pelatiah Mason and Ezra Hutchins, Esq., were commissioned to build the bridge but unfortunately it was soon carried away by high water, not being built "workman like," which involved the town in fresh difficulty and arbitrations.

Killingly was much interested in the mooted question of county seat, favoring her opposite neighbor in preference to any other competitor. Captain Luther Warren as agent, was vested with power to sign any petition that was thought best for the time, provided he did not burden the town with any expense for public buildings. In 1802, the town positively declined to sign a petition for removal to Brooklyn, but would sign for Pomfret under the former proviso. Captain Luther Warren succeeded Sampson Howe as town clerk and treasurer, in 1804. Aaron Arnold, Remember Ingraham, Joseph Adams and Samuel Anderson, were selectmen at this date. Captain Warren and Hobart Torrey, constables; Eleazer Moffat, James Danielson, Ezra Hutchins, Luther Warren, Esq., justices. Sampson Howe, James Danielson, Zadoc Spalding, Eleazer Moffat, Luther Warren, Aaron Arnold and Shubael Hutchins were sent as representatives during these years. James Danielson, after serving for some years as lieutenant-colonel of the Eleventh Regiment, became general of the Fifth Brigade in 1806. Hobart Torrey took his place as lieutenant-colonel. Robert Grosvenor served as surgeon; Darius Hutchins, surgeon's mate. Luther Warren, Joseph Buck, William Torrey,

334 HISTORY OF WINDHAM COUNTY.

David Chase, John Kelly, Pearley Day, were captains and lieutenants. The ample accommodations offered by the broad common on Killingly Hill, made it a favorite place for general trainings and other military parades, and the tavern kept by Captain Warren rivalled in popularity its famous predecessor. Taverns were also kept by Aaron Arnold, Thomas Medbury and Silas Hutchins.

The Middle Society of Killingly occupied a somewhat anomalous position, having little to do with the religious affairs of its inhabitants. Its stated church had virtually ceased to exist, its few remaining members worshipping with other churches, and its meeting-house used for town-meetings and secular purposes. The Baptist church within its limits experienced the usual vicissitudes and trials. In 1784, Elder Robinson was dismissed by his own request from his pastoral charge, and recommended to the Baptist church in Attleborough, " as a member in good standing with us, whose moral and christian character is good both as a preacher of the Gospel and member with us." Notwithstanding this recommendation, reports derogatory to his character were circulated and a root of bitterness was left in the church. In the following year the society reorganized, a number of persons* voluntarily agreeing to form themselves into a society, attend on divine service, contribute to the support of the Gospel and settle a Baptist minister to preach in this place. This movement was made needful by the efforts made to procure the sum promised Mr. Atkins in settlement, as unless they could certify to their attendance upon some place of worship, residents of the North Society would have been assessed for that object. Descendants of old families formerly active in supporting the established worship, and some new and substantial residents, were among the subscribers. Others belonged to the poorer class and some were residents of Rhode Island. The society, October 17, voted to buy a farm for a ministerial farm. A rude meeting-house had already been erected, but probably no farm had been procured, as Elder Robinson in his own name purchased an

---

* MEMBERS OF BAPTIST SOCIETY IN KILLINGLY, ON CHESTNUT HILL, OCTOBER 5, 1785.—Caleb Colgrove, David Law, Eliphalet Corbin, Ebenezer Talbot, Josiah Brown, Jun., Seth Babbit, Ezekiel Mitchel, Nicholas Smith, Cornelius Walling, Obed Winsor, William Leach, William Harrington, George Law, Elisha Warner, Jared Talbot, Ezekiel Brown, Peter Cutler, James Lawrence, Isaac Cutler, Jun., Thomas Bickford, Gideon Burgess, Ezekiel Young, William Mitchel, Samuel Sparks, Benjamin Capron, Benjamin Talbot, Levi Aldrich, Zachery Brown, Chase Hix, Perley Whitmore, John Pike, Job Leach, Benjamin Whittemore, David Robinson, William Basto, Ezekiel Blackmar, Edward Babbit, Jun., Nathan Bowen, John Herinton, Ephraim Fisk, Pelatiah Mason, Richard Tucker, Ebenezer Coud, Jonathan Herinton, Richard Bartlett, William Carder, Loren Carpenter, Benjamin Seamans, Thomas Burgess, Jeremiah Herinton, Benjamin Brown, Oliver Bowen, Benjamin Bateman, Edward Babbit, Sampson Covell, Jonathan Herinton, Daniel Covel, Ebenezer Leach, Wyman Cutler.

hundred acres of land of Robert Baxter, near Brown's, Moffat's and
Mitchel's. David Lamb was procured the following spring to preach
for a year, and was succeeded by John Cooper. The society voted,
1788, "that each man deliver his subscription at Ezekiel Blackmar's for
John Cooper." Pelatiah Mason, David Law, Ephraim Fisk and Jonathan Herinton, Jun., were appointed a committee to meet the delinquents :—

"*March* 10.—Met to hear the report of the committee that was to consult
with Mr. John Cooper to preach with us one year, and that was that Mr.
Cooper told us his sircomstances, and that was, he was poor and needy; the
committee was Pelatiah Mason and Ephraim Fisk. *Voted*, 1. That we will
contribute to fix up the meeting-house; 2. That we will have Mr. Cooper to
preach with us this year; 3. That what is wanted when all is signed that we
will make it up £15."

While the society was thus taking the initiative, and providing for
public worship, the church appears to have been inactive, and did not
even maintain its seasons of communion. Robert Baxter who had served
as its first deacon had removed to Pomfret, and prominent members
had been aggrieved by the dismissal of Elder Robinson. After Mr.
Cooper's year had elapsed, his place was filled by Elder Campbell, an
irregular preacher or itinerant, who was acceptable to the church. A
church meeting was held, July 11, 1789, when it was "proposed,
1. To see whether they was agreed to travel together. 2. To have
the debates between Edward Babbit and Ephraim Fisk on the difficulty about Elder Robinson." The difficulty with the brethren was
satisfactorily settled, and the church resumed its efforts "to travel."
Elder Campbell's preaching was very successful, a large number professed conversion and were baptized by him, but not admitted into the
church, which indeed was not in condition to receive members, having
lost its standing among sister churches by failing to maintain Gospel
ordinances. The society in 1790, voted to subscribe for the support
of Elder Campbell, and deputed Thomas Burgess and William Carder
to provide a place for him to live in the ensuing year. The church
proceeded with its endeavors to bring its members to penitence and
confession, and at a meeting June 24, to learn "how each one stood
as to the unitation we had begun, as to come round our Father's table
once more if we can agree." Ezekiel Blackmar, Jonathan Herington
and Ephraim Fisk were appointed to go to Elder Martin's, and see if
we can regain our fellowship. The result of this effort is not clearly
recorded. The church was censured, and according to one report
"rejected" by the ministers representing the Association. Elder
Campbell's proceedings in baptizing converts and administering the
ordinances were severely rebuked, and he was dis-fellowshipod by a
committee probably of Warren Association, after which it is said "the

church was restored and went on again—" It was sufficiently restored at least to grant letters of recommendation, and administer discipline, nor did it apparently lose its standing in following years though destitute of a stated pastor. This "Campbell split," as it was called, left injurious consequences. Most of his converts fell away and members of the church were alienated. Elder Moffat was employed to preach in 1791, after which there is no entry upon the records for several years.

In 1796, church and society again united in chóice of Elder Peter Rogers of Hampton—whose preliminary labors proved so satisfactory that the three parties entered upon a formal covenant. Elder Rogers agreed upon his part:—"That he would remove his membership and unite with them ; that he will serve them in the Gospel, 1. By supplying as their pastor the pulpit. 2. By administering the ordinances of the Gospel among them as God shall enable him. 3. By visiting the sick in the church and society as duty may call ; and 4. To watch for souls as those that must give an account ; and the church covenanting to receive him as their elder and pastor, give him fifteen pounds a year in money or equivalent articles, and labor to maintain a gospel union with him so far as they had light and grace—this covenant to be binding on both parties equally till it be violated or broken, the society assenting to the same, and agreeing to the stipulated salary." Notwithstanding this fair beginning, the pastorate was not happy. Discordant elements were at work. Deacon Herrington thought the church too hasty in settling Elder Rogers, and even the excellent Deacon Fisk* who had been one of the pillars of the church, became estranged for reasons not manifest, and was finally cut off from it. Another prominent brother was cut off for setting up and holding meetings in opposition to the fellowship of the church, and many others were disciplined or excommunicated for reasons of more or less importance. In the great majority of cases no restoration was effected, but the brother who was accused of *carrying a bottle of rum to the house of a sister*, and "insisting and persuading her to drink," acknowledged he was wrong and said he was sorry for it. It was agreed that no member should act with the church who was not in full communion ; also, not to admit any person to attend our church meetings excepting brethren in good standing in fellowship, without toleration of the church. After the dismission of Deacon Fisk, it was voted to nominate a brother to serve as a deacon at the next church

---

* Deacon Fisk is especially memorable in Killingly as the father of that harmonious quartette of female infants whose names were suggested by the epithets that greeted their simultaneous advent—" Wonderful ! " " *Admirable ! !* " " REMARKABLE ! ! ! " " STRANGE ! ! ! ! "

meeting, and give the *sisters* an invitation to attend. Brother Chase Hicks was nominated to serve on trial. At the same meeting, September, 1799, Elder Rogers and Nicholas Aldrich were requested to write a letter to the Association, and with other brethren represent the church. Notwithstanding its many trials and difficulties this church on Chestnut Hill maintained a good standing among other Baptist churches, and doubtless was the means of doing much good on this remote outpost, reaching a class who had no other religious privilege. Elder Rogers enjoyed a good repute as a preacher, and his meetings were attended by a goodly number of hearers. The meeting-house becoming unfit for use, a movement was made in 1802, "to form a constitution" for building a new one on land purchased of Captain Joseph Cady, which was successfully accomplished within a year or two by private effort and subscription. The society machinery so uncongenial with the Baptist polity had now fallen into disuse, the covenant made with Elder Rogers set aside, and after hiring him for two or three successive years he was peaceably dismissed in 1803, laboring for a time successfully in the adjoining country. "March 15, 1805, a few brothers and sisters on Chestnut Hill met at the house of Brother Levi Aldrich, in conference on our scattered and broken situation, and felt ourselves under obligation to renew covenant and take up our cross and follow Christ in the pathway of duty." These brethren, viz.:—Deacon Herrington, Ebenezer Leach, Levi Aldrich, Sampson Covill, Abner Aldrich, Caleb Colegrove, Oliver Bowen, and eight sisters, continued to meet together and exercise discipline in some degree till they were again so fortunate as to unite in a pastor.

The church in the South Society enjoyed a good degree of prosperity and harmony. Upon the death of its beloved pastor, Rev. Eliphalet Wright, August 4, 1784, within six days of his decease it was voted:—

"1. That it is the mind of this church to exert themselves in resettling the gospel ministry. 2. That for the future we will support the same by an equality according to our several estates. 3. That it is the desire and choice of this church that our brother Israel Day should take the charge of them as their pastor."

Mr. Day was ordained and installed in office, June 1, 1785. Rev. Ebenezer Bradford of Rowley, with whom he had studied theology, preached the sermon. Rev. John Cleveland of Ipswich, and Joshua Spalding, a son of the Killingly church, assisted in the services. Mr. Day's preaching was very satisfactory and forty persons were ere long added to the church. Deacon Spalding, Anthony Brown and Ezra Hutchins, were appointed a committee to take care of the church in relation to breaches of discipline, which was still administered with

43

exemplary strictness. Members were admonished for "going to law contrary to gospel rule." A colored sister excommunicated for indulgence "in stealing and lying." The church was exercised many years by a very grievous difficulty between the pastor and Deacon Spalding, requiring the intervention of many councils and committees. Each was certain that he was in the right and very persistent. The deacon was at length led to perceive that he had been somewhat at fault and arising before sunrise went straight to the pastor and made acknowledgment. Mr. Day listened most benignantly, and graciously granted pardon, but made no counter confession. "Ah," said the wounded deacon, "I have brought a whole bullock to the sacrifice. Have you not as much as a turtle dove to lay upon the altar?"

In this remote corner of Killingly innovation made slow progress and its residents long retained their primitive customs and character. The sturdy old Separates who laid the foundations of society were much opposed to worldly pomp and vanity and ruled their families with rod of iron, yet with all their strictness the world crept on. Sons and daughters of rigid priest and deacons would steal away from their beds at night to join in dance and frolic, and young ladies managed in some way to learn and follow the fashions of the period. A daughter of Deacon Spalding, married in 1785 to Joseph Gay of Thompson, "appeared out" on the Sunday following her marriage in a peach-colored silk most jauntily made, and hat and head-dress trimmed with the marvellous quantity of *sixteen yards* of white ribbon, while her husband walked by her side in smallclothes of white broadcloth. According to the custom of the congregation they took their place in the middle seat of the front gallery, and some time in the course of the service deliberately arose for inspection, turning slowly around and standing in different positions so that the whole effect of the costume might be exhibited. The young bride of Dr. Penuel Hutchins, who "appeared out" the following year, met a somewhat cold reception. The meeting-house was very cold and the light wedding dress unfitted for the season. The good minister's wife after the service invited the shivering bride to her warm fireside, but she was scarcely seated there when a sharp-faced good-wife ushered in three matrons. "You sit there, and you there, and you there," she promptly ordered; "and you, young woman, may sit back; *your fine clothes will keep you warm.*" With such exhibitions it is not to be wondered at that some of the brethren should be troubled with "wandering thoughts on the holy Sabbath." An aged church member so unfortunate as to lose his wife was forced to confess his infirmity to his pastor during intermission—"You preached a very good sermon to-day; but right in the midst of it I could not help reckoning up *nineteen* smart young *widders* within the limits of this ecclesiastical society, and I've thought of another since I came here, and that makes *twenty!* Now what *shall I do?*" Whether he was advised to *lessen* the number as speedily as possible is not reported.

The South Killingly settlement though but a mere hamlet, three or four houses and a shop clustering around the meeting-house, had a very imposing aspect in the eyes of that generation, and by common consent was dignified as "The City"—a name that clung to it for many years. Its one tavern was well patronized by the surrounding population, and its company trainings were carried on with more than ordinary spirit. An eye-witness* reports for us :—

"Nearly everybody attended them either as soldiers or spectators. The boys were often on the ground before a soldier made his appearance. After the company was organized, the captain, escorted by two subaltern officers, with slow and measured step marched forward. We have seen presidents of the United States, Doctors of the Divinity and Law, yet sure are we that we have never felt such awe in the presence of any man as we have in looking upon a South Killingly militia captain. We used often to hear of Bonaparte's army, but thought it would stand but little chance in a contest with this company. Calling the roll was the first business. The sergeant read over the names in this wise—"Elam Howlet"—"Here!" "Abel Adams"—"Here!" "John Owens"—a solemn pause—"John Owens"—no response—"Prick him," cried out the captain, whereupon a pin was inserted into the name of the delinquent. Our sympathies were often wrought to their highest pitch for the unfortunate absentee. The bottle was frequently passed during the military exercises. By night nearly half of both soldiers and spectators were more or less intoxicated. . . . . . . We claim there were good and substantial reasons for our youthful admiration for a fully-equipped military officer, especially *a general.* His russet-topped boots, long white stockings, short breeches with gold buckles, a ruffled shirt, a blue and crimson coat and vest, beautifully wrought with fine twist and linen of divers colors, with powdered hair and long queue hanging down behind! His head surmounted by a hat somewhat in the shape of half the head of a hogshead and well nigh as large. Above this an enormous feather of brilliant colors was perched. He was placed astride an elegant and thoroughly disciplined horse apparently as proud as his rider. Can any one censure our admiration?"

Jacob Rood, captain of this admired company, was succeeded in 1803 by Samuel Sprague; Isaac Day, lieutenant; Simon Spalding, ensign. Shubael Hutchins was at this time lieutenant-colonel commandant of the Twenty-first Regiment with which it was connected; Rev. Israel Day, chaplain; Daniel Kies, paymaster.

As business gravitated more and more to the centre of the town, the question of church removal was again agitated. Dr. Penuel Hutchins and other prominent residents of Central Killingly were active in this movement, and proposed that a new house of worship should be erected that would accommodate both sections. A majority of the church opposed the change, voting, May, 1797, "That all things and circumstances considered, the old meeting-house is the place

* Isaac T. Hutchins, Esq., Danielsonville, 1878.

where we ought to continue to meet for the worship of God." In July, however, a vote was obtained, "that it is the opinion of this church that it does not belong to us as a church to determine where our meeting-house ought to stand, but to the community at large who are at the expense of a meeting-house and support of the ministry." Under this vote a number of individuals proceeded to build a house in the western part of the middle society. The church was troubled and dissatisfied—"did not wish to be dictated to, or controlled by the congregation," and finally, August, 1798, refused "the request sent by the proprietors of the new meeting-house to have our pastor preach to them half the time." A new church was thereupon organized after some delay in the central society and the old South church left to pursue its way unmolested. The piety and strong character of Mr. Day gave him much influence over his people and brought them by degrees into conformity with the orthodox churches. In 1799 he was admitted into the Ministerial Association of Windham County. The church, two years later, virtually abjured its original Separatism by accepting Consociation with other county churches, and thenceforward maintained a respectable standing among them, the only Separate church in Windham County that achieved a permanent existence. A remarkable religious revival was then in progress, which added over sixty to the church membership. The first meeting of the Association at South Killingly was made especially memorable by the ordination of Thomas Williams of Brooklyn, late preceptor of Woodstock Academy, "as an evangelist to go out as missionary." Doctors Benjamin Trumbull and Levi Hart, and Secretary Abel Flint appeared in behalf of the Missionary Society of Connecticut. The Association resolved itself into an ordaining council, and after a satisfactory examination of the candidate, voted, "To consecrate him to the work of the Gospel ministry with reference to his laboring as a missionary in the new settlements in the United States of America." The solemnities were attended in the meeting-house, May 16, 1804. Secretary Flint made the opening prayer. Mr. King of Pomfret preached. Dr. Benedict offered the consecrating prayer. Dr. Hart gave the charge; Mr. Dow the right hand of fellowship. Mr. Lyman offered the concluding prayer. Mr. Williams labored for a time in New York. Rev. Israel Day had previously served as missionary in Vermont. Most of the Windham County ministers engaged for a time in missionary labors.

The meeting-house built in West Killingly, was probably occupied more or less from the date of its erection. Dr. Penuel Hutchins and Mr. Robert Howe gave the ample and eligible building lot. The few church members residing in the vicinity now decided to organize as a distinct body, and summoned an ecclesiastic council which met at the house of Dr. Penuel Hutchins, August 25, 1801. Reverends Josiah Whitney, Joel Benedict, Israel Day, Elisha Atkins, were present. " After reading and approving confession of faith and articles of agreement, the council adjourned to the meeting-house to meet those about to confederate. Prayer was offered by Mr. Whitney. It was voted that the moderator, Mr. Whitney, after sermon from Mr. Benedict, should lead the confederated brethren to the confession of faith, the unbaptized to baptism, and the whole to the covenant, and then to acknowledge them a new church of Christ, and consociated with Christ's churches by fellowship and communion." Abigail, wife of Boaz Stearns, and Anna Kies, were baptized before signing the covenant. The other signers were Zadoc Spalding, Boaz Stearns, Zadoc Hutchins, James Danielson, Penuel Hutchins, Samuel Stearns, Shubael Hutchins, Mrs. Elizabeth Hutchins, Mrs. Mary Stearns, Mrs. Abigail Stearns, Mrs. Sarah L. Danielson, Mrs. Hannah Spalding— recognized as the church of West Killingly. This part of the town was yet but sparsely settled. General Danielson occupied the site and privileges which a hundred years before had been taken up by his name- sake. Dr. Hutchins, Boaz Stearns, Robert Howe, and one or two other families, were living in the vicinity of the new meeting-house. Blacksmithing was carried on by Mr. Howe. Captain Silas Hutchins' tavern was a place of popular resort for travelers and merrymakers. The church made but slow advances for several years. Its first pastor was Gordon Johnson of Farmington, ordained December 12, 1804. No deacons or other church officers are reported. The only additional members in eleven years were the pastor and four women.

In the great movement westward initiated during this period, Killingly was deeply interested. Not only did she send many valued citizens to the western wilds, but one of her own sons was largely instrumental in opening the Western territory to emigration and settlement. Dr. Manassah Cutler, Hamilton, Mass., a man of unusual breadth and solidity of character, deeply interested in the develop- ment of the Nation, assisted in the organization of the Ohio Com- pany in 1786, served as one of its directors and counsellors, urged its claims before Congress, and by his forcible arguments and commanding influence aided very greatly in securing the purchase of one-and-a-half millions of land for the Ohio Company, and the famous Ordinance for the Government of the Territory northwest of the Ohio River. Emigrants were urged to take immediate possession. Dr. Cutler's son Ephraim, then residing with his aged grandfather in Killingly, acted as agent for the company, and prevailed upon some twenty Windham County citizens to take shares in the purchase. Jervis, son of Dr.

Cutler, Captain Daniel Davis, Theophilus Larned and Samuel Felshaw, were with the party that left Hartford, January 1, 1788, under the direction of General Rufus Putnam, crossed the Alleghanies by the old Indian pathway, descended the Youghiogheny by the boats they paused to build, landed at the mouth of the Muskingum, April 7, and there began the settlement of the township of Marietta and the future state of Ohio. They were followed when the spring opened by other men from the same vicinity, *i. e.*, Theophilus Knight, Benjamin Converse, John Leavens, George, Jeremiah and David Wilson, Aaron Clough and John Russell, who went out not as members of a company, but as one reports,* "on our own hook, according to our own roving disposition and desire to see the world. We had a team of four horses and a baggage wagon for clothes, farming tools and provision, and off we set and had a very merry journey through the country. Part of the way we had eleven of us in company, and sometimes we were as merry as people need to be. Sometimes we met with disagreeable things, bad luck, bad traveling, but upon the whole we did pretty well." They were just forty days upon their journey, landing at Marietta, May, 18, 1788. Mr. Knight witnessed many interesting scenes during his sojourn in the territory—the arrival of the first women and children, the funeral of the first white man, the organization of the first court, the celebration of the Fourth of July, when Dr. Cutler delivered the oration and all partook of a twenty-five pound *pike*, barbecued for the occasion, the magnificent parade at the funeral of Judge Varnum, escorted by the officers of the garrison and a company of United States troops, together with "old Revolutionary officers and Indian chiefs in abundance—a very long procession to travel in a forest"—and they also help build the first houses in Ohio. Most of his companions made their homes in the new country, but two after twenty months returned with him to Connecticut, "not thinking it was so much better than any other country, that it would pay a man for carrying a large family to such a wilderness, inhabited by savages and wild beasts of the forest." Their report and example had no apparent effect upon their fellow-townsmen. So many other families emigrated westward from Killingly and adjoining towns, that it seemed as if "New Connecticut" would drain the life blood of its namesake. Many of these Killingly settlers were strong, intelligent men who had great influence in moulding the institutions and character of Ohio. Ephraim Cutler who removed to Waterford in 1795, was a member of the convention that formed the State Constitution in 1802. Captain Perley Howe, who left Killingly at the

---

* Diary of Theophilus Knight.

same date, Captains Daniel Davis and John Leavens, were men of wisdom and experience whose counsels were held in high esteem. Benjamin Converse died the year after settlement in Waterford, having already manifested such "genius, public spirit and enterprise," that his death was mourned "as a serious loss to the whole community." The adventures of his second son, Daniel, who was taken captive by the Indians in 1791, and after suffering great hardships managed to escape, and work his way through Canada and Vermont to Killingly, made a deep impression upon his former townsmen but did not deter them from following the narrator back to Ohio, where he became one of the most respected citizens of Zanesville.

XI.

TOWN ORGANIZATION IN THOMPSON. BUSINESS ENTERPRISE. ORDINATIONS OF DANIEL DOW AND PEARSON CROSBY. REPORT OF SCHOOL INSPECTORS. SALE OF THOMP- SON TRACT. IMPROVEMENTS AND EXCITE- MENTS. COUNTERFEITING.

THOMPSON did not secure town privileges without the customary contest. After voting unanimously in the north and south societies of Killingly, that Thompson Parish should be a distinct town, and also voting in general town meeting, that it be the mind of the town to have said town divided, Killingly repented and remonstrated :—

"That should a division take place it would be attended with many bad consequences, and be very detrimental to the State in general, and this town in particular. 1. As to State it will increase its taxes already so large that the inhabitants groan under the burden, for the increase of the number of the Legislative body, which at present your Honors are sensible is large enough, will increase its taxes. 2. As to the town in its best estate it is very poor and indigent, not more than £26,749 upon its list, and the length of town so much complained of not exceeding sixteen miles, and width not more than seven, and the place where public meetings are held near the centre— which accommodates the people as well or better than any of the neighboring towns. Plan for dividing the town concocted in the extreme parts of the town, and the two central parishes being destitute of preaching at the time the warning was up but few of the inhabitants were apprized, and at the town meeting when the vote was passed there was much dispute and the house was divided which did not satisfy, and it was carried by a vote to take the yeas and nays in writing, and the yeas being first called for the nays withdrew without giving their names; furthermore, about one half the voters present were new made that took the qualifications at that meeting—and beg Assembly not to pass resolves whereby said town shall be divided which we conceive will be injurious to town and State and against the public peace and tranquillity."

This memorial, signed by a large number of citizens, delayed the inevitable division for a season, but upon a renewal of agitation three years later the town found farther resistance useless. At a General Assembly holden at Hartford, May, 1785, it was enacted, "That the north society of Killingly and the inhabitants thereof should be constituted a distinct town, by the name of Thompson, with powers and privileges—said town to be responsible for its share of State taxes, pay one-half the debts, and share one-half of the credit and stock of the former town and support the poor belonging within its limits; that the first town-meeting should be holden in June following—Simon Larned, Esq., justice of the peace, and two of the principal inhabitants to warn the same—said Justice Larned to preside at said meeting and lead said inhabitants to the choice of moderator and clerk."

In obedience to this act and lawful warning, Thompson's first town meeting was held June 21, 1785, "at the Rev. Mr. Russel's meeting-house," on Thompson Hill. Simon Larned, Esq., deacon of Mr. Russel's church, now advanced in years and honors, presided as directed, and led the people to the choice of Jason Phipps, Esq., for moderator; Jacob Dresser, town clerk. The freeman's oath was administered to seventy-eight inhabitants.* "They then voted and chose" Thomas Dike, Esq., Capt. Pain Converse, Simon Larned, Esq., Jason Phipps, Esq., Mr. Stephen Brown, selectmen; Jacob Dresser, town-treasurer; Simon Davis, Peleg Corbin, constables;

---

*The names of those that took the Freeman's oath at the first Town meeting held in Thompson, June 21, 1785 :—Simon Larned, Esq., Jason Phipps, Esq., Thomas Dike, Esq., Stephen Brown, John Jacobs, Ivory Upham, Captains Obadiah Clough, Pain Converse, Daniel Larned, Jonathan Ellis, Capt. Peter Keith, John Whitmore, Capt. John Green, Jacob Dresser, Simon Davis, Lieut. Amos Carrol, David Barritt, John Leavens, John Younglove, Captains Stephen Keith and Benjamin Merriam, Peleg Corbin, Nathan Bixby, Ensign John Whitmore, James Paull, Ebenezer Bundy, Jesse Brown, Ensign Joseph Brown, Moses and Lemuel Barritt, Mr. Jonathan Nichols, Luke Upham, Joseph Prince, William Copeland, Lieut. Jacob Converse, Clement Corbin, Daniel Barrett, Elijah Converse, Amos Green, Jun., Seth Green, Samuel Haley, Joseph Deamon, Joseph Watson, Richard Brown, Robert Plank, Edward Paull, Joseph Gay, Lieut. Davis Flint, William Alton, William Dwight, Lieut. Benjamin Larned, Capt. Issacher Bates, Matthew Watson, Jesse Bixby, Hezekiah Bellows, John Bates, Ensign Daniel Perrin, Isaac Lee, Joseph Jewett, John R. Watson, Capt. Jonathan Nichols, Elijah Nichols, John Flint, Thomas Grant, Joseph Flint, John Cooper, Asa Bastow, Alpheus Converse, Walter Everden, Samuel Fay, Jonathan Russel, Elijah Bates, Joel Converse, Joseph Town, Jun., Daniel Alton, Jeremiah Haskell, Thaddeus Larned, John Alton. These were followed within a few years by Noadiah Russel, Jun., Samuel Wilson, Asa Jacobs, William Whittemore, Elijah Crosby, Roger Elliott, William Richards, Jun., Benjamin and Ebenezer Green, Joseph Lee, Marshall Keith, Israel Munyan, John Robbins, Nathaniel Gregory, Daniel Robbins, Ephraim Houghton, Aaron Robinson, Jonathan Converse, Jason Phipps, Jun., James Keith, Abel Prince, Asa Dresser, Jacob Bixby, Jonathan Clough.

Jason Phipps, Samuel Barrett, Jacob Converse, Ebenezer Prince, John Bates, John Jacobs, Dea. William Richards, highway surveyors and collectors; Amos Carrol, William Richards, fence-viewers; Henry Larned, Jonathan Ellis, Samuel Palmer and William Richards, listers; Simon Davis and Peleg Corbin, town-collectors; John Wilson, leather sealer; Ebenezer Cooper and Jeremiah Hopkins, grand-jurymen; Nathan Bixby, Peter Jacobs and Edward Paull, tithingmen; Amos Carrol, sealer of weights and measures; Joseph Watson, key-keeper. Captains Daniel Larned and Pain Converse and Thomas Dike, Esq., were appointed a committee to join such gentlemen as Killingly should appoint, to settle all debts and charges and divide debts and credits as directed. Jacob Dresser was authorized to purchase books for the town records.

At the annual town meeting held December 12, these officers were replaced by others, viz.:—Selectmen, Lieut. Amos Carrol, Henry Larned, Jonathan Ellis; constables, Alpheus Converse, John Bates; highway surveyors, Ensign Joseph Brown, Daniel Russel, Samuel Palmer, Roger Elliott, Captain Jonathan Nichols, Edward Joslin, William Smith; grand-jurymen, Asa Bastow, James Paull; fence-viewers, Amos Carrol, Pain Converse; listers, Joseph Gay, Captain Simeon Goodell, Jeremiah Hopkins, John Carrol; tithingmen, James Hosmer, Ephraim Ellingwood, Peter Stockwell, Elijah Bates; leather sealer, John Wilson; Joseph Watson, key-keeper. Jacob Dresser was retained for many years as town clerk and treasurer. Deacon Simon and Major Daniel Larned were chosen to join the gentlemen committee of the town of Killingly to run the line between the towns. A due east and west line from Rhode Island colony line to the middle of the Quinebaug River, bisecting "a heap of stones about two feet south of the garden wall owned by Mr. John Mason,* upon the east side of the great road leading through said towns to New London," was affixed by the committee. Residents in Thompson who had been formerly set off to the First society in Killingly remained the same as though said town had never been divided. Lands belonging to Nathan and John Mason, Joseph Richards, Bernard Hix, Samuel Haly, Resolved Johnson, Aaron Mason and Darius Sessions, claimed by both townships, were awarded to Thompson by Act of Assembly, October, 1789. Accounts between the towns were settled with great promptness and harmony, the "credits" allowed to Thompson happily out-balancing the debts by some twenty-five pounds.

One of the first cares of the town was to look out for the numerous

---

* Mr. Mason's mansion house north of the boundary line is now owned and occupied by Mr. William Converse of Putnam.

44

poor people set off with it.   There were two or three helpless families
upon their hands, ailing women with drunken husbands and families of
children, besides old people, chronic invalids and imbeciles.   After
long debate upon the matter it was voted, February 16, 1786, " That
there should be two workhouses provided for the poor ; That Deacon
James Dike's house should be one and he master of the same ; That
Mr. Ebenezer Bundy should provide a house, and be master of the
same "—but the measure failed of accomplishment.   Messrs. Dike and
Bundy, as " masters of the poor," provided places for them with
different families at prices ranging from four shillings to one and sixpence per week.   They also provided clothing, medical attendance
and occasional supplies of rum, metheglin, sugar and molasses on
extraordinary occasions.   Selectmen were desired to give notice to
the inhabitants " that those shall have the poor of said town to keep
that will keep them the cheapest."   Children were bound out whenever
practicable.   Much time and money were expended in transporting
doubtful residents to other towns and contesting their claims by legal
process.

The privilege of laying out and making its own highways was
joyfully assumed by Thompson.   Roads "from Thompson meeting-
house to Muddy Brook-line by the way of Mr. David Jewett's," and
from Child's Mills (now Wilsonville) to Dudley line, that may lead to
Dudley meeting-house, were at once allowed.   Captains Nichols and
Clough were appointed agents to prefer a memorial to the General
Assembly for liberty to mend the highways by a tax, and also "to
give the town of Thompson the name of PRINCETOWN."   The latter
request if preferred was certainly not granted, and would not have
been at all agreeable to the tenants of "the Thompson Land," and
those descendants of old settlers who still exercised a certain romantic
fealty towards the English proprietor.   The family were always
reputed to take great interest in this ancient inheritance, and children
are known to have been named in their honor, so that if any representative should chance to visit his domain he would find that their
connection with the town had been recognized and appreciated.   The
usual highway privileges were promptly accorded.   William Copeland,
Clement Corbin and others having "flung in a complaint to the
selectmen," on account of the shutting up of their road to mill and
meeting by Asaph Bowen, were appeased by the privilege of having
gates and bars that they could pass.   Other roads were allowed and
repaired in various quarters, and a committee appointed to view and
repair bridges.   The line between Thompson and Woodstock was
perambulated and renewed by a committee from each town.   School
affairs were left as before in the charge of society and districts.

General public affairs were not neglected. Jason Phipps, Esq., was sent as Thompson's first representative to the General Assembly. Major Daniel Larned was elected in special town meeting, November 5, 1787, delegate to represent the town in the State Convention called to ratify the Federal Constitution. A committee was sent to consult with committees from other northern towns with regard to obtaining a new county or half-shire, and upon receiving their report the town voted, " that our deputies should join Pomfret deputies with regard to making Pomfret a half-shire, with this proviso that we may be free of cost of a court-house and jail." The young town looked sharply after *cost* in all its expenditures, and kept its accounts most carefully balanced. An execution served upon it in behalf of the State for an unsettled war claim—fifty pounds with the interest from May, 1777— gave it a deal of trouble. For some obscure cause this claim had been disputed. Assets sufficient to meet it had been allowed by Killingly in settlement but could not be collected. September 20, 1786, it was " voted to choose a committee to inspect the collectors and look into the matter of executions, said committee to carefully inspect the collector's bills, and look carefully into the circumstances of those that are delinquent in payment and wherever there is any *personal estate* by no means take the land, and farther assist the collectors by calling on the delinquents and urging the absolute necessity of payment, and endeavour to make the matter as easy as possibly may be every circumstance considered." This delicate service was assigned to Amos Carrol, Henry Larned and Captain Peter Keith. They found the collection of the ancient rate-bills made over to them by Killingly extremely difficult. After procuring a list " of those that hant paid," a committee of five was appointed " to visit every man described in their bill of balance," find out the abatements that had been applied, and also the bill of overcharges and absconderies. Sixty-five pounds were allowed them in abatements and the remainder apparently secured by taking possession of land. Captain Carrol and his associates continued on duty, going with the collectors when they posted up lands for taxes and deciding if it was best to bid the lands off for the town, and as soon as the law allowed applying for payment, and " if not paid, either let the improvements out for the town, or sell in case they can raise the money nearly to the value of the land—or if they can get stock for part or all to take it at the value in money, and to show as much lenity as the nature of the case will admit." By shrewd management the difficulty was surmounted, all accounts with the mother town and State government settled in full, and a balance reported in the treasury in 1788. Relieved from this incubus the town could now condescend to some minor details, consider the condition of the pound, forbid swine " to run on the commons without a good wire ring in the nose and a yoke three inches below the neck and four inches above," and offer a bounty of six-pence for the head of each crow that shall be killed " within its limits. A rise to ten cents a head so stimulated juvenile enterprise that quite a large sum was distributed year by year in bounty money. Nathaniel Mills was chosen town clerk and treasurer in 1798.

In business for several years there was little activity. Times were hard and money scarce. The various mills for grinding, sawing and cloth dressing, supplied indispensable wants. Ebenezer Bundy had now succeeded the Eatons at the Upper Fall of the Quinebaug, and entered into brisk competition with old Captain Cargill, half a mile below. " Larned and Mason " continued their business in the South Neighborhood, and as trade revived prosecuted it with redoubled energy. A road was laid out for their especial accommodation in 1782, running east of Fort Hill through the Thompson Land, which considerably shortened the distance to Boston—" so much advantage no damage laid to owners of land." An attempt was made to secure a more direct road to Bundy's mills. A nail manufactory was now set up. Potash and pearlash were made in large quantities. Produce was taken in from all the surrounding country, and even from neighboring States. Finding that the transfer of so much merchandise in hired ships was costly and inconvenient, the firm decided to build a ship for themselves. A body of men was straightway dispatched to cut and hew timber in Thompson forests, and Quaddic saw-mill engaged for the season. Captain Jonathan Nichols, an ingenious mechanic, had charge of the work, competent workmen were obtained, and in a few months a tight little brig or sloop met the eyes of the many spectators flocking to Quaddic to admire so rare a specimen of inland enterprise and architecture. After being taken in sections to Providence, it was carefully refitted and launched as the sloop *Harmony*, amid much gratulation and rejoicing. It proved a valuable acquisition to its owners, conveying produce and goods back and forth between Providence and the West India Islands, and furnishing the good people of Thompson and its vicinity with abundant supplies of what were deemed most vital necessities. Under the stimulus afforded by this flourishing business, South Neighborhood proudly maintained its position as DISTRICT NUMBER ONE, and was universally regarded as the business and social head of the town, while Thompson Hill was set apart for religious gatherings, trainings and town meetings. Nothing like a village could then be found at this centre. The meeting-house and red tavern house, a pound and blacksmith's shop held sole possession of the common. A fine house* had been built at the north extremity of the hill by Mr. Samuel Watson, in 1767; "Priest Russel's" pleasant residence† overlooked its southern slope. Esquire Dresser's house on an adjacent hill-top was long famed as a place of public resort and entertainment. His second wife, the widow of Thomas Dyer, Esq., of Windham, was a lady of much dignity and presence, remembered for long years by awe-struck neighbors as "the proudest woman that ever lived in Thompson." Her honored husband, Jacob Dresser, Esq., the first white male born within Thompson territory, died in 1783, respected and mourned by all. He had long served as deacon of the church and filled many public offices. Of his six children only one lived to maturity, who bore the name and succeeded in time to many of the offices held by his father. He was one of the first captains of the regiment of light infantry, attached to the Fifth Brigade. Amos Goodell, William Dwight, Peleg Corbin, William Smith, Abel Prince, Augustus Larned, David Wilson, Isaac Davis, Moses Bixby, George Keith, Eli Starr, were also officers in this company or in the militia. Daniel Larned, after serving as major and colonel of the Eleventh Regiment, succeeded General Gordon in charge of the Brigade, in 1793. His promotion led to increased activity in military affairs, and the company trainings on Thompson and Brandy Hills, and the annual "muster" in the autumn, were observed with redoubled spirit. The hill tavern was now kept by Samuel Fairbanks. David Nichols, Jason Phipps, John Bates, John Jacobs had taverns in other parts of the town.

Religious matters were now left to the respective churches and societies, but "Mr. Russel's meeting-house" was claimed by the town as the place for public meetings. Many interesting services were held in this honored house which still retained its place in the affection of the inhabitants. Amasa Learned of Killingly, was licensed to preach in this house at a meeting of the Association, in 1773. Dr. Cogswell in his journal gives a pleasant picture of a meeting of the Association here in 1790. Jogging slowly along on horseback over the rough hills from Scotland, picking up one ministerial brother after another, tarrying for the night with Mr. Whitney, dining with Mr. Atkins, they reached Thompson Hill Wednesday afternoon, October 12. Eight ministers were present and one candidate. Brothers Putnam and Judson were detained at home by ill health. Johnson of Woodstock, after much wrangling had been dismissed with comfortable circumstances. Mr. Russel in the evening gave an excellent discourse "upon the question, Whether God chose our first parents

* Now occupied by Judge Rawson.
† Site now occupied by William H. Chandler, Esq.

should eat the forbidden fruit. He proved the negative incontesta-
bly." On the following day Mr. Lee gave an excellent sermon. A
pretty full attendance and people very attentive. The Association had
a very friendly meeting and were very hospitably entertained. Exercises were concluded by a prayer from Mr. Russel, "worthy of an
ancient Puritan divine," and after an affectionate parting the brethren
ambled peacefully homeward.

Mr. Russel's health was now failing and measures had been taken
to procure a colleague when he was suddenly removed. A cotemporary thus records his decease:—

"Died at Mendon, Mass., Tuesday, October 27, 1795, Rev. Noadiah Russel of
Thompson, Conn. On the Thursday preceding, Mr. Russel, his wife and son
entered upon a journey from their house to Boston; proceeded leisurely;
arrived at the Rev. Mr. Alexander's on the following Monday. Towards
evening sat down at table for refreshment. Then, Mr. Russel was suddenly
seized with apoplexy, and continued with little or no sense or motion till
about eleven the next evening, when he expired. The remains were brought
back to Thompson for interment on Friday, on which very mournful occasion
a sermon was delivered by Rev. Josiah Whitney of Brooklyn, from Hebrews
VII. : 2, 3."

"An early, long and particular acquaintance" enabled Mr. Whitney
to speak of the deceased with great fullness and tenderness. "His
mental powers were excellent. He thought and reasoned well, was
careful and critical in examining things, capable of forming a good
judgment, agreeable and edifying in conversation. His house and
heart were open to friends and acquaintances—a lover of mankind,
faithful in his friendships, ready to do good and communicate, exemplary in relative duties."

Mr. Pinneo, afterward of Milford, was supplying the pulpit at this
time, but was soon succeeded by young Mr. Daniel Dow of Ashford,
already favorably known to the churches and ministers of Windham
County. After graduation from Yale College in 1793, Mr. Dow
maintained himself by teaching psalmody while pursuing the study of
divinity, was licensed by the Windham County Association at its
spring session in 1795, and—"to be further qualified for the office of
a bishop—became the husband of one wife, the daughter of Deacon
Jesse Bolles of Woodstock." These superior qualifications were
promptly recognized by the good people of Thompson, and after a
few months' probation a call was given and accepted, and the new
minister ordained and installed, April 20, 1796, amid much rejoicing
and mutual congratulation. The neighboring County ministers composed the ordaining council. Private preliminary examination was
held at Captain Dresser's tavern. It was a time of great doctrinal
debate and agitation. High Calvinism was coming into fashion.
The shrewd young candidate, who was suspected of Arminian tenden-

cies, was subjected to a most searching inquisition. His adroitness in reply called out all the controversial resources of his assailants, and the debate waxed so warm that Mr. Dow was fain to throw off his coat and stand parrying their thrusts " with sweat raining down from him like a farmer in a July hay-field." Whatever his theological sentiments were at that period, he maintained them triumphantly, one good deacon of his church as persistent as himself voting alone against him. In performing the public exercises at the meeting-house, " Mr. Pond preached the sermon, Mr. Lee made the consecrating prayer, Mr. Whitney gave the charge, and Mr. Graves the right hand of fellowship." Entering with much zest upon his ministerial labors, Mr. Dow began at once to experience the trials of the ministry. In his own words half a century later :—

" The church I found to be in a very cold, backslidden state; very few of them willing to converse upon experimental religion, or ready to give a reason of the hope that was in them, if they had any religion at all. The congregation seemingly intent upon nothing but vanity and folly. My flock scattered over the whole town, an area of about eight miles square, various denominations of Christian people contending with each other about the shells and husks of religion, while they appeared to pay little or no attention to the substance. Intemperance greatly prevailing, and moderate drinkers as they were called, drinking most immoderately. Errorists of every kind running to and fro, and many, having itching ears, running after them. Some openly avowing their infidelity; while others were proclaiming what they called good news and glad tidings; by which they meant that impenitent sinners, drunkards and all, were sure to go to Heaven. . . . My people were all very friendly to me. They filled the old meeting-house well, heard what I said to them with as much satisfaction as they would listen to a song, and gave me as much, and even more commendation, than what I sometimes thought I deserved. But there was the end of it. They were friendly to the preacher, and satisfied with his performances, but generally speaking, they had no love for Gospel truth, nor any concern for their own salvation. Nor was it in my power to awaken them. I preached what I thought good sermons, great sermons, sermons full of excellent speech and moral suasion, sermons good enough to convert anybody, and yet they had no more effect in awakening and converting sinners than a pop-gun discharged against an impenetrable rock. I was greatly disappointed; and the condition of the people who manifested so much friendship for me appeared so deplorable that I sat down discouraged and wept. But in all this the Lord taught me a very important lesson. I was brought to see that nothing short of the power of God can either awaken or convert a sinner. . . . From that time I preached the doctrines of grace more plainly and more constantly than I had ever done before. I expurgated my system of divinity of all Arminian notions, and my language of all such phrases as were capable of misconstruction; (for though orthodox in the main, I had fallen into some mistakes and inconsistencies in consequence of having read many erroneous books in my early days); and I now determined to preach all the doctrines of grace, if I possibly could, as plainly as Christ and his apostles preached them."

This plain and faithful preaching produced a very different effect. People " began to awake from their slumbers." The church was greatly quickened and within a few years many were added to its membership. A new interest was aroused in all the secular affairs of the society. A singing school was opened, and Dudley Holmes, Captain Augustus Larned, Ensign Isaac Davis and George Keith appointed choristers. Enterprising young men now bestirred themselves to improve and adorn the house of worship, and crowned it with steeple and bell "free from any expense to the society." The hanging of the bell was safely accomplished amid a great number of spectators, June 2, 1798, the society thereafter voting, "To get a conductor to said meeting-house steeple, and authorizing its committee to procure and hang said conductor." The last vestige of the old body of seats was now replaced by fashionable pews, and the son of the late minister empowered for twelve shillings a year "to sweep the house once in two months and clear off the cobwebs." To make sure of keeping up with the times, a town clock was procured and instated in office, and "twenty dollars a year allowed for ringing bell and taking care of clock." Notwithstanding the general prosperity of the society it was found very difficult to raise the three-hundred-dollars-salary for the minister, and efforts were early made to establish a fund, "the interest to be for the support of the gospel." Deacon Simon Larned after many years service as clerk of the society, was succeeded in 1789 by his son Thaddeus, who gave place the following year to Captain Jacob Dresser. The deacons of the church in 1796 were Simon Larned and Lusher Gay, in advanced age, and Thomas Dike and Joseph Gay in active service.

The sudden death of General Larned, who had been so prominent for many years in public and military affairs, was made the occasion of the greatest military and masonic display ever witnessed in the old meeting-house. The *New London Gazette* thus reports the funeral solemnities :—

"The General was buried under Arms. His corpse was attended by the Brethren of Moriah Lodge to the meeting-house, where a sermon was preached by the Rev. Daniel Dow; a Masonic Address and prayer followed by the Worshipful Master of Moriah Lodge. A procession was then formed, and moved to the grave in the following order, viz. :

Military;
Masons, clothed with the Badges of their Order;
Clergy;
Pall (corpse) Bearers;
Mourners;
And Strangers.

The corpse being interred, Mr. Daniel Putnam pronounced an Eulogium of which the following is an extract :—

' Here have we deposited to mingle with their kindred earth the Relics of an Husband, a Father, a Brother, a friend. To the Dead this is the last kind office we can perform. Larned now rests from his labors.' . . . . .

As a neighbor, a member of society, a citizen, he cultivated Peace, order and harmony. Faithful to his Trust, persevering in pursuit, accurate in Calculation, he inspired a Confidence that was unbounded.

Engaged in active business and commercial life, punctuality in the performance of engagements he practiced as a virtue, Educated in habits of industry and animated with a Spirit of Enterprise, he was ever prompt to undertake and encourage plans of public utility, domestic convenience and of private and social happiness.

Learning by his intercourse with mankind the aimable virtues of Hospitality and generosity and assiduously cultivating the social and benevolent feelings of the heart, he was ever ready to receive and welcome to his hospitable dwelling, the Indigent, the stranger and the storm-worn or benighted Traveler.

Rambling among these Tombs, the Poor will point and say, There were interred the remains of Larned, our generous benefactor: the neighbor and citizen, There we buried the body of a good, a worthy, an honest man: the soldier, There lies our General: the Sons of Moriah, There we placed the ashes of a beloved Brother, who seeking to obtain *more Light* left our Lodge to join that of the Supreme Architect, the General Master of the Universe, There to flourish like the ever-verdant Cassia in immortal Bloom.

After which the Ceremonies were closed by a masonic prayer by the Worshipful Master, and a sprig of cassia deposited on the coffin.

December, 1797."

Baptists were increasing in the northeast part of the town. Their church gained in strength and numbers though disturbed for a time by difficulties with its pastor, whose mind became somewhat unsettled with advancing years. After long labor and grievous trouble, it was agreed, October 12, 1797, to divide the church into two parts, and for each individual, male and female, to have full liberty to join which party they chose. Eleven males and sixteen females adhered to Elder Martin and set up worship by themselves in an obscure corner east of the Great Pond, known as Oxford Gore. The standing majority soon happily united in choice of one of their own brethren, Deacon Pearson Crosby. The son of Captain Stephen Crosby of Revolutionary fame, his native strength and energy had been early consecrated to Christian service. Uniting with the Baptist church, he had been chosen deacon in 1792, and furnished with credentials four years later, "for to go forth to preach." His preaching had proved so satisfactory that it was now the mind and desire of all "that he should be ordained and qualified to administer the ordinance of the Gospel." Resigning himself wholly to the judgment of his brethren, a council was called, November 7, 1798. Rev. Daniel Dow was invited to sit in council with the Baptist ministers present, and took an active part in the examination of the candidate, who succeeded in satisfying all parties as "to the work of grace on his heart, his call to the ministry and system of doctrine." "Appointed Brother Abel Palmer to preach the sermon, Brother Zenas L. Leonard to make the consecrating prayer, Brother John Rathburn to give the charge, Brother Amos Wells to give the right hand of fellowship, Brother Robert Stanton to make the concluding prayer—all of which was attended to with a degree of becoming solemnity." At the same date, November 8, the church voted to unite with the Stonington Association, and thenceforward maintained connection with that or some similar body and attained an honorable position among its sister churches. Elder Crosby's labors were crowned with abundant success, and in a few years the church

45

was greatly enlarged and strengthened. The religious deadness that had prevailed during the Revolutionary period was succeeded by a general interest and awakening at the beginning of the new century. The Thompson churches with these able and earnest young ministers were well fitted to engage in this work and received large accessions. In the Baptist as in the Congregational society material progress kept pace with spiritual. Aversion to anything like compulsory rate-paying had always made it very difficult to raise a suitable support for the minister. After two-and-a half years of faithful service, Elder Crosby was voted forty dollars in payment. Ebenezer Green, one of the first deacons, had left a legacy of nearly three hundred dollars to the church. Liberal subscriptions from others enabled the society to purchase a farm* in the vicinity for the use and occupation of the minister, which, with an annual salary of eighty dollars, furnished a comfortable support. In 1803, a new meeting-house was erected on land purchased from Noadiah Russel and Jonathan Converse, fronting "on the great turnpike road from Boston to Hartford." More than a hundred men assisted at the raising, May 19, putting up a good frame, "40x42 and 22 feet posts, and having dinner, supper and liquor enough provided." Elder Crosby, Deacons Jonathan Converse and Thomas Day, Captain David Wilson, Joseph Dike and Abel Jacobs, served so efficiently as building committee, that in the latter part of August the new meeting-house was opened to entertain the Sturbridge Association of Baptist churches upon its second session. Pews sold to ready purchasers helped defray the cost of the house. The "former

* "We, the subscribers of the Baptist society find in our minds that it is needful for every religious society for to have a leader or teacher in order for good regulation, and for the keeping up of public worship, and feel ourselves in some good measure free for to provide a place of residence for our minister or teacher near our meeting-house, and furthermore we have concluded and agreed to buy of Deacon Jonathan Converse, his farm that he now lives on, for our minister to live on, so long as he or they shall give good satisfaction to said Baptist society, etc. . . . . . .

Lemuel Knap	$60.00	Elisha Converse	$ 65.00
William Smith	25.00	David Wilson	60.00
Jonathan Converse	60.00	Thomas Ormsbee	30.00
Abraham Green	30.00	Aaron Robinson	60.00
Thomas Day	40.00	John Luther	20.00
Joseph Town, Jun.	30.00	John Keith	30.00
John Burril	20.00	Nathaniel Jacobs	40.00
Simon Burril	10.00	John Pratt	10.00
John Jacobs	50.00	Israel Stockwell	10.00
Asa Jacobs	15.00	Jesse Joslin, Jun.	4.00
Samuel Kimball	10.00	Widow Lidia Woodwart	5.00
Elijah Bates	50.00	David Robinson	14.00
Thomas Davis	30.00	John Bates	133.33
William Town	30.00	Legacy of Dea. Ebenezer Green	298.67

$1,250.00

January 5, 1801."

lot with an old meeting-house on it" was also sold by the committee to John Martin, 2d.

The offshoot on Oxford Gore maintained existence with some difficulty. After the removal of Elder Martin it enjoyed the ministrations of Solomon Wakefield, a member and licentiate of the mother church. He was a pious and godly man, but somewhat eccentric withal, refusing to accept the slightest compensation or even a friendly gift in return for his services, and warmly opposed to Calvinistic doctrines. An earnest and faithful preacher, he did a good work scattering seed in a field remote from other religious influences. Another licentiate of the First Baptist church was John Robbins, who also held meetings in his own neighborhood and obscure school-houses—a light in the far-off corner bordering on Massachusetts and Rhode Island.

Methodists had become quite numerous in the opposite corner of the town, dating back to the early preaching of John Allen and Jesse Lee. A class of six members was formed in the southwest part of Thompson in 1793, closely connected with that of Pomfret, and having often the same leader Joseph Buck, Shubael Cady and Jonathan Allen, were prominent among these early Methodists A notable accession to their ranks was Captain Jonathan Nichols, who opened his house for the reception of the New England Conference, in 1796. This was the sixth Methodist Conference held in New England; the first and last in Windham County. Bishop Asbury, Joshua Hall and many distinguished fathers of Methodism were present, and the sermon preached by the eloquent Bishop was heard with deep emotion by a crowded assembly. A meeting-house was built in what is now the village of West Thompson, about 1800, under the supervision of Captain Nichols. John Gove, Dyer Branch, Joshua Crowell, Elisha Streeter and Thomas Perry, were among the early Methodist preachers in this vicinity.

Schools in Thompson which had hitherto been left to the management of the several districts were brought under more stringent dis cipline by the Legislative enactment of 1798. A State School Fund had now been created by sale of Western Reserve; school societies had been endowed with executive functions, and now each society was obliged to appoint overseers or visitors who should examine the teachers, visit the schools, and assume their general superintendence and direction. In compliance with this enactment, Rev. Daniel Dow, Noadiah Russel and Daniel Wickham were appointed "inspectors." Their report throws some light upon the condition of public schools at this date :—

"The Inspectors of Schools for the town of Thompson, beg leave to present the school society the following report, viz. :—Being impressed with the importance of having our schools subjected to better regulations, and convinced of the wisdom of the law made and provided by the Legislature of Connecticut for that purpose, we cheerfully entered upon the discharge of our office, and took as we trust a faithful view of the present state of the schools in the town of Thompson. We failed not in our determination to respect the law of the State, and we did whatever at the present time in our judgment seemed serviceable to be done. But, the regulating of schools in this place being an object entirely novel, and our work of reformation in this respect being somewhat extensive, we did not find ourselves in a capacity to make all those alterations for the present year, which in other circumstances we should have thought expedient. For the year ensuing, however, we entertain a hope that something more will be accomplished than what we have been able to effect; and, in order that the districts may receive the benefit of the inspection which we have made and of that plan of conduct upon which we have entered, we beg leave to propose the following recommendations :—

We earnestly recommend that for the future it will be generally understood that the inspectors will enter upon a faithful examination of school-masters before their fall schools commence, and that all masters and teachers be requested to make application for that purpose.

We recommend that all masters offering themselves for examination, consider it as a necessary requisite to *be able to read and pronounce English with propriety, to be able to explain the spelling book, and to perform common arithmetic;* that a moral character be considered indispensable; and a *knowledge of English grammar though not absolutely requisite as very desirable.*

We recommend that it be made a serious question with those districts that do not provide for themselves a school-house, nor any suitable and convenient place where the scholars may receive the benefit of instruction, whether they ought to have any certificate *that they have had any school as the law requires, merely because they have hired a master to lose his time.*

We also recommend, considering the large extent of this school society and the requisitions of the law, that the number of visitors be increased so that the burden of inspection be in some way lessened as your wisdom shall direct. And—

Finally, whereas it has seemed good to the Legislature of the State to order by express statute that the visitors insist upon some approved catechism to be taught in every school; that the Bible be read by the higher classes who are able to read therein, at least once a day; and also that it be recommended to all masters and teachers that they conclude the instructions of each day by prayer—we cordially acquiesce in recommending the same. Accordingly, we hereby give notice that all schools are expected to be furnished with, and statedly instructed in The Shorter Catechism as compiled by the Assembly of Westminster divines, provided, nevertheless, if any district shall be better satisfied to make use of Dr. Watts' catechism for children, in the sentiment of which we trust every Christian mind must certainly acquiesce, we recommend that they exercise their own choice to adopt either the one or the other.

The whole is submitted to your wise consideration by

DANIEL DOW.
NOADIAH RUSSEL.
DANIEL H. WICKHAM.

Thompson, May 1, 1799."

This report was accepted and thenceforward teachers were obliged to submit to examination and schools to visitation. Innovation made slow progress. Girls were still expected to spend a part of their time in plying the needle, and were not supposed to know "their letters" thoroughly till they had acquired the art of affixing them upon samplers. Geography was administered in the most economic fashion, the older scholars reading in it instead of other afternoon reading exercise, and

making one or two copies of Morse's Geography suffice for the whole
school. Saturday afternoons they were allowed as a great treat to
read aloud by turns in the County newspaper, received at noon-time
from the weekly courier, before submitting to the catechetic recitation
prescribed by State authority. Mr. Dow was accustomed to visit and
catechize each school in town once or twice during a season—the
church coöperating in the work by requesting "that the brethren
residing in each district should attend together with the pastor at the
catechizing of the schools." Notwithstanding this strictness the
children had their diversions. Spelling schools were frequently held,
and public exhibitions with dialogue and declamation were coming
into fashion. The last day of the school was celebrated with appropriate festivity, the boys contributing pennies for the purchase of
spirit to be made into flip, and the girls bringing home-made dainties.
Captain Copeland, a popular teacher in the South Neighborhood,
was accustomed to close his winter school by a grand *ball* given to the
children in his own house in the evening.

Thompson was greatly favored in the matter of turnpikes. Captain
Jonathan Nichols, Israel Smith and Jacob Dresser were appointed in
1796, "to wait on the committee appointed by the General Assembly
to view and lay out a stage road from Hartford to Massachusetts or
Rhode Island line." Captain Nichols and his associates were incorporated the following year as "The Boston Turnpike Company," and
to him was intrusted the charge of constructing the road. A large
number of men were employed and the work pushed rapidly forward.
The much desired road between Larned's store in the South Neighborhood and Bundy's Mills was now allowed, and carried thence westward to intersect the new turnpike at the stage tavern kept by Abel
Alton. A bridge was built over the French River for the turnpike,
and a new bridge over the Quinebaug at Eaton's Falls for the latter
road. These enterprises made business lively but brought a heavy
burden, increasing the town expenses from seven or eight hundred
dollars a year to over two thousand. A proposal to lay another turnpike from Rhode Island line to Dudley met with very strong opposition from unwilling tax-payers. Lemuel Ingalls, Sampson Howe and
Eleazer Moffat were appointed a committee to view and lay out such
road—Captains Nichols and Davis and Roger Elliott to wait upon
them. The town rejected their report and refused liberty to proceed
in building. Persistent agitation finally overcame opposition and in
1803, the town refrained from choosing an agent to oppose petition.
Elijah Crosby, Joseph Watson, Nathaniel Jacobs, Peleg Corbin,
Thomas Chaffee, Noadiah Russel, John Nichols and associates, were
thereupon incorporated as "The Thompson Turnpike Company," and a

second turnpike was soon opened, intersecting the Boston turnpike on
Thompson Hill. This new road became the main thoroughfare between
Providence and Springfield. Stages were run daily over both lines
and a vast amount of travel passed over them. The tide of business
and population now turned to the hill-top, and soon built up a flourishing village. Pound and horse-sheds were summarily banished to
make way for building lots.

The first "store" on Thompson Hill is believed to have been opened
about 1794 by Daniel Wickham, who married a daughter of Captain
Dresser and purchased of him a building lot* east of the common,
adjoining the pound, where he soon put up a dwelling-house and
business accommodations. His partner, George Keith, purchased the
lot adjoining southward, and built a large house† which he opened for
public entertainment prior to 1798. A handsome house‡ on the
opposite side of the common was built at about the same date by Mr.
Joseph Watson. Enterprising young men from other parts of the
town were drawn to the growing village. John Nichols, 2d, and
Theodore Dwight entered into business partnership, serving their
customers in a new building at the northwest intersection of the turnpikes. Sylvanus and Joseph Coan succeeded to the business of Daniel
Wickham, who removed to Newport, New York. Paul Dudley and
Nathaniel Jacobs bought building lots on the Providence Turnpike,
east of the common, and several houses were built upon them by
Captain Joel Taylor. The first resident physician was Dr. Daniel
Knight, who also received in 1805 the position of postmaster, relieving
Thompsonians from the troublesome necessity of a seven miles' drive
to Pomfret for their letters. Among other improvements a handsome
row of poplar trees adorned the south end of the village.

The new business impulse was felt in all parts of the town. Labor
came into demand; land increased in value. The farms owned by the
heirs of Robert Thompson, were crossed by the Providence turnpike
and brought nearer market. Substantial houses had been built upon
these farms, which were now leased to Daniel Graves, Ebenezer
Covell, Simon Davis, Jonathan Copeland, Jabez Whitmore, Nathaniel
Gregory, Noadiah Russel, Thomas Dike, Hosea Sprague. A fine
farm upon the Quinebaug owned by the same parties was occupied
by Ephraim and Sylvanus Houghton. Thaddeus and Daniel Larned
entered into negotiations for the purchase and succeeded in procuring
a quit-claim deed from its English owners for the sum of fourteen

* Site now occupied by Dr. Lowell Holbrook.
† House still standing and owned by Mr. John Wilkes.
‡ Still occupied by children of Mr. Watson.

thousand dollars, a hundred and twenty years from the date of the
original purchase. These farms were immediately sold out to lessees
and other purchasers—Mr. Thaddeus Larned retaining a fine farm on
the southwest corner for his personal occupation. Many large and
commodious houses were built along the line of the turnpikes, and in
other localities. The various mills in different neighborhoods were
extremely active. Josiah Perry and Elijah Child carried on grinding,
sawing and dyeing on the French River in the extreme north of the
town. Rufus Coburn and Alpheus Corbin purchased the Houghton
farm on the Quinebaug—now a part of New Boston—and set up
clothiery and potash works. Stephen Crosby, a young man of much
mechanical ingenuity, served apprenticeship under Captain Cargill in
the art of clothiery, and established himself at the French River on
the site of the present Grosvenordale, dyeing and pressing cloth, and
grinding grain for a large section of the country. Joseph Joslin,
who returned from Rhode Island to the home farm in 1797, was very
active in setting out trees, laying wall, getting out potash, running
mills, and did much to stimulate improvement in the northeast part of
the town. Through his efforts the first road was laid out over Buck
Hill early in the century. The little hamlet of Brandy Hill, whose
name is believed to have accrued to it from the bursting of a brandy
hogshead, now boasted two taverns kept by Ebenezer Starr and
Charles Cady. It had also two physicians, Doctors Cleveland and
Weaver, and a fine new row of fashionable poplar trees set out by
a new resident—Captain Isaac Davis. His brother Simon Davis
engaged in the practice of law. Thompson's first practicing lawyer,
was George, the second son of General Larned, who after studying
his profession at Canterbury and Litchfield, opened a law office in the
South Neighborhood, in 1801. The foreign trade of Larned and
Mason had been assumed by the Masons. The store and local trade
had passed into the hands of Augustus and Daniel Larned. Daniel,
the third son of General Larned, was a young man of uncommon
energy and business capacity, abreast with the age and ready to do
his part in it. His fellow-townsmen manifested their confidence in
his judgment and ability by intrusting him at a very early age with
important services. Business interests and public convenience demanded
yet a third turnpike, a road from Woodstock through the south part
of the town connecting with the Providence turnpike. By persistent
effort and representation, Daniel Larned succeeded in procuring a
charter for this road, and assumed the oversight of its construction.
Straight-forward, up-and-down roads were now the fashion. The
old circuitous ways winding around to every man's door were con
sidered as much out of taste as out of compass. The building of this

straight road through the granite hill-range of western Thompson proved a most arduous and laborious enterprise, costing not only much money and toil but the valued life of its projector, who fell a victim to disease contracted by over-exertion and exposure, dying in December, 1806, at the early age of twenty-six. The previous October he had served the town as representative, and he was long remembered as one of the most promising and capable young men ever reared in Thompson. The death of his younger brother Otis, who was drowned in crossing the French River after a sudden freshet, also made a deep impression upon the community. So also that of George Keith, the jovial landlord of the new tavern, a leader in sport and revelry as well as in business enterprise, who was suddenly stricken down by disease. The great change wrought in this young man upon his death-bed, his clear conviction of those religious truths which he had previously rejected, his regrets for his wasted life, and his penitent acknowledgments to those young converts whom he had delighted to ridicule, greatly affected the young people of the town, and had much influence in checking the tendency to undue excess in merry-making and deepening the religious interest that prevailed for several years.

Thompson indulged like its neighbors in a *murder* alarm and trial, occasioned by the instantaneous death of a noted inn-keeper while angrily disputing. It was generally thought that " passion was the cause," producing rupture on the brain, and legal investigation acquitted the arraigned offender of overt complicity but sentenced him to a public whipping and branding on the hand, on account of his assumed agency in rousing such angry passions. The giving way of the tavern floor during the funeral of the deceased, precipitating mourners and body into cavernous depths below, suggested untold horrors to terrified spectators and deepened the impression left by this " tragical occurrence." The detection of a fraudulent money coinage at about the same date created also much excitement. An expert from New Hampshire brought down die and tools, and persuaded a simple-minded youth to engage with him in this unlawful art. Good silver money was obtained from a large number of persons under various pretexts, some undoubtedly conniving at its disposition. One good dollar was made to cover a number of spurious coins, which were chiefly expended by an accomplice in buying horses in the new countries. The work was carried on in a hut near King's Pond for a time, and then for greater security removed to a cave in Buck Hill woods, and brought large profits to all concerned till the younger partner brought the hidden deed to light. Intoxicated with the rare delight of plenty of spending money, he came down to Thompson Hill, treating all the loungers at the several stores and taverns, throwing out at each place a new silver dollar in payment. Such unexampled flushness and freeness aroused suspicion and the cheat was discovered. The young man was arrested and packed off to Windham for trial, to the great consternation of many aiders and abettors, who stowed themselves away in old barns and meal-chests until the search subsided. The prisoner evaded trial by forfeiture of bonds, and took a journey out West, whence after many months he returned a sadder and wiser man to his own town and settled down into a sober and law-abiding citizen. His tempter went into banishment and bankruptcy. A few years later a larger gang in the same vicinity engaged in counterfeiting bank-notes which also ended in exposure and punishment, the leaders suffering prolonged imprisonment.

Though business in Thompson was brisk and offered many inducements, it did not check the increasing rage for emigration. Honored names borne by early settlers were no longer represented. Many families had emigrated to Vermont, New York and far Ohio. A number of young men went out soon after 1800 to seek their fortunes in the opening South. James H. Converse after graduation from Yale removed to Tennessee. Elijah Jewett, Jonathan Ellis, Augustus, William and Noadiah Larned, Jacob Dresser and many others, engaged in business in different parts of the south. Some died from country fever; one, David Whitmore, was *murdered* at Augusta, Georgia. Some achieved wealth and good positions, and only returned to their old homes for matrimonial or business partners. The summer visits of these successful adventurers with their dash, display and lavish expenditure caused much fluttering and excitement among the fair belles of the town, and generally resulted in weddings and new departures.

Federalism ruled the councils of the town with little apparent opposition till after the advent of Jefferson's administration. Joseph Joslin, who brought up from Rhode Island a strong proclivity for "State Rights," was one of the leaders in organizing a Republican party, which in 1803 numbered but sixteen voters. Their ranks were now strengthened by Dr. Knight, the Jeffersonian postmaster, and the leading Baptists and Methodists, so that in 1806 they cast ninety-six votes, only thirteen less than the Federalists. A grand Fourth of July celebration was thereupon held at Thompson Hill in honor of this marvelous increase. Dr. Knight, Captain Jonathan Converse and Joseph Joslin were committee. A bower was built upon the common, a band of music procured, and Jesse Jacobs authorized to prepare appropriate toasts. Joseph Wheaton, Esq., was president, and Dr. Knight vice-

46

president of the day. Elder John Nichols read the Declaration of Independence and offered prayer, "and there was a good entertainment, and a good oration delivered by Elder Amos Wells of Woodstock." Under this ministerial patronage the affair passed off with great decency and propriety in spite of the glum looks and disparaging comments of the unsympathizing Federalists. Thompson sent as representatives during its first twenty years, Obadiah Clough, Jonathan Nichols, Paine Converse, William Dwight, Israel Smith, Thaddeus, Henry, George and Daniel Larned, Simon Davis, Joseph Gay, John Jacobs, Jun., Noadiah Russel, Wyman Carroll, and Isaac Davis.

XII.

TOWN AND CHURCH AFFAIRS IN WOODSTOCK. ACADEMY FOUNDED. THIEF-DETECTING SOCIETY. MURDER OF MARCUS LYON. LOSSES AND CHANGES.

WOODSTOCK, during this period, was alert and active. State and town boundaries, change of county seat, the condition of schools and roads, excited much interest. Almost immediately after the close of the war a committee was appointed to confer with Massachusetts respecting the colony line. Noah Mason and Darius Ainsworth were instructed to re-settle Ashford bound "upon the old and established line, without any regard to the proposal of Ashford committee." The lines between Union and Thompson were also perambulated and renewed. At the annual town meeting in 1785, Captain Nehemiah Lyon served as moderator. Jedidiah Morse was chosen town clerk and treasurer; Captains Amos Paine and Ephraim Manning, Daniel Lyon, Thomas May, Noah Mason, Shubael Child, Darius Ainsworth, selectmen; Captain William Lyon, Benjamin Heywood, constables; Ebenezer Smith, collector; David Sprague, John Holbrook, Ebenezer Coburn, Nehemiah Clark, Silas May, Davis Carpenter, General Samuel McClellan, grand-jurors. It was ordered that a decent sign-post and stocks be erected in the most convenient place near the town pound, also, that the selectmen should hire a place for a workhouse. Each society was allowed to provide a pound for its own accommodation. A revival in business was indicated by requests for building spots in various localities. Hezekiah Bugbee had liberty to erect a blacksmith's shop near his dwelling-house on the common under a large black oak; John Flynn to build a black-

smith's shop and coal-house on the highway near his dwelling ; Asahel
Marcy, a cooper's shop on the highway near his residence ; Elijah
Hurlbut a house on the highway.   Elijah Williams of Pomfret, having
purchased a house on Woodstock Hill of Asa Bishop, was allowed by
the proprietors in 1784, " to set up a store " near the same, paying for
land rent the sum of six and eight-pence annually.

This prosperity was somewhat checked by a providential visitation.
A tornado swept through the town, August 23, 1786, reported as
"amazing, awful in its consequences.   It entered the town at the
northwest corner, proceeded in a southeasterly direction about ten
miles, and a quarter of a mile in width, destroying and damaging
everything that lay in its wake.   General estimation of damages as
appraised by nine of the principal gentlemen of the town included
twenty dwelling-houses damaged; sixty-three barns and outhouses
destroyed and damaged; 2,478 apple trees destroyed and other fruit
trees not numbered ; a thousand acres of wood-land damaged; walls,
fences, English grain, standing corn, pulse, hay, wool, flax, household
furniture and lumber, destroyed and damaged."   A petition was preferred for a charitable contribution in behalf of the sufferers.

After many years of seclusion and suffering, Rev. Abel Stiles,
senior pastor in Woodstock, had passed away.   The *New London
Gazette* reports:—

"In him uncommon strength of mind and superior capacity were refined
and brightened by a learned education. His classic knowledge was extensive; his acquisitions in natural and moral philosophy, considerable; in
divinity, eminent. As a preacher, clear, weighty, solemn; hasty in his
natural temper. His soul for many years before his departure waded in
clouds and temptations."

Captain Samuel Chandler—the last surviving son of Colonel John
Chandler (save Thomas of Vermont)—died in 1781.   His distinguished son, Hon. Charles Church Chandler, died suddenly in the
height of professional success and eminence in 1787.   A cotemporary
makes this record:—

"Died on the 8th instant [August], the Honorable Charles Church
Chandler, Esq., of Woodstock, of a malignant cynanche, and on Friday
following, attended by a numerous procession, his remains were interred.
He was an eminent practitioner in the law; he sustained several important
public characters with reputation and ability—as Judge of Probate, representative of the town to the General Assembly, and had been elected a
member for Congress. As a man of genius and ability, he was universally
known and respected; as a man of philanthropy and goodness, he was
universally beloved. He needs not the soft hand of flattery to portray his
virtues; his best and most honorable epitaph is ingraven in the memory of
all who had the pleasure of his acquaintance. A widow with six children
and an aged mother, and numerous more distant relations with the public at
large, regret his loss."

Dr. Thomas B. Chandler, eldest son of Captain William and Jemima (Bradbury) Chandler, one of the earliest champions of Episcopacy in the Colonies, a devoted adherent to the Crown and Church of England, died in 1790, at his home in Elizabethtown, New Jersey. "He possessed an uncommonly vigorous and highly cultivated intellect," and was ranked among the leading men of his generation. His brothers, Captain Samuel and Winthrop Chandler, died the same year. The latter had inherited the fine taste of his mother and was widely celebrated for his skill in portrait painting. The *Worcester Spy*, August 19, 1790, reports him :—

" A man whose native genius has been serviceable to the community in which he resided. By profession he was a house painter; but many good likenesses on canvas shew he could guide the pencil of a limner. He left a manuscript that discovers he had merit as a botanist; many plants, the growth of his native county, are in his manuscript not only well delineated but are accurately and botanically described. The world was not his enemy, but as is too common, his genius was not nurtured on the bosom of encouragement. Embarrassment, like strong weeds in a garden of delicate flowers, checked his usefulness and disheartened the man."

Although the poverty of the times compelled extreme economy in expenditure, Mr. Chandler's merits were not unrecognized at home, and many family portraits of his execution preserve the memory of this first Windham County artist. The portraits of Judge Devotion of Scotland, his wife and children, though crude in execution, give a strong impression of the individuality of each subject, and compare favorably with the ordinary portraits of that date. The widow of Captain Samuel Chandler married Dr. Whitney of Brooklyn. His only surviving brother, Theophilus, still occupied Chandler land within the limits of Thompson.

Samuel McClellan, appointed in 1784 general of the Fifth Brigade, relinquished his mercantile traffic for the care of his land and public duties. His sons, Samuel, William and Lemuel, went out early into the world. John, oldest son by his second wife, Rachael Abbe, fitted for college with Reverends Stephen Williams and Eliphalet Lyman, was graduated from Yale in 1781, studied law with Governor Huntington, and his neighbor Hon. Charles C. Chandler, was admitted to the bar of Windham County, August, 1787, before attaining his majority, and remained for a time at the family homestead, succeeding to the practice of his honored instructor. His early associates and fellow-students, Abiel Holmes and Jedidiah Morse, were graduated in 1783. Holmes, after preaching for a time in Georgia, was installed pastor of the First Church of Cambridge, Mass. ; Morse had distinguished himself as a teacher and compiler of Geography, before accepting a pastoral charge at Charlestown. The brothers of Abiel Holmes, other sons of General McClellan and Deacon Morse, and many other descendants of old Woodstock families, remained in their native town, engaging in trade, farming and mechanical pursuits, and doing their part as good citizens. The old Chandler homestead passed into the hands of Christopher and Philip Arnold, who operated mills and opened a store. Several Providence families, removing to the south part of Woodstock during the war, became permanent and valuable residents. The eccentric Samuel Dexter maintained a residence on Woodstock Hill, journeying often back and forth to attend to business interests in Massachusetts, though never braving the perils of Douglas woods without a shudder. Rufus Kingsley, a later immigrant, was allowed to erect a shop, sufficient to inclose his clothiery works. Jesse Bolles of Ashford, engaged in shoe manufacture at Quasset. This little hamlet, quaintly perpetuating Woodstock's aboriginal designation, was favored with flourishing pottery works, established in 1793, by Thomas Bugbee, Jun. The clay deposit was found available for finer purposes than chimney-building and stone-cementing. With the aid of a skilled artisan, Mr. Bugbee succeeded in constructing a great variety of needful pottery ware—milk-pans, pudding-pots, jars, jugs, mugs and inkstands—which were sold all over Windham County. All the store-keepers in the several towns patronized Mr. Bugbee, and his pottery cart was one of the most familiar and useful institutions of the period when tin-peddlers' carts were yet far in the future. The demand for milk-pans alone kept the kiln burning through the summer. After preparing the clay by grinding, moistening and kneading, each separate piece was fashioned into shape by hand and turning wheel, sized with a glazing mixture and subjected to a week's baking. Six bakings were usually accomplished in a summer, turning out in the aggregate some five thousand pieces, including perhaps two thousand milk-pans. The coarser parts of the clay were made into brick which found a ready market. Mr. Peregrine White, of East Woodstock, greatly distinguished himself in the construction of clocks, with cases six and seven feet high and the face of a full moon upon the dial-face. Elijah Williams' store and other business enterprises gave life to Woodstock Hill, which as the place for general town meetings, public trainings and gatherings, took precedence of the other villages. Town meetings were conducted with all their ancient formality, being opened by prayer and the reading of the law for their regulation. On the day of the annual spring election for governor and deputies, a sermon was preached in the meeting-house by one of the standing clergy. Deacon Morse, as town clerk, delighted in recording text and name of preacher, often characterizing the sermon as "excellent," "suitable," "very suitable." Party spirit sometimes raged fiercely in these meetings. It was the custom for voters to express acquiescense in a nomination by remaining on their seats, and only rising when they wished to express opposition to a candidate. It was said that the Rev. Mr. Lyman was once so carried away by zeal against a nominee of doubtful orthodoxy as not only to rise up and violently declaim against him, but actually to lay hands upon his less excitable brother minister, Rev. Stephen Williams, and "fairly lift him up from his seat and make him vote against the gentleman nominated,"—a report which called out a furious onslaught from Judge Swift. Mr. Lyman denied the charge, adducing certificates from thirty-eight freemen present at the meeting, who *did not see* the transaction, which was rebutted by the direct and positive testimony of *fifteen* respectable citizens that they *did see it*, and so the question was left unsettled.

In religious affairs there was much agitation and rivalry. Baptists, Methodists and Universalists disputed the field with the three established churches. Despite these opposing influences and the prevailing religious declension, Woodstock's First church and society maintained its leading position and even gained in strength and numbers. Many influential families were connected with this church. Mr. Lyman was a resolute and aggressive leader, a staunch supporter of established institutions, and the Federal and Ecclesiastic constitutions. His boldness in refusing his pulpit to Oliver Dodge, and in opposing the election of irreligious candidates, subjected him to vexatious prosecution and a fierce assault in the columns of the *Windham Herald*, but he was comforted and sustained by the approval of a majority of his own people and the cordial sympathy of ministerial brethren. The worthy deacons of the church—Jedidiah Morse and William Skinner—continued to exercise their office with much fidelity and acceptance, their exemplary conversation, benevolence and public spirit giving them much influence in the community. Deacon Morse served at this date as clerk and treasurer for town, society, and south proprietary, justice of peace, notary public, and was usually sent as deputy to the Assembly. The first society was at this time much engrossed in repairing its meeting-house, "which being by Divine Providence, much shattered and broken by thunder and lightning," April 30, 1787, necessitated immediate attention. Elias Mason, Matthew Bowen, and Amos Paine, society committee, were impowered to procure proper materials and workmen. " *Voted*, that the turret of the meeting-house be all taken down and the place where it stands boarded and shingled up as the other parts of the roof." The work, however, did not go forward. More thorough repairs were needed; pews and body seats must be taken up, and as a number of the pews had now no legal owner or proprietor, it was proposed that all the pew-holders should give up their claim to the society. A vote "that those persons who

have legal right to the pews take them up at their own expense and
replace them in good order" was revoked, and the matter intrusted to
"a judicious, disinterested committee, to ascertain the number of pews
in the meeting-house which have now legal owners according to the
first grant or stipulation of the pews. . . . And to abide their
judgment thereon." Thomas Grosvenor, Daniel Larned and Amasa
Sessions, appointed to this service, met at the house of David
Williams, July 6, 1789, and having heard and fully considered the
difficulties as stated, and the several town and parish votes at the
time of building and repairing said house, were of opinion :—

"That the Grantees of the floor or ground whereon to erect pews, their
heirs and assigns, are the legal owners of the pews they have erected, and
[which] are now standing thereon; and do adjudge and determine that they
have right to continue their ownership upon making such repairs in uniform-
ity with other parts of the house as the original grantees were expected to
do and did . . . . or otherwise that the right shall revert back to said
society."

This point being settled, in the following March it was voted "to
go on to repair the meeting-house"—Captains Joseph Peake and
Hezekiah Bugbee, committee—the proprietors of the pews on the
lower floor to advance their proportion of the cost according to the
dignity of their pews, and four new pews to be built in place of
the hindmost body seats. This action raising uneasiness in the
minds of some individuals, another meeting was warned to see if they
would order further repairs which were much wanted, and "also new
color the outside, which it was thought would be a great saving," and
also if any persons have any reasonable objections that they might
offer the same, "that if possible the society may be united and harmonious; which is greatly to be desired in repairing the house of
God." The desired harmony not appearing, and a majority declining
to accept the report of the committee, the work was again delayed,
and no thorough repairs accomplished. Four new pews were built in
time on the ground floor, which was repaired under the direction of
Captains Joseph Peake and William Lyon; the singers had liberty to
alter the gallery in order to accommodate said singers with separate
seats; Jedidiah Kimball, William Chapman, Amos Paine, Alvin
Peake, Sanford Holmes, Samuel Torrey, Benjamin Lyon, Jun., and
Israel Williams, had each of them liberty to build a pew in the back
part of the gallery; *blacks* were allowed the use of the hindmost seat
in the front gallery; Samuel Torrey, Daniel Bottom and David
Williams, Jun., were appointed to act as choristers for the congregation when assembled, and in 1795, the body of the meeting-house was
painted white and the roof also painted. The annoyance caused by

the irruption of Mr. Dodge called out the following vote, April, 1796 :—

" That for the future the society choose a suitable person to keep the key of the meeting-house, to sweep it, &c.—and to open the doors thereof at any time and at all times on Sabbath days and other public days, such as town meetings, society meetings, public Fasts, Thanksgivings, public lectures appointed by the pastor of said society, and at no other time without the voice or consent of the society."

Mr. John Bartholomew was first appointed to this responsible office. Deacon Morse having served the society faithfully for twenty years as clerk and treasurer, his resignation was accepted with suitable acknowledgments. William Bowen, David Williams, Jun., Israel Williams and Amos Paine, succeeded successively to this office. In 1802, a new stone pound was erected, and also a new sign-post and stocks, the post "to be square and painted white and the stocks to be painted red." The society was also called to consider "some method to repair the horse-block." In 1806, the society was asked to agree with some suitable person to ring the Academy bell, the use of which was now allowed them, and joined with the North society in procuring mortuary accommodations. The surplus rate collected for the latter object was divided between the societies, "to be appropriated for the use and benefit of promoting singing."

Mr. Johnson continued in charge of the church in East Woodstock after the decease of Mr. Stiles, but his usefulness was impaired by unpleasantness in his domestic relations. Whispered insinuations resulted in a ministerial investigation which acquitted Mrs. Johnson of overt offense, but recommended greater prudence. Farther developments confirming the wisdom of the ancient adage, that " Cæsar's wife should be above suspicion," a council was again called to consider the question of dismissal. This was at first refused, but it appearing on farther evidence that there had been some collusion between husband and wife, Mr. Johnson was censured " for not acting with that simplicity that becomes a gospel minister, and betraying a degree of human infirmity that was to be lamented," and formally dismissed from his pastoral office in Woodstock. Happily for the church it was soon able to extend a call to "a very worthy character," Mr. William Graves of Hatfield, who was ordained and installed, August 31, 1791, his pastor, Dr. Joseph Lyman, preaching the ordination sermon. Few events disturbed the even tenor of his faithful pastorate. The church maintained its ground if it did not make advances. Its first deacons, Caleb May and Nehemiah Lyon, were·succeeded by Elias and Charles Child, chosen respectively in 1782 and 1789. Singing received the usual attention and was early noted for its uncommon excellence.   The house of worship required little attention for many years.

The singing in West Woodstock or New Roxbury society, was less easily regulated.   Society concurred with church in 1782 in voting :—

" That inasmuch as there are but few psalm-books amongst us, the singing be carried on by reading the portion line by line till the last singing in the afternoon, and then a whole verse to be read at a time : also, That Stephen Johnson and David Perrin be added to the choristers already appointed (*i. e.*, Lemuel Child, Joseph Carpenter, Ebenezer Paine, Abraham Perrin)."

In 1785, a meeting was called to hear the request of a number of the inhabitants, " to see if ye church and congregation will agree as to the mode of singing, whereby they may all rest easy," and after "largely being debated on," voted :—

" That ye mode of singing for the future, that the deacon read the portion line by line in the forenoon; and in the afternoon to read a verse at a time; except the Double verse Tunes; and them to be sung through without reading; and that to be the standing rule till ordered otherwise by the committee."

November 17, 1785, also voted :—

" To repair the meeting-house on the whole of ye outside; To choose a committee to prepare stuff to cover the meeting-house.   The committee chosen are as follows, viz. :— Nathaniel Marcy, Elijah Perrin, David Perrin, Ebenezer Smith, Jacob Child, Henry Bowen, Noah Mason, Ebenezer Coburn, Jun., Eli Bruce, Asa Goodell, Amos Lyon, Ashael Clark.   3. To have ye body-seats below in ye meeting-house made into pews both on ye men's and women's sides—except ye two foremost seats on each side."

It was farther voted at an adjourned meeting to sell the appropriated pew-ground to the highest bidder, each buyer building his pew thereon within a year from date of purchase.

These votes were carried out with much difficulty.   The "great separation" from the pastor and established church left "a very heavy burden upon a small number of people."   Captain Nathaniel Marcy, Captain David Perrin and Stephen Paine, were deputized to inform Mr. Williams that notwithstanding he had considered his people sundry times with respect to his salary, yet remaining a broken people, and attempting to repair the meeting-house with other extra charges, would make it extremely difficult to pay him his full salary. Mr. Williams responded by remitting five pounds of his salary "in case the society will take speedy care to settle arrearages, and seasonably to get me a supply of fire-wood."   Under these circumstances the society was compelled to reconsider its vote to prepare stuff for the needful repairs, and content itself with an assessment of forty pounds to be expended by Lieutenants Mason and Peabody, and Ensign Elijah Bugbee, in the best and most prudent manner.   Pew-ground was sold to Captain Benjamin Howard, Zephaniah Lincoln, Sylvester

47

Smith, Caleb Bugbee, William Pierce, Noah Mason, Jesse Cutler, Isaiah Perrin. In 1791, it was voted that the meeting-house shall be painted when finished fit—the roof with a Spanish Brawn; the sides and ends with a stone color so called, and money granted to complete the same, the former grant being insufficient.

Many other burdens oppressed these western residents. A vote to build a new pound upon Ensign Bugbee's land excited much opposition. Upon petition from Thomas, Lemuel and Elias Child, Elijah Perry, Caleb and William Bugbee and other aggrieved parties, the question was reconsidered. A committee was chosen to discourse with the widow Lydia Morse, to see if leave could not be obtained to set the pound upon her land and not succeeding, asked the privilege of Rev. Stephen Williams, who " had no particular objections in his mind against it," and a vote was passed to build the pound upon his land fronting the road and adjoining land of Lieutenant Peabody. Noah Mason, John Goodell and Deacon John Morse were appointed a committee to procure or build a carriage for the decent burial of the dead. The regulation of the six school districts involved much debate and trouble. Each district had its one committeeman to hire its teachers and collect rates for payment, but the choice of this committee and the general ordering of affairs was referred to the society. After long delay and many fruitless efforts, the southwest district succeeded in accomplishing a school-house in 1790, receiving liberty to tax itself for that object—Ebenezer Stoddard, Daniel Perry and William Bugbee, committee. The West and Northwest districts, taking into consideration the importance and necessity of schooling and their disconnected situation, obtained leave to be united in one entire district in order that they might build a proper school-house in some suitable place to accommodate the whole of the inhabitants—but when immediately after the question was put if the united district should have liberty to *tax* itself for building such school-house, to the great bewilderment and disappointment of the petitioners, " it passed in the negative." Part of these inhabitants were afterwards reinstated into the Northwest district. The east centre district was severely tried at the same date in the conduct of its committee :—

" 1. The mode and method he took to sustain his said office. 2. His not giving the district full warning as is usual for a district meeting in order to choose a schoolmaster, so that said district might get the knowledge where the moneys lay, and how much and in what position, that they might conduct these matters prudently. 3. His hiring a master without the consent of said district, and agreeing to pay the master *in neat stock at a future day*, and putting our moneys into his own pocket. 4. His not attending the school meeting though duly notified."

Notwithstanding these charges, " the reasonable request" of Elijah Bugbee, Elijah Perrin, William Ainsworth, Rhodes Wilkinson, Nathan

Abbot and William Johnson, "that he might be dropped and another chosen in his room and stead," was dismissed after a "lengthy hearing." Thaddeus Gage, Amos Shumway, John Fox, Alfred Marcy, Peleg Corbin, Marvin Clark, Simeon Wight, Levi Perrin, Pardon Morse, Hannah Bugbee, Lois Ainsworth, Apphia Perrin, appear as teachers during this period.

Uneasiness respecting Mr. Williams increased the embarrassments of the society. "The infirmities by reason of advanced age of that venerable person who had ever been dear" to them, made his services less acceptable to the congregation, and new certificates daily came in till it seemed likely that few would be left to bear the burden of his support. Negotiations from time to time, conducted with rare courtesy and consideration on both sides, led to no specific result. Repeated deductions of salary were received with appropriate thanks for the kindness and condescension. In 1790, Mr. Williams agreed to take up with twenty-five pounds and half his fire-wood in case the society procured a suitable colleague; four years later he sends the following letter:—

"*Friends and Brethren:*—Understanding by your committee that some appear desirous of introducing a young minister among us as an assistant to me in the ministry; this is to inform that if you see fit to introduce a young gentleman of good character, of the standing order, of a liberal education; I consent to drop the salary for the term such supply shall be afforded; and wishing peace, truth and righteousness may be and abound among us, I subscribe your aged pastor. STEPHEN WILLIAMS.
March 17, 1794."

The society declining to act upon this suggestion, Mr. Williams continued in charge till his death in the following spring. Sustaining through life "a very amiable and worthy character," he died in a good old age, much esteemed and respected. "A good classical scholar, a serious practical preacher," he held a high position among his ministerial brethren. Mrs. Martha (Hunt) Williams had preceded her husband a few years. Their sons Stephen and Timothy were graduated from Yale College in 1783 and 1785, and both had studied for the ministry. The oldest son Andrew, after teaching school for a time in Cambridge, settled for life on the paternal homestead.

Several years passed before the settlement of a second minister. Arrearages due to the estate of Mr. Williams were made up after some delay and difficulty. Renewed attempts were made to procure the relinquishment of pew-ground so that a fund might be secured and the meeting-house thoroughly repaired. During this interval the pulpit was supplied by various licentiates, viz.:—Messrs. Timothy Williams, Daniel Dow, Averill, Witter, Thatcher, Watson and Wight. The preaching of Amos G. Thompson was much liked by some while others made objections "on account of his professing to be of the

Methodist order or principle." In 1799, it was agreed by nearly an universal vote to call Mr. Stephen Williams to settlement. Amos Lyon, Timothy Perrin, Elias Child, Ebenezer Smith, Jacob Child, Haviland Morris, Henry Martin, David Perrin, Philip Howard, in behalf of the society, offered suitable terms upon the express condition that the relation should terminate upon six months notice from either party. Expressing "affectionate gratitude for this testimony of regard in requesting him to settle amongst so respectable and numerous a people in the place of his nativity," and in the pulpit so long filled by his reverend and honored father, Mr. Williams felt constrained to return a negative answer. More urgent entreaty and liberal offers failing to secure his acceptance, the society made choice of another fellow-parishioner, Mr. Alvan Underwood, a recent graduate from Brown University, who was ordained and installed to great public satisfaction, May 27, 1801, ministers from Woodstock and neighboring towns officiating in the services. John Fox, Elias Child, 2d, and Philip Howard, represented the society on this occasion. John Austin, Parker Morse and John Paine served as committee "to attend on and see to seating people, and to keeping order and regularity in the assembly of spectators."

The meeting-house question now obtaining more exclusive consideration, a committee was appointed to look into the matter of ownership and make a plan of the dimensions of pews to be built. Two pews on the ground floor and twelve in the galleries were laid down by committee, to be held on the same footing as the previous wall pews, agreeably with the original vote passed in 1749. After further delay and complications these pews were erected and formally made over to the subjoined lawful owners, viz.:—on the ground floor one to Luther Baldwin, one to Abraham W. and John Paine. Gallery pews. 1. Taken back by society. 2. Thomas Corbin. 3. John Howlett. 4. John R. Wilson, Benj. Lyon, 3d. 5. William Fargo, David Allen, 3d. 6. Andrew Williams. 7. Charles Smith. 8. Walter Bicknell, William Shepard. 9. Daniel Lyon. 10. Solomon Corbin. 11. A. Abbot Phillips, A. Perrin. 12. Walter Bicknell and William Shepard. A new pound was now built on land of John Fox, Esq. A four-wheeled carriage or hearse was next procured together with a good harness for the same, and a suitable building erected wherein to deposit said carriage. In 1806, Wareham Lyon was chosen sexton; Abraham W. Paine, to have charge of carriage-house, carriage, harness and palls. Dr. Haviland Morris was now chosen clerk; John Fox, treasurer; Parker Morse, collector; Alfred Marcy, David Perrin, Stephen Johnson, committee. Darius Barlow, Danforth Lyon and Benjamin Lyon were also chosen to serve the society as choristers.

The Baptist church in West Woodstock had meanwhile suffered many vicissitudes. "After a long day of desertion and heavy trials," the Lord was pleased to awaken some souls "by means of the uncommon darkness" in May, 1780,* which resulted in a general revival of religion, many converts, and a large addition to the membership of the church. Jesse Bolles, Thomas Bugbee and other newly received members were residents of the First society of Woodstock. David Bolles and John Morse, the active and fervent deacons of the church, had "come to a stand" about granting certificates in compliance with the law, and several of their brethren were thus included in the rate list of the above society and exposed to distrainment. The Baptist brethren, after largely debating the subject of giving certificates finally concluded:—

"That we could not give them, for we believe that no one body of people have right of jurisdiction over another in religious matters; and therefore cannot comply with the demands of our Pedo-baptist brethren and neighbors in demanding certificates as they say according to law; but we are willing to do all that we can with a good conscience in the matter, and therefore passed the following vote, viz.: That we will send to our above described neighbors the names of our brethren and friends who belong to our society that live within the limits of their lined society, in order to take off their grand plea for taxing our brethren, as that they might know who they are, i. e., Christopher Whipple, William Earl, Paul Tew, Elijah, Isaiah and George Lyon, William Underwood, Green Rogers, William Spears, Thomas Bugbee, Zephaniah Cole, Abner Harris, William Martin, Benjamin and Noah Chaffee, Jesse Bolles, John Green, Moses and Peleg Easterbrook, Prentice Chubb, William Apley, David Sprague, John Bolster."

Deacons Bolles and Morse, Jacob Leonard and Silas Corbin, were then appointed to inform the First society what they had done. That body had previously voted to exempt these Baptists from rates, provided they would produce certificates according to law, and after long debate with the delegates the following form of a certificate was proposed and accepted:—

"It is hereby certified that the above-named persons statedly attend worship with us on Lord's days and contribute to the support of the Elders in the

* Joseph Joslin of Thompson thus reports "the dark day" in his cotemporary journal:—"1780, May 15. Dull, thick air. 16. Sun red and dry and very thick air. 17. Very thick, close air, as it were to the bottom round, sun red and moon, very dry now, very smoky. 18. Cloudy and warm. 19. Now let not this day be forgot. In the morning it was cloudy and we laid a little wall. I see the sun in the morning. 8 o'clock, I guess, it rained a fine shower or two; then we went to work. Wind S. West. (Some say the wind was in every point, but not to my knowledge). About 10 o'clock it seemed to come up from the southwest and looked dark, and I expected it would rain in a minute or two, and it grew darker and darker. We worked, laid wall till we could not see to range the wall ten rods right. We went into the house, and it was about 12, it was reconed. The fire shined like night. They light a candle for to get dinner. The air or clouds looked like brass, yellow, and things too, I guess. About 12 was the darkest. About one it grew lighter. It grew lighter once and then was darker; rained a shower at night. 20. That night was as much darker than usual as the day, but I see it not. Was asleep."

Baptist society in Woodstock. Certified by us. JOHN MORSE, deacon. DAVID BOLLES, deacon."

This persecution, as it was called, increased the energy and zeal of the church, so that it reported to the Warren Association in 1781 a membership of a hundred and forty, and flourished greatly for a season. Embodying, however, many discordant and insubordinate elements, "a great fire of contention" presently broke out. Incited at first by a complaint lodged against one of the church members by a member of the Congregational church, it soon enflamed the whole church. There were difficulties and disputes between Elder Ledoyt and some of his members, and many councils and church meetings, until a number of the church withdrew, and "set up by themselves in an adjoining town and called themselves the church," and at the request of their pastor, April 24, 1790, proceeded to vote his dismission and "recommended him to the charity of their sister churches in particular and the world in general as an able and faithful minister in good standing."* A council called the following July under the direction of Thomas Baldwin and Isaac Backus, failed to heal the breach. Elder Ledoyt removed with his family to Newport, N. H., "leaving his flock in a very broken and divided condition." A colored brother, Samuel Webster, fervent in spirit if weak in knowledge and wisdom, labored as an evangelist for a season and received many into the membership of the church. In 1796, the church reported itself to the Warren Association with Robert Stanton, a licentiate from Stonington, as preacher, and three years later he was ordained its pastor. A rough, ignorant man, his labors were not without some fruit. Nearly fifty were added to the church during his nine years ministry, and a movement made for replacing the barn-like meeting-house by a more suitable structure. This work was completed in 1806 after the return of Elder Ledoyt, who found a door opened by God in his providence, "whereby he must return and labor with the church of his youth." A testimonial from the church of Newport certified the value of his service in that vicinity and recommended him as a faithful brother and able minister of the New Testament. He found the Woodstock church still suffering from the evil effects of long dissension, nor did his earnest efforts restore the ancient harmony. Nehemiah Underwood and Samuel Crawford served faithfully as deacons of this church.

A Baptist church was gathered in the southeast part of Woodstock, June 29, 1792. Services were held in the house of Jesse Bolles. Representatives of the Baptist churches in Stonington, Thompson and

* Manuscript of Jedidiah Morse, Esq., 1798.

Hampton, were present. Minutes of the conferences of the brethren who had summoned the Council, together with their Covenant and Articles of Faith, and a relation of their minds towards each other, were heard and approved, and they were received into the fellowship of Baptist churches. August 3, Brother Amos Wells was called to take charge of this church as a particular watchman or elder, and six days later " was regularly set apart by ordination." Mr. Wells was a native of Stonington, a man of piety and eloquence, much engaged in the establishment of religious liberty. Under his faithful administration the church gained rapidly. A number of brethren from Brookfield, Mass., were received into fellowship A decent meeting-house was soon made ready for occupation on land given by Mr. Bolles, and when the Stonington Association met with the church in 1795, it found a membership of seventy-six, and " it was a good time with them." This auspicious opening was not without its clouds. Some scrupulous members stopped going with the church, alleging as cause :—

" 1. Their taking in persons without relating their experiences before the church. 2. Things being carried in the church by the major vote. 3. The restoring Brother —— upon the confession which he made."

The church after much deliberation and prayer for wisdom to direct, and long labor with the aggrieved parties, thus answered allegations :—

" 1. As to receiving into our fellowship the Brookfield brethren, we think we did it upon good grounds, as they first came into covenant among themselves, and then drew a petition to this church requesting our particular fellowship . . . . . and as our Elder and a number of our brethren heard all of them give a relation of their experience, we thought, and still think, we were in duty bound to receive them as we did. 2. We think the church must of necessity govern by a majority. 3. As Brother —— confessed all the church requested him to, we thought in all good conscience we ought to forgive and restore him."

Unable to satisfy the delinquents, the church " with sorrow of heart " was forced to withdraw from them the hand of fellowship. Other offenses demanded more summary " dealing " and punishment. Many young men were called to account " for forsaking the church and going into the world," dancing, playing cards, " assembling with the vain world in the ball chamber " and still more flagrant offenses. Some having seen the evil of such practices confessed and were restored, while others rejected admonition and were finally cut off. In 1802, the church after conference and deliberation instituted a committee to act in behalf of the church in inquiring into scandalous reports, attend to difficulties between members, and settle them if possible by gospel measures, and to hear and advise any member that might be at loss about his duty. Deacons Robert Baxter and Jesse

Bolles, James, Jeremiah and Childs Wheaton, Charles Chandler, Robert Aplin, Artemas Bruce and Thomas Bugbee were appointed to serve for one year in this capacity. In 1801, the Third church of Ashford was received into fellowship as a branch of the church; brethren in Pomfret and Killingly were recognized in 1803 as a branch of this Second Woodstock church. Deacon David Bolles of Ashford was one of its early friends and counsellors, and often attended its service. In 1801, the church considered the propriety of setting him apart by ordination and appointed a committee to lay the matter before the next Association. That body "fell in with the request," and "accordingly Deacon David Bolles was regularly set apart to the work of the ministry by the Stonington Association, October 20—21." Deacon Jesse Bolles, soon after removing to Providence to fill the office of steward for Brown University, and Deacon Baxter requesting a dismission, it was thought expedient to supply their place. The brethren having brought forward their votes in writing, August 20, 1803, it was found that they had made choice of William H. Manning and Childs Wheaton. Deacon Manning was now elected church clerk in place of Thomas Bugbee, Jun. In 1806, the Pomfret Branch was recognized as an independent church. A committee, appointed to attend to all matter of labor with the Brookfield Branch, found "that the greater part of them had moved to distant parts, but a small number still remained steadfast," and were retained in membership. Deacons Baxter and Manning, Henry Wells, Edmond Chamberlain, Thomas Bugbee, Jeremiah and James Wheaton, Charles Chandler and Augustus Bolles, continued to serve as church committee.

The care of schools long borne by the located ecclesiastical societies was remitted to school societies about 1795. The south society met in the meeting-house, October 19, Jesse Bolles, moderator, Jonathan Morse, clerk, Thomas Bugbee, collector. Benjamin Lyon, Jun., Amos Paine, John Albe, Thomas Lyon, Jun., Jedidiah Kimball, were chosen committee. Elias Child was first clerk and treasurer of the North society. Ephraim May, collector. Although the character of the public schools was gradually improving with increasing outlay and more thorough oversight and inspection, they were still very inadequate to the need. Teachers were poorly qualified and the range of instruction very limited. Occasional private schools maintained a few weeks or months in the several villages were no great benefit, and the cost of sending their children to the academies of Plainfield or Canterbury was beyond the means of the great mass of the population. The successful establishment of such institutions in other towns incited the envy and emulation of the enterprising citizens of Woodstock.

General McClellan and his sons, Mr. Lyman, Deacon Morse, David Holmes and other influential men, believed it practicable, to support a High School among themselves, and after careful discussion brought the question before the public. At a meeting of the proprietors of the south half of Woodstock, January 12, 1801, liberty was granted to the proprietors of an academy, to set a building on the common, north of the meeting-house, near Major Elijah Williams' land for said purpose. How to raise funds for an academy building was the next problem. There were no rich men in those days able to spare their thousands for such an object, but there was a deep sense of the need of the community and an earnest spirit of self-sacrifice. It was proposed that thirty-two men should each contribute the worth of a hundred dollars. "Priest Lyman," having himself headed the list, rode on horseback all about the town and by persuasion and argument readily secured the requisite subscribers. An efficient building committee was appointed and the work begun with much heartiness. As the spring opened farmers brought in their best white oak timber, many selling it for half its market value in their eagerness to help forward the academy. It was said there were boards enough brought in to build a shed from Woodstock to Providence. The corner-stone was laid with appropriate rejoicing. The day of the raising was marked by one of the "notable meetings" for which Woodstock was ever famous. Men, women and children from all parts of the town, together with volunteers from Thompson, Killingly, Pomfret, Brooklyn, Ashford and even distant Hampton, flocked to this "Hill of Science," and assisted in the work. "So great was the crowd that a good slice of the common was filled with people, ox-teams and horses.* Old men, too feeble to do heavy work, kept their sons supplied with framing-pins," which were carried about by their grandsons. Major David Holmes particularly distinguished himself by coolness and dexterity, volunteering to be raised up with the eighty-foot timber to adjust the frame of the steeple. The front door-sill being left some ten feet above the ground, the farmers turned out again in a few days with seventy ox teams, and labored all day gratuitously, hauling dirt in front of the building—men too old to shovel smoothing it with their hoes. Under such favorable auspices the building went on prosperously. An ample doorstep was dragged up from the old hearth-stone quarry and a bell of five hundred pounds weight carted from Norwich. A committee sent meanwhile to New Haven had secured for principal Thomas Williams of Pomfret, who was graduated from Yale College in 1800, with a high reputation for scholarship and acuteness. "The event of

* Historical Address of Clarence W. Bowen.

48

establishing a seminary of learning, superior to any other which had been previously enjoyed," was deemed worthy of special commemoration, and on February 4, 1802, the new building was formally opened and dedicated. Suitable addresses were made by John McClellan, Esq., and Mr. Lyman, the latter closing with these words addressed to the prospective teacher :—

"I do therefore on this occasion in the name of the Trustees, and with the approbation of the Proprietors, commit to you, Mr. Williams, the key to the ACADEMY and the office of PRECEPTOR."

Mr. Williams entered upon his duties the next day with nearly an hundred pupils, gathered from all parts of Woodstock and neighboring towns. Board was obtained in the best families for five shillings a week. A petition from John McClellan, Esq., secured from the Assembly in the spring an enactment, that Samuel McClellan, Eliphalet Lyman, Nehemiah Child, Ebenezer Smith, William Potter, Hezekiah Bugbee, Ichabod Marcy, Jesse Bolles, David Holmes and others, who are or hereafter may be proprietors of Woodstock Academy, are erected and made a body corporate, with needful power for its well-ordering and governing. Five trustees annually appointed by the proprietors were to superintend the affairs of the corporation. Mr. Williams retained his office for only a single term and was succeeded by another brilliant son of Windham County, Hezekiah Frost of Canterbury. Jason Parke, his usher, was also from Canterbury. Aaron Dutton, Seth Norton and Phinehas L. Tracy, youthful Yale graduates, followed in quick succession, neither of them remaining long enough to give character or stability to the school. Despite this drawback, interest and attendance were well maintained. A public exhibition every autumn increased its popularity. Teachers and pupils formed in line at the academy and marched with much ceremony into the church. Declamations and orations were followed by entertaining dialogues. On one occasion an elaborate tragedy was performed, embracing fifteen or twenty performers, and Philadelphia's future surgeon was desperately wounded by a pistol shot and carried off the stage by armed soldiers to the intense delight of the applauding audience. Most of the young people of the town enjoyed the privilege of at least a term's attendance at the Academy. Charles Morris, afterwards commodore in the United States Navy, Dr. George McClellan, the distinguished surgeon (son of James McClellan), William Larned Marcy, Secretary of State, and governor of the Empire State, Ebenezer Stoddard, lieutenant-governor of Connecticut, and representative to Congress, David Young, judge, and Congressional representative, Prescott and David Hall, distinguished in law, art and literature, were among its early pupils. Yale College gave it counsel and encouragement. A literary association, called the "Society of Columbian Brothers," was soon formed in connection with the school, each proprietor contributing a number of books as a foundation for its library. A Fourth of July Celebration was held under its patronage in 1803, when Mr. Jason Parke delivered an eloquent oration, whose closing flights must have deeply thrilled the youthful Columbians :— "If you would maintain your Independence inviolate, be prepared for Peace or War. With UNION for your motto extend with one hand the OLIVE BRANCH OF PEACE, and with the other brandish the FLAMING SWORD OF POWER. Be resolved that you will never behold the AMERICAN EAGLE checked in its towering flight and *unfledged*, to decorate a BRITISH CORONET or a FRENCH CAP with its brilliant plumes, but that your INDEPENDENCE shall be commensurate with your *existence*." A library of a hundred volumes had been formed in the First Society a few years previous. The United Lyon Library still flourished in the North Society, numbering some two hundred and fifty volumes. The West Woodstock residents procured a valuable library in 1806.

Improved traveling facilities brought business and gave impetus to the town. Turnpike projects had been carried through after the customary contests. The Norwich and Woodstock Turnpike, with branch to Sturbridge, the turnpike running direct through Thompson to Providence, were great accommodations. Elijah Williams' establishment had now passed into the hands of Mr. William Bowen, whose tavern under its row of poplar trees, received a large share of public patronage. Major Williams' advertisement exhibits the varied capabilities of this business location :—

"For Sale, a few rods north of the meeting-house in the First Society in Woodstock, A PLEASANT COUNTRY SEAT, situated on the great road from Hartford to Boston, and on the road from Providence to Albany; with a large dwelling-house and barn thereon, also a large merchant's store, nailor's and cooper's shop, with tools complete for each. Also, a large convenient slaughter-house for killing and packing provisions. . . . . . It is a very good stand for trade. The house is used as a tavern and has been ever since it was built, etc.
WOODSTOCK, *March* 6, 1797."

Major John, son of Elijah Williams, was for a time partner with Mr. Bowen. Jedidiah Kimball, Chester Kendall and Amos Paine were also engaged in mercantile traffic. Woodstock Hill had now its lawyer—John McClellan, Esq., who had removed hither in 1796, marrying a few months later, Faith Williams, the only daughter of Hon. William Williams of Lebanon. Dr. Ephraim Carroll of Thompson, was established in medical practice in the south end of the street. Dr. Lathrop Holmes engaged in trade and medical practice, Elias Childs and Charles Webb opened a store in West Woodstock. Increasing development in this part of the town had raised the question of division. A number of westward residents, viz.:—Ashael Corbin, David Howard, Joel Gage, Daniel Lyon, Jun., Caleb Bugbee, Daniel Perry, Elias Child, Andrew Williams, Ebenezer Stoddard, Abishai Washburn, Luther Baldwin, Parker Morse, William Shepard, "in great measure divested of the privilege of free and legal inhabitants of the town of Woodstock, and a participation in the election of town officers, as well as the General in the State Legislature, owing to their remote distance"—petitioned town and General Assembly for redress of grievances and independent organization, but after discussion and consideration, division was indefinitely deferred. The "new county scheme" called out more energetic action. Again and again the town deputies were instructed to use "their utmost endeavors" in its behalf. The removal of the Courts to Brooklyn was strongly opposed as "no accommodation." A half-shire with itself for shire-town was Woodstock's aspiration, to further which she promptly voted to be at the expense of erecting all needful buildings. A house for the poor was ordered in 1799. In politics Woodstock continued mainly federal though an earnest minority were followers of Jefferson. The growth of republicanism and anti-federalism was manifested by a vote passed in 1798, that the several ministers in town should take their turn in opening Freemen's meetings—by which the pulpit of the orthodox meeting-house on Woodstock Hill was thrown open to Baptist and Methodist invaders. Deacon Morse straightway reports "that Rev. Mr. Thompson prayed and delivered a discourse," but when the following year *Elder Amos Welles* took his turn as preacher his pen failed to make the accustomed record in the town book! Elder Welles' discourse upon the words—"But I was born free"—an earnest but temperate plea that all Americans might enjoy their birthright without legal preference, free from "the unnecessary and unreasonable trouble of lodging certificates to clear them from paying taxes where they do not belong"—was however so acceptable to a large body of his hearers that they procured its publication. The matter apparently excited much commotion and ill-feeling. Deacons Morse and Lyon and John McClellan were appointed a committee by the First Society "to examine the writings of a certain sermon delivered by Mr. Amos Welles of this town and printed, and for said committee to call on said Welles to see what he will do respecting supposed misrepresentations made by him and printed in said book, and for said committee to treat the matter as they shall judge best." Notwithstanding strong opposition, radicals like Jesse Bolles were sent occasionally to the Legislature. Other representatives were Eliphalet Lyon, Stephen Paine, Ebenezer Smith, Nehemiah Child, Noah Mason, John McClellan, John Fox, Charles Child, Elijah

Williams, William Bowen, Samuel Dana, Silas May, Ebenezer Skinner, Chester Child, Ephraim May. Jedidiah and Jeremiah Morse, John McClellan, Nehemiah Child, John Fox and Ebenezer Smith, served as justices. In 1793, Woodstock resumed jurisdiction over Middlesex —a strip of land on the north which she had previously relinquished as clearly within Massachusetts limits—but finding it impossible to collect taxes from the inhabitants of this gore, she yielded it finally in 1796 to Dudley and Sturbridge.

Among other public enterprises the citizens of Woodstock engaged with much spirit in an association for the detection and punishment of thieving. It does not appear that any especial pilferage led to this organization, whose office was rather preventive than redressive. A meeting of subscribers was held, May 20, 1793, at the noted house of Elijah Williams, "for the purpose of detecting thefts." General McClellan was elected chairman, Major Ebenezer Smith, clerk. Messrs. Elijah Williams, Ebenezer Smith, Hezekiah Bugbee, William Graves and Silas May, were deputed "to form and draw articles for the society." At its second meeting June 3, the constitution was presented and adopted, thirty-eight persons subscribing to the same, each paying six shillings. The meetings were held quarterly, alternating between the Williams tavern and that of Silas May, in East Woodstock, at which pleasant reunions new members were always admitted. A little toddy was furnished out of the rapidly growing fund but no carousing permitted. Five or six efficient members were kept in office as "pursuers"—minute-men to rally out on any alarm. Through their agency stolen goods were from time to time recovered, and doubtless much thieving was prevented by dread of speedy detection.

The shocking fate of one of Woodstock's most worthy young men, must have increased its interest in any crime-detecting association. Returning with his summer's earnings from Cazenovia, New York, in November, 1805, Marcus Lyon was attacked by ruffians in Wilbraham, robbed and murdered. The riderless horse led to the discovery of the body, sunk in Chicopee River. Taken out and identified, it was borne to his home in West Woodstock. An immense number of people accompanied the mournful procession and attended the funeral in the Baptist meeting-house. The assembly was addressed by Rev. Abiel Ledoyt. "The grief of the mourners, the numbers convened, and the tears that profusely flowed, presented a scene which we conclude has never had a parallel in these our inland towns." Mournful ballads and elegies, dolefully droned by many a Woodstock fireside, kept alive for many years the memory of this lamented youth :—

"My blood runs cold, when I am told
In Wilbraham at mid-day,
That blood is shed, Marcus is dead,
Murdered on the highway."

Another mournful tragedy, calling out the deepest interest and sorrow, was the shipwreck of Doctor and Mrs. Lathrop Holmes on their return voyage from Georgia, April, 1801. The April storm that shook the very hills in its fury, seemed doubly terrible to the aged mother and friends, who feared that their loved ones might be exposed to it on the pitiless ocean, but weeks of weary waiting passed before they knew that the reality surpassed their fears. Their only daughter was happily safe in Woodstock, left behind at the earnest entreaty of her grandmother, and there were few children in Windham County whose tears did not flow when they heard of the sad bereavement of "little Temperance Holmes." When taken to Cambridge by her uncle and guardian, Dr. Abiel Holmes, her yearly visits in her old home were joyfully welcomed, and she was ever regarded with special interest and tenderness as one by early orphanage made the child of humanity.

The yearly pilgrimages of Dr. Holmes and Dr. Morse, their acceptable services in Mr. Lyman's pulpit, and familiar intercourse with their old friends, afforded much pleasure and profit to the people of Woodstock. By the recommendation of Dr. Morse, they were among the first to engage in the Quarterly Concert of prayer for the conversion of the world—holding a "concert-lecture," reported as agreeable and well attended. Deacon Morse was able to reciprocate these pleasant visits till advanced age, riding back and forth on horseback, and taking great delight in the dawning promise of his son's remarkable family. The venerable fathers of Woodstock's First Church— Deacons Morse and Skinner—stood together in official relation to the church for forty-three years, "as brothers in harmony and good agreement." By remarkable coincidence their wives were both removed by the stroke of death in April, 1805, after a happy marriage life of nearly sixty years. Mrs. Sarah (Peake) Morse, mother of Deacon Morse, died in 1801, aged 99 years lacking 44 days—the oldest person that had then died in Woodstock, and having the most numerous posterity. Deacon William Skinner died January 30, 1807, in his 87th year, revered and lamented—an eminently devout man and "mighty in the Scriptures," a wise counsellor and a faithful friend. Woodstock lost the same year her most prominent and distinguished public citizen, General Samuel McClellan, who died October 17, aged 77 years. His funeral was attended with the usual masonic and military demonstrations.

XIII.

ORGANIZATION OF STERLING. MEETING-HOUSE ASSOCIATION. TOWN AND CHURCH AFFAIRS IN VOLUNTOWN. LINE MEETING-HOUSE.

STERLING obtained town privileges without the customary struggle. The inconvenience arising from the peculiar elongation of ancient Voluntown was abundantly manifest, and a proposition, April 25, 1793, to divide into two towns met immediate acceptance. John Gaston and Samuel Robbins, from the north and south extremities of the town, were appointed agents to petition the Assembly. Response being delayed, the town by a majority of two to one again voted for divison—Lemuel Wylie and Benjamin Dow, committee. The Resolve incorporating the new town was passed May, 1794, viz. :—

" *Resolved by this Assembly*, that all that part of the ancient town of Voluntown within the following bounds, beginning at the northwest corner of said ancient town of Voluntown, at the south line of Killingly, thence running southerly on the east line of Plainfield until it comes to the southeast corner of Plainfield, thence east ten degrees south, to the division line between this State and the State of Rhode Island, thence by said State line to the southeast corner of Killingly, thence westerly on the line of Killingly to the first-mentioned bounds, be, and the same is hereby incorporated into a distinct town by the name of ' *Sterling*,' and shall be, and remain in, and of the County of Windham."

It was also provided that the new town " shall not have more than one representative," should maintain its proportion of poor and be liable for its portion of all debts due from the mother town, and be entitled to its proportion of public money and all other corporate property. John Gaston, Esq., justice of the Peace, was authorized to warn a meeting for the choice of town officers and act as moderator.

In response to this summons a town meeting was held at the house of Robert Dixon, Esq., on Sterling Hill, June 9, 1794. Benjamin Dow, a respected citizen of the town, was elected town clerk and treasurer; Captains John Wylie and Asa Montgomery, George Matteson, Anthony Brown and Lemuel Dorrance, selectmen; Captain Thomas Gordon, constable and collector; Noah Cole, James Dorrance, Jun., Nathaniel Gallup, Dixon Hall, fence-viewers; Nathaniel Gallup, grand-juryman; John Hill, Nathaniel Burlingame, Matthias Frink, tithingmen. Following their previous custom, John Douglas, Jun., was chosen grand school committee man, and a committee of one for each of the seven school districts, viz. :—1. Jencks Mason; 2. Noah Cole; 3. Elisha Perkins; 4. Lemuel Dorrance; 5. Asa Whitford; 6. Nathan Dow; 7. Nathan Burlingame. Benjamin Dow, Lemuel Dor-

rance and John Wylie were appointed a committee to make division
of all the corporate property that did belong to Voluntown; also, to
settle the line with Voluntown gentlemen and make division of the
poor. Sheep and swine were allowed liberty " to go on the common."
The dwelling-house of Robert Dixon was selected as the place for
holding town meetings until the town saw cause to make other arrangements. Nearly a hundred inhabitants were soon admitted as freemen.
The original Voluntown families, Dixon, Dorrance, Dow, Douglas,
Cole, Smith, Gaston, Gordon, Gallup, French, Frink, Montgomery,
Wylie, were still represented. Patten, Perkins, Vaughan, Young,
Bailey, Burgess, Burlingame, Hall, Mason, and other later residents,
appeared among the inhabitants. The name of the town was given
by a temporary resident, Dr. John Sterling, who promised a public
library in return for the honor.

Sterling entered upon its new duties with the usual spirit and
energy. Its population was about nine hundred. Though much of its
soil was poor, and its shape inconvenient, it had some peculiar advantages. It had fine water privileges, an excellent stone quarry, a great
post-road running through its centre, and sterling men of good Scotch
stock to administer public affairs. One of their first duties was to
examine the circumstances of that stage-road " that leads from Plainfield to Providence by Captain Robert Dixon's." The Turnpike Society, then recently constituted, was about to lay out a large sum of
money in alterations and improvements, and the selectmen of Sterling
were cited to do their part. " Taking into consideration the circumstances and liabilities of the town, and the consequences that might
follow any failure or neglect," they proceeded to notify the inhabitants
and make the proposed alterations, viz., from Archibald Dorrance's
fence through Kenyon's field and so to old post-road; also, another
piece near the Burying-ground and Captain Colgrove's. A bridge
was built over Moosup River near Smith's mill—Lemuel Dorrance,
John Gaston and John Douglas, committee. A turnpike gate was
erected near the western line of the town. To facilitate its fishing
interest, it was ordered that obstructions should be removed from the
river.

The lack of a suitable place for holding town meetings was an
annoyance and mortification to the leading men of the town, publishing to the world their lamentable destitution of that most essential
accommodation—a *public meeting-house*. This surprising deficiency
in a Connecticut township was due in part to its peculiar conforma-
tion, making it more convenient for residents of either extremity to
join with neighboring churches in other towns than to unite in a
common centre, and in part to the prevalence of sectaries, and

Rhode Island propinquity and example, which led many of its inhabitants to eschew all church-going and rate-paying. Congregationalists in the south part of the town were included in the North Society of Voluntown, and now engaged in building a new meeting-house upon the boundary line between the townships; those in the North or Bethesda Society united with the South church of Killingly. The Baptists in the west of the town were connected with the church in Plainfield; the east-side Baptists joined in worship and church fellowship with their Rhode Island neighbors. As no religious society was ready to lead in erecting a house of worship at this juncture the town might very properly have arranged to build a house or hall for its own especial accommodation, but such repudiation of the peculiar legislative influences supposed to inhere to a regularly established meeting-house was not apparently even taken into consideration, and its public spirited citizens hastened to supply the deficiency by erecting a house of worship upon their own expense and responsibility. Possibly the chief movers in this enterprise might not have cared to intrust decision to the uncertainties and delay of town vote and action. Their favorite site on the north extremity of Egunk was quite aside from the centre of the town, and might not have obtained the suffrages of the majority of voters. But Sterling Hill, as it was now called, was virtually the head and heart of the town, the centre of business, the residence of the most influential citizens, and the members of the Sterling Hill Meeting-house Association* could not think of erecting the projected edifice in any other locality. Titus Bailey, David Gallup, Thomas Gordon, Joshua Webb, Philip Potter, committee for the subscribers, procured from the heirs of Samuel Dorrance the deed of a building-lot, "east side the Great Lane (now called Green), ... for the purpose of setting a meeting-house and that only, and the convenience of a green." Funds were procured without apparent difficulty, and the house completed with more than ordinary expedition, the freemen adjourning thither from the house of Robert Dixon during the autumn of 1797. It was voted that the town and freemen's meetings be held at the new meeting-house. Each subscriber had pew shares according to his

---

* *Original Proprietors of the Sterling Hill meeting-house:*—Francis Smith, Levi Kinney, David Gallup, Joshua Frink, Isaac Gallup, William Gallup, George Madison, Charles Winsor, Nathan Burlingame, Philip Potter, Archibald, Lemuel, James and John Dorrance, Stephen Olney, Pierce Smith, Robert and Thomas Dixon, Joshua Webb, Benjamin Tuckerman, Reuben Thayer, David Field, Caleb Cushing, Andrew Knox, Titus Bailey, Joseph Wylie, Reuben Park, Moses Gibson, Azael Montgomery, Dixon Hall, Archibald Gordon, Thomas Gordon, William Vaughan, Captain Gaston, Andrew and Samuel Douglas, Thomas and Samuel Cole, John Kenyon, Sen. and Jun., George Hopkins, Asa Whitford, Benjamin Bennett.

49

subscription and occupied his seat with great satisfaction. Other public meetings were held in it, and occasional religious services, but no regular worship maintained for several years.

Improvements in schools were gradually effected. Ten school-districts accommodated with good convenient schools were reported in a few years. Efforts were made to establish an academy, a company formed, and a suitable building erected, "standing near our new meeting-house, nearly in the centre of the town," where "a man-school was maintained throughout the year, teaching reading, writing, mathematics and grammar." With these public buildings, Robert Dixon's well-known tavern stand, and several large substantial houses built by the Dorrances and other thrifty residents, Sterling Hill presented a fine appearance, and received especial commendation from Dr. Dwight. After noting the lean soil and imperfect civilization of Western Rhode Island, he proceeds:—

"At Sterling we were pleasantly advertised that we had come to Connecticut by sight of a village with decent church and school-house and better houses. A beautiful prospect from Sterling Hill."

Dr. Sterling failed to make good his promise, but a library was obtained by private benefactions. Jeremiah Parish and Artemas Baker attempted legal practice. Dr. Isaac Backus of Plainfield removed his residence to Sterling and pursued his medical practice. John Wylie and Captain John Gaston served many years as justices. Sterling's earliest representatives were John Wylie, Nathaniel Gallup, Thomas Gordon, Noah Cole, Archibald Gordon, Isaac Gallup, Lemuel Dorrance. The proposed change of county seat enlisted the sympathies of the town, and committees were maintained to unite in conference and action with other aggrieved towns.

Voluntown was seriously affected by the loss of its northern territory and population. Many of its ancient families had removed to more attractive regions, and it became still more difficult to maintain its public standing and religious worship. Joseph Wylie, William Briggs and Nicholas Keigwin were appointed to settle the new boundary line; Joseph Wylie, John Stewart and James Alexander to make division of the town property. James Alexander was elected town clerk; Ebenezer Campbell, treasurer; Moses Campbell, grand school committee man. Town meetings were held alternately in the old and Nazareth meeting-houses. Renewed efforts were now made to complete a new house of worship. An attempt to meet the expense by a tax upon the society "to be paid in timber, boards, shingles, corn, wheat, rye, flax, tow-cloth," had been unsuccessful. The subscription method was now tried with better results. A number of proprietors, i. e., Daniel, Benjamin, Nathan, Ebenezer and Aaron

Dow, Samuel and William Gallup, Samuel and James Gordon, John Douglas, Kinne, Keigwin, Tucker, Frink, Campbell, Adams, Burgess, and John Stewart, agreed, February 24, 1794, to give certain sums for the erection of a new meeting-house. A convenient site on the *line* between the towns was given by Mr. James Gordon. In 1797, it was voted to sell the pew ground at vendue to raise money to finish the house. This being accomplished after two years' labor, a new disappointment awaited the society. Rev. Micaiah Porter, their pastor for nineteen years, decided upon removal. Mr. Porter, like his predecessor, had married one of his congregation, Elizabeth, daughter of Captain Isaac Gallup, and it was hoped that he would spend his days amongst them; but continued losses and changes made it difficult to support a Congregational pastor. The old Presbyterian element had nearly disappeared, a large proportion of the existing population was Baptist, and the remnant of the standing church joined with them in worship. Elder Amos Crandall, an Open Communion Baptist, occupied the Line meeting-house every alternate Sabbath for several years, preaching to a small congregation. The Nazareth church gradually wasted away. Mr. Morgan was dismissed in 1782, after a ten years' pastorate. In 1793, "taking into consideration their destitute and broken state, destitute of a pastor and deprived of the regular administration of ordinances, a large proportion removed by death,"— the few remaining members reunited in covenant and made an earnest effort to maintain public worship. Brother Allen Campbell was permitted to preach and expound, and the sacrament was administered from time to time by Separate ministers. A company of subscribers now erected a small meeting-house "at the cross-roads west of John Campbell's"—Moses Campbell, John Stewart, Jas. Wylie, committee; James Alexander and James Campbell, Jun., to apportion out to each subscriber his part of building material. This house was long used by the town for public meetings, but the church became extinct before the close of the century.

In town affairs there was little occurring of special interest. Allen Campbell, James Alexander, Joseph Wylie served as justices; Moses and Samuel Robbins, Nicholas Randall and William Gallup were sent as representatives. With other towns Voluntown was interested in the proposed change of county seat, and appointed delegates to consult measures for removing the place for holding courts to Brooklyn. Increasing attention was given to the utilization of its woods and water privileges, and a forge established for the manufacture of iron. A library association was formed in 1792, and a hundred volumes procured.

XIV.

WINDHAM COUNTY IN 1800. POPULATION. BUSINESS. MORALS.
RELIGION. SCHOOLING. SOCIAL CONDITION.

IN the preceding pages we have carried our Windham townships
from the close of the Revolutionary War to the dawn of a new
era of development. In this twenty-five years there had been growth
and advancement, though the constant outflow to new countries had
checked the increase of population. The census of 1800* showed a
loss of 699 since 1790, and a gain of only 728 since 1774. Ashford,
Brooklyn, Canterbury, Plainfield, Voluntown and Windham had been
losers. The largest gains were in Killingly and Thompson. Business
enterprise had been stimulated by the opening of new avenues of
trade, turnpike roads and mechanical inventions. Several business
firms traded directly with the West India islands, owning their own
vessels and buying up much surplus produce, whereby the farming
interests of many towns had been greatly benefited. Towns with
fewer farming facilities had turned attention to manufactures. Keen
eyes watched with eager interest the various attempts now made to
supersede by machinery the slow and painful processes of hand labor.
Machines for carding wool were brought into the County in 1806.
The manufacture of paper, potash, pottery ware, bricks, boots, shoes
and hats was carried on to a considerable extent. Yet notwithstanding
the apparent briskness of business, and the laborious industry of the
great mass of the population, money was not plenty. Rich men were
rare. The farmer who owned land free from incumbrance, professional men and traders, might indeed secure a competence, but it is
doubtful if a majority of the population could do more than make a
scanty livelihood. Children were numerous, trades few, wages low.
Three shillings a day, paid in produce, was the common price for farm
laborers, and a working woman would drudge through the week for

---

* Ashford, 2,445. Brooklyn, 1,202. Canterbury, 1,812. Hampton, 1,379.
Killingly, 2,279. Plainfield, 1,619. Pomfret, 1,802. Sterling, 908. Thomp-
son, 2,341. Voluntown, 1,119. Windham, 2,644. Woodstock, 2,463. White
population of the towns now forming Windham County in 1800, 22,013.
Slaves, 31. Free negroes and Indians not given.
Rate list in 1800 :—

Windham	$64,272 20	Pomfret	55,154 54
Canterbury	48,037 48	Sterling	20.873 12
Ashford	61,367 41	Thompson	50.932 95
Brooklyn	35,600 90	Voluntown	20,923 20
Hampton	38,321 01	Woodstock	62,821 04
Killingly	41,027 32		
Plainfield	39,826 22	Amount	$539,157 39

two and six-pence. A faithful "hired man" carried on General Cleveland's farm, managing all his out-door affairs, for seventy dollars a year. A poor man has been known to walk miles with his little boys and work hard all day digging potatoes for one bushel out of ten. Ten dollars a month for a school-master and five shillings a week for a school-ma-am, was deemed ample wages. Young men roved about in spring, swingling flax and tow on shares, and picking up any odd jobs they could find. The few ways for earning money made it very difficult for a young man to make his way in the world, and after years of hard labor he would hardly save enough to stock a farm without the closest economy. General Cleveland's man, with bare feet, tow cloth frock and breeches, and no family to support, accumulated quite a fortune, but those who married young found it very difficult to provide for their families. The poverty of the Notts of Ashford, who are reported to have worked their one cow upon the farm because they could not afford horse or oxen, and lived chiefly upon brown bread and milk and bean-porridge, was not without its parallel in other households. So difficult was it in many cases to provide even such seemingly indispensable articles as shoes and stockings, that it was a common practice for young girls to walk barefoot to meeting, donning those hoarded treasures just before entering the house of worship. Numberless instances are reported of men who made one "Sunday suit" last a life-time. Quaint old figures toiling up to the meeting-house could be identified as far as the eye could reach, by the old cocked hat, many-caped great-coat, or some other striking peculiarity of their time-honored costumes.

In accordance with the statutes of 1783, forbidding slave importation and providing for the gradual emancipation of children of slave parentage, slavery had nearly died out. An abnormal excrescence, incongruous and uncongenial, it dropped off without apparent notice. Blacks who had served during the Revolution generally received their freedom at that time. General Putnam freed his body servant, Dick, and bought a farm for his Indian servants. "General Job" of Canterbury lived to receive a pension for his services. Many born in slavery were manumitted by their owners. The old house servants were generally retained for life and comfortably supported. Deacon Gray of Windham kept his old negroes in a cabin, where he supplied them with food. Many of the younger negroes sought employment in large towns. The aboriginal inhabitants were fast disappearing. Remnants of ancient tribes might yet be found on reservations in Woodstock and Brooklyn, as alien from the people around them as if they belonged to another order of beings. Almost every town had its one Indian family, familiar to all, and regarded as a common charge. The Mooch sisters of Scotland, Josh and Martha Sonsamon of Killingly, "Old Quanto," of Pomfret, were well-known characters in their respective towns, and assumed something of the habits of civilization—the Mooch's and Sonsamons uniting with Christian churches. A few wandering Indians with no fixed home roved about from town to town extorting tribute of food and cider. Noah Uncas, Little Olive, Eunice Squib and Hannah Leathercoat, were familiar figures, grim, gaunt and taciturn, stalking in single file along highway and turnpike. Mohegans still made their annual pilgrimages up the Quinebaug. These various representatives of a fallen dynasty were usually treated with kindness and consideration, strongly seasoned with contempt—the "Injun" of that date holding much the position of the succeeding "nigger."

In morals there had appeared at the beginning of this period a marked deterioration. Rum was used without stint; Sabbath-breaking, profanity and loose-living were increasingly prevalent. Yet there were now indications that the supreme ebb had been reached and the tide was slowly turning. The public had awakened to a sense of its condition. Intemperance in drinking was denounced and plans discussed for the suppression of vice and immoralities. The *Windham Herald*, while advertising in its columns the usual variety of tempting liquors at astonishingly low prices, would often balance the sheet by such advanced temperance documents as "The Drunkard's Looking-glass;" "The Moral and Physical Thermometer of the Vices, Diseases and Punishment" resulting from Intemperance, and a new "Drunkard's Catechism,"* prepared expressly for the instruction of

---

* *Question.* What is the chief end of Rum? *Answer.* The chief end of Rum is to make toddy, flip and punch. *Q.* What are the benefits which tipplers receive from toddy, flip and punch? *A.* Peace of conscience, joy in the comforter, increase of love thereto, and perseverance therein to the end. *Q.* Who is the comforter? *A.* RUM. *Q.* Into what state will the love of Rum, and a perseverance in the use of it, bring mankind? *A.* A drunken state. *Q.* What office doth a man execute who is a drunkard? *A.* The office of a *beast* both in his state of humiliation and exaltation. *Q.* Wherein consists a drunkard's exaltation? *A.* In a triumph over reason, fear and common sense, in the prostration of dignity, reputation and honor, and in contempt of Death and the Devil. *Q.* Wherein does a drunkard's humiliation consist? *A.* In his being senseless, and that in a low condition, lying under the table, rolling in the dirt and wallowing in uncleanness. Then follow pain, loss of appetite, trembling hands, with idleness, inattention to business, want, poverty and distress. Friends neglect him, diseases torment him, executions vex him, creditors tease him, sheriffs seize him, and the prison opens its doors to take him in—Surely it is an evil way and the end thereof is sorrow.

The "punishments" accruing from the use of rum as noted by Dr. Rush's thermometer, were:—"Debt, black eyes, rags, hunger, alms-house, work-house, jail, whipping-post, stocks, Castle Island, Newgate, gallows. And unless repentance should prevent they will share in the punishment prepared for the Devil and his angels." As a substitute for this pernicious beverage,

youth. A religious revival had preceded this attempted reformation in morals. Methodism had done a good work in reaching a class removed from religious and restraining influences, and the ministry at large was awakening more and more to the demands of the hour, and striving to arouse the churches to a higher sense of individual responsibility and more general coöperation in aggressive Christian labor. The number of religious societies in 1806, with each its church organization and place of worship, was about forty, viz.: Congregationalists, twenty; Baptists, thirteen; Methodists, four; Separate, two; Episcopalian, one. About forty families, mostly in Woodstock and Thompson, were connected with the Universalist Society of Oxford, under the charge of Rev. Thomas Barnes and his successors. Though other denominations were now rapidly gaining ground, the original churches in their established parishes still kept the lead, and the Windham County Association of ministers continued to exercise their official prerogatives as guides and guardians of the churches and censors of the public morals. Many knotty points of doctrine and practice were discussed and settled in their frequent meetings. They were called to consider in 1786 that most searching question then widely agitated:—"Whether a person ought to be willing to be damned for the glory of God?" "The negative ingeniously and learnedly supported by arguments from Scripture and reason." It was voted at the same date, "That the neglect of family prayer is a censurable evil," (i. e., amenable to public censure by the church) In 1799, it was "judged inexpedient without urgent necessity to travel on the Sabbath from one parish to another for exchanging ministerial labors." "Deacons ought to be ordained by prayer and imposition of the hands." Increasing ministerial assumption was manifested in change of title. At first they had simply styled themselves the associated pastors or ministers of the County; now they met on several occasions as an "Assembly of Bishops," while their Judaizing parishioners loved best to consider them as "Priests." The Hopkinsianism and High Calvinism of the younger generation of clergy led to a division of the Association in 1799, not by lines as in some cases, but each choosing to which of the associations he would be annexed. The Rev. Messrs. Cogswell, Whitney, Staples, Atkins, Putnam and Lee were recognized

the use of that excellent liquor, cider, was strongly recommended, containing indeed "a small quantity of spirits, but so diluted and blunted by being combined with an acid and a large quantity of saccharine matter and water as to be perfectly inoffensive and wholesome. It disagrees only with persons subject to rheumatism, but it may be rendered inoffensive by extinguishing a red hot iron in it or by diluting it with water." Beer was also suggested as "a wholesome liquor, abounding with nourishment." Extracts from *Windham Herald*, 1797—1800.

as the Eastern Association of Windham County. The original Association proposed the following May to effect a more formal consociation according to the provisions of Saybrook Platform. Messrs. Welch, Sherman, Waterman, Ely and Dow were appointed a committee " to collect from the Scriptures and throw light on the subject as they may be enabled." Fifteen ministers with delegates met in convention at Mansfield, November, 1800, to consider the report. "The Plan of Consociation" embraced the following articles:—

"I. The Consociation shall consist of those Pastors and Churches, by delegation, who agree to adopt this and the following articles; which shall be the constitution of Church Government for the Consociation of Windham County, and shall go into operation when nine churches shall agree to and adopt the same.

V. The Consociation shall have cognizance of all things that regard the welfare of the particular churches belonging to the body. Particularly,

1. They shall be considered as having the right at all times to originate and adopt for themselves, and propose to the churches any rules or regulations, which they may judge to be calculated for the edification and well ordering of the same.

2. It shall be considered as their duty to assist the pastors and churches of the body by their counsel and advice in any cases of difficulty, when applied to for the purpose.

3. They shall have a right to censure irreclaimable pastors, churches, or individual members of the churches of the body who fall into heretical sentiments or scandalous immoralities, upon complaints regularly laid before them.

4. A complaint can not be received by this body, or considered as coming regularly before them, unless the previous steps have been taken pointed out by our Lord in Matt. XV., 15, 16, 17.

5. When a member of any particular church belonging to this body shall view himself aggrieved or injured by his being laid under censure, he shall have the right of appeal to the Consociation.

VI. Pastors elected by churches belonging to the Consociation shall previously to their ordination be approved by the body of their committee. The Consociation shall also examine and approbate candidates for the Gospel ministry.

X. The foregoing articles may be amended by calling a special convention whenever a majority of the churches shall signify their desire for the same to the Consociation.

Voted, unanimously, in convention, that we agree to the foregoing articles as a system of church government agreeable to the Word of God; and they are accordingly recommended to the several churches for their concurrence and adoption."

It was also voted "that the committee prepare this plan for the press, together with some arguments and Scripture proof in support of it, adding thereto a serious address to the churches on the subject of christian union and fellowship." Seven churches adopted the plan and were formally consociated. The Eastern Association looked with much suspicion upon this hierarchical combination and declined to transfer to it any proper Association business. Deprecating the High church and High Calvinistic tendencies of the times, it made little apparent effort to influence public sentiment, its members enjoying the pleasure of sympathetic fraternal intercourse varied by occasional sparrings with their western brothers. Highly conservative in usage they suggested one innovation, "That when sermons are delivered at the meeting-house at funerals, prayers at the house of death before carrying out the body are improper." The sympathies of these ministerial brethren were deeply touched by the trials and loneliness of their venerated father, Dr. Cogswell, and through their intercession he was removed to Hartford, where he survived till January 2, 1807. For more than sixty years he had been intimately associated with ecclesiastic and public affairs in Windham County. Pacific and even timorous by nature, he had been called to take a prominent part in most fierce and bitter controversies, and men of more positive convictions had not scrupled to question the genuineness of his christian experience. But to "patient continuance in welldoing," was added a remarkable dying testimony. When mind and memory were so impaired that he had ceased to recognize his dearest friends, ONE NAME could still arouse him. His most beloved son tried in vain to extort a word of recognition, but when he asked—"Do you know the Lord Jesus Christ?"—the aged face brightened and with confidence and rapture he replied—"I *do* know *Him:* He is my God and my Saviour." Monuments in the North Burying-ground of Hartford preserve the memory of Dr. Cogswell with his more distinguished son,* and the beloved granddaughter, whose deprivation of speech and hearing led to the foundation of the American Asylum for the instruction of the deaf and dumb, while his prolonged ministerial service, his connection with the Separate movement and his faithful chronicle of cotemporaneous events, have insured him a lasting place in the annals of Windham County.

The educational interests of Windham County were now receiving more intelligent consideration. Public schools had received a new impulse from the creation of the school fund and more stringent supervision. The district system was more fully carried out, bringing a school within the reach of every family, and schools were maintained

---

* "United in death here rest the remains of Mason F. Cogswell, M. D., who died December 17, 1830, aged 69 years—and of Alice Cogswell, who died December 30, 1830, aged 25 years—the Father distinguished for his private virtues and public spirit and his professional worth, and the daughter (though deprived of hearing and speech) for her intellectual attainments and loveliness of character. The American Asylum for the deaf and dumb which under Providence, owes its origin to the father's tenderness towards his child and his sympathy for her fellow-sufferers, will stand an enduring monument to their memory, when this shall have perished."

with greater regularity and efficiency. The ordinary school-house was yet very rude and primitive. A sufferer* thus reports :—

"It was a wooden building about twenty feet square, underpinned at the four corners with common stones. It was boarded, clapboarded, the roof shingled, and an outer door, no porch or entry, at the southeast corner. It had a loose floor made of unplaned boards, and a ceiling of the same, a chimney in one corner built of rough stone. There was a long writing-table, reaching across one side and one end of the room, and the scholars sat on both sides of the table, facing each other. They had no desks or drawers, nothing of the kind. The idea of being comfortable there never entered our minds. While we wrote our ink would freeze in our pens so that we were frequently obliged to hold them up to our mouths and thaw it with our breaths."

The qualifications required in teachers were still very limited, but the necessity of passing examination involved some degree of fitness and preparation. Yankee utilitarianism insisted upon instruction in reading, writing, arithmetic, sewing and catechism, leaving less vital knowledge optional with the teacher. Notwithstanding this narrow range and the low price paid the teachers, these schools were more efficient than might at first be supposed. In Windham County as a rule the brightest and most capable young men secured the envied position of schoolmaster, and were generally very successful in rousing the energy and ambition of their pupils. The few things taught were thoroughly learned and fixed in the mind, and often a thirst for knowledge was incited which found gratification in the solid, standard works of the various town libraries. Increasing interest in education and mental development was manifested in the establishment of academies and high schools, and the multiplication of these useful libraries. An unusual number of newspapers were taken in Windham County. S. G. Goodrich in his recollections of his boyhood reports not more than three newspaper subscribers in the village of Ridgefield, Fairfield County. Joseph Carter of Canterbury, post-rider, carried the *Hartford Gazette*, in 1778, to twenty-five families in Scotland Parish; forty-three in Westminster Parish, and forty-five in the First Society of Canterbury. The Providence papers were also widely circulated, and the *Windham Herald* had twelve hundred subscribers early in the century. Almost every town had its "newspaper class," neighbors joining together that so they might have a large variety.

In social and domestic life there had been gradual improvement. Each generation built better houses than the preceding. Comfort and conveniences had been sparingly introduced. Foreign goods had been brought in, and many articles once unknown were now in common use. And yet the main features of ordinary domestic life were

* Eliashib Adams, Bangor, 1854. Born at Canterbury, 1773.

unchanged. Things needful for existence had still to be wrought out of the raw material by the separate labor of every household. Time and energies were almost wholly expended in evolving food from the flinty soil and raiment from the sheep's coat and flax stalks. Class distinctions were made in consequence far more definite and irreversible. Those who by inherited wealth or successful trading were freed from the necessity of daily burdensome labor were as distinctly separate from the great mass of the population as the nobility of foreign lands. In Windham County this class was but a unit, scarcely an "upper ten" among its thousands. Its true nobility were the sons of Revolutionary fathers, the hundreds of stalwart men who stood at the head of its public affairs, the farmers, traders and artisans, who earned their bread by the sweat of their brow, and the homes of these men differed little from those of their grandfathers. The great kitchen with its log fire in the huge chimney and high-backed settle keeping the draughts out, its bare, sanded floor, and round-top table tipping back into an arm chair, its wheels and reels and various working appurtenances, its porridge kettle on the crane and dye-pot in the chimney corner, was still the general abiding-place of the whole family—for there alone could be conveniently carried on the multifarious domestic operations. The fabrication of cloth taxed the united energies of the household. Strong arms were needed to break and swingle the stubborn flax fibre, cleanse and separate the matted fleece, ere feminine hands could undertake the hatcheling and carding. Children, grandparents and feeble folk could wind the quills and turn the reel while the sturdy matron and her grown-up daughters accomplished their "day's work" at the loom or spinning wheel. The various kinds and grades of cloth needful for family use, sheeting, toweling, blankets, coverlets, heavy woolen cloth for men's wear in winter and tow-cloth for summer, woolen stuff, linsey-woolsey and ginghams for women and children, were still mainly manufactured at home. And when to this Herculean labor was added the making of butter and cheese, the care of pickling and preserving a year's supply of beef and pork, the cramming of chopped meat into skins for sausages, the running of candles, and other vital necessities, little time was left for ordinary domestic affairs and household adornment. The homespun gowns were made up in the simplest fashion. Perambulating tailors cut and made the heavy garments for men, and revolving cobblers fashioned the family shoes from its own cowhides and calfskins. Bean porridge, baked pork and beans, boiled meat and vegetables, rye and Indian bread milk cheese and cider, with plenty of shad and salmon in their season, and a good goose or turkey at Thanksgiving, made up the bill of fare. Butchers and markets were yet almost unknown but a self-regulating meat exchange was found in every community—neighbors "slaughtering" in turn, and lending to each other so that the supply of fresh meat might be indefinitely prolonged. Even their salt was bought in the rough and had to be taken to the mill for grinding, millers from time to time setting apart a day for this specific purpose.

This toilful life, hard as it seemed, had its pleasant phases. No man or woman was ashamed of working. Matron and maid exultingly displayed their webs of cloth and notable pieces of handicraft, and never thought of apologizing when found in short-gown and petticoat at the loom or spinning-wheel by an afternoon visitor. Community in toil developed mutual sympathy and helpfulness. Neighbors and friends joined together in such jobs of work as involved great outlay of strength, and found that more could be accomplished by working like *bees* in company, and so husking, wool-picking, apple-paring bees came into vogue, in which old and young delighted to participate. Spinning matches and quiltings relieved the monotonous routine of home duties, the afternoon pleasant rivalry followed by dance and frolic in the evening. Work was made easy, good-fellowship and neighborly intercourse promoted by these informal labor-associations. Rural, social life was never more brisk, buoyant and enjoyable than during the years following the Revolution. As in the parallel rebound after the Restoration in England, the long period of darkness and repression was followed by an extravagant outburst of gayety and frolic. Notwithstanding the poverty, embarrassment and anxieties of many, a certain stir, and spring and hopefulness permeated the popular mind. Social requirements as to dress and entertainment were not burdensome, and these hard-working men and women could always find time to help each other in sickness and need, and participate in unnumbered public festivities. Training days and General Musters, Fourth of July and Masonic celebrations, dedications, ordinations, funerals of distinguished men, never failed to bring together great throngs of people, eating, drinking and making merry, even on the latter occasions. The abundance and cheapness of liquor had much to do with the universal jollity. Everybody drank on all these festive occasions, the minister before his prayers no less than the soldier upon review, and the good-wife at every roll of the quilting-frame. Excess in drinking and merry-making led on to dissipation and revelry. Intemperance and kindred vices greatly prevailed. The neighborly "bees," so friendly and helpful in their original design, were often turned into disgraceful orgies. The freedom allowed to young people, the unrestrained intercourse between young men and women, was greatly abused, and lapses from morality and virtue were common even among the most respectable families. Society was in a rudimental state. It had the vices as well as the virtues of immature development. The masses were yet far from being civilized. Their speech was rough; their fun was coarse and broad. Practical jokes were very common. Nicknames were often given, especially to mark some personal defect or peculiarity. Young people were very fond of playing tricks and prying into the future. The ordinary mode of living was unfavorable to health and morals. Promiscuous occupation of kitchen and sleeping-room was incompatible with cleanliness. Contagious diseases often raged with great violence, and offensive cutaneous eruption was so common that an annual "inting" or anointment was more inevitable than house-cleaning. Fleas and other vermin were prevalent in every household, and no head of hair could be secure from unwelcome intruders.

Social life in the last century had thus its good and evil, its sunshine and its shadows, but whether light or dark predominated it was soon to be left behind. The Nineteenth Century had come. New elements, revolutionary forces were already at work. The spirit of the age had even reached Windham County, and though home and social life flowed on for a time in its old channels, it had led hundreds of valuable families and scores of enterprising young men to seek more favoring chances in wider fields. As it became increasingly evident that a large population could not be supported by agriculture alone, that six or eight hearty boys and girls could hardly find sustenance, much less a life settlement upon a Windham County homestead, it might have been a question whether the County had not reached its maximum of attainment and was destined to premature depopulation and decrepitude, but for the opening of new sources of business and prosperity. The great law regulating demand and supply brought relief just when the time was ripe for it. The invention of machinery and the introduction of manufactures solved the problem, stayed the ebbing current and opened a new era of growth and development.

BOOK VIII. 1807-1820.

I.

THE CARDING MACHINE. POMFRET MANUFACTURING COMPANY. MANUFACTURING *FUROR*. WAR OF 1812-14.

THE first harbinger of the new mechanical era was a machine for facilitating the manufacture of woolen goods. Arthur and John Scholfield, who came from England in 1793, succeeded after ten or twelve years of experimental effort in making ready for market "double carding machines, upon a new and improved plan, good and cheap." "A machine for carding sheep's wool" was set up by John Scholfield, Jun., in Jewett's City, in 1804, who accommodated numerous customers by picking, breaking, carding and oiling wool at twelve cents per pound. Families in adjacent parts of Windham County hastened to avail themselves of this most welcome aid and service, and in two years Scholfield advertised a second machine already in operation. But he was not long allowed to enjoy a monopoly of this invention. Its benefits were too great to be restricted to one town or neighborhood. June 20, 1806, Cyrus Brewster thus advertises in the *Windham Herald*:—

"CARDING MACHINE.

NOTICE is hereby given that the machine for picking, oiling and carding wool, erected on the Falls of Willimantic River in Windham, at the Mills of Messrs. Clark & Gray, is now ready to do business. Those gentlemen that will favor the proprietors with their custom may depend on having their work done with neatness and dispatch, and all favors gratefully acknowledged. Price for breaking and carding, cash in hand, seven cents per lb., eight cents other pay; for picking and oiling, two cents per lb. cash in hand—other pay, three cents."

Swift and Brewster at the same date advertised a machine ready for work in Mansfield, and others were soon put up in all parts of the County. Few inventions have brought more instant and general relief and emancipation. The saving of time and labor and the greatly improved condition of the wool were universally admitted. The most niggardly farmer, accustomed to work himself and family to the bone rather than spend a penny, found that it paid to pay out money or barter for wool-carding, while women everywhere exulted in the beautiful white, soft, clean fleecy rolls which made spinning and weaving a positive enjoyment.

In this same summer of 1806, when carding machines were making their way all over Windham County, the foundation of another industry that was to work a radical change in the mode of life and labor was also laid. Wool and flax were to lose their ancient supremacy. A boll of pulpy cotton with its deep embedded seeds did not seem a formidable rival, but when freed from those seeds and drawn out into cohesive filaments by the arts of Gin and Jenny, and when those ductile threads were woven into fabrics far more suitable for domestic use than rough tow cloth and heavy woolen—cotton was welcomed as a most helpful ally if not yet recognized as a claimant for royal honors. Experimenters in Rhode Island after much labor and cost had constructed machines for spinning cotton by water power. Samuel Slater with his father-in-law, Ozias Wilkinson and others, had erected the second cotton mill at Pawtucket, in 1798, and now the Wilkinsons sought a more independent position and selected the Quinebaug Falls in Pomfret, as a most eligible site for such an enterprise. January 1, 1806, Ozias Wilkinson, his sons, Abraham, Isaac, David, Daniel, Smith, his sons-in-law, Timothy Green and William Wilkinson, together with James, Christopher and William Rhodes, formally associated as "The Pomfret Manufacturing Company." A deed of the mill privilege, and about a thousand acres of land adjoining, was secured from James Rhodes for the sum of $25,000. The site now occupied by the thriving village of Putnam, with its mammoth mills, intersecting railroads and multifarious business operations, was then a little mill village nestling between rocky hills, still covered with dense forests. "A wilderness" indeed it looked in the eyes of the young Smith Wilkinson, who came in March to superintend the preparations for building. The youngest son of the house, fond of books and home, his mother and sisters deeply mourned his banishment to this sequestered corner of Connecticut. Saw and gristmills, clothiery works, the dilapidated gin distillery, a blacksmith's shop, a three-tenement block built by Captain Cargill west of the river, and two or three small houses, comprised the settlement. Roads of more or less antiquity led to Bundy's mills and the surrounding towns. Land in Thompson, east of the Quinebaug, was purchased by Mr. Wilkinson, who prosecuted his mission with a spirit and energy that left little time for homesickness. Timber and stones were procured, ground prepared and everything set in motion. The raising the frame of the "factory" on the Fourth of July was a happy stroke of policy, not only getting a hard job of work out of the national holiday but enlisting popular sympathy and co-operation in behalf of the enterprise. As many as two thousand people came together to help and look on, and as free punch was furnished to all it was a most agreeable change from the customary formal " celebration." The "solitary walk " laid out by his predecessor was less attractive to Mr. Wilkinson than a brisk ride to Killingly Hill, where he found agreeable society in the hospitable home of Captain Sampson Howe. In the following winter he was married to Miss Elizabeth Howe, and set up family life in a small house west of the river. Building went on rapidly, machinery was hauled up, and on April 1, 1807, the first cotton factory in Windham County was set in operation. It was a four-story wooden building, a hundred feet long and thirty-two in width. Nine boys and girls picked up in the neighborhood, with three or four men to help and oversee them, comprised its working force. The children were delighted with the new occupation and thought the glittering machinery " the prettiest thing in the world." When on the second Monday morning they found the roads snow-blocked, the little girls put on men's boots and waded nearly a mile through the drifts rather than lose a few hours labor.

It was not children alone who welcomed the new dispensation. The Jennies like good Genii brought with them innumerable blessings. All that they did was to spin yarn for their sister workers. Domestic labor picked and cleansed the cotton and wove the yarn into coarse cloth and bed-ticking. No greater boon could have been brought to the women of Windham County. Nearly every house had its loom, with its active, capable women skilled to use it, and eager to add to the comforts of their family by weaving cloth for Pomfret Factory. Hard labor had heretofore merely brought them food and raiment; with little additional labor they could now earn much better clothes and many other comforts and luxuries. Young girls obliged to stifle their natural craving for pretty dresses and ornaments, hastened to improve the privilege thus afforded. A store promptly opened by the company, offering all manner of useful and ornamental goods in exchange for labor, greatly stimulated feminine enterprise and enthusiasm. Women from all the surrounding towns, even the wives of the ministers, doctors and lawyers, entered with alacrity into the lists and looms in competition with their more needy neighbors. The impulse given by the new industry was felt in every direction. Many workmen were employed in tending mill, hauling cotton and goods, preparing ground and putting up buildings. A handsome house opposite the factory was built for Mr. Wilkinson's residence, and other houses for operatives and incoming residents. Much money was thus brought in and put in circulation. Farmers found a new demand for produce and lumber.   Labor received a more bountiful recompense and land increased in value.

Other towns and companies hastened to follow this inspiriting example.   In August, 1807, James Danielson, Zadoc and James Spalding asked liberty to build a dam on the Quinebaug between Brooklyn and Killingly, while Rhode Island manufacturers sought privileges in other towns.   The relation between the Windham towns and their eastern neighbors, had been always most intimate and friendly. Providence was their most accessible market.   Their first public work was to open a way to that town.   In the days of their own weakness and poverty they had joined in efforts for sending it missionaries.   In the Revolutionary struggle they had furnished it with soldiers and supplies as well as a patriotic governor.   They had taken Providence boys to school while its own institutions were suspended, and sent back hundreds of their own boys to engage in business and useful labor. In trade and barter a most helpful reciprocity had long been established, and now they joined purse and hand in manufacturing enterprise.   The Narragansets in aborignal days had claimed rights in the Quinebaug Country, and Moosup had affixed his name to a large branch of the Quinebaug River.   Modern Narragansets now invaded the land and took possession of old Moosup's River, but they paid for their right in lawful wampum or barter.   Windham gave what she could best spare—land, water-privilege, labor—and received what she most needed—*money*, and business openings.   Asa Ames, Isaac Pitman and Alexander Tefft of Providence, associated with John, Archibald and Samuel Dorrance and Dixon Hall of Sterling, in 1808, as Sterling Manufacturing Company, buying land "at a ledge of rocks, called the Devil's Den chimney thence west by and down a small brook to Moosup River."   Thomas Rhodes of Providence, Peter B. Remington of Warwick, "Holden and Lawton" of Rehoboth, united with Obed Brown, Dyer Ames and others of Sterling, as the American Cotton Manufacturing Company, securing a privilege "near Ransom Perkins' fulling-mill on Quandunk River."   Rufus Waterman, S. G. Arnold, Joseph S. Martin, David and Joseph Anthony of Providence, Peter Cushman of North Providence, David King of Newport, united with Anthony Bradford, Henry Dow, John Dunlap, Walter Palmer, Christopher Deane, Jonathan Gallup, Joseph Parkhurst, Edward Hill, John Lester, Jeremiah Kinsman, James Gordon, Jun., Nathaniel Medbury, James Goff, John Freeman, Elias Deane, Edward Clark, all of Plainfield, Calvin Hibbard and Lemuel Dorrance of Sterling—"for the carrying on the manufacture of cotton under the name of Plainfield Union Manufacturing Company," buying very valuable privileges and land on the Moosup.   Jos. K. Angell with Nathan

Burgess, Humphrey Almy and other non-residents, arranged to occupy the privilege long owned by Nathan Angell, under the name of Moosup Manufacturing Company. Walter Paine and Israel Day of Providence, William Reed, Ira and Stephen Draper of Attleborough, Ebenezer and Comfort Tiffany, John Mason and Thaddeus Larned of Thompson, William Cundall, senior and junior, joined with Danielson and Hutchins in the Danielsonville Manufacturing Company of Killingly. With all possible expedition these various companies constructed dams and buildings and made ready to join in the spinning-race. The greatest hurry and bustle prevailed throughout the favored towns. The Sterling Manufactory and Plainfield Union were ready for work in 1809; Danielson's took the field in 1810, and others in Thompson, Killingly and Plainfield opened in quick succession. As the increasing difficulties with England shut out foreign goods and raised the price of domestic fabrics, the manufacturing interest increased in fervor. The river question, so perplexing in early times, was settled forever. No more conventions were needed to discuss what should be done with them. Those "tedious" and turbulent streams which had caused so much expense and contention, could be made to run mills instead of running off with bridges. Cautious men foreboded over-production and financial disorder. The *Windham Herald* raised its warning cry:—

"*Nov*. 1811. In Nov. 1809, there were within thirty miles of Providence 26 cotton mills in operation, containing 20,000 spindles and 13 erected not then ready to run. At the present time there are 74 mills within the same distance containing 51,454 spindles, making an increase of 36 mills and 31,454 spindles in less than two years! Are not the people running *cotton-mill mad?*"

In spite of these dolorous forebodings and warnings, the people went on setting up manufactories of woolen and cotton goods on every fall that could turn a mill wheel. The larger establishments were carried on by foreign capital; small factories in several towns were built and managed by their own citizens in joint stock companies. The benefits accruing from these manufactories more than counterbalanced the disastrous influences of war. Hundreds of men and women found remunerative employment, the raising of sheep, stock and all farming products was greatly stimulated, the tide of western emigration sensibly checked. Even the revulsion following the return of peace and renewed importation from England did not permanently injure the wealthier companies, nor weaken confidence in the ultimate development and triumph of manufacturing interests.

The War of 1812–14, with preceding events and discussions, excited great interest in Windham County, intensifying party spirit and enkindling sectional and political animosities. The old Federalists as a body denounced the war and its advocates, and quite overbore for a time the influence of the sympathizing Jeffersonians. In the "alarming crisis" following the Embargo Act of 1807, the citizens of Windham County were called to meet at its Court-house. Believing that "the same patriotic spirit which conducted us to LIBERTY and INDEPENDENCE will now animate us when that Liberty and Independence are in danger, and that the American Nation are prepared to sacrifice their lives and fortunes in defence of the only Free Republican Government on Earth against the insidious wiles or the open attacks of any foreign power,"—delegates from the several towns expressed their reprobation of this arbitrary and suicidal Act. The position of the leading Federalists at this time is best shown in the following resolutions passed in Brooklyn in 1809, when after urgent remonstrances from Connecticut, Massachusetts and other New England States, Congress had determined "to enforce and make more effectual" the hated Embargo :—

"Deeply impressed with the dangers which threaten our common country :—

Resolved, that while we will support the Constitution of the United States as the supreme law of the land, we view all acts contrary to and not warranted thereby as usurpations of power to which we are not bound to submit, and that committing their execution to a military force is an attempt to establish a despotism on the ruins of Liberty.

Resolved, that we view the several acts laying an Embargo, more particularly the last, with indignation and horror for various reasons—lastly, to fill up the measure of oppression it creates a DICTATOR, whose unpublished edicts become the laws of the land, and their execution is committed to creatures of his own appointment with the aid of military force.

Resolved, that we will hold in detestation and abhorrence every officer or soldier of the militia of this state who will shed the blood of his fellow citizens in attempting to execute laws by force, which are subversive of those rights of the people secured to them by Constitution.

Resolved, to request the Governor to convene a General Assembly.

Resolved, that Connecticut is a free sovereign state, and when powers ceded to the General Government are perverted, and their political existence as a state in danger of being overwhelmed in the vortex of consolidated power committed to individual hands, it is their duty to proclaim it in the face of the Nation."

Notwithstanding the dominance of the Federal party and the strong influence of such men as Swift and Goddard, personal experience of the exactions and insolence of Great Britain, as well as the spirit of party, led many to welcome the prospect and declaration of war. Windham sailors had been taken from American ships under false pretenses and made to serve for years in the British Navy. The brisk little *Windham* and other craft had been seized and confiscated under Berlin Decrees and Orders in Council. The military spirit, kept alive by reports of Revolutionary exploits and frequent military exercise, flamed up anew at the report of actual encounter with their ancient foe. Young men of bravery and patriotism, desirous of redressing the wrongs of the country and gaining renown in arms, yielded to the inducements held out by recruiting officers of good pay, clothing and living, with the prospect of retiring "to private life with a handsome property," and being "hailed with enthusiasm as the supporter of the rights and liberties of his happy country." The *Windham Herald*, while loudly denouncing the folly and madness of those reckless men who were leading the country to ruin, opened its columns to tempting inducements,* viz.:—

"RECRUITING SERVICE!!"
TO MEN OF PATRIOTISM, COURAGE AND ENTERPRISE.

EVERY able bodied MAN, from the age of 18 to 45 years, who shall be enlisted for the ARMY of the United States, for the term of five years, will be paid a bounty of SIXTEEN DOLLARS; and whenever he shall have served the term for which he enlisted, and obtained an honorable discharge, stating that he had faithfully performed his duty while in service, he shall be allowed and paid in addition to the aforesaid bounty, THREE MONTHS PAY, and ONE HUNDRED AND SIXTY ACRES OF LAND;—and in case he should be killed in action, or die in the service, his heirs and representatives will be entitled to the said three months pay, and one hundred and sixty acres of land, to be designated, surveyed, and laid off at publick expense.

HENRY DYER,
Lieut. U. S. Infantry.

Rendezvous. Windham,
May 11th, 1812.   tf6

N. B.   A good DRUMMER and FIFER are wanted immediately."

The refusal of the government of Connecticut to order the militia of the State into the service of the United States on the requisition of the Secretary of War and Major-General Dearborn, was approved and sustained by a large majority of the voters of Windham County. So unpopular was the war at the outset that in the election following this refusal only thirty-six Democrats were elected out of about two hundred representatives. Yet they did not hesitate to raise troops and provide munitions of war, subject *only* to the order of the Governor of the State. Daniel Putnam was made Colonel of the Second Regiment raised for special service. Second Company, Asa Copeland,

---

* Recruits for the regular army had been previously secured from Windham County under the following " New Inlisting Orders " :—
"THE Subscriber gives this public notification to all young Gentlemen who have an inclination of serving their country and gaining immortal honor to themselves and their posterity, that he has lately received fresh orders of Inlistment from government, which are much more favorable than those he formerly had. The period for inlistment is now fixed at five years, unless sooner discharged; after which time an honorable discharge will be given, where it is merited. Let no male or female disorganizer discourage you from engaging in this most laudable undertaking, but voluntarily step forth and tell the world that no usurpers shall maintain ground on Columbia's shore, but that America is, and shall be a distinct republic. Come, my good souls, come forward, let me see you at the rendezvous at Mr. Staniford's, where you will get further information, and something good to cheer the heart.
WILLIAM YOUNG, jun. Capt."

Pomfret, captain; Ebenezer Grosvenor, first lieutenant; Jonathan Copeland, Jun., Thompson, second lieutenant; Jeremiah Scarborough, Brooklyn, ensign. Third Company, George Middleton, Plainfield, captain; Elkanah Eaton, first lieutenant; George W. Kies, second lieutenant; Jared Wilson, Sterling, ensign. Third Company, cavalry, Thomas Hubbard, captain; William Trowbridge, first lieutenant; William Cotton, second lieutenant; Ralph Hall, cornet. Citizens exempt by years or official position from military service were enrolled as the First Regiment of a Volunteer Brigade under command of General David Humphreys. Hon. Thomas Grosvenor, colonel; Eliphalet Holmes, lieutenant-colonel; James Danielson, first major. Such men as Lemuel Ingalls, Chester Child, Hobart Torrey, Abel Andrus, Moses Arnold, Shubael Hutchins, Ebenezer Eaton, Sylvanus Backus, John Davis, Luther Warren and Jeremiah Kinsman, were officers in this regiment. The first summons to arms occasioned no little excitement. June 21, 1813, men were ordered to rendezvous in the central taverns of their respective towns, "complete in arms to go to New London as there were British there." Arthur Joslin, Joseph Munyan, "most of the infantry and all the militia *that did not abscond,*" met at Dwight's tavern on Thompson Hill, were marched into the meeting-house in old Revolutionary fashion, and up into the front seats of the gallery where they were treated to a stirring address from Rev. Daniel Dow. Some timid youth were said to have left their homes weeping, but the most that had faced the music went bravely forward. James Lyon went around to notify the militia of Woodstock, and when he returned from his mission found two companies already drawn up on the common ready to follow Adjutant Flynn, to the scene of action. These with companies from other towns marched on foot to New London and remained on guard there about three weeks. Another call came in September, when Artemas Bruce, Stephen Ricard, Charles Howard and some twelve or fifteen other Pomfret boys, went out under Captain Copeland and Ensign Grosvenor. Meeting others from Ashford, Windham and other towns in Norwich, they formed a company of 96. Slept in a barn, and proceeded next day by sloop to New London; marched a mile south where they pitched their tents; kept guard seven weeks and saw no fighting. A detachment of cavalry from the Fifth Regiment was stationed at New London and Groton, from September 1 to October 31, 1813—Comfort S. Hyde, Canterbury, lieutenant; John C. Howard, Jacob Dresser, sergeants; John Kendall, David Hutchinson, corporals; Rhodes Arnold, Henry Angell, Charles Barrows, Elisha P. Barstow, Zachariah Cone, Ichabod Davis, Abial Durkee, John Gallup, Arnold Hosmer, Jonathan Hammet, Jun., Edward S. Keyes, Dana Lyon, Hezekiah Loomis, William Morse,

Zeba Phelps, Elisha Paine, Bela Post, Shubael Strong, Otis Stoddard, Jasper Woodward, privates.

Reports of brilliant naval victories and achievements aroused more and more of the old martial spirit of Windham County. Many young men had gone out as soldiers and sailors in the army and navy. Dr. James Tyler of Brooklyn, was one of the first surgeons received into the United States navy. Septimus, son of Captain Daniel Tyler, joined the army in 1812, commissioned as assistant-quartermaster-general. Amasa Trowbridge of Pomfret, left a lucrative practice at Watertown, New York, to serve as surgeon in the American fleet on the Lake. His letters describing important naval engagements excited much interest. May, 1814, he writes to Mr. John Trowbridge of Pomfret:—

"I should not trouble you with a letter was it not for the purpose of transmitting information which must be pleasing to every person who will be pleased with the success of the American arms over our enemies. A secret expedition was fitted out at Sackett's Harbor under the command of Commodore Chancey, Generals Dearborn and Pike. The fleet consisted of a ship of 26 guns, 32's; a brig of 24 guns, 24's; eleven schooners varying from four to eight guns each, manned by 200 marines and 700 sailors; 2,370 troops consisting of infantry and artillery, embarked on board of this fleet on the morning of April 25, at Sackett's Harbor, and the fleet immediately put to sea. I embarked at the same time as surgeon on board the brig *Oneida*. I soon perceived that the place of our destination was Little York, about 300 miles up the Lake, the seat of government in the upper province of Canada. Winds proved favorable and we arrived before that city about 6 a. m. on the 27th. The fleet came to anchor about two miles from the town, and within half a mile of the shore at a very favorable spot for debarking the troops. We unmanned in a few minutes, and three hundred riflemen commanded by Major Forsyth reached the shore. They were met with 300 British Regulars and 150 Indians. A severe contest ensued; other troops soon landed, which together with the guns of the schooners which commenced cannonading obliged the enemy to retreat. Our troops then all landed and formed in battle array, commenced their march against the forts near the town. Our vessels hauled up at the same time within 300 yards of three batteries and a strong fort; a general cannonading commenced and was carried on with spirit on both sides for one hour. At this moment one of the enemy's strongest batteries blew up, and 40 of their men were seen flying in the air, accompanied by three cheers from our brave Yankees; about the same time our troops came to the charge with the enemy in line, and obliged them to retreat to the block-house and fort. The well-directed fire from our vessels soon obliged them to leave their strongholds, and our troops were advancing upon them when their *magazine* blew up, containing, as *by their own statement*, 500 barrels of powder. I cannot describe to you the sublimity of the scene! It seemed that the heavens and earth were coming together. The magazine was placed deep in the earth and surmounted by an immense body, of stone, *probably for the purpose* of injuring an enemy *in case* it should be necessary *to explode it*. Our troops were within 200 yards when the explosion took place, and were leveled with the ground in a moment, and covered with stones. About 40 were killed and 200 wounded, General Pike and several other officers fatally. The enemy did not escape the destruction of their own works. Hundreds were killed and wounded. Our men soon recovered and marched on, took some prisoners, and the town soon capitulated on condition that private property should be respected. They had set fire to a new ship carrying 30 guns; to the store-house containing £320,000 of public property. Gen. Schaffe, their commander, made his escape with about 300 Regulars and the principal part of the Indians. We took two schooners and about one million of public stores and property, 28 pieces of cannon. We continued in the city four days. The people were polite and treated us very well. We have many real friends among them. We left the place May 2, and proceeded to our fort at Niagara, opposite to Fort George, and there landed our troops and wounded."

Another letter written a few months later, gave details of farther action:—

"The battle at the Falls, our retreat to Fort Erie, the desperate attack and shocking slaughter of the enemy in their attempt to storm this place, and the tremendous fight at the batteries on the 17th inst., you have undoubtedly seen official accounts of. In these actions the American arms have been triumphant, and our haughty foe completely humbled. More real courage and heroism could not be displayed than was shown by the troops on these occasions. I never expected to witness such scenes, but it was my fortune to be called to the head of the surgical department in this branch of the army, and I have the proud satisfaction to believe that I have met with the approbation of the whole army in conducting the surgical department. I feel a peculiar pride in being placed in a situation where I can exercise the medical and surgical talents which I have labored a number of years to acquire. . . . . The battle at Chippewa, at the Falls, at Fort Erie, and the siege of that place which lasted 57 days, furnished a large number of the most important cases in surgery. General Gaines mentioned my name in his official account of the action at the Fort. Here were 400 wounded, principally of the enemy, in the most shocking manner. I was constantly at my dressing and amputating table for 36 hours. Our force here is respectable, and we shall in a few days attempt to drive the enemy from this part of Canada. I have no doubt but we shall do it if Chauncy keeps the ascendancy on Lake Ontario.

AMASA TROWBRIDGE, *Surgeon, U. S. A.*
Fort Erie, U. C., September 30, 1814."

Such reports of victory were hailed with joy by all parties, and served to enlist public sympathy more and more in behalf of the war. Woodstock was particularly gratified by the continued successes of her young townsman, Lieutenant Charles Morris, who had already greatly distinguished himself by naval exploits in Tripoli, where her Eaton had won such brilliant laurels. As first lieutenant of the *Constitution* he bore a prominent part in the achievements of that famous frigate, evading a British squadron after three days chase, and assisting in the capture of the *Guerriere*, when he received a severe wound. Promoted to the command of the *John Adams*, he performed important service, till finding it impossible to avoid capture he destroyed his ship and managed to effect escape with every man of his crew.

Reports of false alarms and ridiculous panics brought back by the militia put the people in better humor. Abner Reed, a Windham drummer, had an amusing experience at Stonington. Foraging one night for provisions, he espied to his consternation a British sloop coolly working its way up the harbor. Judging with Yankee calculation, that to go back to his company would be traveling over the ground twice, he hastened on to town and gave alarm. It made a terrible scare; there was only one old iron ship cannon at hand, no cartridges ready and but a few cannon balls. Volunteers emptied their powder-horns and rifled the stores; paper was mustered out, but no heavy wadding could be found. Reed like a true patriot stripped his coat into wadding. Vest and—pantaloons?—followed suit and still the greedy cannon asked for more. Finding that no one else was ready to make sacrifices, Reed swore, yes! *swore* roundly, "That he would not use his shirt nor shoes if all Stonington was burnt." Failing in fire, strategy was next attempted. Cart-bodies strapped on logs were dragged into position by some twenty or thirty men; and finding that the inhabitants were awake and preparing to meet them, the British quietly withdrew. Other versions of this or some other alarm ascribed relief to Mrs. Bailey's red flannel petticoat, but however apochryphal these stories may have been, they had an inspiriting influence. The summons to the relief of New London when invasion actually came, August 9, 1814, awakened something of the old Revolutionary enthusiasm. Lieutenant Hough of Canterbury, with a small body of militia, helped defend Stonington from the attack of the British fleet, and he was himself knocked down by a shell and taken up for dead. David Fuller of Scotland begged leave of Captain Palmer to lead the first company, warned the men at sunrise and at 3 P M marched off with seventeen men direct for New London. Other companies, drafted from the militia of different towns, followed as soon as possible. Marvin Adams, David Walden, and others from Scotland, reached Norwich town, August 23, and lodged in the old Court-house. Joining other companies in Norwich they proceeded next day to New London, running races nearly the whole distance with little regard to military order. "They remained in New London about six days, living in tents and drawing rations of salt pork and sea-biscuit." Those who did not like this fare bought milk of the inhabitants. They then proceeded to Stonington, and were placed on guard there, watching the British ships and keeping a general look-out. For most of the men it was a pleasant experience. Duties were light and discipline lax. One valiant Windham County captain was court-marshaled and sent home for embezzling the soldiers' flour for the use of his own family. Captain James Aspinwall of Canterbury, took the place of the delinquent and gave universal satisfaction, especially as a disciplinarian, "booting" his first lieutenant before the whole company for slowness of motion.* Part of the men were furnished with uniforms; the remainder figured in their Sunday suits. Substitutes in standing guard could always be obtained for a pint

---

* J. Q. Adams, Natick, R. I.

of whisky. A white cow challenged one night was allowed to retire unmolested. An old scow loaded with lumber raised an alarm another night, but all perils were surmounted at last, and after various terms of service the several companies returned home in safety.

The increased travel during the war, the troops and carting passing over the public roads, the arrival of huge loads of cotton from the South for the use of the factories, kept alive a pleasant excitement. Woodstock Hill was the scene of a remarkable conjunction between two government cannons—one ordered by the Secretary of War, the other by the Secretary of the Navy—which toiling over the turnpike from opposite points of the compass drew up before the door of Bowen's tavern at the same moment, to the great wonder and delight of the attendants and spectators, who celebrated the auspicious meeting with the usual treating and cheering.

The "glorious news" of Jackson's triumphant victory at New Orleans reached Windham simultaneously with that of signing the Treaty of Peace. The *Windham Herald*, February 16, 1815, announced the joyful events:—

"We congratulate our readers on the heart-cheering news which they will find in our paper of this day. The rumor of the glad tidings of PEACE reached this place Monday afternoon. It was immediately announced by loud peals from the belfry of the meeting-house. In the course of the evening this gratifying news was fully confirmed by hand-bills from Hartford, &c. No event since the peace of the Revolutionary War could have diffused such general joy. Every countenance appeared glad and mutual gratulations were reciprocated without distinction of party. The rejoicings were resumed, the next day, by the ringing of the bell, firing of cannon and other demonstrations of joy."

The immediately succeeding offer of " good Gin at Peace price," increased the general hilarity. Appropriate celebrations were held in most of the Windham County towns—the old field-piece of the Brooklyn Matross Company doing triple service in honor of the occasion. All parties rejoiced alike that the war was ended, and the bluest Federalist could not but exult in the triumph of his countrymen. Amidst the general rejoicing a few families were called to mourning. Septimus Tyler, the most dearly beloved son of his father, died of yellow fever, while bearing Governmental dispatches to Hayti.

[It is pleasant to know that many Windham veterans of 1812 still remain to tell their own story, and reap the benefit of their country's latest enactment in their favor. As these good men received fair pay and a generous land bounty, had a very pleasant time while on service and suffered no damage, their experience belies the common impression as to the *gratitude* of Republics. It is well that our great Nation is so prosperous as to be able to reward men who are willing even to expose themselves to danger in her service.]

II.

WINDHAM ENTERPRISE AND DIFFICULTIES. FUN AND FISHING. CHURCH AFFAIRS.

PARTY spirit raged fiercely in Windham town during this period. Colonel Dyer died in 1807,* but Swift, Perkins, Clark, Gray and other prominent men, upheld the Federal banner. Peter Webb, Elisha Abbe, and others, whose commercial ventures had been destroyed by British invaders, hotly supported the administration. Recruiting officers found no lack of response in Windham. Henry, son of Col. Thomas Dyer, a graduate of West Point, was captain in the regular army. The business losses occasioned by the destruction of shipping and the suspension of foreign traffic were partly made up by increased activity in manufactures. Clark and Gray's paper-mill at Willimantic Falls was now under full headway. A carding-machine, grist-mill, saw-mill, blacksmith's shop and coal-house were reported in the same locality, while Reuben Peck carried on the clothiery business in its various branches, having large experience in the art of dyeing and dressing. The Spaffords and Allens at South Windham were experimenting in various directions. Jesse Spafford and Amos D. Allen procured a patent for an ingenious planing-knife, making bonnet-chip out of shavings. Joshua Smith carried on clothiery works at South Windham,

---

* The *Windham Herald*, May 21, thus notices the death of its most distinguished citizen:—"Died on the 13th inst., after a short illness, the Hon. Eliphalet Dyer, aged 86, late chief justice of this State. He early took a decided part in favor of the American Revolution; was a very active and useful member of Congress during the most difficult period of the war. He was then appointed a judge of the Superior Court, and continued to fill that station with respectability until the year 1799, and during several of the last years of that period presided in the court. He then left public life at an advanced age to enjoy retirement; the powers of his mind continued with unusual vigor to the last. Though disconnected from civil life during his retirement, he ever remained a firm Federal republican; uniformly maintaining the principles or the American Revolution. He constantly attended all public meetings, and gave his advice and support to such measures as in his opinion had ever been productive of civil liberty and happiness to the State; and bore a firm and honorable testimony against that spirit of innovation, which he plainly saw was attempting to destroy our valuable institutions. He left the world with great cheerfulness and composure, enjoying the supports of that religion of which he had for a long time been an exemplary professor."

assisted by his son-in-law, George Spafford, and made cloth for the army, which had a high reputation for the excellence of its indigo blue. Amos D. Allen carried on furniture manufacture at the family homestead. A very excellent and thorough workman he trained his workmen to conform to his own high standard, and specimens of his work were distributed through the surrounding country. Hundreds of tall clock cases, embellished with many quaint and curious designs, were sent out from this establishment and found a ready market, especially at the South. The Taintor brothers with George Abbe and Edmond Badger, associated about 1810, for the manufacture of paper, building a mill on the Nachauge in the north part of the town, then called New Boston. They made writing paper in three grades, of strong texture but course finish. Elijah M. Spafford, in 1814, set up new clothiery works at Willimantic Falls, carrying on carding, water-spinning and weaving, as well as cloth-dressing and dyeing.

At Windham Green, trade and business continued lively. Ripley and Baldwin engaged in carriage-making at their shop near the meeting-house in 1808, making and repairing carriages of all kinds at short notice. The introduction of wagons into general use was not accomplished without some difficulty. The first brought into town was owned by Roger Huntington, and was sent to Leicester in September, 1809, for hand and machine cards. The lads who drove it, George Webb and Thomas Gray, found themselves the objects of great curiosity. People on the road everywhere stopped to look at them, and women and children flocked to the doors and windows, as if a menagerie was passing. At Woodstock quite a crowd gathered around them to examine the new vehicle that was to kill all the horses. One man had seen such a thing before in Hartford, "and the horse drawing it was fagged nearly to death." When the lads reached Leicester at 3 P. M., having driven from Pomfret that morning, they found to their surprise that the horse was not dead nor even tired. On their return the next day, Esquire McClellan and other Woodstock people came out to see them, and as the horse had traveled over twenty miles with a load of cards and still appeared fresh, they decided "that perhaps such wagons might come into use after all."

Peter Webb, Timothy Warren, John and Charles Taintor, Jonathan Jennings, George Abbe, John Clark, Joseph, Gurdon and Eliphalet Huntington, continued to advertise great variety of goods, and take in country produce. Wait Stoddard offered the highest price for sheep and lambs' skins. Burgess traded in sole leather and skins and took in men's knit stockings for market. All the merchants offered "plenty of cotton yarn for weaving." Money earned by knitting and weaving could be expended in adornments as well as in useful articles. Mary

B. Young kept a large assortment of millinery and fancy goods, and
Mrs. Carey, milliner, assured the ladies of Windham "that it was her
care to watch the earliest dawn of every rising fashion." Joseph Allen
"removed his Goose and shears to No. 4, Cheapside," where tailoring
business was executed in the neatest and best manner. Howes was
now associated with Dr. Benjamin Dyer in his drug store, which flourished greatly during the war, the thousand-dollar stock furnishing supplies when fresh importations were impracticable. Projects for village
improvements excited much discussion and interest. Jabez Clark,
Benjamin Dyer, Elisha White, John and Charles Taintor, John Staniford, Jun., Benjamin Brewster, Samuel Gray, John Byrne and Henry
Webb, associated as an Aqueduct Company in 1807, which by bringing water into the town street by subterraneous pipes, accomplished a
great public benefit. Finding it difficult to procure consent from the
town to needful improvements, the centre district obtained an act of
incorporation in 1814, with power to enact by-laws and maintain a
clerk. Cattle and geese were now forbidden the roads, and encroachments removed. Ancient grants allowing tan-works, shops and houses
on the public highways were revoked.

The necessity of keeping pace with expansion and development
weighed heavily upon the fathers of the town. Five great bridges
requiring constant supervision and renewal did not meet the demand.
The growing village around Taintor and Badger's paper-mill asked
for a new bridge and better road to Willimantic. A new turnpike to
Killingly and other roads, were demanded. There was great need of
a new house for the poor and better school-houses. Scotland Parish
clamored for town privileges; the central district insisted upon incorporation; the war brought special taxes and burdens—and harder
than all was the continued necessity of fighting for the maintenance
of its prerogatives and Court-house. Jabez Clark, Hezekiah Ripley
and John Baldwin, were continued in service as agents for the town.
All parties agreed in providing for this disbursement. Other demands
were not granted without a protracted contest. The motion to divide
the town met a curt refusal. The selectmen in 1815, were impowered
to hire or purchase a house for the poor. Agents were appointed to
oppose petition of John Taintor, and ask relief from the Assembly
from their great burden of bridges. But in spite of opposition they
were obliged to yield to necessity, and in 1818, the selectmen were
authorized "to contract for Horseshoe Bridge over and across
Nachauge River on road leading to paper-mill, ordered by County
Court." The six bridges were thus cared for:—Manning's Bridge,
Nathaniel Wales; Newtown, Zenas Howes; Iron Works, Alfred

Young; Horseshoe, Waldo Cary; Badger's, Edmond Badger; Island Bridge, Joshua Smith. John Staniford, Hezekiah Ripley and John Fitch served as town clerks during these years; Elisha Abbe, Zacheus Waldo, John Baldwin, Ebenezer Bass, Jonah Lincoln, John Burnett, David Young, were among its selectmen; George W. Webb, Andrew Baker, Ashael Kimball, Matthew Smith, grand-jurors. A captain elected to this office was excused from service "because he was afraid his company *would swear* training days." The Probate office was administered by Hezekiah Ripley, judge; Samuel Gray, clerk. Judge Swift as chief justice was much absorbed with the duties of his position and less prominent in town affairs. Jabez Clark served as state attorney. Samuel Perkins, David Young, John Baldwin, John Fitch and Philip Howard, were actively engaged in legal practice.

With all its cares and burdens the town maintained its jovial reputation. Liquor drinking increased during the war, and Bacchus claimed more votaries than ever. Shad and salmon triumphed as yet over attempted obstructions and made fishing at Willimantic a most exciting pastime. The tavern was thronged during the fishery season, and fun and flip were as plentiful as shad and salmon. "What *shad-ers* we are, and what shadows we pursue," exclaimed a disappointed wit, who came too late to supper. A quick retort was never lost in Windham. A most respectable citizen chanced to be once "overtaken" at a festive gathering, and was carried home to his wife, unconscious. Ordinary women give way to grief on such occasions; the lofty Windham dame only ejaculates—"Thank God, that he is not a blood relation!" A returned sea-captain on a visit to his early home indulged in such tremendous oaths that he was arrested by a justice and fined a small amount. Handing out a ten dollar bill he replies with astounding prefix, "By —— —— —— I'll swear that out." As might be expected there was yet no improvement in morals. Not only did the old drinking club bring many a man to ruin, but a Quizzical Club formed among the young people had a most demoralizing influence. A large number of young men associated in this society, had their pass signs and laws and met every week for entertainment. On one occasion they gave a public exhibition in the meeting-house, when the young West Point graduate, Henry Dyer, delivered an appropriate oration. Unfortunately their meetings were marred by such excessive use of liquor, that the more sober-minded youth themselves denounced it, declaring that they only "got together to make drunkards of themselves and encourage dissoluteness." Windham Academy maintained a fair standing under the instruction of "Master Abbott," Roger Southworth, Socrates Balcom and others. The district schools were maintained with more or less efficiency. A down town school-teacher was reported to keep the boys in order by administering Mayweed tea as a punishment. "Manners and dancing" were taught by a gleeful succession of dancing-masters.

Religion was at a low ebb during the early part of this period. Rev. Mr. Andrews—ordained pastor of Windham's First Church, August 8, 1808—was distressed and discouraged by the lack of religious earnestness among his people. Himself a very serious and devout Christian, the general tone of society, the levity and Sabbath-breaking, so pained and grieved him that in 1812, he asked a dismission, and though this was opposed on the very pertinent ground "that ministers were not to leave their people because they were wicked," his dismission was effected the following year. The modern term "incompatibility" sufficiently explains the withdrawal but the people were so annoyed by it as to stipulate in calling a successor, that if either party wished to dissolve the relation the case should be referred to three judges of the Superior Court, or to such other referees as they should mutually choose. The ministry of Cornelius B. Everest, ordained November 22, 1815, happily allayed all storms and had a most invigorating and healthful influence. Many united with the church and the standard of christian character and obligation was greatly elevated.

The death of Elder Benjamin Lathrop left the scattered Baptists without pastor or stated worship, so that they were again exposed to the exactions of the rate collector. Old Andrew Robinson when in Windham town one day had his horse taken from under him for a "priest tax." The old man shouldered his saddle and trudged manfully homeward, revolving relief from farther impost. The great kitchen in the new house he was building was made convenient for holding meetings, and thrown open for that purpose. It was announced that every alternate Sabbath the people might assemble there and that any minister or exhorter, of any creed or denomination, race or color, could have the privilege of preaching to them. Whether this would satisfy legal requirements was a debatable question. The stanch old reformer abhorred society organization as unscriptural and idolatrous, and would countenance no such movement, but those who wished to assure themselves of relief from parish assessment took hold of hands and marching around the room, solemnly pledged themselves to attend worship in this home sanctuary. Baptists, Methodists, and Separates of every shade of opinion, found refuge here, and as it became noised abroad the semi-monthly minister was never lacking.

In Scotland Parish the troubled ministry of Rev. Elijah G. Welles, was succeeded by that of Jesse Fisher, a graduate of Harvard. The ordaining sermon, May 22, 1811, was preached by Dr. Lathrop of

Springfield, then eighty years of age, with whom Mr. Fisher had pursued his theological studies. Exhibiting as a preacher, " soundness of doctrine and manly strength of intellect," and laboring earnestly " for the conversion and salvation of his flock," Mr. Fisher had the satisfaction of seeing his church built up and strengthened, and the evil effects of long dissension gradually disappear. The Brunswick Church did not long survive the loss of Elder Palmer and Deacon Walden. Some members drifted away to the Baptists and Methodists. In 1812, an attempt was made to maintain worship—Enoch Allen being commissioned to get the communion vessels, provide for sacrament and carry about the same. Failing in this effort, he makes this closing record :—

" *May* 24, 1813. *Voted*, That the church will join with and become a part of First Church in Canterbury, on condition we may meet by ourselves when expedient, except on communion days; also, that Canterbury Church approve of improvement of gifts of the private members on the Sabbath, not interrupting common exercise. Each individual have liberty to unite with any regular church where they will best advance the interest of Christ's Kingdom. *June* 11, 1813, met at Canterbury meeting-house. A part joining with Canterbury and a part did not.   ENOCH ALLEN, *Clerk*."

In public affairs Scotland maintained its interest. One-third of the town meetings were held in its well preserved meeting-house. The increasing burden of taxes raised the question of separation and local independence. Judge Devotion though advancing in years retained his interest in public questions nor did his lapse to Jeffersonianism impair his influence or popularity. His oldest son, Ebenezer, died early while on a voyage to the West Indies. John, a Yale graduate, a life-long invalid, held a Government position in Boston; was distinguished for elegant penmanship and high talents. Jonathan, after embarking in various business enterprises, returned to Scotland in 1813. Louis became a merchant in Boston. The mercantile establishment of the village fell into the hands of Philetus Perkins. Saw, grist and fulling-mills upon the various privileges, were carried on by the Devotions, Zacheus Waldo and others. Dr. Cheney was succeeded in medical practice by Dr. Hovey.

III.

TOWN AND CHURCH AFFAIRS IN HAMPTON. CHAPLIN SOCIETY. CHURCH ORGANIZATION. MEETING-HOUSE AND MINISTER.

HAMPTON as a farming town was little affected by war's alarm and manufacturing projects. The introduction of carding-machines so stimulated domestic industry that three fulling-machines were kept busily at work in dressing and dyeing the woven fabrics. Woolen and tow cloth still found a ready market. Cotton-yarn goods found little favor in the eyes of Hampton matrons. Colonel Mosely, the Taintors, Elijah Simons and others, still engaged in trade as far as practicable. A flourishing hat manufactory was established after the war by Luther D. Leach. Town affairs were administered with customary alertness. Dr. Brewster succeeded Colonel Mosely in the town clerk's office. Colonel Simons, Roger Clark, John Tweedy, Daniel Searls, John Loomis, served as selectmen ; Philip Pearl, James Burnett, Ebenezer Griffin, Joseph Prentice, as justices ; Luther Burnett, constable ; James Utley and Jonathan Clark, collectors. Colonel Mosely, Ebenezer Griffin, Roger and Solomon Taintor, William Burnett and Joseph Prentice, were sent as representatives. The latter was now established as Hampton's first lawyer, and a young man in the east part of the town was making ready to compete with him. Captain Silas Cleveland, Mr. Amasa Clark and other wise men, were thought capable of giving legal advice though not formally initiated in the legal profession. Though Hampton was pre-eminently healthy it abounded in physicians. The Doctors Brewster had an extensive practice. Doctors Jacob Hovey and Charles Moulton, were also active in the profession.

The stated church enjoyed peace and privileges under the wise administration of Mr. Weld, a man of culture and fine abilities. His wife, a daughter of Dr. John Clark, was a very intelligent and accomplished woman, though somewhat distinguished for *eccentricities* as well as " excellencies of character." Four sons of much promise grew up in the Hampton parsonage. Lewis graduated from Yale College in 1818, became the principal of the American Asylum for Deaf and Dumb; Theodore D. Weld won a name among the early anti-slavery agitators. The Baptist Church on Grow Hill suffered from the lack of stated ministry, and the developing of a new religious order. A sect of Christian reformers under the leadership of Elders Smith and Varnum obtained a strong foothold in this section of Windham County. For a time they followed in the footsteps of the

53

previous Abbe-ites, washing each other's feet and rolling on the floor to express their humility and lowliness, but after the removal of Varnum and his more ardent proselytes to Ohio, they renounced these excesses and adopted ordinary forms of worship. Elder Roger Bingham was ordained as a Christ-ian minister, and officiated in the Goshen and Burnham meeting-houses which were built for the accommodation of these Christ-ians. William Burnham served as deacon of the church in his neighborhood. After several years of irregular service under the occasional ministrations of Elders Rogers, Palmer, Bennett and Davis, the Baptist church was greatly revived by the preaching of Elder John Paine, a native of Abington. Uniting with this church in his youth, he now came back in maturity to labor with it. "Ordained at the Baptist meeting-house in Hampton, October 28, 1819, Mr. John Paine, to the work of the gospel ministry in that place: and also at the same time brethren Asahel Elliott and Gurdon Robinson, to the office of deacons. Rev. William Palmer, delivered a discourse, founded on 1 Timothy, iii: 1. Rev. James Grow, offered the consecrating prayer; Rev. Jonathan Goodwin, gave the charge; Rev. Esek Brown, presented the right hand of fellowship; Rev. John Nichols, prayed at the ordination of the deacons."

Residents of the western part of Hampton with those of Mansfield and Windham, who by local position were entitled to the privileges of Deacon Benjamin Chaplin's bequest, after an ineffectual effort to obtain immediate possession, delayed farther action till October, 1809, when in response to a petition from Matthew Smith and others, they were incorporated as "an Ecclesiastic Society by the name of Chaplin." William Perkins, Esq., of Ashford, grandson of the legator, was appointed to enroll the names of all the persons within the prescribed limits who should elect to become members of said new society, and to act as moderator at its first meeting to be held December 4, at the dwelling-house of the late Benjamin Chaplin. In compliance with this act, a goodly number assembled at "the old Chaplin House" to organize as a religious society. Rev. David Avery opened the meeting with prayer. The names of Israel, John, Thomas and Francis Clark, James Clark, Sen., and Jun., Ebenezer Cary, Jared and Joseph Huntington, Joseph and Elisha Martin, Roswell Bill, Chester Storrs, Matthew Smith, Daniel, Nathaniel and Joseph Mosely, Jun., Rufus Butler, John Rindge, William Moulton, Elkanah Barton and Nathaniel Cutler, residents in the east of Mansfield, west of Hampton and north of Windham, were enrolled by Esquire Perkins members of the Chaplin society. John Clark, Esq., was chosen clerk and treasurer; Joseph Martin, Matthew Smith and Francis Clark, society committee. Notices for society meetings were to be set up at Howard's and Mosely's mills, Chaplin and Tower Hill school-houses. At its second meeting, December 11, the Chaplin Society proved itself in advance of the age by voting, that Mrs. Lois Robbins be admitted member by enrollment. The widow thus honored had shown great wisdom and executive ability in training up a large family and administering an encumbered estate, and as she expected to share the burdens of the society was wisely allowed a voice in its counsels. It was also voted, to open our meetings by prayer. Measures were promptly initiated for securing and taking care of the funds. According to the terms of Deacon Chaplin's will, when "there should be a corporate society for the support of the public worship of God, according to the faith and practice of the churches now known and distinguished by the denomination of Congregational churches in New England, the place of public worship within one mile and a quarter of my dwelling-house in what is now Mansfield before the first day of January, 1812, there shall be given to such Incorporation, delivered by executor the amount of three hundred pounds . . . and my will is that such Incorporation fund said estate so that it may be safe and permanent, and apply the annual interest of it toward the support of a learned minister, professing and preaching the doctrines of the Gospel according as they are explained in the Westminster Confession of Faith in such society. . . . Provided also, that such preaching shall be kept up steadily, that is to say, there shall be at least forty Sabbaths such preaching in a year in order to be deemed *steady preaching*." The will farther provided that if preaching should cease for seven successive years this sum should revert to the heirs, and should the heirs oppose or discourage setting up such preaching, they should forfeit all rights to the legacies in case of reversion. In the Act of Incorporation it was also provided "That the interest on all moneys heretofore or hereafter subscribed to a fund for the support of the Gospel should be inalienably applied to the support of such minister upon the plan said Benjamin Chaplin of Mansfield, deceased."

"To set up steady preaching" was therefore the first object of the society. Rev. David Avery, who with his family then occupied the Old Chaplin residence, was the first supply secured. The school-house in Chaplin District was selected as the place of public worship till a meeting-house could be erected. Mr. Avery, Captain Erastus Hough, recently removed from Canterbury, Josiah Hendee, John Hovey, Enoch Pond, Jun., Jonathan Ashley, Perley Butler, Hosea and Charles Clark, Stephen and William Ford, were soon enrolled as members of the society. Five hundred dollars were added to the fund by voluntary subscription. May 31, 1810, a council convened at the house of

Rev. Mr. Avery. Reverends Nathan Williams, Moses C. Welch, D. D., and Hollis Sampson, were present with delegates from their respective churches, and after the usual religious services, David and Hannah Avery, Israel, James, Hosea, Francis, Jerusha, Zerviah and Sally Clark, Ebenezer and Sarah Cary, Elkanah Barton, Nathaniel and Esther Mosely, subscribed a confession of faith and were recognized as the church in Chaplin Society. This body almost immediately proceeded to make choice of Rev. David Avery for their pastor, the privileged "sisters affectionately and sentimentally uniting with the brethren" in a unanimous call, but the more worldly-wise society "fearing that it might injure them essentially," refused to concur. The stringent provisions of Deacon Chaplin's bequest made great caution necessary. Mr. Avery, though a brilliant and powerful preacher, was somewhat unsteady and erratic. In previous pastorates at Bennington and Wrentham, he had been accused "of a leaning towards Socinianism," and though this charge had not been sustained it behooved the Chaplin legatees to be on their guard and not incur the risk of losing their legacy by any sentimental preference for the testator's son-in-law. After mature deliberation the society voted, June 3, 1812, "not to concur with the church in the vote for giving the Rev. David Avery a call," and, to make assurance doubly sure, they farther enacted, that the trustees be directed not to pay over any money to any minister until they obtain to their satisfaction the opinion of Windham Association, respecting his answering the requirements of Deacon Chaplin's will. With these precautions Mr. Avery was allowed to remain in charge.

The meeting-house made slow progress. The selection of a suitable site occasioned as much discussion as the requirements of the minister. Matthew Smith was appointed agent to apply to the County Court for a committee to affix a spot, but the vote was rescinded and a vote passed that the meeting-house be placed on the spot contemplated by Mr. Howard, called Wells' Hill. Also, to build a meeting-house upon the plan of that of the North Society of Mansfield, excepting the steeple. Still the work did not go forward. Money was lacking and the society was debarred from making the needful assessments by the terms of its incorporation. April 11, 1813, it was voted, "to petition the General Assembly for the privileges of other located societies, provided there can be money enough raised by subscription to defray expenses," but whether the needful sum was raised or not further privileges were not then obtained. The delay in building a house of worship made it a little doubtful whether the society could lawfully appropriate the interest of the fund for the hiring of a minister, and its committee was directed to lay its condition before Windham Association, and to consult with Judge Root. September, 1812, another effort was made to go on with the meeting-house. Captain Hough, Matthew Smith, William and John Clark and Joseph Martin, were deputized to superintend the getting out of timber. In January a committee was appointed to contract for building, and for the use of Mrs. Howard's saw-mill. Logs were cut down and sawed during the summer, stuff at the mill being placed in charge of Captain Bill. October, 1813, the committee was directed to make a contract to build as soon as may be, but it was not till the following January that the work began in earnest. Daniel Martin was then appointed agent to superintend the getting of materials, collect and apply all subscriptions for that purpose—receiving a compensation of ten cents an hour for his services. Chaplin now again manifested its progressive spirit by enacting, that *seven hours* should constitute a day's work, pay for a man's labor, ten cents an hour; oxen, six cents; for use of cart, six cents; sled, three cents. May 9, 1814, "voted unanimously to apply to County Court for alteration of meeting-house spot—James Utley, agent; August 1, to raise the meeting-house as soon as possible after the 21st—Daniel Martin, Enoch Pond, David Avery, Jun., Chester Storrs and Samuel Tracy, committee of arrangements." Even then the site had not been affixed, and on the 15th, the committee was directed, "To apply to the County Court, Tuesday next, to affix a spot thirty-five rods north of that now established, west side of road, west of the gate letting into Captain Hough's north pasture, on the rise of ground called Chaplin's Hill." This being effected, the meeting-house frame was formally raised, Thursday, August 25, amid great public rejoicings. Another year passed before it was ready for occupation. September 14, 1815, the society voted, to accept the meeting-house as finished, and to apply to their honored friend and father, Mr. Jonathan Clark of the First Society, to appoint a day for dedication and to choose a minister to preach. Rev. Samuel P. Williams of Mansfield's First Church, was appropriately chosen, who preached a suitable sermon from Genesis xxviii: 17, and all the exercises were conducted with the solemnity and ceremony befitting the occasion.

Though Mr. Avery had now ceased to supply, preaching was statedly maintained though it might be doubtful whether it attained the requisite standard of *steadiness*. Rumors having reached the society that the church had become Socinian, the church addressed the society a letter, asking for a good understanding between them, and solemnly averring, "that they were constituted a regular Congregational church upon the foundation of the Westminster Confession of Faith, and have never one of us departed or deviated therefrom."

The society responded, "That we view said church as standing on the ground required by Deacon Chaplin's will." Full society privileges were obtained in 1815, inhabitants residing on the lands owned by Nathaniel Linkon being at the same time restated to Windham. Pew ground was now sold to pay for building expenses and Joseph Martin engaged to sweep the meeting-house and keep the key for $2.32 a year. The Rev. Messrs. Treat, Finney, Nichols and Nathan Grosvenor were among the various supplies procured for the pulpit. In 1818, it was "voted to hire preaching for the year provided it can be done for six dollars a Sunday, including ministers board and horse-keeping." An effort was now made to complete the meeting-house, such super-fluities as pews and pulpit not having been included in the previous "finishing." In the following year Mr. Jared Andrus of Bolton, was called to the pastorate, the society offering a salary of $300 and twenty cords of wood for ten years. Mr. Andrus accepted the call with some addition to the salary. May 3, 1820, it was voted that the body of the house be finished by slips in lieu of pews—slips to be finished with banisters provided it costs no more. Painting the house was left to the judgment of the committee. In November, Abel Ross, Darius Knight and Erastus Hough were appointed to provide for the ordaining council; Jonathan Ross, James Utley, Abel Ross and James Clarke, committee of arrangements, and on December 27, more than ten years after organization, a pastor was installed over Chaplin church and society. Among the many candidates none could have more fully answered the requirements of Deacon Chaplin. Mr. Andrus was a man of unusual sobriety and earnestness, who had entered the ministry when past his thirtieth year from a deep conviction of duty, and labored faithfully to discharge every obligation.

IV.

ENTERPRISE IN CANTERBURY. FATAL ACCIDENT. CHURCH AFFAIRS IN FIRST AND WESTMINSTER SOCIETIES.

DESPITE its heavy losses by death and emigration, Canterbury maintained its buoyancy, hastening to take advantage of manufacturing and mechanical inventions, and yielding its best water privileges to experimenter and capitalist. Carding-machines were soon busily at work on Little River, and cloth-dressing and hat-making carried on with increased vigor. Capt. Joseph Simms removed his business stand to Canterbury Green, and with the aid of four or five journeymen was

able to supply many business firms in Windham County, and even a
distant Southern market, with heavy black woolen hats, made in three
sizes, so firm and stocky that one might last a lifetime. James Burnet
also engaged in the hatting business in Westminster society, and invented
a process or forming hat bodies "by placing the material in a hollow
sphere and subjecting the same to a revolving motion," by which it
was evenly deposited on the form, but not succeeding, "kettles,
basons, blocks and Irons" were advertised for sale, and he retired
westward to experiment in other directions. Some six or eight stores
were still needed to supply the wants of the town. Thomas Coit, Gad
Buckley, Jedidiah Johnson, Luther Paine, Fenner and Harris occupied
the block on the Green. Energetic young men took the places of
those who had gone. Andrew T. Judson of Eastford had already
gained a flourishing legal practice. The old class of physicians, which
had attended to patients when nothing more important was on hand,
was giving place to younger men, who had won by study the title
prefixed to their names and devoted themselves to their profession
with more singleness of purpose. Dr. Andrew Harris at Canterbury
Green and Dr. Elijah Baldwin in South Canterbury, harmoniously
occupied the field, the former practicing more especially with the
knife and the latter carrying round the saddle-bags. Dr. Johnson continued his daily rounds through Westminster Parish. Dr. Hough
retained his dual office, administering pills and whippings with equal
excess and alacrity. Dr. Gideon Welles, so long prominent in town
affairs, died in 1811. Elisha Paine, Esq., (or Payne, as he wrote his
name), died early. Rufus Adams and Daniel Frost continued in the
practice of law, the latter serving as town clerk. These lawyers, with
Isaac Backus, Asa Butts and Luther Paine, were often sent as representatives. Gad Bulkley administered the post-office and David Hyde
served as mail-carrier, supplying the newspaper class that held its
head-quarters at Samuel Barstow's much-frequented tavern. The
tavern at the Green enjoyed its accustomed patronage and popularity—
Jacob Bacon, Samuel Hutchins and Capt. Bicknell serving successively
as landlords. Its previous incumbent, Jedidiah Johnson, was made
general of the Fifth Brigade in 1809. His brief term of command
was marked by great military activity. War rumors had re-kindled
the flame of martial enthusiasm, for even those who disliked the war
delighted in military parade. Mounted on a stately steed, and attended by a negro servant in appropriate uniform, General Johnson
added great lustre to those popular pageants. Canterbury at this date
furnished most of the officers for the Twenty-first Regiment, viz: William Kinne, adjutant; Samuel Hutchins, quartermaster; Isaac Knight,
pay-master; Rev. Erastus Learned, chaplain. Its company of Light

Infantry was one of the best drilled and equipped in the State. Its officers in 1809 were Joseph Simms, captain; Nathan Fish, lieutenant; in 1815, James Aspinwall, captain; Samuel Hough, lieutenant; Amos Bacon, ensign. This company and officers, together with other companies drafted from the militia, rendered efficient service during the war, hastening on several occasions to the relief of New London, and remaining many months on guard. Canterbury was also enlivened by frequent Masonic parades and demonstrations. The Festival of St. John the Baptist was observed June 26, 1811, with unusual ceremony—brethren from Putnam and East Star Lodges assembling at Moriah Lodge, marching about the streets in resplendent regalia, and after listening to an eloquent oration in the meeting-house, returning to a good dinner and appropriate festivities. Luther Paine, Darius Matthewson, Nathan and John Williams, and Capt. Eleazer Mather served as committee of arrangements. Those debarred from participation in this esoteric entertainment, caught bursts of uproarious merriment and snatches of convivial song, quite out of keeping with the ordinary demeanor of these most respectable citizens.

In cotton-spinning Canterbury made no great pretenses, and only achieved one small mill, erected by Fenner, Harris and Bulkley on Rowland's Brook, which did a good business during the war. The clothiery works of Captains Kingsley and Spafford enjoyed abundant patronage. Tanneries, cooperage, pottery and potash works were maintained with creditable energy, and the various saw and grist-mills continued to improve their privileges. Freshets and floods still exercised their ancient prerogatives, subjecting the town to serious outlay and impost. The great flood of 1807 damaged Butts' Bridge and destroyed Bacon's (formerly Nevins') Bridge, occasioning a fatal accident and loss of life. The ferry-boat used as a substitute for the latter bridge was overloaded and swamped. Luther Paine, Esq., though a large and heavy man, succeeded in swimming ashore. Dr. Isaac Knight, unable to swim, sprang upon his horse and safely breasted the furious current. Erastus Barstow with his two-horse team also gained the shore. All on board were saved but Nathaniel Kinne of Black Hill, a man of great height and vigorous strength, who was in some way disabled and life was extinct before assistance could reach him. His ghastly figure stretched out upon the grass made a deep impression upon all who saw him, and his untimely end was much lamented. Ten years later, the town was again called to rebuild or repair both Bacon's and Butts' bridges. The selectmen were enjoined to confer with Plainfield respecting building a good boat to convey passengers and teams across the Quinebaug near Bacon's bridge. In case of refusal they were directed to build the same and have it well tended at the expense of the town: also, to petition the County Court to divide the charge of this bridge.

The vacancy in the ministerial office that had so long afflicted the First church and society of Canterbury was happily filled in 1808 by the Rev. George Leonard of Middleborough, Mass.,—called to settlement "without a dissenting voice." The ordaining services, February 3, were conducted with all the ceremony befitting so joyful an event. Captain Bacon and Messrs. Samuel Carter and Thomas Coit provided suitable accommodations for council and delegates, Luther Paine, Rufus Adams and Asa Bacon, Esquires, waited upon the same, while Captain Bacon and five others served as ushers at the meeting-house to preserve order and furnish strangers with seats. But though so auspiciously inaugurated, this ministry was of short continuance. Mr. Leonard was feeble in health and somewhat inclined to Arminianism in doctrine and in a little more than two years sought and obtained dismission. His successor, Rev. Asa Meech, installed October 28, 1812, succeeded in harmonizing various conflicting elements, "not only increasing the number of the church, but establishing its faith and order," but he, too, lost favor after a time. It was somewhat difficult for an earnest minister to avoid giving offense. The horse-racing at Butts' Bridge race-course, the revelries at Masonic Hall, the all-night dances and promiscuous frolicking, could hardly fail to escape reprobation. And if while denouncing amusements as sins he limited the chances of obtaining forgiveness to "about one in a million," the Canterbury people might be pardoned for adopting the conclusion of the old negro upon a similar close calculation—"If only so few are to be saved I think we had better not putter any more about them."

The Westminster church continued to prosper under the faithful ministration of Rev. Erastus Learned. Increasing interest in religion and frequent accessions to the church greatly cheered the heart of the good minister. He reports:—

"*November* 3, 1816.
This was an interesting, refreshing and solemn day. To behold the trophies of Zion's King come forward to the church caused the children of Zion to rejoice. Fifteen admitted to full communion. *January* 5, 1817. Another joyful communion. Seventeen admitted to the church. *March* 2. Blessed be the Lord for his continued goodness to this branch of Zion. Eight persons came forward and entered into covenant with God and His people. *May* 4. Blessed be the Lord for his marvelous grace and mercy in continuing to build His Zion here. Nine persons received to full communion. Dr. Rufus Johnson was baptized and his family. *July* 6. Eight persons admitted to full communion."

The temporal affairs of the church were wisely administered. In 1809, a committee was appointed to provide money for new covering and painting meeting-house, build a steeple and procure a bell; also, a decent hearse or carriage; also to promote decency, good order and regularity at funerals. These improvements were not effected till 1813, when a building was ordered in the burying-ground "to contain, store and shelter the hearse." The coveted bell was given to the society by a son of the minister, Seth P. Staples, Esq. Highway repairers were warned not to encroach upon the meeting-house green. The salary of the minister was increased to four hundred dollars. William Carew, one of the early members of the church, bequeathed the reversion of forty-five acres of land for the support of the Lord's table. The deacons continued " to line out the psalms " till 1815, when Deacon John Barstow was allowed to convene the singers and lead them to the choice of a chorister. This innovation opened the way for singing schools and other modern devices. Deacon Stephen Butts served as society clerk till 1816. Asa Butts and David Walden also served the church as deacons.

In business Westminster held its own fairly, supporting at least one store and tavern, and various industries. Rufus Johnson & Co. gave place in 1811, to "Smith and Morgan" who offered a handsome assortment of West India and European goods, taking in produce and putting out " weaving in the cotton-line." The efficiency of its schools was increased by the organization of a school society in 1812. Isaac Backus, moderator; Josiah Park, clerk and treasurer. To each district was assigned one committeeman and one inspector, viz.:— 1. Amasa Park, committee; Rev. Erastus Learned, inspector. 2. Daniel Meech, John Barstow. 3. Horatio Pettingill, Nathaniel Clark. 4. Nathan Allen, Ebenezer Waldo. 5. Daniel Storer, Asa Butts. 6. James Cary. 7. Samuel Chad, Isaac Backus. 8. Curtis and Samuel Barstow. 9. Roger Smith, Asa Burgess. Youth from both societies still sought the privilege of academic and collegiate instruction. Zedekiah S. Barstow was graduated from Yale in 1813. Archibald and Anson Burgess and Samuel Backus were graduated during this period. The religious interest that prevailed in the churches led these and other Canterbury young men to enter the ministry. Simon Barstow was debarred by ill health from pursuing ministerial studies. The ministerial aspirations of another Canterbury youth was one of the concurring influences in the formation of the American Education Society. A pious young man gone out from this town, Thomas L. Paine, joined with others in "The Young Christian Fraternity" of Boston, in 1814. Visiting Canterbury soon after he found a great revival in progress and one young convert in particular, " who had a strong desire to get an education and devote his life to the Christian ministry." The Fraternity was greatly moved in his behalf and planned to form a society to give him definite aid, and seeking advice from their ministers it was found that similar calls were coming from all parts of the land, and a national society was soon organized to meet it. Whether the young man in question became a beneficiary is not apparent.

The old Separate church after the death of Rev. William Bradford, maintained a feeble existence, its members carrying on the services. Captain Ephraim Lyon died in 1812. Dr. Hough and "old Esquire Felch," long known and respected in Canterbury, died in 1818.

V.

PLAINFIELD MANUFACTORIES. DEATH OF DR. BENEDICT. HIGHWAYS AND BRIDGES. STERLING AND VOLUNTOWN.

PLAINFIELD was much favored by manufacturing enterprise. The Union Manufacturing Company with its solid phalanx of citizens and non-residents, the Central Company under the charge of John Lester and Job Angell, the Moosup and Andrus Factory companies, carried on their various mills and business operations during the war with great spirit and energy. Abel and Benjamin Andrus, Thomas and Andrew Gibbs, Levi Robinson and Joseph Hutchins of Plainfield; Charles Townsend of Norwich; Titus Adams, John Baldwin and Joseph Farnham of Canterbury, associated as the Andrus Factory Company in 1811, buying "land in Plainfield and Canterbury, south of grist-mill on brook" of Stephen and Joseph Farnham, and putting up a small building on the site of the present Packersville. Adjoining residents in both towns were much interested in this manufacturing experiment and freely gave their aid in clearing up land and digging the cellar. The frame-raising called out the customary crowd and frolic. A jolly youth climbed to the top of the ridgepole, and pouring out a bottle of spirits, named the building in honor of its chief proprietor the excellent Deacon Andrus. Woolen factories were also set in motion by Darius Lawton of Newport, and Joseph Eaton. Carding-machines and fulling-mills were run by John Kennedy and others. Mr. John Lester and Dr. Fuller engaged largely in wool raising. The manufacturing depression following the return of peace occasioned much embarrassment in Plainfield. Several companies were forced to suspend work, and many changes were effected.

Plainfield Academy retained its place in public interest. Nathan Hewitt, Samuel Backus, Samuel Phinney and Archibald Burgess, officiated as principals during Mr. Burleigh's withdrawal to Woodstock. Jonathan E. Chaplin, Evan M. Johnson, John Bronson, James B. Dorrance, Luther Spalding, William Danielson, Nicholas Brown of Providence, William M. Benedict, John Witter, John A. Stevens, Elisha B. Perkins, Frederick Morgan, Merritt Bradford, Lemuel Smith, Jonah Spalding, George Sumner, and many others who filled honorable positions in various departments, were graduated during these years. Mr. Burleigh returned to his charge in 1816, in time to supply in some degree the loss of Dr. Joel Benedict, the faithful friend and counsellor of the school. Though suffering greatly from weakness and disease he was able to preach till the Sabbath before his death. "In his approach to the grave he evinced the most unqualified resignation and even joyful triumph." A monu ment "reared by filial affection among the graves of his attached people," commemorated the virtues of this great and good man, who for over thirty years had so worthily honored his calling and profes sion, and identified himself with every scheme for public advancement. Doctor's degrees had been given him by Union and Dartmouth Colleges.

Plainfield had lost the presence of her distinguished lawyer, Hon. Calvin Goddard, who was drawn away to Norwich in 1809. Joseph Eaton and Job Monroe now shared the legal practice. Town officers were much engrossed in keeping up their roads and bridges, and smoothing the way for manufacturers. Highway districts were remodeled in 1808, and re-entered as, No. 1, Southwest; No. 2, Middle District, with three bridges, including bridge over west turn- pike by tan vats; No. 3, North meeting-house—begins at the Great Gate; No. 4, Green Hollow, extending north to Killingly line on the road to Elder Cole's meeting-house; No. 5, Shepard Hill; No. 6, Moosup, extends north by Hartshorn's mills; No. 7, Black Hill— includes Nevins' and Cutler's bridges; No. 8, Pond Hill—extending to Sterling line; 9, Snake Meadow, north to Killingly line; 10, Mill Road; 11, Goshen; 12, Walnut Hill; 13, Kinne Road; 14, Howe Hill; 15, Dow Road; 16, Spring Hill; 17, 18, East and West Flat Rock. Roads were laid out near Union Factory, and from the Andrus Factory over Butts' Bridge, but a road was refused from the latter factory to Plainfield village on the ground "that there was no house on the way and never would be." In 1818, Benjamin Bacon, William Kinne, Nathan Burgess, Erastus Lester and Lot Morgan, were appointed a committee to confer with Canterbury upon building a bridge across the Quinebaug on the Plainfield and Canterbury road. The selectmen were meanwhile authorized to establish a method of crossing by boat. They were also called to join with Brooklyn in providing for bridge repairs and with means of crossing the Quinebaug. Bridges over Moosup River were also replaced.

"The September Gale," so famous in New England meteorologic annals, swept with great violence through Plainfield and Canterbury, damaging and destroying many buildings, and uprooting fruit and forest trees. The accompanying rain, which fell in torrents, was said to be as salt as the distant ocean. The special mission of this tempestuous visitant in Windham County was apparently the demolition of dilapidated meeting-houses, three at least yielding to its fury. Plainfield's Congregational church edifice was entirely prostrated, and the materials for a Friends' meeting-house then collected on Black Hill were scattered and in part destroyed. These losses were repaired with great promptness. A substantial stone meeting-house was completed by the Congregational society in 1818. Under the auspices of the Monthly meeting of Quakers at Greenwich, R. I., a simple house was also erected for the Friends' worship. Several of the non-resident manufacturers were of this order, and aided in this work. Forty-five acres of land on Black Hill were conveyed by John Monroe to Sylvester Wicks and Dea. Howland in presence of Rowland Greene—to whom was committed the charge of establishing a Friends' boarding school. Some forty or fifty pupils from some of the most influential Quaker families of Rhode Island were received into this quaint and primitive family school under the fatherly care of Dr. Rowland Greene, aided by his good wife, and his brother, Dr. Benjamin Greene. The Quaker school and worship seemed to lend a calm and tranquil radiance to this ancient hill. "Green Hill," it might have been more appropriately called now that the avenue of trees set out by William Kinne were offering such grateful shade and verdure. Dr. Isaac Knight still occupied a pleasant homestead on this hill. John Monroe and Lot Morgan were among its residents. A new house of worship was built in 1813 on land "near the dwelling-house of Silas Bailey, extending east four rods across the Black Graves, so called . . . . said meeting-house to be called the Friends' or Baptist meeting-house and lot held for no other purpose."

Sterling's manufacturing facilities were well improved during this period. Its first factory, built by Dorrance, Hall and others, was destroyed by fire soon after its completion, but its site was soon occupied by a larger building under the more exclusive management of Samuel Ames of Providence, which was described in 1818 as "one of the largest manufacturing establishments in the State, running sixteen hundred spindles." The buildings for the accommodation of the workmen were built of stone, taken from the ledge of rocks included in the company's purchase. This "Devil's Den Chimney," as it was previously called, possessed according to *Niles' Gazetteer* "very singular and curious features," viz:—

"It is situated within a ledge of rocks and has a circular area of about 100 feet in diameter. The rock is cleft in two places, forming at each a chasm or fissure of about 50 feet deep, through one of which there runs a small stream of water; the other communicates with a room of about twelve feet square, at the interior part of which there is a fireplace and a *chimney* extending through the rock above, forming an aperture of about three feet square. In another part of the rock there is a natural staircase, winding around it from the bottom to the top. In the cold season of the year a large mass of ice is formed in the room above described by the dashing of water through the chimney which continues there through nearly the whole of the warm months; the sun being almost excluded from this subterraneous recess."

The American Factory upon the Quanduck, and a small cotton factory upon the Moosup, were also carried on. Three grain mills, one carding-machine, one fulling-mill and clothiery works, two tanneries, four mercantile stores and two taverns, were reported in 1818. A post-office had then been opened—Benjamin Tuckerman, postmaster. The Academy and public library were still maintained. Calvin Hibbard of Windham had engaged in the practice of law. Thomas Backus, John Partridge and Oliver Howlett were reported as practicing physicians. Pierce Smith succeeded Asa Montgomery as town clerk. John Wylie, Thomas Backus, Dyer Ames, Richard Burlingame, Dixon Hall, Jeremiah Young, John Gallup and Calvin Hibbard served as justices. Other town offices were filled by Lemuel Dorrance, Obadiah Brown, Asa Whitford, Jonah Young, Archibald Dorrance, John Hill, John and Azel Cole, Elias Frink, Amos Perkins, Joseph Gallup, John Keigwin, Artemas Baker. Good bridges were built and roads altered for the convenience of the manufacturing companies. Half of the town meetings were held in the house of Azel Cole, and later in that of William Fairman "on the new road near the American Cotton Factory."

The meeting-house on Sterling Hill continued to be used for public meetings and occasional religious services till about 1812, after which date it was statedly occupied by the Baptists. Under the preaching and labors of Elder Amos Welles, previously of Woodstock, a new religious interest was developed. Baptists in Coventry and Sterling united in a new church organization February 13, 1813. Its pastoral charge was assumed by Elder Welles. Public worship was held alternately a Coventry and Sterling Hill. Asa Montgomery was chosen deacon in 1816; Philip Keigwin assistant. Nearly fifty were added to the church during the ministry of Elder Welles, which continued till his death, in 1819. The Plainfield Baptist church, and a neighboring church in Rhode Island, united with this church in the Sterling Hill Association, holding a general meeting once a year, which was largely attended and excited much interest.

The church worshipping in the Line meeting-house was greatly broken and scattered. Rev. Elijah Welles after his dismission from Scotland labored with it for a year but did not succeed in uniting the flock. Worship was kept up in intermittent fashion by a few brethren who in 1817 sought relief from the Windham Association. That body referred their case to the Domestic Missionary Society for Connecticut, which from time to time extended much-needed aid.

In business affairs Voluntown reported some progress. One small cotton factory, two carding-machines, two fulling-mills, four grain mills and two tanneries, were in operation. Charcoal burning was also carried on to considerable extent. James Alexander served many years as town clerk. Allan Campbell, James Alexander, John Wylie, Storry Kinne, Amos Treat and Benjamin Gallup, justices. Doctors Allan and William Campbell were widely known as medical practitioners.

VI.

EXCITEMENT IN KILLINGLY. INVENTION AND DISCOVERIES. CHURCH AFFAIRS. WOMAN'S TRACT SOCIETY.

THE manufacturing *furor* raged with great violence in Killingly, its numerous rivers offering such convenient facilities that her own citizens were able to embark in such enterprises with less foreign aid than was requisite in other towns. "Danielson's Factory" at the Quinebaug Falls enjoyed a high place in popular favor, its twenty liberal-handed stockholders, mostly town residents, prosecuting its various business affairs with much energy. William Reed served most efficiently for many years as its agent. Its well-filled store was managed by the Tiffany brothers from Rhode Island. Once a year, proprietors and managers met to report progress and divide profits, when business was followed by a jovial good time and supper. The "Stone Chapel" on the present site of the Attawaugan, was built by Captain John and Ebenezer Kelley for John Mason of Thompson in 1810, but did not get into successful operation for some years, when John, James B. and Edward Mason, Jun., were incorporated as the "Stone Chapel Manufacturing Company." Messrs. John Mason and Harvey Blashfield had the oversight of this establishment. The tallow candles needed for its morning and evening service were dipped by Miss Harriet Kelley, in batches of forty dozen at a time. The privilege on the Five-Mile River long occupied by Talbot's Grist-Mill passed into the hands of the Killingly Manufacturing Company in 1814. Its constituent members were Rufus Waterman, Thomas Thompson, John Andrews of Providence; David Wilkinson, Henry Howe of North

Providence, Dr. Robert Grosvenor, Jedidiah Sabin, Elisha Howe, Benjamin Greene of Killingly, Smith Wilkinson, Eleazer Sabin of Pomfret. The Howes had charge of the business, and the factory soon built was called by their name. The remarkable descent of the Whetstone Brook furnished privileges quite out of proportion to its volume of water. The first Chestnut Hill Company to take advantage of this fall was constituted by Joseph Harris, Ebenezer Young, Calvin Leffingwell, Asa Alexander, George Danielson, Lemuel Starkweather, whose wheels and spindles were soon competing with those of other manufacturers. The greatest spirit and activity prevailed in these growing villages. Everybody was hard at work, building, digging, planting, carting, weaving, spinning, picking cotton, making harnesses, dipping candles, and attending to the thousand wants of the hour. The wives and families of the manufacturing executives entered into their work with jubilant enthusiasm, helping everything forward. Mrs. John Mason was a lady of wonderful energy and vivacity, one who would be a social light in the darkest corner. Very pleasant intercourse was kept up between the families of the several villages, who seemed bound together in a common aim and fraternity. The intense mechanical activity of the time was manifested by a remarkable feminine achievement, the exercise of the inventive faculty, hitherto dormant in the female mind. Mrs. Mary Kies of South Killingly invented "a new and useful improvement in weaving straw with silk or thread," for which she obtained in May, 1809, the *first patent issued to any woman in the United States,* and she is also said to have been the first female applicant. Mrs. President Madison expressed her gratification by a complimentary note to Mrs. Kies. The fabrication of this graceful and ingenious complication was thus added to the other industries of Killingly.

The impulse given by manufacturing enterprise was manifested in other activities. The mineral resources of the town were sought out and brought before the public. The old Whetstone Hills were found to enclose valuable quarries of freestone, suitable for building purposes. Rare and beautiful detached stones as well as extensive quarries were found on Breakneck. "A rich bed of porcelain clay" was discovered on Mashentuck Hill, "pronounced by competent judges to equal the best French or Chinese clay." Indications of lead and still more valuable ore were also reported. Many new roads were demanded to facilitate the opening industries. The town accepted a road laid out from Danielson's Factory to the country road near the dwelling-house of Solomon Sikes (declining responsibility at the same time for the bridge over Five-Mile River), and voted not to oppose a road from Danielson's to the house of Rev. Israel Day, and thence to Rhode Island line. This new road to Providence was very needful for the transportation of goods and cotton. The mercantile operations of Captain Alexander Gaston, who had removed from Sterling to South Killingly, were also greatly benefited thereby. His flourishing store added greatly to the importance of this miniature "city." He was accustomed to buy large quantities of goods at auction in New York market, and farmers would hurry down to Providence with their teams when his ships were expected, that they might reap the profit of hauling them up to Killingly. A new turnpike project forcibly urged by some citizens was most vigorously resisted, and called out the following successful manifesto :—

"Whereas a contemplated branch of four miles to the Connecticut and Rhode Island turnpike (petition by Evan Malbone and others) is to meet about a thousand dollars expense upon Killingly without enhancing the interests of the town, or facilitating a convenience to the public; and, whereas, such an obtrusion upon the town would be considered as truly extraordinary and unprecedented as it would be derogatory to its interests; and, whereas it is the unquestioned privilege of a town at all times to defend and protect its interest against that principle of invasion which would sacrifice the interests of town and individuals to its own accommodation—therefore voted, that the town of Killingly will never submit to such an invasion upon these rights while protection can be claimed by the laws of the State."

So heavy was the burden brought upon tax-payers by public improvements that an effort was made to secure town division by an east and west line through the centre. Sampson Howe, Captain Gaston and Ezra Hutchins appear frequently as moderators of town meetings ; Daniel Buck, John Day, Samuel Sprague, John Kelly, Tiffany and John Adams, Jacob Spalding, as selectmen ; Ezra Hutchins, Joseph Adams, Anthony Brown, Ebenezer Young, Penuel Hutchins, Luther Warren, Arba Covill, David Chase, as justices ; Luther Warren, town clerk ; Hezekiah Howe, constable. Ebenezer Young had now opened a law office in the rising village of Westfield, which with its meeting-house, doctor's office and tavern, was becoming more and more of a town centre. A fine house near the meeting-house was occupied by Captain Evan Malbone and his establishment. Captain Solomon Sikes' popularity as a military officer added much to the fame of his tavern, especially during war-time. Killingly's artillery company was very efficient at this date, commanded by Captain David Bassett. Laban and Barzillai Fisher served as its lieutenants. William Alexander, Calvin Day, David Chase and Charles Buck were rising officers. The admired South Killingly company maintained its standing under Simon Hutchins, John Eaton, 2d, and Aaron Rood. Increasing centralization and other causes gave a new impetus to the West Killingly church. Mr. Johnson was dismissed from the pastorate in 1809. His successor,

55

Roswell Whitmore, the son of an old Killingly family removed to Ashford, was ordained January 13, 1813. Ordination services conducted with due form by Reverends Moses C. Welch, Walter Lyon, Israel Day and Elisha Atkins, were very satisfactory as was also the Ordination Ball held the same evening at Captain Silas Hutchins' Assembly Room under the management of the Messrs. Malbone and Hutchins. Many of the young people who graced the Assembly Room on that joyful occasion were among the subjects of the almost immediately succeeding revival and became pillars in church and town. Mr. Whitmore was a man of much life and energy, ready to engage in any form of christian labor and the church was rapidly built up. James Danielson and Shubael Hutchins were elected and installed as deacons in March, 1813. The South Killingly church also enjoyed religious revivals and under its respected pastor peacefully kept the even tenor of its way.

Killingly Hill received its share of the new impetus. Mr. Smith Wilkinson, the Howes, Masons, with many of their managers and operatives, attended worship with the North Killingly church, and identified themselves with its religious and social interests. Very agreeable society was found upon this hill in the families of Captain Howe, Captain Arnold, Dr. Grosvenor and others, and it was a matter of doubt whether the many frequenters at Captain Arnold's were attracted by the new post-office or the charms of his blooming daughter. A select school or class taught by Mr. Atkins was an additional attraction to young people. While performing the ordinary ministerial duties with great fidelity and acceptance, this good minister accomplished much for education and public culture. His skill in stimulating the intellect and raising the tone of character was especially recognized, and young people going out into the world needed no other recommendation than a certificate from Mr. Atkins. Young men went out from his training well prepared for college, business and public life; young women, fitted for any station that might await them. Some of the latter became very successful teachers, perpetuating the impress received from their revered instructor; others adorned high social positions at home and in distant States. The first voluntary benevolent associations in Windham County were greatly forwarded if not originated by pupils of Mr. Atkins. The careless merry-making of the olden time had given place to a more earnest and thoughtful spirit. Young women of culture and aspirations felt that they had some other mission in the world than to dance and frolic. Balls and merry-makings were now less in vogue than reading-clubs and debating societies. A tendency to unhealthy sentimentalism was happily checked by an opportunity to engage in works of practical benevolence. The development of missionary enterprise, the formation of the American Board, the sailing of the first foreign missionaries, the fervent appeals for aid and co-operation, awakened the warmest sympathies of thousands of Christian women. "Choice spirits" on Killingly Hill were among the first to give their talents and energies to missionary work. Appeals from Windham Association and their own minister met immediate response. Interest in a foreign field opened their eyes to home demands and necessities. They found that mission work was needed in their own community, that could be best accomplished by the associated efforts of women. It was proposed that the ladies of Killingly North Society and Thompson "should unite on principles of true Christian charity and liberality in a Society that is to be formed for the purpose of communicating moral and religious instruction by the distribution of tracts." A meeting was accordingly held in the South District in Thompson, July 20, 1816. A constitution, prepared for a similar association of ladies in Providence, was unanimously adopted. It declared the present period "distinguished by very uncommon and important occurrences. While there are passing before us many scenes which are extremely disastrous and gloomy . . . . nothing can be more interesting and encouraging than that spirit of benevolent exertion for extending the knowledge and enjoyment of the Gospel which has been extensively excited in the hearts of Christians . . . . . not merely by particular denominations but by Christians of all denominations . . . . in every section of the earth which is favored with the light of divine truth." The object of the society was to promote the interests of evangelical piety and liberality ; its title, The United Female Tract Society of Thompson and Killingly. Mrs. Martha Whitman Mason, wife of Mr. William H. Mason—a lady of great intelligence and force of character—was elected president ; Miss Mary Atkins, Killingly, treasurer ; Miss Nancy S. Gay, Thompson, secretary ; directors, Misses Susan Bishop, Lucina Converse, Penelope W. Sessions ; receivers, Misses Rebekah Gleason, Elizabeth Copp, Hope B. Gay. A hundred and twenty-two ladies enrolled themselves members of this society. It was then voted that the first annual meeting should be holden at the Presbyterian meeting-house in Thompson, on Wednesday, July 24, and that the Rev. Messrs. Dow, Crosby and Atkins be requested to attend, and that Mr. Dow be requested to preach a sermon on the occasion. "Agreeable to the previous resolution a large number of ladies assembled at Mrs. Dow's at one o'clock, P. M., and at two repaired to the meeting-house where an appropriate discourse was delivered by Mr. Dow, and the exercises concluded by a very pertinent and impressive address to the Throne of Grace by the Rev. Mr. Crosby."

A large number of tracts were promptly distributed among its members, and sent to destitute places. The receivers were required to "peruse the tracts" previous to circulation, and approbate or suppress them according to their judgment. Every family in the two societies was visited by some zealous distributer and supplied with this form of religious literature. After flourishing for two years the society resolved itself into an auxiliary Bible Society, for the general object of disseminating the Holy Scriptures in all languages throughout the earth. Its first meeting was held in Killingly, October, 1818. It was arranged to hold two public meetings a year, one in each meeting-house, on which occasions sermons should be ordinarily preached, and such reports from societies and accounts of the progress and success of the Gospel be read as the officers of the society should think proper to communicate.

A new meeting house had been completed previous to this date. A vote not to repair but to build, had been obtained in 1815, but the difficulty of raising money without resort to direct taxation delayed the work till the September gale so damaged the old building that repairs were no longer practicable. Proprietors now consented to relinquish their rights. Smith Wilkinson, Robert Grosvenor and Ebenezer Kelly were appointed to exhibit a plan and report expense. "Plan" was more easily agreed npon than *site*, which excited much discussion. A committee sent by the County Court affixed a place that was rejected. January 28, 1818, the remains of the old meeting-house and step stones were sold at auction—Mr. Wilkinson officiating as salesman. It was then voted that the names of the proprietors should be called; those who wished to have the meeting-house erected on the hill south of Mr. Atkins should answer—"Hill"—and those who wished it on the common—"Common." Twenty two declared for common, eighteen for hill. The accepted site was "that part of the ancient meeting-house lot lying between Providence and Killingly Turnpike and the road leading to the new factory so called, near the east side of said lot." This point decided, the house was built during the following summer under the supervision of Elias Carter. "Spirits" used in raising the frame cost twenty-five dollars. Prosper Alexander, Josiah Deane, Asa Cutler, served as society committee; Augustus Howe, clerk; Joseph Adams, treasurer. Its dedication was attended by all the élite of the County.

The Baptists on Chestnut Hill happily united in choice of Calvin Cooper, a native of Northbridge, who brought a suitable recommendation from the Second Baptist Church of Sutton. The day of his ordination, October 14, 1807, was marked by the gathering of all the leading Baptists in the vicinity, viz: Elder Abel Palmer of Hampton ; Dea. Henry Wells, Robert Baxter and James Wheaton from Woodstock ; Elder Pearson Crosby, Deacon Lemuel Knapp, Thomas Day, James Brown and Joseph Town from Thompson ; Elder Zenas Leonard, Deacon Fish and Reuben Stone from Sturbridge ; Jeremiah Field, Thomas Brown and Stephen Chapman from Pomfret ; William Bachellor and Deacon Whipple from Sutton.   Elder Palmer was chosen moderator.   The council was " measurably satisfied with the relation of the candidate relative to his conversion from nature to grace, his call to the work of the ministry, and his views of the Gospel, and concluded to proceed to ordination."   Agreeably to arrangement, " the several parts were performed at the Baptist meeting-house," and Mr. Cooper solemnly set apart to the work of the ministry with earnest prayer for his success and usefulness.   These good wishes were " measurably satisfied."   Elder Cooper's ministry was the longest enjoyed by the church, and perhaps the most harmonious and prosperous. The building up of many factory villages in its vicinity brought a large accession to population and church membership, but as had been previously the case many of these members were unreliable and disorderly and the church was constantly agitated with questions of discipline.   Many were excluded for neglect of ordinances and open misdemeanors.   In 1817, " Brother John M. Hunt was unanimously set apart for ordination to the evangelical ministry of the Gospel."   The first council called for this purpose thought the church had been too hasty in this movement, but after farther trial of the young man he was formally ordained to this work by Elders Crosby, Grow, Dwinell and Coles.   Elder Cooper, Deacons Jonathan Harrington, Sampson Covill, Edward Chase and Silas Slater, and Brethren Edward Bartlett, Ezekiel Smith and Samuel Bullock, represented the church before this council.   During this year it was voted that deacons should be ordained in their offices, but after hearing those then standing in nomination " relate the leading traits of their minds as to the deaconship," the vote was reconsidered and rescinded.   The actual membership of the church during this period cannot be ascertained, but the character of its officers and leading men would indicate a good standing and gradual improvement.

Killingly's excessive activity during the war was followed by corresponding depression.   Mills owned by men of moderate means were generally closed, and those that still kept at work did so to the pecuniary loss of the proprietors.   Experiments in machinery and modes of work were meanwhile tested, power-looms introduced and many improvements effected.   A strong conviction in the ultimate success of manufacturing enterprise, and its peculiar adaptation to their own town, encouraged these pioneers to continue their efforts during the darkest days.   Companies were re-organized, new men and capital brought in, and when business revived Killingly mills were soon under fresh headway.   In 1819, the town had so far recovered from its losses as to report four factories in operation, "all of which contain about five thousand spindles, and were erected at an expense, including buildings, machinery, &c., of nearly $300,000. . . . . . At the Danielson Manufactory, water-looms have been introduced, and in general the business is carried on upon the most improved principles and very advantageously.   Besides the cotton factories there are one woolen factory, one gin distillery, one paper-hanging manufactory, four dye-houses, three clothiers' works, three carding-machines, three tanneries, eight grain mills, eight saw-mills."   There were also in the town six mercantile stores, four social libraries, five clergymen, six physicians and one attorney.   A post-office had been opened at Killingly Centre.   Experiments in straw weaving were brought to an untimely end by a sovereign decree from the supreme arbiter of fashion, and hopes of pecuniary profit proved as brittle as the straw with which Mrs. Kies had wrought out her ingenious invention.   Her son, Daniel Kies, Esq., of Brooklyn, as well as friends at home, lost heavily by investing in a manufacture which by a sudden change of fashion became utterly valueless.

VII.

THOMPSON'S MANUFACTURING COMPANIES.   VILLAGE GROWTH
AND IMPROVEMENTS.   THE GREAT REVIVAL OF 1813-14.

THE Thompson Manufacturing Company was formed in 1811— John Mason, John Nichols, Jun., Theodore Dwight, Rufus Coburn, Nathaniel Crosby, all of Thompson, and James B. Mason of Povidence, associating for the purpose of establishing a so-called cotton manufactory.   Land on the French River—a swampy hollow, "near the old bridge-place below Stephen Crosby's mills"—was purchased of Willard Whittemore and John Elliott.   As soon as possible buildings were put up and machinery set in motion, but ere the establishment was fairly under way a change of base had been effected.   Rhode Island capital again secured the prize.   Land, water-privilege, buildings, machinery, stock of yarn and cloth, were made over to Mr. James B. Mason, April 17, 1813, for the sum of $11,000. The Mason Brothers, James B., Amasa, William H. and John, now joined in company—John Nichols also retaining a share. Mr. William H. Mason assumed the management of affairs and soon the factory was in successful operation. Laboring men with their families, young men and girls, hastened to engage work in its various departments, and the lonely valley was transformed into a brisk little village, known for many years as "The Swamp" and "Swamp Factory"—names derisively given by rival manufacturers in other parts of the town. The Connecticut Manufacturing Company was also formed in 1811, buying a Quinebaug privilege near the Boston turnpike bridge. Its constituent members were John Nichols, Jonathan Nichols, Jun.; Daniel Dwight, William Dwight, Jun., Benjamin Arnold, Samuel Perrin. A substantial brick edifice built under their direction was soon equipped and ready for action, and the Brick Factory took its place among eager competitors. The bricks used in constructing this factory building, and many substantial dwelling-houses in different parts of the town, were manufactured at Allen's flourishing brick-works in West Thompson. Meanwhile Rhode Island adventurers had also appropriated a privilege on the Five-Mile River in the east of the town. Emor Angell, Nehemiah Knight, Thomas Burgess, John Mackie, all of Providence, Stephen Matthewson of Johnson, associating with Josiah Sessions and Joseph Waterman of Thompson, under the name of the Quaddic Manufacturing Company, and buying land of Deacon Jonathan Converse. Quaddic Factory was built in 1813, and devoted at first to manufacturing woolen hats. A carding machine on the Quinebaug in the northwest of the town accommodated many customers in Thompson and Woodstock. These manufacturing enterprises were followed by the usual results, general quickening and activity, and development in every direction. The Swamp Factory establishment was particularly enterprising and helpful. Many men were employed in out-door labor, filling up the hollows and draining the malarious swamps. Many teamsters were needed to draw the cotton from distant marts. It was said that one load brought from Philadelphia during the war cost the company $1,400. The town showed its appreciation of the new industries by favoring them with needful roads and bridges. A road was laid out from Swamp Factory to Woodstock, and roads leading to Pomfret Factory improved and altered. The bridges pertaining to the Thompson Turnpike Company were now assumed by the town. A bridge contractor whose work was not satisfactory, was suspended from town privileges till defects were remedied. In 1811, the town voted to encourage inoculation, and appointed two men in each school district to assist Dr. Fanshear in performing the service. A public burying-ground having now been laid out in the Jacobs District, the town ordered the selectmen to provide two hearses for public use. James Wheaton, Abel Jacobs, William Lamson, Pardon Luther, Joel Chaffee and Theodore Dwight, were licensed by the civil authority in 1813, to keep houses of public entertainment.

Thompson village, which had been somewhat straitened by scarcity of building lots, received a new impulse in 1814, when land belonging to the heirs of Samuel Watson, was thrown into market. Eligible building sites on both sides the turnpike north of the common were quickly secured. The present tavern-stand at the intersection of the two turnpikes and houses north of it, were built by Stephen E. Tefft, Dr. Webb, Noadiah Comins and Hezekiah Olney. The latter engaged in hat manufacture; Comins opened a saddler's shop. Dr. Webb unfortunately miscalculated his balance sheet and was obliged to take unceremonious leave of patients and creditors. His unfinished house was completed and occupied by Dr. King, while Dr. Horatio Holbrook built a new house nearly opposite. Esquire Larned, who bought out the Watson land, retained the family homestead at the north extremity of the village. The handsome brick house on the corner below built by John Nichols, was further improved by setting out trees in the little triangular green opposite, commonly termed "The Heater Piece." Meanwhile a new church edifice had been completed. After much opposition from time-honored fathers who insisted that the old house was good for another century, that discriminating gale (which gave so many gala-days to Windham County by opening the way for the erection of new meeting-houses), came to the aid of Young America, and so dismantled it that repairs would cost as much as re-building. At a society meeting the week after that remarkable providential visitation, September 25, 1815, it was voted "not to repair, but to build." Thaddeus and George Larned, Elijah Crosby, Zadoc Hutchins, Isaac Davis, John Nichols, Noadiah Russel, David Town, Daniel Dwight, John Brown, Roger and Joseph Elliott and James Bates, were appointed committee for building. An association was formed, subscribers agreeing to build a meeting-house not expending over $6,000. Mr. Ithiel Town, son of Archelaus Town of Thompson, a promising architect then settled in New Haven, presented the plan ; Elias Carter had charge of the work ; Harvey Dresser of Charlton, furnished the painting below the lofty pulpit, which so artfully simulated a stairway with curtained drapery that it was a perpetual wonder to children that Mr. Dow did not make use of it. The dedication of the new house was observed, September, 1817, with the usual ceremonies and rejoicing. The singing under the direction of that renowned choir leader, Mr. Charles Sharpe, was greatly admired, as were also the very handsome young ladies, who occupied the front seats of the gallery on that occasion.   The old meeting-house was taken across the street and reconstructed into a town house with stores underneath, where its prolonged public service in various capacities justified the good opinion of the venerating fathers, and still bears witness to the *solid character* of its *builders* and *timbers*.   Its post-office was then administered by John Nichols, Esq.   The stores were run by the Tefts, "Nichols and Dwight," and others.   A very satis-factory house of entertainment was conducted by Theodore Dwight, in the central tavern.

This era of growth and business prosperity was also marked by a very powerful and wide-spread religious revival, pervading both churches and extending into the adjacent towns.   Elder Pearson Crosby sent to the *Baptist Magazine* in 1814 a very interesting ac-count of this work.   Beginning the previous autumn " at a conference meeting in Rev. Mr. Dow's society," it soon spread to the Baptist church.   " Conference meetings were generally well attended and the life and energy displayed on these occasions made a means of con-tributing to advancement."   Elder Crosby gives a most unflattering picture of the Swamp Factory village as a place " where for two or three years Satan had seemed to reign with almost sovereign and despotic sway.   Vice and immorality permitted to riot without con-trol.   The sound of the violin, attended with dancing, the sure prelude to greater scenes of revelry for the night."   Conference preaching and meetings were held there and impressions made.   Elder Crosby reports —" Convictions of the most pungent and powerful character.   Some wrought upon in the most sudden manner—one moment swearing, cursing and ridiculing religion; the next, calling upon God to save their souls.   In less than a week instead of the violin, the songs of Zion, and preaching and conference every evening."   The preaching of Elder Thomas Paul " had a most blessed effect in awakening, convicting and converting souls."

" Eighteen baptismal seasons," all characterized by the greatest solemnity, were observed by Elder Crosby during this remarkable revival, and a large number added to his church.   A corresponding religious interest prevailed for several years in the Congregational church and about ninety added to its membership.   The Methodist society was also quickened and strengthened.   Many were added to the church.   An earnest brother, Shubael Cady, labored with much zeal and effect, and gathered the children into a class for instruction— perhaps the first attempted Sunday school in the County.   The meet-ing-house was much improved by galleries and pews brought from Southbridge.

This revival, so gracious and beneficial in its general results, was

56

unhappily marred by the sectarian strife and bitterness unavoidable at a time when all these good people most firmly believed that every iota of their own doctrinal tenets was right and every opposite shade of belief heretical, and that it was their duty to use every possible endeavor to convince their opponents of their errors. Ardent Methodists, aglow with revival fervor, could not speak gently of those who upon any ground would limit the freeness of salvation and the freedom of the will. Self-denying Baptists, glorying in their obedience to the literal command and example of their Master, could not sit idly down and see precious young converts fail to follow that Divine example, and to receive what they deemed the only true baptism and communion. And the valiant leader of the Congregational forces, equally positive in his own convictions, returned their assaults with interest, and even carried the war into the enemy's country. Keen, witty, logical, eloquent, with all his resources at instant command, Mr. Dow was a most formidable antagonist, but fortunately for his opponents his audacity sometimes led him to acts of rashness which gave them the advantage. Such an act was his appearing upon the platform at the first camp-meeting in Windham County, where hundreds of zealous Methodists were preaching, praying, exhorting, singing and shouting after their peculiar fashion, and when asked to speak, boldly denouncing in most straightforward terms their whole method of procedure. Young people of his own congregation, timidly questioning the validity of their baptismal sprinkling in infancy, and humbly seeking clearer light and evidence, were little helped by a discourse upon "vain jangling" and the keen home thrust, "Have not some of you been *jangling* about your *baptism?*" Though so staunch an advocate of sprinkling, Mr. Dow of course consented to immerse any candidate not previously baptized in infancy. On one such occasion a great crowd had gathered, including many Baptists, curious to witness an immersion performed by such an uncompromising believer in sprinkling, and as the two came up together out of the water they broke out spontaneously into their usual triumphant song;—

> "How happy are they
> Who their Saviour obey,"—

"Stop, stop!" said Mr. Dow, "there's another subject!"—and taking a little girl who stood by from the hands of her parents, he dipped the flowing water and touched the brow of the child, repeating the formula of baptism. "Now," he remarked to the astonished spectators, "you can go on with your hymn,"—but the zeal of the discomfited Baptists was thoroughly quenched.

Wrong-doers in his own congregation found little mercy from the out-spoken pastor. Young people who had attended a dance or merry-making would be greeted the following Sabbath with the expressive query—"How long ye simple ones will ye love simplicity?" A house-warming frolic in which some of the most prominent men in the congregation had been led to great excesses, called out a most scathing rebuke from the words—"Who hath woe? who hath sorrow? who hath contentions? who hath babbling?" &c.—the first temperance sermon ever delivered in Thompson. Answering the objection that some could not live without the use of liquor, he thundered out in his most emphatic manner—"Well, *die* then! better *die sober* than *live drunk!* Better die *now* and die *sober*, die *penitent*, than die *ten years hence* and *lose your souls!*"

Mr. Dow's peculiar characteristics were sometimes unpleasantly manifested on funeral occasions. Believing only in imputed or engrafted righteousness, he gave small praise to natural graces. "Ho, ye who ride upon white asses!" furnished the text for discourse upon the death of General Washington, in which he pronounced judgment upon that great and good man with all the freedom and plainness of Isaiah or Jeremiah. Still less complimentary was a sermon preached at the funeral of one of his most prominent parishioners, who had done more than any one in the society for its temporal prosperity, but was not a member of the church. "A wise man's eyes are in his head, but the fool walketh in darkness," afforded little comfort to mourning friends. With such a strongly-marked character, great natural ability and clear conviction of duty, Mr. Dow made a very strong impression upon the community, and even those who disliked his doctrines and preaching were forced to acknowledge him as a power. His own people while sometimes wincing under his darts, regarded him with great pride and affection, and he was still looked upon as in a certain sense minister of the town, remote residents craving his services at weddings and funerals. Explicit "Articles of Faith and Covenant" were adopted by the church in 1818. Deacons Aaron and Moses Bixby were now in active service, whose venerable figures seated beneath the lofty pulpit inspired the deepest reverence in youthful minds. The children supposed that their appropriate names belonged to them *ex-officio;* that all deacons were called Moses and Aaron.

The Baptist church continued to increase in numbers, order and stability. Elder Crosby was a strict disciplinarian and less democratic in his views of church administration than was common among Baptists at that date. This was shown by approval of a standing committee, disapproval of women's preaching, and consenting that the amount needful for his support should be raised by an "everedge" upon each member which differed only in name from the obnoxious rate-bill of the standing order. "A Rule for the Management of its Temporal Concerns" was adopted by the church in 1818, which provided, "That all Delegated power in things of a temporal concern shall be vested in the Deacons except in such things as the church shall think proper to add other brethren." It was to be the duty of the Deacons "to make out the Everage Bill," lay it before the church for ratification, receive payment, warn and report delinquents, and if any should neglect to pay within a month of the time specified, church fellowship would be withheld till satisfaction was given. Thomas Day and Stephen Crosby were the much-esteemed deacons, entrusted with such momentous duties. Dishonest dealing, intemperance, family contentions, and giving away to passion, were among the offences rebuked by formal letter and admonition. During the absence of Elder Crosby the church allowed a zealous sister from Vermont to occupy the pulpit, but the pastor on his return "whipt us smart* for hear ing a woman," and lamented that "grievous wolves" should have been allowed entrance to his flock. In 1819, Elder Crosby, having decided to follow his children to Fredonia, New York, resigned his charge, to the great grief of his people. Three hundred and fifty-four had been added to the church during his ministry. His immediate successor was Elder John Nichols of West Thompson, received into the fellowship of the Baptist church and ministry in presence of a large and attentive assembly, May 19, 1819.

VIII.

THE REVIVAL IN POMFRET. BUSINESS AFFAIRS. MORAL AND AGRICULTURAL SOCIETIES. GENERAL PROGRESS.

THE religious revival of 1813–14, extended to Pomfret, "that worthy character, Elder James Grow, being exercised with the tenderest feelings of regard and concern" for the spiritual welfare of his flock, and his unwearied "exertions productive of much good." Many were converted and united with his church, which in time was able to erect a house of worship on Pomfret street. Very great religious interest was excited in Pomfret Factory village and down the Quinebaug valley. Most impressive and awakening meetings were held in the Brick and Gary school-houses. The Methodists were very active in this vicinity, holding meetings in the Perrin House and other private dwellings. Mr. and Mrs. Elijah Bugbee, Noah Perrin, Mrs. Lucy Perrin Gary, had long been known as prominent leaders and ex-

---

* Diary of Joseph Joslin.

horters. A nephew, brought up by the latter, George Gary, was converted at the age of seventeen, and almost immediately began preaching with remarkable power and efficiency. The first Methodist camp-meeting in Windham County, was held in Perrin's Grove, in 1808. Throngs came from all parts of the country and great excitement prevailed. The presence and avowed disapproval of Rev. Daniel Dow added to the commotion, and he was tauntingly reminded that as according to his theory the camp-meeting had been divinely fore-ordained he should not presume to find fault with it.

The affairs of the Pomfret Manufacturing Company were most efficiently administered by Mr. Smith Wilkinson. Wild land in the vicinity of the Factory was bought and brought under cultivation. Population increased steadily, respectable families moving to the village to find work for their children. The old Cargill grist-mill was still kept busily at work, and the Cargill tavern was kept up under Malachi Green and other landlords. The old gin distillery was turned to better uses, and a neat brick school-house built in 1812, adorned a sightly eminence east side the river. A new road was laid out to the Brick Factory intersecting with the Woodstock and Thompson Turnpike, facilitating travel and trade with both those towns. A road was also cut through the woods over Park's Hill in 1818, and the previous road pitching down to Bundy's mills discontinued. Other roads were altered and improved leading to Pomfret and Killingly, Mr. Wilkinson helping them on with land and labor. The financial affairs of the Company were very flourishing. Yarn was sent out for weaving all over the country even as far as Brimfield, Mass. A dividend of $36,000 was made in one of the years of war, and so well established was the company that it was able to continue work during the succeeding embarrassments. Mr. Wilkinson was a strict disciplinarian, and looked carefully after the morals of the community. At his especial request the Windham Association furnished "religious instruction" at stated intervals, holding meetings in the Brick school-house. A Pomfret Woolen Manufacturing Company was incorporated in 1817, and erected buildings upon the Mashamoquet, but it suffered severely from the great flood the following year, and other causes, and disbanded after a time with pecuniary loss to its associates. Bridges and dams at Pomfret Factory and Bundy's mills were carried away by that most destructive freshet, which inflicted great damage upon all the manufacturing corporations of the country.

In general town affairs there was little deserving record. The town opposed the war vigorously, but did its part towards maintaining it, sending skillful surgeons to the regular army and lively militia companies to the relief of New London and Stonington. Its influence in State and County was strengthened by the public spirit and intelligence of its prominent men—Judge Thomas and General Lemuel Grosvenor, Sylvanus Backus, John Holbrook, Lemuel Ingalls, Doctors Hubbard and Hall, and other men of weight and character who occupied less conspicuous positions. Sylvanus Backus served for many years as speaker of the House of Representatives at home, and was elected representative to Congress in 1817. Ebenezer, son of General Lemuel Grosvenor, was graduated from Yale in 1807, and after completing legal studies also settled in Pomfret—a man of much culture and ability, giving promise of future eminence. Dr. Hubbard's surgical skill was becoming widely noted, attracting many students, who followed him on horseback on his daily rounds, striving to keep pace with his swiftly running sulky, and thinking themselves most favored if they could ride a few moments by his side, catch his oracular opinions and enjoy his humorous anecdotes. Other young men were studying law with Esquire Backus. Probate and post-offices enjoyed abundant patronage. A flourishing business was carried on by Charles L. Webb. Dr. Darius Hutchins and Samuel Lyon engaged in trade in Abington Society. Several other stores were supported in town, together with three fulling-mills and clothier's works, two carding-machines, three small distilleries, four grain mills and six tanneries. The Killingly and Pomfret Turnpike was discontinued after a time and the bridge built for its accommodation removed. The great flood of 1817, compelled the erection of new bridges at Pomfret Factory. One of Pomfret's casualties was a raid of thieves, stealing clothing from Deacon Payson and others. Ten dollars was allowed by the town, expended in horse ride and pursuit.

Rev. Aaron Putnam, second pastor of Pomfret's first church, died in 1813, and was buried with all the accustomed solemnities, ministers serving as pall-bearers. The pastorate of Rev. Asa King was harmonious and fruitful. The prayer and conference meetings quietly introduced by him were greatly blessed to spiritual quickening and growth. A special revival season was enjoyed in 1808, when seventy members were added to the church. A most radical and thorough work, "it changed the character and habits of the place and laid the foundations of good for future generations." An imposing addition was now made to the great meeting-house—a lofty tower or steeple and a spacious porch. An unfortunate casualty while raising the frame, turned that day of festivity into one of mourning. Barnard Philips, a youth of nineteen, who had eagerly sought a place in the honored band who were allowed to assist in this hazardous service, was thrown from the top of the frame and fatally injured, dying in a few days. Benjamin Duick, Thomas Hubbard, Peter Chandler, Peregrine Gilbert, Ebenezer Fitch, Sylvanus Backus and Payson Grosvenor, had charge of these additions, which were accomplished in 1810–11, greatly enhancing the dignity of that venerated sanctuary and inspiring the deepest awe and admiration in many who came to worship. A bell was placed in the tower by the generosity of Mr. Benjamin Duick, chairman of the committee and clerk of the society, too modest to record his own benefaction. It served for town clock as well as church purposes, being rung three times a day by Lloyd Williams.

Mr. King was dismissed from his charge in 1811, and after three years interval Rev. James Porter was inducted into the pastorate. Though feeble in body he abounded in labors and most successfully carried forward the good work begun by his predecessor. It was said by a successor* that "no man ever wrought out and set in order so many ways of doing good in this parish as Mr. Porter. He was in advance of his time in every good work. He established the first Sabbath school in this region. He began the first monthly concert for prayer—took a collection and paid into the treasury of Foreign Missions the first money that was collected at a monthly concert in Connecticut. He set on foot and arranged plans for our various charitable contributions which have continued as model schemes to the present time." He was also one of the first ministers in the country to engage in Temperance work, and most heartily seconded the efforts of those good men who organized in 1812, the "Connecticut Society for the Reformation of Morals." A branch organization called "the Moral Society" was speedily formed in Pomfret, enlisting the co-operation of Mr. Porter, and some of the best men in his church and congregation. The suppression of gambling, lottery-dealing, Sabbath-breaking and the excessive use of liquor, was the aim of the Pomfret Moral Society. Its members were expected to drink no more than was good for them, and to use their influence in discountenancing intemperance in drink and other specified immoralities. Decanters were banished in many houses from their prominent position on the sideboard, and the social glass no longer urged upon visitors. At public meetings and dinners, Judge Grosvenor and other members now declined to partake of the proffered liquor, but the former would leave his money upon the table that his comrades might not attribute his abstinence to niggardliness. This self-denial excited much wonder and comment. One of its junior members, Charles P. Grosvenor, took a journey into New York State, and where-

* Rev. Daniel Hunt.

ever they stopped on the way his companion while sipping his sling or toddy would remark--"Here is Charles! He belongs to the Moral Society—he don't drink!" In response to a request from the State Society, that the Branch Societies should pledge themselves to secure a better observance of the Sabbath, the laws forbidding Sabbath profanation were more rigidly enforced. Deacon Grosvenor as grandjuror frequently stopped travelers on that day, compelling them to wait till Monday and pay the allotted fine, and townspeople who presumed to work on Sunday were also arrested and fined.

Rev. Walter Lyon continued in charge of the church in Abington Society. Fifteen were added to its membership in 1809, and the same number in 1819. William Osgood and Wyllis Goodell were chosen deacons in 1811. Captain Elisha Lord continued to lead the singing. Mr. Abishai Sharpe was excused from paying his assessment for meeting-house repairs on condition that he teach a singing-school two evenings a week through the season. One of the most note-worthy events occurring in this society was the formation of a Ladies' Library in 1813. George Sumner, Lemuel Ingalls, Jun., and other Abington young men, went out to college and business, gained broader views and higher culture, and through their influence the young ladies were moved to associate for mutual improvement and higher literary privileges. A meeting was called; Alathea Lord, Maria Gordon and Nancy Ingalls deputed to form a constitution. Susan and Nancy Cunningham, Alathea Lord, Sophia Sharpe, Delia and Olive Goodell, Sarah Sumner, Eliza and Delia Ingalls, Peggy Holbrook, Dolly and Delia Dresser, Dolly Allen, together with one matron, Mrs. Payson Grosvenor, accepted the constitution and organized as a Ladies' Library Association. Delia Goodell was chosen clerk; Alathea Lord, librarian; Nancy Cunningham, treasurer. Admission fee was three dollars; annual tax, twenty-five cents. Seventy dollars was promptly raised and expended—George Sumner selecting the books with excellent taste and judgment. The young ladies delighted greatly in this peculiar Abington institution and sustained it with much spirit. New members were from time to time admitted to its privileges, and many valuable books brought to their knowledge. Stimulated perhaps by this example, the previous libraries were made more efficient. At a meeting of the Junior Library, October 22, 1815, George Sharpe, Samuel Dresser, John Holbrook, Roswell Goodell and George S Ingalls were empowered to confer with the committee of the Social Library, for the purpose of joining the two libraries in one. The conference was successful, and Social and Junior happily merged in the United Library of Abington—the difference of value in the two collections making no obstacle.

Both Pomfret and Abington societies met with serious losses. Their young men went out into the world ; older men passed away. Dr. Elisha Lord died in 1809. Major John Wilkes Chandler, so active in military and political affairs, died suddenly in 1808. His father, Peter Chandler, lived till 1816. The unhappy death of Mr. Benjamin Duick, who removed from Boston to Pomfret and manifested much public spirit and generosity, was greatly lamented. A still greater loss was that of Sylvanus Backus, in February, 1817. Activity of mind and brilliancy of imagination combined with much solidity and strength, made Mr. Backus one of the most influential men of the time—"a strong pillar of society and state." As a " peculiar testimony of the people's love, he was chosen a member of Congress by the united vote of all parties." His friends anticipated much from him in that position, but ere the time came for him to take his seat, he had been summoned to the Supreme Tribunal. " A widow and five children were left to weep over a grave bedewed by the tears of the whole community." He was followed in a few months by his brother practitioner, one of Pomfret's most promising sons, Ebenezer Grosvenor, Esq., whose death was caused by imprudence in eating after fatiguing exertion. Elisha B. Perkins who had studied with Esquire Backus succeeded to his practice. Other new residents took places made vacant. Mr. Darius Matthewson of Brooklyn, Deacon Henry Sweeting of Boston, Judge Rossiter of New Haven, Eben Thompson, and other families from Providence, were valuable acquisitions. Peter Thompson, of Massachusetts, opened a tavern near the business centre, a famous place for courts, masonic meetings, and other public gatherings. Possibly Pomfret's astonishing enterprise in the formation of an agricultural society had some influence in attracting such men. The first existing notice of this organization is found in the *Hartford Courant*, viz:—

" *A SOCIETY* has been formed by the name of *The Pomfret United Agricultural Society*, consisting of members residing in the towns of Pomfret, Woodstock and Brooklyn. At a meeting of said society held in Pomfret, December 19, 1809, the following gentlemen were elected officers for the year ensuing, viz:—Benjamin Duick, president; Amos Paine, John Williams, vice-presidents; Sylvanus Backus, Esq., treasurer; Darius Matthewson of Brooklyn, Benjamin Duick of Pomfret, James McClellan of Woodstock, committee of correspondence. Communications upon subjects relative to the institution addressed to either of the committee of correspondence will be thankfully received.
A true copy from the minutes.
THOMAS HUBBARD, M. D., *Secretary*."

Nothing farther is heard of its progress till 1818, when reinforced by in-coming residents it takes a step forward. A meeting was held at the house of Peter Thompson; articles exhibited and premiums
57

awarded.* Stimulated by this society, new inhabitants and fresh importations of stock, the dairy business was now " pursued to an extent and with a success that is scarcely surpassed. Not only cheese and butter, but pork, lard and beef, are among the surplus productions of the farmers of this town. . . . Wool has been added to its agricultural products, and considerable rye, corn and oats are raised."

Deacon Sweeting was responsible for another innovation—the introduction of a grand musical organ, which made a great noise all over the County. Pomfret's First Society was induced to purchase this instrument for its capacious meeting-house, banishing the primitive pitch-pipe and tuning fork then used by Peter Grosvenor in leading the singing. Deacon Sweeting's son, Nathaniel, served as the organist, and many were the comments called forth by his orchestral performances. " Hear them pump thunder !" exclaimed a wondering youth. The plain old Quakers and Methodists of the town, so averse to worldly pomps and vanities, were not a little scandalized by what they deemed the unhallowed aspirations of this degenerate church, and the elaborate church edifice with its tower, bell and Papal organ, seemed hardly less offensive than the typical Babylon of the Revelation. This feeling was illustrated in the remark of a Quaker lad, suffering from undue repression, who desperately declared that when he was big enough, he meant " to drink rum, swear and "—as the climax of excess and enormity—" go to the steeple meeting-house." Notwithstanding this sectarian reprobation the church went quietly forward under Mr. Porter, engaging with much interest in any progressive movement. A Duick Charitable Society was organized in 1817, having for permanent fund a legacy left for charitable purposes by Mr. Duick. A Bible class met every week at the parsonage. In 1819, Mr. Porter had succeeded in establishing a Sabbath-school, with one class of boys and two classes of girls—Major Copeland, superintendent.

Pomfret's select coterie retained its preëminence, though dancing parties were less in vogue than more intellectual entertainments. Culture and art now claimed their votaries. Dr. Hall's young people were

---

* " PREMIUMS proposed by Pomfret Agricultural Society for the year 1818; — For the largest and best fattened animal for beef, $10.00; next best, $5.00. For the best or most valuable crop of flax, $5.00; next best, $2.50. For the greatest quantity of clear spring wheat on a piece of ground, not less than one acre, $5.00. For the largest crop of barley on the same quantity of land, $5.00. For the largest or most valuable crop of potatoes, giving an account of the quantity of seed and the manner of planting, $6.00. For the best pair of working oxen, not exceeding five years old, $5.00. For the best lot of pork made from spring pigs, not to exceed ten months old when killed, and not less than six in number, $6.00. For the best fattened and largest ditto, two in number, of a different lot, $4.00.

WILLIAM WILLIAMS, Secretary.
Pomfret, August 24, 1818."—Connecticut Courant.

remarkable for high breeding and accomplishments. Miss Ann Hall had distinguished herself in drawing and portrait painting, and works of her execution compared favorably with the highest art that had been attained in America. Other family circles shone with scarcely inferior lustre. Distinguished visitors from abroad graced their social reunions. Hidden from vulgar gaze, these gatherings of Pomfret élite might easily have been rated beyond their deserts, but a discriminating visitor who had seen much of the world gave this testimony:—
"That the Pomfret assemblies were remarkable for elegance and distinction, and that the dress and demeanor of Miss Ann Hall would have done credit to any court in Europe."

IX.

BUSINESS IN WOODSTOCK. CHURCH AFFAIRS. ACADEMY. THEFTS AND WHIPPING. LAND CASE.

"AGRICULTURE" reports the *Gazetteer*, "affords employment for most of the industry of this town excepting what is employed in domestic or household manufactures, which receive general attention, there being a loom in almost every house. Most of the primary and substantial fabrics of clothing are the product of domestic industry." Woodstock "shuttles merrily went flashing through the loom" in those days of weaving cloth for factories. The six mercantile stores of the town offered every variety of goods in exchange for weaving. "Asa Pierce and Co." carried on a very flourishing business in West Woodstock, keeping on hand "a large assortment of cotton yarn to be woven, for which the best encouragement would be given for good weavers;" having also a lumber yard with great variety of building stuff, wrought and cut nails, etc., and the general run of European and West India goods. Colonel Jonathan May was equally active in East Woodstock or Muddy Brook, running a store, slaughter-house and distillery. Ralph Malbone of Pomfret opened a store at the junction of the Southbridge turnpike with the road leading to Muddy Brook, near the little shop occupied by Peregrine White in the making and repairing of fashionable six-feet clocks, adorned with full moons and other appropriate figure-heads. Theophilus Bradbury Chandler, surveyor and justice, had a store at the Muddy Brook bridge, a mile north of the Lake. A post-office added to the popularity of Bowen's store and tavern. These Woodstock stores and hostelries must have been extremely attractive, as church members in Thompson were impeached and censured for

intemperance in "Bowen's and Chandler's shops." Captain Judah
Lyon built a large and convenient tavern house in Muddy Brook
village in 1818, which was also popular and well sustained. Taverns
were also kept by Rhodes Arnold, Thomas Lamson, Chauncey Kibbe,
Abiel Fox and David Button. While agriculture was the leading
interest, the farmers raising not only their own corn, rye, oats and
barley, but sufficient spring wheat for the consumption of the town—
manufactures were not neglected. The useful pottery works kept up
the supply of domestic earthen ware. Two blacksmith shops and
large trip-hammers, two wheel-wrights and one goldsmith, one carding-
machine, one fulling-mill, one oil-mill, seven grain-mills, twelve saw-
mills and two distilleries, found abundant patronage. In 1815, Chester,
Willard and Rensellaer Child, Amasa and Judah Lyon were incorporated as "the Woodstock Manufacturing Company for the purpose
of manufacturing cloths and other fabrics of wool and cotton," which
erected suitable buildings in the north part of the town. Walter and
Royal Paine of Providence, Job Williams of Pomfret, Jonathan and
William May, John Paine, William Lyon and others, were also incorporated as the Muddy Brook Cotton Manufacturing Company, erecting a factory building a little north of the village. The *Gazetteer*
reports them as both upon a large scale and doing business extensively.
Moses Arnold, Thomas Hubbard, Benjamin Duick and William Bowen,
were incorporated as "The Arnold Manufacturing Company in Woodstock," in 1814, and were soon underway in what was known as
Arnold-town or South Woodstock.

Woodstock's First Society was much occupied in providing for Mr.
Lyman's salary and discussing meeting house repairs. It was found
very difficult to raise the nominal amount specified while its real
value had greatly depreciated. Taxation had become so offensive to
many that an attempt was made to raise the amount by subscription
but it was probably found too unequal in its working. Money received
from the State in 1818, was appropriated for the foundation of a
permanent fund for the support of the ministry. In 1819, Mr. Lyman
consented to accept an annual salary of $275, in lieu of the original
contract, which provided £70, and twenty cords of firewood. The
society received a bequest of land upon the demise of Mr. Samuel
Dexter, to be improved for the use and benefit of Rev. Eliphalet
Lyman and his successors in office, forever, upon the condition that no
building should ever be erected nor tree suffered to grow thereon;
that it should be kept a separate piece by itself forever, and only be
used for mowing, pasturage and tillage; that he should be buried
in the centre of the land, in such manner "as that not the smallest
appearance of a grave may be visible after the earth shall be settled

down." "*Nor let any stone tell where I lie.*" A sum of money was also given by Mr. Dexter for the use of the poor of the society. Captain Frissell was appointed to receive and hold the same ; Amos Paine, to fulfill the conditions of the landed bequest. Hezekiah Palmer succeeded Amos Paine as society clerk in 1814. The latter with Samuel Mashcraft, David Frissell and Jedidiah Kimball, served as society committee. The service of William Flynn as chorister was so efficient that four substitutes (viz., Hezekiah Palmer, Amos Paine, Jacob Lyon and Abram Peake) were needed during his absence in New London. Deacon Jedidiah Morse survived till 1819. His declining years were greatly comforted by the consideration of the prosperity of his surviving children who were not only comfortably settled in this world, but "had devoted themselves and their children to God and walked in some good measure agreeable to their profession."* William Lyon, 2nd, and Jedidiah Kimball now served in the deacon's office, reluctantly taking the place filled by such honored predecessors.

The church in East Woodstock was called in 1813, to part with its excellent pastor, Rev. William Graves, "a pious and faithful man of God, dear to his people while he lived and after death universally lamented." Mr. Lyman in his funeral discourse pronounced him "so distinguished for his prudence, modesty, candor and fidelity, that he might with great propriety be said to be an example to the flock ; " possessed to an uncommon degree of the requisite qualifications of a gospel bishop. "Wonderfully supported and comforted with the presence of Christ, he met death with a sweet and placid frame ; it seemed as if he had nothing to do but to die." He was succeeded in office by Samuel Backus of Canterbury, grandson of the Baptist church historian, Rev. Isaac Backus, ordained in East Woodstock, January 19, 1815. A powerful revival was soon after enjoyed by the church, enlarging and strengthening its membership. Nathaniel Briggs and William Child succeeded to the deacon's office.

The "*Presbyterian* church" in West Woodstock (as it was usually styled) enjoyed much peace and harmony under the ministrations of Mr. Underwood, who by evenness of temper and urbanity of manner greatly endeared himself to his people. It was said that while the East Woodstock church without a pastor Mr. Underwood was invited to attend all the weddings and Mr. Lyman the funerals—the former excelling in convivial and the latter in mortuary occasions. Even

---

* Piety would seem to be an inherent characteristic of this renowned branch of the Morse family if we may judge from the younger brother of Deacon Jedidiah, who, dying at the age of three years and four months, had "read the Bible twice through, committed many passages, *led the devotions* of the family and given satisfactory evidence of piety."

HISTORY OF WINDHAM COUNTY.

the singing question was harmoniously decided, and a bass-viol introduced without exciting discord. Benjamin Lyon, 3d, Abiel Fox and
Abraham Paine, serving as committee to see that the new instrument
be kept in order. Darius Barlow, Charles Skinner, Dolphus Child,
Thomas Corbin, Benjamin Lyon, 3d, Benjamin Child, Danforth Lyon,
Andrew and John F. Williams, Russel Stead and Stephen Johnson,
were among the numerous choristers year by year appointed. An
" instructor to teach singing " was frequently employed under the
charge of a competent committee.

Elder Ledoyt continued in charge of the First Baptist Church till
his death in 1813. While preaching a funeral sermon he was seized
with malignant fever, and carried home to die, as he at once foreboded. The father of the Baptist church order in Windham county,
his memory has ever been held in honor. The church soon united in
choice of Nicholas Branch of Providence, a recent proselyte to the
Baptist belief, who was ordained its pastor, June 25, 1815,—Elder
Gano of Providence preaching the ordaining sermon. This pastorate
was " successful and profitable in a very desirable degree ;" being characterized by " peace, love, union and prosperity." With a strong and
active intellect and much native force of character, Elder Branch took
a high position in the Baptist ministry, and was made instrumental in
the conversion of many souls and the building up of churches. Many
were added to the Woodstock church during his ministry. A ministerial lot was also procured and a parsonage erected. Elder Amos
Wells was dismissed from the charge of the Second Baptist church
about 1811. The ordaining of his successor, Brother George Angell
of Southbridge, in 1813, was a very interesting and solemn occasion,
conducted by Elders Wells, Crosby, Grow and Dwinell. An earnest
and devout Christian, much good was anticipated from his ministrations, but after three years he decided to remove to Sturbridge, when
Elder Isaac Dwinell " came to take care of the church." One of the
first Windham County Sunday schools was organized in this church
in 1816.

Woodstock Academy retained its place in public favor. Liberty to
erect a boarding-house on the common near the powder-house was
granted in 1807. In 1810, the town gave bonds to the proprietors for
some twelve hundred dollars, the interest to be applied in supporting
the school, entitling any resident to six weeks' tuition annually. Mr.
Burleigh's two years' administration was efficient and profitable, bringing the institution to the culmination of its early prosperity. Succeeding teachers did not succeed in keeping up its standard, though the
Messrs. Burgess of Canterbury are believed to have been fully competent for the position. The yearly exhibitions were maintained with

accustomed spirit. The brilliant exploits of a former pupil, Lieut. Charles Morris, excited much martial enthusiasm among the boys, which found vent in sounding declamations and pistol-shooting trage- dies. The military parades upon Woodstock's famous common were greatly enjoyed by these youthful patriots. A mock fight was carried on at company-training in Muddy Brook village, in 1818, when a party dressed like Indians seized upon astonished children and tri- umphantly bore them to their rock fortress. These performances were more enjoyable than some others to which the academicians were treated. Notwithstanding the vigilance of the Thief Detectives, thefts were occasionally committed. A poor family emigrating from Ash- ford, crossing Woodstock Hill at dusk, was tempted by the universal "Monday washing," left out for spring whitening. It took but a few moments for two stout pair of masculine arms to strip the lines, and stow away the stolen clothes, and on they went rejoicing ; but their joy was soon turned to mourning. Awakening in the morning to a sense of its loss, all Woodstock Hill arose in indignation. The "pursuers" were quickly routed out, and following the tracks they soon came up with the slowly moving teams, and brought thieves and booty in tri- umph back to the village. There is no doubt that the rogues richly deserved the legal penalty—a public whipping—but the judgment of the Trustees or teachers in making it serve as an "object lesson" to the Academy pupils is a little questionable. That the moral influence of such exemplary punishment for misdemeanors might not be lost upon the youthful mind, the scholars—girls and boys—were marshalled up to the whipping-post and made to look on while Constable Flynn administered the stripes with vim and vigor proportioned to the enor- mity of the offence, and deluged the bleeding backs with cider brandy immediately after the infliction. It is to be feared that abhorrence of theft was less stimulated than sympathy for the sufferers and hatred of vindictive justice. A youth found guilty of abstracting money and cloth in East Woodstock under somewhat peculiar circumstances, escaped his doom by forfeiture of bail and precipitate flight. With such proofs of its being needed, Woodstock Thief Detecting Society was kept up with unbated interest, its members being sure of having a good time if they did not always forestall theft or recover stolen property. The oyster supper provided from the general fund for their annual meeting served as an additional attraction, and most of the active men of the town gave their names and patronage to this society. The Pomfret Agricultural Society was encouraged by leading farmers, Amos Paine and James McClellan serving among its early officers.

Among the excitements of this period was a legal controversy in- volving the homes and farms of a number of Windham County resi-

dents. Governor Joseph Dudley of Massachusetts owned extensive
farms in Woodstock and Thompson, which he had entailed upon his
oldest son, to descend according to the English law of primogeniture.
Joseph Dudley, the legal representative of Governor Dudley at this
date, conveyed these farms by deed to previous tenants. His brothers,
and other representatives of the family claimed that this sale was illegal, and brought suit for their recovery. The defendants, Obadiah
Child, Captain John Chandler, Chester Brown, Captain Ephraim May,
Captains William, Chester and Jonathan May, Stephen, Nehemiah and
Charles Child of Woodstock, Peter Reccard, David Nichols, Jason
Phipps and Simeon Buxton, of Thompson, associated together for the
defence of their claim as "The Woodstock and Thompson Land Company," engaging for their counsel, John McClellan, George Larned and
William Perkins, Esquires. Sylvanus Backus served in behalf of the
plaintiffs. Trials were held before the Superior Court at Windham and
before the United States District Court at Hartford, without gaining a
satisfactory verdict. The magnitude of the interests involved, and the
intricacies of the legal points at issue, made this suit the most exciting
and important ever brought before the Courts of Windham County,
and its long delayed decision was waited with eager interest. John
F. Williams of West Woodstock was now enrolled among the lawyers
of the town. Its list of physicians embraced Doctors Haviland Morris, Ebenezer Bishop, Joseph Seagrave, Thomas Morse, Daniel Lyman,
Amasa and Amos Carrol. Dr. Lyman gave his attention more particularly to surgery. Dr. Thomas Morse, now settled in West Woodstock,
was noted as the third Dr. Morse who had practiced within the town.
His grandfather, Dr. Parker Morse, Sen., was graduated from Harvard
College about 1735, and settled in East Woodstock immediately after
acquiring his profession, and was succeeded by his son of the same
name. The grandson maintained the medical reputation of the family,
and served many years as clerk of the County Medical Society.

X.

TOWN AND CHURCH AFFAIRS IN ASHFORD.

ASHFORD kept pace with the times in internal improvements.
The Woodstock and Somers Turnpike was now completed, and
the Tolland County Turnpike intersected with Boston and Hartford
two miles west of Ashford village. Travel on these thoroughfares
was stimulated by the war and manufacturing; stages were daily passing to and fro over the various roads, and at the junction of the Boston and Providence Turnpikes, a continuous line of vehicles as far as

the eye could reach, was frequently seen. The numerous taverns kept by Clark, Richmond, Palmer, Preston, Burnham, Howe, Woodward and others, had abundant patronage. Four carding-machines were set up in different parts of the town. Rufus Sprague, Edward Keyes, John N. Sumner, Benjamin and Mason Palmer were incorporated in 1815 as the Sprague Manufacturing Company for the manufacture of cotton wool into yarn or cloth. Read, Stebbins & Co., engaged in a woolen factory, advertising the same year "for eight or ten young men (to whom good encouragement would be given) for the purpose of learning to card, spin and weave." Benjamin Palmer also engaged in the novel manufacture of tin ware, and offered tin ware of any description, plain and Japan, as low as any one in the State.

Eight mercantile stores, six grain-mills, nine saw-mills and five tanneries were reported in 1818. Josias Byles continued in the office of town clerk ; David Bolles and his son had charge of the post-office. The former was made judge and the latter clerk of the County Court in 1817. William Perkins, Esq., served as State attorney and councillor.

The "seven churches" of Ashford were more or less prosperous. The First Congregational church was severely afflicted in the death of its honored pastor, Rev. Enoch Pond, August 6, 1807. His epitaph, composed by Rev. David Avery, gives a just estimate of his character :—

"Generous in temper, correct in science and liberal in sentiment, the gentleman, the scholar, and the minister of the sanctuary, appeared with advantage in Mr. Pond. The church and society in Ashford were favored with his Gospel ministry eighteen years."

Rev. Philo Judson of Woodbury was ordained and installed as his successor, September 26, 1811, and enjoyed a successful ministry for a still longer period.

The Eastford church, after five years' vacancy, made choice of Mr. Hollis Sampson, a former "deacon of the Methodist Episcopal church." After a candid conference with Mr. Sampson at the house of Esquire Bosworth, upon Christian doctrines and discipline, and the relative duties of pastor and church, the Church expressed its satisfaction with his sentiments and preaching, and invited him to settlement—the Society offering three hundred dollars salary and making suitable provision for the entertainment of the Council. Ordination took place December, 1809, in the presence of a numerous and attentive assembly. Rev. Mr. Lyman made the opening prayer. Mr. Dow gave one of his characteristic sermons from Malachi i : 1—4. Dr. Welch of Mansfield, Messrs. Storrs and Weld, assisted in other services. Though the pulpit had a new incumbent, the society thoughtfully provided " That

Mary Judson may have the ministerial pew so long as she remain Mr. Judson's widow." The number of choristers was now greatly reduced and a singing-master employed. Mr. Sampson's pastorate was unhappy. Shrewd, witty and eloquent, he was deficient in steadiness and moral principle, and after much unpleasantness was dismissed from his charge at his own request, May 13, 1816—the council withholding recommendation. This omission led to a more thorough investigation, in which part of the charges were owned by Mr. Sampson, "who blamed himself and made satisfactory confession," but did not succeed in gaining the desired approbation. With characteristic aptness he chose for his parting text:—"For with me it is a very small thing that I be judged according to man's judgment." During the vacancy following his dismissal, Rev. Asahel Nettleton labored for a time with great effect in Eastford and its sister churches, and very many professed conversion. More than fifty were added to the membership of the Westford church, which still enjoyed the ministrations of Mr. Storrs. The list of pew-holders* in 1815 indicated a steady growth and material prosperity. The meeting-house was faithfully repaired and made comfortable, and furnished with one of the first *stoves* in the County, the society in 1820 allowing one to be set up and "a fire in the same, provided the expense can be raised by free donation."

The First Baptist church, in the Knowlton neighborhood, after improving for two years the gifts of Frederic Wightman, voted to call a council for his ordination :—

"*Ashford. First Wednesday in October*, 1807. Then met with the church from other churches—Elders Biel Ledoyt, Abel Palmer, Amos Wells, James Grow, David Lillibridge, and ordained our brother, Frederic Wightman, to administer Gospel ordinances. Elder Palmer preached from these words:— 'Holding forth the word of life;' Elder Grow offered the consecrating prayer; Elder Wells gave the charge and Elder Lillibridge the right hand of fellowship. *December* 1. The church met according to appointment. *Voted*, To call Elder Frederic Wightman to administer the ordinances of the Gospel in this church for the future. Even while the fellowship continues between the church and said Wightman."

Elder Wightman cordially accepted this call. John Weston was chosen to the office of deacon ; Deacon Abraham Weston, church clerk. It was agreed to have four church meetings a year and a committee appointed to look up brothers and sisters that are delinquent In 1813, the Deacons Weston and Amos Knowlton were appointed a

* Dr. Andrew Huntington, Abner Chaffee, Ashael Kendall, David Sears, Amos and Elias Kendall, Ezra Smith, Stephen and Elijah Whiton, Eli Hawes, John Bosworth, Calvin Warren, William Bicknell, Rufus Pearl, Joab Cushman, Shubael Preston, Joel Ward, Caleb Seagrave, Gurdon Robinson, Phinehas Burchard, Medinah Preston, Peleg Russel, John Loomis, Allen Bosworth, Joseph Woodward, Harvey Preston, Timothy Walker, Johnson Amidon, Boaz Whiton, John Whitmore, Nathan Lamb, Jedidiah Amidon, Josiah and Amos Chaffee.

committee to sell or exchange the farm that belonged to the society, which was accomplished to general satisfaction. Elder Wightman "continued with this lovely church eleven years. All this time few churches prospered more. A state of perfect harmony the whole time." Justus H. Vinton, afterward missionary in Burmah, was baptized by Elder Wightman; Matthew, son of David Bolles, a useful and honored Baptist minister, received the following certificate from his hand :—

"ASHFORD, *May* 10, *A. D.* 1811.

The First Baptist church in Ashford to the strangers scattered throughout Pontus, Galatia, Cappadocia, Asia and Bothynia:—These lines may certify that our beloved brother, Matthew Bolles, is in good standing with us, and we recommend him to any church of the same faith and order. And we shall consider him dismissed when joined with you. Also believing to have a public gift that ought to be improved."

Matthew Bolles began to preach at Lyme the following year, and was afterwards widely known as an eloquent and effective preacher. His brother Augustus was ordained pastor of the Baptist church in Tolland in 1814; was afterward for a time editor of *The Christian Secretary.* Lucius Bolles was early identified with the Foreign Mission work, and served most faithfully and efficiently as the Corresponding Secretary of the Baptist General Convention for Foreign Missions. The father of this remarkable ministerial triad—Elder David Bolles—so widely known and honored in Connecticut, rested from his labors in 1807.

In 1816, the First Ashford Baptist church reluctantly resigned Elder Wightman to the church in Upper Middletown, and was not able to induce him to return to this field. The Westford Baptist church continued in charge of Elder Rathburn. The North Ashford church was favored for three years with the ministrations of a gifted young brother, William Palmer of Hampton, whose winning eloquence attracted large and delighted congregations. The society was now able to complete its meeting-house, adding fourteen new pews to the gallery. After an interval of supplies Mr. Stephen Haskel was ordained pastor, "a man of fine personal appearance with a voice of great harmony and power," when the house was again filled with delighted hearers. Twelve were baptized during the first year of his ministry.

The Methodist society in Eastford gained in strength and popularity, and enjoyed the usual succession of earnest and faithful ministers.

XI.

TOWN AFFAIRS IN BROOKLYN. UNITARIAN CONTROVERSY. THE
    NEW CONSTITUTION. CHANGE OF COUNTY SEAT.

BROOKLYN was much interested in public and home affairs.
    While earnestly reprobating Embargoes and approbating the
course of the Executive of Connecticut, ordering a copy of Constitutional amendments distributed to every inhabitant at the expense of
the town, keeping up her matross and military companies and entertaining Brigades, steadily working and planning for securing the removal of the court-house, she was equally alert in the administration
of local government. In her by-laws she expressly enjoined "that
only two neat cattle to a family should be allowed to run at large." A
Health-committee was instituted in 1810, which was instructed to
procure the most skillful physician in case the spotted fever should
appear. As a farther preparation, perhaps, for this dreaded visitant,
a hearse-house and harness were procured, and also a pall or grave-
cloth and trunk to keep it in, and a committee appointed in each district to superintend at funerals, and form rules for promoting order
and regularity on such occasions. The selectmen were required to ascertain by personal investigation "who are and who are not furnished
with Bibles as the law directs," and if any families were found deficient
and not able to procure them, to provide and distribute the same.
With such precautions and a corps of watchful physicians the threatened visitation was probably averted.

The Brigade Review, September, 1812, was a very notable and
brilliant affair. Five regiments of foot and one of horse participated
in military exercise, comprising it was said, "at least 2,500 troops, and
four times as many spectators, presenting something of a warlike
appearance." It was considered the greatest gathering in point of
numbers and glittering array ever witnessed in Windham County, and
doubtless had its influence in stimulating the war spirit and encouraging enlistment. The manufacturing excitement only affected Brooklyn
indirectly by furnishing a nearer market for its abundant dairy products. No town of equal magnitude in the State, it was confidently
asserted, "makes an equal quantity of cheese and pork." One carding-
machine, two tanneries, three grain and two saw-mills were also
reported. Captain Mather had relinquished his hat-making for tavern
keeping in the village, which now contained about twenty dwelling-
houses and two mercantile stores. Adams White, Jun., had charge of
the first post-office. John Parish and Daniel Kies divided the legal
practice, though the latter had met with great loss in attempting to

utilize the ingenious invention of his mother, Mrs. Mary Kies of
Killingly. John Gallup served as deputy sheriff. Dr. Waldo
Hutchins was established in medical practice. Joseph Scarborough,
John Parish, Roger W. Williams served as justices; Samuel Scar-
borough, town clerk. Noted taverns were kept by Phinehas Searls
and P. P. Tyler. Though so energetic and prosperous, Brooklyn
continued to lose by emigration. Mr. Darius Matthewson removed to
Pomfret. The younger sons of Captain Tyler, and representatives of
Cady, Spalding and many other old families, went out into the world.

The faithful rector of Trinity Church, Rev. Daniel Fogg, died in
1815, after forty-three years service. A monument erected by Colonel
Daniel Putnam bore fitting testimony to his exemplary life and
character. His funeral was attended by Rev. Philander Chase, rector
of Christ Church, Hartford. The church then numbered thirty-one
communicants. Its strongest pillar was Colonel Daniel Putnam, who
had married a niece of its founder, Godfrey Malbone. After three
years of irregular worship, Rev. George S. White accepted the charge.
An Englishman of strong character and native eloquence he was at
first very popular and drew a large congregation—but difficulties soon
arose, the building a new parsonage was suspended, and the two years
engagement ended in alienation and detriment.

In consequence of the increasing years and infirmities of Dr. Whitney, Mr. Luther Wilson of New Braintree, was ordained colleague
pastor of the Congregational Church and Society in 1813, which
position he filled with fidelity and acceptance till it was found that he
had embraced the Socinian or Unitarian views then becoming so
prevalent in Massachusetts. Although the Brooklyn church was but
moderately Calvinistic in belief and very liberal in its practice, these
views broached by Mr. Wilson fell so much below its standard as to
awaken apprehension of disastrous results, and he was advised by Dr.
Whitney and leading church members "to ask dismission and leave in
peace and not rend the church asunder." But already a strong party
sympathized with Mr. Wilson in his belief and desired his continuance,
the liberty allowed in religious matters having developed in the community an unusual independence of thought and expression, and it
soon became evident that a conflict was irrepressible. After much
private agitation and discussion, a church meeting was called February
16, 1816, to consider the erroneous opinions supposed to be held by
Mr. Wilson. Esquire Parish was chosen moderator. Interrogation
drew from Mr. Wilson the distinct statement—"That he believed the
Lord Jesus Christ not a divine person, equal and eternal with the
Father, the supreme, self-existent God." The church thereupon proceeded to vote:—"That it considered the doctrine of the Trinity to be

an essential and fundamental doctrine "—yeas, 13 ; nays, 5 ; neutral, 5. In a public discourse soon after, Mr. Wilson more fully defined his position, and called upon the church to explain their vote and make known their wishes. The church accepted his proposal to call a mutual council to consider existing matters of difficulty and advise to measures for terminating them. The Reverends Joseph Sumner, D. D., of Shrewsbury, Andrew Lee and Abiel Williams, with delegates, obeyed the summons, and after due consideration " did not see that Mr. Wilson had forfeited his ministerial character, or that the church wished his removal." The church accepted this result by a small majority (ten *versus* eight) but was unable to abide by it. The breach became every day wider ; the controversy more bitter. Those hard-headed, strong-minded men and women, accustomed to think and speak with great freedom, found the situation very serious and critical. Belligerent "old Captain Tyler" held up the orthodox banner; Esquire Parish, keen, cool, wary, led the opposition forces. A majority of the church favored Dr. Whitney and Captain Tyler ; a society majority sympathized with Mr. Wilson and Esquire Parish. As the decision of the council composed in part of members of the Eastern Association had proved unsatisfactory it was but natural that church and pastor should meditate a return into her original association relations, and an appeal to that august judicial body the WINDHAM COUNTY CONSOCIATION. To forestall such appeal the society made the following proposals :—That the church should entirely disconnect themselves from Windham County Consociation ; annul their vote respecting the Trinity, and put themselves on the Covenant as before said vote was passed. To which the church made answer—January 26, 1817—" As respecting Consociation not the proper time to discuss the subject considering the varieties of opinion. As to annulling Trinity vote nothing more meant in it than to recognize what was contained in our ancient covenant, and express our intention strictly to adhere to it ; but were willing for the sake of peace to vary the mode of expression and adopt words of our original church covenant, Article I."

So far was the church from *disconnection* from Consociation that it had already decided to submit its difficulties to its consideration and decision. This Unitarian controversy was exciting very great interest and alarm all over the land and the ministers of the County joyfully hastened to join in the fray. February 5, 1817, the County Consociation accordingly met at the house of Captain Tyler. Moses C. Welch, D. D., the great champion of orthodoxy, was chosen moderator. Mr. Wilson and the church minority, obeyed the summons to appear before the Consociation but challenged its right of jurisdiction. Dr. Whitney had deliberately withdrawn years before from the County Association, and with Mr. Wilson was member of another body, and the Brooklyn church had dropped its connection with other churches of Windham County. After full hearing and discussion, the Consociation decided :—

" That the church of Brooklyn was originally voluntarily consociated and has acknowledged this relation by a series of subsequent consociational acts and has neither forfeited these privileges nor surrendered them. The Constitution of the churches does not admit that a consociated church may be deprived of its privileges by the act of the pastor or of an association of pastors, but subjects the pastor of such church to its discipline. It supposes every person entering into connection with such church acquainted with its government and solemnly covenanting to operate with it in carrying its system of discipline into effect. Consociation are of opinion that they not only have jurisdiction, but are imperiously bound since all other attempts have proved abortive to listen to its complaint and endeavor to restore its peace."

These complaints being fully presented, and the accused heard at length in his own vindication, the Consociation decided :—

" 1. That the charge against Mr. Wilson was supported; 2. That the denial of the Trinity is a departure from the faith; and, 3. Disqualifies Mr. Wilson from the office of teacher as it is a rejection of an essential part of the Counsel of God.

Accordingly his pastoral office in churches in our fellowship is now declared to be ended, and his pastoral relation in Brooklyn in particular, ought to be and is hereby dissolved."

The adherents of Mr. Wilson declined to accept these decisions, and as a majority of the society proceeded to exercise control of the meeting-house. At a society meeting, March 3, 1816, it was voted that no persons except the ministers of the society, and those belonging to the Eastern Association should be allowed to hold a religious meeting in this house without a written permit from its committee. Mr. Wilson was requested to preach whenever Dr. Whitney did not occupy the pulpit, without regard to the action of Consociation. Much confusion and strife followed. The aged pastor went far beyond his strength in attempting to preach twice on every Sabbath to keep out the deposed colleague, and when at his special and urgent request Mr. Preston of Providence occupied the pulpit without obtaining the requisite order, the intruder was prosecuted by the society. A council was called in September by Mr. Wilson and his supporters, " to examine and give their opinion whether the result of the Consociation was agreeable to ecclesiastic usage, and to the maxims and precepts of the Christian religion." However unfavorable their verdict upon this much disputed question, they agreed upon the propriety of dismissing Mr. Wilson from his unpleasant position, expressing at the same time their entire satisfaction with his pacific and charitable temper, theological attainments and ministerial qualifications. The church discharged this parting volley :—

" Whereas, Mr. Luther Wilson has been found guilty of a charge of HERESY by the Consociation of this County, and has been frequently admonished by the members of this church for that crime and also by Consociation—it is the opinion of this church that he ought to be and is suspended from the communion of this church till he retracts and reforms."

The departure of Mr. Wilson only increased the breach and difficulties. The society procured an avowed Unitarian from Massachusetts, placed him in the pulpit and levied taxes for his support. A number of his opponents not liking to pay for heretical preaching withdrew from the society, weakening their own ranks and adding to the strength of the Unitarians, who now openly asserted their right to the house of worship and other parochial privileges. The aged and infirm pastor, greatly afflicted by this defection and strife among a people who were so dear to him, labored painfully to discharge all the duties of his office and maintain what he believed the rights of the church, until the doors of the meeting-house were barred against him. It was on a communion Sabbath, nine were to be admitted to the membership of the church, when the gathering congregation was denied admittance. Dr. Whitney was a man of great equanimity and self-control. Jokes were to him more natural than tears, but on this occasion his feelings wholly overcame him and as bowed down with grief he re-entered his dwelling he repeated with deep emotion the words of David :—

> " O Lord! how many are my foes,
>   In this weak state of flesh and blood;
> My peace they daily discompose,
>   But my defence and hope is God."

The distressed church hired the unfinished attic of a common dwelling-house for a place of worship, and called upon the County Association to supply them with preachers. Among others who volunteered their friendly services was Mr. Dow of Thompson, whose quaint texts afforded merriment as well as consolation. Glancing at the bare walls and rafters with his keen, sarcastic eye, he queried— "And wherefore have ye made us to come up out of Egypt, to bring us in unto this evil place?" Nor was the afternoon selection less appropriate—"The conies are a feeble folk and dwell among the rocks." Efforts for conciliation were still considered and at one time seemed likely to prove effectual—a mildly orthodox candidate gaining the suffrages of both parties. "For the purpose of healing divisions and promoting christian peace and harmony," the church agreed, "to give up the jurisdiction of Consociation and Saybrook Platform, and establish the following tribunal as a mutual council impowered to settle all matters of difficulty i.e. Dr. Lee of Lisbon, and delegate; Rev. Jesse Fisher of Scotland, and delegate; Rev. Philo Judson of Ashford, and delegate; Rev. Abiel Williams of Dudley, and delegate." Also "voted, that no member of

Josiah Whitney

this church shall be called in question for any religious sentiments avowed during our unhappy condition ; also, not to expunge any vote." September 15, 1818, the church proposed to society "to unite with them in procuring some suitable person for minister ; in event of society not accepting, church requested them to repeal or to modify their votes, that the church may improve the meeting-house without molestation or disturbance, provided they procure preaching without any expense to the society." But the difference was too deep and radical for healing, party spirit had raged with too great fierceness, words and blows had been too freely exchanged, and after a final council, March 3, 1819, all hopes of reconciliation were abandoned The church voted a formal Remonstrance to Deacon Roger W. Williams, John Parish and John Williams, and withdrew from them its watch and care, and with diminished numbers, unabated courage and greatly stiffened doctrinal orthodoxy, continued its meetings in the upper chamber, and instructed a committee to procure aid in preaching "if a suitable place can be found."

While this sectarian controversy was raging in Brooklyn, the great religious question which for nearly a hundred years had so deeply agitated Connecticut was forever settled. By the adoption of a new Constitution all previous enactments and restrictions had been swept away, and religious worship and maintenance left to the judgment of the individual conscience. Windham dissenters, so active in the early days of agitation, battled on to victory. Baptists, Methodists, Universalists, Freethinkers, took up the war-cry of the vanquished Separates —"Down with the priest tax, the certificates, the Standing Order, the Saybrook Platform, the whole Ecclesiastic Establishment of Connecticut." Roger Huntington of Windham printed and circulated at his own expense "A Review of Ecclesiastic Establishments in Europe," which struck most forcible and telling blows upon the Connecticut system. Judge Bolles wrote and spoke with equal vigor, and was the first Baptist permitted to argue the Baptist petition before the two houses of the Legislature. As the struggle drew near its close it increased in intensity. The ministers and brethren representing the original churches of Connecticut—those churches which had done so much in the building up and developing character and institutions—the rulers of the State, the wise men, the councillors, clung to their system with the tenacity of men who believed that religion was the great end and aim of all human affairs, and that it was their supreme duty to provide for its universal observance. Political combinations added fury to the flame. The conservative and dignified Federalist stood by the ecclesiastic constitution ; the progressive Jeffersonian Republicans offered aid and sympathy to the champions of religious liberty. The war of 1812 hurried on the inevitable result. The unpopular course of the Federalists in refusing to call out troops and instituting the Convention at Hartford, and their unwise and unequal distribution of public funds, hastened their downfall. The stately Episcopalians declared against them and joined with other sectaries into one great Toleration Party, which gathered into its ranks every opposing element and carried the State by overwhelming majority. At the May Session of the General Assembly in 1818, a bill was passed recommending, that on July 4, the freemen should meet in their respective towns to choose delegates to aid in the formation of a Constitution of civil government. A Baptist clergyman present simply said:—"I withdraw my petition," for he knew that the day was won. Windham County sent as delegates:—Windham, Peter Webb, Zaccheus Waldo; Ashford, Josias Biles, William Perkins; Brooklyn, Roger W. Williams; Canterbury, Luther Paine, Daniel Frost; Columbia, Silas Frost; Hampton, Ebenezer Griffin; Killingly, Luther Warren, Ezra Hutchins; Lebanon, Stephen D. Tilden, Thomas Babcock; Mansfield, Edmund Freeman, Artemas Gurley; Plainfield, Elias Woodward, John Dunlap; Pomfret, Darius Matthewson, Lemuel Ingalls; Sterling, Dixon Hall; Thompson, George Larned, Jonathan Nichols, Jun.; Voluntown, Daniel Keigwin; Woodstock, John McClellan, Elias Child, 2d. The convention met at Hartford, August 26. Peter Webb, George Larned and Edmund Freeman were chosen from Windham County to act with three members chosen from each other county in drafting a Constitution. Another distinguished son of Windham, Amasa Learned, represented New London County. Day after day the committee made reports which were discussed and amended by the whole body. The Bill of Rights declared, that the exercise and enjoyment of religious profession and worship shall forever be free to all persons in this State, and that no preference shall be given by law to any christian sect or mode of worship. In Article VII. it was affirmed:—

"It being the duty of all men to worship the Supreme Being, the Great Creator and Preserver of the Universe, and their right to render that worship in the mode most consistent with the dictates of their consciences; no person shall, by law, be compelled to join or support, nor be classed with, or associated to, any congregation, church or religious association. But every person now belonging to such congregation, church or religious association shall remain a member thereof, until he shall have separated himself therefrom, in the manner hereinafter provided. And each and every society or denomination of Christians in this State, shall have and enjoy the same and equal powers, rights and privileges."

Section Second provided that any person could separate himself from society relations by a written notice to the clerk of the society. The draft of the Constitution, as amended and approved when read by sections, was read through for the last time before the final question of acceptance or rejection, at 5 P. M., September 18. But even on this closing day it was moved "to strike out the Seventh Article relating to Religion," but determined in the negative by majorities of thirty-five upon Section First and forty-two upon Section Second. The Constitution was accepted by 134 yeas, *contra* 61 nays—(five of the Windham County delegates voting against it)—and submitted to the respective towns for their approbation and ratification. Town meetings were held, October 5, when the assembled citizens of Windham County heard the new Constitution read and expounded, and thus pronounced their verdict :—

	Yeas.	Nays.		Yeas.	Nays.
Windham,	182	127	Mansfield,	210	178
Ashford,	189	161	Plainfield,	101	87
Brooklyn,	103	42	Pomfret,	91	116
Canterbury,	69	161	Sterling,	58	44
Columbia,	62	65	Thompson,	174	95
Hampton,	89	120	Voluntown,	53	32
Killingly,	174	144	Woodstock,	133	147
Lebanon,	86	152			
				1,777	1,671

These votes would seem to be irrespective of party lines, nor can they be explained by the religious status of the towns—strong Federal towns like Brooklyn and Thompson voting acceptance, and Canterbury and Woodstock, with their vehement Separate and Baptist element, giving judgment against it. The probability is that in the disintegration and confusion of parties the question was met upon its own merits, and decided according to individual bias and conviction.

The adoption of the new Constitution was followed by the settlement of another vexed question, that for nearly an equal period had excited much contention in Windham County. The northern towns carried their point and obtained the removal of the Courts from Windham. Hampton, as holding the exact geographical centre of the county as then stated, was exceedingly active in the later movements. Ebenezer Griffin, Elijah Simons, Philip Pearl, James Burnett and Joseph Prentice, were continued in service as committee. In December, 1817, a committee was sent to Hampton by the General Court to consider the situation. A very animated meeting was held at the house of Luther D. Leach. Every town in the County sent its best men to join in deliberations. Windham was well represented by its lawyers, Samuel Perkins, John Baldwin and Jabez Clark. Hampton's committee of six employed "an able lawyer" to plead their cause, but were unable to secure a report in their favor. After careful deliberation and other meetings, the committee reported in favor of BROOKLYN

The Assembly accepted their report and provided for its execution, viz:—

"An Act, approved, May 27, 1819, provided that so soon as a convenient court-house and jail should have been erected in the town of Brooklyn, at a place to be fixed by three persons or any two of them, to be appointed by the County Court for said County a committee for this purpose, within forty rods of the meeting-house, to the acceptance of any two of the judges of the Superior Court for the time being, the County and Superior Courts within and for said County of Windham shall thereafter be holden in said town of Brooklyn, any law, usage or custom to the contrary notwithstanding : Always provided, that said buildings should be erected without any expense to said County, and within three years from the rising of this Assembly. That whenever said court-house and gaol shall be completed as aforesaid, then the court and county-house with the land adjoining and on which they stand belonging to said County, situated in said Windham, shall belong to the town of Windham."

Brooklyn immediately bestirred herself to take advantage of this enactment. At a town meeting, June 8, Dr. Ebenezer Baker was chosen moderator. A committee was chosen to correspond with other towns, and a thousand dollars out of the town treasury pledged for court-house and jail. In response to Brooklyn's summons, Darius Matthewson, Lemuel Ingalls, John H. Payson, John Davis, Judah Lyon, John F. Williams, Luther Warren, Penuel Hutchins, William Read, George Larned, Jonathan Nichols, Jun., Benj. Gallup, Joseph Eaton, John Dunlap, Sessions Lester, Jonathan Hammet, delegates from their respective towns, met in conference June 19, with Vine Robinson, John Parish, Charles Dabney and Eleazer Mather, to consider the location, size and expense of the necessary buildings. Judge Ingalls was chosen moderator ; Jonathan Nichols, clerk. John Parish, Darius Matthewson, Luther Warren, George Larned and Joseph Eaton were deputized to affix the size of the public buildings and estimate the probable expense. They reported "that six thousand dollars would be needful, of which Brooklyn guaranteed twenty-five hundred, and that the balance must be raised by the other towns or there would be no chance for establishing the county buildings at Brooklyn, and recommended that measures be immediately taken by each town to raise its reasonable proportion of this money."

This amount was not raised without considerable effort. Thompson, Killingly, Plainfield, Canterbury, Sterling, voted their appropriation without demurring, but towns whose ambitious aspirations had been blighted withheld their quota. Pomfret positively and repeatedly declined "to raise any money to assist Brooklyn to erect the county buildings at that place." The Woodstock committee vainly urged the matter upon their fellow-citizens—"had supposed that Woodstock from its well known liberality and ability would raise at least five hundred dollars ; considered it very important to render assistance ; Brooklyn, small, divided; the town had worked for fifty years, and should the object be lost for want of funds?" Unable to secure an appropriation, John McClellan and Elias Child were appointed a committee to draft a subscription paper, and a much larger committee was appointed to receive the money thus collected. Public spirited citizens in Brooklyn and Canterbury subscribed liberally in addition to the sums pledged by their towns. At a meeting of the County Court, July 20, "on motion of John Parish, Thomas Kinsman of Lisbon, Elisha I. Abell and Alexander Stewart, Jun., of Griswold, were designated to fix the place whereon a Court-house and jail shall be erected in the town of Brooklyn, according to act of General Assembly." The proposals of Charles Dabney and Benjamin E. Palmer were accepted, and Vine Robinson, Adams White, Captain Elisha Adams, Captain Eleazer Mather, Dr. Ebenezer Baker and John Parish, appointed to take said building agreement from the contractors in behalf of the town.

BOOK IX. 1820-1845.

I.

TRANSFERRENCE OF COURTS. BROOKLYN ENTERPRISE. DEATH
OF DR. WHITNEY. MINISTRY OF SAMUEL J. MAY.
EXECUTION OF WATKINS.

WINDHAM County's first court session was holden in Windham town, June 26, 1726. On the 26th of July, 1820, Chief-
justice Stephen T. Hosmer and Judge John T. Peters, having found
that a convenient court-house and jail had been erected at Brooklyn,
approved and established the same. A special court of common pleas
was holden, Judge David Bolles presiding. His associates were James
Gordon, Jun., Artemas Gurley; David C. Bolles, clerk. Andrew T.
Judson was present as state attorney; Edmond Freeman as sheriff.
Ebenezer Baker was appointed as keeper of the jail, and jail limits
were assigned. At the following session, August 18, William Tyler
was appointed keeper of the jail; Cyrus H. Beardsly, Azel Utley and
Jared W. Williams were admitted attorneys. Business opened with
much animation. Two young lawyers had already appeared in Brook-
lyn, ready to compete for clients and honors. The Bar of Windham
County at this time boasted a very creditable array of legal talent, and
held a good position in the State. It reported from Brooklyn—John
Parish, Daniel Kies, Jonathan A. Welch (son of Dr. Moses C. Welch),
Uriel Fuller; Ashford, David Bolles, Philip Hayward, Samuel Ashley;
Canterbury, Rufus Adams, Andrew T. Judson, Daniel Frost, Jun.;
Hampton, Joseph Prentice, Chauncey F. Cleveland (admitted at the
last court session in Windham); Killingly, Ebenezer Young; Lebanon,
William T. Williams, Denison Wattles, Jun., Henry Huntington;
Plainfield, Joseph Eaton, Ira Case; Pomfret, John Holbrook, Elisha
B. Perkins, Jonathan Prescott Hall; Sterling, Calvin Hibbard;
Thompson, George Larned, Simon Davis; Windham, Jabez Clark,
Samuel Perkins, David Young, John Baldwin, John Fitch, Thomas
Gray, Edwards Clarke; Woodstock, John McClellan, Ebenezer Stod-
dard, John F. Williams. A newspaper was on hand to report their
proceedings. The Press had taken precedence of the Bar. Monday,

July 1, 1820, the *Independent Observer and County Advertiser* sent out its first issue—Henry Webb, printer and publisher. Samuel and Horatio Webb were also associated in this enterprise—the former having previously published newspapers in Norwich and Windham. The *Observer* surpassed the waning *Herald* in size and general appearance. The paper was fairer, the print clearer. It manifested a good degree of enterprise in securing public and local intelligence. Literary readers were regaled with a variety of original and selected poems, and one of Brockden Brown's most harrowing complications administered as a serial. Samuel Webb acted as general agent. Its circulation was reported, as "pretty general in all parts of the County."

Bar and Press were soon followed by other institutions. Associated enterprise and effort sought the County centre. The Agricultural Society hitherto limited to Pomfret and adjacent towns now embraced the whole County. An act incorporating Windham County Agricultural Society, was passed in May, 1820, and in the following January the society was formally organized—Thomas Hubbard, president; Darius Matthewson, vice-president.; Amos Paine, 2d vice-president; Samuel Howard, treasurer; James McClellan, secretary. Its first meeting was held at the house of Peter Thompson, but arrangements were soon initiated for transferring its meetings to Brooklyn. In 1822, Windham County Bank was incorporated—Joseph Eaton of Plainfield, president; Adams White, Brooklyn, cashier. Among its first directors were Joseph Eaton, Vine Robinson, John McClellan, Andrew T. Judson, E. C. Eaton, Ebenezer Young, James Gordon, Rufus Adams, William Putnam, Bela P. Spalding, Herbert S. Williams. A neat new building soon accommodated this institution, which was regarded with much pride and favor by Windham County citizens. A close communion bank it was wittily called, as the privilege of stockholding was restricted to county limits. Upon petition of Vine Robinson, Adams White, Jun., Daniel Tyler and many other prominent men, the Windham County Mutual Fire Insurance Company was incorporated in June, 1826. Vine Robinson was chosen president; Adams White, secretary; Joseph Eaton, Andrew T. Judson, George Larned, John McClellan, directors. This institution met with general favor and secured patronage from all parts of the County.

The new impulse was manifested in the quickening of business and development of manufacturing enterprise. Young men were drawn to the town to engage in various avocations. Daniel C. Robinson, William Storrs & Co., C. W. Jenkins, advertised large assortments of merchandise at their fashionable stores. Edwin C. Newbury of Mansfield, having served apprenticeship in Hartford, opened shop as a silversmith, finding a ready market for serviceable spoons and spectacles. Others experimented in making tinware and furniture. Projects were broached for utilizing the clay deposit east of the village. A great cotton manufactory was built up on the Quinebaug in East Brooklyn by the Tiffanys of Killingly. B. E. Palmer, the architect of the court-house, removed his residence to the village. Two young physicians from abroad, William Hutchins of Killingly, and Thomas Huntington of Norwich, both very promising and public spirited young men, took the place of Dr. Ebenezer Baker, deceased. Daniel P. Tyler, after a short trial in Pomfret, returned to practice law in his own village. Among other new residents was Mr. George Benson of Providence, a man of advanced years and out-reaching philanthropy, who with his large and influential family of sons and daughters was welcomed as a valuable acquisition to the aggressive force of the town.

Brooklyn did not gain all these advantages without labor and self-sacrifice. Even the sum pledged for court-house and jail was not secured without a struggle. Sectarian strife interfered with plans for public improvement. Unitarians and Trinitarians could not unite even in building a court-house. Wealthy members of the latter society refused it was said to subscribe even one cent for that purpose. A basement was built below the court-rooms intended for business purposes which was rented for a few weeks to the Trinitarian congregation. The town called an indignation meeting and declared that the Court had no power to control the use of this room, and if they had it would be highly inexpedient to allow it to persons who had refused to aid in building it, especially as there was a meeting-house in town sufficiently large for all its inhabitants, and such indulgence would only have a tendency to prolong the difficulties, and requested Vine Robinson, John Parish and Samuel Scarborough to present the respects of the meeting to the Court, and request them not to permit said inhabitants to occupy said room for religious service. This act aroused some merriment as well as indignation all over the County. A humorous ballad was widely circulated, giving a ridiculous account of the whole controversy :—

> " On subjects dark they raised a rout,
> And what they nothing knew about,
> They talked upon till all was blue,
> And split their body right in two.
> Then Fate in pity kindly sent 'em
> A handsome Court-house to content 'em,
> That by this means, o'er-flowed with money,
> Their bitter gall might turn to honey.
> But what to them this gift will do,
> Time and experiment will shew—
> They now contend in spirit odd
> That none therein shall worship God."

Farther collision with the Court was prevented by ceding to the County the town's right in these public buildings—David C. Bolles, Uriah Fuller and J. A. Welch, committee for that purpose. Accounts were finally settled by the aid of Pomfret and Woodstock, who found it necessary to join forces with other northern towns against Windham's most earnest and persevering agitation for a half-shire and county division. Brooklyn opposed these efforts with her usual spirit and liberality, and sustained the various demands with patience and good temper. Vine Robinson now usually served as moderator in town meetings. Elisha Adams, Adams White, Jun., Philip Searls, selectmen; Zachariah Spalding, town clerk and treasurer; Bela P. Spalding, constable; John Weaver, Uriah C. Prince, Shubael Brown, William Putnam, Elias Blanchard, Nathan Witter, Jun., Jesse Fuller, Timothy Herrick, John Williams, 2d, highway surveyors for their respective districts. Delegates from Woodstock, Thompson, Pomfret and Killingly, were invited to confer at Champion's tavern in Pomfret, April 26, 1825, about a County poor-house and house of correction. A more direct road to Hampton was laid out the same year—damages laid to William Cundall, John Ashcraft, Galen Hicks, Havilah Taylor, Amasa Pooler, Richard Carder, Ebenezer Witter, Elijah Witter. In the following year the Brooklyn and Windham Turnpike was constructed.

As broader interests occupied the public mind religious animosities gradually subsided. The Trinitarians were able to complete a chapel for divine service in 1821, kind friends of the church assisting in its equipment. Different ministers aided Dr. Whitney in his labors, and quite a number were added to the church. In the following summer through the efforts of lady visitants, a Sabbath-school class was gathered, and a suitable children's library procured. Its first superintendent was Amos Prince, recently removed from Promfret. In April, 1824, Ambrose Edson of Stafford, was ordained and installed colleague pastor, on which pleasant occasion the use of the great meeting-house was magnanimously tendered by the First Society. The most conspicuous figures in Brooklyn at this time, were those of Captain Tyler and his wife, and their venerable pastor. Though in his ninety-fourth year Dr. Whitney was still erect and vigorous, his eye not dimmed nor his natural force abated. With flowing wig and antique garb he still was often seen upon the street, exchanging pleasant greetings and happy repartees with his dear friends and neighbors. His face beamed with animated expression, his playful sallies were tempered by christian dignity. As he entered the house of God, the congregation rose to receive him, and remained standing in reverential attitude till he had taken his seat. The fatal illness that seized him in September, found him in full possession of all his faculties, at peace with God and man, and as he drew nearer the end his mind grew clearer and brighter and his spirit seemed to soar above this world. Scripture, hymns and long passages from Young's Night Thoughts, were repeated by him with great animation and expression. He was able to see and converse with all his dear people, and many precious words of counsel, trust and triumph were treasured in their hearts. Colonel Daniel Putnam who called to see him on one of the last days found the chamber filled with the old and young of his flock, and was received with equal warmth and friendliness and with touching allusions to the death-bed of his honored father, his "constant and faithful friend; an Israelite indeed, in whose heart there was no guile." Young mothers brought their children to him for baptism as if the touch of those dying hands and prayer from those dying lips would bring an especial blessing. Yet amid all this rapturous elevation when it seemed at times as if the very gates of Heaven were opened to him, the native humor would flash out with its wonted brightness. To Judge Hosmer as an excuse for keeping his bed in his presence, he explained—"You know I am not of the rising generation." Some anxiety was expressed about the funeral arrangements as several of the ministers were absent or ailing and Mr. Atkins was suggested, when Dr. Whitney burst out—"He durstn't plead inability seeing he has got a new wife." "His voice soon after failed and he sunk gradually and most serenely into the arms of death." The funeral sermon was given as was suggested by his old friend, Mr. Atkins, other ministers bearing part in the services. Mr. Edson continued in charge as sole pastor of the church.

The Unitarian church was so fortunate as to secure for their pastor, Mr. Samuel J. May, a young man of vigorous intellect, good education and wide, philanthropic sympathies, most earnestly and honestly striving to learn the exact truth upon every question and teach the same to others, who was ordained over them, March 13, 1822. The ministry of Mr. May was most acceptable and beneficial to his own people and the community at large. Entering with his whole heart and soul into all of the great questions of the day, he carried others with him. It was a period of wonderful growth and quickening, when men's eyes were opening as never before to the sins, miseries and wants of the world. Himself a born reformer, and personally connected with the leaders of various aggressive movements, it was his privilege to initiate most vital and salutary reforms in Windham County. Through his efforts "The Windham County Peace Society" was organized, August 16, 1826. A larger number of gentlemen was present than had been expected. George Benson, moderator; Elisha B. Perkins, clerk. Rev. James Porter moved that a society be organized. A committee of five reported a constitution for a society, whose object was to discountenance by all *lawful* and *justifiable* means the anti-Christian and inhuman practice of war. A subscription of fifty cents a year, or five dollars for life, was authorized—funds to be exclusively employed in diffusing information upon the uselessness, miseries and criminality of war, and in cultivating the spirit of peace. Dr. Thomas Hubbard was chosen president; Mr. George Benson, Rev. Hubbel Loomis of Willington, Samuel Perkins, Esq., of Windham, vice-presidents; Rev. Samuel J. May, corresponding secretary; Rev. Ambrose Edson, recording secretary; Dr. Thomas Huntington, treasurer. A board of trustees was chosen, made up of gentlemen from different towns, who it was hoped would favor the undertaking, viz: Rev. James Porter, Pomfret; Rev. Roswell Whitmore, Killingly; Darius Matthewson, Pomfret; Ingoldsby Crawford, Union; George Sharpe, Abington; Rev. Orin Fowler, Plainfield; Amos Paine, James McClellan, Woodstock; Samuel Scarborough, Brooklyn; Dr. Minor Grant, Ashford; George Larned, Thompson; John Salter, Mansfield; Dr. Orrin Witter, Chaplin. Messrs. Benson, Porter and May were chosen a committee to prepare and publish an account of the formation of the society and a statement of its views and principles. Samuel Perkins was appointed to deliver an address upon the subject of peace at the Rev. Mr. Porter's meeting-house in Pomfret; Dr. Thomas Hubbard to deliver the first annual address to the society. Thus efficiently organized the society secured a respectable standing and did a good work in disseminating information and enlightening the public conscience.

The onward movement of temperance reform in 1826, found in Mr. May a most earnest and effective advocate. Happening to attend a business meeting of the Massachusetts Society for the Suppression of Intemperance, when it was proposed to meet the evil by entire absti nence from intoxicating liquors, he came home fired with zeal to pro pound the new doctrine and practice to the people of Brooklyn. Mrs. May cordially joined with her husband in heart and effort. They con signed a hamper of delicious wine to the service of the sick, emptied the cider barrel into the vinegar cask, and treated callers to cake, cold water and expository explanation, which brought the question into im mediate discussion. With his usual directness Mr. May proceeded to investigate, ascertained from every retailer in town the various sorts of intoxicating drinks sold in the course of a year, and the number of avowed inebriates; gathered from physicians, sextons, poor-overseers, jailor and well-informed citizens an estimate of the sickness, death, poverty and crime caused by these drinks, and much to his surprise found that the frightful statements made in society reports "were

abundantly sustained by the facts of the case found in our own town."
The results of his investigations were laid before the public in eloquent
discourses, which made a deep impression upon his hearers. Many
adopted the principle of total abstinence, a society was organized and
the cause of temperance made rapid headway throughout the town.

The educational interests of town, County and State were greatly
promoted through Mr. May's efforts. Placed on the school committee,
he was astonished to find that the public schools were even inferior to
those of Massachusetts; that the much-vaunted school-fund was actually detrimental in its workings; that people generally took little interest in schools which cost them nothing. By greater strictness in
the examination of teachers, and more thorough supervision, he gave a
new stimulus to the Brooklyn schools, and so aroused the attention of
other public-spirited citizens that they agreed to unite with him in
bringing the question before the consideration of the general public.
Accordingly a committee was appointed, and circulars sent throughout
the State, asking the towns to send delegates to Brooklyn for the purpose of considering the character and condition of our common schools.
This educational convention was held in May, 1827—its novelty elic-
iting a large attendance from Windham and adjoining counties. Reports by letter or delegate from nearly an hundred towns, revealed
such deficiency in teaching and administration, in conveniences and
attendance, as to surprise and mortify the citizens of the State, and
lead to the initiation of measures that effected in time an entire revolution. Windham continued her efforts by organizing a Society of
the Friends of Education for Windham County, George Sharpe,
president, which held meetings and circulated information.

With equal readiness and heartiness Mr. May espoused the cause of
those heroic men who felt themselves called by God to agitate for the
overthrow of American slavery. His pulpit was at once thrown open
to them and their principles, and having won, almost to a man, his own
congregation, they joined with him in promulgating their views in
other towns. In the controversy respecting the colored school at Canterbury, Miss Crandall found in Mr. May her most efficient and devoted
coadjutor, ready to face obloquy and loss of friends and position in
defence of equal rights and humanitarian interests. In these various
efforts Mr. May enjoyed the hearty sympathy and coöperation of his
own church, and also of many leading citizens of Brooklyn and other
towns. Especially in the Peace and Temperance movements he was
aided by the Rev. Mr. Edson, Vine Robinson, Uriel Fuller, Doctors
Hutchins and Huntington, and other Congregational brethren, all laboring earnestly for the public good, forgetful of the recent sectarian
division.

These public interests did not interfere with pastoral duties. Abounding energy and vital power enabled Mr. May to feed his own flock and all that needed help outside. He performed the usual pulpit ministrations to great acceptance, he knew the character and needs of every resident of his parish, he edited newspapers—first, *The Liberal Christian*, and later, *The Christian Monitor*, a weekly sheet open to the discussion of all moral and religious questions, and earnestly advocating the promotion of peace, temperance, education, civil and religious liberty—he joined in establishing a village lyceum, and delivered many lectures before it, and he held religious meetings in school-houses all over the County, in behalf of what he deemed a simpler and purer Gospel than that taught in the orthodox churches. Yet notwithstanding his efforts and eloquence Unitarianism made little advance. "The soil of Connecticut was so saturated with Calvinism that it was uncongenial to the true vine." Few were won to his church, but many welcomed his reforms, and men and women in different parts of the County still gratefully affirm "that no other had so marked effect in awakening and maturing resolves for a life of usefulness, earnest activities and high moral aims," as the genial and large-hearted Christian philanthropist and reformer, Samuel J. May.

Incessant calls to varied fields induced Mr. May to leave his pleasant home and work in Brooklyn, to the great regret of many devoted friends. His immediate successor, Rev. George W. Kilton, was followed in 1837 by Rev. William Coe. Trinity church, after a long period of irregular service, entered upon "a new lease of life" in 1828, in connection with the labors of Rev. Ezra B. Kellogg. Glebe and parsonage were now redeemed to the use of the parish, and the church edifice repaired and remodeled. Col. Daniel Putnam, senior warden, and one of the staunchest friends of the church, died in 1831. This great loss was in some degree made up by gradually increasing numbers and a higher tone in church life and public worship. When the Rev. Josiah M. Bartlett succeeded Mr. Kellogg in 1835, the parish was self-supporting with thirty-one families and forty-five communicants. Rev. Riverius Camp entered upon the rectorship in 1837. A Baptist element long existing in Brooklyn was farther developed under the preaching of Elder Bentley and revival influences, so that a Baptist church was gathered in 1828. The accession of Dr. Thomas Huntington after a remarkable religious experience, added strength and influence. In 1833, it secured the chapel vacated by the Congregationalists, and thenceforward maintained regular services. Dr. Huntington was ordained as an evangelist and served as pastor for several years. Mr. Edson's useful pastorate closed in 1830. He was soon followed by George J. Tillotson of Farmington, ordained and installed May 25, 1831. The church was almost immediately visited by one of the intensely emotional revivals peculiar to that period, and many were added to its membership. The chapel became too strait for the enlarged congregation, and a new house was erected the following year. A noteworthy event in Mr. Tillotson's early ministry was his official connection with Brooklyn's only execution—the hanging of Oliver Watkins, for the murder of his wife in August, 1831. This event was marked by the usual accompaniments, an immense crowd of people, drinking and jangling. It is said that the tavern-keepers were so fearful of losing their anticipated rush of custom by the self-destruction of the criminal, that they hired an extra guard the night preceding, who had him removed to the debtor's room where they could watch him more closely. Before break of day the roads in every direction were thronged with people coming in from distant counties and States. The gallows was erected in a hollow east of the village, a natural amphitheatre whose sloping sides acommodated the vast concourse of spectators. Roger Coit of Plainfield officiated as high sheriff—Captain David Keyes of Ashford having resigned to escape the painful duty. Dr. Harris of Canterbury attended as surgeon. Prayer from a neighboring minister was followed by an impressive discourse from Mr. Tillotson, founded upon the words—"Be sure your sin will find you out." The "amen" of his closing prayer was the signal for the fatal launch and was pronounced with remarkable composure and distinctness, so as to be heard "by the thousands who listened with the most absorbing interest, in stillness that seemed of the dead rather than that of the living." Perfect order prevailed during the services, which made a deeply solemn impression upon sober-minded spectators, preparing in some degree the way for the almost immediately succeeding religious revival. The vast throng present, the abundant supply of liquor and scarcity of food, made the afternoon and following night a scene of confusion and disorder.

The *Observer* was superseded in 1826 by *The Windham County Advertiser*, published by John Gray, who gave place in a year to Mr. J. Holbrook. This paper attained the greatest age and most general circulation as a County organ of any published in Brooklyn. It was followed in 1835 by *The Windham County Gazette*, published by Messrs. Carter and Foster, which was maintained for several years. Public exigencies and rising reforms called out several short-lived newspapers, viz: *The People's Press*, devoted to the advancement of Anti-masonry; the misnomered *Unionist*, an Anti-slavery journal, edited by C. C. Burleigh and supported by Arthur Tappan; *The Windham County Whig*, *The Harrisonian*, a campaign paper, published by Edwin B. Carter, in 1840, and one or two others whose names have perished with them. Mr. Joel Davison of Killingly served as news-carrier during the latter days of these papers, taking them and other periodicals all over his route in baskets and bundles suspended from his stalwart shoulders.

A High School was maintained intermittently during all these years, and in 1829 an academy was formally incorporated—Benjamin E. Palmer, Vine Robinson, Philip Scarborough, Daniel P. Tyler, William Hutchins, proprietors. A suitable building was procured, and considerable pains taken to build up a flourishing school. Scholars came freely from surrounding towns, but were apparently more impressed by the Court sessions and social attractions of the village than by the instruction administered. The standard of scholarship was higher than that of *teachership*, if we may judge by the success and accomplishments of those same ungrateful pupils who make disparaging reports of their alma-mater. Ex-Governor Gaston of Massachusetts, Hon. Abraham Payne of Providence, William S. Scarborough of Cincinnati, Brigadier General Tyler of Montgomery, Alabama, and very many other notabilities abroad and at home, may owe something of their fame to their training in Brooklyn Academy. Brooklyn's youth continued to go out in the world to fill places of credit and usefulness. Much enterprise was manifested by those who remained in the home field. New stores were opened by Sam'l H. Webb, Charles W. Jenkins and William Storrs. Edwin Newbury accepted an agency for the sale of fruit and ornamental trees and bulbs. Dr. James B. Whitcomb engaged in medical practice after the death of Dr. Waldo Hutchins.

II.

TEMPERANCE WORK IN WINDHAM COUNTY. ORGANIZATION OF COUNTY TEMPERANCE SOCIETY. EFFORTS AND RESULTS.

THE temperance movement initiated by Mr. May in Brooklyn was followed or perhaps accompanied by similar agitation in other Windham County towns. As in corresponding popular movements it is difficult to assign priority to any one section; it seemed rather to burst out spontaneously and almost simultaneously in various quarters. The fact of the excessive use and evil effects of liquor-drinking had been long admitted. Drunkenness was condemned with greater severity than at the present day. A common drunkard was the butt of derision, ostracized by society, and cast out from the churches. The

Pomfret Moral Society, ministers and philanthropists, expended an immense amount of logic and eloquence in urging men not to drink too much. Men denounced drunkenness and kept on drinking. The Windham County Association passed temperance resolutions—"talked *well*, talked *right*, but spoiled it all by taking their grog afterward." The temperance of those days was much like that of an old toper in Thompson whose reformation was attempted by a good landlady. Moved by his misery and destitution, she promised to find him work and keeping if he would restrict himself to two glasses of rum a day, which she would furnish. Old Darius accepted the terms and the work was assigned. "But now," he hiccoughed, "I must have a glass *to begin with*." A temperance reform begun with a glass was very sure to end with one.

It was not till after many years of apparently useless effort and experiment that the friends of temperance awoke to the conviction that the only cure for drunkenness was to quit drinking. A series of articles was published in *The Connecticut Observer* by Rev. Calvin Chapin, in 1826, entitled "Entire Abstinence the only Infallible Antidote," which had great effect, and in that same memorable year, auspiciously opening the second half-century of the Republic, Lyman Beecher delivered his famous "Six Sermons" at Litchfield, and the American Temperance Society was formed at Boston. The new watchword and pledge to keep it, served as a rallying cry to unite the temperance sentiment of the land into a mighty force and onward aggressive movement. Temperance societies sprang up as if by magic in every community and in a marvellously short time a revolution had been effected. Mr. May was perhaps the first to openly advocate Total Abstinence in Windham County, yet there were others who soon engaged in temperance work. The first pledge offered in Killingly was drawn up by Mr. William H. Fisher, superintendent at Howe's Factory. His three little boys attended the public school and not returning home at the usual hour he went to look for them, and found that the master had been treating the scholars with liquor as was customary in that district on the last day of the term, and that many of them were under its influence. His two older boys were partially intoxicated and the youngest one too far gone to speak—"the breath of life was in him and that was all." They took him home at once and used every means to restore him but he gave no signs of consciousness for many hours and was alarmingly ill for several days. The indignation excited by this occurrence put an end to the custom of "last day treats" in that district. The death of one of their employés, a promising young man prematurely cut off by liquor-drinking, strengthened Mr. Fisher in his temperance sentiments, and he declined to conduct the funeral unless liquor was banished from it. As soon as he heard of the invention of the temperance pledge he drew one up, and called upon Mr. Atkins and a number of his parishioners for advice and co-operation. Mr. Atkins at first refused to give his name, thinking his health required the daily use of liquor, but one of the deacons and another church member fell in with Mr. Fisher's views, and aided in calling a meeting and organizing a society.

It does not appear that temperance societies were formed in any of the towns till 1828. The older ministers, Messrs. Atkins, Lyman, Dow, and perhaps others, looked with some suspicion upon the movement as arrogating a power that ought to be controlled by the churches. Mr. Fowler of Plainfield, Mr. Edson, and young ministers generally, entered into the work with great zeal, but probably no man in Windham County exerted so much influence as Daniel Frost, Jun., of Canterbury. Unsuspected by himself he was on the very verge of ruin. The warnings of faithful friends, the expositions and arguments of Mr. May, with concurrent domestic influences, led him to abandon the use of liquor, and come out boldly on the side of temperance. Church-goers, who on Sunday noon had been hitherto regaled with rum, gin and brandy from his well-furnished sideboard, were now treated with cold water and exhortations to total abstinence. He became so engrossed in the subject, so convinced of its overwhelming importance, as to renounce his legal practice and devote himself entirely to temperance work. Through his influence a temperance society was organized in the meeting-house on Canterbury Green, August 25, 1828. The following constitution was presented:—

" *Resolved,* That this meeting do cordially approve of the principles and objects of the American Society for the Promotion of Temperance, and that we will cheerfully co-operate with them and all other associations whose object is the suppression of Intemperance.

Resolved, That in the opinion of this meeting there is abundant evidence that ardent spirits are not necessary as a refreshment or support to the strength during labor; but on the contrary absolutely injurious to health, and that to the *general moderate use* of them is to be chiefly attributed the prevalent *habit of Intemperance,* that an entire abstinence from them except when prescribed by a physician as a medicine, is the only sure remedy against this alarming evil.

Therefore, *Resolved,* that we will entirely abstain from the use of *ardent spirits,* except as an article of medicine, that we will not furnish them for persons in our employment, or provide them for our friends as an article of refreshment, and that in all suitable and proper ways we will discountenance their use in the community.

Voted, That any person may become a member of this society by signing the foregoing Constitution."

This constitution was immediately signed by thirty-two* of the leading citizens of Canterbury, men whose position and character guaran-

---

* *Names of constituent members.* Thomas Coit, Daniel Frost, Jun., John Barstow, James R. Wheelock, Israel G. Rose, Anson S. Cobb, Samuel L.

teed the success of any movement. Daniel Frost, Esquire, was chosen president ; Samuel L. Hough, vice-president ; Isaac Clark, secretary ; Stephen Coit, treasurer. By-laws were then passed, and William Dyer, Isaac Backus, Anson S. Cobb and S. L. Hough appointed to circulate a copy of the Constitution, persons signing the same to be considered in the same standing as if they signed the original. A large number of signatures was obtained in all parts of the town and the work went on with much spirit. A special meeting was held in the meeting-house, November 12, when neighboring clergy and citizens from other towns were present, and listened to a most effective address from the president, which was published by request of the society and widely circulated. A public meeting was held as often as once a month rotating among the different societies and school-houses. Three or four members of the society were appointed to deliver addresses or read dissertations on these occasions. Much local talent was thus elicited and a great variety gained. Ministers and physicians, lawyers and merchants, farmers and mechanics, gave in their testimony against the common enemy. Aged deacons and youthful students were among the speakers and equally engaged in helping forward the work. Dr. Clarke's addresses showing the physical effects of alcohol were very instructive and valuable. Rev. George S. White, who had recently removed his residence to Canterbury, proved a most efficient aid, entering into temperance work with much ardor and speaking with great eloquence and power. A Woman's Temperance Association was organized during this winter, which secured the names and sympathy of nearly every woman in the town. This too had its officers, and business meetings, and exchanged sympathetic and congratulatory addresses with the parent society.

In August, 1828, a temperance society was also formed in North Woodstock with thirty male members. Brooklyn followed in October. In December, "a few individuals in Abington started the plan to form a temperance society in the town, and proposed to meet those of the First Society who would unite with them at the school-house. Mr. Porter gave notice from the desk. About forty were present but none of Mr. Porter's church except Mr. John Williams." A committee was appointed to prepare a constitution, and a town society was organized early in January, 1829. Darius Matthewson, Esq., " who seemed to be more interested about it than others," was appointed

Hough, Isaac Morgan, Allen G. Clark, Stephen Coit, Isaac Backus, Chauncey Brown, William R. Morgan, Elijah Dyer, Jun., Isaac P. Morgan, Daniel Morgan, Enoch W. Waldo, William Dyer, S. G. Adams, Isaac Clark, O. Hudson Butts, Daniel C. Frost, Sylvanus Shepard, Job Rood, Andrew Harris, Nathan Adams, Joseph Bond, John Brown, Harvey R. Dyer, George L. White, John D. Clark, Asa F. Clark.

president. Charles P. Grosvenor, an early member of the defunct "Moral Society," was much interested in the new organization and by his personal persuasion induced one or more of the village store-keepers to abandon the sale of liquor. Societies were organized in other towns, and on April 20, 1829, a convention was holden at the Court-house in Brooklyn, to consider the expediency of forming a county temperance society. Delegates were present from Brooklyn, Canterbury, Chaplin, Hampton, Killingly, Pomfret, North and West Woodstock. After preliminary exercises the following resolution was adopted :—

"*Resolved*, That in our opinion the question whether intemperance is to be suppressed is no longer problematical, and that the time when it will be suppressed is rapidly approximating. That it is expedient for the various temperance societies in this county to concentrate their forces by uniting in a County Society."

Daniel Frost, Esq., John Holbrook, Esq., and Dr. Darius Hutchins, were appointed a committee to report a constitution, and after delibe ration their report was accepted. The constitution adopted closely resembled that of Canterbury. The society then proceeded to make choice of officers, to retain their position till July 4, 1830, viz:— Darius Matthewson, president; Daniel Frost, George Benson, Hon. Ebenezer Stoddard, vice-presidents; Rev. Ambrose Edson, secretary; Edwin Newbury, treasurer; Rev. Samuel J. May, Thomas Hough, Uriel Fuller, Esq., John Holbrook, Esq., Major Asa May, executive committee. The society* held its first annual meeting the following fourth of July in Brooklyn. Much interest was manifested. A large number of delegates assembled at Mather's tavern, now transformed into a temperance "coffee-house," and at 11 o'clock, formed a procession and marched with much ceremony to the Unitarian meeting-house. Devotional exercises were conducted by Rev. Messrs. Dennis of Massachusetts, and Whitmore of Killingly. An appropriate and impressive

---

* Societies represented at the organization of the County Society :—

	Male Members.	Female Members.
Canterbury	70	90
Brooklyn	40	22
Pomfret	70	42
Killingly	22	20
Hampton	8	14
Chaplin	33	..
North Woodstock	30	..
West Woodstock	14	..
	287	188

Number of members 475

At the July meeting, four additional societies were represented, viz :—Ashford, Eastford, North Killingly, Plainfield; bringing in some three hundred members.

address was delivered by Mr. Frost. Messrs. Parish, Whitmore and Fuller were then appointed to express to Mr. Frost their thanks for his address, and request a copy for publication. It was also voted that Mr. Frost be appointed agent for the society to visit the towns and bring the subject of temperance more fully before the public. Also, that the society should hold quarterly meetings in the several towns. The society then adjourned "to partake of an excellent dinner" at Mather's coffee-house, and rejoice over the approaching triumph of temperance and peace. A Fourth of July celebration transformed into a Temperance ovation seemed indeed the harbinger of an immediate millennium. Inspired by such prospects the members cheerfully submitted to close their exercises "by taking up a collection for the Colonization Society."

Thus efficiently organized, the temperance reform swept onward. Wherever he went Mr. Frost found a ready welcome and thoughtful hearing. The first phase of the movement was comparatively simple. It was only administering a remedy to those who felt the need of it. The thriftlessness, poverty, crime, disease and death caused by intemperance, were manifest in every community. Every neighborhood had its death-roll of victims; its shocking casualties—drunken men and women frozen and burnt to death; children starved, women beaten and murdered, promising young men brutalized and lost. Nor were the evil effects of what was called moderate drinking less obvious upon closer examination. The great mass of sober-minded conscientious men and women needed little persuasion or argument. Especially did the wives and mothers, who had borne such unspeakable burdens, welcome with full hearts the new gospel of temperance, while the economic side of the question appealed with great force to the shrewd sense and pockets of their more worldly minded husbands. The *folly* of furnishing drink to workingmen, paying out good money for that which only made them less efficient, was quickly recognized by the Yankee mind. It was true that many said that men would not and could not work without the accustomed stimulant, but that point was quickly tested by successful experiment. Mr. Matthewson, the Grosvenors, and temperance men generally, promulgated the law that no liquor was to be furnished to hired help, and a single summer's work settled the question forever. Equally prompt and summary was its banishment from the household circle. The time-honored custom of treating visitors to a friendly glass disappeared as if by magic. A woman with her mind fully made up can indeed almost work miracles. She can at least set aside *social* laws and customs. The tempting array of decanters vanished from the sideboard, the offering of liquor became as disreputable as its previous omission, and its use was interdicted in thousands of families. So radical a social revolution has probably never been effected as that achieved in an incredibly short period by the temperance reform.

Such results could not be accomplished without exciting opposition. Sellers and drinkers stared aghast at this temperance onset and scoffed at the proposition to sign away their liberties. Stage-drivers refused to bring newspapers that advocated temperance. Organized opposition once confronted Mr. White in Canterbury. Having appointed a lecture in the old Red Meeting-house he found a company of hard-looking men, sitting around a table spread with rum and glasses. The quick-witted Englishman saw and met the situation. Walking straight to the desk he instantly began :--" It is said that we ought not to engage in any act upon which we cannot ask the blessing of God—O Lord, thou knowest that thy servant has been in all parts of the world, among Indians, Cannibals, Jews and Turks, but never has he seen such miserable, God-forsaken wretches as those now before him "—and went on praying for them with a zeal proportioned to their needs—and the cowed bullies dared not lift a finger, and heard perforce all that he had to say to them. There was opposition also from men who professed to favor temperance. There were doubters and croakers who questioned the hygienic effects of total abstinence and the expediency of pledge and society. Reports from the different societies gradually satisfied honest objectors. All testified that labor was performed with much more care and efficiency without liquor. One man reported a very laborious task of wall-laying, drilling and rock-blasting most successfully and safely carried through " with no drink at all but pure cold water." Others had found that they "could even wash their sheep much quicker and cleaner without rum." Nobody found any difficulty in getting in their hay and grain without spirit, and it was solemnly asserted after repeated experiment " that death is never the result of the strictest temperance." The moral influence quickly perceptible, the greater quiet, the disappearance of loafers and loungers from stores and taverns, and above all the change wrought in men who had been induced to give up drinking, brought over those good ministers and church members who at first distrusted the movement. Mr. Lyman thought it absurd if he could not keep from drinking without signing a paper, but when he heard that one of his most prominent men who drank more than was good for him had promised scoffingly to sign when his pastor did—he at once called for a pledge and signed it, and was rewarded by the total reformation of a much-valued citizen, and the rapid spread of temperance sentiments in the town. Finding that the temperance societies were actually doing what the churches had failed to accomplish, Mr. Dow gave up his opposition, and accepted the presidency of the society formed in Thompson. The first lecture in this town was given by Mr. Frost. The people who had expected something in the "spread-eagle" style of the ordinary Fourth of July oration, heard instead a plain statement of facts to which their own experience furnished abundant testimony. A week before they had attended the funeral of a once respected citizen who had died of rum-consumption. Another victim lay at the point of death in the village. The earnest words of the lecturer, enforced by such examples, had great weight. Many signed the pledge, and a strong society was organized. A very hopeful work was carried on in the factory villages. Owners and agents were mostly temperance men. Mr. William Fisher was very active in temperance effort, allowing no liquor sold at hs new village, Fisherville, urging his employés to sign the pledge, and maintaining interesting meetings. Mr. Smith Wilkinson gave his strong influence to temperance, aiding and encouraging the society and discountenancing in every way the use and sale of liquor. Similar efforts were made in most of the factory villages. The Canterbury society extended its labors to Packerville. At the first meeting they gained forty-nine signatures. Daniel Packer and the young Baptist minister, Elder Kneeland, were very efficient workers. Messrs. Fowler and Burleigh labored with much energy in Plainfield, where they gained a large membership. From the new village of Willimantic and the young towns, Chaplin and Sterling, from ancient Windham, Voluntown and Killingly came alike cheering reports. Stores and taverns did not sell one-half the quantity of spirits. No person had been known to contract a relish for drink after joining the societies, and very few had broken their pledge. Improvement in order, industry and thriftiness was reported from every town. Brooklyn continued its labors with much zeal, reinforced by such speakers as Mr. Tillotson, Mr. Vine Robinson and Dr. Hutchins. The proposed public quarterly meetings were held at Ashford, Pomfret, Woodstock and Canterbury. The meeting at Pomfret was especially memorable from the delivery of Dr. John Marsh's celebrated lecture—"Putnam and the Wolf, or the Monster destroyed," which was immediately published and very widely circulated. Dr. Hewitt spoke with much effect at the Ashford meeting. A spice of opposition gave zest to the work in that town. The Eastford people were called to take their old meeting-house down a steep hill-side—a very difficult and delicate operation. A great crowd gathered, and with three strings of oxen, thirty-three in a line, had fairly launched the building on its perilous descent when a chain broke. The leader of the day demanded treat according to the usual custom, which Esquire Bosworth, the purchaser of the house, as a temperance man, promptly declined. High words and threats had no influence, and, getting their temper up, men and oxen forthwith decamped, leaving the meeting-house suspended. But there were too many good temperance men then in the ranks to allow a brother to suffer loss in such a cause. President Matthewson with a corps of sturdy Abington men came to the rescue, and completed the removal without a single drop of liquor. Their spirit and efficiency cheered the hearts of their Ashford brethren, and brought many of the wavering and desponding to take a firmer stand.

The Windham County Temperance society kept its second anniversary, July 4, 1830, with even more animation than on the preceding year. Rev. Daniel Dow was the orator of the day. The third anniversary was held in Pomfret, where a most stirring and eloquent address was made by Dr. Wilbur Fisk of the Wesleyan University, which made a very deep impression upon all who heard it.

With unabated spirit the work went on for several years. The great religious revivals of 1830–31, in which a large number of young men were brought into the churches, added strength to the temperance ranks. A converted young man was sure to be a temperance man. "Coburn's store" on Thompson Hill had continued to furnish liquor, but the morning after his son's conversion not another drop was to be had there. The quarterly temperance meetings in the different towns continued to be well conducted and attended. No town carried on its specific work with more regularity and interest than Canterbury. George S. White succeeded Mr. Frost as president; Daniel Packer, vice-president; Stephen Coit, treasurer; Abijah Dewing, Rufus L. Dimmick, Benjamin Delop, executive committee. Meetings were held alternately at the different school-houses, and were always addressed by one or more competent and interesting speakers. Temperance publications were scattered through the town, committees were from time to time appointed to circulate the constitution in each school district. In 1834, a membership of 635 was reported and it was further resolved that:—

"*Whereas*, Divine Providence has crowned with signal and unparalleled success every effort which has been made to stay the ravages of intemperance, we are encouraged by the success of the past to make greater effort in future to promote the cause of temperance."

Mr. Isaac Backus, the owner of Foundry works in the north part of the town, was very active in his neighborhood, a vexatious litigation to which he was subjected for some statement respecting a liquor-vender, only making him more zealous in the work. Mr. Solomon Payne, who served as president for several years, received an especial vote of thanks for his fidelity and perseverance in discharging the duties of his position. Messrs. Frost and White, though much occupied with general temperance work, were frequently present at the Canterbury meetings. Young men from other towns, Dr. Hutchins, Rev. George Tillotson, John B. Young, George H. Middleton, helped to maintain their tone and interest. The public meetings of the County society were well sustained. Mr. Matthewson was retained as president for several years. Public sentiment had so advanced in Pomfret that in 1837 more than a hundred voters petitioned the Civil Authority "not to grant license to any person to retail spirituous liquor the ensuing year." The request was rejected on the ground " that the law imperiously requires them to recommend for license a suitable number of proper persons "—four of the Board dissenting from the decision. Measures initiated the following year to amend or repeal the law, and remove as far as possible all means of intoxication, met the approval and support of advanced temperance workers in all the towns. Much indeed had been already accomplished, but it became increasingly evident that the evil was "only *stayed*" and not suppressed. Men who had acquired an appetite for drink had not been reached. Societies refrained from urging "such persons as had made great proficiency in the Bacchanalian school to join our association, believing that their *sense of moral obligation* is impaired in proportion to their advancement ; consequently will break over all restraint, and injure the cause we would promote." Stop making new drunkards and intemperance will gradually die out—was the favorite theory of the first reformers. Take care of the children, dissuade men from forming the habit of drinking, and as the old drunkards die off we shall have temperance communities. But somehow the process of extermination was less rapid than had been expected, and men who indulged in the permitted wine, beer and cider, sometimes acquired a taste for stronger liquors. After some twelve or fifteen years of earnest effort temperance workers were fain to fall back from their theory, and admit that more stringent methods were needed. Total abstinence from all alcoholic liquor, and the suppression of licensed liquor-selling, was now the rallying cry of the vanguard. At the annual meeting in Canterbury, August, 1836, Andrew T. Judson was chosen president ; Isaac Backus, secretary and treasurer. The president, with Reverends King and Whiton, were appointed delegates to the Temperance convention at Hartford. After hearing their report at the November meeting, the propriety of circulating a pledge of abstinence from all intoxicating drinks was largely discussed, but public sentiment was yet unequal to it. A committee of one in each school district was, however, appointed to obtain signatures to the Constitution, giving liberty to subscribers " to signify their resolution to abstain from the use of all intoxicating drinks."

62

III.

MISS CRANDALL'S SCHOOLS—WHITE AND COLORED.   CANTER-
BURY IN DANGER.   EXCITEMENT.   EXPULSION.

THE advent of the Temperance Reform was cotemporary with
another great popular agitation in which Windham County
took a very different position, and the town most active and prominent
in temperance effort especially signalized itself by its most bitter and
determined opposition to the Anti-slavery movement.   Canterbury was
a very influential town at this period, and was particularly noted for
the public spirit and high character of its leading men, and its cultivated and agreeable society.   Andrew T. Judson, State attorney and
successful lawyer, Dr. Harris, the skillful surgeon, Esquire Frost, the
devoted champion of temperance, Rufus Adams, with his fund of dry
humor, George S. White, with his strong character and multifarious
knowledge, Luther Paine, John Francis, Thomas and Stephen Coit,
Samuel L. Hough, all solid men interested in public affairs—had their
homes at or near Canterbury Green, and gave tone and prominence
to the town.   Few country towns could boast such social attractions.
Dr. Harris was one of the most genial and hospitable of men, and his
new model house with its rare appendage of a conservatory and choice
flower-garden, was the wonder of all the County.   Mrs. Harris had inherited the social characteristics of her distinguished father, General
Moses Cleveland, and received their unnumbered guests with all his
ease and heartiness.   A handsome new house had been also built by
Mr. Judson, in which much company was entertained, although it was
said that Mrs. Judson as a Windham lady assumed superiority over her
neighbors.   Her husband, who liked to rally her upon this weakness,
once called her down to the parlor to receive a Windham visitor, and
most blandly presented to her an intrusive *frog*, which had hopped
into the hall.   His own tact and courtesy made ample amends for
his wife's reputed deficiencies.   Pleasant familiar intercourse was
maintained among the village residents.   All united with uncommon
unanimity in plans for village improvement and public benefit, and
it was in carrying out one of these projects that they struck
upon the rock which foundered them.   The school question was
one in which Canterbury felt great interest.   Her young people
sought education at home or abroad, and an unusual number of young
girls then growing up in the village families awakened parental solicitude.   The proposition of Miss Prudence Crandall to open a young
ladies' boarding-school at Canterbury Green was received with much
favor.   A large house left vacant by the death of Esquire Paine was

secured for her, and in the autumn of 1831 the school was opened under the most favorable auspices. A goodly number of young ladies from the best families in town were enrolled as pupils. Messrs. Judson, Harris, Frost, Adams, Hough, Packer, Kinne, and Rev. Dennis Platt, were constituted a board of visitors, and bore most flattering testimony to the character of the school and the ability of its teacher. The cordiality and friendliness of her reception were gratefully acknowledged by Miss Crandall, her relations with pupils and patrons was most agreeable and harmonious, and it seemed likely that this much-needed institution would become permanently established. Circulars were sent out commending it to public patronage, scholars came from neighboring towns and even from distant cities, and everything was going on pleasantly and prosperously when—a crash came. Without premonition or warning, before the patrons of the school had dreamed of any real danger, a new element had been introduced, a change of base effected, and their daughters dismissed from school to make way for *negroes!* Was it strange that the community should flame out in indignation? The causes that led to this revolution are thus detailed by Miss Crandall:—

" The reason for changing my school of white pupils for a school for colored pupils is as follows: I had a nice colored girl, now Mrs. Charles Harris, as help in my family; and her intended husband regularly received *The Liberator.* The girl took the paper from the office and loaned it to me. In that the condition of the colored people both slaves and free was truthfully portrayed, the double-dealing and manifest deception of the Colonization Society were faithfully exposed, and the question of Immediate Emancipation of the millions of slaves in the United States boldly advocated. Having been taught from early childhood the sin of Slavery, my sympathies were greatly aroused. Sarah Harris, a respectable young woman and a member of the church (now Mrs. Fairweather, and sister to the before-named intended husband), called often to see her friend Marcia, my family assistant. In some of her calls I ascertained that she wished to attend my school and board at her own father's house at some little distance from the village. I allowed her to enter as one of my pupils. By this act I gave great offence. The wife of an Episcopal clergyman who lived in the village told me that if I continued that colored girl in my school it could not be sustained. I replied to her, *That it might sink, then, for I should not turn her out!* I very soon found that some of my school would leave not to return if the colored girl was retained. Under these circumstances I made up my mind that if it were possible I would teach colored girls exclusively. I made the attempt, and the result is before the public."*

Before acting upon this decision, Miss Crandall consulted with leading Abolitionists in Boston and New York, who gladly pledged their coöperation and assistance. Had she also consulted her generous friends and patrons in Canterbury, or even given them notice of her intentions, they would have had less ground of complaint, but their indignation when the proposed change in the complexion of the school was suddenly announced to them was greatly hightened by what they

* Private Letter, May 15, 1869.

deemed an inexcusable breach of good faith in one they had so encouraged and befriended. As soon as the young ladies took to their
several homes the news of their dismissal to make room "for young
ladies and little misses of color," Messrs. Rufus Adams, Frost, Fenner
and Harris visited Miss Crandall and endeavored to persuade her "to
give up her project so far as Canterbury was concerned," but found
all argument and persuasion useless. Having made up her mind to
this step from a clear conviction of her duty to the colored race,
nothing could change her. The people of Canterbury saw to their
supreme horror and consternation that this popular school in which
they had taken so much pride was to be superseded by something so
anomalous and phenomenal that it could hardly be comprehended. A
public meeting of citizens was at once called and the previous visitors
delegated to convey their sentiments and wishes to Miss Crandall.
They found her as before, firm as a rock. Esquire Frost, as spokesman
of the committee, "in a most kind and affecting manner" labored to
convince her of the impropriety and injustice of the proposed measure,
and delicately hinted at the danger that might ensue from "these lev-
eling principles and intermarriage between the whites and blacks."
"Moses had a black wife," bluntly replied the lady, opening to the
prophetic eye dark visions of forthcoming amalgamation and disorder.
Reports of these unsatisfactory interviews increased the pervading excitement to actual frenzy. The people of the town with scarce an
exception were united in horrified antipathy to the colored school and
a determination to prevent its opening. South of Dixie's line, Judge
Lynch would probably soon have settled the matter, but this Connecticut town knew no better way to accomplish its purpose than by the
familiar agency of a town-meeting hastily summoned, "to devise and
adopt such measures as would effectually avert the nuisance, or speedily
abate it if it should be brought into the village." This meeting was
held March 9, 1833. It was a very memorable occasion. Reports of
the proceedings in Canterbury, now noised far and wide, brought many
from other towns to the scene of action. Mr. Samuel J. May, who
drove over with Mr. Benson from Brooklyn to aid and support Miss
Crandall, found the village in furious excitement, and was warned of
personal danger, but the lady who had excited all this commotion was
still "resolved and tranquil." By the advice of Mr. May and Arnold
Buffum—agent of the Anti-slavery Society who had also come to the
rescue—Miss Crandall consented to remove her school to some less
public part of the town if her opponents would take her house and
cease to molest her. Armed with this proposal and power to negotiate
a compromise, Messrs. May and Buffum repaired to the meeting-house
at the hour appointed, and with difficulty made their way through the

crowded aisle to a seat near the moderator. A strange spectacle greeted them—the great house filled to its utmost capacity with hundreds of anxious, angry citizens intent to devise some scheme of escape from the crushing calamity of "a school of nigger girls." The "prodigious descent of devils" recorded by Cotton Mather could not have inspired more preternatural dread and horror. After the reading of the warning by the moderator, Judge Adams offered the following resolutions :—

"WHEREAS, it hath been publicly announced that a school is to be opened in this town, on the first Monday of April next, using the language of the advertisement, 'for young ladies and little misses of color,' or in other words for the people of color, the obvious tendency of which would be to collect within the town of Canterbury large numbers of persons from other States whose characters and habits might be various and unknown to us, thereby rendering insecure the persons, property and reputations of our citizens. Under such circumstances our silence might be construed into an approbation of the project;

Thereupon, Resolved, That the locality of a school for the people of color at any place within the limits of this town, for the admission of persons of foreign jurisdiction, meets with our unqualified disapprobation, and it is to be understood, that the inhabitants of Canterbury protest against it in the most earnest manner.

Resolved, That a committee be now appointed, to be composed of the Civil Authority and Selectmen, who shall make known to the person contemplating the establishment of said school, the sentiments and objections entertained by this meeting in reference to said school—pointing out to her the injurious effects and incalculable evils resulting from such an establishment within this town, and persuade her to abandon the project."

Messrs. Adams and Judson supported these resolutions with great earnestness and vehemence, filling their hearers "with the apprehension that a dire calamity was impending over them; that Miss Crandall was the author or instrument of it; that there were powerful conspirators engaged with her in the plot; and that the people of Canterbury should be roused by every consideration of self-preservation as well as self-respect to prevent the accomplishment of the design." Others with much warmth urged the resolutions; but Mr. George S. White, who alone attempted to oppose them, was frequently interrupted by calls to order, and his proposal to assist in the purchase of Miss Crandall's house received no attention. Messrs. May and Buffum then stepped forward with Miss Crandall's letter, authorizing them to speak and act in her behalf, whereupon Mr. Judson broke forth with greater violence than before, accusing them of insulting the town by this interference, while other excited citizens gathered around them, and with "fists doubled in their faces" poured out tirades of wrath against Miss Crandall and her accomplices, threatening the utmost penalty of the law if they dared to open their lips, if not a more immediate vengeance. Thus effectually silenced the gentlemen sat down, and the resolutions were presented and passed by unanimous vote, but the instant of adjournment Mr. May sprang upon his seat and besought the audience to listen to a plain statement of the circumstances that had led Miss Crandall to take this step, and the true character of the proposed school. Mr. Buffum followed with a few impressive words upon the great question at issue and might have gained a hearing but the more violent leaders drove the people from the meeting-house with cries of "out," "out," and the society committee ordered the speakers to leave and closed the doors against them.

Five days after this meeting a formidable array of town officers presented the Resolutions "in a formal and becoming manner," and earnestly besought Miss Crandall to relinquish her scheme, "responsible individuals offering and urging upon her the sum she had paid for the house upon condition that she would abandon the proposed school." This she positively declined though willing to remove to a less public location, and went on her way making preparation for her pupils, "with a firmness of design and a decision of action worthy the holiest cause." On the appointed day the school actually began. Some ten or twelve quiet, harmless little colored girls or young ladies, from the very best colored families in the Northern cities, had found their way to Canterbury, and were receiving instruction from Miss Crandall. If the Canterbury people had quietly accepted the situation and left them in peace the difficulty would soon have ended. Even if the children had remained they would have given them little annoyance. Twenty *Indian* lads were received into Plainfield Academy a few years later, and few outside the village ever heard of them. But such submission at that date was entirely out of the question. The sudden outburst of the Abolition movement and the unscrupulous audacity of its leaders had frightened people out of their senses. The Crandall school was an outgrowth of Abolitionism. At a later town meeting it was placed on record, " That the *establishment* or *rendezvous* falsely denominated a school was designed by its projectors as the *theatre*, as the place to promulgate their disgusting doctrines of amalgamation, and their pernicious sentiments of subverting the Union. Their pupils were to have been congregated here from *all quarters* under the false pretence of *educating them*, but really to " SCATTER FIRE-BRANDS, *arrows and death* among brethren of our own blood." With such suspicions and apprehensions it is not surprising that the people of Canterbury should use their utmost endeavors to suppress and crush out this obnoxious institution, especially, when to terror of Abolition aim and effort was added a sense of personal injury and a very natural desire "to have their own way." "Every argumentative effort" having failed them, they were forced to resort to other measures. The oft-read lesson in the spelling-book came home with peculiar emphasis—"When neither words nor grass would answer they were forced to try what virtue there was in *stones*." If these stones could have been thrown by lawful authority they would have much preferred it, but the legal State armory was wholly inadequate to the occasion, legislation in Connecticut having hitherto always aimed to *build up schools* and *protect women and children*. The old pauper and vagrant law was however pressed into service and a warrant served upon Ann Eliza Hammond of Providence, warning her out of town unless her maintenance was guaranteed, "to be whipped on the naked body not exceeding ten stripes" in default of satisfaction or departure. Meanwhile Andrew T. Judson, William Lester, Chester Lyon, Rufus Adams, Solomon Paine, Andrew Harris, Ashael Bacon, George S. White, Daniel Packer and Isaac Backus, were appointed agents by the town to draw up and circulate a petition to be laid before the General Assembly, "deprecating the evil consequences of bringing from other States and other towns people of color for any purpose, and more especially for the purpose of disseminating the principles and doctrines opposed to the benevolent colonizing system," and praying it to enact laws to prevent this evil. Inhabitants of other towns were also requested to prefer "petitions for the same laudable object." While waiting for legal power to break up the school, Canterbury did its best to make scholars and teacher uncomfortable. Non-intercourse and Embargo Acts were put in successful operation. Dealers in all sorts of wares and produce agreed to sell nothing to Miss Crandall, the stage-driver declined to carry her pupils, and neighbors refused a pail of fresh water, even though they knew that their own sons had filled her well with stable refuse. Boys and rowdies were allowed unchecked if not openly encouraged to exercise their utmost ingenuity in mischievous annoyance, throwing real stones and rotten eggs at the windows and following the school with hoots and horns if it ventured to appear in the street. Not only was Miss Crandall herself assailed with threats of coming vengeance and ejection, but her father in the south part of the town was insulted and threatened. "When lawyers, courts and jurors are leagued against you," said one to him, "it will be easy to raise a MOB and tear down your house." Poor Mr. Crandall, the meekest of non-resistant Quakers, was greatly terrified by these warlike demonstrations and besought his daughter "to give up her school, sell her property and relieve Canterbury from their imagined destruction," but that high-spirited woman very kindly but positively declined to follow his suggestions. The calmness and fortitude with which she met this furious onslaught astonished her friends and exasperated her enemies. Her chief ally and supporter, Mr. May, always found her firm and tranquil, prepared for any emergency. Her father and an old Quaker brought them fresh water. Packerville dealers furnished household supplies, and a colored driver from Norwich took the school-girls back and forth, and accommodated Abolition visitors.

As soon as possible Canterbury's petition was brought before the Legislature. It was a difficult and delicate matter to legislate but Connecticut was equal to it. Public opinion strongly favored the petitioners. That peculiar rabies which had transformed the genial, jovial gentlemen of Canterbury into malicious persecutors was not confined to that town. "We should not want a nigger school on *our* common," was the universal sentiment and expression of every town in Windham County. Many towns in all parts of the State had seconded Canterbury's request and would have opposed the establishment of such a school with equal bitterness. Slavery was the unsolved problem in American destiny. The Abolitionist was the fuse thrown among combustibles and the great mass of the people shrank with dread from the inevitable explosion. The Legislators of Connecticut were fully persuaded of the necessity of closing this pernicious school, but did not see exactly how to accomplish it. Ninety years before when asked by the standing clergy and churches to devise some means for keeping out irregular preachers and itinerants, their predecessors had enacted that a minister from out of the State preaching without the invitation of a stated minister or society should be sent like a vagrant by warrant out of the bounds of the Colony, but the civilization of the nineteenth century eschewed this process as too summary and preferred to levy a tribute from the offender's pocket. After suitable discussion and deliberation it was enacted, "That no person should set up a school or educational institution for the instruction of colored persons who were not inhabitants of the State, nor instruct in such a school nor harbor or board any colored person instructed in such a school, without the consent in writing first obtained of a majority of the civil authority and selectmen in the town in which such school is situated under penalty of a fine of a hundred dollars for the first offence ; two hundred for the second, and so double for every subsequent offence of which such person should be convicted." In vain did poor Mr. Crandall humbly entreat the Assembly, to remember these self-evident truths, that all mankind are created free and equal, and implore them "not to grant the prayer of any petition, nor pass any act that will curtail or destroy any of the rights of the free people of this State or other States whether they are white or black." "Mr. Crandall," said Mr. Judson afterwards, "when you sent your printed paper to the

General Assembly, you did not injure us; it helped very much in getting the bill through. When they received it every man clinched his fist, and the chairman of the committee sat down and doubled the penalty. Members of the Legislature said to me—'If this law does not answer your purpose, let us know, and next year we will make you one that will.'"

The receipt of the legislative devise for the relief of Canterbury was welcomed in that town by the ringing of bells, firing of cannon, and every demonstration of popular delight and triumph. A more orderly and systematic opposition was now enforced against the school. The new dispensation was thus promulgated in Mr. Crandall's household by two of the leading citizens :—

"Mr. Crandall, if you go to your daughter's you are to be fined $100, for the first offence; $200 for the second, and double it every time; Mrs. Crandall, if you go there, you will be fined and your daughter Almira will be fined, and Mr. May and those gentlemen from Providence (Messrs. George and Henry Benson), if they come there will be fined at the same rate. And your daughter, the one that established the school for colored females, will be taken up the same way as for stealing a horse, or for burglary. Her property will not be taken but she will be put in jail, not having the liberty of the yard. There is no mercy to be shown about it!"

But while this law encouraged Miss Crandall's enemies it increased the number and strengthened the determination of her friends and supporters. Among many letters of approval and sympathy addressed to Mr. May came one from Arthur Tappan, expressing his entire approbation of the course that had been pursued, encouraging Miss Crandall to maintain her position, and offering to bear all the forthcoming legal expenses. These friendly offers were followed by personal intercourse, giving great aid and comfort. Finding that the little band with all its heroism was almost overborne by the storm of abuse and invective, and especially by misrepresentations which they were not allowed to rectify, Mr. Tappan made immediate arrangements for the publication of a newspaper in Brooklyn, "to the advocacy of all human rights in general, and to the defence of the Canterbury school and its heroic teacher in particular." Mr. Charles C. Burleigh of Plainfield was secured as its editor, and under his able leadership the fiery little *Unionist* soon took the field and struck most telling blows for Miss Crandall and Abolitionism. Thus encouraged and supported Miss Crandall went calmly on with her school, unterrified by the threats and denunciations of her adversaries. Previous to this she had skillfully foiled their first legal approaches. On June 27, she had been summoned before Justice Adams on charge of violating a statute law of the State of Connecticut. Her counsel gave in a demurrer to the complaint, admitting the facts true, and submitted to the finding of the Court without argument. The sum

63

498 HISTORY OF WINDHAM COUNTY.

needful to be pledged as surety for her appearance before the County Court for trial was named by the Court, but to the astonishment of her accusers no one appeared to give bonds for her, and they were forced to the disagreeable necessity of taking her to Brooklyn jail, to the very room occupied by Watkins the night preceding his execution. The result of this ingenious stroke of policy was far more favorable than had been anticipated by its projectors. Miss Crandall immured in a murderer's cell for the crime of teaching colored girls made a most vivid and startling impression upon the popular mind. Many who had before blamed her for disturbing the peace of Canterbury, were shocked at this alleged outrage. An intrusive, troublesome woman was thus transformed into a martyr. It was in vain that her accusers protested that the imprisonment was entirely voluntary and nominal, the cell a good room furnished with every comfort, that a female friend passed the night with her and both were released the following day. The story of her unjust imprisonment was noised in every direction, and unquestionably had great influence in awakening sympathy in her behalf and strengthening anti-slavery sentiment.

The anger and mortification of the Canterbury leaders at having their weapons thus turned against them made them more bitter in opposition, and more zealous in preparation for the approaching legal contests. The first trial was held before the County Court, August 22. Jonathan A. Welch conducted the prosecution, aided by Andrew T. Judson and Ichabod Bulkley. Calvin Goddard, W. W. Ellsworth and Henry Strong appeared for the defence, retained by Mr. May at the expense of Mr. Arthur Tappan. The constitutionality of the law under which Miss Crandall was arraigned was the point at issue. It was claimed by the defence that this newly enacted law conflicted with that article of the Federal Constitution, which allowed to citizens of each State all the privileges and immunities of citizens in the several States. The prosecution denied that blacks were or could be citizens of any State. Both positions were defended with much ability and adroitness. In his charge to the jury Judge Eaton gave as his opinion, " that the law is constitutional and obligatory on the people of this State," but the jurors were unable to agree. In October, the case was tried before the Superior Court of Windham County upon the same grounds and with the same counsel. In an able and elaborate charge, Judge Daggett maintained the constitutionality of the law, and declared that to his mind " it would be a perversion of terms, and the well known rule of construction to say that slaves, free blacks or Indians, were *citizens* within the meaning of that term as used in the Constitution." His overpowering influence gained the verdict and judgment was pronounced against the defendant. Her counsel then appealed to the Court of Errors, before which tribunal a final trial was held July 22, 1834, when the arguments on both sides were reiterated with all possible ingenuity and eloquence. The Court reversed the decision of the Supreme Court upon the ground of "insufficiency of the information," which omitted to allege that the school was set up without the requisite license. The legal question as to the constitutionality of the law was thus left undecided.

During this period affairs in Canterbury had remained in the same vexed and unhappy condition, the opponents of the school waxing more impatient and violent, and teacher and scholars bearing indignity and annoyance with unabated spirit and fortitude. So far as can be ascertained the school was well-sustained and prosperous. The pupils were docile, affectionate and studious, eager to improve their hardly-won advantages. William H. Burleigh and his sister assisted for a time as teachers, and it is their testimony as well as Miss Crandall's that these colored girls "made as good if not better progress than the same number of whites taken from the same position of life." Miss Crandall's sister Almira, was constantly with her and assisted in teaching, a very lovely, active and efficient young woman, "possessing a great heart, loving everybody and being loved by all." Storms might rage without the walls but all was peace and harmony within. They had like other scholars their "gala-days" and exhibition exercises. On one such occasion, called a Mental Feast, four of the youngest pupils dressed in white sang with great sweetness this story of their trials, composed by their teacher :—

> " Four little children here you see,
>   In modest dress appear;
> Come, listen to our song so sweet,
>   And our complaints you'll hear.
>
> 'Tis here we come to learn to read,
>   And write and cipher too;
> But some in this enlightened land
>   Declare 'twill never do.
>
> The morals of this favored town,
>   Will be corrupted soon,
> Therefore they strive with all their might,
>   To drive us to our homes.
>
> Sometimes when we have walked the streets
>   Saluted we have been,
> By guns, and drums, and cow-bells too,
>   And horns of polished tin.
>
> With warnings, threats and words severe
>   They visit us at times,
> And gladly would they send us off
>   To Afric's burning climes.

Our teacher too they put in jail,
   Fast held by bars and locks!
Did e'er such persecution reign
   Since Paul was in the stocks?

But we forgive, forgive the men,
   That persecute us so.
May God in mercy save their souls
   From everlasting wo!"

As time went on they gained. some outside sympathy. Esquire Frost and others who embraced anti-slavery principles, ceased to molest if they did not openly encourage. Debarred by public sentiment and the voice of the trustees from the Congregational house of worship, they found admission and friendly welcome among the Friends at Black Hill, and the Baptists at Packerville. Religious services in their own house were exposed to unseemly interruption, as when the Rev. Mr. Potter of Pawtucket was preaching, and a clamorous rabble assailed the house with volleys of rotten eggs and other missiles.

But however harmless and even praiseworthy the Canterbury school may have appeared to a dispassionate spectator, to the great majority of the people of the town it was the embodiment of all evil and blackness. When after all their efforts and months of wearisome delay the suit at law so eagerly prosecuted had come to naught, and all prospect of legal relief was indefinitely postponed, they felt that they could endure it no longer. Legally, if we can; forcibly, if we must—was the prevailing sentiment. One morning early in September, Miss Crandall's house was found to be on fire but the flames were more easily extinguished than the resultant controversy which like the constitutionality of the Black Law was never definitively decided. Miss Crandall and her friends insisted that from the position of the fire when first discovered it could not have been kindled from within, and her opponents were equally positive in maintaining that it could not have been done outside. A very respectable colored man from Norwich, who had been mending a clock in the room in which the fire broke out, was made the victim of popular vengeance. To his utter astonishment he was seized by a writ and brought before Judge Adams, and though the evidence against him was utterly trifling was committed for trial, the enemies of Miss Crandall insinuating that she had instigated this act as a pretext for abandoning the school which had become burdensome to her.

But while there were some who professed to believe that Miss Crandall had set fire to her house no one ever accused her of breaking in her own windows. This occurred September 9, 1834. It was late in the evening, the family was preparing for bed when a number of men armed with heavy iron bars stole noiselessly around the house and at a given signal simultaneously raised the bars, and with all the force they could muster beat and dashed in the windows. The suddenness and violence of the assault, and the exposure to which they were subjected, completely unnerved this household of defenceless women, and even Miss Crandall quailed at this manifestation of deadly hatred and unscrupulous ruffianism. After a night of sleepless agitation, Mr. May was summoned "to the scene of destruction and the terror-stricken family." A consultation was held. It was evident that Miss Crandall's enemies were bent upon breaking up the school. In the absence of any security against further assault it seemed useless and fool-hardy to prolong the unequal contest. Mr. May announced the decision to the trembling pupils, and as soon as possible they dispersed to their several homes. A short time before Miss Crandall had married Mr. Calvin Philleo, and as soon as she could dispose of her property and make needful arrangements, she too left Windham County forever. "Thus ended," says Mr. May, "the generous, disinterested, philanthropic Christian enterprise of Prudence Crandall."

Canterbury's exultation over its downfall was somewhat marred by the method of accomplishment. With the object probably of justifying her course in the eyes of coming generations, an elaborate "Preamble and Resolutions" was prepared the following year, adopted by vote of the town and inscribed within its records. After expressing their views as to the dangerous nature and tendency of Abolitionism, and the character of the institution located within their town "by the combined efforts and energies of Buffum, Tappan, Garrison and May," . . . .

"*Resolved*, That the Government of the United States, the Nation with all its institutions, of right belong to the white men who now possess them, they were purchased by the valor and blood of their Fathers, and must never be surrendered to any other nation or race of men.

Resolved, That our appeal to the Legislature of our own State in a case of such peculiar mischief was not only due to ourselves but to the obligations devolving upon us under the Constitution. To have been silent would have been participating in the wrongs intended. The manner that protection was afforded by the Legislature of the State is a sure guaranty that in future should the imposing attempt be repeated here, or elsewhere within our State, that attempt would be met with protection to our fellow-citizens as it has been afforded us. In the open defiance of the laws of the State, and in the abusive manner we have been assailed because we sought that protection, we see displayed the *temper* and *motive* which hitherto have characterized this organized foe of our common country.

Resolved, That the effects produced by such efforts upon the peace of the Union are exactly those which every reflecting mind must have anticipated when it beheld the spirit of *oppression* and IMPOSITION with which this combined force erected their standard of rebellion upon our soil; and when their counsel in a Court of Justice in their behalf declared as a matter of right that they would fix their establishment upon Canterbury in defiance of law, we saw more than ever the necessity of the appeal we had made, and now we rejoice that the appeal was not in vain."

Looking back upon this memorable episode after nearly half a century, we also can rejoice that in this as in numberless other instances " the wrath of man" so signally subserved the purposes of God and the highest interests of humanity. Miss Crandall did not succeed in teaching many colored girls but she *educated* the people of Windham County. Not only did every act of violence awaken corresponding sympathy but in the resultant agitation and discussion mind and conscience were enlightened. The law by which blacks were debarred from educational privileges in Connecticut, was a most powerful motor in effecting their final emancipation. The statement enforced and reiterated with so much clearness and decision that by the constitution of the United States blacks never could be citizens, awoke a spirit of inquiry and resistance that was never satisfied until an amended Constitution gave them the rights and privileges of citizenship. As the slavery question came into politics it was found that many in Windham County were opposed to its further extension. A large majority of her citizens supported the Free Soil and Republican parties. Her vote gave to Connecticut many a Republican victory, and her voters were the first in the State to repudiate Judge Daggett's decision, and give to its colored inhabitants the rights and privileges of freemen. Connecticut's final verdict upon the constitutionality of the Black Law was shown by its quiet disappearance in a revision of her Statutes.

IV.

CANTERBURY. PLAINFIELD. VOLUNTOWN. STERLING.

THE business interests of Canterbury were not unaffected by these agitations. Previous to the Crandall outbreak they had received much attention from public-spirited citizens. Projected business enterprises were largely discussed. In 1825, the representatives were instructed to use their influence in favor of a petition for liberty to erect dams across the Quinebaug for manufacturing purposes. In the following year the town voted:—

" That we highly approve of the contemplated *canal** on the Quinebaug River, connecting our manufacturing and agricultural interests, opening a ready market for our surplus productions, and calling for our energies and enterprise."

To be ready perhaps to take advantage of the expected opening,

---

* Calvin Goddard, Esq., was president, Esquire John McClellan, vice-president, Adams White, Jun., secretary and treasurer of the "Association for constructing a canal from Norwich to Massachusetts," which was much

Capt. David Butts, Solomon Payne, Elisha Chaffee, Isaac Backus and
Rufus Adams, were appointed a committee to inquire what measures
can be taken to promote domestic manufacturing and agriculture.
Their report, April 6, 1829, reveal a touch of *Morus Multicaulis* epidemic. It strongly recommended the cultivation of the mulberry tree,
as well adapted to the soil and not impoverishing it; labor required in
the production of silk performed by hands not suitable for ordinary
farm work; also the reclaiming of hedges and sterile pastures—the
shade of the maple tree being supposed to impart both sweetness and
nutriment to the grass beneath—also, the manufacture of wagons,
plows, scythes, hoes, rakes, pitchforks, chairs and cabinet work, buttons, wire-sieves, bricks, hats, augers, combs, corn-brooms, cards, saddles, harnesses, spools and bobbins. Aiding the spirit of enterprise,
and encouraging honest industry by example as well as precept, the
committee entertained the confident hope that they should see the
town rising into a more prosperous condition, honorable to themselves
and profitable to their children. Confused perhaps by the multiplicity
of objects presented, the town contented itself with offering a reward
of fifteen dollars "to the first person who shall produce upon any
single farm in Canterbury in one year the greatest quantity of silk not
less than fifteen pounds from mulberry trees, raised in this town from
the seeds." Several manufactories were already in successful opera-

---

favored by the river towns. Various obstacles delayed the work till a more
efficient mode of communication was suggested. *The Windham County Advertiser*, January 25, 1832, after publishing a list of projected railroads in
other States, thus summons Connecticut to action:—

"Are the citizens of Connecticut to sit idle while these stupendous
operations are going forward and do nothing? Massachusetts may extend
her road to our line on the north, and Rhode Island, to our line on the east,
and here they must stop. Passengers must leave their flying machinery, and
pass through the *land of steady habits*, at the rate of two miles an hour. Is
there no enterprise here? Is this sleep to be perpetual? Remember fellow-
citizens, that unless Connecticut *does something* evincing a regard for the
good of our population, that population will take up their march, and will go
onward until more congenial spirits are found. The people of New England
have a work to perform, or lose their glory. Where can this work be commenced with more propriety than down the valley of the Quinebaug? Suppose a Rail Road were constructed from New-London to Worcester, what an
intercourse would be opened between Boston and New-York? The expense
will be but little, compared with that of a canal, and the means are adequate,
and the object is worthy of deep consideration. We now have a Canal
Charter, why not convert this Canal into a Rail Road? *Norwich* has an
interest which should call out her citizens, and every other town on the route
has an interest which ought to secure their operation. During the winter a
meeting will be held at some convenient place, to take up this subject in
earnest."

In the following May the Boston, Norwich and New London Railroad
Company was incorporated, and the Act of 1827, incorporating the Quinebaug
Canal Company repealed.

tion. Flourishing foundry works were carried on in the north part of Westminster Parish by Isaac Backus and Nathan Allen, which were facilitated by the Brooklyn and Windham turnpike. Samuel Hough and D. F. Eaton engaged successfully in axe-making; George Justin fabricated scythes and axes in his blacksmith's shop in South Canterbury; Perez Austin made and repaired wagons and carriages; Phinehas Carter continued his cooper's work; Stillman G. Adams carried on the hat-manufacture in place of Deacon Simms now removed to New York State. Job Rood, the ingenius coffin-maker, exercised his inventive powers upon window-blinds. Sufficient domestic cloth was yet made to keep Kingsley's and Foster's fulling-machines and clothier's works in active operation. Cotton manufacturing was still carried on in Fenner's factory, and Canterbury shared with Plainfield the rising promise of Packerville. Local improvements received due attention. A house and farm to furnish a home for the poor was purchased in 1829, and a committee chosen to direct improvements in the burial-ground. Canterbury Probate Court was constituted in 1835, Chester Lyon, judge.

Innovations and projects were little favored by residents of the more remote districts, who long preserved the customs of preceding generations. Farmers who came to church with fine horses and carriages and were rated as men of large substance, still lived in primitive fashion, wearing home-made clothing and eschewing household luxuries. The "meeting-suit" was expected to serve for many years, if not a lifetime. One quaint resident was married *three times* in the same blue, brass-buttoned coat, and after sixty years' service he was finally buried in it. His economy was matched perhaps by that of the good woman who made a single nutmeg last a lifetime, keeping it done up in velvet which she *shook* over her cake and pudding. Among Canterbury eccentricities was Capt. John Clark, who lived nearly 101 years. He retained to the last his autocratic authority, governing his elderly daughters as if they were children.*

---

* This venerable person, who is said to have assisted in turning out the tea at Boston Harbor, preceded by nine years another distinguished Revolutionary veteran who had done good service at Bunker Hill. A tablet in Cypress Avenue, Mount Auburn Cemetery, commemorates the virtues and public services of Captain Josiah Cleveland, born at Canterbury, Dec. 3, 1753, "He served his country faithfully through the whole war of the Revolution. He fought her battles at Bunker Hill, Harlaem Heights, White Plains, Trenton, Princeton, Monmouth and Yorktown. He sustained an unblemished reputation, and lived in the practice of every christian virtue. He loved, feared, and served God. In the ninetieth year of his age he journeyed nearly five hundred miles from his home (Owego, N. Y.) to be present at the celebration of the completion of the monument on Bunker Hill. He lived to witness that remarkable spectacle. He was satisfied. He laid down quietly and yielded up his breath near the scene of his first conflict with the enemies of his country." He died at Charlestown, Mass., June 30, 1843.

Mr. Meech was succeeded in 1822, by Rev. Thomas J. Murdock—"a model of a man, a scholar, a Christian and a minister,"—who exerted a most salutary influence in the community. Thomas Coit, Luther Paine, Fitch Adams, John M. Francis, and other influential men, now united with the church. Acute disease terminated this valuable life and ministry in 1826, to the great grief of church and society. A marble slab in the North Burying Ground still testifies their "respect for his memory and exalted virtues." His name was also preserved in the fine library of books left for public use. Rev. James R. Wheelock was installed in 1827, but only remained in charge two years. Rev. Dennis Platt, somewhat noted as a revival worker, served a somewhat longer period, and received many into the church. The pastorate of Rev. C. J. Warren was equally brief. Episcopal service was frequently performed by Rev. George S. White after his removal to Canterbury, and in 1827, "St. Thomas Parish" gained a name but scarce "a local habitation." Its existence was however recognized for several years. Westminster Society was called to part in 1824 with its beloved pastor, Rev. Erastus Larned, in the fiftieth year of his age and twentieth of his ministry. The succeeding pastorate of Rev. Israel Rose was marred by exceptional unpleasantness, but with the advent of the Rev. Asa King, the former harmony returned. His faithful labors were blessed as in previous fields, by the upbuilding of the church and the strengthening of good influences. His efforts in behalf of temperance were ably seconded by leading men in his society, especially Isaac Backus, Esq., the enterprising manager of the Foundry, now one of the leading men of the town, and by Dr. Isaac Clark, a man of fine education and most excellent spirit, who had succeeded to the medical practice of Dr. Johnson. Westminster's first post-office was opened by Peter Spicer in 1836. The old Separate church had now breathed its last and its meeting-house was falling to pieces. Methodists maintained worship in the centre of the town.

A new religious interest had developed in the southeast corner of the town in connection with the building up of Packerville. The Andrus Factory privilege passed in 1818 into the hands of Daniel Packer and Daniel Lester of Preston, and after a few years manufacturing operations were resumed under the management of Mr. Packer. Buildings were repaired and enlarged, new machinery introduced, a village started into life. As usual in such rapid up-growths bad elements at first predominated. Sundays were given over to drinking, horse-racing and kindred amusements. Captain Packer was greatly impressed by the prevailing irreligion and vice, and resolved "that he would use the utmost of his exertions and influence, not only to have the word of the Lord regularly dispensed but a house of worship

64

erected." Applying to the Baptist Home Missionary Society, he secured the services of a recent graduate from Hamilton Seminary, Levi Kneeland. A nephew of the able editor of *The Boston Investigator*, he was as earnest in promulgating the Gospel as his kinsman in opposing it. "In homes and school-houses, in barns and groves," he proclaimed the message of salvation with great power and effect. A congregation gathered quickly around him, and October 8, 1828, the Packerville Baptist church was organized and Mr. Kneeland ordained to the ministry. Beginning with twenty-one brothers and sisters, its membership was rapidly increased. Scarce a Sabbath passed without a baptismal service, and in eight months a hundred and one had been received into the church. A house of worship was soon prepared for it (mainly by the efforts and means of Captain Packer) whose doors were opened wide for all Christian and philanthropic enterprise. Most interesting temperance meetings were held in this house in 1829, Messrs. Kneeland and Packer engaging with great earnestness in this much needed reform. Here Miss Crandall was received with her troop of colored girls when other church edifices were closed against them. The wholesome influence of this church was felt throughout the surrounding country. Mr. Kneeland extended his labors into Voluntown, Scotland, Preston, and aged men would journey many miles on Sunday to join in worship with this Baptist church and its earnest pastor. Laboring with such intensity his life work was soon accomplished. A painful illness closed his life and ministry, August, 1834. The immense crowd gathered at the funeral witnessed to the wide and deep impression made by this faithful Christian laborer.

> " Some still survive who yet remember well,
> What earnest words he spoke, how sweet his life,
> How prayerful was the spirit that he bore,
> What love for souls, what zeal for Christ he felt.
> Who of all those that ever heard his words
> Can e'er forget the holy zeal he showed,
> The blessed unction that he ever bore,
> God's witness evident on face and mood,*
> Heaven's high approval of his honest work."

Captain Daniel Packer, the founder of the village, Kneeland's worthy coadjutor and supporter, died in 1838. His continued thoughtfulness and generosity had left the church free from debt, and provided it with a comfortable parsonage. Rev. Tubal Wakefield succeeded in pastoral charge. Walter Williams, T. J. Gates and Ephraim Browning were faithful officers and helpers in this church, which zealously maintained its early standing and efficiency, and exerted a most marked and beneficial influence.

---

* Rev. Lucius Burleigh.

After many changes and failures, Plainfield's numerous cotton and woolen manufactories were again in motion. The Moosup Company had its factory burned up and went down after the war. The Central Manufacturing Company in 1827 passed into the hands of Richard and Arnold Fenner of Cumberland, and Holden Borden of Smithfield. Buildings, machinery, privileges of land and water, occupied in woolen manufacture by Joseph Eaton, Darius Lawton and Co., were made over in 1826, to one of Rhode Island's shrewdest manufacturers, the plain old Quaker, William Almy. A large new factory building was erected the following year, improved machinery introduced, tenement houses built, adjoining land purchased and brought under cultivation, and soon one of the largest woolen manufactories in Connecticut was under full headway. Another smaller factory eastward on the Moosup was built and run by Joseph S. Gladding. The Union Factory, owned mostly in Plainfield, was also flourishing—Henry A. Rogers acting as its agent in Providence. Four "little manufacturing villages," known as Almyville, Unionville, Centerville and Packerville, were thus growing up in the town. The former was under the charge of Sampson Almy, nephew of its chief proprietor. Packerville distinguished itself in the organization of the first fire engine company, July 5, 1830, and in great zeal for temperance. All were managed by good men, ready to promote order and improvement. A small settlement also grew up around Kennedy's mill, near the mouth of the Moosup.

The town showed its interest in the manufactories by ordering its fishery laws repealed for their benefit so that its citizens might avail themselves of the natural powers furnished by our water streams. It also took into consideration the canal proposed from tidewater to Worcester, and expressed the universal sense of the town that such canal would be highly beneficial to agricultural, commercial and manufacturing interests and requested its representatives to further the same. Joseph S. Gladding, Elkanah C. Eaton, Allen Harris, William Kinne, Colonel Lester, were successively called upon to investigate the subject of a workhouse and the condition of the poor, and in 1832, the house of Amos Witter was established for a workhouse and house of correction. Its interest in public morals was manifested by voting that lotteries have a pernicious influence, and enjoining upon its representatives to use their influence for their suppression. They were also to oppose the appointment of any lawyer to the office of justice of the peace unless he shall recede from the bar rule in said County which provides that all writs shall be filled and signed by a lawyer or his student. Francis B. Johnson engaged in legal practice in place of Ira Case, deceased. William Dyer of Canterbury opened a law office in Centerville. Sessions Lester, Ebenezer Young of Killingly, and Joseph Eaton, successively administered the Probate office, which after 1830, was reduced in territorial jurisdiction. The latter was now chief judge of the County Court. Squire Cady, F. B. Johnson and Nathaniel French, served in the town clerk's office. Plainfield was very forward in establishing a Savings Institute, successfully opened in 1839.

Mr. Burleigh filled the position of principal in Plainfield Academy till compelled to resign by increasing optical disease. Plainfield was most fortunate in securing for his successor, Mr. John Witter of Preston, an experienced and competent instructor, under whose pro tracted administration the Academy maintained a high reputation. A handsome stone edifice now replaced the old Academy building*, erected in 1825, on a beautiful and commanding site given by Mrs. Lydia Farlan, other public spirited residents subscribing funds for the building. About a hundred students were usually connected with the school, of whom nearly one-half pursued classical studies, fitting for college or professional life. Mr. Witter was a careful and thorough teacher, training his pupils to habits of critical exactness, which enabled them to take high positions in college, and to fill with credit their various callings in life. Failing health obliged him to withdraw for a season, and finally to resign his position in 1837, but he continued for several years to prepare young men for college. The long list of his pupils embraces many distinguished men who have passed away and many still active in public affairs in different parts of the land. In modest boast he was wont to say recalling his arduous labors—"I think I must have added about six acres to the field of intellect." The Quaker School on Black Hill was maintained for a number of years, giving a peaceful home and competent instruction to many willing pupils. Gentle and serene beyond even ordinary Quakers, Father Greene and Master Benjamin maintained excellent discipline, and exercised a marked and salutary influence. Susan Anthony, Phebe Jackson, Samuel B. Tobey, Elisha Dyer, and many others famed in public life, or benevolent enterprise, were trained in this Quaker school. First-days and Fifth-days they marched in pairs to the plain meeting-house, the boys first and the girls at proper distance behind them, and enjoyed a quiet session. Here sometimes came Miss Crandall with her school of colored girls, sure of a friendly welcome. Abolition leaders shut out from other church edifices here enjoyed

---

* This historic edifice, so associated with the early educational enterprise of Windham County, enters upon its second century in good preservation, and is now appropriately owned and occupied by Mr. Roswell Ensworth, a professional teacher, descended from one of the first settlers of the "Quinebaug Country."

freedom of speech. The Anti-slavery influence emanating from Black Hill may have stimulated the Burleigh brothers in their early championship of the hated cause, which gained them such disrepute in other quarters. The *Advertiser* reports that " the everlasting great William H. Burleigh, the verse man, the schoolmaster, had turned traitor to his native State . . . located himself at Schenectady, New York," and was " pouring forth the most villainous abuse upon the people and laws of this State "—and was at a loss to conjecture what his fate might be, " so soon as his bitter and wicked spirit shall come in contact with the virtue and intelligence of the people." Other brothers of this remarkably gifted family engaged in the promotion of various reforms.

After a short vacancy, Rev. Orin Fowler of Lebanon was installed pastor of the Congregational church, March 1, 1820. Deacons Rinaldo Burleigh and John Douglas, James Gordon and Elias Parkhurst, with forty sisters, constituted the membership; but under the stimulating influence of the new pastor a new religious interest was awakened and their number was soon greatly increased. A brief season of prosperity was unhappily followed by a very unpleasant controversy, injurious to church and community. Mr. Fowler's eminent abilities may not have been accompanied by equal discretion, and he had the misfortune to incur the ill-will of prominent church members, who professed to believe reports derogatory to his character. Mr. Fowler insisted upon a public investigation by the Windham Association which decided that it was satisfied with his confession and recognized him as a member in regular standing. A succeeding council agreed " That unhappy dissatisfactions on the part of some individuals rendered the continuance of the connection so unpleasant as to justify separation, and dismissed him from his charge, January 27, 1831." Mr. Fowler was installed the same year in Fall River, Mass., where he filled a highly respectable position as minister and representative to Congress. His successor in Plainfield, Rev. Samuel Rockwell, harmonized conflicting elements and remained in charge nine years. Elder Nathaniel Cole continued to officiate as pastor of the Baptist church, till compelled to resign in 1833, by advancing years and infirmities. He was succeeded by Charles S. Weaver, who after three years gave place to Daniel Tilden.* Plainfield was still abundantly favored with competent physicians, the young Doctors Burgess and Cogswell sharing the field with Dr. Fuller, and Doctors Baldwin and Harris of Canterbury.

*In 1840, the church was re-organized as the Union Baptist Church of Plainfield, and removed to Moosup, where a new house of worship was soon erected.

The Baptists worshipping in Sterling Hill meeting-house enjoyed for five years the ministry of George Appleton. In April, 1829, they received Elder Peleg Peckham, as their pastor, who continued in charge for many years. The great revivals soon following brought more than fifty into the church. Connection with Coventry was no longer recognized, the church assuming the title of the First Baptist church of Sterling. John Gallup succeeded Thomas Douglas as clerk. Ira Crandall was chosen deacon upon the death of Deacon Asa Montgomery. Philip Keigyan also served as deacon. Like many Baptist churches it did not for a time unite with Temperance societies but voted to discountenance the soul-destroying sin of intemperance and as christians felt bound by the Word of God as adverse to the same both in and out of the church. The local association of neighborhood churches continued to hold their annual meetings, which were largely attended and greatly enjoyed. After nearly thirty years of intermittent worship, the church pertaining to the Line meeting-house secured the services of a stated pastor, Rev. Otis Lane, who was installed over it October 29, 1828. Infirm health compelled his removal after a few years but he was quickly succeeded by Rev. Jacob Allen, installed, October, 1837, who with a brief inter- mission remained in charge for nearly twenty years. A branch Baptist church was formed in the south part of Voluntown, in 1829, in con- nection with the labors of Elder Kneeland, which gained an independ- ent standing in about ten years.

Sterling's several cotton factories continued in operation with the usual beneficial results, furnishing employment to male and female operatives, and a ready market for farmers. The Sterling Company manifested much enterprise, and was one of the first in the country to whiten their cloth by the use of chlorine instead of a sun bath. Mr. William Pike effected this invention, and also experimented in wood distillation, extracting for the use of the dyer the first Pyroligneous acid made in the country. His success encouraged him to further enterprise. Brandy and gin distilleries had fallen into disrepute, but the transformation of wood into various chemical agencies met with nothing but favor. Three of these "sap works" were in time established—two in Sterling, one in Voluntown—requiring some five or six thousand cords of hard wood annually and at least a score of men to prepare the wood and aid in the working. Pyroligne- ous and citric acids, sugar of lead, tincture of iron, naphtha, fine charcoal, were among the products of distillation. Mr. Pike had his residence on Sterling Hill in one of the fine old Dorrance houses, and was much respected as one of the leading men of the town. He was the first to introduce one-horse wagons into use, paying for them in cotton yarn. Dr. William H. Campbell engaged in medical practice, having his residence near the hill. Dr. Nathan S. Pike was widely known in the profession. Calvin Hebard continued in legal practice. Pierce Smith served as town clerk and treasurer. Calvin Hebard, Jeremiah Young, John Gallup, John Thurston, justices. Benjamin Tuckerman retained the charge of the post-office.

The privilege on the Pachaug in the west part of Voluntown, was purchased by an Industrial joint stock company, which in 1828, had erected factory buildings and engaged in the manufacture of cotton goods. Mr. James Treat with his son-in-law, Donne, came into possession of the establishment, and Voluntown village was built up in a few years. A meeting-house was built by the company which was afterwards purchased by the Baptists. A second cotton factory was built before 1835, and a woolen factory was also established. Charcoal-making was carried on quite extensively both in Voluntown and Sterling. Dr. Harvey Campbell had now an extensive medical practice, and was an active and useful member of church and society. Voluntown Probate Court was constituted in 1830. Sterry Kinne, judge ; Minor Robbins, clerk.

V.

WINDHAM. WILLIMANTIC VILLAGE. CHAPLIN.

WINDHAM did not yield to the inevitable without farther resistance. Ere courts and jail were removed she was agitating for half-shire privileges. On the very day that delegates from other towns were planning Brooklyn Court-house, she was instructing her own delegates—Messrs. Clark, Perkins, Roger Huntington, Charles Taintor, Jonah Lincoln—to confer with Lebanon, Mansfield, Ashford and Columbia, in regard to retaining the courts half the time. In October, 1820, her selectmen were directed to take charge of the former Court buildings, and the committee to continue their efforts to regain lost privileges. Other changes were vigorously resisted. The incorporation of Chaplin, Scotland's petition for town privileges, Brooklyn's demand for turnpikes to Windham and Colchester, were curtly refused. Even the project for procuring a fire-engine and establishing a fire company in the Centre District, was allowed to rest in abeyance after procuring a charter. Land south of the Willimantic was remitted to Columbia, and two new bridges over Merrick's Brook granted to Scotland—one near John Burnett's called Church Bridge,

one near Zaccheus Waldo's Mill.   Petitions for roads and bridges urged
by Willimantic manufacturers in 1826, were dismissed as of little
moment while the town was preparing for a final grapple for the Court-
house.   Lebanon had already lapsed to New London County ; other
towns were discussing withdrawal.   Resistance and appeal were useless ; Mansfield and Columbia were transferred to Tolland County, and
Windham reluctantly gave orders to sell the vacant jail and court-
house.   Even then, in 1828, many would have continued the strife for
a half-shire, but increasing internal demands absorbed all the town resources.   The manufacturing epidemic had broken out in Windham.
Cotton factories had been built at Willimantic ; unique industries were
developing in North and South Windham.   Old Windham with its
courts, lawyers, newspapers and political influence ; its stores, workshops and noted taverns, was rapidly declining—but a young Windham with yet more vital force and multifarious energy was pushing
itself into notice.   The privileges of "the fair, full-watered stream,"
so long given over to droning mills and jolly fishermen, had been
snatched up by eager competitors.   The "Old State" had come under
a new dominion.   Providence with its usual avidity was first to seize
the prize.   In September, 1822, Perez O. Richmond bought of Waldo
Cary and Anson Young, land and privilege on the Willimantic near
its junction with the Nachauge, and soon built up a factory and village.   The brothers Jillson of Dorchester in 1824 purchased a site just
above the old paper and grist-mills, west of the Iron Works bridge,
and put up more substantial buildings.   The Windham Company was
next in the field, led by Hartford Tingley and Matthew Watson of
Providence, occupying a privilege farther westward.   A small factory
in the same vicinity was built and carried on by Deacon Charles Lee
of Windham.   The almost simultaneous irruption of so many clashing
enterprises and interests was quite overpowering.   It came like a
spring freshet, tearing down the old land-marks and sweeping everything before it.   The few previous residents of the hitherto quiet valley were almost dazed by the onset.   Hibernians settled down upon it
like an army of grasshoppers.   Shanties were set up wherever they
could find a footing.   The first public building erected was a two-story
grog-shop called "The Light-house," which diffused a most lurid light,
especially on Sundays.   The first village erected around Richmond's
mill was known for a time as "Sodom," and the self-seeking proprietor
was mockingly designated "Poor Old Richmond."   Chaos and confusion seemed to reign supreme for a time, but after the buildings were
completed, and the factories fairly at work, law and order began to
assert themselves.   People came for work or traffic, built houses and
settled down into citizens.   A new stone school-house was built, and

opened for school and religious services. The first preacher there was a young Baptist licentiate, Chester Tilden, who was aided for a time by the Baptist Convention. Mr. Asa Jillson, who built a handsome residence east of the river, Mr. A. E. Tingley, agent of the Windham Company, who removed to Windham Green, interested themselves in the growth of the settlement. The town was compelled to build a new bridge to accommodate the Windham Company, and the old public highway was widened and transformed into Main street. Buildings for stores and public uses soon sprung up along this street, and a very pretentious new hotel was built and opened by Guy Hebard.

Willimantic's first public demonstration was made July 4, 1826. It was a great occasion—the day on which the Nation commemorated its fiftieth birthday. Public celebrations were held in Scotland, Chaplin and Hampton, and the rising village at Willimantic Falls did the honors for Windham. A numerous and united concourse of citizens formed in procession on Main street, and cheered by sounding cannon and a large band of martial music marched to Stone Chapel, where they heard an oration from Daniel Frost, Esq., of Canterbury, and other services by Reverends Brown and Tilden, "followed by a sumptuous entertainment at the Willimantic Hotel, prepared by Guy Hebard." Its exhilarating influence was manifest in the twenty-four toasts served for dessert, which surpassed the usual flights attained on such occasions.

"4. The TREE OF LIBERTY planted on Columbia's broad plains, of but fifty years' growth, its massing branches have reached the centre and this day are more than *twelve millions* of souls basking under its shade."

"8. RIVER WILLIMANTIC : Like the autumnal harvest is constantly bringing in its rich treasures to repay the labors of industry and art, and opens her wide extended arms to embrace the farms, manufactures and mechanics through the country which it flows."

"12. WINDHAM CENTRE DISTRICT, who has long since immortalized her name by her glorious struggle for independence when her territories were invaded by *Bull-frogs*—May her ancient glory never be sullied by a vain attempt to sway her proud and haughty sceptre over the destinies of Willimantic!"

Insubordination at home was quite as subversive to progress as Windham's resistance. Heterogeneous elements refused to blend. Boys were so rampant that the school committee sent expressly to Sterling for a master with will and hand strong enough to keep them from marring the school-house. Temperance workers complained of "bitter and violent opposition," and Christians found it difficult to find a place in which to hold religious meetings. Sectarian strife raged fiercely. The school in the first district was forbidden to the Baptists, and persistent efforts made to drive them from that in the second district. Opposers even threatened to *blast the rock* that served for its

65

foundation. Locked out on one occasion, they formed in procession and marched singing to the private house opened to them. "They have done more mischief than they would in the school-house," sighed the discomfited opposer. A Baptist church was organized October 20, 1827, with twenty constituent members. Rev. Chester Tilden, ordained the preceding August, remained in charge. George Byrne was elected clerk and treasurer. With aid from abroad a church edifice was completed and dedicated, May 27, 1829. A Sabbath-school was immediately organized. Samuel Barrows, Jun., and Eliphalet Martin were chosen deacons. The Congregational church was organized at the house of A. C. Tingley, January 22, 1828, sixteen persons signing the covenant. The uniting brethren, were Charles Lee, Nathaniel Robinson, John, Eliphalet and Joseph Brown, Azariah Balcom and Seth Jillson. Mr. Dennis Platt, a Yale Theological student, who had labored several months previous as a missionary among them, supported by the Domestic Missionary Society, and the Ladies' Missionary Society of Tolland County, was continued in charge. On the following Sabbath the sacrament was administered by Rev. Mr. Atwood of Mansfield, "when sixty communicants, members of different churches in the Congregationalist and Methodist communion, sat down at the table of their common Lord." Efforts were at once made for building a house of worship. A plan very popular for a time of building a large house conjointly with other denominations, was successfully opposed. A building site was given by Messrs. Tingley and Watson. Funds were procured from various sources, abroad and at home, and the house was completed the following autumn, Dr. Hawes of Hartford preaching the dedication sermon. Mr. Platt labored on for two years with much zeal and efficiency till worn down by care and anxiety he was forced to leave the field. The membership of the church had increased to fifty, but it met many obstacles and difficulties, especially in meeting its pecuniary obligations. Its first deacons were Charles Lee and Nathaniel C. Warren. An efficient Sabbath-school was soon established. Methodists organized a class in 1828, Jonathan Fuller, leader. A house of worship was erected in 1829, and a society located, and a stated preacher secured the following year. The Universalists, who were very numerous in those early days, effected society organization and maintained regular services. Earnest men and women from all the churches joined in temperance work, which indeed demanded extreme efforts. A flourishing society was reported in 1831—George S. Catlin, president; N. C. Warren, vice-president. It was not without unceasing labor and vigilance that these churches and societies were maintained. The constant influx of population from the surounding country made it difficult to keep pace with the needs of the hour. The inconvenience of voting at Windham Green, and Windham's opposition to needful outlay, soon incited efforts for local independence. Petition for town privileges was successfully resisted, but in May, 1833, Willimantic Borough was constituted. Its first meeting was held in July. Loring Carpenter was chosen warden; Silas Walden, Asa Jillson, William Witter, burgesses. Liberty was thus gained to regulate its own highways and institute local improvements. The material growth and prosperity of the village was thereby greatly promoted but its progress in other directions was slow. The character of its early population was unfavorable for healthy development and assimilation. It was largely made up of persons of small means from many different communities who came to the factories to get a living, with no thought or care for the public good. The immense "teaming interest," the vast number of persons employed in hauling goods and cotton back and forth over the Norwich Turnpike, and the accompanying taverns and low drinking places, occasioned much disorder and drunkenness, and bad elements seemed for a time to greatly predominate. Yet notwithstanding these drawbacks, Barber in 1835 reports Willimantic "a flourishing village," with three houses of worship, six cotton factories, a satinet factory and a paper-mill. A post-office was opened as early as 1827—Henry Hall, postmaster. The Willimantic Fire Engine Company was organized in 1830.

North Windham had undergone various vicissitudes. The paper-mill to which it owed its growth was abandoned by Badger in 1825, and after farther failures fell into the hands of an Englishman, Joseph Pickering, who with great labor and difficulty had succeeded in bringing to America the first imported Fourdrinier machine for the manufacture of paper. Associating with J. A. H. Frost of Boston, they bought the dilapidated paper-mill at North Windham at a low price, in 1827, and there set up the machine which was to effect a revolution in paper-making. But as often occurs, those who introduced this invention received no profit from it. The firm lacked steadiness or business capacity, and soon became bankrupt. Boston creditors who attempted to carry on the business were equally unsuccessful. In 1831, the mill property came into the hands of Mr. Justin Swift, who transformed it into a cotton manufactory and the rejected Fourdrinier moved on to Andover, Conn., and finally ended its wanderings at York, Pa. But though not permanently retained in Windham, its brief sojourn led to important consequences. George Spafford of South Windham, a man of much mechanical insight, employed to refit the North Windham mill and aid in setting up the new machine, was much impressed by its remarkable capabilities, and the certainty that it would in time supersede the very inadequate paper-making process then in use. Forming a partnership with James Phelps, an experienced paper-mill builder, they set to work to construct a duplicate. Selecting New Furnace in Stafford for its foundry accommodations, they hired a loft and with much caution and secrecy pursued their difficult enterprise. Nine men under charge of young Charles Smith constituted the working force with only ordinary hand tools and a single power lathe. The curiosity excited by their mysterious operations was allayed by plausible inventions. Yankee ingenuity triumphed over every obstacle and completed an improvement upon the original Fourdrinier which was sold to Amos D. Hubbard and put in successful operation at Norwich Falls, May, 1829. Soon a second was accomplished and sold to Henry Hudson of East Hartford. "Both yielded such excellent results that the projectors were encouraged to make preparations for the permanent continuance of the business," and erected suitable accommodations on the site of the old fulling-mill at South Windham, which were ready for occupancy early in 1830. Here they built mills for customers in many States and supplied machinery. In 1831, they invented and constructed *dryers*, which performed in a few minutes the work of previous hours. Mr. Spafford also devised a *cutter* for dividing the continuous web into sheets of uniform size. "Phelps and Spafford" as partners carried on a flourishing business till the great crash of 1837, when their losses compelled them to suspend work. A new firm, Smith, Winchester & Co., succeeded the following year. Charles Smith, son of Joshua Smith, brother-in-law to both Spafford and Winchester, assumed the general management.

"By the death of his father, Charles Smith was left an orphan at the age of fourteen, when the cares and responsibilities of manhood at once devolved upon him. Before attaining his majority he directed the operations of large gangs of men proving equal to every task as it came. Uniting rare executive ability to mechanical talent both natural and cultivated of a high order, he started the company upon a career of prosperity which it has since pursued undeviatingly through all the vicissitudes of the general business of the country. It has been a fundamental rule of the establishment to knowingly permit only thorough work to leave its doors, while the integrity of its dealings has won the universal confidence of its patrons."

So great was the demand that the firm was again and again compelled to enlarge their works and build new conveniences for storage. The little Pigeon Swamp Brook running dry half the summer was made permanently effective by the construction of reservoirs covering the former swamp. A prosperous village grew up around this establishment. Other industries were introduced. Amos D. Allen continued his furniture manufacture. His son Edwin, inheriting a large share of the inventive genius of the family, distinguished himself by the construction of machinery for making wood type. Strolling casually into a newspaper office in Norwich his attention was excited by a font of wood type, and a scheme for making it by mechanical process seized his mind with such force that in three days it was embodied in wood and iron, and a perfected machine was turning out its specimens of finished workmanship. In 1837, Mr. Allen entered into partnership with George F. Nesbit of New York City, who under his own name introduced the wood type to the trade, while his partner had charge of the manufacture in South Windham. Such was his skill that he was able to fabricate every part of his machines even to imparting to the steel-cutting apparatus the exquisite temper required. The business made fair progress though encountering the opposition incident to new inventions, but in time it gained ground and the use of large metal type was entirely superseded.

Under the administration of Mr. Justin Swift, North Windham was able to maintain a successful manufacturing establishment, to the benefit of the surrounding country as well as the proprietor. The Lincolns* of this neighborhood had transformed their fulling and card ing-mill into a manufactory of felting used in working the Fourdrinier machine, having acquired the art by picking to pieces and reconstruct ing the English specimens first imported. In 1838, Mr. Ralph Lincoln was invested with the office of postmaster, which he retained for many years.

Windham Green though deprived of official honors kept its place as head of the town, exercising its ancient sway over the border vil lages. Their growth at first added to the importance of the mother settlement. Proprietors and managers of Willimantic factories found pleasant homes at Windham Green. Windham's six stores, bank, probate and town clerk's offices, accommodated all the villages. The first fire-engine in Windham County was purchased by resi dents of Windham Green, and made over to the committee of the Centre District, June 18, 1825, for the sum of $180.00. George W. Webb, Henry Webb and Eliphalet Ripley were chosen fire-wardens, with power to enlist a fire-company. A suitable company was soon organized, which met monthly for practice and exercise. Fines for absence or tardiness, rigorously enforced, were expended in an annual supper at one of the modern hotels, which had superseded the primitive tavern, while the tutelary Bacchus now swung aloft in Staniford's elm

---

* This was the family so remarkable for its longevity. Samuel Linkon or Lincoln, born 1693, lacked but a few days of completing 101 years. His son, Captain Nathaniel Lincoln, lived 105 years, 3 months and 18 days. His son of the same name had nearly completed 94 years—making an average of one hundred years to the three generations. It was said that when a Lincoln died, " they wore out a new bell-tongue, tolling his age."

tree. Windham Bank was incorporated in 1832. The first meeting was held August 8. John Baldwin, George Spafford, Justin Swift, Levi Johnson, Stephen Hosmor, Thomas Gray, Wm. R. Dorrance, John Webb, Jun., Chauncey F. Cleveland, John C. Rockwell, Abner Hendee were chosen directors; John Baldwin, president; J. A. White, cashier; Thomas Gray, attorney.

Mr. Joel W. White, who had now removed his residence to Windham, was an active business man, much concerned in staging and transportation movements. Another acquisition was George S. Catlin, a lawyer of brilliant promise. John Baldwin, Esq., was sent as representative to Congress, 1825–29. Windham maintained its political interest, though its influence was diminished by party division, Peter Webb and other prominent Democrats declining to support Jackson, and Anti-tariff principles. Judge Swift died in 1823, his sons having previously removed to Ohio. Samuel Gray, Esq., after a long life of public usefulness, dating back to the breaking out of the Revolution, and officiating as clerk of Windham County Courts for more than forty years, died in 1836, in his 86th year. His son, Thomas Gray, admitted to the Bar in 1819, served as clerk of Courts, town and probate office. Hon. Jabez Clark, chief-justice for a time of the County Court, also died in 1836, and was succeeded in his profession by his son, Edwards Clark. Eliphalet Ripley served as town treasurer. Town meetings were much occupied in resisting demands and encroachments. Willimantic having secured borough privileges furthered the movement for a new town-house. Selectmen were authorized to purchase site within fifty rods of Windham Green. George Spafford, Justin Swift, Joel W. White, Hartford Tingley, joined with them as committee, and the house was completed in 1836. It was voted that all town meetings should be held in this house.

Windham's First church resigned many members to the Willimantic church. Mr. Everest was dismissed in 1827, after a peaceful and prosperous ministry. Rev. R. F. Cleveland's three years' service was equally acceptable. J. E. Tyler of East Windsor was ordained and installed, October 11, 1837. Samuel Perkins, Esq., elected deacon in 1796, continued in office during his ministry. Deacons Charles Lee and Thomas Welch were dismissed to other churches. Abner Follet was chosen deacon in 1840. An Episcopal society was formed in 1832, and a house of worship erected the following year. Mr. Asa Jillson aided largely in supporting this worship. Religious services were stately maintained in the Robinson house—Elder Roger Bingham often officiating there, and chance preachers. Lorenzo Dow and other famous itinerants found open doors and willing hearers. Rev. Jesse Fisher remained in pastoral charge of the Scotland Congregational church till his lamented death in 1836. His successor, Rev. O. T. Whiton, was dismissed after four years' service. Thomas Tallman of Middle Haddam, was ordained and installed pastor, March 20, 1844— the society reluctantly consenting to less stringent provisions for the dissolution of the contract. Judge Ebenezer Devotion so long prominent in Scotland affairs, died in 1829, in his eighty-ninth year. The "old Devotion house" was long occupied by his son. Scotland Parish was greatly burdened by excessive imposts and inconveniencies brought upon it by Windham's growth and aspirations, and devoted much of its energies to efforts for separation. No special business enterprises were developed within its limits. The old saw and grist-mills were kept up, and brick-making carried on near the line between the parishes. Timothy Tingley advertised remarkable trading advantages for a time, but mercantile operations were gradually transferred to Willimantic village, which absorbed more and more of the life of the town. Colonel George Spafford assumed the paper-mill after the demise of "Clark and Gray." The adjacent grist and saw-mills were kept busily at work. Richmond's village, now known as Wellesville, was somewhat poorly managed and less flourishing than the other establishments. The Jillsons showed much business enterprise, operating cotton and duck-mills, and building many substantial stone houses. Mr. John Tracy, who succeeded A. C. Tingley as agent for the Windham Company, was very successful as a manager. The Willimantic Savings Institute, organized in his office in 1842, had a most beneficial effect, encouraging operatives to lay up their earnings and make solid investments. Mr. Tracy served as secretary and treasurer for a time without compensation. The Company's store exceeded any in the village. In 1839, Amos D. Smith and James T. Smith (afterwards governor of Rhode Island), initiated manufacturing operations which led to the organization of the Smithville Company, and the building up of large factories and accommodations. The "Lee Mill" was absorbed by this company—Deacon Lee having removed to Norwich. Its management was entrusted to Mr. Whiting Hayden, who manifested much business capacity and public spirit. Doctors John Hill, Jun., and William Witter engaged in medical practice. Lawyers preferred as yet the vicinity of the former forum.

In spite of remonstrance from Windham, Chaplin Ecclesiastic Society obtained town privileges in May, 1822. The bounds of the ecclesiastic and school societies were soon after made identical with those of the town. Town government was organized on the Fourth of July following, Erastus Hovey, moderator. Orin Witter was chosen town clerk and treasurer; John Ross, William Martin, Origen Bennett, Luther Ashley, Nehemiah Holt, selectmen; Abel Ross, James Utley, constables; James Mosely, Jun., Elisha Bill, Judson Metcalf, grand-jurors; Enoch Pond, Darius Knight, Heman Clark, Isaiah Geer, tithingmen; Jonathan H. Ashley, sealer of weights and measures; Erastus Hough, Matthew Smith, John Clark, fence-viewers. Chaplin's population was about eight hundred. It showed its loyalty to the mother town by almost immediately joining in effort to secure half-shire privileges. Its business development was quickened by town organization. Peter Lyon set up a paper-mill in the south of the town. Major Edward Eaton engaged in lumber operations, and built new houses in Chaplin village. Boot-making was carried on to a large extent. A tannery was actively maintained and attempts made to establish an iron foundry. The culture of silk received considerable attention, and palm-leaf hats were successfully manufactured. Mr. Andrews labored faithfully as pastor of the Congregational church for ten years. He was followed successively by Reverends Lent S. Hough and Erastus Dickinson. The Register of 1826 reports four other ministers in Chaplin—Roswell Bill, Ebenezer Clark, Baptist; Elias Sharpe, Joshua Abbe, Christ-ians—but it does not appear that local churches were organized. Its only physician, Dr. Orrin Witter, was greatly esteemed. Darius Knight was chosen deacon in 1822.

VI.

HAMPTON. ASHFORD. EASTFORD PARISH.

WHILE in the manufacturing towns there was life and growth, the farming towns were losing ground. The great out-flow of population to the opening West sapped their vital energies. The western tier of towns suffered severely from this constant drain though Hampton escaped deterioration by the energy and public spirit of those who staid behind. Its farmers maintained its agricultural reputation, and its young men engaged in business and public affairs. Edward S. Mosely succeeded to the mercantile business so long carried on by his grandfather and father, Colonels Ebenezer and Samuel Mosely. Promising sons grew up to take charge of the business enterprises of the Taintors. The Cleveland brothers entered early into the political arena and gained much influence in town and county. Chauncey F. Cleveland won immediate success at the bar, by his intuitive skill in seizing upon the salient points of a case and presenting them before a jury, and was equally successful in winning the suffrages of his fellow-citizens. A radical by training and conviction,

he soon became a power in the Democratic party. In 1826, he was
sent as representative to the Legislature and thenceforward was
retained in public service. He was made judge of Windham Probate
District, and prosecuting attorney for the County. Mason Cleveland
was chosen town clerk in 1825, and employed in various public
capacities. William Durkee, Edmond Badger, Hezekiah Hammond,
now served as selectmen; N. F. Martin, C. Moulton, C. F. Cleveland,
Roger Taintor, Daniel Searls, Jonathan Clark, justices; Philip Pearl,
deputy-sheriff; James Abbott, William Martin, David Fox, grand-
jurors. Elijah and Lucius Greenslit, William Brown, Harvey Fuller,
William Durkee, Alonzo Martin, Charles Griffin, Charles C. Button,
William Bennett, were among later town officers. Ebenezer Griffin,
judge of the County Court, was a man of weight and influence.
Jonathan Clark was a much respected citizen, earnest in forwarding
temperance and anti-slavery movements. Doctors Brewster and Hovey
were succeeded in practice by Dr. Dyer Hughes, assisted later by his
son and Dr. Clark, previously of Canterbury.

Infirmities brought on by close application and sedentary habits
compelled Rev. Ludovicus Weld to seek a dismissal from his charge in
1824. The church was so fortunate as to unite almost immediately in
choice of Daniel G. Sprague of Killingly, who was installed May 26th,
of the same year. Mr. Sprague's interest in the reform questions then
agitating the public mind made him a valued acquisition to the
County ministry. Through his influence, the Hampton Temperance
Society was promptly formed and efficiently maintained, although
impeded in its growth by the convivial hospitalities for which the
town had long been noted. Hampton's enterprising young men were
greatly interested in the condition of its meeting-house, now a venerable edifice. Successive committees were appointed in 1837–38, comprised of leading men, viz.: Josiah C. Jackson, William Brown,
Henry G. Taintor, Uriel Hammond, David Searls, Mason Cleveland,
Harvey Fuller,—to consider the question of building a new house, and
solicit subscriptions, but after much discussion it was decided to repair
the old house. Committees were appointed, the building was moved,
thoroughly remodeled and equipped, and made ready for dedication
May 9, 1840. Mr. Sprague had previous to this date been succeeded by
Rev. Daniel C. Frost of Canterbury, who was followed in 1842, by
Rev. William Barnes. Rev. John Paine continued in charge of the
Baptist church till 1827. After his dismissal the church lost ground
rapidly, and became extinct about 1844. Worship was still regularly
maintained in the Burnham and Goshen meeting-houses.

In military matters Hampton retained its early interest, its regular
trainings and occasional "musters" being kept as gala days by the

whole population. The pure air, generous living and social amenities of this pleasant town, were eminently favorable to health and longevity, and an unusual number of Revolutionary soldiers welcomed the semi-centennial commemoration, July 4, 1826. Hampton's celebration of this auspicious day was almost as preternaturally impressive as the "Midnight Review" of Napoleon's grand army, portrayed by an imaginative poet. Not the *phantoms* but the very men themselves who had marched to Lexington and braved unnumbered battles—*forty-two hoary veterans*—under their old leader, Abijah Fuller, with Nathaniel Farnham as drum-major ; Joseph Foster and Lucius Faville as fifers, and all the subalterns at their posts—appeared in Revolutionary costume on Hampton Hill, took arms of the military company, formed in line, and marched up and down the length of the street to the drums and tunes of " '76." Joseph Foster, not a member of the original company, excited much interest as one of *twelve sons*, who with their father had borne a part in Revolutionary service. Other military companies present did homage to the veteran corps, who were treated to a free dinner by their admiring fellow-citizens. So great was the military enthusiasm awakened by this unique company that ordinary speech-making was apparently omitted as quite inadequate to the occasion. Samuel Mosely now served as lieutenant-colonel of the Fifth Regiment. Eleazer Litchfield, surgeon's mate. Chauncey F. Cleveland was captain of the Hampton company. His military bearing and affable manner gave him great popularity as an officer, and he was rapidly promoted, rising from the ranks to the highest military office in the State. In 1836, Hampton was made a distinct probate district, Edward S. Mosely, judge. In the following year, when bank commissioners were instituted, General Cleveland was one of the first to fill the office. For two years he had now served as speaker of the House of Representatives to great public acceptance, and by his personal influence and persistency had aided largely in securing the appropriation of the greater part of Connecticut's share of the surplus revenue for the benefit of public schools. Elected in 1838, the only Democrat from Windham County, with but thirty-eight from the whole State, he yet managed to defeat leading measures urged by the dominant party. The Democratic party warmly recognized his services and enthroned him as their leader. In the following year he received an unanimous nomination to Congress, but was defeated with all Democrats. Yet notwithstanding the great Tippecanoe excitement, and the temporary prostration of the Democrats, so great was General Cleveland's popularity and personal influence that in 1842, he was elected governor of Connecticut by a plurality of nearly two thousand, although the Whigs had carried the State for Ellsworth the year preceding by about five thousand majority. Even the stanch old city of Norwich with a large Whig majority yielded to the fascinations of Windham County's Democratic champion. Governor Cleveland's administration was radical and aggressive. He recommended the abolition of imprisonment for debt—"taking the honest poor man out of the hands of the unfeeling rich, and carried it through in spite of the opposition of almost if not quite the entire Whig members and of the creditorial interest of his own party." He also "recommended and carried through the first appropriation ever made by the State for the support and care of the insane poor. He also recommended and the Legislature passed the law which secured to children worked in factories under fourteen years of age the ten-hour system, and schooling for three months in each year, under suitable penalties. In short his recommendations were always made for the benefit of that class who are more or less at the mercy of the rich, and a legislature which was in reality as well as name Democratic nobly responded." His course with relation to the famous Dorr Rebellion was somewhat unsatisfactory, Whigs insisting that he should have surrendered the *pseudo* Governor upon Rhode Island requisition, and ultra Democrats complaining that he did not retain and defend the fugitive who sought his protection. But notwithstanding some murmurings excited by that remarkable imbroglio, Governor Cleveland again carried the State triumphantly in 1843, against so powerful an antagonist as Roger S. Baldwin, and was only beaten by Connecticut's enthusiasm for another popular favorite, Henry Clay—the Whig spring-tide of '44, sweeping all before it. Hampton Hill had greatly enjoyed its honors as the seat of Government, and the county at large exulted in its first resident governor. Other citizens of the town were favored with important public offices. Mr. Mason Cleveland, who was highly esteemed for sound judgment and integrity, officiated as school commissioner and comptroller. Messrs. Griffin, Mosely, Clarke and Taintor filled public offices at various dates with credit and fidelity.

Ashford village was still a place of considerable importance with its much-frequented taverns, its stores, lawyers' offices and popular physicians. To these accommodations a Probate Office was added in 1830, David Bolles, judge, but this honored citizen of the town died during this year. Ichabod Bulkley, Esq., a very able young man, succeeded to his legal practice, and also to the administration of Probate. He won a high position at the Bar, was employed on the Crandall case and in other important suits. After his death in 1838, Abner Richmond of Westford Parish established himself in Ashford village, and practiced law for many years. Dr. Nehemiah Howe died in a good old age.

A second Dr. Joseph Palmer succeeded to the extensive medical practice of his father. His brother was equally well-known as general of the Fifth Brigade and proprietor of one of the popular Turnpike taverns. A third Dr. Palmer practiced for a time in Ashford and then removed to Canterbury. After a long and useful pastorate, Rev. Philo Judson was released from his charge in Ashford in 1833. His immediate successor, Rev. Job Hall of Pomfret, remained but three years. Rev. Charles Hyde of Norwich was installed as pastor of Ashford's First church, February 21, 1838. Matthew Reed and Elisha Byles were chosen deacons in 1825. After the death of Deacon Kendall in 1829, his son of the same name was chosen to fill his place, the third Isaac Kendall who had occupied the deacon's seat, and the fifth of the name in direct succession to occupy the Kendall homestead, of 1714. A new meeting-house was erected on the previous site in 1830. Rev. William Storrs remained in charge of the Congregational church in Westford Parish till his lamented decease in 1827, after a pastorate of thirty-four years. His place was worthily filled by Rev. Luke Wood, a successful worker in various Home Mission fields. After his dismissal in 1831, no stated pastor was ordained for several years, the great emigration from Ashford seriously affecting its numerous churches.

The First Baptist church enjoyed a revival of its early prosperity under the pastoral care of Dr. Ezekiel Skinner of Lebanon, a man of varied ability and wide-reaching influence. Settling at first as a physician in the little village, then known as Pomfret Hollow, he united the care of this church with professional practice.

"*December* 3, 1822.—Then met with the church from other churches, Elders Frederic Wightman, Jonathan Goodwin, David Lillibridge, John Paine and Esek Brown, and ordained our brother Ezekiel Skinner to administer gospel ordinances."

Under such efficient leadership the Baptist interest was greatly strengthened. New members were received into the church and absentees cut off. In 1824, Ashford Baptist Association was organized. A committee to make arrangements met at the house of Dr. Skinner, and its first meeting was held in the Knowlton meeting-house. Ten churches, viz: First and Second Ashford, First and Second Woodstock, Thompson, Pomfret, Killingly, Tolland, Andover and Stafford— were dismissed from the Sturbridge Association. Sermons appropriate to the occasion were delivered by Elders Bloss and Cushman, and constitution adopted. Third Ashford, Mansfield and Hampton were admitted the following year. Dr. Skinner was a forcible and eloquent preacher, aggressive and radical, a leading Democrat, a co-worker in every progressive and reformatory movement. Under his stimulating influence other Ashford young men were roused to join in effort with those previously gone out to labor. November 17, 1825, the First Baptist church voted, "That Brother Justus H. Vinton has a gift for public improvement as a preacher of the gospel, and that the church will give him a letter to enable him to improve his gift as such wherever there is a door open." A life of most successful missionary work among the Karens of Burmah was the door opened to this graciously gifted youth. Brothers William Chaffee and Amos Babcock were also licensed to preach. Interest in mission work was hightened by the influence of the Bolles brothers, now actively connected with denominational agencies.

Dr. Skinner was much interested in the development of the African race, at home and abroad, and his son, Benjamin Rush Skinner, a most thoughtful and conscientious young man, who had early consecrated himself to mission work, sailed for Liberia in 1830, under appointment of the Baptist Board of Missions, but with wife and child soon fell a' victim to the climate. His father, though nearly sixty years of age, felt impelled to occupy the place thus vacated, and in 1834 accomplished his desire, and labored for four years with great efficiency in Liberia, tending the sick, preaching, and serving as colonial agent and finally as governor, when the whole administration of government rested upon his hands. "Nothing could exceed the energy and industry with which he labored to promote the temporal and spiritual interests of the Colonists." A daughter of like spirit aided him in his labors, and engaged in teaching. Exhausted by such severe labors he returned to Ashford, resuming the charge of the Westford Baptist church, and his professional practice.

The First Baptist church steadily declined after the loss of Dr. Skinner. Elder David Bennet served as pastor for two years—the church manifesting its wonted independence of judgment by voting, "That we disapprove of unscriptural titles to ministers of the Gospel; also, of the practice of Baptist ministers *reading* their sermons instead of preaching." Brother Amos Babcock took the place left vacant by Elder Bennet and maintained worship and ordinances. The Westford Baptist church gained ground under the charge of Dr. Skinner, though somewhat reduced by the increasing lapse to the Christ-ian order. A new meeting-house was built in 1840, chiefly by the efforts of Messrs. Michael and Ichabod Richmond, now engaged in a flourishing business in Westford village. The North Ashford Baptist church after a period of depression was revived through the faithful labors of Elder Leonard Gage. A Sabbath-school was organized, services made more attractive, and soon many were added to the church. The first convert baptized by Elder Gage, Isaiah C. Carpenter, became a successful minister. Two other young men from the same class in Sabbath-school went out as evangelists and ministers. Illness and loss of voice compelled Elder Gage to retire from active service, but under the charge of faithful men the church maintained standing and influence. A new house of worship was completed in 1843.

Eastford Parish was now agitating the question of local independence, but its aspirations were thwarted through the influence of Mr. Bulkley and other leading men. Business was thriving and villages building up in this section. Captain Jonathan Skinner's cotton factory gave life to Eastford village; the Sprague mills were maintained on the site of Phenixville. Tannery works and wagon-making were also carried on, giving employment to many young men, who were less inclined to roving than those in the western section. Eastford was especially noted for its lively and agreeable society, its balls, parties and sleigh-rides, and frequent hilarious festivities. This gayety was not incompatible with desire for mental improvement. The school maintained year after year by "Master John Griggs" never lacked intelligent pupils. Nathaniel Lyon and other future notabilities were among the three thousand scholars instructed by this Eastford pedagogue, who is reported to have taught over fifty terms in Ashford and neighboring towns. The temperance cause gained a good standing here, notwithstanding the "strike" in moving the meeting-house. Esq. Bosworth, Mr. Torrey, Captain Nichols, were strong temperance men and used their influence in its behalf. The Congregational church was so fortunate as to retain Rev. Reuben Torrey as their pastor for twenty years. A new house of worship was erected in 1829, after arduous effort. Benjamin Bosworth, John N. Sumner, Calvin Whitney and Esek Preston, served as building committee. Claims with dissenters holding rights in the previous house were peaceably settled and sufficient money subscribed for the new edifice, which was dedicated Dec. 23, 1829. The unlucky old meeting-house, left by Temperance volunteers at the foot of the hill, was caught by a storm and ice-bound through the winter, obstructing travel till people talked of petitioning for an Act of Legislature "forbidding meeting-houses to run the roads." A legacy of a thousand dollars was left by Esq. Bosworth to help support a settled orthodox minister approved by Consociation. Methodists had become so numerous that Ashford circuit was instituted in 1826. The refusal of the Congregationalists to allow their new church edifice to a distinguished Universalist minister, incited his followers to unite with the Methodists in building a house for their joint accommodation. A Methodist society was located in Eastford village in 1831, and a chapel built the same year, used alternately by Methodists and Universalists.

VII.

WOODSTOCK. THOMPSON.

WOODSTOCK was chiefly occupied these years in building meeting-houses and carrying forward religious and secular controversies. The Dudley-land Claim was happily settled in her favor by the decision of the Supreme Court of the United States in 1822—the first case carried up from Windham Courts to this tribunal. The defendants secured the services of a rising Boston lawyer, Daniel Webster, to plead their cause, promising him a thousand dollars if they gained a favorable verdict. The trial was not only memorable for the magnitude of interests involved in it, but for its connection with the death of the "distinguished orator, lawyer and statesman," William Pinkney of Baltimore, who argued against Webster. While "exerting himself in the discussion of a great cause before the Supreme Court," he was stricken down by sudden illness and lived but a few days. Woodstock was also deeply interested in the long delayed settlement of the boundary line between Connecticut and Massachusetts, accomplished in 1826. Ebenezer Stoddard, Moses Warren and Andrew T. Judson served as commissioners for Connecticut. Jonathan Nichols of Thompson, surveyor. The bound established in 1834, was maintained as far as practicable.

West Woodstock was first in the field in securing its meeting-house. At a meeting held at the tavern of Abiel Fox, November 29, 1819, John Austin, Andrew Williams, Ebenezer Stoddard, Jacob Child, Elias Child, 2d, Eleazer Litchfield, Lathrop Clark, Benjamin Lyon, 2d, John Chandler, were chosen to fix a place for meeting-house; Darius Barlow, John Fox, Abram W. Paine, Elias Child, 2d, Benjamin Lyon, 2d, to circulate subscriptions. A site between the elm tree and house of Abram W. Paine, was designated and accepted, and some twenty-four hundred dollars promptly subscribed. Benjamin E. Palmer, Brooklyn, agreeing to build the house for $3,100, farther subscriptions were obtained. The good, genial minister, Mr. Underwood, appropriated his year's salary for the meeting-house. To Ebenezer Skinner, Benjamin E. Palmer, William Lyon was assigned the responsible duty "to stick the corner stakes for the foundation." The building committee "having taken upon them the burden" of viewing the site, were constrained to make it front more easterly. This being accepted the work went on rapidly, marred only by an unfortunate casualty and loss of life at the raising, and the new house was ready for dedication in the autumn of 1821. The number of choristers was now reduced to five; treble singers seated in the north half of the front gallery; tithing-men to eject boys from side gallery seats east of the separation. In the following year a new bell was procured by subscription, and Gurdon Marcy appointed to ring bell, unlock meeting-house and sweep once a month for $4.80 a year, taking twenty-five cents tollage for each mortuary tolling. The First church began its work with equal harmony and spirit, May 21, 1821, voted to accept of the plan for a new meeting-house—Captain William Lyon, General David Holmes and William K. Greene, committee to superintend the building; Rhodes Arnold and James Lyon, to take down the old house in a prudent manner, so that everything valuable may be saved; Jedidiah Kimball, to procure subscriptions to defray expenses of building. Four June days were devoted by the society to gratuitous labor upon the foundation. Pausing through haying, in August they proceeded to prepare for the raising, voted to have a dinner on the common for those who assist and for spectators, to be furnished by donation, and to accept Mr. William Bowen's proposal to give a supper the first day and a dinner the second to the workers; also, to give eighty-nine cents a gallon for the necessary spirit and eighteen cents a pound for loaf sugar. Provision was made for transporting Captain Babcock and an assistant with blocks and ropes from Norwich and back. Punctually, at 7 A. M., August, 1821, the citizens assembled from all parts of the town, and after an opening prayer from Mr. Lyman, proceeded to business. Again the second day they assembled with equal alacrity, food and spirits holding out with the workmen, "and finished raising about noon—and in view of the goodness of God in preserving the lives and limbs of all those who were engaged in this perilous business the meeting was closed by prayer and an anthem of thanksgiving." Gratuitous service was again rendered in November, when the society met several times at a place called the Hearthstone Lot for the purpose of getting out door-stones for the meeting-house. Notwithstanding this auspicious inauguration the work was delayed. Money and patience gave out. In December, 1821, "the vote was unanimous in favor of Mr. Lyman's continuance among this people as a gospel minister," and his contribution, and promised deductions from his salary were received with thanks. Difficulties, however, almost immediately followed. A back debt was due him as well as heavy bills for the meeting-house, the bell purchased of the academy was to be recast, disaffected members withdrew names and help, and the society fairly broke down under its burdens. Feeling unable to fulfill the contract with Mr. Lyman, they desired him now to ask his dismission that he might be employed in a place more profitable to himself. Some time passed before these difficulties were surmounted. Mr. Lyman declined to desert the post to which the

Great Head of the church had assigned him, choosing to remain at least till another minister or colleague had been engaged. The deficiency of $1,300 was made up in part by the liberality of members of the society and a committee appointed to make arrangements for dedicating the meeting-house. *Voted*, "That Mr. Flynn be requested to select such tunes as he may think proper, and with the rest of the singers learn and sing them on the day of dedication." Thursday, July 11, 1822, was selected for this interesting service. James Lyon, Dr. Daniel Lyman, John McClellan, Esq., Spalding Barstow and Rhodes Arnold, had charge of seating the congregation. The thanks of the society were formally tended to Mr. William Flynn and his associates for their good performance on the day of dedication and at other times ; also to Major George Holbrook, for his liberality in casting the bell and making gratuitous addition. A communion table was given by Jedidiah Kimball ; ladies of the society with their accustomed public spirit had assumed "dressing the pulpit." Mr. Lyman was dismissed from his charge, December 15, 1824, after some farther unpleasantness concerning remuneration for his closing years of service. William W. Hunt and Tertius S. Clarke supplied the pulpit for a time, and each declined to assume the pastorate. Ralph S. Crampton of Madison, was ordained and installed pastor, May 23, 1827.

Woodstock's Third or North Society indulged in *two* new meeting-houses. Its northern and southern residents favored different locations, and the ensuing "contention was so sharp between them" that like Paul and Barnabas-they parted company. It is said that the original disagreement concerning its site had never been forgotten, and that the children had been trained to hold fast to the traditions and feuds of their ancestors. The northern residents took the initiative in building a new church edifice upon their own responsibility at Village Corners, in 1830, and by most urgent efforts secured from the society and church a vote to occupy this house, and took possession of the same with church and society records. The Muddy Brook residents claimed that these votes were unlawfully obtained, and the pretended transfer a fraud and usurpation. A meeting of the County Association was called, April 19, 1831. The Rev. Messrs. Dow, Lane, Underwood, Whitmore, Sprague, Rose, Platt, Fitch, Torrey and Atwood were present. Denison Wattles served as counsel for the plaintiffs ; Asa Child, recently admitted to the bar, defended the claims of North Woodstock. Question before the council :—

"Which part of the church that choosing to remain at the East or old meeting-house, or that choosing to assemble at the West or new meeting-house habitually for worship and ordinances, is, or shall remain the church?

After due hearing the council decided:—Whereas it appears that at the meeting when the vote was taken to remove to the new meeting-house three of those who voted in favor of removing were minors, and two others were non-residents, and whereas in our opinion a church ought not to be moved by a bare majority—therefore, *Resolved*, That the Congregational church in North Woodstock has not been divided nor removed."

Committees appointed to attempt to effect a union were wholly unsuccessful. The North Woodstock branch retained the records and gained a legal verdict. A council called to ordain Foster Thayer as their pastor, June 29, 1831, recognized it as a distinct church, and its delegate, Mr. Peleg Child, was admitted to a seat in Consociation the same year. One unhappy result of this "ever-to-be-lamented difficulty" was the loss of an excellent minister, Rev. Samuel Backus, dismissed in 1830. The ninety-four church members left in Muddy Brook met the situation with much spirit, proceeding to erect another edifice on the site for which they had so bravely battled. The ordinary dedication services, April 25, 1832, were made more impressive by the ordination of Orson Cowles to the vacant pastorate.

The Baptists during this period erected a house of worship in South Woodstock, removing their church organization from Quasset. Brother John Sanger, chosen to take the place of Deacon Wheaton on account of his advanced age and infirmities, was approbated as a lincentiate in 1831, the church manifesting that they were edified under his improvement. Elder Albert Cole, served as pastor for some years. Previous to its removal the church was greatly reduced in numbers, having suffered much from the lapse of its members "to the sentiments and practices of a people called Millerites." West Woodstock Baptist church suffered a period of depression after the removal of Elder Branch, but enjoyed a remarkable revival season in 1824, when sixty were added to its membership. Among these converts was one most useful and honored in after life, Calista Holman, who as the wife of the Ashford licentiate, Justus H. Vinton, accomplished a most efficient missionary work in Burmah. Continued prosperity was enjoyed during the nine years' pastorate of Rev. George B. Atwell. Another powerful revival was experienced in 1834, under his successor, Rev. Nathan D. Benedict. The pastorate of Rev. Bela Hicks, 1840–43, "was also one of prosperity and success." Universalists in Woodstock, long connected with the Oxford Society, insisted in a local organization in 1839, Charles Wood, George Sumner, John G. Marcy, John Fox, John Weaver, committee. A house of worship was soon erected and public services maintained. A Methodist class formed in East Woodstock, in 1827, prepared the way for a located society in 1846.

Woodstock's ecclesiastic harmony was seriously affected by the Ma-

sonic excitement, which raged therein with unusual violence, leading
to the dismissal of Mr. Crampton from the First church, and the suspension and censure of prominent church members. William K. Green,
then engaged in business on Woodstock Hill, was a valiant champion
of Anti-masonry. Interesting conventions were held upon the Hill,
largely attended by Anti-masons from all parts of the County. Rev.
Daniel Dow's sermon upon the text —" If ye will inquire, inquire ye "—
a very temperate and logical plea for liberty of inquiry into the principles and practice of Masonry, as of other popular organizations —was
severely censured by Masons, while Masonic utterances were denounced
with even greater bitterness by their opponents. The spirit with
which belligerents carried on this most vituperative warfare is sufficiently illustrated by the remark of a prominent Anti-mason—"That
it was a question with him whether an adhering Mason should be allowed to draw water out of his well." Few controversies have called
out deeper personal animosities or accomplished less obvious results,
except in its connection with political changes and developments. The
old Toleration Party, through which Ebenezer Stoddard, Esq., had
served four years in Congress, was now defunct and many of its
former supporters were prominent Anti-masons and Democrats. Esq.
Stoddard was elected Lieut.-governor in 1833–35, and subsequent years.
John F. Williams, who still practiced his profession in West Woodstock, was also a leader in the Democratic ranks. His brother, Jared
W. Williams, who had settled in Lancaster, N. H., gained much
political influence, filling the offices of governor, congressional representative, and senator. Amasa, grandson of Capt. Phinehas Walker,
after successfully engaging in business in West Brookfield and Boston,
had turned his thoughts to questions of political economy and progressive science. His cousins, Reverends Charles and Aldace Walker,
had won a high position among the ministry of Vermont. Willard,
son of Deacon Luther Child, was also a successful pastor. Asa and
Linus, sons of the much-respected Rensellaer Child, Esq., after graduating from Yale College, engaged successfully in legal practice in Norwich and Southbridge. Their younger brother remaining in Woodstock was an active Democrat, and so prominent in the Muddy Brook
meeting-house controversy that people thought his name must have been
prophetically suggested.—" And they called his name Peleg: for in his
days was the earth divided." Esquire McClellan, now advancing in
years, was less prominent in politics, but continued his various professional and public services, and by his courteous manners and tempered judgment exercised a healthful and beneficent influence, softening the asperities that were wont to prevail in this town. John
Paine, Sen., appointed judge of the Woodstock Probate Court in

1831, was much respected as one of the sterling men of the town. Amos Paine was an influential and public-spirited citizen, noted for "open-handed generosity." He was the especial friend and patron of Woodstock's few remaining Indians, who knew that food and shelter could always be found at his ample farm-house. The Nedson family still occupied their reservation near Hatchet Pond, swingling flax, chopping wood, weaving baskets and chair-bottoms, when not too full of liquor. It was perhaps one of the progenitors of this family who shouldered a barrel-full of cider and trudged home with it. A pail-full at a gulp was nothing for them. One by one they succumbed to drink or disaster. Jim Nedson was killed by a falling tree; his aged mother Meribah was thrown in the fire by a drunken savage. John, the last survivor, ended his days at the town poor-house, and the land they had so long occupied was sold by the town authorities.

Cotton and woolen manufacturing enterprises were not particularly successful in Woodstock, suffering severely from stress of freshet or business panic. Other industries met with better fortune. A carriage manufactory was initiated at Village Corners in 1835 by L. M. Deane and Co., which became very celebrated. Occupying at first the former foundry building and batting-mill, it soon demanded especial accommodations. Messrs. Lane, Morse, Torrey and Ezra C. Deane, were successively partners in this establishment, which achieved a high reputation, supplying a large section with excellent wagons and carriages. Woodstock also engaged with much zeal in the shoe-manufacture, so popular for a time in rural New England. Lyman Sessions in West Woodstock, the brothers P. O. and Z. D. Wight in Woodstock Valley, employed very many masculine and feminine hands in closing and binding shoes. A great amount of leather was furnished from Mr. Elias Mason's extensive tannery, which flourished greatly for a time. The financial storm of 1837 prostrated Sessions and Wight, but the carriage factory and tannery managed to weather it, and continued to furnish employment. Amasa Carpenter and others engaged later in shoe business, which flourished to such an extent that Woodstock in 1845 reported the manufacture of 5,651,580 pairs of shoes and fifty bushels of shoe pegs, accomplished by 4,918 males; 4,907 females. Six thousand wooden pails were also reported. Sewing-silk and thread were manufactured. The little Baptist meeting-house in Quasset was transformed into a twine factory. Pottery-making was kept up until the death of Mr. Thomas Bugbee in 1843. William Bowen, Esq., died in 1837, his son George succeeding to his various business and public offices. Rev. Eliphalet Lyman died in 1836. Rev. John D. Baldwin, who succeeded Mr. Underwood at West Woodstock, did good service in collating and preserving the church records. Doctors Lorenzo Marcy, Eleazer Litchfield, Milton Bradford and Asa Witter were enrolled in 1846 among Woodstock physicians. Its academy had greatly declined in standing and continued at a low ebb for some twenty years. The Thief Detecting Society having eaten up its fund in oyster and turkey suppers, re-organized in 1824 upon a new basis. Incorporation was secured, and the annual dinner restricted to such members as chose to pay for it out of their own pockets.

Thompson's cotton manufactories were now its dominant interest. A second factory and village were built up at Masonville, where Mr. Thomas Thatcher, as superintendent, maintained strict discipline. "Who is governor of Connecticut?" queried a passing traveler. "Mr. Fracher," lisped a little maid, echoing popular belief. Rough land and water privilege a mile north, were purchased in 1828 by Messrs William Fisher, John Nichols and Darius Dwight, and a factory soon built and working. Westward on the Quinebaug a mill and village were built, which mocking wits ironically dubbed New Boston, while Fisher's rocky settlement was long known as "Mount Hunger." Farther north on the French River, Laban T. Wilson and Josiah Perry were experimenting in satinets and woolen fabrics. Brick Factory enjoyed new prosperity under the management of William Reed, Esq., removed from Killingly—his son-in-law, George Larned, 2d, having charge of the usual factory store. An interesting manufacturing experiment was initiated in 1827, near the junction of the Quinebaug and French Rivers—Erastus Buck, Augustus Howe, Thomas and James Dike, Jude Sabin, John Chollar, Jacob Leavens, James Cunningham, associating as the Mechanics Company for the manufacture of woolen goods. A three-story woolen-mill was soon erected, also a saw-mill, and eight-tenement block for operatives. Mr. Howe served as agent; Messrs. Dike and Cunningham ran the machine-shop; Mr. Buck drove the mules, and Mr. Leavens the weavers. A work-shop bought with the land was turned into a school-house. Coöperative labor for some reason failed of immediate success, and after three years the association dissolved. Mechanicsville mills were operated for a time by different individuals and passed in 1838 into the hands of Mr. Smith Wilkinson.

Thompson Hill continued brisk and lively. The stages and cotton-teams passing daily over its turnpikes furnished abundant patronage for its excellent taverns; factory operatives sought needed supplies at its numerous stores. Mr. Erastus Knight opened a temperance store in the present post-office building in 1829. Captain Humphrey Almy and Talcott Crosby kept the usual assortment of goods in a new building opposite. The jeweler's store established by Mr. Edward Shaw of

Providence in 1830, was a very great novelty and attraction, factory girls delighting in its shining array of ornaments and trinkets, and men coming miles from all the surrounding country to buy new watches or have their old ones regulated. Coburn's well-known store was succeeded after a time by a very extensive millinery establishment, kept by Mrs. C. C. Dow. Mr. Hezekiah Olney, high-sheriff of the County, built a brick block between the tavern and town-house, and opened a fashionable "New York Hat and Cap store." Mr. Horatio Paine engaged largely in the manufacture of boots; Albert Whipple and James O. Mills enjoyed much celebrity and custom as fashionable tailors. Messrs. Baldwin, Hutchins, Kinney and Bates engaged in the manufacture of carriages and furniture. These business enterprises found financial accommodation in the Thompson Bank, incorporated May, 1833, and managed by an efficient board of directors.* Harvey Blashfield, president; Joseph B. Gay, cashier. Mr. William H. Mason succeeded to the presidency in a few years. This bank was largely patronized by manufacturers in Thompson and adjoining towns, and gained a high reputation for financial shrewdness and soundness. Able young lawyers from abroad were attracted by the growing fame of the village—George H. Middleton of Plainfield, Thomas E. Graves of Hebron, and a few years later, William S. Scarborough of Brooklyn.† Young editors sought it out as a favorable field for news paper enterprise. George Roberts, the somewhat famed publisher of the first cheap daily paper in Boston and the originator of the *Mammoth* newspaper, entered upon his journalistic career in a dainty little semi-weekly, called *The Thompson Transcript*. This was succeeded by *The Windham County Gazette*, published by another newspaper celebrity, the J. P. Chapman, told "to crow" in the Tippecanoe campaign, whose flapping rooster shared the honors of victory with "log cabins" and "hard cider." Thompson proved too narrow a sphere for such soaring spirits and their village newspapers had but a brief existence. Some interesting local events were recorded by them—the Probate Court constituted 1832, John Nichols, judge;

*THOMPSON BANK.—At a meeting of the stockholders of the Thompson Bank, held this day, the following gentlemen were elected Directors for the year ensuing, viz:—Harvey Blashfield, John Nichols, William H. Mason, William Reed, William Fisher, Robert Grosvenor, Franklin Nichols, Jonathan Nichols, Simon Davis, Talcott Crosby, George B. Slater. And at a subsequent meeting of the Directors, Harvey Blashfield, Esq., was re-elected President, and J. B. Gay, Cashier.
January 6th, 1835.

† These young lawyers showed excellent taste, not only in selecting so pleasant a site for their first legal ventures but one of them in almost immediately choosing for home partner the prettiest young lady that could be found in town. Mr. Middleton married the very charming daughter of Mr. Dow, and after a few years removed to Newark, New York, where he achieved a high position.

the Thompson Fire Engine Company, organized the same year, and the purchase of its jaunty little engine ; the organization of the Masonville Fire Engine Company in 1833, with twenty-four members ; the formation of a Thompson Society for Mental Improvement, the following year—Simeon Davis, Esq., president ; Joseph B. Gay, vice-president ; George Roberts, secretary. This society was well sustained for several years, discussing and deciding many debatable and highly important questions in morals, science and politics. Here the young lawyers met in debate with their seniors, Esquires Larned and Davis, and Doctors Holbrook and Bowen enjoyed the privilege of friendly combat. The latter, who came to Thompson in 1824, was extremely radical and versatile, alive to all new issues and "isms," while the former was eminently cautious and conservative. Both were good physicians and citizens, widely known throughout the surrounding country, and each had his devoted adherents, ready to take up arms in behalf of their own doctor.

One of the Thompson notabilities of this date was Captain Vernon Stiles, now in charge of the central tavern, who claimed that "more stage passengers dined there every day than at any other house in New England." Captain Stiles was the beau-ideal of a landlord, distinguished in person and manners, a genial host, a graceful speaker, an adroit politician. His bar-room was the headquarters of the Democratic party, now very powerful in town, and his spacious hall the scene of many a festive entertainment. Stiles' tavern was especially noted for its matrimonial facilities. Thompson's local position, cornering upon two States, afforded some peculiar advantages. Its "Line-taverns" enabled legal fugitives and liquor-sellers to dodge back and forth into Rhode Island and Massachusetts, and its convenient access tempted youthful lovers to evade the prolonged publishment required in the above States. A single notice read before or after church service satisfied legal requirements in Connecticut, and so it became very much the fashion for affianced pairs to drive to Thompson Hill on a Sunday and there celebrate their wedding. At first Mr. Dow, and other ministers performed the ceremony, but the occasions became so frequent and the consequent "Sabbath-breaking" so alarming, that they resigned the office to Captain Stiles as justice, who administered the vows with a grace and dignity that charmed all the participants. Scarce a Sabbath passed without bringing its wedding parties to partake of the wedding cake that was always made ready for them. "Run-aways" were united on more than one occasion, and Thompson Hill and its hymenial landlord were as celebrated for a time in the adjoining section as Gretna Green and its famous blacksmith in Great Britain. Thompson post-office was for many years administered by

Simon Davis, Esq., whose museum of curiosities and Indian relics shared public favor with "Mr. Shaw's shop" and "Stiles' tavern." He also administered the pension bureau for a large section of country to great acceptance, his tact and native kindliness peculiarly fitting him for that somewhat difficult position. Amongst all these notable residents of Thompson village, none probably made so much noise in the world as Mr. Obadiah Stone, the time-honored sexton, who was thought to bring more music out of a church bell than any man in Windham County.

Mr. Dow retained his physical and mental vigor, preaching indeed with increasing ease and animation. Though opposed to what were called "new measures" and revival machinery, he entered with great heartiness into the religious interest initiated through the agency of several succeeding "protracted meetings" when many were added to the church. Keenly alive to any taint of doctrinal unsoundness, he was still more aroused by questions relating to the growth of the church and the coming triumph of the Redeemer's Kingdom. He loved to preach upon the prophecies, the "shaking of the dry bones in the valley of vision," the restoration of the Jews, on which latter subject he would sometimes dilate till hearers thought they would return before he had finished his sermon. He was particularly opposed to the Millerite delusion, and delivered a series of sermons, which were largely attended and had very great influence, not one of his own congregation embracing the belief. His long experience and familiarity with the circumstances of every family, made him in his latter years most effective and impressive at funerals, which occasions he valued as special means of grace, reaching many who attended no other service. Softening with declining years, Mr. Dow relaxed somewhat from denominational exclusiveness and enjoyed pleasant fraternal intercourse with Baptist and Methodist ministers. A doctor's degree was conferred upon him by Williams College in 1840. Deacons Moses and Aaron Bixby were succeeded in office by Josiah Thayer and Charles Brown. After some years of unsuccessful experiment Elijah Crosby, Jun., Harry Gleason and Noadiah Wellington were chosen a committee to "report whether it be expedient to set up a Sunday school," and reporting in favor a school was established in 1825. Deacon Thayer was appointed superintendent in 1830. The public service of singing was now made more impressive by musical accompaniment on single and double bass-viols, and the scientific instruction of Watson, a very celebrated singing-master. A choir full of accomplished singers did credit to his training, and carried through a most successful Oratorio at the close of his school, May 28, 1823. Anthem and Chorus from Handel and Haydn's Creation, and

Daniel Dow Pastor of the Consociated Church in Thompson. —

many other popular pieces, called forth enthusiastic plaudits from a large and appreciative audience. Mr. James O. Mills succeeded Mr. Sharpe as leader of this choir, which maintained for many years a high reputation.

Elder James Grow assumed the charge of the Baptist church, in 1823, and served for eleven years with much fidelity and acceptance. The question of building a new meeting-house was now agitated, and increasing centralization led to its location on Thompson Hill. Deacon Stephen Crosby gave much care and oversight to its construction, and in 1836 it was occupied by Elder Bela Hicks and part of the church and congregation. Elder Harvey Fittz succeeded in charge the following year when a pleasant revival was enjoyed and a number added to the church. During the succeeding pastorate of Rev. Silas Bailey the church continued to prosper and received large accessions. Jason Elliott and George Davis were ordained as deacons in May, 1840. The house on Brandy Hill was still occupied by a part of the church. Elder Grow continued in charge till laid aside by increasing infirmities. He was succeeded by Elder James Smither, an earnest worker, much interested in temperance and kindred reforms. Elder Branch followed for two years, during which time his flock essayed to worship in the central house, but after a year's trial it returned to its old home, and soon after erected a new house of worship. April 8, 1846, by mutual consent of both branches the church was divided and two new churches formed. Elder Charles Willett had succeeded Rev. L. G. Leonard in charge of the Central church. The venerable Elder Grow was able for a time to minister to the East Thompson Baptist church. Thompson was now so strong a rallying point of Methodism as to give its name to the former "Pomfret circuit." Methodists in Pomfret Factory and Rhodesville, as well as in all parts of the town, repaired to the West Thompson meeting-house, which was bisected and enlarged to accommodate the increasing congregation. A convenient new meeting-house was erected in 1840, when Thompson and Eastford were united in a circuit, embracing seven hundred members. New societies were soon after formed and church buildings erected in Fisherville and East Thompson. Messrs. Faxon and George Nichols, and Jonathan Nichols, Esq., were very active and efficient in building up the Methodist interest in the town. So also was their brother-in-law, Rev. Hezekiah Ramsdell, who made his home in West Thompson, while preaching in various fields with much eloquence and acceptance. He was greatly interested in education and horticulture, and did good service in town, raising the character of the schools and stimulating the cultivation of flowers and choice fruit. Mr. Faxon Nichols was the first postmaster in West Thompson. Jonathan Nichols served

68

for many years as county surveyor, and as judge of Probate, and public offices were also filled by his son-in-law, Joseph Perrin.

The decline of Woodstock Academy gave Thompson an opportunity to indulge in intermittent High Schools. A select school was taught by Miss Caroline Dutch, more especially devoted to polite accomplishments. Its influence was doubtless perceptible on that very interesting occasion when the ladies of the town presented an elegant banner to the newly-uniformed popular Rifle Company—John J. Green, captain; Herbert A. Reed, lieutenant; Stephen Crosby, ensign. The ease and address of the young ladies who made the presentation were no less conspicuous than their exceeding grace and beauty. Select schools were also taught by Messrs. Wilmoth, Cooley and Matthew Mills. A High School opened by Thomas P. Green of Auburn, Mass., in 1837, gained a more permanent standing and wider reputation. Many pupils came from neighboring towns and States. Its exhibitions held in the Congregational church edifice were very notable and largely attended. The old tavern-house, now fallen into disrepute, was purchased by Messrs. Joseph B. Gay and William H. Mason in 1840, and transformed into an academy and boarding-house. In this convenient domicile, the school flourished proportionably and boasted an unusual number of bright and promising pupils.

The temperance reform, which at first made slow advances in Thompson, received a new impulse through the labors of John Hawkins, who spoke for many nights in the central meeting-house with his usual power and effect. Several men long known as common drunkards and considered beyond the reach of effort came forward and signed the pledge, and Captain Stiles closed his bar, and made his popular tavern a *temperance house.* The town temperance society was now reorganized with Mr. W. H. Mason for president, and other prominent men for officers. The adjacent manufacturers, Messrs. Fisher, Thatcher and Reed, the ministers, deacons, merchants, lawyers, doctors, and hundreds of other citizens, attended the temperance meetings and helped carry forward the movement. In 1843, John B. Gough was engaged for a week's labor, speaking to large and deeply affected audiences in the newly-completed town-house* and various school-houses throughout the town. His earnest words made a deep and lasting impression, and

---

* This town-house was the first building erected on the south side of the street. Mr. Whitman Jacobs broke ground on the north side about 1835, and was soon followed by Messrs. Kinney, Knight, Shaw, Graves and Comins, who built a row of neat houses, and set out a line of maples. Mrs. Thatcher built the first dwelling-house on the south side of the street. These residents were greatly annoyed by vicinity to the famous "Ponog," which with house, barn and blacksmith's shop, in linked squalor, long drawn-out, occupied the western apex of the adjacent common.

had much influence in arousing and intensifying temperance sentiment. Only one drinking-place was left in the village, the well-known "ponog" on the western point of the common, occupying the site of a former gravestone manufactory. This peculiar name, brought up from Rhode Island by some of Dorr's fugitives, was derived from Apanogue, supposed to indicate "a place of fair water," but the eliminated "ponog" meant a place for *fire-water*, and was used to designate the lowest species of rum-hole. The Thompson Ponog fully sustained its name and reputation, and in spite of all the efforts and eloquence of temperance workers remained for many years a disgrace to the village.

VIII.

KILLINGLY. POMFRET. POMFRET FACTORY.

KILLINGLY is reported by Barber in 1836—"the greatest cotton-manufacturing town in the State." Its reputation and resources had been magnified by the building up of Williamsville on the Quinebaug and Dayville on the Five-Mile River. Dayville was commended "for its neat appearance, and for a bridge composed of two finely constructed stone arches, each 25 feet broad and 12 feet high." Captain John Day sold two-thirds of this privilege to Prosper and William Alexander, and joined with them in building and equipping a cotton factory in 1832. Caleb Williams of Providence purchased the Quinebaug privilege and erected a handsome stone building in 1827. This village was also attractive for its neat appearance and good order. Danielson's Mills had passed into the hands of the sons of General Danielson, and began to be noted "as a thriving village." The temperance reform had swept away the distillery at Mason's factory, and "Gin-town" was transformed into Ruggles' Factory. The Killingly Company owning Howe's Factory was reorganized in 1828. Smaller factories on the Five-Mile River were run by Ballou and Amsbury. The carding machine on the outlet of Alexander's Lake had been superseded by a woolen factory. Great activity prevailed in the east part of the town, where some half-dozen mills were propelled by the lively little Whetstone, under the patronage of Ebenezer Young, Richard Bartlett, Prosper Leffingwell, Asa Alexander, John S. Harris, Thomas Pray, and others. An aggregate of twenty-five thousand spindles was reported, with three woolen mills, one furnace, one axe factory. In 1840, Killingly boasted the largest population in Windham County, having gained upon Thompson which stood at the head in 1830.

As business gravitated to the valleys and centre, Killingly Hill was forced to resign the leadership, though the flourishing stores of "Ely and Torrey," opened in 1835, and its competitor, A. A. Austin, prolonged its business activity for several years.   Mr. Ely afterwards removed to Norwich, while his younger brother, Edwin, established business in Danielsonville in 1837.   Flourishing stores and shops were maintained in East Brooklyn where the Tiffanys carried on extensive business in various departments.   Isaac T. Hutchins' store accommodated Westfield residents.   A second lawyer was now established in this village—Mr. Thomas Backus of Sterling, a graduate of Brown University, who was made judge of the newly-constituted Probate Court in 1830.   His father-in-law, Hon. Ebenezer Young, was much occupied with public duties, serving six years as representative to Congress, 1829-35.   He was also actively concerned in the organization of reformatory agencies, co-operating with the friends of peace and temperance in their public efforts.   Killingly's justices at this date were Arba Covill, David Chase, Thomas Backus, William Alexander, Daniel Brown, George Warren, Jedidiah Leavens, Leonard Ballou, George Danielson, Norman Kelley, N. A. Durfee.   Jeremiah Field and Jonathan Dexter, served as town clerks.   It was remarkably well accommodated with post-offices having five allowed in 1836, viz:—North, Luther Warren, Postmaster; Centre, J. Field; East, H. Peckham; South, Cyrus Day; West, George Danielson.   It also showed much spirit in organizing fire companies, meeting at the house of Silas Hutchins, June, 1829, to enlist not more than sixteen persons resident in Westfield Society as "The Enterprise Fire Engine Company."   Liberty was given four years later to add eight men from "the factory village in Brooklyn."   " Williamsville Fire Engine Company was organized in 1833."   After many efforts Killingly succeeded in procuring a specific residence for the poor whose keeping was intrusted to the lowest bidder.   A *very poor* house it was according to the testimony of old Martha Sonsamon, taken there to end her days after her wigwam was blown over.   "How do you like your new home?" asked a visitor sympathetically.   "Pretty well, 'cos we live just like Injuns," was the quick reply.   This last representative of Killingly's aboriginal inhabitants lived to a good old age, losing much of her ancient ferocity, and was treated with great kindness.

Westfield retained for many years its energetic pastor, Mr. Whitmore, who engaged with much zeal in temperance work and other reforms.   Its church increased proportionably with the growth of the surrounding villages, and enjoyed many seasons of special religious interest. Its Sabbath-school ante-dated nearly every other in Windham County, being organized and well-established in 1820. Isaac T. Hutchins, one of some fifty converts who joined the church during this year, was elected superintendent. Testaments furnished by the town Bible Society served for text-book and library. The session was chiefly occupied in repeating Scripture verses committed to memory the previous week. Some ambitious children could repeat two hundred verses, and several during the first year had stored up half the New Testament. The revival of 1832 brought into the church about 150 members. Adam B. Danielson and Warren Stearns were chosen deacons in 1828. The various benevolent societies connected with this church were well sustained. Rev. Israel Day resigned his charge in 1826. His mortuary record kept for forty years showed a great mortality, three hundred and seventy-eight having died out of the church and congregation. Emigration also weakened the South Killingly church so that it was no longer able to settle a pastor. Forty were added to the membership in 1832, through the labors of John H. Whipple, who held the charge for three years.

The East Killingly Baptist church added largely to its members in 1821, but suffered afterwards a serious declension. Through the friendly mediation of advisory brethren difficulties were healed and aggrieved parties restored. Elder Cooper resigned his charge in 1828, but continued active in the church. Elder George Appleton was succeeded in 1830, by Albert Cole of Plainfield, called to the pastoral work by the unanimous voice of the church. Delegates from Thompson, Pomfret, Brooklyn and Plainfield, were invited to join in a council with the former pastors of the church, Elders Cooper and Appleton, and Brethren Silas Slater, Sampson Covill, Samuel Bullock, Benjamin Brown and Nicholas A. Durfee. After some delay Mr. Cole was ordained pastor, December 1, 1830, sermon by Rev. Thomas Barrett, consecrating prayer, Rev. James Grow, charge, Rev. G. B. Atwell. Revival influences continued, and the church gained in strength and numbers. The succeeding pastorates of Elders Oatley and Doty were marred by renewed strife and disagreements, which were happily allayed in the three years ministry of Elder Branch. A new church edifice was now built in the vicinity of the factory villages, which was enlarged during the succeeding ministry of Elder Smither. A somewhat heterodox element which had long existed in this vicinity was absorbed into the Free Will Baptist church organized previous to 1840. The old Field tavern near the town-house was now occupied by Kingsbury. Doctors Justin Hammond and Daniel Hovey engaged in medical practice in East and South Killingly. The former "city" had lost its ancient prestige, with the decline of Captain Gaston's store and the growth of new villages.

Mr. Atkins continued in sole charge of the church on Killingly Hill till 1832, when after nearly a half-century's service he was compelled to employ a colleague. Reverends William Bushnell, Sidney Holman and Henry Robinson were successively installed in office—the latter remaining in charge several years after the death of the venerable pastor in 1839. Dr. Grosvenor, now advancing in years, was aided in his extensive practice by his son, Dr. William Grosvenor. The old hill tavern, now kept by Captain George Warren, was still a place of much public resort, and the village had not lost its social standing. Among its social acquisitions was Mr. Joseph Torrey, one of the promising young men instructed by Mr. Atkins, who engaged in legal practice in Detroit with bright prospect of professional eminence. Suddenly disabled by an unfortunate accident resulting in paralysis, he returned to his old home, a crippled invalid. But though often suffering intense pain his mind retained its vigor and brilliancy, and his varied learning and remarkable conversational powers, his patient submission to Providential dealings, made his prolonged life a rich blessing to those around him. Other young men who went out into the world from Killingly accomplished most dissimilar destinies. The sons of Messrs. Tiffany and Young engaged in business in New York city, establishing a house and name, since famed throughout the world. Frank Alexander gained a place in the foremost rank of American artists. His success was not achieved without a struggle. A farmer's son, brought up to work on the farm without even knowing the existence of art, his inborn genius early asserted itself. As a boy he was always "picturin' out sunthin." Barn-door and walls were ornamented with chalk-drawn birds and fanciful creations, and noon-time spent in making "curious" sketches for little girls while his mates were playing. His passion for color was first excited by the beautiful tints of freshly-caught fish, and he wrought out imitations that old fishermen said might have been taken for real perch and pickerel. Praise received for these and other copies from nature impelled the embryo artist to sally forth to New York "to learn to paint." Calling on the way upon Mr. Prescott Hall in Pomfret, he gave him letters to his brother, Mr. Charles Hall, who received him very kindly, took him to galleries of paintings and recommended him to instructors. Some time passed before he succeeded in finding willing and competent teachers, but he continued his practice and ventured an experiment in portrait-painting. Rude pictures painted on old chest-lids astonished every one by vividness of representation. His fame soon traveled to Thompson, where he was engaged to paint the portraits of several families, receiving "three dollars a head and his board." With the money thus earned he again sped to New York for further instruction. Colonel Trumbull and his fellow-countyman, Samuel Waldo, gave him counsel and encouragement. Portraits painted after his return for the extravagant price of eight dollars, were taken to Providence and greatly admired. "That's a *very vigilant* old lady," remarked a critic of one of these rough sketches. These early efforts were indeed characterized by a life-likeness that he never afterward surpassed. Through the kindness of Mrs. James B. Mason, Mr. Alexander obtained access to some of the best families in Providence, and her untiring efforts in his behalf were ever remembered by him with affectionate gratitude. From this time his progress was rapid. He was received most kindly in Boston by Gilbert Stuart, who pronounced his pictures "very clever," lacking things that might be gained by practice and study, but having "that which could not be acquired." Fastidious Boston confirmed this verdict. His fine personal appearance and engaging manners gave him access to the higher circles, and fortune now lavished her favors. Marrying a lady of beauty, wealth and high family connection, he went abroad in 1831 upon an extended tour, returning to pursue his art with extraordinary dexterity and success. Boston may thank Killingly for some prominent celebrities—Joseph Howe, the admired pastor of New South Church, Alexander the popular portrait-painter, and a recent popular mayor—also governor of Massachusetts.

As other towns gained post-office and probate privileges, Pomfret declined from its pristine prominence, its population diminishing each succeeding decade after 1820, when it had attained its maximum, 2,042. Its prominent men passed away. Col. Thomas Grosvenor* died in 1825; Dr. Hall, Judge Lemuel Ingalls, General Lemuel Grosvenor, followed in a few years. Dr. Hubbard was called to surgical professorship in Yale's medical college. Elisha B. Perkins was compelled by ill health to seek a milder climate. The sons of Dr. Hall, and other enterprising young men, went to New York and other cities; the Rossiters and Sweetings removed from town. New families came in, young men grew up to fill the vacant places. Dr. Holt

* Another honored son of Pomfret, the late David Hall, Esq., New York city, bears ample testimony in his Grosvenor Genealogical notes to the distinguished merit of Colonel Thomas Grosvenor, as "a patriot pure and unsullied, a soldier, who by his justice, firmness, strict adherence to principle, and nobleness of character, shed lustre on the military name—who adorned society by his example and virtues: a valued counsellor, most venerable and respected." The various important public offices intrusted to him had been filled with credit to himself and satisfaction to his fellow-citizens. His kinsman, Gen. Lemuel Grosvenor, had also honored many important offices in town, filling a high position in militia service, and for nearly forty years administering the post-office to universal acceptance.

of Hampton succeeded to much of the medical practice of his former instructor. Thomas M. Grosvenor served as town clerk and treasurer and probate clerk. The three great needs of the town were poor-house, town-house, meeting-houses. "The house of Col. Calvin Day," was made a work-house in 1824. Elisha B. Perkins, Darius Matthewson and Lemuel Ingalls were directed to consider the condition of the poor, and consult with other towns. The town-house was a very serious question, prolonged for many years. The great meeting-house in the First society had now become too large for the congregation, and it was proposed to rebuild it with basement accommodations for secular use. The town declined to aid, *particularly* in building basement. A proposed road from West Woodstock to Brooklyn excited much opposition. At a meeting in Abington meeting-house, August 8, 1831, Deacon Joshua Grosvenor, moderator: "refused to accept road laid out through lands of Ingalls and others; refused to build a town-house; agreed to meet in Abington till the town provided a more suitable place." In the following year, Thomas M. Grosvenor, George Sharpe and Smith Wilkinson were appointed committee to confer with the societies, and see on what terms they could obtain their meeting-houses for the use of the town. A committee of one from each school-district, viz: George Cady, Hiram Holt, Samuel Underwood, Smith Wilkinson, William James, Charles Chandler, Lemuel Holmes, William Osgood, Robert D. Sharpe, George Randall, John Williams, Orin Morey—was chosen to make inquiries as to the cost of a town-house, which resulted in farther postponement. Meanwhile the First Society had achieved a new church edifice. A hundred pairs of stockings knit by the deft fingers of Pomfret matrons and maidens secured a building lot east of the former site from Dr. Waldo, a temporary resident, who also furnished the wool from which the yarn had been previously spun by the nimble knitters. Col. Zephaniah Williams, Harvey Holmes and George B. Matthewson served as building committee; Lemuel Holmes, master-builder. Materials taken from the old house were freely used in its construction. Mr. Porter asked dismission in 1830; Rev. Amzi Benedict installed pastor the following year; the meeting-house dedicated, October, 1832. The still phenomenal organ was played by Miss Elizabeth Vinton, the only person in town, it is said, competent for the service. A deep and powerful religious revival was experienced during Mr. Benedict's short pastorate, bringing many into the church, and impressing the whole community. His successor, Rev. Daniel Hunt, was ordained, April 4, 1835, and most worthily filled the place of esteemed predecessors. He was especially interested in the collation and preservation of town and church history, and compiled a "History of Pomfret" for a Thanksgiving discourse, 1840, remarkably full, clear and accurate. The church enjoyed at this time the services of two excellent deacons—the brothers Zephaniah and Job Williams. The former died in 1838, not having "attained unto the days of the years" of the fathers who preceded him. Deacon Simon Cotton died in 1819; Deacon Hayward in 1823, aged 91 years; Deacon Grosvenor in 1829, aged 81. Deacon John H. Payson in 1825. Lewis Averill was elected in place of Colonel Williams.

Episcopalians in Pomfret worshipped with those in Brooklyn till 1828, when the parish of Christ Church was organized. A church edifice was built the following year. Rev. Ezra Kellogg officiated in Christ and Trinity churches. Rev. Roswell Park assumed the sole charge of the Pomfret church in 1843, and opened a select school which gained a very high reputation. Dr. Park was a thorough scholar, a strict disciplinarian, and his nine years' incumbency left abundant fruits. The Baptist church maintained service and pastors during this period, though weakening by the constant outflow to the valleys. Rev. Walter Lyon remained in charge of the Abington church till his death in 1826. His habits of order, discipline and exactness continued through life, his clock and desk were never moved from the spot selected for them on his first occupation of the ministerial homestead. He left a generous bequest to the society and gave liberally to benevolent objects. Rev. Charles Fitch, a noted revivalist, was installed pastor in 1828. A very powerful revival was experienced in 1831, in connection with "a four-days'-meeting." Thirty-three persons united with the church the following January; fifty-nine during the pastorate. He was followed in 1834, by Rev. Nathan S. Hunt, who retained the charge eleven years. Abington's usual placidity was greatly disturbed during his ministry by a controversy about building a new meeting-house. "Two* strong parties were formed and drawn up in battle array; the one desiring a new location on the hill a few rods east of the parsonage; the other preferring to have the house built on the old foundation. After the heat of the controversy had passed away, a compromise was effected, and the society voted to repair thoroughly the old meeting-house." Alanson Peck, Samuel P. Sumner and John R. Holbrook served as committee. Repairs were accomplished to general satisfaction, and the renovated house has since been maintained in excellent condition, the oldest church edifice now occupied in Windham County. George Sharpe succeeded to the position of chorister. Elisha Lord and William Osgood, Jun., were chosen deacons in 1831. A Sabbath-school was organized in 1826, Deacon Wyllis Goodell, superintendent. Abington was very active

* Historical Discourse, delivered by Rev. H. B. Smith.

69

in temperance work, taking the initiative in forming the first society in town. Judge Lemuel Ingalls, so respected for integrity and sound judgment, died at an advanced age. Captain Elisha Lord died in 1826, having led the choir till the Sunday before his death. A Second Advent church was formed in Abington about 1840—Dr. Thomas Huntington of Brooklyn officiating as its pastor.

Renewed agitation of the town-house question was followed by a most spirited controversy. At a meeting at the south school-house, April, 1840, voted, to build a town-house—Smith Wilkinson, George Sharpe, Lemuel Holmes, G. S. Ingalls, George Cady, committee. The site of the new edifice was next discussed, which elicited almost as many different opinions as there were voters. One clique advocated "a spot near Haskell's tavern;" another, "a spot near the south school-house;" a third, "place near Stebbins' store." A motion "to erect on land of Colonel Day, near the house formerly occupied by Capt. E. Fitch," was carried by a vote of 47 to 37, but on proposing to levy a tax it was at once reconsidered and rescinded by 46 to 26. Pausing through the summer, hostilities were resumed in December. Meeting after meeting was held. Propositions to build "on south end of burying-ground near Mr. Lemuel Hayward's;" "near Larned Haskell's;" "near Stebbins' store;" "on land of Sessions near Stebbinsville," were successively rejected. An interesting meeting was held, January 2, 1841—George Sharpe, moderator. Proposed to build "near dwelling-house of William Segur," nays 161, yeas 61; "near Averill's," nays 128, yeas 81; "near house of Larned Haskell, he offering to give land," yeas 138, nays 83. Lewis Averill, Charles Chandler and George B. Matthewson were continued committee and instructed to proceed to build immediately, but at the next meeting the vote was rescinded, Col. Calvin Day's land selected, and new committee appointed, viz: George Cady, Edward Eldredge, John Williams. April 12, rescinded vote and affixed a spot between Segur's and Four Corners. April 24, "rescind last vote and locate on land of William Sabin between school-house and Quaker meeting-house." George A. Dresser and Pitt Sharpe added to committee. It was next decided to invite Jonathan Nichols of Thompson, Philip Pearl of Hampton and Arba Covill of Killingly "to hear and decide," and "*rescind former vote*." Fortunately for all, this was the last act of *rescission*. At a town-meeting, June 8, voted to accept committee's report affixing site on land of Frederic Averill, committee to lay foundation and proceed. Greatly to the credit of all parties, this long contention had been carried on without acrimony, if not with positive sportiveness, and all united in hastening the erection of the new town-house, which was opened to the public, October 4, 1841. Deacon Job Williams now

Smith. Wilkinson

served as town clerk and treasurer, John Williams as judge of Probate. Its only lawyer was John Holbrook of Abington. Doctors Lewis and Elisha Williams engaged in medical practice. Dr. Alexander Vinton practiced for a short time in Abington before entering the Church ministry. With the multiplication of newspapers and magazines, Pomfret libraries were less needed and patronized, though the Abington Ladies' Library still retained its place in the affection of its founders. New books were added and old ones carefully conned, stimulating the intellectual proclivities of the daughters of Pomfret. Miss Abby Allen was now quite noted as a writer, publishing a volume of poems and contributing to newspaper and magazine. Miss Anne Hall was most successfully pursuing her art in New York city, her miniatures characterized "by the most exquisite ideality of design and coloring." Groups of children executed by her are among the finest specimens of ivory miniatures. She was the first woman elected member of the American National Academy of Design, and was ranked among the first American artists. Her reputation had extended to other countries and some of her works were honored in France by preservation in enamel.

Pomfret Factory pursued its way in very independent fashion, asking little of the mother town but postal facilities and occasional road or bridge outlay. Mr. Wilkinson was emphatically the autocrat of the village, and his strong will and marked individuality gave it a peculiar character. Everything went on like clock-work. Accounts and morals were looked after with equally keen scrutiny. No man was allowed to overrun his credit, get drunk or misbehave on Sunday. Religious services were held in the brick school-house whenever practicable, and operatives encouraged to attend church in the neighboring towns. Pomfret Factory was remarkably exempt from the immoralities and disorders incident to the ordinary factory village of the period. Houses and yards were kept neat, loafing prohibited, children sent to school as the law required. Respect for legal authority was indeed one of the leading characteristics of Mr. Wilkinson. Even the annual Fast-day must be kept as sacredly as the Sabbath, and young men who presumed upon their position to indulge in the "vain recreation" of ball-playing as by "law forbidden," were arrested and fined with none the less promptness because the son of a venerated minister, his own relatives, and favorite clerks, were among the transgressors. Yet notwithstanding this severity of discipline, there was much that was pleasant and enjoyable in life at the old Pomfret Factory. The master was the owner, having his home with his people, taking a personal interest in all their affairs, and that home was one of the most cheerful and attractive in Windham County. Not only did it offer a

most cordial and graceful welcome to throngs of visitors from the adjoining towns, but its light and warmth seemed to permeate the village, tempering the austerity of autocratic authority, and bringing its
residents into a family connection, with a common head and interest.
As yet the operatives were native families, drawn from the surrounding country, taking pride in the place and even in the peculiarities of
its master, which furnished inexhaustible discussion and anecdote.   A
man born to rule will always find willing subjects, and Mr. Wilkinson
was none the less esteemed because he could command obedience.
Young men employed by him in store or office acquired good business
habits and were almost sure to succeed in after life.   William K.
Greene, afterwards of Woodstock, Lemuel Elliott, the faithful steward of Brown University, Davis and Jedidiah Leavens, and many other
young men who engaged successfully in manufacturing and other enterprises, served business apprenticeship for a time in Pomfret Factory.
The impression left upon these young men by its varied social and
local attractions as rhythmically expressed by J. Erskine Dow, who
served as clerk for a time, gives a pleasant picture of the Pomfret Factory of other days :—

> "Sweet vale of Pomfret! 'tis to thee
> I offer now my poesy.
> The spot which boyhood hallowed dear
> Has lived in memory many a year,
> And still within the minstrel's breast
> It gives to his dark hours a zest.
> His fancy paints thee now so bright,
> With thy broad stream of liquid light,
> Thy rocky caves, thy shady bowers,
> Thy meadows carpeted with flowers,
> Thy waterfall, thy busy mill,
> The little school-house on the hill,
> The village bursting into view,
> With its old inn beneath the yew—
> Till ages seem to roll away
> And thou stand forth as yesterday.
> Yes! lovely vale!   Oh, who can tell
> How memory loves with thee to dwell?
> How sweet the thoughts that thou recall,
> Thou never-ceasing waterfall!
> Though years have rolled themselves away
> Since last I heard thy waters play,
> As down thy craggy rocks they rolled,
> A sheet of purple, white and gold,
> Still when the woes of life assail
> I sigh for thee, sweet Pomfret vale."

In 1826, Mr. Wilkinson became chief proprietor as well as manager,
associating with Mr. James Rhodes in place of the former company.
A substantial stone building was now erected, and the old factory devoted to manufacturing woolen goods.   More houses and workmen
were thus demanded, and business operations extended.   The Rhodes

village, northward, grew up rapidly, successfully competing with Pomfret Factory.   In 1835, a road was laid out from South Woodstock, intersecting the Hartford Turnpike near Simeon Allen's brick works, and
thence to the Quinebaug near the north house of Rhodesville, and on
through the South Neighborhood to the Woodstock and Thompson
turnpike, in the vicinity of Sawyer's store—which greatly facilitated
communication with Providence and the adjoining towns.   Yet with
all the skill and good management of Messrs. Wilkinson, Rhodes and
other Windham County manufacturers, development was restricted by
the cost and difficulty of transportation.   The supply of cotton was
limited ; expansion in other directions was impeded.   The villages
built up by them were merely " factory villages," communities of
working-men and their families appended to the inevitable cotton-mill.
The men at the head, the owners and managers, influencing and sometimes controlling the votes of the operatives, were gaining power and
political influence, but their villages as such were of no account
compared with those which looked down upon them from their several
hill-tops.   "The gods of the hills were yet stronger than the gods of
the valleys."   The old hill-top villages with their meeting-houses,
academies and social privileges ; their turnpikes, taverns and dashing
stage-coaches ; their trainings, town-meetings and great public gatherings ; their lawyers, doctors, stores and mechanical enterprises—were
still the dominant power.   The manufactures established in other
parts of the town had brought them business and prosperity.   In
many respects there had been great improvement since the advent of
the century.   Business had developed, money had become more plentiful, comforts and conveniences had multiplied, great reforms had
been effected, new institutions had grown up, the mode of living had
greatly changed—but numerical strength had diminished.   The increase in manufacturing villages had not made up the loss of the southwest towns and the constant westward outflow.   After a period of
growth and activity there came, after the financial revulsion of 1837–38,
a pause if not a retrogression, and again the question was raised if
development had not reached its maximum, and again was answered
by the introduction of new agencies and motors.

BOOK X. 1840-1880.

THE PRESENT OUTLOOK.

MODERN Windham dates its birth from the first whistle of the steam engine. That clarion cry awoke the sleeping valleys. Energy, enterprise, progress followed its course. At every stopping-place new life sprung up. Factory villages received immediate impetus, and plentiful supply of cotton. Larger manufacturing enterprises were speedily planned and executed, foreign help brought in ; capital and labor, business and invention, rushed to the railroad stations ; innumerable interests and industries developed—and in less than a score of years the County was revolutionized. The first had become last and the last first. The turnpike was overgrown, stage-coach and cotton team had vanished, the old hill villages had lost the leadership, and new railroad centres held the balance of power, and drew to themselves the best blood and energies of the towns. As other railroads were opened and business facilities increased its progress became more rapid, and the Windham County of 1880 is far more populous and prosperous than that of 1840. It has within its limits four railroads and admirable business facilities. A few hours easy ride connects it with Norwich, Worcester, Providence, Boston and New York. It has five or six newspapers of its own, and leading city dailies; telegraphs, telephones and other modern improvements. It has manufacturing establishments unsurpassed in the country. It has its graded schools, elaborate church edifices, public cemeteries, lofty town buildings, its summer visitors, its market gardens, its Roseland Park—and it has also its trotting parks, its grog-shops, its foreign element, its "rings," its town debts, and all the usual accompaniments of modern civilization. The Windham County of to-day as typified by its business centres is wide-awake, progressive; a true child of the Nineteenth Century.

PUTNAM.

One of the most characteristic and prominent of these later up growths is the village of Putnam. Sleepy Rip Van Winkles who stray in occasionally to take a peep at Cargill's Falls and the long-gone Pomfret Factory are sorely bewildered. Old landmarks have vanished, the forests are gone, the hills leveled or built up with houses, the very graves of their fathers removed to an ornamented cemetery. The roar of the Falls is drowned in the clatter of machinery and steam engine. The homes and workshops of an enterprising and varied population crowd the narrow vale, and stretch out over the hills on every side. Gradually and naturally the transformation has been effected. The Pomfret Factory station on the Norwich and Worcester *Railroad opened in 1839, was the outlet for Pomfret, Woodstock, parts of Killingly and Thompson, and a wide radius inland. A depot village sprang up at once, business flowed in. Enterprising men saw the great natural advantages of the site, bought up land and built houses. Young men from the hill towns experimented in store-keeping. Lawyers and doctors doubtfully hung out their signs. Asa Cutler of Killingly, was one of the first capitalists to invest in the growing village, building a brick block for stores and many dwelling-houses. Its first physicians were Doctors Hough, Plimpton and Perry; its first lawyer, Harrison Johnson. L. K. and C. Perrin, Manning and Searls, Williams and Ely, were among the first to engage in trade. J. O. Fox, postmaster in West Thompson, moved his office to Putnam Depot and set up a grocery store. Mr. Wilkinson, now old and cautious, foresaw the coming tide but did not care to engage in new enterprises. Rhodesville was greatly favored by manufacturing development. Handsome stone factories were erected between 1846-48, by Hosea Ballou of Woonsocket, G. C. Nightingale and Co., M. S. Morse and Co., of Providence, bringing great influx of foreign help as well as capital. As usual in such rapid growth there were clashings and rivalries between the different villages, business interests and religious denominations. Baptists were first in the field, holding services in the Brick school-house and afterwards in the depot building. A Baptist church was organized August 24, 1847, with forty members, and the following year a church edifice was erected on land given by Mr. Wilkinson. Congregationalists worshipped in the school house and Quinebaug Hall, organizing a church in 1848, with twenty-seven members gathered from twelve churches. Their house of

---

*The first cars ran from Norwich to Worcester, Thanksgiving Day, 1839. The first survey of the road was made by William Lester of Norwich, afterward surveyor of Windham County. He also had charge of building the New England Road from Putnam to Willimantic. Mr. Lester merits remembrance, also, for his admirable " Map of New London and Windham Counties," published in 1833, with a Geological Map on the same sheet, prepared by Lieut. W. W. Mather, son of Capt. Eleazer Mather of Brooklyn, Conn., afterward State Geologist of New York. Mr. Lester spent his closing years in Woodstock.

worship was completed in 1852, on land given by Messrs. Wilkinson and Dorrance. Methodists worshipped for a time with the society in West Thompson. Reverends Lucius Holmes, Charles Willett, G. J. Tillotson, E. B. Huntington, D. D. Lyon, Solomon Gale, Hezekiah Ramsdell, Sidney Deane, Charles Morse, were associated with these early religious efforts.

With increasing business and population difficulties multiplied. A double-headed village with half a dozen names, embraced within three distinct towns, was anomalous and hard to manage. It was very agreeable to supply these out-lying towns with railroad and market privileges, but extremely *disagreeable* to resort to them to vote and consult records. Expansion and improvement were restricted by dependence upon their sovereign will and pleasure. Voting places and borough privileges suggested as modes of relief would fail to meet the difficulty, as inhabitants of separate towns with alien interests might not unite harmoniously in efforts for the public good of this particular section. The proposal to consolidate as a distinct, independent township, broached in 1849, met immediate favor. Mr. Wilkinson and his son heartily approved the project and joined with other citizens in petition and effort. Vehement opposition from representatives of four towns readily procured the rejection of the first petition. Leaving out Woodstock land, the petitioners in 1851 endeavored to secure parts of Pomfret, Thompson and Killingly. Beaten again and again, they still kept heart and returned to the charge. The old towns fought with great valor and persistency, especially Thompson, whose relative position in wealth and population would be greatly changed by the loss of Rhodesville and her old South Neighborhood, but were forced to submit to the inevitable course of progress and "manifest destiny." Taking PUTNAM for their name and pattern, the new-town champions battled bravely on. The rise of the Know-nothing party and political combinations turned the scale in their favor. The final trial in May, 1855, excited unusual interest in the State. Very able counsel was employed on both sides. The closing arguments were heard in one of the largest halls in Hartford, which was crowded with eager listeners. Hon. Charles Chapman made one of his most brilliant efforts in behalf of the old towns. He was answered by one of Windham County's own orators, Ex-Governor Cleveland, whose sympathies were strongly enlisted in the development of manufacturing enterprise and railroad centralization, and who carried committee, assembly and audience with him in his masterly exposition of the true sources of municipal power and prosperity, and his plea that the petitioners should be allowed their reasonable request for expansion and independence. Six years of arduous conflict were rewarded by

70

triumphant victory, which was joyfully celebrated on the succeeding
Fourth of July.   Town organization was effected the day preceding ;
George Warren, moderator ; James W. Manning was chosen town clerk
and treasurer; George Warren, Horace Seamans, L. Hopkins, selectmen.
Putnam's subsequent career was typified in the result of this struggle.
Her energy and unconquerable resolution have overborne every opposing obstacle.   Built up mainly by the gradual drawing in of men of
moderate means, her growth has been steady and healthful.   With
few large capitalists, she has had the good fortune to attract many
sterling men of energy and public spirit, ever ready to bear their
share in schemes for public improvement.   The junction of the "New
York and New England railroad" with the "Norwich and Worcester,"
has greatly stimulated her later growth and development, and few
inland towns manifest greater business activity and more varied enterprise.   Its admirable manufacturing facilities are very largely improved.   The mart and market of many thriving towns its trade is
lively and extended, and its importance as a manufacturing, business
and railroad centre is every year more manifest.   It has had to contend with unwise radicalism and overwise conservatism, with large out-
goes and limited incomes, with conflicting land and road titles, with
floods, fires and the rapid growth of evil influences.   With great labor
and cost she has established an excellent school system with a High
School of exceptional character and standing, and provided suitable
buildings for school accommodation.   Her churches are strong, active,
aggressive, guided by competent pastors and officers, and furnished with
convenient and elegant edifices.   Methodists organized as a distinct
society and erected a house of worship in 1857.   St. Mary's Catholic
Church, a very elaborate and costly edifice completed in 1870, and burned
down after a few years, has been already replaced.   The graceful St.
Philips Church accommodates Episcopalians.   The square left vacant
by the great fire of 1877, is already filled up with finer blocks, hotels
and stores.   In newspaper enterprise Putnam yields the palm to her
rivals, contenting herself for many years with a broadside of the
County Transcript, edited by Dr. Plimpton.   The *Putnam Patriot*,
established in 1872, by Mr. Everett C. Stone, now fitly represents the
interests of the town.   The *Putnam News*, edited by sons of Dr.
Bronson, had a brief existence.   The modern town pre-eminently of
Windham County, Putnam is not without historic interest and land-
mark.   Within its borders are the old mother church of Killingly Hill
(now known as Putnam Heights), the first Killingly burying-ground,
given to the town by Peter Aspinwall, and the Revolutionary Elm of the
old "South Neighborhood."   Many prominent men have been associated with her past history—Captain John Sabin, the first settler of

Pomfret, Deacon Benjamin Eaton at the Upper Falls (now Rhodesville), Captain Cargill at the Great Falls. She has grateful memories
of the honored names connected with her later development—Mr.
Wilkinson, the Messrs. Cutler, Dr. Plimpton, Messrs. Horace Seamans,
Lewis Williams and others, already passed away. She can boast what
all old towns cannot, a town clerk that has served a quarter of a century, and she has celebrated in advance that interesting anniversary by
an unique exhibition of antique relics and art that would do credit to
the oldest town in the Republic.

DANIELSONVILLE.

West Killingly has been greatly changed by railroad facilities;
Westfield village, Danielson's and Tiffany's mill-villages compacted
into a flourishing and influential Borough. Danielsonville Depot was
the nucleus which gathered around it new business elements, and after
the usual fermentative and formative period, united the various villages and interests in a common centre. Ely and Co., G. C. Segur,
L. Thompson, I. T. Hutchins, were first to meet the urgent demands
of trade. A Windham County Cash Store, opened in East Brooklyn
by J. S. Curtis of Hampton, offered great inducements to in-coming
customers. Business and manufacturing enterprises initiated in Brooklyn crossed over to the Railroad station. Edwin B. Carter after several unsuccessful newspaper ventures in the shire-town transferred his
press to Danielsonville in 1844, and tried his luck in *The New-England
Arena*—a spicy little sheet, which did good service in advertising the
new business centre. Abiel Converse of Thompson opened a lawyer's
office and succeeded in time to the office of State attorney. Samuel
Hutchins and D. E. Hall essayed medical practice. The Killingly
Institute, conducted by Joseph S. Winsor of Chepachet in 1840, developed into a superior High School, which flourished for a number of
years under competent and successful teachers, sending out young men
to college and ministerial service, and giving many young women
accessible educational privileges. A suitable academy building was
erected by private liberality. A Methodist class of thirteen members
was formed in 1840, and a church two years afterward. Its first pastor was Elder George May. A house of worship was completed in
September at a cost of three thousand dollars, including the building
lot. The great revival of this year helped build up the Methodist
strength and added nearly an hundred and fifty members to the Congregational church.

The cotton manufacturing interests of the village were greatly promoted by the new impetus. Danielson's mills, which had run back-

ward, were sold out in 1845 to a new company, Messrs. Foster, Sherman and Remington of New York and Providence, who built a large and commodious brick mill, and manufactured print cloths. Tiffany's Mills and accommodations passed into the hands of Providence proprietors, who inaugurated extensive improvements, building new dam, factories, dwelling-houses, with most thorough and substantial workmanship, and running a greater number of spindles than the dozen factories of the previous generation. An iron foundry, machine-shop, plough and shovel manufactory, brass foundry, tin factory, establishments for making saddles, harnesses, carriages, furniture, congregated in the vicinity of the station. The incorporation of Danielsonville Borough in 1850, stimulated local growth and enterprise. New business blocks, Minitexit and Attawaugan Houses, were built up and opened. An elegant church edifice was erected by the Congregational society, south of the former site in Westfield, in 1856. The pastorate of Mr. Whitmore was succeeded by that of Rev. T. O. Rice, who was followed successively by Rev. Messrs. T. T. Waterman and James Davenport, now deceased, and later incumbents. The Methodist house was repaired and enlarged in 1868 at a cost of seven thousand dollars. Episcopalians and Adventists have erected houses of worship. Last in the field, the Baptists organized in church estate in 1875 and erected a suitable church edifice. Danielsonville's local position and consequent aspirations have given it prominence and importance. The *key* to Court-house and County administration, it has seemed not unlikely that these privileges might in time be transferred to it. Lawyers and newspapers have sought it as the virtual or prospective centre of the County. The short-lived *Arena* was succeeded in 1848 by *The Windham County Telegraph*, which struggled for life under various editors. *The True Democrat*, and the *Windham County Gazette* failed to survive the perils of infancy. In 1859 the *Telegraph*, with some four hundred subscribers, was purchased by J. Q. A. Stone. Changing its name to *The Windham County Transcript*, Mr. Stone entered upon his editorial work with much energy and perseverance, aiming to establish a true county paper, "devoted to the best interests of Windham County." The character and standing of this paper upon attaining its majority is sufficient proof of his success. Faithfully advocating all measures and influences that would tend to public elevation and benefit, *The Transcript* has been for many years *a power* throughout the County, and has not only helped carry forward and accomplish many good works, but has stimulated county feeling and strengthened the bond of union between the several towns. To its persistent efforts Danielsonville is greatly indebted for the achievement of her graded school system, and the elegant and commodious High School building of which she is justly proud. The dedication of this fine building, December 6, 1871, was observed with appropriate rejoicings.

A somewhat faint-hearted *Herald* after a few years' effort was succeeded by a very wide-awake *Sentinel*, which maintains an advanced position on the Democratic vanguard. Westfield's honored lawyers had retired from active life before the consolidation of the villages. Hon. Ebenezer Young, after filling many useful and prominent positions, died in 1851. Feeble health prevented Judge Backus from assuming many public duties which were urged upon him, but he served several years as judge of the County Court, and also as State Senator, and was one year lieutenant-governor. After some years of sickness and infirmity he died in 1858, greatly respected and beloved. Abiel Converse, Esq., removed to New London. Elisha Carpenter, Esq., of Eastford, after some years of successful practice in Danielsonville, was called to judicate in the Superior Court of Connecticut, the only Windham County lawyer thus honored, save its distinguished jurist, Chief-Justice Swift. His successor, Edward O. Oundall, serves as clerk of the County Court. Earl C. Martin, Thomas E. Graves, Esquires, are among the later lawyers of the enterprising borough. The former has also been made a judge of the Superior Court. A large number of physicians have ministered to the public health. Among Danielsonville's latest achievements is a public hall, which claims to be the finest in the County, and which furnishes many enjoyable musical and intellectual entertainments to large and appreciative audiences. The general tone and character of the village has been greatly raised within the past decade, and to business activity and facilities are added the advantages of refined and agreeable society.

WILLIMANTIC.

Three railroads have helped bring this important village to its present status. Asa Jillson and other public citizens labored earnestly to awaken public sentiment to the importance of these enterprises, and aided in carrying them into execution. *The Willimantic Journal*, established by John Evans in 1848, quickened local interest and agitation. The Hartford and Providence and New London and Northern Railroads opened at nearly the same date, in 1854, inaugurated a new era. "Cotton-teaming" was killed at a blow, the turnpike gates were thrown open, and laden trains from the four quarters of the globe brought goods, trade, money and prosperity to the Willimantic Valley. The old "Air-Line" from Boston to New Haven, passing through the heart of the village, early discussed and surveyed, after many delays and misadventures, was finally carried through, and as the "New York and New England"' thoroughfare has greatly contributed to the later growth of Willimantic, and the development of business and manufacturing interests. Centralization has wrought great changes. The varied mills and industries that once clustered around the Falls and the Oven Dam, the paper, grist and saw-mills, the site of "Sodom," Wellesville, Jillson's cotton and duck-mills, the old "stone schoolhouse," "the Light-house," and other historic landmarks, are now swallowed up and absorbed by that great "Willimantic Linen Company," whose line has gone out through all the earth, and whose *thread* is known throughout the world. The Windham and Smithville cotton manufacturing companies still occupy their former sites with greatly extended facilities. In addition to the ordinary industries called out by the daily wants of a large population, the manufacture of twisted silks, established by J. H. and G. Holland, and of silk machinery by W. G. and A. R. Morrison, employ nearly three hundred workmen.

The general growth of Willimantic has kept pace with its business development, though its chaotic elements were somewhat slow in taking permanent form. Its moral and educational interests were much promoted through the agency of *The Willimantic Journal*, which under the charge of Mr. William L. Weaver, assumed a high moral and literary character. A native of Windham, and an early resident of Willimantic, he was deeply interested in its past and future development. A valuable series of papers published in *The Journal* preserve priceless data concerning the early settlers of old Windham and its vicinity, while his earnest efforts in behalf of temperance, education and all elevating influences, and his broad and enlightened patriotism, left their mark upon the present generation. His death, December 8, 1866, was a great loss to Willimantic and Windham County, but the labor performed by him amid great bodily infirmity and obstacles, will give him lasting remembrance. Mr. Weaver had collected materials and made considerable progress in compiling a Genealogical History of Ancient Windham, comprising all the families embraced within its original limits. Through his efforts the dilapidated town records were collated, repaired and copied. He served the town for many years as registrar and school visitor, and in 1856 was sent as its representative. *The Willimantic Journal* under successive editorial administrations has continued to represent the interests of the village; other newspaper enterprises have been called out by increased demands.

Business facilities and expansion gradually drew in a more substantial class of citizens, who helped to raise the character of the village and carry forward needful public improvements. By persistent labor and effort, schools and roads were graded, suitable school-houses, church edifices and town buildings constructed, a tasteful cemetery laid out, boggy swamps reclaimed into fruitful fields ; desert and waste places made to blossom with roses and cheerful homes. And when to these residents was added the vast throng of foreign operatives, the BOROUGH was soon able to outvote the town, and the various public offices were gradually transferred from Windham Green to Willimantic, till even the solid old "Windham Bank" was forced to yield to the pressure, and take its securities and trusts to the all-absorbing business centre. Within the last decade its progress has been increasingly rapid. The enlarged operations of the Willimantic Thread Company, and their enlightened public spirit in beautifying their grounds, and providing for the intellectual improvement of their employés, has been a great benefit to the village. A hall devoted to public purposes occupies the upper part of the unique Company store-building, where lectures and gratuitous instruction in singing have been provided, and a library open to the use of all has found abundant patronage. Increasing pride and interest in the village is manifested by improvements in stores and public buildings. Plate glass windows and marble fronts are coming into fashion, and the "Opera House" of Willimantic threatens to quite overshadow and surpass Danielsonville's Music Hall. Next to its Thread Company, Willimantic's most famous institution is probably its annual camp-meeting, which attracts many thousand visitors from all parts of the land. From small beginnings this has become a noted resort. The first land for a camp-ground was purchased in 1860 by leading Methodists, and conveyed the following year to the trustees of the Willimantic Camp Meeting Association. Other purchases were made, till now the ground comprises about thirty acres on a sloping hill-side, covered with natural growth and commanding an extensive view, with an audience circle capable of seating five thousand people, streets regularly laid out, tents, cottages, boarding-house, and every convenience for accommodating the great multitude, who enjoy its æsthetic and spiritual privileges. The various religious societies in Willimantic have grown with the village and are well sustained and influential. Sabbath-schools have received much attention, and an annual gathering of the children on the evening of Fast-day from the Baptist, Congregational and Methodist schools, excites much interest. The Universalist society has been superseded by a Spiritualist organization, the largest and most prosperous in Windham County. Regular services are maintained in Excelsior Hall, erected by the society in 1868. A Children's Progressive Lyceum organized about the same date is in a very flourishing condition. Many of the best speakers in the State have lectured upon its platform. A Catholic mission ministered to the foreign

residents at an early date. The former Baptist church, re-christened
as St. Joseph's, became too small for the increasing number of
worshippers, and a very elegant edifice was completed in 1874,
the High Altar built in Munich, Bavaria. Father De Bruycker,
its pastor for sixteen years, is now the patriarch among Willimantic clergy, and cares for his large flock with most unremitting watchfulness and fidelity. Willimantic's numerous churches have been
favored with a competent succession of faithful ministers, who have
aided in all good enterprises. It has also had its full share of professional aspirants. The lamented Catlin had his residence for a time
in this village. Dr. William Witter died after some years of professional service. Numerous lawyers and physicians have essayed the
field with varying ability and success.

Windham Green yielded slowly to the demands of her aspiring offshoot, but was forced to submit to the will of the stronger. Gradually
her stores, public offices and business interests lapsed to the Borough.
Her Fire-company dissolved, and its engine was stored away, her
taverns were reduced to the minimum, and Bacchus himself tumbled
off his post and was ignominiously pitched into a wood-shed.* The
Windham Bank meantime retained its place and integrity. In 1840,
Mr. Samuel Bingham was chosen cashier. Ten years later Henry S.
Wolcott was elected president in place of John Baldwin, deceased ;
Thomas Ramsdell succeeded to the office in 1872, upon the decease of
Mr. Wolcott. The venerable Deacon Perkins died in 1850. George S.
Catlin, after a brilliant career, died young. The last of the old Windham lawyers, Judge Calvin Hebard, died at an advanced age. The
Congregational Society completed its fourth house of worship in 1849.
The church celebrated its one hundred and fiftieth anniversary December 10, 1850, when the several churches that had gone out from it took
part in the interesting services. Rev. George I. Stearns of Killingly,
who succeeded Mr. Tyler in the pastorate, died in 1862. A Baptist
church was organized in 1846. The Windham Bank was removed to
Willimantic in 1879, retaining its respected officers. Though shorn of
its ancient honors and business prosperity, Windham Green is a wellpreserved and attractive village, a pleasant home for public-spirited
citizens, and a favorite summer resort for many of its wandering children, who enjoy its pure air and historic associations. The late Hon.
A. A. Burnham, so prominent in public life for many years, speaker of
the House of Representatives, lieutenant-governor, congressional repre-

* This time-honored Revolutionary relic was not left long in such ignominious quarters, but after narrowly escaping demolition for kindling-wood,
it was rescued by appreciative friends, and finally transferred to the city of
Hartford, where it occupies a conspicuous position in a window on Main
street, exciting much admiration and remark.

sentative, had his residence at Windham Green.   Lieutenant Colonel Rufus L. Baker, U. S. A., after many years of professional service, returned to a beautiful home in Windham.

South Windham retains its manufacturing enterprise.   Large reservoirs recently constructed increase the working power of Smith and Winchester's establishment, which not only supplies an increasing home market with paper-making machinery, but fills orders for Cuba, Mexico, England and other foreign countries.   The manufacture of wood type, introduced by Mr. Edwin Allen, was transferred to John G. Cooley, and afterwards to William H. Page, who acquired the art at South Windham and pursued it there for a time in partnership with James Bassett.   Becoming satisfied that the use of wood type could be greatly extended, Mr. Page removed to Greeneville, found a wealthy partner, and has built up an extensive and flourishing business, supplying the trade throughout the country.   The ingenious and costly machinery perfected by Mr. Page preserve the principle of the original machine thought out in three days by Mr. Allen, who like many other inventors has failed to reap the golden harvest.   Educational Tables, combining amusement with instruction, machinery used in making government envelopes, are among his many achievements.   The "type-mill" in South Windham, purchased by Guilford Smith, and used for a time as a felt manufactory, now manufactures wood type in the service of "The American Wood Type Company."   "The Adams Nickel Plating and Manufacturing Company" has a prosperous establishment in this busy village, and many thousand tons of fertilizing gypsum imported by the ship-load from Nova Scotia have been ground out in Elisha Holmes's grist-mill and distributed over an extensive region.

The pleasant village of *North Windham* with its convenient railroad accommodations is thriving and prosperous.   The cotton factory built by Mr. Swift, after twice burning and re-building, is now employed in thread manufacture.   The felting works have been for some time discontinued.   Mr. Ralph Lincoln maintained the ancient reputation of the family name by administering the post-office department till past his eightieth year.   A Christ-ian church has long existed in this locality, dating back to the days of Joshua Abbe.   The various industries of the several villages, and the great manufacturing interests of Willimantic, make Windham now the richest town in the County, and notwithstanding the loss of Scotland Parish, she is second if not first in population.   Her central position on the great thoroughfares of travel, and distinguished manufacturing advantages, would seem to augur continued growth and prosperity, and despite her loss of

71

territory and dignity we may well believe that the modern business town will yet far. exceed the glories of the ancient shire-town.

SCOTLAND.

This ancient parish after repeated struggles achieved its independence in 1857. Its first town meeting was held on the morning of July 4th, in the vestry of the Congregational house of worship. Jephtha Green, moderator. Benjamin Hovey was chosen clerk and treasurer; John P. Gager, Zephaniah Palmer, John P. Webb, selectmen; Henry Webb, constable. A pleasant social gathering was held in the afternoon, when patriotic and congratulatory addresses were made by Governor Cleveland, Rev. Mr. Tallman, and native citizens. Change of status made little practical difference in local administration. A slight change in the former west bound brought the Main Brick works and the old Robinson house with its monthly religious services within the town. Rev. Thomas Tallman resigned the pastorate of the Congregational church in 1861. A meeting-house had been built in the village in 1843, by the Universalist society, H. Slade, pastor. Dr. C. H. Bromley practiced medicine for many years. No special events have occurred since town organization. Youngest and smallest of Windham County towns, with no special business facilities, Scotland can hardly be expected to take a conspicuous position. The sons of David L. Fuller, Esq., engaged about 1850, in a clothing manufacture, sending out garments to be made throughout all the adjacent towns, and conducting a branch establishment in Thompson, but they followed the westward movement, and devoted their energies to building up St. Paul and Minnesota, while other young men have won success in varied fields. Restricted in present compass and population, Scotland abounds in historic memorial. She can show us the birthplace of Hon. Samuel Huntington; the early homes of Daniel Waldo,* the famous centenarian chaplain of Congress, and the more distinguished artist, Samuel Waldo† ; the old Devotion homestead with its Revolutionary associations, and the homes of other ancient families which sent out names now known throughout the land. Inspired by

* Born in Scotland Sept. 10, 1762; drafted into the Continental army in 1778; pastor of West Suffield, Cambridgeport, and several other churches; served as chaplain of the House of Representatives in 1856-58; died in Syracuse, July 30, 1864, aged 101 years, 10 months and twenty days.

† Born in Scotland in 1783. Incited to art by the example and instructions of Rev. Joseph Steward. Success in Litchfield enabled him to visit England where he studied portrait painting in the studio of Benjamin West. Returned in 1809, and for 53 years pursued his art successfully in New York and Hartford; was one of the best art critics as well as artists of his day; very highly esteemed by a large circle of friends.

such illustrious examples the inherent genius of the little town can hardly fail to assert itself in present and future generations, and we may be sure that she will maintain her previous reputation, and perhaps send out names yet more noted and honored.

Chaplin is a brisk little town, with one river, one village, one church and one town minister, who in date of service has become the patriarch of the Congregational clergy in Windham County. Its chief apparent characteristic is a certain homogeneousness and sociability as if all its residents constituted a single family. Its seniors live on to almost immemorial age; its deacons serve some fifty or sixty years with apparently unabated vitality. The manufacturing facilities offered by the Nachauge in its diagonal course through the town are somewhat sparingly improved. A paper-mill has been kept at work many years; spindles and plow-handles are manufactured. Silk culture receives some attention. Agriculture is the leading interest of the town. Requiring the services of but one physician they take care that he shall be a good one. Doctors Orin Witter, father and son, have occupied the field for many years. Rev. Francis Williams, the "one minister" was installed in 1858. He has been distinguished for especial interest in temperance work, and the fruit of his labor in that and other directions is seen in the good order and sobriety of the town, and its general intelligence and prosperity.

Hampton was left for many years remote from railroad station and business centre, and gradually declined in business and population, but was brought back into the world through the agency of a railroad thoroughfare for which she is largely indebted to the untiring energies of a distinguished citizen. Governor Cleveland was greatly interested in this as in other railroad enterprises and labored most effectually to secure its laying out through that section of country which most needed its benefit. After two years service in the State Legislature, devoted more especially to the encouragement of railroad enterprise, he was sent as Congressional representative in 1849, where he gave his vote and influence against the extension of slavery. Disaffecting the leaders of his own party by this course he received the warm support of the Free Soil party, was re-elected by a trebled majority and fought slavery extension two years longer. Faithful to his own radical convictions of right and justice, Governor Cleveland felt constrained to continue his opposition to slavery, joined in the organization of the Republican party, and was nominated at the head of the Presidential electors who gave Mr. Lincoln the vote of the State. He was appointed by Governor Buckingham one of the delegates to the Washington Peace Convention, March, 1861, and did all in his power to avert the threatened collision, and with equal earnestness supported the administration throughout the War.   Whenever practicable Governor Cleveland has resumed his professional duties as an advocate, winning continued success.   His peculiar art was best exhibited in a case of legal complications where equity and natural justice were on the side of his client, and rarely failed to convince the jury.   Governor Cleveland's happy and honored life "among his own people" in Hampton was shadowed by heavy bereavements—the death of his most promising son, John J. Cleveland, in early manhood, followed in less than two years by the decease of his only surviving child, Delia Diantha, the beloved wife of Hon. Alfred A. Burnham.   Hon. Mason Cleveland died in 1855, greatly respected by all, leaving sons who now represent the name and family.   Hampton has also mourned the loss of a most excellent minister, Rev. George Soule, who served as pastor of the Congregational church for several years, whose vacant place it was not easy to fill.   Worship is still maintained in the Christ-ian churches.   A new church edifice, conspicuous on Hampton Hill, illustrates the change now going on in many parts of rural New England.   A large Catholic church in the heart of a small farming population is indeed a strange and suggestive sight.   Thrifty Willimantic operatives, hoarding their wages in convenient savings banks, invest finally in a permanent homestead, and take with them their families and religion, and the homes and churches of Puritan ancestors are thus gradually replaced by those of alien blood and worship. Industrious and orderly in the main, it yet remains to be seen whether they will sufficiently assimilate to take their place as good citizens. This Catholic church built in 1878, is attended by a considerable congregation gathered from Hampton and adjacent towns.   Vicinity to the railroad has proved a great convenience to this town, and brings each year a larger number to enjoy the fine air and out-look of Hampton Hill, and the cordial hospitality of its many agreeable residents.

ASHFORD.

No town has suffered so severely from modern changes as Ashford. From being one of the great public thoroughfares between New York and Boston, it is left as it pathetically asserts "fourteen miles from anywhere."   Eastford Parish has gone from it; various industries flourishing for a time in Westford Parish have been abandoned, emigration has continued to rob it of its vital forces, business and population have diminished, till the churches that once so proudly sent forth missionaries, are themselves subjects for mission help and threatened with dissolution.   One ancient church indeed, the senior

Baptist church of Windham County, has fairly given up the ghost and suffered legal administration. It is seldom that a defunct church leaves so handsome an estate. When from increasing emigration and the building up of other Baptist churches it was found that the Knowlton Church could no longer maintain worship, the ministerial farm was sold and the avails deposited in Shetucket Bank, Norwich. Rolling up in some twenty years to about two thousand dollars, it was drawn out under legal rescript and distributed among the heirs of the original donors, according to the terms of the gift. This somewhat difficult service was successfully accomplished by Mr. Edward Knowlton, who succeeded in unearthing some two hundred legatees from all parts of the land, who claimed rights ranging from five shillings to a hundred dollars. The old Knowlton meeting-house after long disuse and decay paid the debt of nature. A new Baptist church gathered in the village of Warrenville in 1846, bears a good name and record. The Westford Baptist church has been succeeded by a Free-Will Baptist organization. The Congregational church of Westford* enjoyed a season of renewed prosperity in 1846, achieving a new church edifice and bell, and installing Rev. C. S. Adams as pastor, who combined the charge of a flourishing High School with his pastoral duties. After some unpleasantness, Mr. Adams was dismissed in 1858, and the succeeding pastorates have been of short duration. The First church of Ashford has steadily declined in numbers and resources, and though still sending out valued ministers to other churches, is pressed to maintain its own worship. Among its later ministry, Rev. Thomas S. Dutton merits special remembrance for his excellent historic discourse, delivered January, 1864. Its present pastor, Rev. Charles P. Grosvenor, is greatly honored as probably the oldest surviving licentiate of the Windham County Association and a faithful minister in many Windham County churches. Warrenville, so named in honor of one who aided largely in building the Baptist house of worship, has some manufacturing and business interests. The making of coarse glass bottles and willow coverings, carried on quite extensively for a time in Westford village has been discontinued. Mr. John L. Deane, formerly connected with this business, and very prominent in town and county politics, has recently deceased. Judge Richmond, Ashford's last lawyer, Major Horace Gaylord, long connected with pension distribution and other public services, and Lorenzo Dow Bolles, the characteristic

---

* Among the many useful men sent out by this obscure church, none have shown a more self-denying and heroic spirit than Samuel J. Whiton, son of Deacon Whiton, who when prevented by illness after two laborious attempts from serving as a missionary in South Africa, returned to labor with great fidelity and success among the freedmen of the South, and in Home Mission fields at the West as long as his enfeebled health would permit.

representative of two remarkable families, have passed away within a few years. It is fitting that Ashford should take as she does such especial care of her several burying-grounds for her record is mostly with the past. Her living sons are found everywhere out of their own town. One of these pilgrims who achieved success and fortune has shown his interest in his birthplace by devising liberal things for its benefit—leaving it the sum of six thousand dollars, whose income is to be expended upon its musical and intellectual culture. The "Babcock Brass Band" with facilities for continued improvement; the "Babcock Library," free for the use of all the inhabitants of the town, have resulted from this considerate bequest of Archibald Babcock, Charlestown, Mass. With such substantial remembrances from those who owe it allegiance, it may be hoped that the home of Knowlton, Dana, the Notts, the Bolleses, and other illustrious sons, will still maintain an honorable position among Windham County towns.

EASTFORD.

This brisk young town was organized, June 21, 1847. James Lyon served as moderator. John B. Adams was chosen town clerk and treasurer; Jairus Chapman, James Trowbridge, Willard Lyon, selectmen; F. Watkins, assessor; Earl C. Preston, board of relief. The basement of the new Methodist house of worship was soon secured for town meetings. Edward A. Lyon was then in charge of the Methodist church. Rev. Francis Williams had succeeded to the Congregational pastorate. Several mills were in operation in Eastford village and Phenixville, and business was lively. Captain Skinner continued his cotton factory till it was destroyed by fire. Woolen stocking yarn was manufactured by J. M. Keith & Co. Twine and cotton batting were made in Phenixville. Extensive tannery works were carried on by Mr. J. D. Barrows. Mattresses, palm-leaf hats, boots, shoes, stockings, shoe-pegs and lasts, were among the various products of the town. Mr. Frederic Hovey opened a law office. Post-office was managed by a well-known military official, Major James Dorset. This hopeful beginning has been well sustained. Though suffering the usual business changes and losses, Eastford maintains a certain youthful spring and buoyancy and is able to retain a fair proportion of her young people, while she has gained much credit for those she has sent out into the world. She has already furnished a judge* for the Superior Court of Con-

---

* Hon. Elisha S. Carpenter.

necticut, and a speaker* for the House of Representatives at Washington—and more than all she has given a LYON to sacrifice himself for his country. The energy and determination with which this Eastford lad secured the education that fitted him for a military career, enabled him to fill every position to which he was called, and "to strike the blow which saved the State of Missouri to the North," and gave fresh impulse and hope to every loyal heart. The funeral of General Lyon, when officers and civilians from all parts of the land gathered with thousands of his own county to pay the last tribute of respect to the dead hero, was one of the most remarkable demonstrations ever witnessed in Connecticut. Buried at his own request beside his parents in the rural cemetery, his fame belongs to the Nation, and the quiet grave in Eastford will be held in grateful remembrance by coming generations.

BROOKLYN.

The prosperity of the shire-town has been checked by the transfer of newspapers, business enterprises and county gatherings to more accessible centres. Its various philanthropic societies gently declined. Even the County Temperance Society suffered decease. The Windham County Agricultural Society, however, took a new lease of life in 1840. Solomon Payne was chosen president; Septimus Davison, secretary; John Day, George S. White, Thomas Hough, Henry G. Taintor, Luther Day, Isaac Knight, Charles Osgood, Hezekiah Ramsdell, Amos Gallup, Henry Campbell, Joel W. White, William Lyon, 3d., vice-presidents. An annual fair was thenceforward maintained, increasing in display and attendance and stimulating a healthy emulation. As agricultural interests have received more intelligent consideration the society has enlarged its borders and accommodations, and its September "Cattle Show and Exhibition" is the great gala day of the present generation; calling together interested exhibitors and spectators from all parts of the County. Chaplin furnishes the present president, J. W. Griggs; Sterling the first vice-president, James Pike. A committee represents its interests in each town. John Gallup, 2d, succeeded to the presidency of the Windham County Bank. Leading citizens in Brooklyn and neighboring towns have served as directors. The Windham County Insurance Company has continued to prosper, making no assessments and suffering few losses, insuring apparently from fire as well as accruing damage, and its surplus fund might excite the envy of more pretentious institutions. John Palmer has served for

* Hon. Galusha A. Grow, Pennsylvania.

twenty-three years as secretary and treasurer; David Greenslit, Hampton, president. In 1851, Brooklyn reluctantly accepted the resignation of her faithful town clerk, Zachariah Spalding, unanimously voting:—

> "That by continued service in that office for the almost unprecedented term of forty-two years, he has in the almost stereotyped plainness and accuracy of our town records given us a memorial of his official fidelity and scrupulous exactness, while his urbanity and uniform kindness have gained for him our entire respect as a citizen and friend."

Bela P. Spalding succeeded in office. The Courts and Bar suffered few changes for many years. Thomas Gray and Uriel Fuller harmoniously interchanged the clerk's office. Daniel P. Tyler engaged ardently in politics and was very popular as a stump speaker in the Harrison campaign. Mr. Welch devoted himself more exclusively to his profession. Gradually the older lawyers, Young, Baldwin, Perkins, Stoddard, McClellan, Williams, Larned, Davis, Backus, Eaton, Judson, Holbrook, Richmond, Welch, grew gray and passed on, and younger men—Catlin, Graves, Penrose, Converse, Johnson, Philips, Martin, Carpenter—contested with the veterans Cleveland, Dyer and Tyler. Changes were made in Court sessions and customs. In prison discipline reforms were instituted. The County jail was made a workhouse and prisoners employed in out-door labor, to the great betterment of their own health and morals and also of the County Treasury, which is able to meet all current expenses, and even extraordinary repairs from their earnings, so that those who break the laws bear the whole cost of judicial administration—a stroke of Yankee policy most worthy of praise and imitation.

Brooklyn's lack of manufacturing facilities has developed enterprise in other directions. Instead of coining gold from cotton she has transmuted it into spectacles, pens and watch-cases. The workshops of Newbury, Bard and Preston, the silk factories of Richmond and Marlor absorbed much labor and capital. She has also shown much interest in horticulture, the nurseries, gardens and greenhouses of Messrs. Dyer, Newbury and Tarbox attaining a wide reputation. Music has added its attraction to town and village, the news-office of F. S. Luther boasting the largest assortment of stringed instruments in the County. Taste and culture are manifested in the many fine residences, the well-kept gardens, the improvements in Court-house, Mortlake House and private houses. An elegant church edifice was built by the Episcopal society in 1866. The hundredth birthday of this society was appropriately celebrated in the "old Malbone Church," April 12, 1871, when an interesting historical discourse was given by the grandson of Rev. Daniel Fogg. A special fund given by the late George Brinley of Hartford provides for the continued preservation of this memorial edifice and its hallowed grave-yard. Dr. Riverius Camp, rector of Trinity Church for many years, died in 1875. Rev. G. J. Tillotson was dismissed from the pastorate of the Congregational Church in 1858. Mrs. Celia Burleigh, widow of the poet and philanthropist, Wm. H. Burleigh, died in charge of the Unitarian Church. Competent pastors have succeeded to the charge of Brooklyn's several churches. Great social changes have occurred within the past few years. Daniel P. Tyler, Adams White, Deacons Newbury and Robinson, Messrs. Davison, Gallup, and many others long prominent in local and public affairs, are gone; business enterprises have been abandoned, and the present outlook in Brooklyn is less favorable than that of other days. Population and business interests are gravitating more and more to the railroad, and legal advocates are warmly urging the removal of the County-seat to some accessible business centre. Distance they tell us is now measured by minutes, not mile-stones, and Brooklyn is at least thirty minutes "behind-time." Fortunately for her, the prize is sought by *three* competitors, and in the division of counsel and effort she may find safety and continuance. To the public at large a change would probably be distasteful. Existing Court accommodations seem to them sufficiently ample and convenient, and the facilities for the care of prisoners exceptionally excellent. It is a question between the Old and the New; Conservatism and Young America; and we may be sure that in this fast-moving generation it will not take *seventy years* to settle it. Danielsonville, Putnam and Willimantic will persistently sue for the golden apple, and the prize will ultimately fall to her who makes the highest bid for it.

Canterbury has changed greatly since the days of Judson, Adams, Frost, Harris, Hough, Coit, Francis, White, Payne, Backus, and other distinguished citizens. No special business interest has drawn in new residents or kept in her young folks. The Foundry works maintained so long by Esquire Backus, Deacon Allen, and other public-spirited men, have been abandoned or transferred to railroad stations. Its farming advantages are not remarkable, and it has not yet attained to market-gardens and summer boarders. The last survivor of the preceding generation was Dr. Elijah Baldwin, who continued to practice in Canterbury and adjoining towns for more than sixty years, dying March, 1867. He was distinguished for "good judgment and sound common sense." A son of the same name has succeeded him in practice. Ashford's third Dr. Palmer practiced for a time in Canterbury village. Among later noted residents are Dr. Walter Clarke of Farmington, who filled the Congregational pastorate for three years to great acceptance, and his successor, Rev. Robert C. Learned of New London, who in addition to faithful pastoral labor compiled a valuable

72

church manual, and a very complete record of the churches and ministers of Windham County. Westminster Society, despite many losses, maintains its early efficiency, receives new members to its church and beautifies its church edifice and burial-ground. Methodist worship is maintained in the centre of the town. The great change wrought in Canterbury was painfully manifest at the late semi-centennial commemoration of the organization of its former flourishing Temperance Society, when one* of the six survivors of the original band gave interesting reminiscences of its early history. But though fallen from its former high estate, Canterbury is still able to accommodate the State with efficient *secretary* and officials, and maintain creditable representatives in various departments all over the land.

Voluntown is fortunately favored with manufacturing facilities. The mills set up by Donne, Treat and other pioneers, passed into the hands of Ira C. Briggs, Spencer, Dixon, Starkweather and Jencks, and have built up quite a lively little village known as Beechdale. Mr. George Weatherhead, a former Killingly manufacturer, engaged in business here, and died lately, much respected. Dr. Harvey Campbell, a very prominent citizen of this town, died in 1877 after long infirmity. He had served many years as town clerk and representative, was an advocate of temperance and other reforms; a leader in every good work. He had a wide medical practice and was greatly esteemed in the profession, serving many times as Fellow of the State Medical Society. Rev. Charles S. Weaver has labored much in this town, filling for sixteen years the Baptist pastorate. Baptist and Methodist churches are sustained in Voluntown village, exerting a good influence. The old Congregational church in the north of the town received a new impetus through the labors of Charles L. Ayer, ordained at the dedication of the new "Line meeting-house," January 6, 1859. Through his efforts funds were raised for the erection of a new parsonage, which furnished a pleasant home for the aged ministerial father† who succeeded him, and later incumbents. Voluntown has now but few representatives of its original families, yet despite its lean soil and local disadvantages it is gaining in many ways and has hopes of farther advancement.

Sterling has been helped by the Hartford, Providence and Fishkill Railroad, which enables her to take her ores and wares to market. The new granite village, Oneco, shows something of her architectural resources. Mr. Henry Sabin of Plainfield was the founder of this village, building a small cotton factory about 1830. Successive owners gave it their names till it was finally re-christened by the Norwich proprietors who now utilize its granite, working its fine quarries to good advantage.

* Rev. Daniel C. Frost, Killingly.   † Rev. Joseph Ayer.

Indications of yet more valuable ore have been found in the vicinity—specimens of plumbago and dendrite, and such large and glittering quartz crystals that their chief depository is known as " the Diamond Ledge." The " Devil's Den Chimney " was blown up in building the railroad. The cotton manufacturing interests of the town have declined; factories burned down have not been replaced, and its natural resources furnish its chief reliance. The " sap works " of Mr. James Pike continue to resolve the forests into their component elements, consuming annually some two or three thousand cords of hard wood, employing a number of workmen, and extracting and re-combining a variety of useful products. A specialty of this unique establishment is the dissolution of refuse tin and iron, battered tin pans, rusty stovepipes, and the like, by which these heretofore indestructible nuisances are made subservient to the will and use of man. Stimulated by these enterprises, Oneco bids fair to become a place of business importance, has a new public hall and public-spirited residents. Of other parts of the town there is no special record. A local interest centres in " the Line Store " in its northeast corner, where there is a Union Free-Will Baptist church, a post-office and frequent social demonstrations. Sterling Hill furnishes as ever a pleasant place of residence for a few families. Robert Dixon's famous tavern passed into the hands of Archibald Douglas, who served for twenty-seven years as town clerk and treasurer. The meeting-house was thoroughly reconstructed in 1860–61, the former " proprietors " relinquishing their rights to a new " Sterling Hill Meeting-house Association" and the Baptist church which had so long occupied it. Faithful ministers have succeeded the venerable Elder Peckham. Messrs. Thomas and J. A. B. Douglas and John Gallup, have served as clerks. The meetings of the Sterling Hill Association are continued with increasing interest and draw a great concourse of people. Like other inland towns, Sterling sends out creditable representatives, helping build States as well as State-houses. Connecticut's present respected lieutenant-governor was born and bred in this town. His older brother, John Gallup, was many years a resident of Brooklyn. Judge Backus of Killingly, and many other Sterling men, have filled honorable positions in various parts of the land. Mr. Amos Gallup succeeded Charles Mason as judge of Probate.

Plainfield. The contrast between this town and its opposite neighbor illustrates the importance of cultivating manufacturing interests. Previous to 1820 Canterbury had the larger population ; to-day Plainfield has at least three to one. Central Village owes much of its growth and prosperity to the enterprise and public spirit of the late Arnold Fenner, Esq., its leading manufacturer, who was for many years identified with its best interests. William Dyer, Esq., was also an influential citizen, much employed in the settlement of estates and public business. Various stores and workshops give life to this village. A Congregational church was organized here in 1846, and house of worship erected. Episcopalians have a society and church edifice. A High School was maintained for a time by Mr. Lucian Burleigh. The town clerk's office, administered for many years by John S. French in the centre of the town, has been removed to a new townhouse in this village. J. G. Penrose, Esq., continues his legal practice. Dr. C. H. Rogers, has been established in medical practice for several years. The Hartford, Providence and Fishkill Railroad has brought prosperity to Moosup. The old Union Factory, after forty years of joint-stock ownership and management, was purchased by Mr. Sampson Almy in 1850, who built a large new stone factory and made many improvements, greatly increasing the working capabilities of the village. Smaller factories were then carried on by Jos. S. Gladding and his successors, and James B. Ames. "Almyville" and "Unionville" were soon absorbed in the growing "Moosup." Many new residents were brought in, substantial citizens as well as operatives. Mr. Almy took great interest in the improvement of his lands and village, bringing his farms under high cultivation. His example was followed by other residents. The Baptists and Methodists have maintained prosperous churches and suitable houses of worship. Father James Quinn ministered for a time to the Catholic church. While Central Village has attracted lawyers, Moosup would seem to have especial charms for physicians. Doctors Morey and Frank S. Burgess, and William A. Lewis have enjoyed extensive medical celebrity and practice in this vicinity. The later prosperity of Moosup has been checked by the burning of the great woolen mill in 1875, and financial embarrassments, but new companies have entered the field and its prospects are again buoyant.

The liberal policy of the non-resident manufacturing company, and the administrative capacity of the superintendent, Mr. James Atwood, have made Wauregan a model village. Beautifully situated on the Quinebaug, removed from the railroad and disturbing influences, it has been able to carry out the design of its founders and realize a high ideal. Everything about it is orderly and tasteful. The manufacturing buildings, houses, store, hall, roads, gardens, green, are all in keeping. The church edifice is an architectural gem, and the residence of Mr. Atwood one of the finest in the County. A Congregational church was organized in 1856, soon after the factory was at work. Charles L. Ayer was its first pastor. The present pastor, Rev. S. H. Fellows, was installed in 1859. Services were held till 1874 in a convenient hall, provided by the Company. A library was soon founded and is maintained through their liberality, and the elegant church edifice is due to the same source. No intoxicating liquors are sold in the village, and great pains are taken to promote the best interests of the operatives and residents.

Packerville has maintained its early standing. Its Baptist church has continued to bring forth good fruit. Reverends J. B. Guild and John Paine, faithful laborers in many fields, have been among its pastors. The village is neat and thriving and bears evidence of careful management and oversight.

Plainfield Junction for many years was nothing but a railroad crossing, but now carries on Foundry works, and steam saw-mills, and is building up into a village. Old Plainfield Village has perhaps the finest avenue of trees in Windham County, and many handsome residences. The Congregational church still worships in the stone meeting-house of 1818, and though greatly weakened by dismissal of members to Central Village and Wauregan churches, is regaining its former strength. Reverends Andrew Dunning and Henry Robinson were greatly esteemed pastors of this church. Elisha L. Fuller has long filled the deacon's office. Plainfield Academy has suffered a permanent decline, but its building is from time to time occupied by hopeful aspirants. Messrs. William A. Benedict, Elijah Perry and Lucian Burleigh are among the later teachers, who did their best to resuscitate the enfeebled institution. Plainfield, like many similar towns, suffers from a multiplicity of interests, its villages being practically independent organizations. The senior village, however, occupies a nominal head-ship, and has still been able to retain the administration of the Probate Court. Its charge was held for twenty-three years by Hon. David Gallup, who removed his residence to Plainfield at an early age, and became very active in town and public affairs. Serving repeatedly in the Legislature, his sound judgment and business capacity gave him the speakership of the House, and a place on many important committees. Spending his winters latterly in Hartford, he has become widely known and respected in business circles, and was elected with great heartiness and approval to fill the office of lieutenant-governor. Judge Gallup continues to pass his summers in his pleasant Plainfield home, and enjoys the confidence and respect of many friends in his own town and County. Plainfield has recently lost its venerable physician, Dr. William H. Cogswell, so widely known in professional and public life. His services as agent for Connecticut in care of sick and wounded soldiers during the late War, were especially valuable. In public and private, in Church and State, he was alike useful and honored. Judge Eaton, Colonel Lester, Joseph

S. Gladding, left an honorable record of past service. Among the many who went out from Plainfield homes, and the instruction of Plainfield Academy, none achieved a more useful life-work than George Shepard, D. D., Bangor, Maine, professor of Sacred Rhetoric, stamping upon many minds the impress of his own high character and deep spiritual consecration. The highest in public life was probably Hon. Edward A. Bradford, who won much success at the Bar in New Orleans, and was honored by an appointment as judge of the Supreme Court of the United States. Connection with the great Anti-slavery conflict, as well as their own genius, have made the Burleigh brothers very widely noted.

KILLINGLY.

Growth and business expansion in this town are not confined to Danielsonville. Dayville is a lively and thrifty village with various mills and interests. Mr. Ezekiel Webster followed the railroad track, building a hotel and many private dwellings. He engaged largely in lumber trade, introducing a steam mill and lumber-working machinery. In 1846, Mr. John Day put up a new brick factory and carried on manufacturing till the destruction of the building in 1858, when privilege and accommodations were purchased by Messrs. S. and H. Sayles, who built up extensive woolen manufacturing establishments. Other industries were developed, stores opened, churches built up. The Dayville Congregational church was organized May 23, 1849. Its constitutent members were mostly dismissed from the three Killingly churches. Rev. Roswell Whitmore* officiated as pastor till 1857, thus ministering to a part of his former flock. Suitable houses of worship were provided for Congregational and Catholic churches. Schools received needful attention, and are accommodated by "a nice house with ample play-ground around it." The neighboring Williamsville Factory has been repeatedly enlarged. In 1849 the company was reorganized, and after refitting the mill with new machinery of the best workmanship, turned out the "Williamsville fine sheetings," so favorably known to connoisseurs in cotton fabrics. Williamsville like Wauregan is "a close corporation," owned and controlled by a single company and interest—a pleasant, isolated working village, well-managed and orderly. Enlightened self-interest as well as public spirit and philanthropy have effected great improvement in the administration of factory villages. Sanitary conditions are studied and observed. Evil influences are kept in abeyance. Compelled by

---

* This venerated pastor, so long and intimately associated with Windham County churches, survived till April, 1861.

the State to educate the children, they voluntarily in many cases provide for the instruction and innocent entertainment of adults by libraries, reading-rooms, lectures, &c. A fine hall has been built by the Williamsville Company for religious purposes and lectures. Attawaugan and some of the smaller factories are maintained on former sites. East Killingly has been aided by increasing centralization and the construction of a capacious reservoir which enables the enterprising little Whetstone to run its mills throughout the year. Messrs. Thomas Pray and Henry Westcott were among the many owners who have helped build up Chestnut Hill villages. Lemuel Elliott, Esq., of Providence, improved another privilege and had a pleasant country seat at the foot of Breakneck. The mineral treasures of Mashentuck and Breakneck are as yet nearly undeveloped, waiting for the construction of the "Ponoganset Railroad" or some kindred enterprise. The well of "porcelain clay" formerly so vaunted has been tested and found lacking in quantity. The East Killingly and Free-Will Baptist churches have maintained their standing under a succession of pastors. Revs. Austin Robbins and David Williams, formerly laborers in both these churches, died on successive days at their homes in East Killingly. Rev. Hubbel Loomis, well-known in the Baptist ministry, compiled an historical sketch while pastor of the former church. The church in South Killingly after reaching the verge of dissolution, was happily revived, and under an efficient ministry has quite renewed its youth. Its house of worship has been remodeled and much pains expended upon Sabbath school and temperance training. The village has recently suffered the loss of its much respected physician, Dr. Daniel L. Hovey, who had pursued his calling there for nearly half a century. He was the oldest member of the County Medical Society at the time of his decease. Having no manufacturing interests, this village is gradually wasting. Killingly's strength lies in her rocks and rivers. Extensive Brick Works have been carried on near Dayville for many years by Colonel L. D. Alexander. The "Nashawaug Farm" and privilege of Hon. Elisha Dyer, promises to bring new business and prosperity to the south of the town.

Thompson, in 1850, the most populous town in Windham County, and one of the wealthiest rural towns in Connecticut, has managed to maintain existence despite the loss of her southern territory and nearly two thousand inhabitants. Since the transfer of Masonville and Fisherville into the hands of The Grosvenordale Company,* two large and elegant brick factory buildings have been erected and many

---

* The present company still represents the Mason interest, Dr. William Grosvenor having married the daughter of one of the constituent members of the former Corporation, Mr. James B. Mason.

dwelling-houses, an immense reservoir constructed, roads built, hills levelled, and many hundreds added to the population. Mr. Lucius Briggs, as manager, maintains strict order and discipline, and the Grosvenordale manufacturing villages compare favorably with the best in other towns. Regular worship is maintained in the chapel under the charge of the pastor of the Central Baptist church. Mechanicsville, has been greatly improved under the administration of Messrs. S. and T. Sayles. A handsome brick building has been erected, a fine green laid out, and much skill and taste exhibited. Smaller factories have been kept at work in Wilsonville and New Boston, and intermitted at Quaddic and West Thompson. Apart from the special industries, the town seems to be generally thriving, its farms and roads are well kept up and its bills paid every season. The character of its rural population is gradually changing— the Puritanic church-going element replaced by foreigners. The attendance to-day of the six Protestant churches does not proba- bly equal that of the two churches of a former generation. A Catholic church in Grosvenordale draws a large congregation, and preparations are made for erecting a second church building between Mechanicsville and West Thompson.

Thompson Hill long since ceased to be a place of business, but it is none the less a pleasant place of residence, and has been greatly improved and beautified. Adjacent residents bought out the "Ponog," swept off the whole establishment, purified and reconstructed the western point of the common. Mr. William H. Mason built a hand- some house in the curve of the crescent. At about the same date, 1845, a lecture was given by Professor William A. Larned* in the town-house, upon Beauty, Taste, Tree-Culture—all now summed up in the term, "Village Improvements." Spontaneous pledges were given by many of the hearers to aid in carrying out suggestions, and in November a day was devoted to setting out elm, maple and ash trees under the especial oversight of Mr. William H. Chandler. Ten years later, the common left bare by the demolition of the old meeting-house was made over to Thomas E. Graves, Esq., for fencing, smoothing and cultivation, which added much to its beauty and with later touches from the recent Village Improvement Society, and the growth and verdure of the trees, has brought it into fine condition. A new and elegant Congregational church edifice opposite the former site, was completed in 1856, Mr. William H. Mason bearing a large share of the cost of construction. Dr. Dow had ere this closed his ministerial and earthly service. The Semi-centennial Commemoration observed April 22, 1846, was a most interesting occasion, when children and friends

* Son of George Larned, Esq., professor at Yale College, 1839-62.

of the church from near and far came together to congratulate the
aged pastor and enjoy his characteristic report of his half-century's
ministry. Original poems from Mrs. Anna S. Larned and J.
Erskine Dow, added interest to the service. A still larger congregation gathered at the funeral of the beloved pastor, August, 1849.
A chance word dropped by him led to the call of a single candidate, Rev. Andrew Dunning, Brunswick, Maine, who won at once
the unanimous voice of the people and was most happily installed,
May 15, 1850. Filling most acceptably the place of honored predecessors, Mr. Dunning died like them in charge after a less prolonged service, acute disease terminating his valued life, March 26,
1872. With him died too the cherished custom of life-long pastorates
and afternoon service—the dismissal of two ministers within five
years showing that Thompson can keep pace with the present generation. Failure to keep may ensue from too ambitious selection, and in
its later ministerial succession the church has faithfully maintained its
early pledge and traditions. Thompson has been also favored in its
medical succession. Dr. Holbrook is worthily represented by the son
who succeeded him. Doctors McGregor and Hosford who followed
Dr. Bowen, like him gained many friends and died much lamented.
The presidency of the Thompson Bank after the decease of Mr.
Mason was intrusted to Mr. Talcott Crosby, a much respected citizen,
also judge of Probate, and has since reverted to Mr. J. Olney, under
whose charge it sustains its financial credit and soundness. The Thompson Savings Bank also receives satisfactory patronage. A Family
and High School was opened in 1851, by Messrs. Alanson Rawson
and Henry Parker, which was well sustained for several years. Among
later village institutions a family hotel kept for some twenty years
by Mr. Stephen Crosby has served a useful mission. Thompson makes
no business pretensions, but its convenient railroad accommodation, pure
air and local attractions draw many summer visitors, especially those
favored with family associations. Young men who go out from it into
business have the good taste to make it a summer residence, building
new houses and adding much to its life and prosperity.* Convenient
parsonages have been built within five years for the Congregational
and Baptist societies. The hundredth anniversary of the parent Baptist church was appropriately commemorated by a pleasant gathering
near the site of the first church edifice on Brandy Hill, Sept. 9, 1873.

* *Erratum.* *Ante*, page 534, please erase from second line of second note
the superfluous " one of them," not *one* but the *three* young lawyers exercising
immediate selection as aforesaid. Thompson is too peaceful in these latter
days to offer much scope for legal practice, but if such lawyers as chance
to make it a home have failed to follow the example of their predecessors, it
is not to be inferred that it is from any lack of *pretty young ladies.*

73

An interesting discourse was delivered by Rev. N. T. Pinkham, pastor of the East Thompson church, and many touching reminiscences detailed by aged church members and former pastors. The Congregational church celebrated its hundred and fiftieth birthday, Feb. 11, 1880, by a social reunion and brief addresses.

Pomfret suffered serious declension after the loss of her factory, but revived with the opening of the New York and New England Railroad, which accommodates her with three stations and a great influx of company. The pleasant scenery and fine old trees and farm-houses of this picturesque town are more and more appreciated, and it is becoming a favorite and fashionable resort. Families from many cities enjoy the coolness and comforts of these airy homes. This summary demand has greatly quickened agricultural enterprise. A flourishing Farmers' Club has been instituted, which discusses improved methods of farming, and puts them in practice. Intelligent and capable men give their time, energies and thoughts to farm-working, which has resulted in increased products and profits, and a higher standard of agricultural attainment throughout the town. Pomfret dairies have gained a higher repute, and her "model farms" excite wonder and imitation. Pomfret is also gaining permanent residents. Children of her old families come back to the old haunts and hearth-stones, and strangers after a summer's sojourn return perhaps to build villa and mansion of their own. Elegant residences going up on sightly hill and shady nook attest the increasing popularity of the town. The tasteful "Pomfret Hall," recently erected, manifests the public spirit of its citizens and their efforts to provide agreeable entertainment for guests and stranger sojourners, while its Book Clubs and Library Associations show that they have not outgrown their literary proclivities.* The Abington United and Ladies' Libraries, dating back as far as 1793, have been extremely well preserved and were recently consolidated into a Social Library, already endowed with some seven hundred volumes, many of them rare and valuable.

The hundred and fiftieth anniversary of the organization of Pomfret's First Church was appropriately commemorated, October 26, 1865. Rev. Walter S. Alexander, recently ordained pastor, welcomed the numerous guests, and gave an introductory discourse. Interesting historical papers were presented by the former revered pastor, Rev.

---

* Pomfret's inherent genius once more asserts itself in the success and reputation achieved by present aspirants who have gone out from its homesteads—Mrs. Caroline F. Corbin and Mrs. Louise C. Moulton—who are thought to have inherited a share of the gifts of their respected great-grandmother, Mrs. Hannah (Sharpe) Cleveland, the heroine of the Revolutionary "Pink Satin" (*ante*, page 200), a woman of rare intelligence and "wonderful gift of language."

Daniel Hunt. Rev. A. C. Thompson brought greetings from the mother church of Roxbury, and pleasant reminiscences and congratulations were given by Reverends C. P. Grosvenor, Andrew Dunning and G. N. Webber. Mr. Hunt survived for several years, a great blessing to all who knew him. The honored church father and deacon, Job Williams, died in 1863. Darius Matthewson, Esq., so prominent in public affairs and temperance work, had preceded him ; and his respected sons, Deacon George and Colonel Charles B. Matthewson, have lately followed. Not only church officers but churches have passed away. The Pomfret Baptist church has been absorbed into the former Branch at Putnam, and Quaker worship has died out. A Second Advent church is maintained in Abington. The Episcopal church is very flourishing and enjoys the ministrations of many distinguished clergymen. Dr. Hiram Holt died in 1870, after a successful medical practice of nearly fifty years. Pomfret's only remaining physician, Dr. Williams, has held the place many years.

WOODSTOCK.

The present generation has seen great changes in Woodstock. Its academy after a long period of depression was resuscitated through the agency of Mr. Henry C. Bowen, who after successfully engaging in business in New York City, made his summer home in his native town, setting out trees, beautifying the Common and stimulating public improvement. The old building was thoroughly repaired and re-opened in the spring of 1847, with John P. Averill for principal, whose popularity soon drew more than a hundred pupils. During his four years' service the academy continued to flourish, and the impetus survived succeeding administrations, especially that of Mr. J. W. Patterson. Renewed depression led to more general and vigorous effort resulting in an Endowment Fund of more than fifteen thousand dollars, and a capacious and elegant academy building costing more than twenty thousand—liberal initiatory pledges made by Mr. Bowen securing a generous response from citizens and friends of Woodstock. The expense of furnishing the house was also mainly borne by Mr. Bowen. Messrs. Abel Child, S. M. Fenner and Joseph McClellan served as building committee. Its dedication, August 21, 1873, was one of Woodstock's "notable meetings." Rev. N. Beach reported in behalf of the Trustees. Congratulatory addresses were made by Governor Buckingham, Professor Northrup and others ; a sprightly historic compendium was read by Clarence W. Bowen, and a delightful reminiscential letter sent by Dr. Oliver Wendell Holmes. Competent teachers have since been instated in office, and it is hoped that the old academy has entered upon a permanent career of prosperity and public usefulness. Scholars find boarding accommodations in Elmwood Hall, which under Mr. Amasa Chandler has been for many years one of Woodstock's "peculiar institutions," furnishing a pleasant summer home to many city-worn refugees, and an excellent annual supper to the perennial Thief Detecting Society, which heartily enjoys the exercise of this official prerogative. Woodstock takes much pride and interest in her modern Agricultural Society, organized in 1859, which has already achieved a long list of substantial members, ample grounds and hall, and annual exhibitions which rival those of the older society. It has also a very wide-awake Farmers' Club, whose essays and discussions upon many practical questions awaken much thought and interest. The changes effected by modern modes of working, the difficulty of finding mechanical employment, and the increased demand for garden products in the growing villages, have stimulated a new interest in farming, and a great departure from traditional practices. Woodstock with its rich soil and vigorous population is preëminently a farming town, and is doubtless destined to make great agricultural advances. Some of its market gardens and fruit farms are already very celebrated and successful, and the superior stock sent out by Mr. Sumner takes the highest prize at every cattle show. Its manufacturing interests are declining from various causes. Its villages are in the main well preserved, though West Woodstock suffers from distance from railroad accommodations, and North Woodstock from the decline of its carriage manufactory, following the decease of Ezra C. Deane, who had been so prominent in business and public affairs. A tasteful new church edifice has been recently erected in this village in place of the former house, destroyed by fire. The feuds of former generations are now so far outgrown that North and East societies unite in one minister, officiating by turns in each house of worship. East Woodstock lost an honored citizen in George Paine, Esq., who had served as school commissioner as well as in many town offices, and more recently has suffered the loss of one still more widely known and honored. Rev. Edward Pratt, the efficient secretary of the Connecticut Temperance Union, had previously wrought a most useful work as pastor of the East Woodstock church. The temperance movement so earnestly begun in this town, had suffered as in other towns a reaction naturally resulting from the discovery that intemperance was far more deeply rooted than at first supposed, and also from the increase of the foreign element and other influences. With characteristic patience and fidelity, Mr. Pratt began anew at the foundation, gathering the children of his own church into societies and thoroughly indoctrinating them with temperance sentiments, and laboring whenever practicable in wider fields. In 1861, he joined with Reverends William L. Walker, Lucian Burleigh and other earnest temperance men, in forming a County Alliance to take the place of the extinct society, and as its chief executive officer succeeded in carrying out plans which resulted in the formation of the Connecticut Temperance Union. The office to which he was then called by the universal consciousness that he was of all others *the man* for the place and time, compelled him to seek dismission from his charge and devote his time and energies to most arduous and responsible labors. The grief felt at his loss, and the spontaneous testimony of hundreds throughout the State, bear ample witness to his fidelity and usefulness. Mr. Pratt was greatly esteemed in every relation, ready to further any scheme for public or individual benefit, a man of rare purity, integrity, self-sacrifice, and whole-hearted consecration to his Master's work. Woodstock's numerous churches have been served by a countless succession of pastors. The hundredth anniversary of the First Baptist church was appropriately commemorated by an interesting historical address from Rev. J. T. Smith, and letters from former pastors and members. Rev. Lemuel Grosvenor of Pomfret, pastor for five years of the church on Wood-stock Hill, prepared an historical sketch of this old church for its Thanksgiving service, 1859. Doctors Asa Witter, Marcy and Bradford lived to advanced years, the former leaving three sons to represent him in the profession.

WOODSTOCK'S NOTABLE MEETINGS.

A prophetic instinct would seem to have impelled Judge Sewall to give New Roxbury the name of Woodstock, "for the sake of Queen Elizabeth, and the *notable meetings* that have been held at the place bearing the name in England," for it may be doubted if any rural town in the country has witnessed more remarkable gatherings. From the day that John Eliot proclaimed the Gospel to the assembled Wabbaquasets in the face of a defiant message from King Uncas till the President of the Free Republic honored it by his presence, it has witnessed a succession of "notable meetings"—meetings for town organization and secession, of preparation for revolt and adoption of Federal Constitution, martial parades and funerals, spirited raisings and dedications, Anti-masonic and Sabbath school con-vocations, mighty musterings of Cold Water Armies, and the great mass-meetings of the present generation. The first of these latter demonstrations occurred in the Fremont campaign, September, 1856, when thousands of adolescent Republicans, fired with the glow of youthful enthusiasm, met as if by spontaneous impulse on Woodstock Hill to be farther electrified and inspired by the stirring words of Raymond and Beecher. Very different was the far greater gathering in the dark autumn of 1864, when after four years of ceaseless struggle and sacrifice the continuance of the War and the Nation hung upon the result of the impending Presidential election. Thousands from Connecticut and adjoining States joined with Windham County citizens upon that memorable day, and the heroic spirit that animated the vast assemblage, and their avowed determination to stand by Lincoln and the Government at any cost till the rebellion should be subdued, gave new hope and courage to despondent Republicans throughout the North, and had a powerful influence in effecting that happy result. Larger in number and more elaborate in preparation and display was the great Grant Mass Meeting of 1868, when from fifteen to twenty thousand gathered on the Common.

> " Through the length and breath of old Windham,
>   An army was marching that day ;
>   An army with torches and banners,
>   In proud and triumphant array."*

The immense town processions, with bands of music, ox-teams, and innumerable banners ;† the " ships with white sails, heavy laden, with cargoes of beautiful girls ; " the " Boys of Blue " with their martial tread and suggestive uniform, formed the most remarkable pageant ever witnessed in the County. Governor Buckingham officiated as presiding officer ; Sheriff Greenslit as chief marshal. Four stands in different parts of the common were occupied by a succession of distinguished and eloquent speakers. Not less notable than the size and spirit of this gathering was its good order and sobriety, the great multitudes dispersing to their homes as quietly as if from a church service.

Later "notable meetings" have been of less partisan and political character. Most emphatically did Woodstock fulfill her prophetic destiny on that memorable July 4, 1870, when she welcomed the head of a far greater empire than that of Queen Elizabeth, and guests who would have brought honor to her royal namesake. The honor of entertaining President Grant and his suite, the Russian minister, Count De Catacazy, and other notables, solely accrues to Mr. Bowen, who carried out all details with his accustomed taste and efficiency. The centennial town celebration, July 4, 1876, was contrastingly noteworthy as an almost strictly *local* gathering, an assemblage of citizens entertained by native speakers. Gilbert Phillips, Esq., the president ; E. H. Bugbee, the historian of the day, were both of Woodstock

* Poem by Mrs. C. N. W. Thomas, Killingly.
† Thompson most particularly distinguished herself as the *banner town*, having in addition to the usual representations, an admirable colossal portrait of General Grant, painted expressly for the occasion by a native artist, then resident in New York, Mr. George Baldwin.

birth. July 4, 1877, witnessed "a new departure." The historic
"Common" was forsaken for the new "Roseland Park" opened by
Mr. Bowen, who had thus thoughtfully provided for the perpetuation
of Woodstock's most cherished institution. Senator Blaine, Ex-
Governor Chamberlain made characteristic addresses on this occasion;
but its distinguishing feature was the presence and poem of an
honored son of one of Woodstock's earliest families, Dr. Oliver
Wendell Holmes, whose graceful reminiscences with their patriotic
prelude will ever be held in grateful remembrance. Other noted
speakers have been provided in subsequent years, and an infinite series
of notable meetings in this picturesque park may be confidently pre-
dicted. Not only is it available for Fourth of July celebrations and
Saturday afternoon concerts but it is found to be eminently favorable
for picnics, family gatherings and various social purposes, and the
experiment of transplanting the European Pleasure Garden into the
heart of a New England community seems likely to be permanently
successful, and deserves to be ranked among the most notable achievements of its ingenious projector.

WINDHAM'S LATEST WAR-RECORD.

In the Revolutionary contest Windham took a leading position;
in the last great struggle she had but to bear her part among many.
But though her resources were relatively limited, her political status
enabled her to extend most hearty aid and comfort to the central
Government. The strong Anti-slavery sentiment early developed,
deepened and strengthened by the repeal of the Missouri Compromise
and concurrent events, overcame partisan and political bias, broke the
supremacy of Democratic influence and made her the strongest
Republican County in Connecticut. Hundreds of honest, earnest
Democrats like Governor Cleveland, were forced to renounce allegiance
to party by their loyalty to the "higher Law," and the general Government. The call to aid in putting down the gigantic rebellion met
immediate response in Windham County. Meetings were at once
held in all the prominent villages, and measures instituted for carrying
out patriotic resolutions. Revolutionary scenes were re-enacted.
Young men hurried to cities to enlist, or joined in company drill at
home; women came together to prepare clothing and lint; towns
hastened to make provision for raising and supplying their prospective
quotas. A County mass meeting was held in Brooklyn, April 22,
1861—Governor Cleveland presiding. Daniel P. Tyler, W. H.
Chandler, B. F. Palmer, H. Hammond, W. Simpson, J. Q. A. Stone,
B. P. Spalding, Jeremiah Olney, committee on resolutions, declared

"that citizens of Windham County would expend their last dollar and exhaust the last drop of their blood ere they would submit to a disruption of the Nation." Stirring, patriotic addresses were made by many earnest speakers. Sixty volunteers offered to take the field at once, and six thousand five hundred dollars was pledged for the support of the Government, W. H. Chandler heading the list with five hundred dollars. Many volunteer companies were formed in the several towns in advance of State requisition. E. W. and Daniel Whitaker of Ashford, and Lester E. Braley of Windham, gained admittance into the First Regiment of Connecticut Volunteers. No man rendered such service in organizing Connecticut's forces as the Colonel of this regiment, Daniel Tyler, of Norwich, a worthy representative of the father and grandfather bearing the same name, so long honored in Brooklyn and Windham County. Educated at West Point and experienced in military discipline, to him was assigned the most arduous task of making an army out of entirely raw material. He was made General of Connecticut's First Brigade, and Brigadier-General of United States Volunteers after his arrival at Washington. Sixteen Windham County residents enlisted in the Second Regiment, Colonel Terry, and a small number in the Third, of which Alexander Warner of Woodstock was major, Dr. John McGregor of Thompson, surgeon. These regiments were hurried on in time to share the defeat at Bull Run, where Dr. McGregor was taken prisoner. This disastrous repulse, tidings of the remarkable career of General Nathaniel Lyon and the great demonstration at his funeral in Eastford, and General McClellan's* assumption of command, all awakened the deepest interest in Windham County and stimulated activity in enlistment and military preparation. Young men kept back by the reiterated declaration that they would not be needed were mustered by hundreds into the quickly forming regiments. About fifty were included in the Fourth Regiment. Company H, Fifth Regiment, Albert S. Granger, Putnam, captain; Company A, Sixth, Thomas K. Bates, Brooklyn, captain; Company K, Seventh, Charles Burton, Killingly, captain, succeeded by Jerome Tourtellotte, Putnam; Company F, Eighth, Elijah T. Smith, Plainfield, captain—were almost wholly filled from Windham County, with many in other companies. The Whitakers and Edwin L. Lyon of Ashford were enrolled in Cavalry Company B. Judson

*Son of Dr. George McClellan, the distinguished Philadelphia surgeon, whose boyhood was well remembered in Woodstock, grandson of James, and great-grandson of General Samuel McClellan, so prominent throughout the Revolution and in later years, the *name* could not but awaken much enthusiasm and hope in Windham County, and only the unwelcome conviction that the modern General lacked something of the fire of his ancestors, and did not share its Anti-slavery views, overcame this early predilection.

M. Lyon of Woodstock was Major of First Regiment Cavalry, and Andrew B. Bowen captain of Company A, with some thirty men from Woodstock and towns adjacent. The Eleventh Regiment was greatly beloved in Windham County, Charles Matthewson, Pomfret, lieutenant colonel; Rev. George Soule, Hampton, chaplain; Dr. James R. Whitcomb, Brooklyn, surgeon; George W. Davis, Thompson, quartermaster sergeant. The companies of Captain Clapp, Pomfret, and Captain Hyde, Plainfield, were mostly made up from the County. Many from the south part of the County enlisted in Company G, "the Lyon Guards," Twelfth Regiment, under the veteran Captain Braley, Windham. Alexander Warner of Woodstock, went out as Lieutenant-Colonel of the Thirteenth. Windham's contribution to this regiment were mostly included in Company E—E. E. Graves of Thompson, first lieutenant. These soldiers received generous bounties from their respective towns and ample provision for their families, and went out hopefully to their varied posts of duty and service. After six months of military vicissitudes, culminating in the withdrawal from the siege of Richmond, the towns were again called to raise their proportion of "three hundred thousand more." Eastern Connecticut responded with such alacrity that the Eighteenth Regiment raised in New London and Windham Counties, though the last summoned was the first to leave, August 22, 1862.* This was most especially Windham's representative regiment. Colonel Ely was of Killingly parentage, Lieutenant-Colonel Nichols, a favored son of Thompson, widely known in other towns; Major Keach, a Killingly veteran, Assistant Surgeons Harrington and Hough, familiar residents of Sterling and Putnam. Captains T. K. Bates, Brooklyn, Joseph Matthewson, Pomfret, G. W. Warner, Woodstock, C. D. Bowen, Windham, E. J. Matthewson, Killingly, commanded companies of county men. Dr. Lowell Holbrook of Thompson, Rev. W. C. Walker of Putnam, went out later as surgeon and chaplain of this favorite regiment. Windham was also well represented in Companies D, J, K, Twenty-first Regiment, Company G, Twenty-sixth. Addison G. Warner, Putnam, having recruited more than a hundred men for the First Cavalry, was commissioned captain, January, 1864. Windham also furnished recruits for the artillery and other regiments, and paid her proportion for the colored regiments, promptly fulfilling from first to last every requisition of government. More earnest in filling her quotas than in seeking for office, she furnished proportionably more

---

* Enlistment in the north part of Windham County was greatly stimulated by the opportune return of Dr. McGregor, after more than a year's captivity. A public reception given him on Thompson Green was very largely attended, and his changed appearance and affecting story made a very deep impression, rousing sober, thoughtful men to a truer apprehension of the nature of the contest.

subalterns than commanders, though many of Windham birth or stock who went out from other places gained a high rank and rendered distinguished service. At home as in other sections there was great outflow of private liberality, money and labor freely expended in sending comforts to friends who had gone to the front, and to the Sanitary and Christian Commissions, Soldier's Aid Societies busily working in every neighborhood, and "prayer made without ceasing of the church unto God" for help and deliverance. Of the service rendered by the men sent out from Windham County it is impossible here to give detailed report, but there is good reason for belief that it compared favorably with that of the great mass of volunteers, and in many instances was signally effective. Still less can we speak of the lives that were sacrificed. The wounds are yet too fresh; bereavements are yet too keenly felt. We remember but too vividly the days that brought the tidings that one and another of those who had gone out so bravely had fallen. Each town has its death roll, and its honored graves which it yearly decorates. Some of these heroes were among the best and brightest young men of Windham County, most worthy to be remembered with those of a previous generation, who like them had given their lives for their country. We need not fear that their names or deeds will be forgotten. Enrolled in the archives of the State and Nation, embalmed in every patriot heart, their fame will but grow brighter with the lapse of years. Mustered into the great Army that from age to age in every clime has raised "the battle-cry of Freedom," the men whose names are inscribed on "Windham's latest War-record" may be sure of imperishable remembrance.

THE ARMY OF EMIGRANTS.

If the record fails to chronicle those who went out to battle much less can it include the far greater army that have gone out from Windham County to plant, to build, to educate, throughout the length and breadth of the land. No muster-roll inscribes their names; no estimate gives even an approximation of their number and achievements. Emigration began early. Westward the son of Windham took his way, bearing with him her impress and institutions. Younger Windhams, Woodstocks, Plainfields, Canterburys, Pomfrets, represent the mother towns in many States, and testify to the filial love of these roving children. Wyoming, Vermont, New Hampshire, Western Massachusetts and New York, Ohio, and territories westward, received large colonies from Windham. Scattered throughout the land in almost every County of every State, are found descendants of these early pilgrims in every rank and position, but usually classed among the solid, sterling citizens, who have built up society and maintain civil and religious institutions. Here and there one especially gifted or fortunate has set his name high up where all may read it. The world has heard of our Morse's and Holmes's, Generals Eaton and Lyon, and Commodore Morris. Dartmouth, Williamstown, Schenectady, Andover, Yale, Middlebury, Bangor, honor the memory of the good men that Windham has given them—Presidents Wheelock, Fitch, Nott, Professors Adams, Kingsley, Hubbard, Larned, Hough, Shepard. Rhode Island will never forget the services of Lieutenant-Governor Sessions. William Larned Marcy and Elisha Williams hold a high rank among the great men of the Empire State. Ohio gratefully remembers Dr. Manasseh Cutler and General Moses Cleveland. Edmond and George Badger won success and honor in North Carolina, and New Orleans still bears witness to the eloquence of Sylvester Larned and Chief Justice Bradford. Colonel Craft of Vermont, Governor Williams of New Hampshire, Senator Ruggles of Ohio, Hon. Thomas P. Grosvenor, of Maryland, has each an honorable record in his adopted State. New Haven owes to Windham her respected Whitings and Whites, and the late excellent mayor, Hon. Aaron Skinner, while Hartford is indebted for distinguished and useful physicians, Doctors Coggswell, Welch and Sumner. Windham is largely represented in the ministerial ranks, sending out the ancestors of the present Dr. Bacon, New Haven, Dr. Storrs, Brooklyn, Dr. William Adams, New York, Dr. George L. Walker, Hartford, and a host of lesser luminaries. She has given to art Miss Anne Hall, Samuel Waldo, Frank Alexander, Henry Dexter* and Ithiel Town, architect, the collector of one of the largest and most valuable libraries in the country. The Grosvenor† Library of Buffalo perpetuates the name and munificence of the son of one of Windham's honored families. The works of E. G. Squier, Alice and Phebe Carey, Mrs. Botta, Mrs. Lippencott (Grace Greenwood), E. C. Stedman, do honor to their Windham ancestry. Other names equally meritorious might swell the list and still a tithe would not be given. Ministers, professors, lawyers, bankers, merchants, farmers, mechanics, tens of thousands of American citizens

*Henry Dexter, sculptor, lately deceased at Cambridge, was born in Nelson, New York, but spent a part of his early years in Killingly, where his native love of art was greatly incited by the example and encouragement of his townsman, Frank Alexander. Ithiel Town was born in Thompson, 1784, one of the "odd boys" who devolop remarkable genius. Beginning his career as a common house carpenter, he accomplished architectural feats at Boston that excited great admiration. Entering into business at New Haven and New York City he became widely celebrated, furnishing designs for many important public buildings in those cities and other large towns. He also invented a bridge, which was very popular for a time.

†Hon. Seth Grosvenor, New York.

in all parts of the land, trace descent from the same old County.
And still the tide sets outward, and still despite all that have gone
before and the reputed decrease of our native population she has a
man ready for any opening.   A goodly proportion of active business
men, to-day, in Providence, Boston, Worcester, Norwich, Hartford,
New York, Chicago, and other cities, went out from Windham County
homes and school-houses.   She accommodates Massachusetts with a
governor, and Rhode Island with leading lawyers, merchants, editors
and instructors.   She furnishes New York with a very *Independent*
editor, and *The Tribune* with a specially sprightly correspondent,
whose charming lyrics melt the most obdurate critic.   She sends to
Chicago an author and editor whose name is a " Woman's Secret,"
and a merchant prince to be president of its Commercial Club, interchange greetings with Boston magnates, and even draw out a witty
response from the speechless ex-president and chief commander.   Let
a son of Windham rove where he will he finds a brother to welcome
him.   In every section, in every position, Windham has to-day its living representatives, its bright, enterprising capable men and women,
ready to bear their part in the battle of life, and winning a fair share
of its honors and victories.

TO-DAY AND TO-MORROW.

And notwithstanding all this outflow there is something left behind.
The perennial fount is full and living.   It is pleasant to believe that
after the vicissitudes of nearly two hundred years Windham was never
more prosperous than at the present epoch.   New interests have developed, new elements are at work, bringing indeed fermentation and
change but giving promise of continued expansion and development.
With a few exceptions the tendency is upward, and great advancement has been made during the present generation, not only in wealth
and numerical strength but in all things that contribute to material
prosperity.   Town affairs are administered with more enlightened
public spirit.   Money is expended more freely for needful uses.   The
poor of the towns are provided with suitable homes and allowed more
comforts than in former days.   Schools receive more stringent supervision.   Ample and convenient school-houses are demanded and teachers receive far more liberal compensation.   A section so well provided
with railroads can hardly fail to be up with the times in all essential
matters, and yet it has enough conservatism to keep it on the track,
and with all its modern impetus it sticks fast to its old traditions,
repudiates the idea of a county debt and never suffers a legally
executed will to be broken.   Windham is essentially a *well-balanced*

county. Its varied business interests work harmoniously for the good of the whole. Manufacturing has developed agricultural enterprise; labor with few exceptions finds its best friend in capital. The resistant gravity of the old hill-top villages and the comparative inertia of the rural districts, happily check the undue momentum of the steam-driven railroad centres, and even those out-lying sections that would seem to be almost dead-weights serve a useful purpose in preserving the equilibrium, and receive a reflex benefit from the general advancement. Its inherent vitality is manifested in the energy and progressive spirit of those who stay at home as well as in the restless ambition that impels so many to leave, while the general intelligence of the people, the demand for books and news-papers, the book clubs and literary societies springing up in almost every neighborhood, argue a good degree of mental activity.* A pleasant feature in latter-day life is the yearly increasing number of out-goers who return to their old homes, and their willingness to aid in schemes for public benefit—a return-tide, bringing back to Windham some of the treasures she has so freely lavished. This hopeful omen, with the general status of the County, its improved business facilities and established manufacturing interests, would seem to augur a bright and prosperous future.† There are indeed as in other sections adverse

---

* While boasting of editors, authors and artists who have gone out from Windham, it is scarcely fair to leave unnoticed those who have won success at home. Well conducted County journals show that Windham boys can edit a newspaper without going to New York or Providence. The poems and stories of Miss Jane G. Fuller of Scotland, and Mrs. C. N. W. Thomas of Killingly, vie in merit with those which have brought honor to Mrs. Corbin and Mrs. Moulton. Miss Fuller has done especial service in her vivid repro-duction of revolutionary incidents, and her charming volume upon our wild-flowers, which has contributed towards "the popularization of science." Mrs. Charles Thompson of Pomfret, has published "The Rectory of More-head," and other pleasant stories. The portraits and sketches of Miss Sarah S. Hall, West Killingly, indicate a share in the hereditary genius so con-spicuous in her distinguished kinswoman, as well as careful study and training. Mr. J. I. Sawyer of Pomfret (now in Putnam), has won a good reputation as an artist, and Messrs. Baldwin of Thompson and Thurber of Putnam, bring back to their early homes the fruits of artistic culture.

† *Population of Windham County according to the United States Census,* 1870:—Ashford, 1,242; Brooklyn, 2,355; Canterbury, 1,552; Chaplin, 704; Eastford, 984; Hampton, 891; Killingly, 5,712; Plainfield, 4,521; Pomfret, 1,488; Putnam, 4,192; Scotland, 648; Sterling, 1,022; Thompson, 3,804; Vol-untown, 1,052; Windham, 5,413; Woodstock, 2,955. Total, 38,535. 8,521 were of foreign birth, of whom 4,606 were born in British America. 460 Negroes. 40 Indians. Grand List for 1880, $17,303,636. Highest on list, Windham, $3,505,309. 81 houses of worship and 77 churches were reported at the same date, viz:—Baptist, 17; Congregationalist, 27; Episcopalian, 6; Methodist, 13; Roman Catholic, 5; Second Advent, 4; Unitarian, 1. One or two Catholic churches have been added. Spiritualists maintain worship in several of the larger villages.

elements. Windham has to face the inevitable accompaniments of rapid growth and expansion—the rowdyism and vice that congregate in thickly-settled communities, the changed character of her rural population. Probably half the foreign-born* operatives who run the mills that bring so much wealth to the County become in time incorporated into its population. An unknown factor of little appreciable influence, representing at present scarcely more than a negative quantity, it may prove a most positive force in working out its future destiny. To these tendencies she opposes the transforming power of her civil and religious institutions, and the stability and sound sense of her native population. The churches that have done so much for her past development are still at work. Not one of her original town churches has become extinct, and very many have been added. While church attendance and strict Sabbath-keeping have declined since they ceased to be compulsory, the number of churches proportionably to the population has doubled. Representing many shades of religious belief, they are all on the side of right living, of moral and spiritual advancement. Its ministry is as of old, able, active, aggressive, eager to labor and to lead in every effort for the elevation and purification of churches and communities, and its hands are strengthened by many faithful men and women, who, discerning the signs of the time, are ready to do their part in helping forward the good and resisting the evil. With such conserving and reformatory forces, and the continued blessing of the kind Providence that has so happily sustained and guided her on her way, it may be hoped that Windham will overcome every threatening or inauspicious element, that her moral and spiritual development will keep pace with material growth, that through coming generations she will increase in prosperity and influence, and maintain an honorable position as a " corner-stone " of Connecticut and the Republic.

---

* The French operatives, with scarce an exception, take their savings back to Canada, and make no attempt to assimilate with the Yankees. The Irish who predominate at Willimantic usually buy small farms and become permanent residents.

APPENDIX.

A.

Inquiry has been made as to the origin of the names of the several towns in Windham County. Judge Sewall's record gives the data concerning Woodstock, and it is believed that the names were generally given by some high official in memory of some special locality in the Mother Country. Governor Fitz-John Winthrop had the honor of naming Plainfield and probably Canterbury. Governor Saltonstall is believed to have named Killingly, Pomfret and Ashford. With other English possessions derived from distinguished ancestry, he held the "Manor of Killingly, near 'Pontefract [Ponfret, Pomfret] in Yorkshire,'" which undoubtedly suggested the names given to the former towns. Ashford was so called from its great number of ash trees. The Volunteer's Land was appropriately called Voluntown. Thompson preserves the name of its early English proprietor Sir Robert Thompson.

B.

It has been a matter of surprise that no account has been discovered in any cotemporary newspaper of Putnam's adventure with the wolf. The first detailed report of that famous exploit would seem to be that in his own biography prepared by Colonel Humphrey, 1788, under the direction of General Putnam himself, and Dr. Albigence Waldo. The following extract found in a copy of the *Norwich Packet*, 1784, shows what extraordinary versions had attained circulation in England :—

["*From a late London Magazine*].

ANECDOTES OF THE LATE CELEBRATED AMERICAN GENERAL PUTNAM.

We read that David slew a lion and a bear, and afterwards that Saul trusted him to fight Goliath. In Pomfret lived Colonel Israel Putnam, who slew a she bear and her two cubs with a billet of wood. The bravery of this action brought him into public notice ; and, it seems, he is one of fortune's favorites. The story is as follows :—In 1754, a large she bear came in the night from her den, which was three miles from Putnam's house, and took a sow out of a pen of his. The sow, by her squeaking, awoke Mr. Putnam, who hastily run in his shirt to the poor creature's relief; but before he could reach the pen, the bear left it, and was trotting away with the sow in her mouth. Mr. Putnam took up a billet of wood, and followed the screamings of the sow, till he came to a foot of a mountain, where the den was. Dauntless he entered the horrid cavern, and after walking and crawling upon his hands and knees for fifty yards, came to a roomy cell, where the bear met him

with great fury. He saw nothing but the fire of her eyes; but that was sufficient for our hero; he accordingly directed his blow, which at once proved
fatal to the bear, and saved his own life at a most critical moment. Putnam
then discovered and killed two cubs; and having, though in Egyptian darkness, dragged them and the dead sow, one by one, out of the cave, he went
home, and calmly reported to his family what had happened. The neighbors
declared, on viewing the place by torchlight, that his exploit exceeded those
of Samson or David. Soon afterwards the general assembly appointed Mr.
Putnam a Lieutenant in the army marching against Canada. His courage
and good conduct raised him to the rank of Captain the next year. The third
year he was made a Major; and the fourth a Colonel. Putnam and Rogers
were the heroes through the last war. Putnam was so hardy, at a time when
the Indians had killed all his men, and completely hemmed him in upon a
river, as to leap into the stream, which in a minute carried him down a
stupendous fall, where no tree could pass without being torn to pieces. The
Indians reasonably concluded that Putnam, their terrible enemy, was dead,
and made their report accordingly at Ticonderoga; but soon after, a scouting
party found their sad mistake in a bloody rencounter. Some few that got off
declared that Putnam was yet living, and that he was the first son of Hobbamockow, and therefore immortal. However, at length the Indians took this
terrible warrior prisoner and tied him to a tree; where he hung three days
without food or drink. They did not attempt to kill him for fear of offending
Hobbamockow; but they sold him to the French at a great price. The name
of Putnam was more alarming to the Indians than cannon, and they never
would fight him after his escape from the falls. He was afterwards redeemed
by the English."

C.

Windham's Frog Battle found a wider place in literature. It was first
noticed in a private letter from Dr. Stiles, June, 1754. Dr. Samuel Peters
gives an absurdly exaggerated account of the affair in his " History of Connecticut," 1781, representing that the frogs "filled a road forty yards wide
and four miles in length," and were several hours passing through the town.
A ballad founded upon his narrative was soon after its publication published
in the *Providence Gazette* entitled " The Frogs of Windham—an Old Colony
Tale founded on Fact—by Arion." Another version of the story, the well-
known "Lawyers and Bull-frogs," was published some years later, aiming
rather to ridicule the prominent men of Windham than to give any authentic
report of the panic. Its authorship was ascribed to "Master Tilden" of
Lebanon, on grounds apparently quite insufficient. Another ballad, called
" The Bull-frog Fight," was given to the world in the *Boston Museum* of
1851.   George Webb, Esq., Elizabeth, New Jersey, sends the following
account received in childhood from old Sinda, wife of Jack, Colonel Dyer's
body-servant :—

" Well it was in June, I think, and the weather was very hot, and Master
had drawn off the Pond to fix the dam. When he came home he did not
think of nothin'—by and by when it became cool there began to be a *rumble,
rumble, rumble* in the air, and it grew *louder* and *louder* and *louder*, and
seemed to be like drums beating in the air. Well, it was in the old French
War, when our men had gone to Belle Isle or Canada to fight the French and
Indians, and some guessed it was the Injuns having a powwow or war dance
on Chewink Plain, and we should all be killed in the morning. But Master
and Colonel Elderkin and Mr. Gray mounted their horses and rode to the top
of Mullein Hill, and as the pond was a little over there beyond, they found
out what it was—and the scare was over. Master said he supposed the frogs
fought each other for the next day there were thousands of them dead. They
croaked some the next night but nothing so bad."

D.

As slavery left behind so few traces that it is hard to believe it ever existed in the County, it may be well to preserve the following advertisement found in the *Connecticut Gazette*, 1774 :—

"TEN DOLLARS REWARD.

RUN AWAY from the subscriber, in Canterbury, on the Night following the 26th instant, a Mulatto Slave, named Sampson, about five Feet eight Inches high, and thirty Years of Age. He is a Slender built Fellow, has thick Lips, a curled, Mulatto Head of Hair, uncut, and goes stooping forward. He had on and carried with him, when he eloped from his Master, a half wore Felt Hat, a black and white Tow Shirt, a dark brown Jacket, with Sleeves cuffed, and Pewter Buttons down before, a Butter Nut colored Great Coat, with Pewter Buttons, a Pair of striped long Trowsers, and a pair of short white Ditto, a Pair of white Tow Stockings, and a Pair of single channel Pumps. Whoever will take up said Slave, and deliver him to the Subscriber, in Canterbury, shall have the above Reward, and all necessary Charges paid by me. DANIEL TYLER.

Canterbury, June 27, 1774."

ERRATA.

Page 137, for "Home," read "Howe."
Page 183, for "Point," read "Parish."
Page 523, for "Abner Richmond," read "Jared D. Richmond."

NOTE.—This son of Abner Richmond of Westford, had established himself in legal practice in Ashford as early as 1831, administered the Probate Office for a number of years to public satisfaction, and, notwithstanding the unfounded allusions, pages 565-68, has survived the professional service of half a century, and is still able to expound the law to others, though not engaged in active practice. Judging from his own vitality, and the well-preserved longevity of his respected brothers in Westford, Ashford may retain its "last lawyer" for many years.

INDEX OF NAMES.

76